ECONOMIC INSIGHTS FROM INPUT–OUTPUT TABLES FOR ASIA AND THE PACIFIC

JULY 2022

ASIAN DEVELOPMENT BANK

6 ADB Avenue, Mandaluyong City, 1550 Metro Manila, Philippines
Tel +63 2 8632 4444; Fax +63 2 8636 2444
www.adb.org

ISBN 978-92-9269-636-8 (print); 978-92-9269-637-5 (electronic); 978-92-9269-638-2 (ebook)
Publication Stock No. TCS220300-2
DOI: http://dx.doi.org/10.22617/TCS220300-2

Notes:
ADB recognizes "China" as the People's Republic of China.
In this publication, "$" refers to United States dollars, ₹ to Indian rupees, and ¥ Japanese yen.

Cover design by John Arvin Bernabe and Gienneen Antonio.

Contents

Tables and Figures

Tables

Figures

Foreword

Since the 1990s, trade liberalization and fragmentation of production processes have made national economies more interconnected and interdependent. Global value chains (GVCs) have created new opportunities and benefited developing economies through enhanced trade, transfer of technology and knowledge, and expansion of services within the manufacturing sector. All these outcomes lead to greater economic growth for low- and middle-income economies. Similarly, advanced economies gain from GVCs by outsourcing to economies that have greater comparative advantages.

Supply and use tables and input–output tables (IOTs) are tools that, when constructed and interpreted correctly, provide a comprehensive view of the world's economy by analyzing economic interdependencies between different sectors and regions. Information captured by IOTs can be used to analyze and address some of the world's most pressing issues (such as estimating the economic impacts of the COVID-19 pandemic), to understand the varying degrees of digitalization across economies, or to measure the extent to which economies are engaged in GVCs.

A multiregional input–output (MRIO) table is an extended version of an IOT that takes intersectoral and cross-border economic flows into account. The Asian Development Bank (ADB) implemented an initiative in 2014 to produce and regularly update its MRIO database in a bid to address the demand for a more comprehensive approach to macroeconomic analysis. The ultimate goal of this initiative is to support research and subsequent policy formulation for economies around the world. Usage of the database has since expanded significantly, from analyzing GVCs to more cutting-edge issues such as the links between technology, trade, and environment, among others.

This publication serves as a central effort to present and collect statistical indicators and analytical results from the various applications of the MRIO database. It is the third in the series *Economic Indicators: Input–Output Tables*, which began in 2018, and covers extensive statistical data and insights on the patterns of trade and production relationships. This release features common economic statistics on production and consumption as well as analytical indicators generated both from established and more novel input–output frameworks. These indicators have a broad range of applications, from identifying important economic sectors to tracing value-added in production chains.

Aside from economic indicators, the publication features three supplementary chapters demonstrating the wide analytical use of IOTs. These chapters introduce a measurement framework to determine the size of core digital economies in the Asia and Pacific region; analyze the economic contribution of the real estate sector in these economies; and document the impact of the COVID-19 pandemic on the performance of these select economies.

I hope that the suite of economic indicators generated in this technical report will enable researchers, decision-makers, and those responsible for formulating policy to create solutions to critical economic challenges.

I want to thank all those who contributed to the publication: the consultants, the industry experts, ADB staff, and the official statistics agencies and other government organizations of economies participating in ADB's statistical and analytical capacity-building initiatives. I commend them for their dedication, cooperation, and hard work. We hope that this report will be a valuable resource for economic research and policy implementation—and will provide a way forward to a sustainable future.

Albert Park
Chief Economist and Director General
Economic Research and Regional Cooperation Department

Acknowledgments

This publication is the third edition of *Economic Indicators for Asia and the Pacific* using input–output tables prepared by the Statistics and Data Innovation Unit (EROD-SDI) within the Economic Research and Regional Cooperation Department (ERCD) at the Asian Development Bank (ADB). The publication is the result of collaboration by government agencies and national statistics offices, made possible under ADB Regional Capacity Development Technical Assistance 8838: Updating and Constructing Supply and Use Tables for Selected Developing Member Economies. This initiative formed the key statistical foundations for building the ADB Multiregional Input–Output Database. Since 2014, ADB has continued to maintain, update, and expand the tables to support economic analysis, operations, and other knowledge solutions. In this year's publication, the initiative is supported by three projects: (i) Knowledge and Support Technical Assistance (KSTA) 9920: Key Indicators for Asia and the Pacific 2021–2023; (ii) KSTA 9646: Data for Development (Phase II); and (iii) KSTA 9624: Supporting Knowledge Solutions in Central and West Asian Countries.

The publication benefited immensely from the contributions of the core publication team, under the overall supervision of Mahinthan Joseph Mariasingham. This team comprised Gienneen Antonio, John Arvin Bernabe, Renz Marion Catapang, Ma. Charmaine Crisostomo, Elyssa Mariel Mores, Kenneth Luigi Reyes, Anna Monina Sanchez, and Eric Suan. Saeda Najafizada and Rai Sengupta provided critical reviews of the manuscript. Technical advice and statistical support were received from Michael Barsabal, Janine De Vera, Julieta Magallanes, Sarah Mae Manuel, Danileen Parel, Ana Francesca Rosales, Michelle Monique Sianghio, and Dean Joseph Villanueva. Early contributions from Samantha Joy Cinco, Clara Delos Santos, Georgina Gonzales, Angeli Juani, Angelo Jose Lumba, and Marcus San Pedro shaped the direction of this report. The chapter on COVID-19 analysis was written by Julian Thomas Alvarez, Samantha Joy Cinco, Jessica Jola, and Elyssa Mariel Mores. The chapter on digital economy was compiled by Faith Balisacan, John Arvin Bernabe, and Jahm Mae Guinto. The chapter on real estate activities was prepared by Ridhima Bahl, John Arvin Bernabe, Arushi Gupta, Christian Regie Jabagat, and Elyssa Mariel Mores. A special word of gratitude is due to Simon Cox of *The Economist*, whose ideas and comments made an invaluable influence on the analysis of the real estate economy.

We are grateful for the valuable contributions made during the initial stages of preparing the publication by the team leaders, coordinators, and specialists in supply and use tables within the participating official statistics agencies and international organizations. These implementing agencies include the Bureau of Statistics, Bangladesh; the National Statistics Bureau, Bhutan; the Department of Economic Planning and Development, Brunei Darussalam; the National Institute of Statistics, Cambodia; the National Bureau of Statistics, the People's Republic of China; the Bureau of Statistics, Fiji; the Census and Statistics Department, Hong Kong, China; the Central Statistics Office, India; Badan Pusat Statistik, Indonesia; the Committee on Statistics of the Ministry of National Economy, Kazakhstan; the National Statistical Committee, the Kyrgyz Republic; the Statistics Bureau, the Lao People's Democratic Republic; the Department of Statistics, Malaysia; the Department of National Planning, Maldives; the National Statistical Office, Mongolia; the Central Bureau of Statistics, Nepal; the Bureau of Statistics, Pakistan; the Department of Census and Statistics, Sri Lanka; the Directorate-General of Budget, Accounting and Statistics, Taipei,China; the National Economic and Social Development Board, Thailand; and the General Statistics Office, Viet Nam.

Eric Suan provided administrative and operational support throughout the course of the publication process. The cover was designed by John Arvin Bernabe and Gienneen Antonio, while Anna Monina Sanchez led the visualization of the economy profiles. Paul Dent edited the manuscript, while Joe Mark Ganaban oversaw the layout, page design, and typesetting process. Proofreading was done by the core publication team. The Logistics Management Unit of the Office of Administrative Services assisted with the printing and distribution of the publication, while the publishing team in ADB's Department of Communications provided general guidance on production processes and organized promotional and awareness activities via the bank's website and social media.

Elaine S. Tan
Advisor, Office of the Chief Economist and Director General,
and Head, Statistics and Data Innovation Unit,
Economic Research and Regional Cooperation Department

Abbreviations

ADB	Asian Development Bank
AEG	Advisory Expert Group on National Accounts
APL	average production length
BATIS	balanced trade in services
BEC	broad economic classification
CAGR	compound annual growth rate
CIF	cost, insurance, and freight
CII	changes in inventories
COVID-19	coronavirus disease
CPA	classification of products by activity
CPC	central product classification
DAVAX	directly absorbed value-added exports
DVA	domestic value-added
ECLAC	Economic Commission for Latin America and the Caribbean
FIGARO	Full International and Global Accounts for Research in Input–Output Analysis
FOB	free on board
FVA	foreign value-added
GDP	gross domestic product
GFC	global financial crisis
GFCE	government final consumption expenditure
GFCF	gross fixed capital formation
GVA	gross value-added
GVC	global value chain
HEM	hypothetical extraction method
HFCE	household final consumption expenditure
HS	harmonized system
ICIO	intercountry input–output
ICT	information and communication technology
IFS	international finance statistics
IMF	International Monetary Fund
IOT	input–output table
ISIC	International Standard Industrial Classification of All Economic Activities
IT	information technology
ITS	international trade statistics
Lao PDR	Lao People's Democratic Republic
LQM	Leontief quantity model
MRIO	multiregional input–output
MRIOT	multiregional input–output table

NAS	national accounts statistics
NAICS	North American Industry Classification System
NBS	National Bureau of Statistics (People's Republic of China)
NIOT	national input–output table
NPISHs	nonprofit institutions serving households
NSC	National Statistical Committee (Kyrgyz Republic)
NSO	national statistics office
OECD	Organisation for Economic Co-operation and Development
PBX	public branch exchange
PDC	pure double-counting
PPI	producer price index
PRC	People's Republic of China
PREDICT	Prospective Insights on Research and Development and Information and Communications Technology
PSTN	public switched telephone network
RCA	revealed comparative advantage
REER	real effective exchange rate
REF	reflection
REX	reexports
ROK	Republic of Korea
SAM	social accounting matrix
SARS	severe acute respiratory syndrome
SDA	structural decomposition analysis
SIC	Standard Industrial Classification
SNA	System of National Accounts
SUT	supply-use table
UN	United Nations
UNCTAD	United Nations Conference on Trade and Development
US	United States
USBEA	United States Bureau of Economic Analysis
VAX	value-added exports
VoIP	voice over internet protocol
WHO	World Health Organization
WIOD	World Input–Output Database

Executive Summary

Economic Insights from Input–Output Tables for Asia and the Pacific presents indicators and analyses covering 25 select economies in Asia and the Pacific for 2019 and 2020. The economies assessed in this publication are Bangladesh; Bhutan; Brunei Darussalam; Cambodia; Fiji; Hong Kong, China; India; Indonesia; Japan; Kazakhstan; the Kyrgyz Republic; the Lao People's Democratic Republic; Malaysia; Maldives; Mongolia; Nepal; Pakistan; the People's Republic of China; the Philippines; the Republic of Korea; Singapore; Sri Lanka; Taipei,China; Thailand; and Viet Nam.

Underpinning all statistics and analyses is the Asian Development Bank's Multiregional Input–Output Database, which contains national and bilateral sectoral flows for 62 national economies. These economies comprised more than 90% of the world's gross domestic product (GDP) in 2020. Anchored on the 2008 System of National Accounts, the structure of the multiregional input–output tables (MRIOTs) is broadly described in the introduction, including the general sources and methods for compilation of these tables. Due to more disaggregated information contained in the MRIOTs, the number of analyses has significantly expanded since 2015, in parallel with major developments in the global economy. As such, this publication serves to centralize this additional knowledge by presenting a consolidated database of all major statistical and analytical indicators based on an input–output framework.

As a preview of these indicators, the chapter on **domestic linkages** describes the basic economic aggregates, multipliers, and linkages from a national input–output table (NIOT). By construction, the orientation of analysis in a NIOT puts emphasis on domestic sectors' supply and use relationships and their capacity to induce economic growth or contraction in the local economy. Variants of multipliers and measures of linkages are presented with the objective of quantifying a sector's impact on, and contribution to, the domestic economy. Findings from this chapter reveal that, while final demand in 2020 generally contracted in the select economies of the Asia and Pacific region, output multipliers expanded on average as a result of increased intersectoral trade. Further, analysis of linkages highlights the economic importance of food and beverage manufacturing and refined petroleum sectors across several economies in the region.

The domestic-based analysis is extended in the subsequent chapter on **international linkages**. This chapter presents indicators that explicitly link domestic sectors to foreign suppliers and consumers. Given that foreign inputs are embedded in domestic outputs and exports, a frequent element in the indicators described is the need to disentangle the sources and uses of value-added embodied in a product. Presented indicators range from simple measures such as trade-to-GDP ratios, to more sophisticated metrics such as global value chain participation rates. Generally, these indicators show the degrees of interdependence of an economy or sector to global trade. Meanwhile, some indicators serve to highlight the dominant features of global production, such as identifying what economies do best (i.e., revealed comparative advantage), how products reach the market (i.e., position and production length), and how supply chain decisions are affecting product sourcings (i.e., agglomeration indices). For example, analysis shows that international trade receded from 2019 to 2020, which meant lower global value chain participation across sectors and economies in the region. However, domestic markets provided some cushion against the global trade slowdown, as evidenced by heightened agglomeration indices in 2020.

Application of the input–output framework is expanded to special chapters on the impacts of the COVID-19 pandemic, the digital economy, and the real estate sector on economic growth in economies of Asia and the Pacific.

The chapter on **estimating the economic effects of COVID-19** uses counterfactual NIOTs to disentangle the observed and unrealized impacts of the pandemic through an input–output framework. The methodology puts emphasis on measuring the output, income, and employment performance of economies in a "no pandemic" scenario. Results highlight that these unrealized effects had a commensurate, if not substantial, impact on economies (as compared to the observed changes) from 2019 to 2020. Value-added impacts ranged from −3.2% to −12.3% for 2020, while employment levels were impacted by −1.6% to −16.7% in select economies.

The chapter on **establishing a framework for measuring the digital economy** operationalizes a proposed input–output approach for capturing the wholesale contribution of digital sectors to select economies. Core digital sectors were first defined and extracted from the NIOTs, thereby enabling the calculation of backward and forward linkages of these identified sectors with the rest of the economy. Statistics reveal that the digital economy in Asia and the Pacific varied across economies, ranging from about 1.5% to 17.9% of GDP in 2019.

The chapter on **determining the economic contribution of real estate activities** demonstrates a fresh perspective on measuring an economy's exposure to changes in the real estate sector. In response to growing concerns about the property sector's vulnerability, the chapter defines the relevant activities, from real estate construction to lease and management of properties, and correspondingly uses the details in the MRIOTs to quantify the share of real estate activities to GDP. Findings suggest that few economies exhibit real estate activity shares of more than 20%, with only Japan and the People's Republic of China achieving this level in 2017, while Thailand posted the lowest rate of 5.4% among the select economies.

In addition to the relevant applications of input–output analysis, the publication's **economy profiles** present a high-level summary of compiled indicators for each of the 25 select economies in Asia and the Pacific. This section is followed by a technical description of methodologies and introduces the standard class of Leontief and Ghosh models, which underlie the suite of input–output indicators referenced throughout the publication.

The datasets, profiles, and input–output tables are accessible through the publication's web page. The data presented in this publication are not official statistics. Production and trade data from various sources are integrated into the input–output economic analysis framework and adjusted as required to conform to specific macroeconomic concepts. As such, data and statistics presented herein could differ from relevant official statistics.

ADB **Full publication datasets can be accessed online:**

National Input-Output Tables for Asia and the Pacific, 2000, 2007-2020

East Asia
- Hong Kong, China
- Japan
- Mongolia
- People's Republic of China
- Republic of Korea
- Taipei,China

South and Central Asia
- Bangladesh
- Bhutan
- India
- Kazakhstan
- Kyrgyz Republic
- Maldives
- Nepal
- Pakistan
- Sri Lanka

Southeast Asia and the Pacific
- Brunei Darussalam
- Cambodia
- Fiji
- Indonesia
- Lao People's Democratic Republic
- Malaysia
- Philippines
- Singapore
- Thailand
- Viet Nam

Economy Profiles

East Asia
- Hong Kong, China
- Japan
- Mongolia
- People's Republic of China
- Republic of Korea
- Taipei,China

South and Central Asia
- Bangladesh
- Bhutan
- India
- Kazakhstan
- Kyrgyz Republic
- Maldives
- Nepal
- Pakistan
- Sri Lanka

Southeast Asia and the Pacific
- Brunei Darussalam
- Cambodia
- Fiji
- Indonesia
- Lao People's Democratic Republic
- Malaysia
- Philippines
- Singapore
- Thailand
- Viet Nam

Analytical Indicators for Asia and the Pacific, 2000, 2007-2020

Click here to access the full dataset of input–output economic indicators

Multiregional Input-Output Tables for 2000, 2007-2020

Click here to access the tables as of July 2021

Highlights

This publication features a broad suite of statistical indicators characterizing the supply-and-use interactions of economic sectors within and across 25 economies of Asia and the Pacific. The indicators include sector- and economy-specific multipliers and linkages, trade orientation and openness, participation in global value chains, patterns of product specialization, and domestic agglomeration, among many others. Supplementing these analyses are special chapters on the economic impacts of the COVID-19 pandemic, the digital economy, and real estate activities.

ADB's Multiregional Input–Output Tables consist of:

62 economies around the world, representing about 90% of the world's gross domestic product (GDP) in 2020, and featuring

25 economies from the Asia and Pacific region.

GDP for the economies of Asia and the Pacific exhibited a slight decline of 0.1% from 2019 to 2020.

2020 **$28,598** *billion in GDP*

2019 **$28,616** *billion in GDP*

East Asia managed to expand its GDP by 1.7% in 2020, while the other subregional groupings suffered losses.

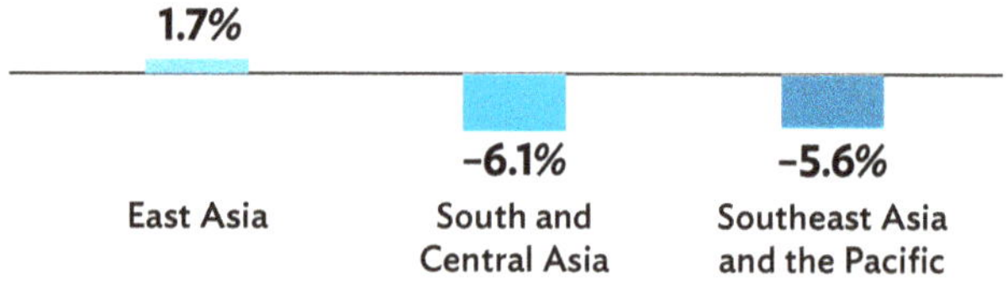

Value-added in Asia and the Pacific was dominated by business services in 2020...

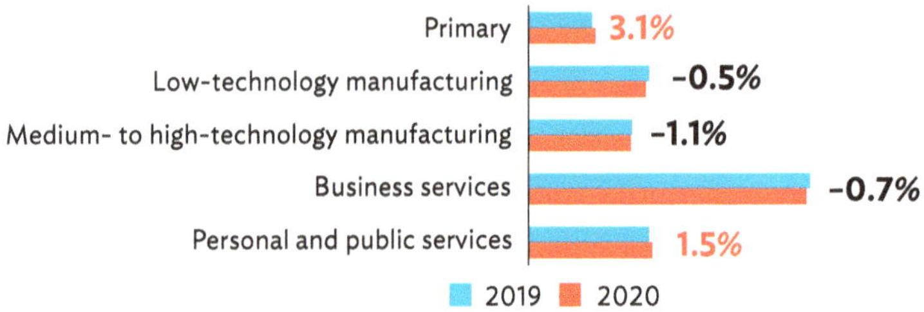

...but the primary sector (agriculture and mining) and personal and public services (government services, community, social, health, education) experienced growth in 2020.

In 2020, economies in the region generally increased their **output multipliers** across sectors.

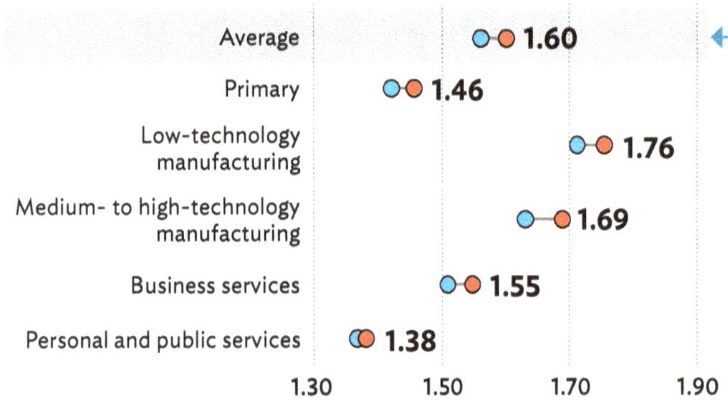

For every **$1** unit of demand, on average, **$0.6** more units were produced economy-wide.

Gross output of the 25 economies in 2020 reached **$72,222** billion.

Direct demand declined by 2.3% from 2019

but *production-induced* effects grew by 3.0%.

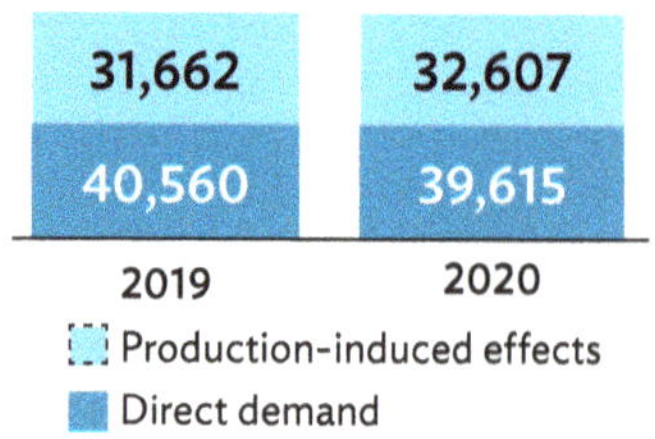

The region's sum of trade contracted by 7% in 2020.

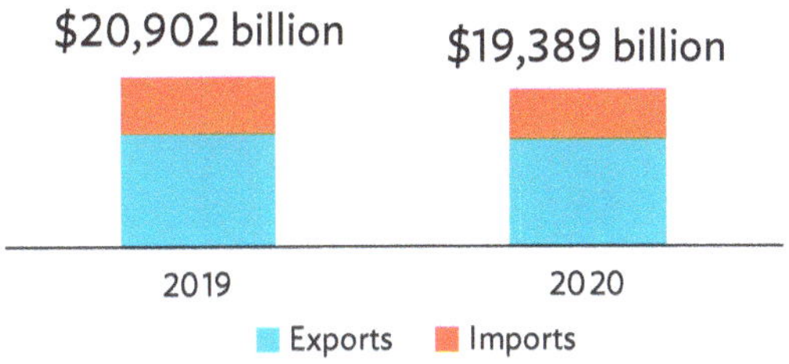

By subregional grouping:
East Asia's total trade declined by **4.5%**,
South and Central Asia by **13.7%**, and
Southeast Asia and the Pacific by **12.5%**.

Similarly, 2020 saw reduced trade-to-GDP ratios across the subregional groupings.

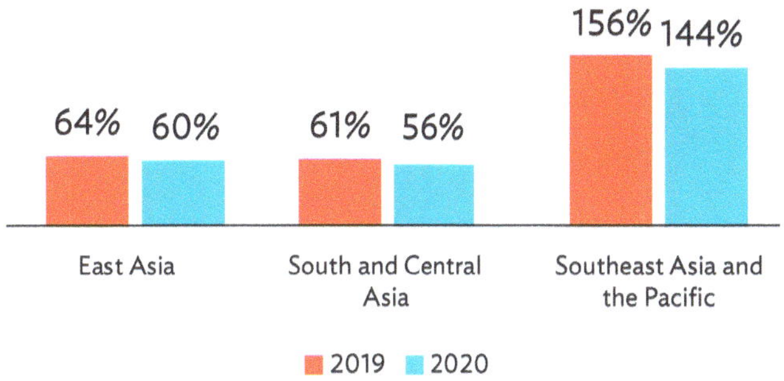

Lower trade in 2020 influenced **participation in global value chains.**

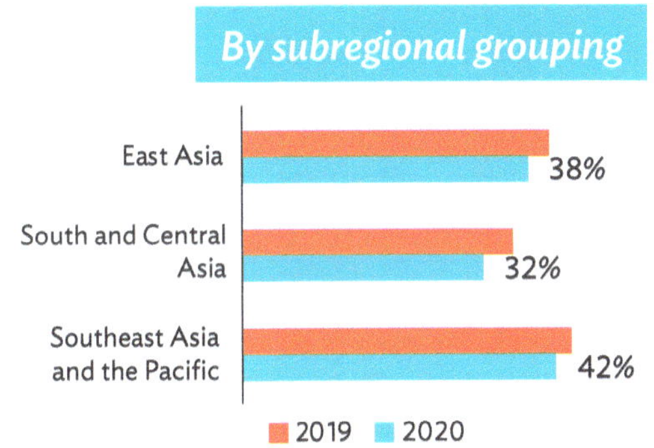

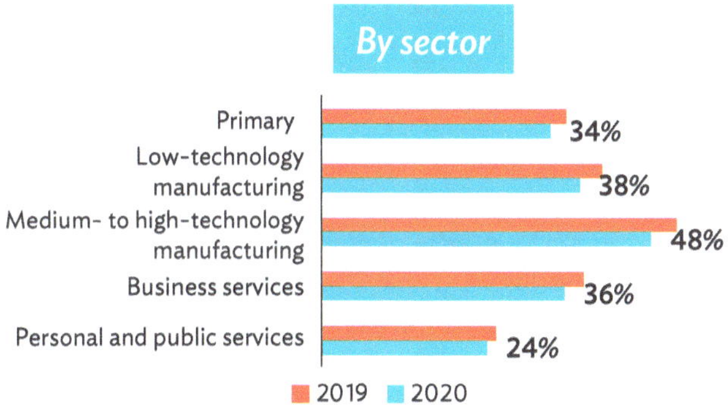

Limited participation led exporting economies to lose some **revealed comparative advantages** (RCA) across sectors, except in primary products.

	Primary sector	Low-technology manufacturing	Medium to high technology manufacturing	Business services	Personal and public services
RCA based on value-added exports in 2020	1.79	**1.23**	0.77	**1.24**	0.83
Difference from 2019	+0.25	−0.03	−0.0	−0.02	−0.07

However, domestic markets compensated for the slowdown in trade as evidenced by average increases in **domestic agglomeration.**

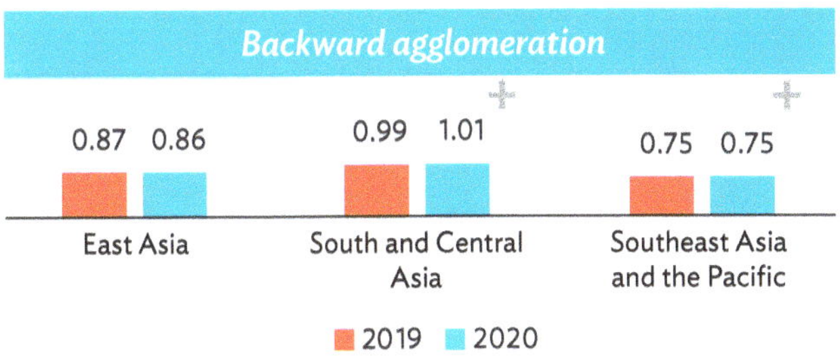

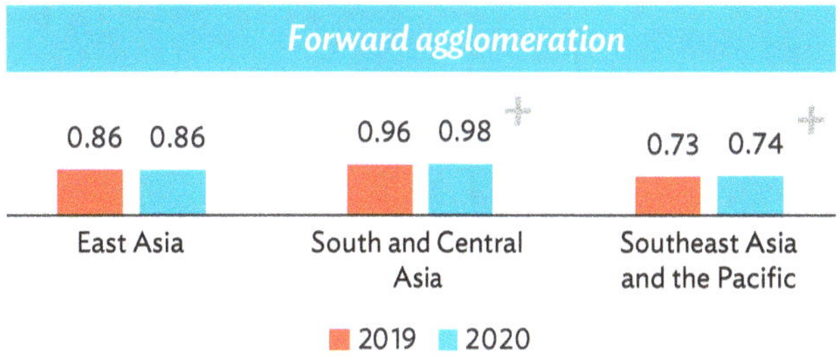

SPECIAL APPLICATIONS OF THE INPUT-OUTPUT FRAMEWORK

COVID-19

While economies in 2020 generally performed worse than the previous year by observed measures, the **COVID-19 pandemic** also disrupted economies' growth trajectories, leaving potential gains in output, value-added, and employment unrealized.

GROSS OUTPUT

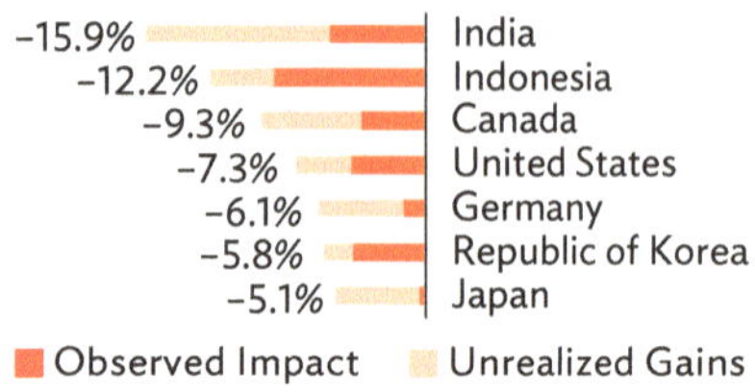

In terms of output, India suffered a decline of **15.9%** from 2019 to 2020, while Japan contracted by about **5.1%**, with the majority of these declines attributable to unrealized gains.

The Republic of Korea showed a modest increase of **0.3%** in value-added, but the economy's potential gains of about **3.4%** in 2020 were *not* realized due to the pandemic, thereby netting a negative impact of **3.2%**.

VALUE-ADDED

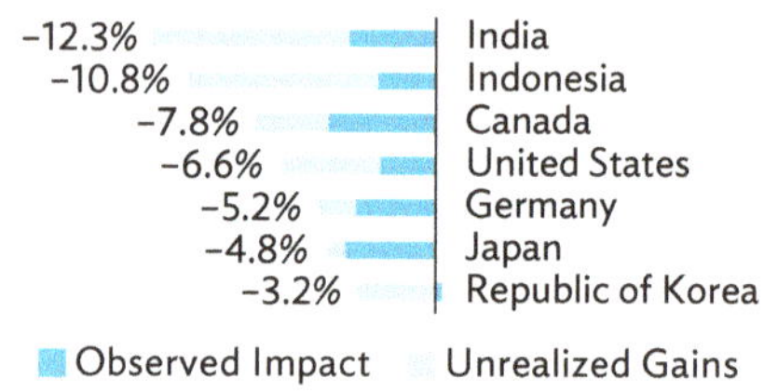

DIGITAL ECONOMY

Digital economies in the region ranged from **1.5%** to **18.6%** of respective economy-wide GDP in 2020.

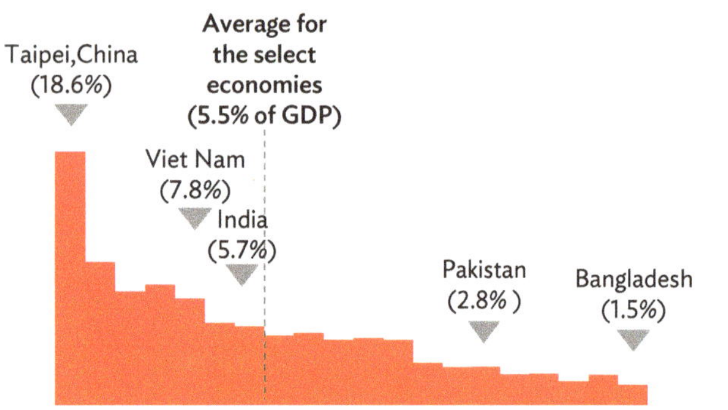

Digital GDP = value-added embedded in supply and use of primary producers of goods and services with the main function of generating, processing, and/or storing digitized data.

Some economies were predominantly **digital goods-producing**, such as:

Taipei,China
Viet Nam

while some were mainly engaged in software and **digital services**, such as:

India
Pakistan

Broadly, economies in the region showed high activities in **telecommunications**.

REAL ESTATE

The real estate sector in economies of Asia and the Pacific exhibited wide-ranging shares of total GDP, with the highest proportion recorded in the People's Republic of China.

On average, shares of real estate activities to GDP were higher in more advanced economies compared to select economies of developing Asia.

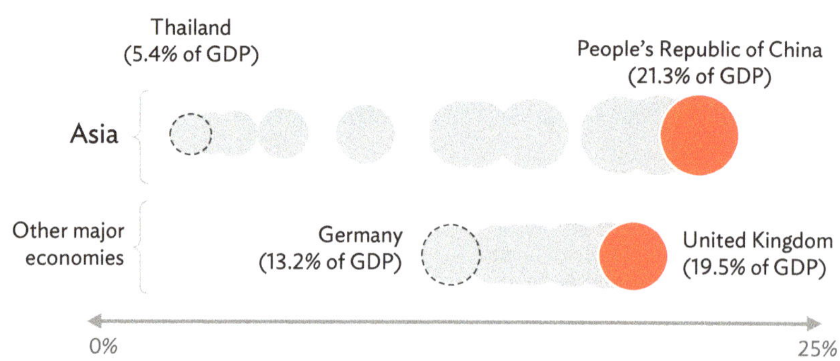

Introduction

1

This chapter introduces the ADB Multiregional Input-Output database, which underpins all statistical and analytical indicators in this report. The sources and methods for compiling the multiregional input-output tables are briefly described, as are some of the key practices for addressing limitations in the data. These tables span economic data on both national and international transactions and are therefore applicable in various analyses of an economy. Results from some of these applications are featured in this publication, including the national input-output tables for 25 economies in Asia and the Pacific.

1.1 Background on the Use of Input-Output Tables

Input-output tables (IOTs) serve many purposes. Accounts of their first use date back to the late 1930s, particularly to assist with post-war recovery and central planning. Wassily Leontief, the pioneer of input-output analysis, used these tables in the 1960s to determine how to sustain employment in the United States economy as the government withdrew from high military spending (Dietzenbacher and Lahr 2004; Mukhopadhyay 2018). Other major economies undertook similar exercises in the early years of IOTs—from production targeting in the centrally planned economies of the Soviet Union to incentivizing predetermined sectors in the market economies of France and the Netherlands (Lequiller and Blades 2014).

The use of IOTs evolved to become a framework for income accounting and they have since been applied to the analyses of issues such as trade, investments, employment, and productivity. At the turn of the millennium, IOTs continued to be relevant in analyzing novel issues, including global value chains, robotics and artificial intelligence, human health and wellness, disasters and pandemics, digitalization, gender equity, and climate change, among many others. While the applications of IOTs can be diverse, the common theme through all the analyses is the concept of intersectoral linkages and how these can define movements of shocks and flows of economic value in a system.

Particularly, IOTs make visible the unintended consequences that certain policy actions can have and, more importantly, determine the mechanisms that underlie these impacts. Insights from the use of IOTs remain relevant and continue to challenge the convention on a wide range of economic issues. For example, unilateral border closures could impact other seemingly unaffected national economies; bilateral trade policies could benefit or disadvantage third-party economies; the imposition of tariffs could impact the host economy. Meanwhile, in modern economies, small domestic producers can be part of large-scale, multinational production. Goods are becoming embedded with more intangibles than physical inputs. Digital service relies as much on hardware as it does on software. Economies can go carbonless, but still account for a sizable portion of pollution. Being able to establish and analyze connections between supply and demand, sources and destinations, and inputs and outputs is the hallmark of input-output analysis.

All these insights originate from the notion of interconnectedness in the modern economy. By constructing a disaggregated picture of the economy, IOTs can be useful in tracing the flows of goods and services that link any one region or sector to another. These linkages emerge from the supply and use relations of each sector with other sectors in the economy. For example, cotton is cultivated as an agricultural commodity. It is then processed to separate the lint and the seed. The lint is then converted into yarn, and the yarn into fabric. As these activities appear across different industries, the IOTs enable users to trace the value-added from growing the cotton to manufacturing the eventual fabric.

The same concept may be applied regardless of where these transactions take place. By identifying not only the specific industry from which value-added originates but also the economy (or region) where value addition takes place, one can easily see how the cotton grown in Pakistan is processed and transformed to fabrics in Viet Nam. This combination of national and international flows of products provides a powerful tool for analysis of global trade, global value chains, and many other extensions. An excellent introduction to input–output analysis is provided in Miller and Blair (2009), while a brief background is explained in ADB's *Economic Indicators: Input-Output Tables* (2018; 2020).

1.2 Objectives of this Publication

Given the relevance and wide range of applications for IOTs, this publication intends to present economic statistics and model-based indicators derived from such tables to stimulate research and collaboration in this field. It is the third release of a compendium of reports that includes *Economic Indicators for East Asia: Input–Output Tables; Economic Indicators for Southeastern Asia and the Pacific: Input–Output Tables;* and *Economic Indicators for South and Central Asia: Input–Output Tables.*[1] In this edition, new statistics on production linkages, multipliers, and global value chains are presented along with the indicators that come with standard input–output analyses. More notably, this release extends the period covered by previous editions to include data for the years 2019 and 2020.

1 To access IOT reports for 2018, 2020, and 2022, go to https://www.adb.org/publications/series/economic-indicators-input-output-tables.

As a statistical compendium, this publication centralizes and documents efforts by ADB to contribute to the growing knowledge of input–output analysis. It is not only intended to complement the study of intersectoral and international production systems, but also to encourage the development and expansion of input–output literature. Overall, the objective is to provide statistical evidence of the complex and dynamic nature of economic production and its interlinked relationships.

Given the extensive applicability of IOTs, the suite of indicators presented in this edition is divided into two major sections: domestic linkages and international linkages. A demonstration of these indicators' potential uses can be found in Chapters 2 and 3.

This release also features special chapters on three topical economic issues. The chapter on COVID-19 documents the observed and unrealized economic performance of Asian economies at the onset of the pandemic in late 2019 through to the end of 2020. This is followed by a chapter presenting statistical indicators that define and measure the size of core digital industries in select economies of the Asia and Pacific region. A third special chapter measures the extent of economic growth that is driven by activities related to real estate in several major economies (both within and outside the region).

These special chapters are followed by economy profiles that present broad statistical results and indicators for each of the 25 participating economies in Asia and the Pacific.

The publication concludes with a technical description and mathematical formulation for each indicator generated for this report. Readers seeking further details and specific directions for replicating these results are directed to the sources indicated in the Technical Notes.

All datasets, including IOTs for each economy, may be accessed electronically by users through the regional input–output tables webpage on ADB.org website. Please note that the data presented in this publication are not official statistics and are intended for research purposes only.

1.3 Multiregional Input–Output Tables

Underpinning all the indicators presented in this publication are IOTs derived primarily from ADB's Multiregional Input–Output (MRIO) database.[2] Since 2014, the MRIO database has been part of regular statistical releases by ADB. It builds strongly on the bank's Regional Capacity Development Technical Assistance (R-CDTA) 8838: Updating and Constructing Supply and Use Tables for Selected Developing Member Economies,

2 These tables produced by the ADB MRIO database team can be accessed through https://mrio.adbx.online/.

from which several economies were able to produce benchmark supply and use tables (SUTs). These official SUTs serve as the core building blocks of the multiregional input-output tables (MRIOTs) and the basis for national input–output tables (NIOTs).[3]

The MRIO database contains a series of MRIOTs that provide a detailed view of economic relationships between 35 sectors of 62 distinct economies (which covered about 90% of global GDP as of 2020) plus a region labeled "rest of the world" (which proxies for all remaining economies). These tables build upon the World Input-Output Database (WIOD) published by the Groningen Growth and Development Centre (Timmer et al. 2015). The original 2016 release of WIOD covered 43 economies (6 of which were from Asia) for periods 2000 to 2014. With outcomes from the RCDTA 8838, the WIOD tables were then augmented to include 19 more economies from developing Asia. This initiative completed the 25 economies from the region that are featured in this publication (6 from WIOD and 19 from the ADB RCDTA 8838).

The simplified structure of the MRIO framework in this release is illustrated in Table 1.1, showing only three regions: economies A and B, and the rest of the world. This basic outline may be generalized for the 62 economies plus one region of the MRIO. In contrast to NIOTs, each use (in columns) is now split into rows separating products from

Table 1.1: Simplified Schematic of the Multiregional Input–Output Table

		Economy A	Economy B	Rest of the World	Economy A	Economy B	Rest of the World	Total
		Intermediate Use			Final Use			
Economy	Industry	c1...c35	c1...c35	c1...c35	F1...F5	F1...F5	F1...F5	
Economy A	c1 ⋮ c35	Intermediate use of domestic output	Intermediate use by B of exports from A	Intermediate use by RoW of exports from A	Final use of domestic output	Final use by B of exports from A	Final use by RoW of exports from A	Output of A
Economy B	c1 ⋮ c35	Intermediate use by A of exports from B	Intermediate use of domestic output	Intermediate use by RoW of exports from B	Final use by A of exports from B	Final use of domestic output	Final use by RoW of exports from B	Output of B
Rest of the World	c1 ⋮ c35	Intermediate use by A of exports from RoW	Intermediate use by B of exports from RoW	Intermediate use of domestic output	Final use by A of exports from RoW	Final use by B of exports from RoW	Final use of domestic output	Output of RoW
		Value-added of A	Value-added of B	Value-added of RoW				
		Output of A	Output of B	Output of RoW				

RoW = rest of the world.

Source: M. Timmer (ed.), A.A. Erumban, R. Gouma, B. Los, U. Temurshoev, G.J. de Vries, I. Arto, V.A.A Genty, F. Neuwahl, J.M. Rueda-Cantuche, A. Villanueva, J. Francois, O. Pindyuk, J. Poschl, R. Stehrer, and G. Streicher. 2012. The World Input-Output Database (WIOD): Contents, Sources, and Methods. IIDE Discussion Papers. No. 20120401. Institute for International and Development Economics.

3 The structure of supply-use tables differs in each compiling economy. As necessary, these official tables are harmonized to a common statistical classification of products and sectors and are subsequently transformed to input-output tables following the industry technology assumption ("Model D") discussed in European Commission (2008).

domestic and foreign origin. Meanwhile, each supply (in rows) is also split according to destination (i.e., domestic or foreign) and use (i.e., intermediate or final use).

This integration of national and international flows of products enables a comprehensive analysis of global production at a sectoral scale. As such, the MRIO database continues to be in demand for a wide range of applications and practical analyses of developments in the global economy. Notably, relevant topics include trade analysis, economic integration, tourism, impact evaluation of development policies and projects, and progress in gender equity, among others. MRIOTs have been used in key reports by international organizations and serve as the main source for regularly producing trade and global value chain statistics in ADB's flagship publication *Key Indicators for Asia and the Pacific*.[4]

1.4 Constructing the Multiregional Input–Output Tables

To better appreciate the statistics in this report, the underlying data sources and methods for the MRIOTs are introduced. Broadly speaking, the MRIOT construction process starts with NIOTs as the core building blocks. These tables are then linked across economies through detailed bilateral international trade statistics to construct the symmetric MRIOTs.

A broad overview of the compilation process of the MRIOTs is provided in Figure 1.1. The compilation starts with the collection of data from national and international sources, which are then processed to ensure consistency with statistical classifications and standard valuations. Once data are harmonized into a common format and valuation, the domestic (or national) and bilateral trade transactions are consolidated into a single compilation framework. This process allows examination of consistency among different statistical sources, thereby providing meaningful feedback on the quality of the underlying data. A preliminary balanced table is produced from a combination of manual and minimal automated balancing. These tables undergo a series of checks, primarily to investigate if the levels and changes in the table reflect economic reality. In addition, analytical models are replicated using these preliminary tables to address any potential errors that users may encounter. An example of these exercises includes checks using the value-added trade accounting discussed in Chapter 3.

Three main types of data are used in the entire process, namely SUTs, national accounts statistics (NAS), and international trade statistics. The data are sourced from officially published releases by national statistics offices (NSOs) as these figures typically undergo thorough validation procedures conducted at each NSO.

4 To access *Key Indicators for Asia and the Pacific for 2015–2021*, go to https://www.adb.org/publications/series/key-indicators-for-asia-and-the-pacific.

Figure 1.1: Simplified Process for the Compilation of Multiregional Input–Output Tables

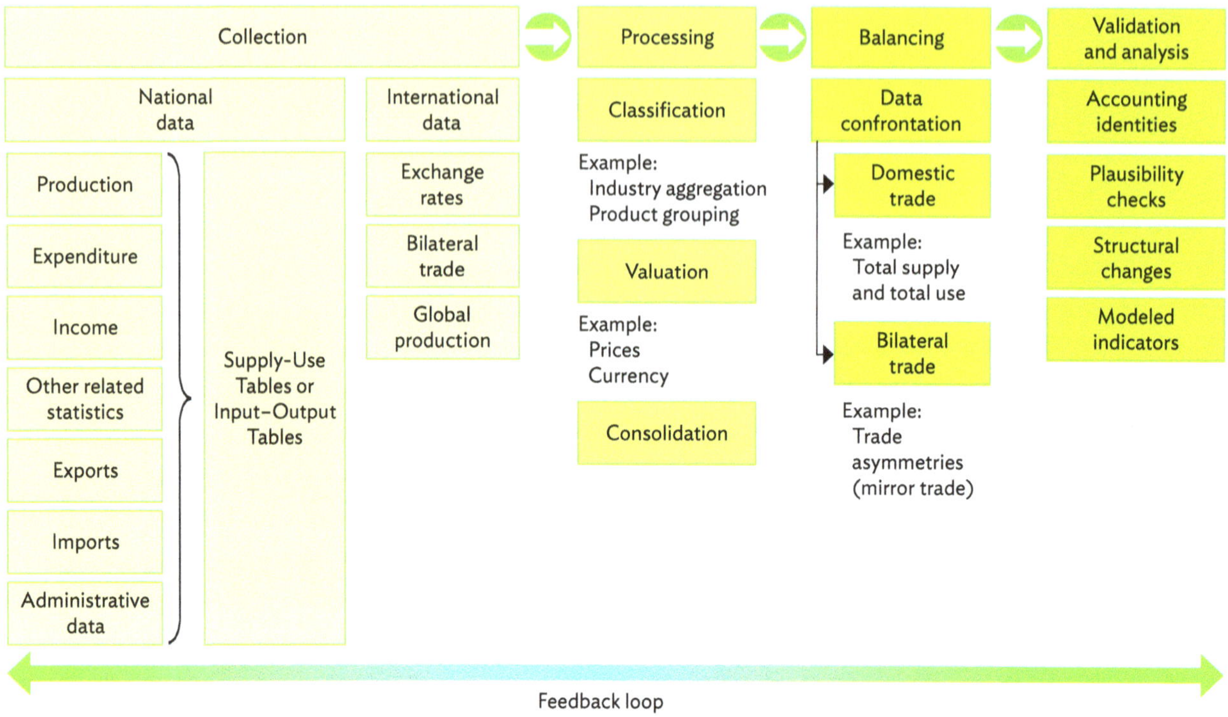

Source: Asian Development Bank Multiregional Input–Output Database Team.

1.4.1 Constructing the Domestic Tables

The first two data types—SUTs or IOTs and NAS—serve to fulfill the main diagonal blocks of the MRIOT in Table 1.1. In principle, these two data sources should be no different from each other, since SUTs serve as a compilation framework for NAS. In practice, however, SUTs are constructed infrequently due to the data- and resource-intensive nature of their compilation. As such, most NSOs undertake SUT-related initiatives every 3 or 5 years.[5] Moreover, when SUTs are available for certain years, these may not necessarily be comparable over time, with changes in the interim comprising both movements in the real economy and revisions in statistical practices. Since SUT compilation takes significant time, revisions might have already taken place in the national accounts, while the historical SUTs have not been updated. Hence, it is not uncommon to see some differences in the gross domestic product (GDP) figures between SUTs and NAS. Intermediate steps are therefore taken to update and harmonize SUTs based on consistent time-series from NAS.

5 A more detailed documentation of the compilation process is provided in ADB (2017) Compendium of Supply and Use Tables for Selected Economies in Asia and the Pacific (https://www.adb.org/publications/compendium-supply-use-tables-selected-economies).

To update SUTs or IOTs, time-series data on gross output, value-added by industry, taxes less subsidies on products, imports and exports, and final use by category are the minimum requirements (Table 1.2). The data are obtained from NSOs and, when available, are compared against international databases of the Organisation for Economic Co-operation and Development (OECD), Eurostat, United Nations (UN) National Accounts Statistics, and ADB. As SUTs and NAS are in national currencies, the figures are converted to a common basis (United States dollars) using official exchange rates from the International Monetary Fund's International Finance Statistics.

Table 1.2: Minimum National Accounts Statistics for Compilation of Multiregional Input–Output Tables

Production Approach	Gross output by industry
	Gross value-added by industry
	Intermediate consumption by industry
	Net taxes on products
Expenditure Approach	Household final consumption expenditure
	Final consumption expenditure of NPISH
	Government final consumption expenditure
	Changes in inventories and acquisitions less disposals of valuables
	Gross fixed capital formation
	Exports of goods
	Exports of services
	Imports of goods
	Imports of services
Main Aggregate	Gross domestic product

NPISH = nonprofit institution serving households.
Source: Asian Development Bank Multiregional Input–Output Database Team.

Further, the data must be harmonized to a common industry classification. The current structure of the MRIOTs observes the International Standard Industrial Classification revision 3.1 (ISIC Rev. 3.1). For each classification variant, corresponding tables are built to link sectors in each national SUT and NAS to the level of detail and classifications in the MRIOT. This process involves aggregation when more detailed (sectoral) data are available. Conversely, disaggregation is needed when data are not published at the desired level of detail. As a general principle, the MRIO database prioritizes the use of published NSO data for disaggregation. Examples of these sources are turnover data from establishment surveys; economic censuses; merchandise, trade, construction, and industry statistics; and extended balance of payments statistics. In other cases, detailed data from other input–output databases are used, such as those from the OECD intercountry input–output tables (ICIOTs), Eurostat ICIOTs, or modeled estimates released in various statistical publications.

The list of these sectors and their relationship to sectoral aggregation is given in Table 1.3 (note that short titles for these sectors are also used in this report for brevity and ease of presentation). The level of detail adopts the detail of the 2013 release of WIOD, which was chosen based on maximum available data at the NSO level while minimizing the need for assumptions to split industries to more granular subsets. Throughout this publication, note that these sectors may be shown at higher levels of aggregation for ease of presentation.

Table 1.3: List of Sectors in the Multiregional Input–Output Tables

Code	35-Sector Aggregation	15-Sector Aggregation	5-Sector Aggregation
c1	Agriculture, hunting, forestry, and fishing	Agriculture, hunting, forestry, and fishing	Primary
c2	Mining and quarrying	Mining and quarrying	Primary
c3	Food, beverages, and tobacco	Light manufacturing	Low-technology manufacturing
c4	Textiles and textile products	Light manufacturing	Low-technology manufacturing
c5	Leather, leather products, and footwear	Light manufacturing	Low-technology manufacturing
c6	Wood and products of wood and cork	Light manufacturing	Low-technology manufacturing
c7	Pulp, paper, paper products, printing, and publishing	Light manufacturing	Low-technology manufacturing
c8	Coke, refined petroleum, and nuclear fuel	Heavy manufacturing	Medium- to high-technology manufacturing
c9	Chemicals and chemical products	Heavy manufacturing	Medium- to high-technology manufacturing
c10	Rubber and plastics	Light manufacturing	Low-technology manufacturing
c11	Other nonmetallic minerals	Light manufacturing	Medium- to high-technology manufacturing
c12	Basic metals and fabricated metal	Heavy manufacturing	Medium- to high-technology manufacturing
c13	Machinery, nec	Heavy manufacturing	Medium- to high-technology manufacturing
c14	Electrical and optical equipment	Heavy manufacturing	Medium- to high-technology manufacturing
c15	Transport equipment	Heavy manufacturing	Medium- to high-technology manufacturing
c16	Manufacturing, nec; recycling	Light manufacturing	Low-technology manufacturing
c17	Electricity, gas, and water supply	Utilities	Low-technology manufacturing
c18	Construction	Construction	Low-technology manufacturing
c19	Sale, maintenance, and repair of motor vehicles and motorcycles; retail sale of fuel	Trade services	Business services
c20	Wholesale trade and commission trade, except of motor vehicles and motorcycles	Trade services	Business services
c21	Retail trade, except of motor vehicles and motorcycles; repair of household goods	Trade services	Business services
c22	Hotels and restaurants	Hotels and restaurants	Business services
c23	Inland transport	Transport services	Business services
c24	Water transport	Transport services	Business services
c25	Air transport	Transport services	Business services
c26	Other supporting and auxiliary transport activities; activities of travel agencies	Transport services	Business services
c27	Post and telecommunications	Telecommunications	Business services
c28	Financial intermediation	Financial intermediation	Business services
c29	Real estate activities	Real estate, renting, and business activities	Business services
c30	Renting of M&Eq and other business activities	Real estate, renting, and business activities	Business services

continued on next page.

Table 1.3 *continued.*

Code	35-Sector Aggregation	15-Sector Aggregation	5-Sector Aggregation
c31	Public administration and defense; compulsory social security	Public administration and defense	Personal and public services
c32	Education	Education, health, and social work	Personal and public services
c33	Health and social work	Education, health, and social work	Personal and public services
c34	Other community, social, and personal services	Other personal services	Personal and public services
c35	Private households with employed persons	Other personal services	Personal and public services

M&Eq = machinery and equipment; nec = not elsewhere classified
Source: Asian Development Bank Multiregional Input–Output Database Team.

After processing and harmonizing the NAS, these figures serve as the basis for estimating unbalanced intersectoral transactions for nonbenchmark years, particularly by using direct input coefficients of benchmark SUTs and/or IOTs. This constructs an initial table that undergoes a series of validation and consistency checks to adhere to accounting identities in the SUT or IOT as well as the control totals derived from NAS indicated in Table 1.2.

1.4.2 Constructing the Bilateral Trade Matrixes

A second crucial component of the MRIOT is the bilateral trade matrix. These matrixes link one economy's export values to a trade partner's import values. The basic data requirement of bilateral trade matrixes are the flows of imports and exports of all economies covered in the MRIOT from all partners in the world at the Harmonized System (HS) 6-digit product level, taken from the UN Comtrade database and OECD Balanced International Trade in Services. However, bilateral trade flows of imports and exports are not always consistent due to time lags and differences in coverage, method, valuation, classification, and reporting procedures across economies. Following Timmer et al. (2015), the MRIOT prioritizes the use of imports data as these are scrutinized by NSOs and central banks.

The HS product codes describe the "sectoral" classification of the product (i.e., which of the 35 sectors exports the product) as well as its use (i.e., how and where the product was used). The codes are mapped out from HS 2002 to ISIC 3.1 classification using conversion and correlation tables published by the UN Statistical Division. The detailed product level codes are also classified based on the "use" categories—intermediates, final consumption, and investment—using the correspondence between HS6 codes and the Broad Economic Categories. While still not at the detailed "use" level desired, the Broad Economic Categories classification allows for a theoretical allocation of intermediate goods flow versus its final consumption.

For services trade, bilateral flows are mainly collected from the World Trade Organization, UN Comtrade, and the OECD's Balanced Trade in Services dataset. This dataset contains detailed trade data for 12 standard services sectors and a total for commercial services. It provides both reported and balanced figures that reconcile previously asymmetrical export and import data. Concordance is set up between balance of payments codes and the MRIOT sector list to allocate the services trade flows.

The datasets from international organizations on goods imports by use and trade partner as well as services imports by trade partner are further disaggregated into receiving industries in the importing economy using the general structure from the import use matrix compiled at the national level. These import use matrixes are obtained from benchmark or annual SUTs and/or IOTs. Analogously, goods and services exports by trade partner are allocated across receiving industries in the importing economy using export matrixes from Eurostat's Full International and Global Accounts for Research in Input–Output Analysis, OECD ICIOTs, Eora MRIOTs, and the UN Economic Commission for Latin America and the Caribbean[6] and Institute of Applied Economic Research's South American IOTs. The combined bilateral trade flows are compared and checked for consistency with the balance of payments statistics published by NSOs and/or monetary authorities as well as other international databases.

Once domestic and bilateral trade matrixes are completed for all products, uses, and trade partners, these trade flows must be reconciled and balanced based on row (i.e., export by product) and column (imports by sector). In most cases, manual balancing is preferred over automated algorithms and iterative proportional fitting methods, as it allows for a closer evaluation of underlying sources, trade asymmetries, and outliers within the time series. The reconciliation process also uses mirror trade figures, while still considering valuation differences. The balancing process is also performed separately for domestic and bilateral trade matrixes to ensure that domestic and international flows are consistent with the control figures. Automated balancing is performed only when the discrepancies are diminished to low tolerable figures. Consistency and plausibility checks are conducted after balancing to minimize potential errors in the data.

1.4.3 Rest of the World

Completing the MRIOT requires a region called "the rest of the world" (RoW), which encompasses all economies in the world aside from the 62 "visible" economies in the MRIOT. This region's "domestic" or intra-RoW transactions are obtained residually. They are estimated by taking the world GDP in a particular year minus the total GDP

6 The UN Economic Commission for Latin America and the Caribbean is also known by its Spanish acronym, CEPAL, which stands for Comisión Económica para América Latina y el Caribe.

of all 62 economies in the MRIO database. The residual GDP serves as a basis for deriving gross output in the region, which is then used to populate "domestic" or intra-RoW intermediate and final uses following the approach of Timmer et al. (2012).

Meanwhile, the external trade of the 62 economies with RoW are derived residually. That is, exports from RoW are simply the imports by each economy from the world minus imports from the 62 visible economies. Similarly, imports to RoW are derived as the total exports from each economy to the world minus exports to the 62 economies. By extension, each economy's exports to 62 other economies plus RoW should sum to its total exports to the world. Adding RoW matrixes to the 62 economies completes the IOT for the world economy.

1.5 National Input–Output Tables

As previously discussed, the MRIOT is structured such that the domestic transactions of each economy fall into the main diagonal blocks of the entire matrix, with the off-diagonals representing the explicit trade links of one economy to another (Table 1.1). These bilateral trade links, both imports and exports, can therefore be aggregated in a standard fashion of a NIOT. These national-based tables are more likely to be used in analysis focusing on domestic industries and their sale and purchase relationships. In contrast, MRIOTs are often used in the analysis of regional trade and analysis of economic events that may have international repercussions. NIOTs, however, are the most available type of IOTs as MRIOTs (or ICIOTs) often require some form of multilateral effort to harmonize and link various national economic statistics.

NIOTs on their own still provide a comprehensive account of the domestic economy by describing the flows of goods and services from one sector to another. As such, these tables facilitate a wide range of industry-based analysis, economic planning, and the statistical compilation of GDP (UN 2018). The following chapter provides a preview of these analyses that can be performed using NIOTs, with particular interest in statistics that characterize the internal structure and performance of domestic sectors in an economy.

References

Asian Development Bank (ADB). 2017. *Compendium of Supply and Use Tables for Selected Economies in Asia and the Pacific*. Manila: Asian Development Bank. https://www.adb.org/publications/compendium-supply-use-tables-selected-economies.

ADB. *Key Indicators for Asia and the Pacific. Manila (7 years: 2015–2021)*. Manila: Asian Development Bank. https://www.adb.org/publications/series/key-indicators-for-asia-and-the-pacific.

ADB. 2018. *Economic Indicators: Input–Output Tables: December 2018*. Manila: Asian Development Bank. https://www.adb.org/publications/series/economic-indicators-input-output-tables.

ADB. 2020. *Economic Indicators: Input–Output Tables: December 2020*. Manila: Asian Development Bank. https://www.adb.org/publications/series/economic-indicators-input-output-tables.

E. Dietzenbacher and M. L. Lahr (eds.). 2004. *Wassily Leontief and Input–Output Economics*. New York: Cambridge University Press, pp. 9–29.

European Commission. 2018. *Eurostat Manual of Supply, Use and Input–Output Tables*. Luxembourg: Office for Official Publications of the European Communities

F. Lequiller and D. Blades. 2014. *Understanding National Accounts*. Second edition. Paris: OECD Publishing.

R.E. Miller and P.D. Blair. 2009. *Input–Output Analysis: Foundations and Extensions*. Second edition. Cambridge, UK: Cambridge University Press.

K. Mukhopadhyay (ed.). 2018. *Applications of the Input–Output Framework*. Singapore: Springer Proceedings in Business and Economics.

M. Timmer (ed.), A.A. Erumban, R. Gouma, B. Los, U. Temurshoev, G.J. de Vries, I. Arto, V.A.A Genty, F. Neuwahl, J.M. Rueda-Cantuche, A. Villanueva, J. Francois, O. Pindyuk, J. Poschl, R. Stehrer, and G. Streicher. 2012. The World Input–Output Database (WIOD): Contents, Sources, and Methods. *IIDE Discussion Papers*. No. 20120401. Institute for International and Development Economics.

M. Timmer, E. Dietzenbacher, B. Los, R. Stehrer, and G. de Vries. 2015. An Illustrated User Guide to the World Input–Output Database: the Case of Global Automotive Production. *Review of International Economics*. 23 (3). pp. 575–605.

United Nations (UN). 2018. *Handbook on Supply, Use and Input–Output Tables with Extensions and Applications*. Studies in Methods. New York: United Nations.

Domestic Multipliers and Linkages

2

This chapter introduces a set of statistical and analytical indicators derived from national input–output tables. At minimum, these indicators characterize the productive structure of the economy from the point of view of its domestic sectors. The discussion progresses from the set of basic economic aggregates to more complex indicators that exploit detailed sale and purchase interactions among domestic industries. These interactions, commonly referred to as linkages, serve as the basis for quantifying the localized economic impacts of a given demand or supply shock.

2.1 Core Economic Indicators

Input–output tables (IOTs) are traditionally used in national economic planning. Applications of IOTs, especially before the rise of global trade activity, have been focused mostly on understanding domestic industries and their interrelationships. At the rudimentary level, an IOT framework divides the economy into several known sectors. Each sector's output and income are presented, along with the sector's intermediate and final demand for its products. National input–output tables model observed data on the flows of products from each of the sectors (as a producer and/or seller) to each of the sectors (as a purchaser and/or buyer) within a single economy for a given period (usually a year). These figures are based on the monetary values of transactions between pairs of productive sectors and from productive sectors to external purchasers (households, governments, foreign economies).

Summing the values of all sectors' value-added or final demand in the economy results in the gross domestic product (GDP). These figures are regularly presented in national accounts statistics and used frequently in the study of an economy's performance and its sources of growth. Since the IOT framework integrates the production- and expenditure-based measures of GDP, one can directly examine and compare the economy's composition from those two accounting methods.

Consider Figure 2.1 below. The chart shows the composition of each economy from the demand perspective, as represented by the shares of private consumption, government consumption, gross capital formation, and exports in the total final demand for each economy for 2019 and 2020.

Figure 2.1: Composition of Final Demand of Select Economies in Asia and the Pacific, by Subregion
(% of GDP)

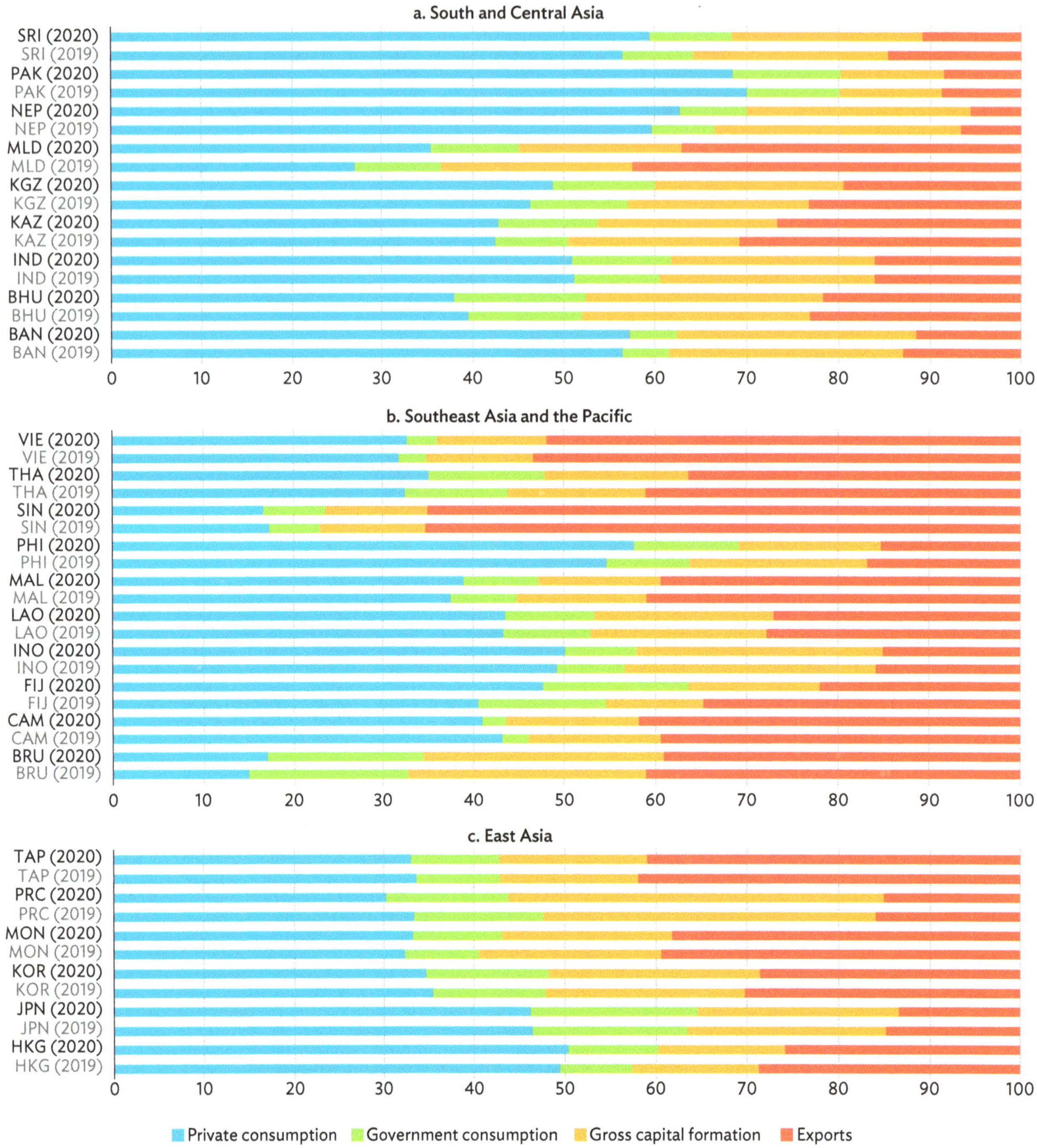

BAN = Bangladesh; BHU = Bhutan; BRU = Brunei Darussalam; CAM = Cambodia; FIJ = Fiji; GDP = gross domestic product; HKG = Hong Kong, China; IND = India; INO = Indonesia; JPN = Japan; KAZ = Kazakhstan; KGZ = Kyrgyz Republic; KOR = Republic of Korea; LAO = Lao People's Democratic Republic; MAL = Malaysia; MLD = Maldives; MON = Mongolia; NEC = Not elsewhere classified; NEP = Nepal; PAK = Pakistan; PHI = Philippines; PRC = People's Republic of China; SIN = Singapore; SRI = Sri Lanka; TAP = Taipei,China; THA = Thailand; VIE = Viet Nam

Note: East Asia is comprised of Hong Kong, China; Japan; Mongolia; the People's Republic of China; the Republic of Korea; and Taipei,China. Southeast Asia and the Pacific is comprised of Brunei Darussalam; Cambodia; Fiji; Indonesia; the Lao People's Democratic Republic; Malaysia; the Philippines; Singapore; Thailand; and Viet Nam. South and Central Asia is comprised of Bangladesh; Bhutan; India; Kazakhstan; the Kyrgyz Republic; Maldives; Nepal; Pakistan; and Sri Lanka.

Source: Calculations using the Asian Development Bank Multiregional Input–Output Table for 2019 and 2020. https://mrio.adbx.online/ (accessed July 2021).

Click here for figure data

Across the 25 economies in Asia and the Pacific that participated in this report, private consumption accounted for an average of 41.8% of the total final demand in 2019; gross capital formation, 19.7%; exports, 29.0%; and government consumption, 9.5%. Private consumption had the largest share in the total final demand of most economies, ranging from 15.0% to 70.0%. In 2020, its shares ranged from 16.6% to 68.5% across all economies. For both 2019 and 2020, Bangladesh, Nepal, Pakistan, Philippines, and Sri Lanka had the highest shares in terms of total final demand accounted for by private consumption. However, exports are also significant in economies such as Brunei Darussalam; Cambodia; Malaysia; Maldives; Singapore; Taipei,China; and Viet Nam.

Figure 2.2 presents the economic composition of the three subregions from the production-side, by calculating each sector's value-added share to the total. This is a common way of describing the sectoral composition of GDP and the activities that generate the most income for the economy. Across all subregions, the business services sector had the highest share in gross value-added (GVA): 40.63.% in 2019 and 40.35% in 2020. In absolute terms, business services in Southeast Asia had the highest value-added among all the subregional groupings for both years, even though the business services sectors share within the subregion decreased from 42.74% in 2019 to 41.92% in 2020. In addition, the shares of business services sectors in the respective GVAs of South and Central Asia and East Asia also decreased from 2019 to 2020.

The low- to high-technology manufacturing sectors also decreased slightly across all subregions from 2019 to 2020. This decline, however, was offset by a slight increase in the shares of the primary sector (e.g., agriculture and mining activities) as well as public and personal services (e.g., government services, social services, and other community services) across all subregions for both years. Primary sector activity rose from 9.16% in 2019 to 9.44% in 2020, while the public and personal services sector slightly increased from 17.49% in 2019 to 17.75% in 2020.

These basic economic indicators presented in the IOT framework offer additional advantages compared to regularly published figures in national accounts. First, figures obtained from the IOT have been compared with other statistics and balanced for any statistical discrepancies. This ensures that the figures are internally consistent in accordance with the accounting identities of the IOT framework. Second, the IOTs present a more disaggregated view of the economy. The final demands of the economy are shown not only by type (e.g., household consumption, government expenditure, fixed investments) but also by product. This product detail is, among other uses, often used to understand the consumption basket of households, composition of exported goods and services, and the most significant fixed assets in the economy.

Figure 2.2: Sectoral Composition of Value-Added of Select Economies in Asia and the Pacific, by Subregion
(% of GVA)

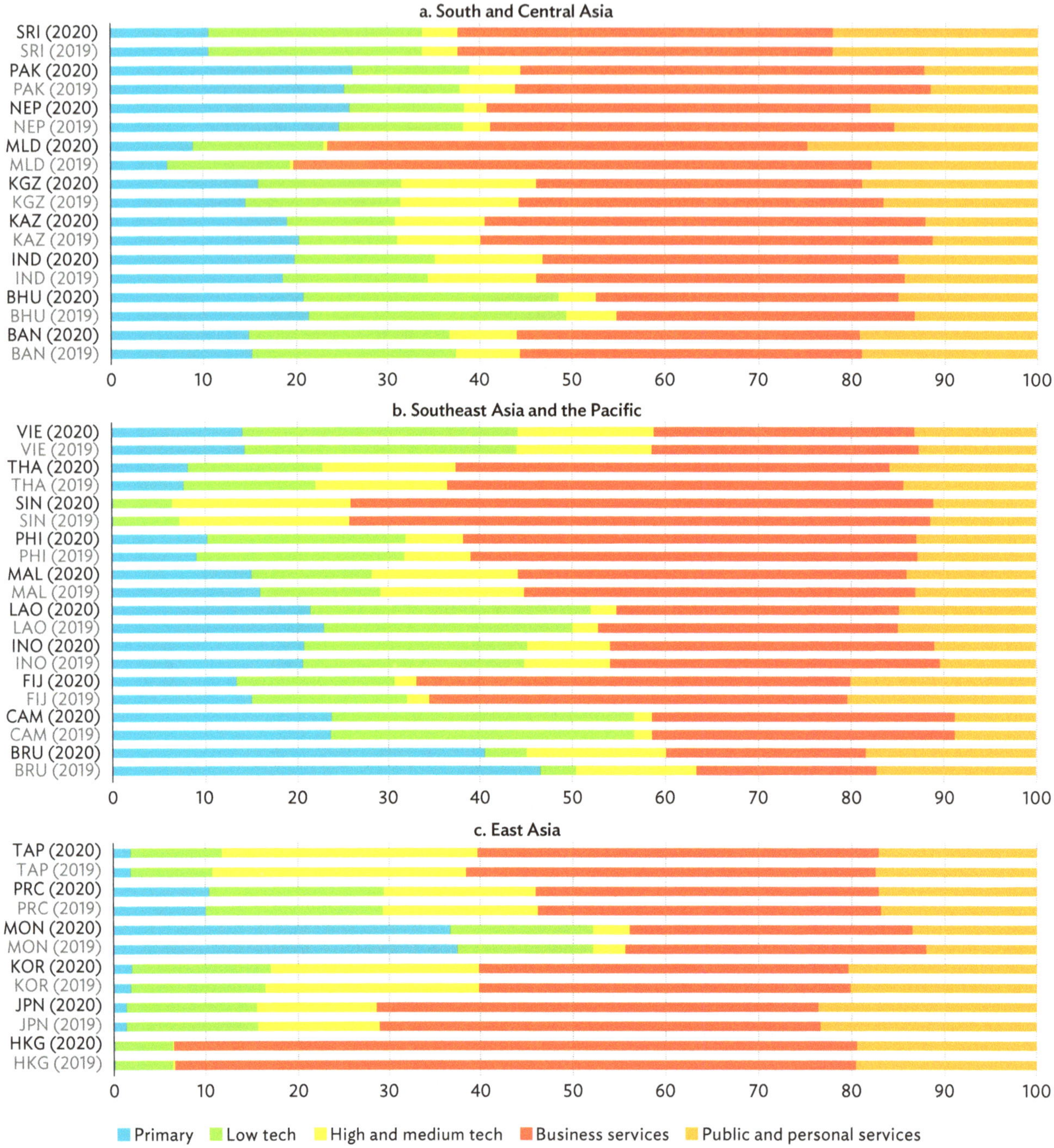

BAN = Bangladesh; BHU = Bhutan; BRU = Brunei Darussalam; CAM = Cambodia; FIJ = Fiji; H GVA = gross value-added; KG = Hong Kong, China; IND = India; INO = Indonesia; JPN = Japan; KAZ = Kazakhstan; KGZ = Kyrgyz Republic; KOR = Republic of Korea; LAO = Lao People's Democratic Republic; MAL = Malaysia; MLD = Maldives; MON = Mongolia; NEC = Not elsewhere classified; NEP = Nepal; PAK = Pakistan; PHI = Philippines; PRC = People's Republic of China; SIN = Singapore; SRI = Sri Lanka; TAP = Taipei,China; THA = Thailand; VIE = Viet Nam.

Note: East Asia is comprised of Hong Kong, China; Japan; Mongolia; the People's Republic of China; the Republic of Korea; and Taipei,China. Southeast Asia and the Pacific is comprised of Brunei Darussalam; Cambodia; Fiji; Indonesia; the Lao People's Democratic Republic; Malaysia; the Philippines; Singapore; Thailand; and Viet Nam. South and Central Asia is comprised of Bangladesh; Bhutan; India; Kazakhstan; the Kyrgyz Republic; Maldives; Nepal; Pakistan; and Sri Lanka.

Source: Calculations using the Asian Development Bank Multiregional Input–Output Table for 2019 and 2020. https://mrio.adbx.online (accessed July 2021).

Click here for figure data

Aside from final demand, IOTs present detailed intermediate consumption by sector (Table 2.1). This square (*nxn*) matrix contains information on the two roles that any given sector performs in the economy. The rows depict the "supply" perspective (i.e., sectors as sellers) by showing the flow of intermediate sales *z* from sector *i* to sector 1 to *n* in the columns, with *n* being the total number of sectors in the IOT. The columns present the "demand" perspective (i.e., sectors as buyers) by detailing what volume of inputs *z* were purchased by sector *j* from sector 1 to *n*.

Table 2.1: Intersectoral Transactions in Intermediate Goods and Services

		Buying Sectors				
		1	...	*j*	...	*n*
Selling Sectors	1	z_{11}	...	z_{1j}	...	z_{1n}
	⋮	⋮		⋮		⋮
	i	z_{i1}	...	z_{ij}	...	z_{in}
	⋮	⋮		⋮		⋮
	n	z_{n1}	...	z_{nj}	...	z_{nn}

Source: Adapted from R. Miller and P. Blair. 2009. *Input-Output Analysis: Foundations and Extensions*. Second edition. Cambridge: Cambridge University Press.

To illustrate, Figure 2.3 combines the nominal intermediate transactions of the 25 economies from the Asia and Pacific region in the MRIOT for 2000 and 2020. One observation from the figure is that these intermediate transactions have grown massively in the span of 2 decades; from $7.9 trillion in 2000 to $40.9 trillion in 2020. This is understandable considering the gap between the two benchmark years, as well as the rise within the region of manufacturing powerhouses such as the People's Republic of China (PRC). Even with the pandemic, these transactions increased by 0.7% from 2019 to 2020. However, it is important to emphasize that these values are in nominal terms and are therefore influenced by price fluctuations. For example, most substantial gain from 2019 to 2020 was recorded in the consumption of primary products (i.e., agriculture, mining, and other resource-based inputs) by low-technology manufacturing sectors. This is partly attributable to the observed price hikes in several oil and petroleum products in 2020, which happen to be an important input to a wide array of producers such as food, energy, textile, paper, rubber, and plastics.

Figure 2.3 also shows the two roles that industries occupy in the Asia and Pacific region. Sectors are described as suppliers at the upper segment of the chart by showing the value of intermediate sales these aggregate sectors have made to other purchasing sectors at the bottom. Notice that sectors such as low-technology manufacturing and personal and public services record larger amounts as purchasers of inputs than as suppliers. This implies that the products of these sectors use relatively higher amounts of inputs and are therefore more dependent on other sectors' supplies.

Figure 2.3: Intraregional Intermediate Transactions of Select Economies in Asia and the Pacific, by Sector
($ trillion)

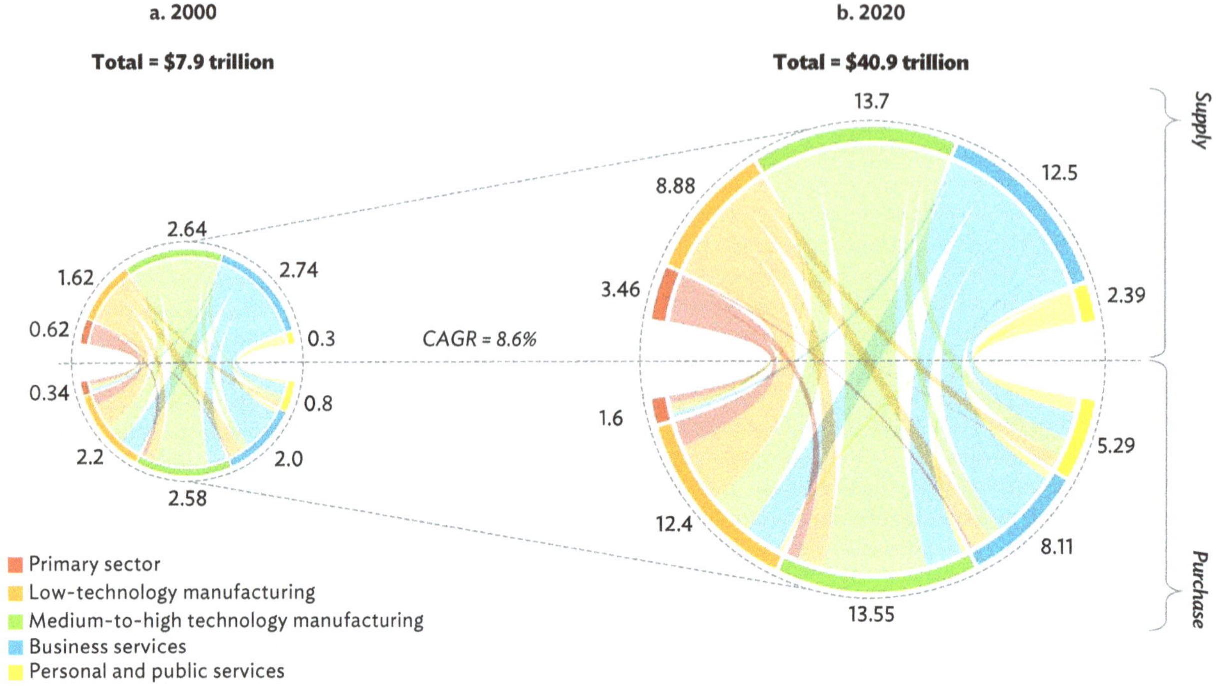

$ = United States dollars; CAGR = compound annual average growth rate.
Note: The data pertain to the economies of Bangladesh; Bhutan; Brunei Darussalam; Cambodia; Fiji; Hong Kong, China; India; Indonesia; Japan; Kazakhstan; the Kyrgyz Republic; the Lao People's Democratic Republic; Malaysia; Maldives; Mongolia; Nepal; Pakistan; the People's Republic of China; the Philippines; the Republic of Korea; Singapore; Sri Lanka; Taipei,China; Thailand; and Viet Nam.
Source: Calculations using the Asian Development Bank Multiregional Input–Output Table for 2000 and 2020. https://mrio.adbx.online/ (accessed July 2021).

Click here for figure data

On the other hand, sectors such as primary sector and business services tend to sell more inputs than they consume. This indicates that these sectors generally enable production in the economy by providing necessary raw materials and services inputs. Figure 2.3 illustrates that the patterns of trade at that level of aggregation are not significantly altered from 2000 to 2020. This rigidity in trade structure indicates that input consumption patterns of producers tend to follow predominant industry processes. Food manufacturing will largely require raw agricultural products, modern buildings rely on steel, footwear products are birthed from rubber materials. As these ways of conducting business tend to be established at the industry level, inputs or cost structures also tend to be more stable irrespective of where the materials come from. Innovations however disrupt these structures; but that too will need an almost universal adoption of new technologies for it to be acutely reflected in the aggregate figures. The subsequent sections will further explore these supply-and-use interactions and demonstrate its utility for constructing a simple model of the economy.

2.2 Economic Sensitivity and Dependency

Relying on the intermediate transactions table, IOTs can model interdependencies among domestic sectors and further measure sensitivity of all producers to a single sector's changes in final demand. Suppose a decline in tourism activities for a particular economy reduced the demand for accommodation services. Rather than lose profits, this sector scales down its operations, which must mean a concomitant decrease in its purchases of inputs such as food, cleaning materials, utilities, and other services. Since these inputs affect other sectors' outputs, the macroeconomic effect of the decline in tourism activities would not come solely from the decrease in the demand for accommodation, but also from the lower demand for inputs to the hotel and restaurants sector. Using what is known as the Leontief insight, input-output analysis uniquely captures this broader impact from final demand changes: that is, supply and demand impacts to economy-wide production may be quantified using an array of multipliers and sectoral interlinkages.

2.2.1 Multipliers

One of the basic indicators that can be derived from an IOT is a multiplier. The multiplier determines which sectors could generate high changes in output or value-added in the economy if their final demand changed by some value. This indicates the sensitivity of an economy to a given sector, thereby providing insights on which sectors should be carefully developed or stimulated in order to induce wider growth in the economy through what is known as the multiplier effect. The effect can also be measured through other economic indicators such as income and employment, or through any analysis of interest (e.g., energy use, carbon emissions, pollution) as long as sector-level data are available.

Output Multipliers

The model starts with the assumption that the intersectoral flows between two sectors depend on the production level of the purchasing sector. This follows the logic that a sector purchases inputs based on its need to produce an output to satisfy demand in an economy. Suppose that a shoe producer demands $400,000 worth of inputs from a leather manufacturer to produce $1,000,000 worth of shoes. This intersectoral transaction between the footwear sector and the leather sector explicitly demonstrates the direct linkage between the two sectors. The share of the leather sector's inputs to the footwear sector's output is: $400,000 ÷ $1,000,000 = 0.4. In other words, $0.4 worth of leather is required to produce $1 worth of shoe. This ratio is known as the direct input requirement coefficient or technical coefficient.

Technical coefficients serve as the basic mechanism through which impacts are modeled in an input–output system, particularly by operationalizing intersectoral linkages. Assume that the shoe manufacturer forecasts double its demand in the following period. In this scenario, the direct economic impact amounts to $2,000,000 (up from $1,000,000). However, to produce this number of shoes, the manufacturer must procure leather as material input. In the Leontief model, technical coefficients are assumed to be fixed, such that if the level of shoe production doubled, the required leather or any other inputs for that matter would also double.[1] In the example, 0.4 multiplied by $2,000,000 is equal to $800,000 worth of leather required to produce $2,000,000 worth of shoes. This is interpreted as the first-round effect of the change in demand for shoes. However, to produce $800,000 worth of leather inputs, the leather sector must in turn demand inputs as well, such as raw materials from livestock producers and chemical manufacturers. This further induces more demand of inputs from supplier sectors until all production requirements are met. These additional demands from leather, livestock, chemical, and all other upstream sectors represent the indirect economic impacts from doubling the demand for shoes.

More technically, the Leontief model captures the round-by-round effects brought by any changes in the final demand, in what is known as the Leontief inverse matrix. This matrix is defined as the inverse of the difference between the identity matrix and the technical coefficients matrix.[2] This gives the total requirements needed by a sector to produce its desired level of output. As suggested, the Leontief inverse coefficient accounts for not only the direct impacts but also the indirect impacts from intersectoral flows, hence also referred to as "total" requirements. In effect, each coefficient b_{ij} in the Leontief inverse matrix may be read as a multiplier, in that it gives the total output required from sector i for every unit of final demand in sector j. This type of multiplier is known as the **sectoral output multiplier**, since impact from a unit of final demand in one sector "multiplies" in the form of induced production in another sector. For example, if the sectoral output multiplier between leather producers and shoemakers is 0.50, this means that for every 1 unit of demand for shoes, the leather sector must produce a total of 0.50 units.

Summing sectoral output multipliers across sectors i to n due to demand in j yields the second (and most common) type of multiplier known as the **simple output multiplier**. Instead of showing the impact of a demand change to only one particular sector, the simple output multiplier gives the total (i.e., direct and indirect) outputs required from all sectors in the economy. It is calculated as the column sum of the Leontief inverse matrix, or the total Leontief inverse coefficients of a purchasing sector. To illustrate, the leather sector of Bangladesh exhibited a simple output multiplier of 1.95 in 2019, as shown in Figure 2.4. This simply indicates that for a $1 increase in the demand for shoes, production from all sectors must increase by $1.95 to provide for the final shoes.

The total production effects can be disaggregated to initial effects, first-round effects, and industrial support effects. The ***initial effect*** is the amount of exogenous change in demand and is assumed as one unit of output for a particular sector. This initial shock determines a new level of production for the affected sector, which must then purchase inputs from its "production recipe" described in the technical coefficients. The ***first-round effect*** provides the direct amount of inputs required for meeting the initial effect. For the leather sector of

1 This fixed relationship implies that producers operate under constant returns to scale.

2 Refer to the technical notes for the derivation of the Leontief inverse matrix.

Bangladesh, the first-round effect for every one unit (initial effect) demand for shoes is $0.60. This is the amount of inputs requirement from all the sectors in Bangladesh to meet the additional $1 in demand for their final shoes.

Further, the ***industrial support effect*** refers to all rounds of induced production from a unit change in demand after the first round. This effect includes all successive production from all sectors to meet the additional input requirements in the production of the additional direct input requirements (first-round effect) due to the one unit (initial effect) increase in final demand for a sector's product. It is calculated as the difference of the simple output multiplier, initial effect, and the first-round effect. In Bangladesh's leather sector, this is calculated as $1.95 (total effect) minus $1 (initial effect) minus $0.60, which is equal to $0.35. The first-round effects and industrial support effects make up the **production-induced effects**. This refers to the amount of output required from all supplying sectors to meet the change in final demand. This can also be calculated as the difference of the simple output multiplier and the initial effect. In the example, the production-induced effect is $0.95, which means that, for every $1 in demand for shoes, an additional $0.95 is needed to be generated in the total economy.

Applying these calculations to the 25 participating economies of the Asia and the Pacific in the MRIOT, the manufacturing sector frequently features the highest simple output multiplier for each economy, most especially food and beverages and refined fuels (Figure 2.4). Note that the private households sector is omitted from the discussion in this chapter as transactions in this sector tends to be less illustrative of the economy's business sector, relative to other producing sectors.[3] In 2019, the Kyrgyz Republic had the highest simple output multiplier of 5.48 units, belonging to the finance sector. If demand for final financial intermediation services increased by $1,000,000, total output in the economy would increase by $5,484,268. This was followed by the PRC's transport equipment sector and its rubber and plastics manufacturing sector, with 3.34 units and 3.30 units, respectively. These large simple output multipliers imply that the economies of the Kyrgyz Republic and the PRC are highly sensitive to final demand changes in these sectors. Meanwhile, in more detailed terms, Mongolia's transport equipment sector had the highest proportion of first-round effects in its simple output multiplier (40% of 2.40 units).

For 2020, the same top three sectors were observed in the 25 economies of Asia and the Pacific as shown in Figure 2.5. The Kyrgyz Republic's finance sector recorded the highest simple output multiplier among the 25 economies, with 69% of its demand impacts being comprised of industrial support effects. This means that an additional demand for final financial intermediation services induces disproportionately higher levels of production in other sectors than in the finance sector. Ultimately, most of the economies in Asia and the Pacific are highly sensitive to the final demand changes of the manufacturing sector, mainly on food and beverages and refined fuels.

3 Examples include services of maids, cooks, babysitters, and tutors.

Figure 2.4: Simple Output Multipliers for the Top Two Sectors of Select Economies in Asia and the Pacific, 2019
(%)

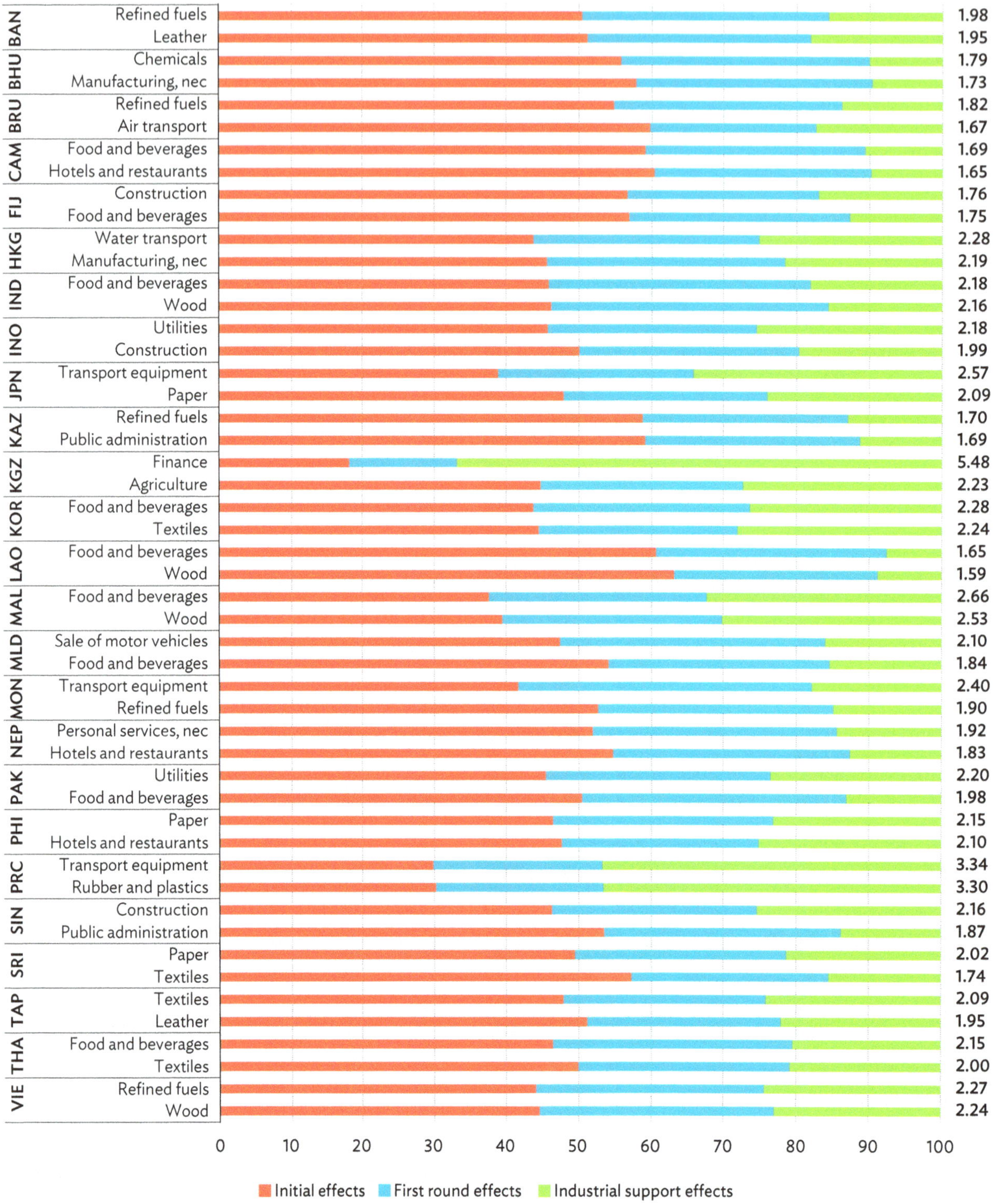

BAN = Bangladesh; BHU = Bhutan; BRU = Brunei Darussalam; CAM = Cambodia; FIJ = Fiji; HKG = Hong Kong, China; IND = India; INO = Indonesia; JPN = Japan; KAZ = Kazakhstan; KGZ = Kyrgyz Republic; KOR = Republic of Korea; LAO = Lao People's Democratic Republic; MAL = Malaysia; MLD = Maldives; MON = Mongolia; NEC = Not elsewhere classified; NEP = Nepal; PAK = Pakistan; PHI = Philippines; PRC = People's Republic of China; SIN = Singapore; SRI = Sri Lanka; TAP = Taipei,China; THA = Thailand; VIE = Viet Nam.

Source: Calculations using the Asian Development Bank Multiregional Input–Output Table for 2019. https://mrio.adbx.online/ (accessed July 2021).

Click here for figure data

Figure 2.5: Simple Output Multipliers for the Top Two Sectors of Select Economies in Asia and the Pacific, 2020
(%)

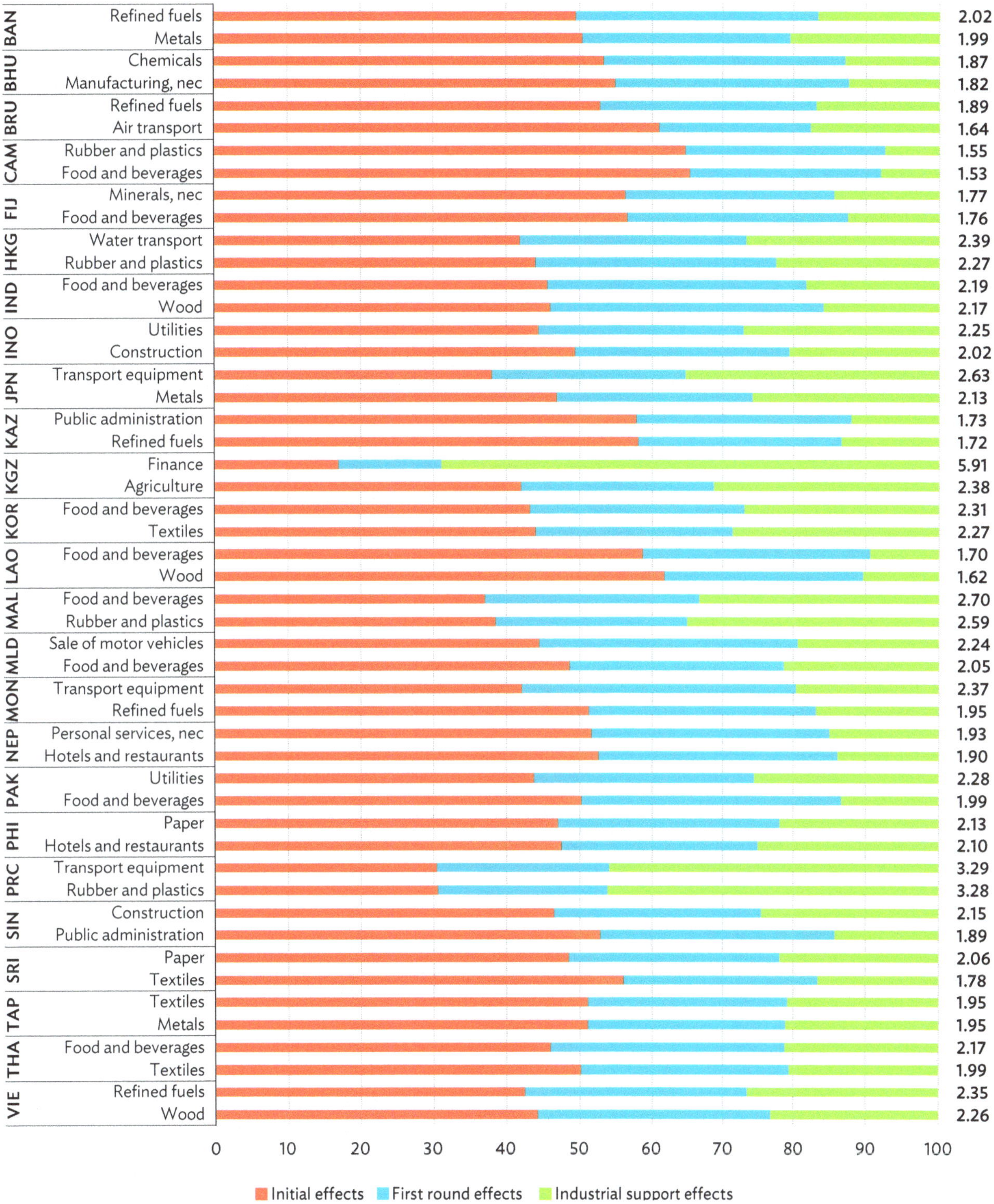

BAN = Bangladesh; BHU = Bhutan; BRU = Brunei Darussalam; CAM = Cambodia; FIJ = Fiji; HKG = Hong Kong, China; IND = India; INO = Indonesia; JPN = Japan; KAZ = Kazakhstan; KGZ = Kyrgyz Republic; KOR = Republic of Korea; LAO = Lao People's Democratic Republic; MAL = Malaysia; MLD = Maldives; MON = Mongolia; NEC = Not elsewhere classified; NEP = Nepal; PAK = Pakistan; PHI = Philippines; PRC = People's Republic of China; SIN = Singapore; SRI = Sri Lanka; TAP = Taipei,China; THA = Thailand; VIE = Viet Nam.

Source: Calculations using the Asian Development Bank Multiregional Input–Output Table for 2019. https://mrio.adbx.online/ (accessed July 2021).

Click here for figure data

Value-Added Multipliers

In some cases, an analyst may want to describe the total impacts in terms of the income or value-added accruing to the domestic economy. In an IOT, the gross value-added vector can be used to measure the total value-added embodied in each unit of final demand. The approach is to convert the components of the Leontief inverse matrix from output into value-added terms through value-added coefficients. This multiplier can then be directly used to express impacts that are more bounded to the value of gross domestic product. To illustrate, suppose the income or gross value-added of the footwear sector is $700,000 on $1,000,000 worth of shoes. This gives an increase to the economy of $700,000 ÷ $1,000,000 or $0.7 per $1 worth of shoes produced. Multiplying this to the Leontief inverse matrix will give the **simple value-added multiplier**, which sums the economy-wide value-added generated to satisfy a dollar's worth of final demand in a sector. A sector's simple value-added multiplier may be lower than 1, suggesting that part of the income does not accrue to the domestic economy, but it should not be greater than 1.

For both 2019 and 2020, the industries with the highest simple value-added multiplier, on average, in the Asia and the Pacific were found in the real estate, education, and finance sectors (Figures 2.6 and 2.7). Pakistan led the 25 economies within the real estate sector, with the highest multiplier for both years. This means that an additional $1,000,000 in final demand for real estate would have generated an income or value-added to the Pakistan economy of about $995,454 in 2019 and $996,298 in 2020. Pakistan also led in terms of the value-added multiplier for the finance sector. For the education sector, Sri Lanka claimed the highest simple value-added multiplier for both years. This implies that, for every $1,000,000 in final demand for education services, the economy could have potentially accrued $993,143 and $994,909 in value-added as estimated in 2019 and 2020, respectively. Also notable are Bangladesh, India, Indonesia, Japan, Pakistan, and the PRC, whose economies recorded simple value-added multipliers higher than the regional average in almost all sectors, as shown in the blue-filled cells in Figures 2.6 and 2.7. Moreover, Viet Nam observably showed low value-added multipliers, since the economy is heavily engaged in the midstream part of value chains for manufacturing (e.g., subassemblies for electronic products) where value-added to output ratios are typically low.

Figure 2.6: Simple Value-Added Multipliers for All Sectors of Select Economies in Asia and the Pacific, 2019

	BAN	BHU	BRU	CAM	FIJ	HKG	IND	INO	JPN	KAZ	KGZ	KOR	LAO	MAL	MLD	MON	NEP	PAK	PHI	PRC	SIN	SRI	TAP	THA	VIE	*Sec. Ave.*
Agriculture	0.90	0.96	0.78	0.85	0.84	0.68	0.97	0.97	0.87	0.82	0.81	0.84	0.95	0.86	0.65	0.83	0.91	0.96	0.92	0.95	0.69	0.89	0.81	0.88	0.60	**0.85**
Mining	0.97	0.89	0.83	0.83	0.70	-	0.89	0.95	0.66	0.86	0.64	0.81	0.79	0.92	-	0.76	0.87	0.98	0.85	0.90	-	0.93	0.77	0.63	0.63	**0.72**
Food and beverages	0.80	0.73	0.62	0.62	0.78	0.46	0.88	0.92	0.88	0.84	0.75	0.77	0.77	0.76	0.56	0.71	0.82	0.92	0.88	0.92	0.60	0.88	0.75	0.77	0.51	**0.76**
Textiles	0.74	0.86	0.82	0.56	0.87	0.67	0.86	0.55	0.89	0.79	0.72	0.68	0.78	0.68	0.73	0.54	0.62	0.90	0.75	0.90	0.56	0.83	0.64	0.72	0.51	**0.73**
Leather	0.88	0.86	0.75	-	0.75	0.45	0.86	0.54	0.86	0.71	0.72	0.62	0.81	0.75	-	0.63	0.67	0.91	0.71	0.88	0.54	0.85	0.73	0.76	0.58	**0.67**
Wood	0.89	0.80	0.63	0.77	0.81	0.67	0.89	0.91	0.86	0.79	0.51	0.72	0.85	0.77	0.70	0.53	0.71	0.86	0.84	0.87	0.65	0.83	0.58	0.79	0.58	**0.75**
Paper	0.71	0.64	0.59	0.58	0.74	0.56	0.82	0.85	0.89	0.71	0.65	0.77	0.83	0.71	0.67	0.47	0.54	0.87	0.80	0.85	0.49	0.77	0.72	0.86	0.46	**0.70**
Refined fuels	0.80	-	0.89	0.27	-	0.32	0.55	0.91	0.47	0.92	0.67	0.40	0.71	0.76	-	0.80	0.59	0.70	0.39	0.78	0.43	0.47	0.25	0.25	0.57	**0.52**
Chemicals	0.89	0.78	0.69	0.67	0.74	0.53	0.81	0.82	0.80	0.80	0.65	0.67	0.81	0.64	-	0.81	0.54	0.79	0.76	0.84	0.54	0.70	0.49	0.57	0.47	**0.67**
Rubber and plastics	0.82	0.60	0.55	0.39	0.55	0.58	0.80	0.77	0.88	0.90	0.68	0.71	0.66	0.54	-	0.72	0.56	0.72	0.68	0.83	0.70	0.82	0.61	0.78	0.41	**0.65**
Minerals, nec	0.93	0.87	0.54	0.70	0.78	0.27	0.78	0.85	0.81	0.79	0.68	0.66	0.78	0.68	0.62	0.52	0.58	0.84	0.64	0.90	0.37	0.77	0.58	0.37	0.69	**0.68**
Metals	0.63	0.66	0.60	0.65	0.68	0.33	0.54	0.83	0.74	0.90	0.83	0.60	0.50	0.53	0.62	0.61	0.44	0.75	0.47	0.80	0.50	0.47	0.56	0.48	0.37	**0.60**
Machinery, nec	0.72	0.66	0.60	0.33	0.76	0.55	0.75	0.69	0.85	0.75	0.66	0.73	0.57	0.60	-	0.32	0.70	0.74	0.58	0.82	0.55	0.53	0.62	0.63	0.36	**0.60**
Electricals	0.89	0.66	0.59	0.60	-	0.56	0.73	0.71	0.83	0.82	0.74	0.76	0.78	0.48	-	0.14	0.40	0.63	0.50	0.75	0.46	0.57	0.62	0.63	0.34	**0.57**
Transport equipment	0.91	0.66	0.60	0.60	0.77	0.55	0.75	0.85	0.81	0.71	0.62	0.63	0.56	0.45	0.66	0.68	0.50	0.56	0.69	0.84	0.55	0.59	0.64	0.63	0.42	**0.65**
Manufacturing, nec	0.85	0.74	0.60	0.59	0.84	0.58	0.75	0.83	0.85	0.65	0.56	0.72	0.77	0.75	0.81	0.54	0.56	0.84	0.75	0.92	0.57	0.79	0.64	0.66	0.56	**0.71**
Utilities	0.88	0.77	0.66	0.43	0.74	0.81	0.66	0.79	0.74	0.81	0.63	0.50	0.90	0.76	0.38	0.59	0.65	0.71	0.89	0.86	0.63	0.82	0.48	0.69	0.90	**0.71**
Construction	0.82	0.72	0.45	0.70	0.76	0.72	0.80	0.88	0.86	0.85	0.61	0.77	0.53	0.71	0.62	0.48	0.60	0.80	0.76	0.87	0.68	0.82	0.64	0.55	0.54	**0.70**
Sale of motor vehicles	0.97	0.93	0.53	-	0.87	-	0.95	0.91	0.92	0.80	0.77	0.89	0.78	0.77	0.66	0.77	0.94	0.90	0.89	-	0.73	0.94	0.88	0.72	0.69	**0.73**
Wholesale trade	0.93	0.93	0.73	0.73	0.84	0.78	0.95	0.92	0.94	0.88	0.82	0.86	0.89	0.82	0.85	0.72	0.96	0.97	0.93	0.95	0.59	0.94	0.88	0.86	0.82	**0.86**
Retail trade	0.98	0.93	0.72	0.70	0.88	0.93	0.95	0.92	0.94	0.89	0.78	0.87	0.86	0.81	0.77	0.79	0.93	0.94	0.94	0.94	0.82	0.93	0.92	0.86	-	**0.84**
Hotels and restaurants	0.84	0.93	0.71	0.77	0.84	0.62	0.65	0.90	0.91	0.88	0.74	0.80	0.83	0.82	0.64	0.73	0.79	0.89	0.87	0.94	0.73	0.89	0.83	0.84	0.62	**0.80**
Inland transport	0.91	0.70	0.65	0.66	0.62	0.88	0.68	0.85	0.91	0.82	0.64	0.77	0.72	0.73	0.69	0.54	0.61	0.83	0.73	0.92	0.80	0.85	0.74	0.76	0.50	**0.74**
Water transport	0.89	0.76	0.61	-	0.58	0.70	0.80	0.82	0.84	0.78	0.77	0.58	0.16	0.77	0.60	0.71	-	0.84	0.72	0.91	0.16	0.86	0.29	0.59	0.38	**0.60**
Air transport	0.70	0.45	0.43	-	0.55	0.74	0.80	0.80	0.86	0.79	0.56	0.60	0.16	0.64	0.67	0.70	0.70	0.82	0.62	0.83	0.44	0.63	0.53	0.65	0.44	**0.61**
Transport activities, nec	0.93	0.96	0.49	-	0.78	0.90	0.83	0.92	0.95	0.85	0.78	0.83	0.28	0.72	0.77	0.65	0.78	0.96	0.86	0.90	0.69	0.90	0.84	0.82	0.77	**0.77**
Telecommunications	0.93	0.86	0.56	0.77	0.80	0.85	0.79	0.92	0.93	0.89	0.71	0.86	0.88	0.79	0.78	0.58	0.81	0.94	0.88	0.91	0.58	0.71	0.86	0.84	0.59	**0.80**
Finance	0.95	0.96	0.85	0.94	0.89	0.94	0.94	0.95	0.96	0.89	0.89	0.89	0.94	0.91	0.91	0.89	0.89	0.97	0.95	0.96	0.64	0.94	0.93	0.93	0.82	**0.91**
Real estate	0.98	0.99	0.94	0.86	0.92	0.97	0.99	0.97	0.98	0.92	0.83	0.94	0.96	0.94	0.88	0.91	0.90	1.00	0.96	0.97	0.87	0.95	0.95	0.89	0.85	**0.93**
Business activities, nec	0.95	0.82	0.57	0.78	0.87	0.92	0.92	0.89	0.96	0.85	0.84	0.87	0.91	0.85	0.83	0.66	0.77	0.98	0.93	0.89	0.57	0.88	0.84	0.82	0.75	**0.84**
Public administration	0.94	0.90	0.73	0.72	0.86	0.96	1.00	0.94	0.94	0.80	0.86	0.93	0.84	0.82	0.85	0.74	0.91	0.85	0.95	0.92	0.72	0.98	0.91	0.89	0.87	**0.87**
Education	0.96	0.92	0.75	0.86	0.92	0.94	0.96	0.90	0.97	0.89	0.91	0.90	0.90	0.91	0.90	0.87	0.94	0.97	0.95	0.92	0.88	0.99	0.93	0.86	0.90	**0.91**
Health and social work	0.83	0.86	0.68	0.79	0.87	0.89	0.88	0.87	0.93	0.78	0.87	0.86	0.82	0.74	0.83	0.72	0.83	0.87	0.90	0.89	0.81	0.95	0.85	0.80	0.54	**0.83**
Personal services, nec	0.96	0.84	0.89	0.82	0.76	0.88	0.95	0.94	0.94	0.90	0.78	0.85	0.86	0.81	0.74	0.79	0.80	0.97	0.86	0.89	0.76	0.89	0.84	0.88	0.75	**0.85**
Economy Average	**0.87**	**0.78**	**0.67**	**0.58**	**0.73**	**0.65**	**0.83**	**0.85**	**0.87**	**0.82**	**0.73**	**0.75**	**0.74**	**0.74**	**0.57**	**0.66**	**0.70**	**0.86**	**0.79**	**0.86**	**0.60**	**0.81**	**0.71**	**0.73**	**0.58**	

BAN = Bangladesh; BHU = Bhutan; BRU = Brunei Darussalam; CAM = Cambodia; FIJ = Fiji; HKG = Hong Kong, China; IND = India; INO = Indonesia; JPN = Japan; KAZ = Kazakhstan; KGZ = Kyrgyz Republic; KOR = Republic of Korea; LAO = Lao People's Democratic Republic; MAL = Malaysia; MLD = Maldives; MON = Mongolia; NEC = Not elsewhere classified; NEP = Nepal; PAK = Pakistan; PHI = Philippines; PRC = People's Republic of China; Sec. Ave. = Sector Average; SIN = Singapore; SRI = Sri Lanka; TAP = Taipei,China; THA = Thailand; VIE = Viet Nam; - = no data available.

Note: The regional average is the average simple value-added multiplier of the 25 economies per sector. The comparison of values is done row-wise. The intensity of the color scale is anchored to the regional average value per sector. The darker the shade the higher it is from the regional average value per sector.

Source: Calculations using the Asian Development Bank Multiregional Input–Output Table for 2019. https://mrio.adbx.online/(accessed July 2021).

Click here for figure data

Figure 2.7: Simple Value-Added Multipliers for All Sectors of Select Economies in Asia and the Pacific, 2020

	BAN	BHU	BRU	CAM	FIJ	HKG	IND	INO	JPN	KAZ	KGZ	KOR	LAO	MAL	MLD	MON	NEP	PAK	PHI	PRC	SIN	SRI	TAP	THA	VIE	*Sec. Ave.*
Agriculture	0.91	0.97	0.77	0.79	0.88	0.73	0.97	0.98	0.88	0.83	0.86	0.86	0.96	0.87	0.73	0.85	0.92	0.96	0.92	0.95	0.72	0.90	0.82	0.89	0.62	**0.86**
Mining	0.97	0.91	0.83	0.75	0.76	-	0.90	0.96	0.69	0.86	0.73	0.83	0.83	0.93	-	0.79	0.89	0.98	0.87	0.91	-	0.94	0.80	0.66	0.64	**0.74**
Food and beverages	0.82	0.79	0.62	0.49	0.82	0.51	0.89	0.93	0.89	0.85	0.81	0.78	0.80	0.78	0.63	0.73	0.84	0.93	0.88	0.93	0.63	0.90	0.76	0.78	0.53	**0.77**
Textiles	0.76	0.85	0.82	0.42	0.89	0.78	0.87	0.58	0.90	0.79	0.79	0.70	0.81	0.70	0.75	0.57	0.66	0.91	0.77	0.91	0.59	0.85	0.67	0.74	0.53	**0.74**
Leather	0.89	0.85	0.78	-	0.82	0.50	0.87	0.59	0.88	0.71	0.78	0.64	0.85	0.76	-	0.65	0.71	0.92	0.73	0.89	0.58	0.87	0.78	0.77	0.59	**0.70**
Wood	0.90	0.84	0.64	0.68	0.85	0.73	0.90	0.92	0.87	0.79	0.61	0.74	0.87	0.79	0.74	0.56	0.74	0.88	0.85	0.89	0.68	0.86	0.61	0.79	0.60	**0.77**
Paper	0.74	0.70	0.61	0.48	0.79	0.62	0.83	0.87	0.90	0.72	0.73	0.79	0.86	0.73	0.72	0.51	0.59	0.89	0.80	0.86	0.52	0.81	0.75	0.87	0.48	**0.73**
Refined fuels	0.81	-	0.89	0.27	-	0.40	0.57	0.92	0.52	0.92	0.75	0.45	0.75	0.76	-	0.83	0.63	0.76	0.64	0.80	0.45	0.52	0.29	0.25	0.58	**0.55**
Chemicals	0.90	0.82	0.68	0.60	0.76	0.59	0.83	0.84	0.82	0.80	0.74	0.71	0.85	0.66	-	0.82	0.59	0.82	0.61	0.85	0.57	0.73	0.53	0.59	0.49	**0.69**
Rubber and plastics	0.83	0.68	0.56	0.50	0.64	0.64	0.82	0.80	0.88	0.90	0.76	0.73	0.72	0.55	-	0.74	0.59	0.75	0.69	0.84	0.72	0.84	0.66	0.79	0.42	**0.68**
Minerals, nec	0.94	0.89	0.56	0.59	0.82	0.35	0.80	0.86	0.83	0.80	0.76	0.68	0.81	0.70	0.65	0.56	0.62	0.86	0.68	0.91	0.41	0.79	0.65	0.40	0.71	**0.71**
Metals	0.65	0.72	0.62	0.66	0.71	0.43	0.57	0.85	0.77	0.90	0.87	0.62	0.57	0.56	0.66	0.68	0.46	0.79	0.52	0.81	0.54	0.48	0.61	0.51	0.39	**0.64**
Machinery, nec	0.74	0.72	0.61	0.45	0.81	0.61	0.77	0.72	0.87	0.75	0.74	0.74	0.65	0.62	-	0.36	0.71	0.78	0.62	0.84	0.58	0.58	0.64	0.65	0.38	**0.64**
Electricals	0.90	0.72	0.61	0.59	-	0.60	0.75	0.74	0.85	0.82	0.80	0.77	0.87	0.51	-	0.14	0.43	0.69	0.52	0.76	0.49	0.60	0.64	0.65	0.36	**0.59**
Transport equipment	0.90	0.72	0.61	0.64	0.82	0.60	0.77	0.86	0.83	0.71	0.71	0.65	0.69	0.48	0.69	0.68	0.53	0.63	0.72	0.85	0.57	0.62	0.66	0.65	0.42	**0.68**
Manufacturing, nec	0.86	0.79	0.61	0.63	0.87	0.46	0.77	0.85	0.87	0.65	0.66	0.74	0.80	0.76	0.84	0.57	0.58	0.87	0.76	0.93	0.60	0.81	0.67	0.68	0.57	**0.73**
Utilities	0.89	0.81	0.64	0.26	0.73	0.85	0.69	0.81	0.77	0.82	0.71	0.52	0.92	0.77	0.49	0.62	0.72	0.73	0.90	0.87	0.66	0.85	0.57	0.71	0.91	**0.73**
Construction	0.83	0.78	0.45	0.57	0.81	0.75	0.82	0.90	0.87	0.85	0.70	0.78	0.58	0.73	0.68	0.53	0.61	0.84	0.78	0.88	0.69	0.84	0.67	0.58	0.56	**0.72**
Sale of motor vehicles	0.97	0.94	0.52	-	0.89	-	0.96	0.92	0.93	0.80	0.82	0.90	0.83	0.78	0.74	0.79	0.95	0.92	0.90	-	0.74	0.95	0.79	0.74	0.71	**0.74**
Wholesale trade	0.94	0.94	0.71	0.65	0.86	0.81	0.96	0.93	0.95	0.90	0.86	0.88	0.93	0.83	0.87	0.74	0.97	0.97	0.94	0.95	0.61	0.96	0.92	0.87	0.84	**0.87**
Retail trade	0.98	0.95	0.71	0.63	0.91	0.95	0.96	0.93	0.95	0.90	0.83	0.88	0.89	0.82	0.82	0.81	0.93	0.95	0.95	0.95	0.83	0.95	0.94	0.87	-	**0.85**
Hotels and restaurants	0.85	0.95	0.68	0.73	0.84	0.64	0.68	0.91	0.92	0.88	0.80	0.82	0.86	0.83	0.69	0.74	0.83	0.90	0.88	0.95	0.75	0.91	0.84	0.86	0.64	**0.82**
Inland transport	0.92	0.77	0.67	0.57	0.70	0.90	0.70	0.87	0.91	0.82	0.72	0.81	0.79	0.75	0.76	0.57	0.61	0.85	0.78	0.93	0.81	0.88	0.78	0.78	0.52	**0.77**
Water transport	0.89	0.81	0.57	-	0.68	0.77	0.82	0.84	0.85	0.79	0.82	0.65	0.32	0.79	0.69	0.73	-	0.87	0.78	0.92	0.18	0.89	0.65	0.61	0.40	**0.65**
Air transport	0.73	0.56	0.40	-	0.66	0.79	0.83	0.83	0.87	0.80	0.66	0.65	0.31	0.66	0.76	0.72	0.73	0.85	0.71	0.85	0.47	0.70	0.63	0.68	0.46	**0.65**
Transport activities, nec	0.93	0.96	0.48	-	0.84	0.92	0.85	0.94	0.95	0.86	0.83	0.85	0.38	0.75	0.81	0.67	0.81	0.97	0.87	0.91	0.70	0.93	0.88	0.83	0.78	**0.79**
Telecommunications	0.94	0.88	0.58	0.70	0.88	0.88	0.81	0.93	0.94	0.89	0.77	0.87	0.92	0.82	0.84	0.61	0.84	0.96	0.89	0.92	0.59	0.77	0.89	0.85	0.61	**0.82**
Finance	0.95	0.96	0.85	0.93	0.88	0.96	0.95	0.96	0.97	0.90	0.92	0.91	0.96	0.92	0.93	0.90	0.91	0.98	0.96	0.96	0.66	0.96	0.96	0.93	0.84	**0.92**
Real estate	0.98	0.99	0.95	0.83	0.92	0.97	0.99	0.98	0.98	0.93	0.87	0.95	0.96	0.94	0.90	0.92	0.91	1.00	0.97	0.98	0.88	0.96	0.96	0.90	0.86	**0.94**
Business activities, nec	0.96	0.86	0.60	0.72	0.87	0.94	0.93	0.90	0.96	0.86	0.88	0.88	0.92	0.87	0.87	0.69	0.80	0.98	0.94	0.90	0.59	0.90	0.86	0.84	0.77	**0.85**
Public administration	0.94	0.92	0.72	0.65	0.91	0.96	1.00	0.95	0.95	0.82	0.90	0.94	0.88	0.84	0.89	0.76	0.93	0.87	0.96	0.93	0.73	0.98	0.93	0.90	0.88	**0.89**
Education	0.97	0.93	0.74	0.82	0.90	0.95	0.97	0.92	0.97	0.90	0.94	0.91	0.93	0.92	0.92	0.88	0.95	0.97	0.95	0.93	0.88	0.99	0.94	0.87	0.90	**0.92**
Health and social work	0.85	0.89	0.68	0.73	0.90	0.91	0.89	0.89	0.94	0.78	0.90	0.87	0.85	0.76	0.86	0.74	0.85	0.88	0.89	0.90	0.82	0.96	0.88	0.81	0.55	**0.84**
Personal services, nec	0.96	0.87	0.89	0.76	0.71	0.90	0.96	0.95	0.95	0.90	0.83	0.86	0.88	0.83	0.81	0.81	0.82	0.98	0.87	0.91	0.77	0.91	0.87	0.89	0.77	**0.87**
Economy Average	**0.88**	**0.82**	**0.67**	**0.53**	**0.77**	**0.69**	**0.84**	**0.87**	**0.88**	**0.83**	**0.79**	**0.78**	**0.79**	**0.76**	**0.61**	**0.68**	**0.73**	**0.88**	**0.81**	**0.87**	**0.62**	**0.84**	**0.75**	**0.74**	**0.60**	

BAN = Bangladesh; BHU = Bhutan; BRU = Brunei Darussalam; CAM = Cambodia; FIJ = Fiji; HKG = Hong Kong, China; IND = India; INO = Indonesia; JPN = Japan; KAZ = Kazakhstan; KGZ = Kyrgyz Republic; KOR = Republic of Korea; LAO = Lao People's Democratic Republic; MAL = Malaysia; MLD = Maldives; MON = Mongolia; NEC = Not elsewhere classified; NEP = Nepal; PAK = Pakistan; PHI = Philippines; PRC = People's Republic of China; Sec. Ave. = Sector Average; SIN = Singapore; SRI = Sri Lanka; TAP = Taipei,China; THA = Thailand; VIE = Viet Nam; - = no data available.

Note: The regional average is the average simple value-added multiplier of the 25 economies per sector. The comparison of values is done row-wise. The intensity of the color scale is anchored to the regional average value per sector. The darker the shade the higher it is from the regional average value per sector.

Source: Calculations using the Asian Development Bank Multiregional Input–Output Table for 2020. https://mrio.adbx.online/(accessed July 2021).

Click here for figure data

In both Figure 2.6 and 2.7, the economies of Brunei Darussalam, Cambodia, Maldives, Singapore, and Viet Nam appear to be below the regional averages across a majority of their respective sectors. As value-added multipliers refer to domestic income content of demand, lower indices are generally due to the increased share of foreign inputs in the production of final products. Consider two of the most trade-exposed economies in the sample: Singapore and Viet Nam. In these economies, the share of foreign inputs to total output is above average, suggesting that substantial value accrues to foreign rather than domestic sectors in the production process. Interested readers may compare the data on simple value-added multipliers and foreign input shares to output, and easily find the strong negative correlation between these two indicators.

Value-added multipliers can be presented as a ratio of the simple value-added multiplier (or direct and indirect value-added generated per unit of demand) to the value-added coefficient (or the direct value-added generated per unit of demand). This multiplier, known as the **type I value-added multiplier**, measures how much the effects of initial demand (normally assumed as one unit of demand or type of activity) are magnified when both direct and indirect effects are considered. Suppose a type I value-added multiplier of a footwear sector is equal to 1.62 units. If a certain amount of final demand is directly responsible for about $150,000 of gross value-added in the economy, then in the event that this demand is realized, the economy should expect a total value-added impact of 1.62 × $150,000 = $243,000. The initial effect would be $150,000, while the difference of $93,000 would be the impact to the economy brought by round-by-round effects through the intersectoral flows present in an IOT.

Looking at Figure 2.8, the type I value-added multiplier of Hong Kong, China's nonmetallic minerals increased from 5.85 in 2019 to 7.35 in 2020. This makes it the third sector with the highest type I value-added multiplier in the region, and indicates increased production chain effects that are possibly attributed to the strengthening of upstream linkages over the year.

Figure 2.8: Type I Value-Added Multipliers for the Top Two Sectors of Select Economies in Asia and the Pacific

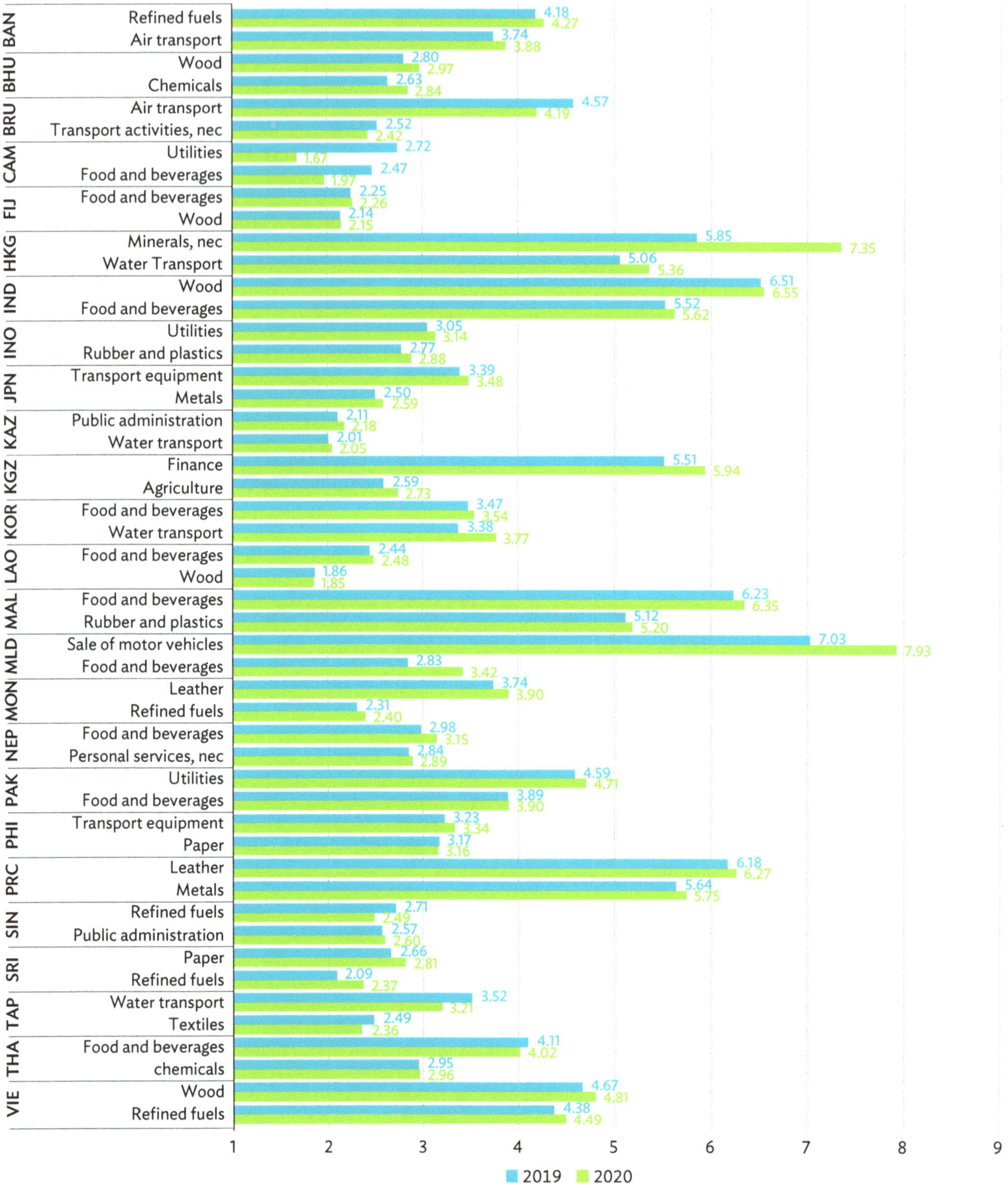

BAN = Bangladesh; BHU = Bhutan; BRU = Brunei Darussalam; CAM = Cambodia; FIJ = Fiji; HKG = Hong Kong, China; IND = India; INO = Indonesia; JPN = Japan; KAZ = Kazakhstan; KGZ = Kyrgyz Republic; KOR = Republic of Korea; LAO = Lao People's Democratic Republic; MAL = Malaysia; MLD = Maldives; MON = Mongolia; NEC = Not elsewhere classified; NEP = Nepal; PAK = Pakistan; PHI = Philippines; PRC = People's Republic of China; SIN = Singapore; SRI = Sri Lanka; TAP = Taipei,China; THA = Thailand; VIE = Viet Nam.

Notes: 1. Top two sectors with the highest type I value-added multiplier in 2019.
2. Outliers removed.

Source: Calculations using the Asian Development Bank Multiregional Input–Output Table for 2019 and 2020. https://mrio.adbx.online/ (accessed July 2021).

Click here for figure data

2.2.2 Intersectoral Linkages

While multipliers are often used in evaluating economy-wide impacts, these indicators can also be used to characterize a sector's importance in the economy by virtue of its interconnectedness with the other sectors. When multipliers are used in this context, "linkages" becomes the more appropriate term. In an input-output framework, a sector supplies (intermediate products) and demands (inputs) from other producers in the market. These supply and demand interactions can be construed as a measure of a given sector's economic connectedness. When compared against all other sectors, one can identify sectors that have maximal effects on the entire framework through their input and output relations with other sectors. The value of these intersectoral linkages signify whether sectors are strongly or weakly connected to either downstream purchasers or upstream suppliers. These linkages are also used as a basis for determining key sectors in the economy.

The demand-side intersectoral flows are measured through backward linkages. This concept looks at the interconnectedness of a particular sector with sectors from which it purchases inputs. Conversely, supply-side flows are measured through forward linkages, considering the interconnectedness of a particular sector with sectors to which it sells its output. There are different proposed ways to measure both backward and forward linkages.

Backward Linkages

The direct backward linkage is defined as the first round of economy-wide impacts induced by changes in the final demand of a sector. It measures the linkages of the purchasing sector to suppliers it transacts with directly. The direct backward linkage is calculated as the sum of the direct input requirements of the purchasing sector, or the sum of the technical coefficients of the purchasing sector. If all rounds of effects are relevant in the analysis, then the total backward linkage may be used. This is the economy-wide impact induced by changes in the final demand of a sector. It includes the direct and subsequent rounds of impacts on interlinked industries due to a demand stimulus. This is the linkage equivalent of the simple output multiplier.

There are different ways to measure backward linkage (Oosterhaven 2019). For one, a sector with a high total backward linkage stimulates a relatively large amount of production in the economy. However, a sector that predominantly uses inputs from its own sectoral group will have less potential of spreading exogenous impulses throughout the economy. Hypothetically extracting a sector (both its demand- and supply-side effects) in measuring its contribution to the economy-wide total output would reveal only such impulses. Hence, the **complete hypothetical extraction backward linkage** gives the total backward linkage of a sector, but is corrected by its self-dependency. It is calculated as the sector's total backward linkage divided by its own simple output multiplier, or the diagonal entries in the Leontief inverse matrix.

A drawback of a complete hypothetical extraction backward linkage is that it is mixed with the supply-side interactions. Thus, for analysts concerned with pure backward linkage, the **partial hypothetical extraction backward linkage** offers a demand-side analog of the complete hypothetical extraction linkage. This index, also normalized by self-dependency, measures the backward linkage of a sector only with the other sectors that it buys inputs from. It is calculated as the total backward linkage less 1 divided by the sector's diagonal entry in the Leontief inverse matrix. These hypothetical extraction backward linkages, both the complete and partial, are not to be confused with the economic impacts from a given sector's hypothetical extraction (discussed in the Hypothetical Extraction section of this chapter).

As observed in Figure 2.9, the direct backward linkage is represented as the lowest base values among the different linkage measures, since it focuses solely on direct sector connections. Conversely, the total backward linkage considers both direct and indirect sector connections. Considering the sectors' self-dependency, the complete backward hypothetical extraction linkage observes different values from the total backward linkage. For example, the Kyrgyz Republic's finance sector's total backward linkage of 5.48 in 2019 drastically reduces to 1.003 after considering the sector's backward linkage within the sectoral group. This stark difference is due to the sector's dependence on financial firms for inputs, which are mostly comprised of implicit charges involved in interbank lending activities. Its partial backward hypothetical extraction linkage further decreased to 0.82 after considering only the upstream interactions in the measurement.

Most of the sectors with the highest total backward linkages per economy in the region remained unchanged from 2019 to 2020, except for Cambodia; Fiji; Kazakhstan; and Thailand. The ranking of sectors also changed per linkage measure, given differences in identifying upstream linkages. For 2019 and 2020, the sectors with the highest total backward linkage were the Kyrgyz Republic's finance sector, the PRC's transport equipment sector, and Malaysia's manufacturing of food and beverages. By considering self-dependencies, different groups of sectors led the sample of economies in terms of backward linkage, such as the transport equipment sectors in Mongolia and the PRC and the sale of motor vehicles sector in Maldives. Finally, using partial extraction linkages registered the same leading sectors as the complete extraction linkages in 2020, although in 2019 the third-highest sector among the sampled economies was Malaysia's food and beverages sector.

The unusually high total backward linkage (also the simple output multiplier) of the Kyrgyz Republic's finance sector is largely due to the high direct operating costs borne by the banking sector, in addition to expenses related to the imputed financial services on its borrowing transactions with other banks. Recall that the Leontief model assumes that these costs reflect direct linkages of the banking sector with other sectors.

Figure 2.9: Variations of Backward Linkages for the Top Sector of Select Economies in Asia and Pacific

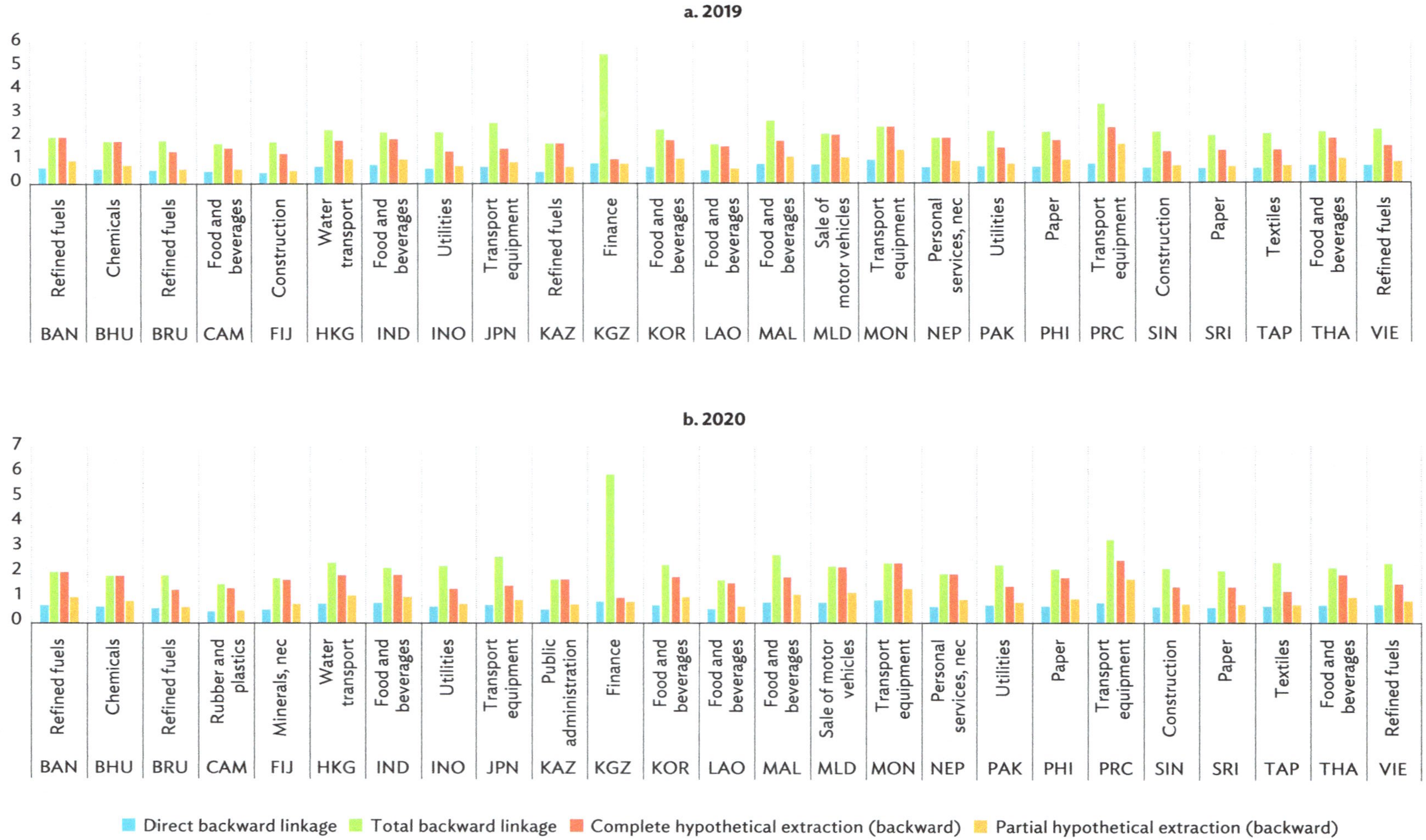

BAN = Bangladesh; BHU = Bhutan; BRU = Brunei Darussalam; CAM = Cambodia; FIJ = Fiji; HKG = Hong Kong, China; IND = India; INO = Indonesia; JPN = Japan; KAZ = Kazakhstan KGZ = Kyrgyz Republic; KOR = Republic of Korea; LAO = Lao People's Democratic Republic; MAL = Malaysia; MLD = Maldives; MON = Mongolia; NEC = Not elsewhere classified; NEP = Nepal; PAK = Pakistan; PHI = Philippines; PRC = People's Republic of China; SIN = Singapore; SRI = Sri Lanka; TAP = Taipei,China; THA = Thailand; VIE = Viet Nam.

Note: The top sector with the highest total backward linkage in 2019 for (a) and 2020 for (b).

Source: Calculations using the Asian Development Bank Multiregional Input–Output Table for 2019 and 2020. https://mrio.adbx.online/(accessed July 2021).

Click here for figure data

This technical[4] relationship of costs to output implies that financial firms are extensively dependent on other sectors in the production of a monetary unit of its service. For example, the National Statistical Committee of the Kyrgyz Republic's official supply-use table for 2019 assessed the intermediate consumption of the finance sector to be at more than 90% of its gross output (NSC 2021a). This figure is near the range of finance sector's ratio of direct costs to gross revenues (at around 80%) derived from the surveys of financial enterprises (NSC 2021b).[5] Looking further into financial statements of sampled public financial companies, calculations by the authors of this report saw ratios of operating profit to income (a crude but informative indicator of value-added ratios) to be low, ranging from 10% to 35%. The bank with the widest reach in the Kyrgyz Republic, for example, registered a 12.5% ratio of profit to its total income, the inverse of which again indicates the high operating costs incurred by the enterprise. In any of these cases, for every $1 worth of financial services produced in the economy, more than $0.8 must be accruing to upstream sectors, significantly impacting the demand for these sectors' outputs. This high cost (input) ratio, combined with it being spread across many different domestic sectors, contributes to the large total backward linkage of the finance sector of the Kyrgyz Republic.

Forward Linkages

Forward linkages are the supply-side counterpart of backward linkages. These linkages are typically observed from the Ghosh family of input–output models (Ghosh 1958; Oosterhaven 1996; Dietzenbacher 1997). This concept assumes that the level of production of a sector is fixed and would be allocated between final consumers and other sectors for their respective productions. Suppose that the leather sector provides $100,000 of its total output of $3,000,000 to the footwear sector, then $100,000 ÷ $3,000,000 = 0.03. This ratio is the sales proportion of the footwear sector (the buying sector) to the total level of production of the leather sector (the supplying sector). It is also known as the direct allocation coefficient. Following the similar solution in the Leontief model for backward linkages, the Ghosh inverse matrix can be derived by using direct allocation coefficients instead of direct input requirement coefficients.[6] The row sum of the Ghosh inverse matrix represents the total output generated in the economy, given a unit supply of primary inputs. This row sum is the analog of column sums in the Leontief inverse.

The direct forward linkage measures the first round of economy-wide impacts induced by a change in the primary inputs of a sector. This limits the measure of forward linkages to sectors that directly purchase their inputs. This is calculated as

4 In this context, it is important to highlight that the technical input coefficients are more accurately termed as accounting coefficients, since these reflect the monetary values of costs rather than physical quantities of technologies and materials (Lequiller and Blades 2014).

5 The difference between the two figures is explained by the inclusion of financial intermediation services indirectly measured in the former.

6 Refer to the technical notes for the derivation of the Ghosh inverse matrix.

the sum of the direct allocation coefficients of the supplying sector. Furthermore, the total forward linkage sums the direct forward linkage and the round-by-round effects induced by a change in primary inputs of a sector. As indicated above, this is calculated as the row sum of the Ghosh inverse matrix.

The **complete hypothetical extraction forward linkage** measures the total forward linkage of a sector adjusted for its self-dependency. This indicator highlights a sector's capacity to spread exogenous impulses to sectors other than itself. It is calculated as the sector's total forward linkage divided by its own Ghosh inverse multiplier, or the diagonal entries in the Ghosh inverse matrix. As with the backward linkage analog, the **partial hypothetical extraction forward linkage** provides the sector's self-dependency-adjusted total forward linkages with sectors it sells inputs to. It is calculated as the sector's total forward linkage less 1 divided by its own diagonal entry in the Ghosh inverse matrix.

Figure 2.10 compares different types of forward linkages across top sectors in select economies of Asia and the Pacific. Notice that total forward linkages exhibit higher values on account of round-by-round impacts from intersectoral flows. The sector with the highest total forward linkage within the region is the Kyrgyz Republic's finance sector, with 5.83 in 2019 and 6.39 in 2020. Adjusting for self-dependence, the same sector's complete hypothetical extraction forward linkage reduces to 1.07 in 2019 and 1.08 in 2020. This implies high intrasectoral transactions (or self-dependency), which indicates that any supply-side stimulus could exert lesser influence on other sectors in the economy. In contrast, Japan's mining sector had a total forward linkage of 2.93 in 2019 and 3.03 in 2020, and its complete extraction linkage did not deviate far, at 2.89 in 2019 and 2.98 in 2020. This indicates low self-dependency and that the mining sector of Japan could spread exogenous impulses to other sectors just as much as to itself. The sector's partial extraction linkage, meanwhile, reduced to 1.90 in 2019 and 2.00 in 2020. These values are considerably lower, since this measure only considers interlinkages of the mining sector with its upstream sectors.

From 2019 to 2020, the sectors with the highest total forward linkage per economy in the region remained unchanged (Figure 2.10). Aside from the Kyrgyz Republic's finance sector, the top sector in the region with the highest forward linkage for all measures is the mining sector, mainly from Indonesia, Japan, the PRC, and Viet Nam. This is expected, since the outputs of the mining sector are predominantly used as intermediate input to other production, such as steel manufacturing.

Figure 2.10: Variations of Forward Linkages for the Top Sector of Select Economies in Asia and the Pacific

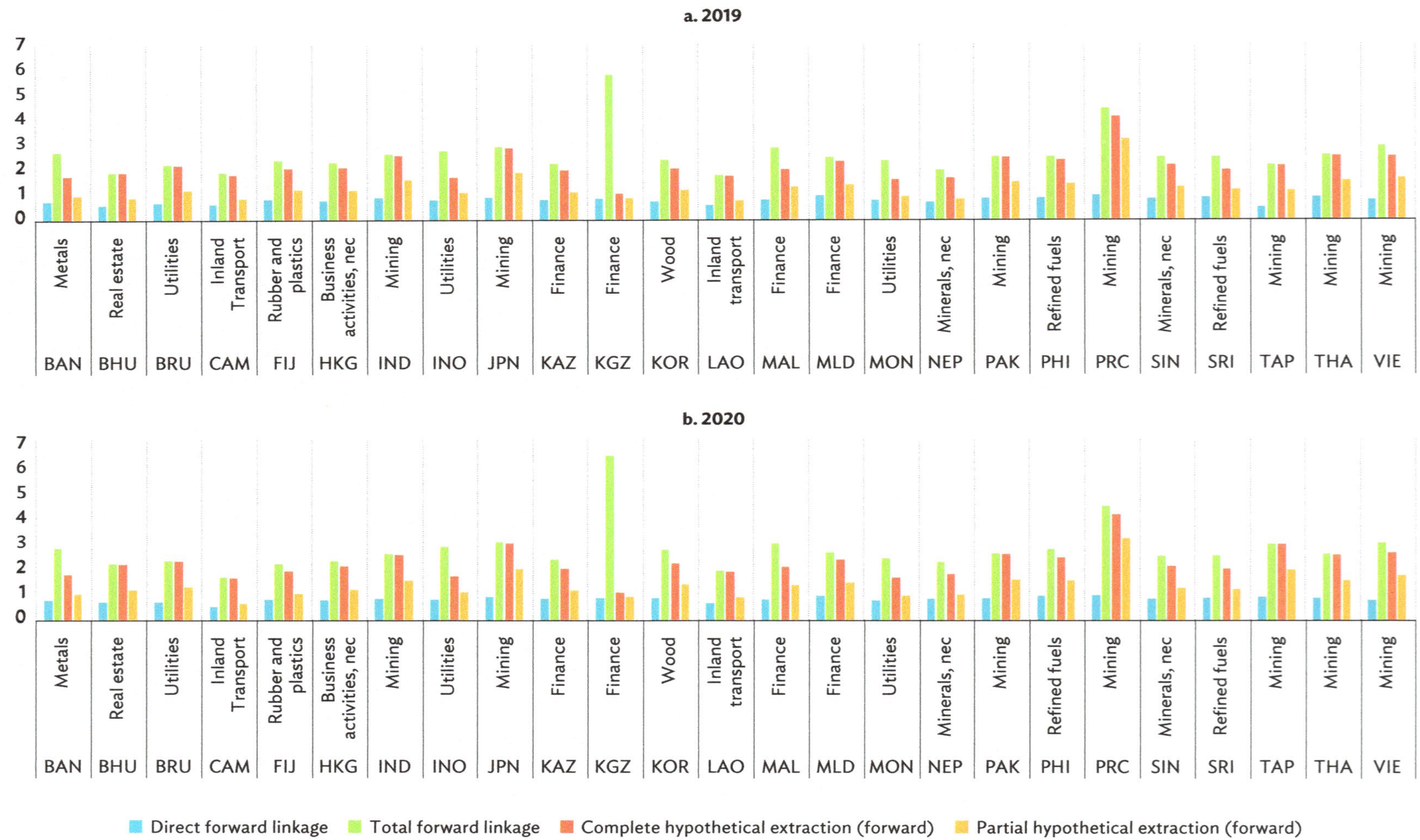

BAN = Bangladesh; BHU = Bhutan; BRU = Brunei Darussalam; CAM = Cambodia; FIJ = Fiji; HKG = Hong Kong, China; IND = India; INO = Indonesia; JPN = Japan; KAZ = Kazakhstan KGZ = Kyrgyz Republic; KOR = Republic of Korea; LAO = Lao People's Democratic Republic; MAL = Malaysia; MLD = Maldives; MON = Mongolia; NEC = Not elsewhere classified; NEP = Nepal; PAK = Pakistan; PHI = Philippines; PRC = People's Republic of China; SIN = Singapore; SRI = Sri Lanka; TAP = Taipei,China; THA = Thailand; VIE = Viet Nam.

Note: The top sector with the highest total backward linkage in 2019 for (a) and 2020 for (b).

Source: Calculations using the Asian Development Bank Multiregional Input–Output Table for 2019 and 2020. https://mrio.adbx.online/(accessed July 2021).

Click here for figure data

Normalized Linkages

The normalization of linkages is performed in order to scale indices by some other measures, such as economy-wide averages of linkages, value-added, and final demands, among others. In previous discussions, this normalization procedure was illustrated for hypothetical extraction linkages, particularly with respect to the self-dependency of a sector. Aside from this, linkages are also normalized to the average linkage of all sectors in an economy.

This normalization measure is often used to identify key sectors, given its high dependence on both upstream and downstream sectors (Miller and Blair 2009).

The **normalized total backward linkage** divides the sector's total backward linkage by the average of all domestic sectors. If the normalized value is greater than 1, then the sector has "strong" or higher-than-average dependence on other sectors' supplies. If this value is less than 1, the dependence is low. Meanwhile, the **normalized total forward linkage** divides the sector's total forward linkage by the average of all domestic sectors. If the normalized value is greater than 1, then a sector has "strong" or higher-than-average dependence on other sectors' demands for its output. The dependence is "weak" if the value is less than 1. Table 2.2 summarizes the interpretation of the normalized backward and forward linkages for each sector.

Table 2.2: Classification of Key Sectors Using Normalized Backward and Forward Linkages

		Backward Linkage	
		Low (<1)	High (>1)
Forward Linkage	High (>1)	Dependent on intersectoral demand	Generally dependent
	Low (<1)	Generally independent	Dependent on intersectoral supply

Source: Adapted from R. Miller and P. Blair. 2009. *Input-Output Analysis: Foundations and Extensions*. Second edition. Cambridge: Cambridge University Press.

The classifications presented in Table 2.2 are visually plotted in the corresponding quadrants of Figure 2.11. This allows for economy-sector classification based on its interdependence with other economy-sectors, whether downstream, upstream, or both. In the 2019 section of Figure 2.11, Japan's mining sector can be found in the second quadrant, wherein it has a low normalized backward linkage of 0.79 and a high normalized forward linkage of 1.49 (referring to Table 2.2, this sector is dependent on intersectoral demand, which is typical for a mining sector). Meanwhile, Mongolia's transport equipment sector is found in the fourth quadrant, given its high normalized backward linkage of 1.68 and low normalized forward linkage of 0.66. This indicates that the sector is dependent on intersectoral supply, which is generally expected of sectors whose outputs are mainly consumed as a final product (or, in this case, as fixed investment). In 2020, Viet Nam's refined fuel manufacturing sector was generally dependent on both upstream and downstream sectors.

Figure 2.11: Normalized Linkages of Select Economies in Asia and the Pacific

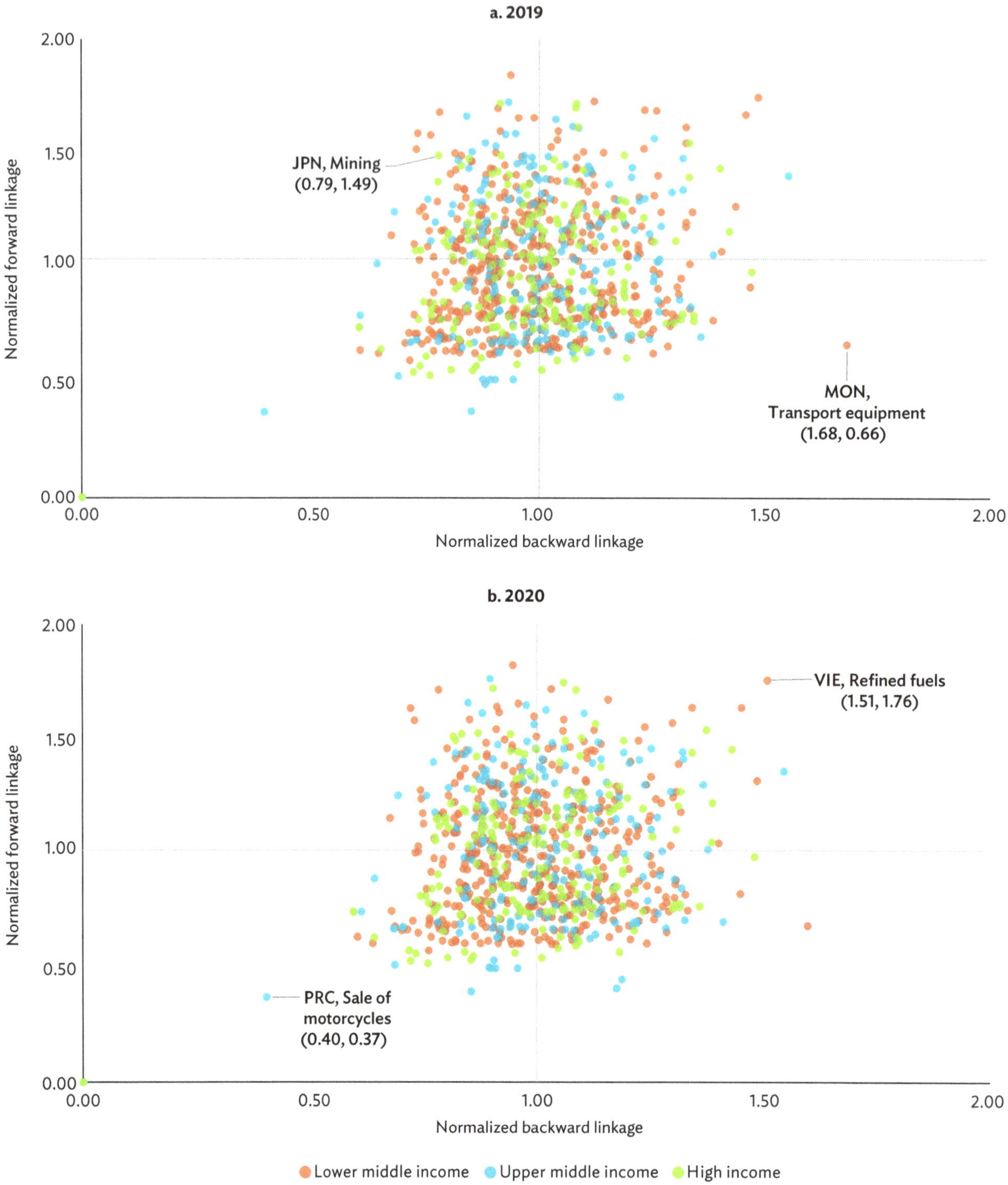

JPN = Japan; MON = Mongolia; PRC = People's Republic of China; VIE = Viet Nam.
Source: Calculations using the Asian Development Bank Multiregional Input–Output Table for 2019 and 2020. https://mrio.adbx.online/ (accessed July 2021).

Click here for figure data

In Figure 2.11, this key sector exhibits a normalized backward linkage of 1.51 and a normalized forward linkage of 1.76. As such, changes in the sector's demand or supply could generate significant ripple effects to the economy. Conversely, the PRC's sale of motor vehicles sector was generally independent of both the upstream and downstream sectors in 2020, having a normalized backward linkage of 0.40 and a normalized forward linkage of 0.37. This sector also tended to show the weakest normalized linkages for other economies in the region. This implies that any change within the sector would exert low influence on the rest of the economy.

Figure 2.11 shows no observable pattern linking the income status of the select economies and the normalized linkages of their respective sectors. This is evidenced by a small average dispersion of 0.35 standard deviation across economies. This implies that sectors' production and sales structures, and by extension their normalized backward and forward linkages, are invariant to the income level of their economies. To further investigate this pattern, a two-way analysis of variance was performed by grouping the economies into quintiles based on gross national income per capita, in keeping with the World Bank's (2021) income classification (Table 2.3). The results indicate that similar sectors' linkages within an income class do not vary significantly from sectors from another income class (*F*-statistic of less than 1 and *F*-critical value of 2.38). However, significant differences were noticeable from one sector group to another (*F*-statistic of 9.15 and *F*-critical value of 1.44). For example, the normalized backward linkages of food manufacturing sectors of the first quintile—namely in Hong Kong, China; Japan; the Republic of Korea; Singapore; and Taipei,China—were not statistically different from those of food manufacturers in Bangladesh, Cambodia, the Kyrgyz Republic, Nepal, and Pakistan. However, food manufacturers' normalized backward linkages were remotely different from other sectors such as textiles or petroleum production.

Further, a supplementary finding is that variances of normalized forward linkages are larger than its backward linkage counterpart. For example, the *F*-value of normalized forward linkages across sectors was 16.86, compared to 9.14 recorded in normalized backward linkages. This stems from the observation that market sales structures tend to be less stable than production structures (Miller and Blair 2009) and that sectors in each economy are often composed of distinct products and occupy different positions in the value chain. For example, mining in different economies generally requires the use of heavy equipment, but the sales structure of the mining sector in Brunei Darussalam would tend to diverge from Kazakhstan's mining sector. The former's oil and gas extraction sector delivers a sizable amount to refineries, while the latter tends to supply to the basic metals sector.

Table 2.3: Results of Two-Way Analysis of Variance of Normalized Linkages, 2019

Source of Variation	SS	df	MS	F	P-value	F crit
			Normalized backward linkages			
Income	1.7764E-14	4	4.4409E-15	1.6685E-13	1	2.38465612
Sectors	8.27695469	34	0.24343984	9.14655212	3.3819E-37	1.44639133
Interaction	4.01818352	136	0.02954547	1.11008597	0.20426591	1.23279137
Within	18.6308336	700	0.02661548			
Total	**30.9259718**	**874**				
			Normalized forward linkages			
Income	4.2633E-14	4	1.0658E-14	1.934E-13	1	2.38465612
Sectors	31.6053233	34	0.92956833	16.8679798	1.1624E-69	1.44639133
Interaction	6.29062624	136	0.0462546	0.83933769	0.89701987	1.23279137
Within	38.5759195	700	0.05510846			
Total	**76.4718691**	**874**				

df = degrees of freedom; F = F statistic; F crit = alpha value; MS = mean squares; P-value = probability that the alpha is the same as the values obtained from F-statistic; SS = sum of squares,

Source: Calculations by the Asian Development Bank Multiregional Input–Output Database Team.

Net Linkages

Another method to normalize a sector's linkage is to consider both (i) how the rest of the economy reacts to changes in the sector's demand, and (ii) how the sector reacts to demand changes in other sectors. This two-sided dependence of a sector is summarized as the **net backward linkage** (Oosterhaven 2019). This variant of backward linkage gives the output generated in all sectors due to the demand for the buying sector's final products, and then normalized by the output generated by the supplying sector due to the final demand of all sectors. If the value is greater than 1, then the whole economy is more dependent on the sector for the purchase of inputs than the sector is dependent on the whole economy, and the opposite is true if the value is less than 1. More specifically, the net backward linkage is given by the following:

$$\text{Net backward linkages} = \left(\text{Leontief column sums} \times \text{Final output coefficients}\right) - \left(\text{Gross backward linkages} \times \text{Ability to generate own demand-driven growth impulses}\right)$$

On the other hand, the **net forward linkage** provides the gross inputs of all sectors that utilize the primary input of the supplying sector, and then normalized by the gross input of the buying sector that utilized the primary inputs of all sectors. If the value is greater than 1, then the whole economy is more dependent on the sector for its supply of inputs than the sector is dependent on the whole economy, and vice versa if the value is less than 1. The net forward linkage is given by the following:

$$\text{Net forward linkages} = \left(\text{Ghosh row sums} \times \text{Primary input coefficients}\right) - \left(\text{Gross forward linkages} \times \text{Ability to generate own supply-driven growth impulses}\right)$$

These relationships are summarized in Table 2.4.

Table 2.4: Classification of Key Sectors Using Net Backward and Net Forward Linkages

		Backward Linkage	
		Low (<1)	High (>1)
Forward Linkage	High (>1)	Sector is dependent on the whole economy as a supplier; Whole economy is generally dependent on sector for inputs	Whole economy is generally dependent on sector
	Low (<1)	Sector is generally dependent on the whole economy	Whole economy is dependent on sector as suppliers; Sector is dependent on the whole economy for inputs

Source: Adapted from J. Oosterhaven. 2019. *Rethinking Input–Output Analysis: A Spatial Perspective.* SpringerBriefs in Regional Science. Springer, Cham.

Figure 2.12 plots the results based on the four-quadrant classification of Oosterhaven (2019). Most sectors of economies in Asia and the Pacific are not located in the first (upper right) quadrant. One of the few sectors found in this quadrant is the Republic of Korea's real estate sector, both for 2019 and 2020. In 2019, the sector registered a net backward linkage of 1.04 and a net forward linkage of 1.05, implying higher economy-wide dependence on real estate services than the reverse. The PRC's agriculture sector, meanwhile, is dependent on intersectoral supply and the economy is dependent on agricultural inputs (upper left quadrant). This characterizes the PRC's agriculture sector as a main provider of raw materials for production by other sectors. Diametrically opposite to this is Thailand's education sector, which recorded high net backward linkage and low net forward linkage in 2020 (lower right quadrant). Using Table 2.4, the economy's education sector may be described as dependent on intersectoral supply, while the rest of the sectors are also dependent on the education sector's demand for inputs. This implies that the education sector is a downstream sector that has mutual dependence with the other sectors, and that education services are mostly consumed as a final product and less as intermediate inputs to production. The Kyrgyz Republic's finance sector exhibited general dependence (lower left quadrant), as was the case under normalized linkages. The same may be said for Bhutan's manufacturing sector (not elsewhere classified), which showed low net forward and backward linkages. This is typical of sectors that require complex and diverse inputs from other sectors, but whose outputs are also further consumed in the production process of other sectors.

Figure 2.12: Net Linkages of Select Economies in Asia and the Pacific

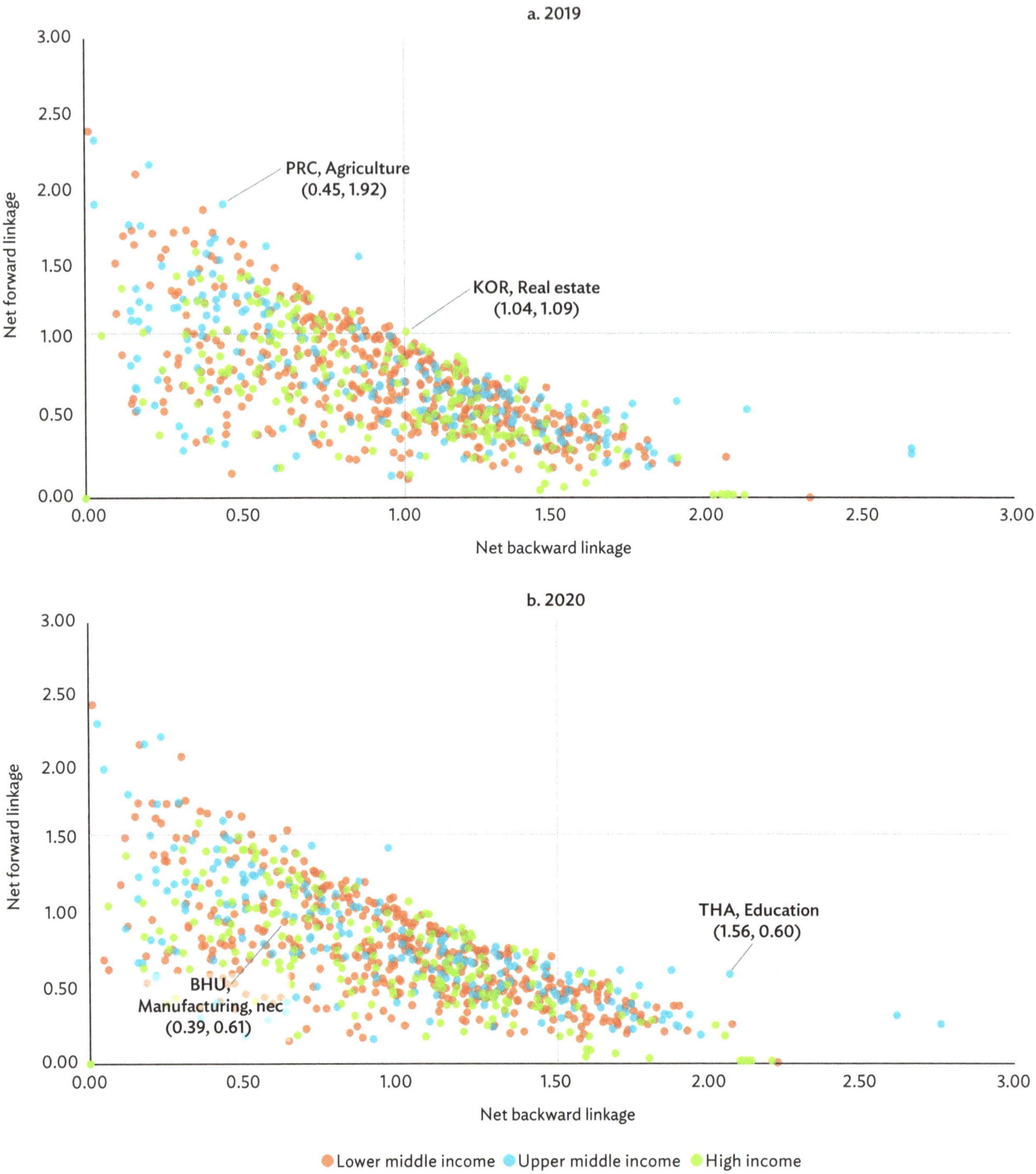

BHU = Bhutan; KOR = Republic of Korea; NEC = Not elsewhere classified; PRC = People's Republic of China; THA = Thailand.
Note: "Net" linkages refer to "gross" linkages weighted by the respective sector's ability to generate own growth impulses (Oosterhaven 2008). Net backward linkages are derived from Leontief column sums multiplied by final demand coefficients, while net forward linkages are derived from Ghosh row sums multiplied by value-added coefficients.
Sources: Calculations using the Asian Development Bank Multiregional Input–Output Table for 2019 and 2020. https://mrio.adbx.online/ (accessed July 2021); and J. Oosterhaven. 2008. A New Approach to the Selection of Key Sectors: Net Forward and Net Backward Linkages. *International IO Meeting on Managing the Environment*. Seville.

Click here for figure data

Similar to the discussion on normalized linkages, one can compare the effect of income levels to the results of net linkages in Figure 2.12. The two-way analysis of variance reveal that differences in net linkages exist across sector groups, but no significant differences are found across income groups. The *F*-statistic across income groups for both net backward and net forward linkages were less than the stated critical values, indicating that no noticeable differences exist across income levels (Table 2.5). The opposite was true, however, across sector groups. This is again consistent with the findings from normalized linkages, except that sector-specific characteristics are magnified in net linkages as evidenced by higher *F*-statistics compared to those observed in normalized linkages. For example, financial and real estate services often exhibit some similarities in their cost structures. Average total backward linkages of these two sectors were not too distant from each other, typically ranging from 1.3 to 1.4. However, net backward linkages showed marked difference between the two sectors. Net backward linkage for the finance sector across economies averaged at 0.52, while the real estate sector was estimated at 0.84. The larger net linkage for the latter reflects the fact that housing services occupy a greater share in (households') final demand than do financial services. However, net linkages of real estate tend to behave similarly across economies irrespective of the income status. As a result, net linkages generally accentuate sector-specific characteristics more than normalized linkages.

Table 2.5: Results of Two-Way Analysis of Variance of Net Linkages, 2019

Source of Variation	SS	df	MS	F	P-value	F crit
			Net backward linkages			
Income	1.32857338	4	0.33214334	2.26667417	0.06056861	2.38465612
Sectors	83.5099807	34	2.4561759	16.7618908	2.9684E-69	1.44639133
Interaction	18.4564169	136	0.13570895	0.92613015	0.70670459	1.23279137
Within	102.57334	700	0.14653334			
Total	**205.868311**	**874**				
			Net forward linkages			
Income	0.24245243	4	0.06061311	0.66234268	0.61831885	2.38465612
Sectors	64.924893	34	1.90955568	20.8664477	2.6091E-84	1.44639133
Interaction	11.7422214	136	0.08633986	0.94346882	0.65764844	1.23279137
Within	64.0592491	700	0.09151321			
Total	**140.968816**	**874**				

df = degrees of freedom; F = F statistic; F crit = alpha value; MS = mean squares; P-value = probability that the alpha is the same as the values obtained from F-statistic; SS = sum of squares,

Source: Calculations by the Asian Development Bank Multiregional Input–Output Database Team.

Hypothetical Extraction

The hypothetical extraction method (HEM) measures the relative importance of a particular sector or activity in the economy (Oosterhaven 2019; Miller and Blair 2009). This method departs from the traditional practice of taking a sector's share of value-added to total GDP. Instead, HEM takes a creative approach by assuming that a sector vanishes from the economy, and the impact from the hypothetical exercise is construed as a measure of the sector's importance and linkages.

In this section, the sector is extracted by zeroing out all its supplies in the rows as well as its demand in the columns in the IOT, thereby effectively nullifying all intersectoral linkages and contribution of this sector. Then, the IOT without the extracted sector is run in the standard Leontief method to project the economy's level of output in the hypothetical scenario. Since supplies of the sector are eliminated, other sectors lose supply of corresponding inputs and final consumers fail to meet their demand for the extracted product. In addition, since the demands of the sector are also eliminated, the economy loses the intersectoral demand from the extracted sector itself (i.e., input-producing sectors experience reductions in sales). In sum, scarcity in supply and demand induced by extracting the sector is in effect a measure of its importance in the overall economy.

Using data for 2019 and 2020, Figure 2.13 shows the sectors that incurred the largest impact to the economy from the HEM exercise. Notice that many economies in the sample registered the agriculture sector as the most impactful from the HEM. Considerable, too, is the size of the potential impacts of mining and quarrying in Brunei Darussalam and Mongolia. Expectedly, Maldives in 2019 showed high reliance on the hotel and restaurant sector until 2020 saw a drastic decline in the sector's contribution to the island economy. Evidently, Singapore and Hong Kong, China displayed the highest economic impacts in wholesale trading activity. Meanwhile, Japan and the Republic of Korea owed a large portion of their economies to real estate activities and business services, respectively. Taipei,China showed concentration in the manufacture of electronics and electrical equipment, while the Philippines and Viet Nam[7] largely manufactured food, beverages, and tobacco products. The neighboring economy of Indonesia was, however, more driven by construction activities as were Bangladesh, Bhutan, and the PRC.

7 Results for Viet Nam showed that the wholesale trade sector registered the highest impact. However, since the IOT of Viet Nam aggregates the wholesale and retail trade activity, the impacts arising from both are combined in the HEM results. As an ad hoc exercise, splitting the trade sector into two downgrades the wholesale sector's overall impact, placing the food, beverage, and tobacco sector to the top rank.

Figure 2.13: Sectors with the Highest Value-Added Impact from a Hypothetical Extraction
(% of total value-added)

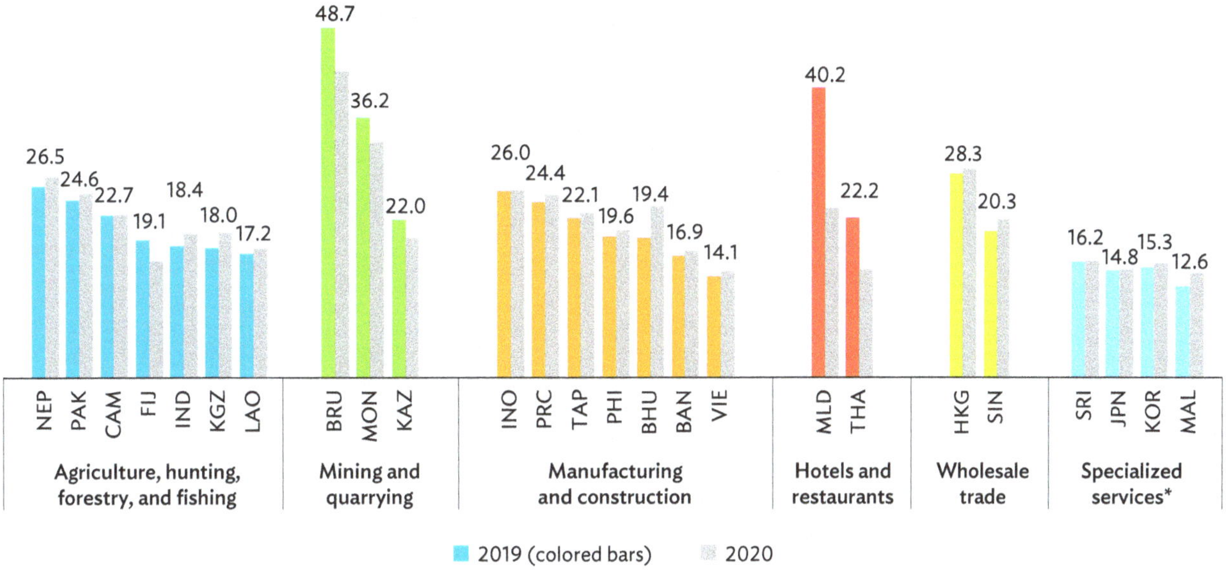

BAN = Bangladesh; BHU = Bhutan; BRU = Brunei Darussalam; CAM = Cambodia; FIJ = Fiji; HKG = Hong Kong, China; IND = India; INO = Indonesia; JPN = Japan; KAZ = Kazakhstan; KGZ = Kyrgyz Republic; KOR = Republic of Korea; LAO = Lao People's Democratic Republic; MAL = Malaysia; MLD = Maldives; MON = Mongolia; NEP = Nepal; PAK = Pakistan; PHI = Philippines; PRC = People's Republic of China; SIN = Singapore; SRI = Sri Lanka; TAP = Taipei,China; THA = Thailand; VIE = Viet Nam.

Notes: 1. Shown for each economy is the sector that recorded the highest value-added impact in 2019 and the comparative result in 2020.
2. The top sector for Japan is real estate activities; for the Republic of Korea, renting of machinery and equipment and other business activities; for Malaysia, public administration and defense; and for Sri Lanka, other community, social, and personal services.

Source: Calculations using the Asian Development Bank Multiregional Input–Output Table for 2019 and 2020. https://mrio.adbx.online/ (accessed July 2021).

Click here for figure data

2.3 Summary

A national input–output table holds vital information on the structure and extent of intersectoral connections within an economy. Input–output-based methods for analysis allow one to measure these connections and determine any key sectors in an economy. In 2019 and 2020, Asia and the Pacific observed waning yet still significant value-added shares of services within the region. However, in terms of linkages, Asian economies exhibited considerable dependence on the manufacturing sector, mainly on food and beverage production and the refining of fuels. This suggests that, while these sectors could have growth-inducing effects on the economy, extensive linkages could likewise spread undesirable impulses to the system in the form of negative shocks. Hence, careful evaluation of policies and market structures of these sectors is warranted. Also observed in Bangladesh, India, Indonesia, Japan, Pakistan, and the PRC are sectors that predominantly generate larger value-added than the regional average, considering intersectoral transactions. In addition, key sector analyses show that only a few sectors in the region exhibited economy-wide dependence for both their supply and demand of inputs. Few sectors found to be highly dependent on both upstream and downstream sectors include the Kyrgyz Republic's finance sector, Viet Nam's refined fuels sector, and Sri Lanka's manufacturing sector for paper-related products.

While there are a myriad of multiplier and linkage indicators to choose from, the use of these statistics depends on the concept and objective for development strategies. As a starting point, Table 2.6 broadly describes different multiplier and linkage indicators that can be employed in research and analysis.

Table 2.6: Applications of Multiplier and Linkage Indicators

Indicator	Description	Some Applications
Simple value-added multiplier	Value-added in the whole economy embodied in one unit of exogenous final demand of sector j.	Analysis of sector's potential to generate economy-wide income
Type I value-added multiplier	Ratio of simple value-added multiplier to the direct value-added embodied in one unit of final demand in sector j.	Same as above, but with more focus on sector's capacity to induce spillover effects relative to its demand stimulus
First-round effects	Direct intermediate inputs required from the whole economy per unit of exogenous final demand of sector j. Also the ratio of a sector's intermediate inputs per unit of output.	Analysis of a sector's dependence on direct suppliers
Industrial support effects	Sum of subsequent rounds of indirect intermediate inputs required from the whole economy per unit of final demand in sector j, excluding the first round.	Analysis of a sector's dependence on suppliers of its direct suppliers
Production-induced effects	Total indirect intermediate inputs required from the whole economy per unit of exogenous final demand of sector j, or simply the sum of first-round and industrial support effects.	Analysis of sector's dependence on all upstream suppliers
Sectoral multiplier	Total production required from producing sector i to purchasing sector j to satisfy one unit of demand for sector j products.	Granular analysis of how demand in one sector can potentially induce production in another sector
Direct backward linkage	Ratio of a sector's intermediate inputs to its total output. This is a direct measure of a sector's dependence on intersectoral supply of inputs. This measure is equivalent to first-round effects and the demand-side analog of direct forward linkage.	Basic measure of a sector's direct dependence on intersectoral inputs per unit of its output
Direct forward linkage	Ratio of a sector's intermediate sales to its total output. This is a direct measure of a sector's dependence on intersectoral demand for its output. This is the supply-side analog of direct backward linkage.	Basic measure of a sector's direct dependence on intersectoral demands per unit of its supply
Normalized total backward linkage	Total backward linkage of a sector divided by the arithmetic average of all sectors' total backward linkage in a given economy and period. Values greater than 1 indicate higher-than-average backward linkage of a sector.	Analysis of sector's dependence on intersectoral supply relative to the economy-wide average
Normalized total forward linkage	Total forward linkage of a sector divided by the arithmetic average of all sectors' total forward linkage in a given economy and period. Values greater than 1 indicate higher-than-average forward linkage of a sector.	Analysis of sector's dependence on intersectoral demand relative to the economy-wide average
Total backward linkage (or simple output multiplier)	Total amount of production required from all input-supplying sectors to satisfy one unit of demand for the sector's output.	Analysis of sector's direct and indirect dependence on intersectoral supplies or its economic relationship to upstream sectors
Total forward linkage	Total amount of production available to all input-purchasing sectors as a result of a unit change in a sector's primary inputs.	Analysis of sector's direct and indirect dependence on intersectoral demands or its economic relationship to downstream sectors
Complete hypothetical extraction linkage (backward)	Total backward linkage divided by the output multiplier of sector j demand to the production of the same sector j=i (or diagonal elements [ljj] in the Leontief inverse).	Analysis of a purchasing sector's ability to transmit a given stimulus' effects to other sectors; conversely, an analysis of how a sector's demand-driven impacts are confined and localized within the sectoral grouping

continued on next page.

Table 2.6 *continued.*

Indicator	Description	Some Applications
Complete hypothetical extraction linkage (forward)	Total forward linkage divided by the input multiplier of sector i supply to the production of the same sector i=j (or diagonal elements [gii] in the Ghosh inverse).	Analysis of a supplying sector's ability to transmit a given stimulus' effects to other sectors; conversely, an analysis of how a sector's supply-driven impacts are confined and localized within the sectoral grouping
Partial hypothetical extraction linkage (backward)	Total backward linkage less the initial effect (=1), divided by the output multiplier of sector j demand to the production of the same sector j=i (or diagonal elements [ljj] in the Leontief inverse). This refers to the strength of production induced in sectors other than the source of exogenous change in demand of final products j.	Same as complete hypothetical extraction linkage (backward), but excluding the sector's initial impact on its demand to solely focus on demand-side interactions
Partial hypothetical extraction linkage (forward)	Total forward linkage less the initial effect (=1), divided by the input multiplier of sector i supply to the production of the same sector i=j (or diagonal elements [gii] in the Ghosh inverse). This refers to the strength of production induced in sectors other than the source of exogenous change in supply of primary inputs i.	Same as complete hypothetical extraction linkage (forward), but excluding the sector's initial impact on its primary inputs to solely focus on supply-side interactions
Net backward linkage	Total backward linkage of a sector multiplied by the ratio of its final demand to the economy-wide gross output. This index scales the value of total backward linkage to the corresponding size of a sector's demand in the economy.	Analysis of sector's demand-driven economy-wide impacts, but correcting for its relative share in the total final demand in the economy
Net forward linkage	Total forward linkage of a sector multiplied by the ratio of its value-added to the economy-wide gross output. This index scales the value of total forward linkage to the corresponding size of the sector's value-added in the economy.	Analysis of sector's supply-driven economy-wide impacts, but correcting for its relative share in the total value-added in the economy
Absolute impact of sector's hypothetical extraction	Total (direct and indirect) amount of value-added lost in the economy as a result of nullifying the sector's supply (forward linkage) and use (backward linkage) in the economy.	Study of a sector's overall dollar contribution to the economy, both as a supplier and source of demand
Relative impact of sector's hypothetical extraction	Share of total value-added lost from the sector's hypothetical extraction to the total value-added in the economy.	Study of a sector's overall dollar contribution to the economy, both as a supplier and source of demand, normalized to the size of the economy's gross domestic product

Source: Compiled by the Asian Development Bank Multiregional Input–Output Database Team.

The analysis of domestic sectors and their interactions is necessary, but the realities of an integrated world economy should also be explored, given that the implications of various policy scenarios run beyond domestic borders. In a globalized setting, domestic sectors are now forming links with production chains across borders, in line with the precipitous decline in transportation costs, the impressive growth of emerging markets, and the rise of digital technologies. Hence, with deepening trade, it is apparent that assessing international linkages is as valuable as considering local linkages, especially in terms of access to key foreign inputs and external markets. The extension of these national input–output-based models to multiregional settings significantly expands the framework's analytical uses to include linkages with foreign economies. This international perspective in analyzing trade and production linkages is explored in the next chapter.

References

E. Dietzenbacher. 1997. In Vindication of the Ghosh Model: A Reinterpretation as a Price Model. *Journal of Regional Science*. 37. pp. 629–651.

A. Ghosh. 1958. Input–Output Approach to an Allocation System. *Economica*. 25. pp. 58–64.

F. Lequiller and D. Blades. 2014. *Understanding National Accounts*. Second edition. Paris: OECD Publishing.

R. Miller and P. Blair. 2009. *Input–Output Analysis: Foundations and Extensions*. Second edition. Cambridge: Cambridge University Press.

National Statistical Committee of the Kyrgyz Republic (NSC). 2021a. *Intersectoral Balance of Production and Use of Goods and Services of the Kyrgyz Republic*. Bishkek. http://www.stat.kg/ru/publications/sbornik-mezhotraslevoj-balans-proizvodstva-i-ispolzovaniya-tovarov-i-uslug-kyrgyzskoj-respubliki-za-2011g-zataraty-vypuska/.

NSC (Kyrgyz Republic). 2021b. Finance of Enterprises of the Kyrgyz Republic. Bishkek. http://www.stat.kg/ru/publications/sbornik-finansy-predpriyatij-kyrgyzskoj-respubliki/.

J. Oosterhaven. 1996. Leontief versus Ghoshian Price and Quantity Models. *Southern Economic Journal*. 62. pp. 750–759.

J. Oosterhaven. 2008. A New Approach to the Selection of Key Sectors: Net Forward and Net Backward Linkages. *International IO Meeting on Managing the Environment*. Seville.

J. Oosterhaven. 2019. *Rethinking Input–Output Analysis: A Spatial Perspective*. SpringerBriefs in Regional Science. Springer, Cham.

World Bank. 2021. World Bank Country and Lending Groups. https://datahelpdesk.worldbank.org/knowledgebase/articles/906519-world-bank-country-and-lending-groups (accessed March 2022).

International Linkages

3

This chapter expands the scope of economic interactions to include the supply and use relationships of domestic sectors with foreign producers and consumers. Given the availability of internationally linked national input-output tables, trade activity can be examined in greater detail, such as facilitating the analysis of global value chains, reshoring, and comparative advantages, among other topics.

A fundamental concept in economics is that supply tends to meet demand. The discussion in the previous chapter emphasized the production of domestic sectors and the role other local sectors may play in fulfilling output requirements. Due to various reasons, however, demand in an economy is not always satisfied by domestic producers. One economy may be endowed with certain resources, while another may lack the capacity to foster and develop its economic advantages. While some economies are rich in minerals, precious metals, or fossil fuels, others experience scarcity in these resources. Some economies have advanced infrastructure or a highly skilled workforce, while others do not.

There has been significant interest, especially in recent literature, as to whether domestic economies are in the position of meeting their own needs (Bohn et al. 2021; Byé et al. 2021; Honsakhone et al. 2021; Ishikawa 2019; Jackson 2020; METI 2011; PSA 2006; Pourrostami 2018; Sim et al. 2007). This is traditionally measured in terms of self-sufficiency.

3.1 Self-Sufficiency

Borrowing from applications in food security and agriculture statistics, the Food and Agriculture Organization of the United Nations (1999) uses self-sufficiency to describe the extent to which an economy can satisfy its own demands. This ratio is useful in determining internal (or intraregional) dependence, domestic supply and demand gaps, and the need to tap foreign sources to meet such gaps. The self-sufficiency index is calculated by taking the proportion of domestic production to domestic consumption. Domestic consumption includes all intermediate inputs and final demand consumed in the domestic economy, irrespective of origin, and excludes exports.

A ratio or index equal to 1 signifies that total production equals total consumption, or perfect self-sufficiency. On an aggregate level, a ratio above 1 means that an economy is deemed to have domestic production levels significant enough to cover domestic demand levels. Conversely, a ratio less than 1 indicates low self-sufficiency. In this case, such economies may require foreign supply of goods and services to meet domestic needs.

These economy-wide interpretations hold if all sectors in the economy are homogenous, which in reality is not always the case. Thus, to offer an alternative perspective on economy-wide self-sufficiency rates, Figure 3.1 shows the percentage change in output (domestic production) and domestic demand from 2019 to 2020 among the sampled economies. Distinguishing between the growth in domestic production and demand allows for a clearer understanding of the decline in self-sufficiency across the 25 economies of Asia and the Pacific. Compared to change in output, a larger upswing (or smaller contraction) in domestic demand signifies whether an economy's self-sufficiency declines versus 2019 levels.

The island economies of Maldives and Fiji experienced the largest declines in output from 2019 to 2020: 29% and 24%, respectively. Further, Fiji's domestic demand grew by more than 28% in 2020. Meanwhile, amidst the pandemic, Bangladesh; the People's Republic of China (PRC); Taipei,China; and Viet Nam posted growth in both output and domestic demand, although only the PRC and Taipei,China saw increases in domestic production exceed growth in domestic demand.

Output either grew by more or contracted by less than domestic demand in 12 economies: Bhutan; Cambodia; Indonesia; India; the Lao People's Democratic Republic (Lao PDR); Mongolia; Nepal; Pakistan; the Philippines; the PRC; Singapore; and Taipei,China. The Lao PDR exhibited a notable growth of 11.5% in self-sufficiency, although this was not due to a remarkable increase in domestic production but by a 9.8% contraction in domestic demand, the largest recorded in Asia and the Pacific.

Figure 3.2 presents the 10 economy-sectors with the highest self-sufficiency ratios. Hong Kong, China's wood manufacturing sector ranks the highest in both years, with a self-sufficiency ratio of 138.5 in 2019 and 141 in 2020. Wood consumption in the economy is not as significant as consumption in other sectors as seen from Hong Kong, China's small demand for domestic and foreign intermediate inputs and final goods. Additionally, in both years, Hong Kong, China produced more wood and wood products for export than for local use. Thus, production of wood outputs geared toward exports drove the economy's self-sufficiency index up.

The sector that mostly appears in both year's rankings is the air transport sector. More air transport services in Bhutan, Mongolia, and Maldives, as both intermediate inputs and final outputs, are exported to the rest of the world than are purchased by domestic firms, households, and governments. Purchases of domestic air transport

Figure 3.1: Change in Output and Domestic Demand of Select Economies in Asia and the Pacific, 2019 to 2020
(%)

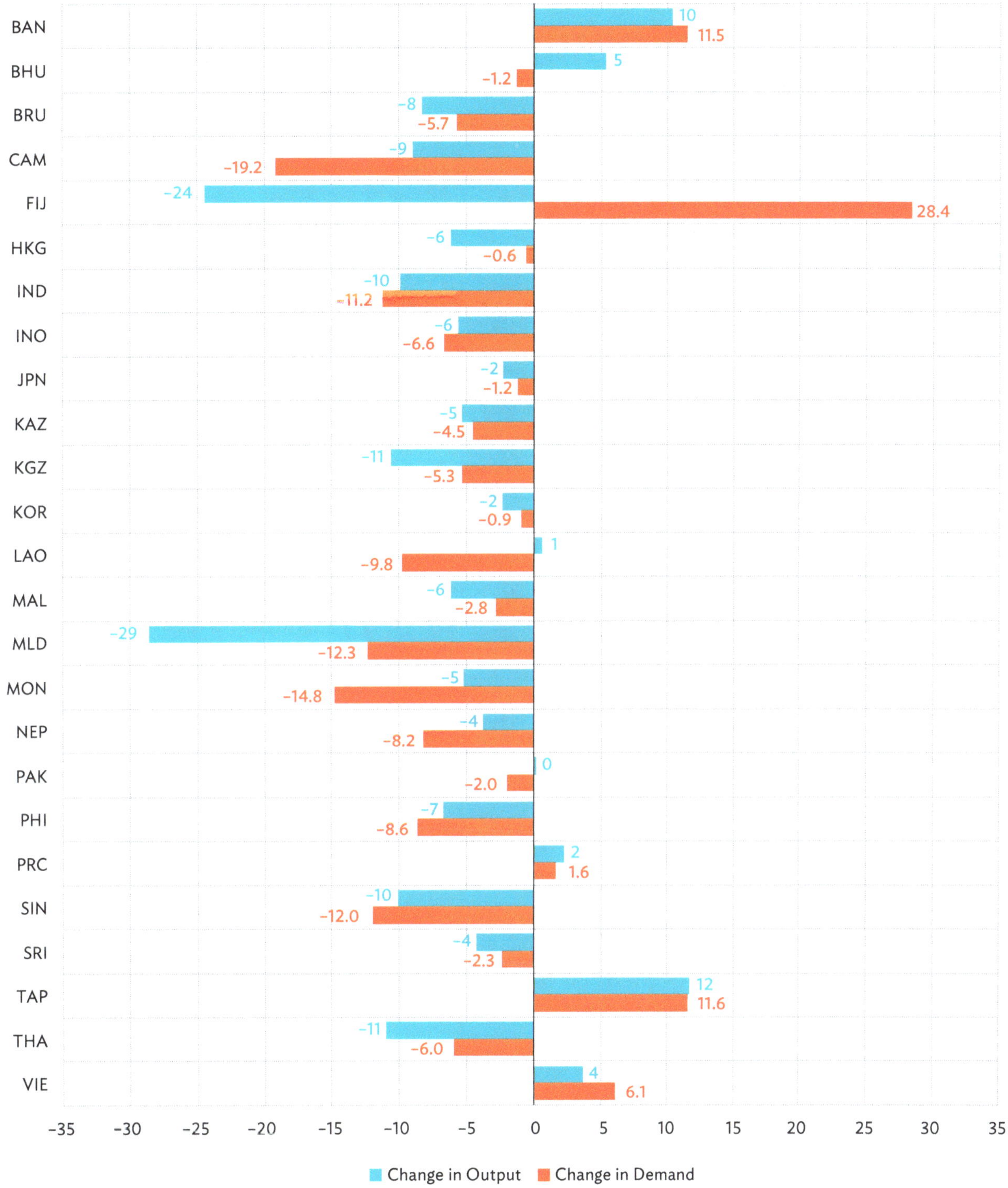

BAN = Bangladesh; BHU = Bhutan; BRU = Brunei Darussalam; CAM = Cambodia; FIJ = Fiji; HKG = Hong Kong, China; IND = India; INO = Indonesia; JPN = Japan; KAZ = Kazakhstan; KGZ = Kyrgyz Republic; KOR = Republic of Korea; LAO = Lao People's Democratic Republic; MAL = Malaysia; MLD = Maldives; MON = Mongolia; NEC = Not elsewhere classified; NEP = Nepal; PAK = Pakistan; PHI = Philippines; PRC = People's Republic of China; SIN = Singapore; SRI = Sri Lanka; TAP = Taipei,China; THA = Thailand; VIE = Viet Nam

Source: Calculations using the Asian Development Bank Multiregional Input–Output Table. https://mrio.adbx.online/ (accessed July 2021).

Click here for figure data

Figure 3.2: Sectors with the Highest Self-Sufficiency Ratios in Select Economies of Asia and the Pacific

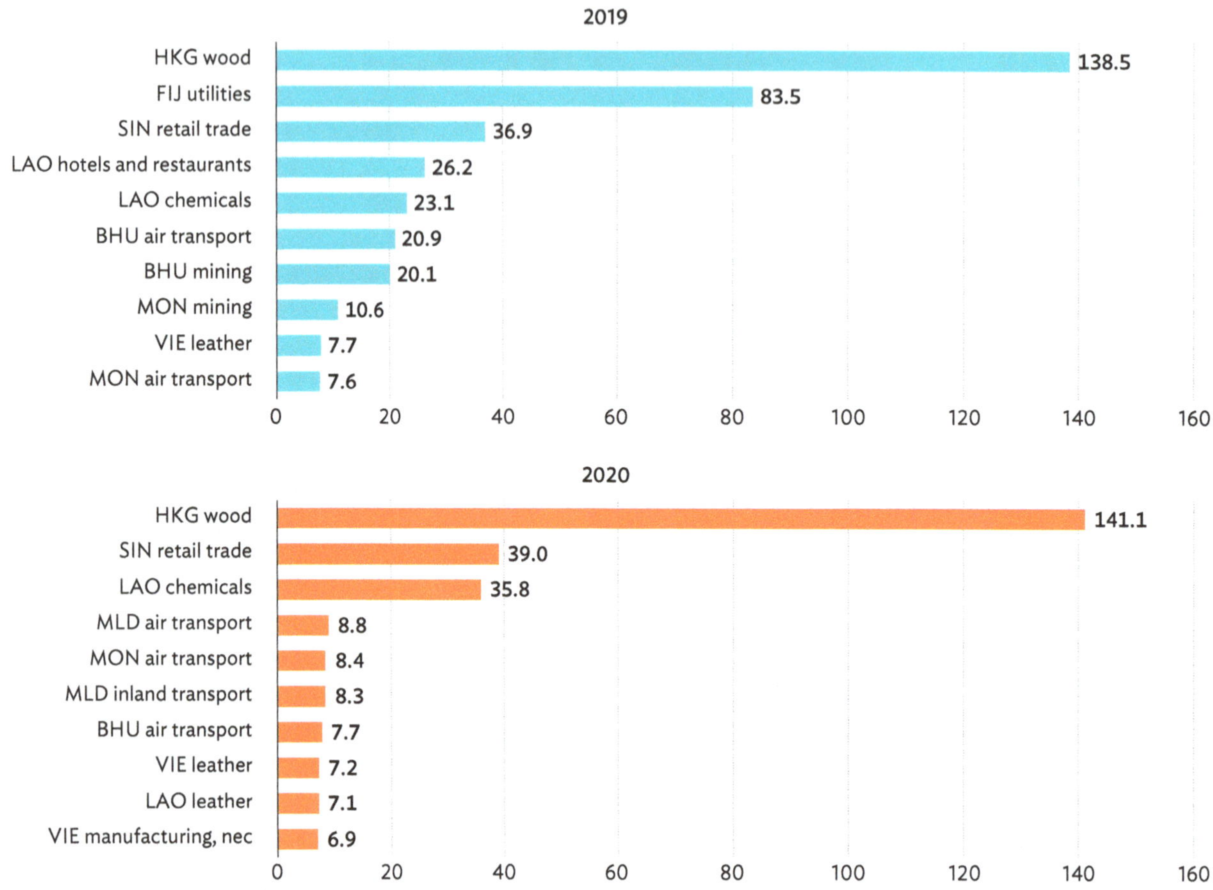

BHU = Bhutan; FIJ = Fiji; HKG = Hong Kong, China; LAO = Lao People's Democratic Republic; MLD = Maldives; MON = Mongolia; nec = not elsewhere classified; SIN = Singapore; VIE = Viet Nam.
Source: Calculations using the Asian Development Bank Multiregional Input–Output Table. https://mrio.adbx.online/ (accessed July 2021).

Click here for figure data

services by local industries and final consumers are much weaker compared to the imports from the rest of the world, which suggests that these economy-sectors service foreign firms, tourists, and travelers more substantially.

Taking the self-sufficiency index on an economy-wide level masks the heterogeneity of each sector in the mix. To illustrate, surplus service outputs certainly could not compensate for deficits in manufacturing output without material transformations in technology, labor, and resources. Firms that are unable to meet domestic and foreign demands would rather source their inputs abroad to be able to produce their goods and services.

3.2 Trade Orientation

In the modern global economy, local sectors do not operate independently. Businesses require access to overseas markets to source and supply their goods and services. Moreover, consumers in an economy also demand certain products that are not produced domestically. As economies develop and modernize, businesses tend to internationalize and consumers expand preferences beyond their own borders. To meet these needs, economies engage in international trade. This allows domestic producers to access inputs from abroad as well as exploit market opportunities for exports, while consumers can purchase products from international suppliers. Each economy may gravitate toward exporting more than importing or vice versa. Understanding the trade orientation of sectors and economies can inform trade and development strategies.

The trade orientation of a given sector within a given economy (described here as an "economy-sector") can be determined by its relative levels of, or dependence on, export and import activity. The **export orientation** (or *export-to-output ratio*) is obtained by dividing the economy-sector's exports to total output. Conversely, **import orientation** (or *import-to-input ratio*) is measured by taking an economy-sector's share of intermediate imports to total intermediate and primary inputs. A unit of output comprises all intermediate and primary inputs devoted to production; thus, total output is the same as total input. By looking at both measures, an economy's trade orientation simply provides the share of its total output (or total input) that is involved in external activities. Export-to-output and import-to-input ratios can similarly be calculated on a national level by taking the economy-wide aggregates of exports, intermediate imports, and gross output.

Figure 3.3 presents economy-wide export and import orientation ratios for 2019 and 2020. Noticeably, both trade ratios shrank in all economies except Cambodia. Singapore, Viet Nam, and Cambodia were the most trade-oriented economies in 2019 and 2020. While the two former economies experienced a slight decrease in trade orientation ratios, Cambodia saw a rise from 0.33 to 0.42 in export orientation and 0.22 to 0.33 in import orientation. The boost in Cambodia's trade orientation ratios was in part due to the economy's increased external trading activity and a lower output in 2020. The economy's non-imposition of exports ban, slight currency depreciation in 2020 against the United States dollar, and a surge in demand for products (such as machinery, electronics, bicycles, and milled rice) were some of the factors which brought trade levels upward. Meanwhile, Japan and the PRC, economies recognized as top importers and exporters, had ratios close to 0, indicating that the majority of their total production is sourced from and supplied to domestic sectors.

Figure 3.3: Trade Orientation of Select Economies in Asia and the Pacific

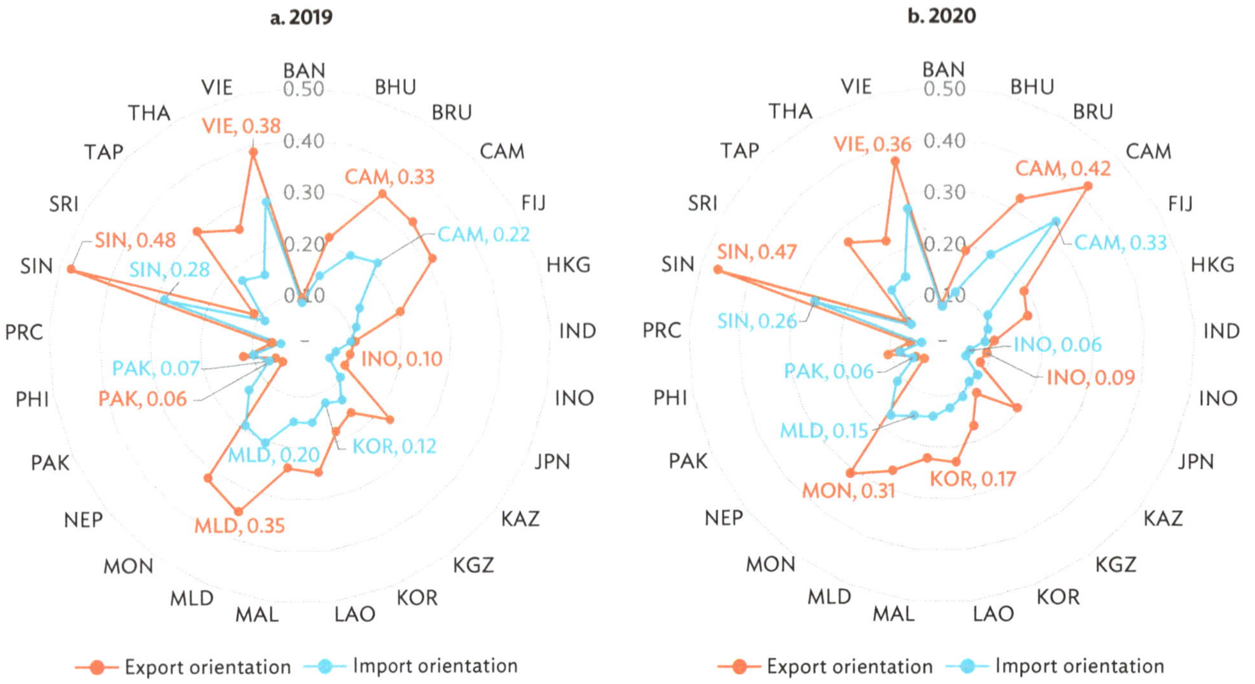

BAN = Bangladesh; BHU = Bhutan; BRU = Brunei Darussalam; CAM = Cambodia; FIJ = Fiji; HKG = Hong Kong, China; IND = India; INO = Indonesia; JPN = Japan; KAZ = Kazakhstan; KGZ = Kyrgyz Republic; KOR = Republic of Korea; LAO = Lao People's Democratic Republic; MAL = Malaysia; MLD = Maldives; MON = Mongolia; NEC = Not elsewhere classified; NEP = Nepal; PAK = Pakistan; PHI = Philippines; PRC = People's Republic of China; SIN = Singapore; SRI = Sri Lanka; TAP = Taipei,China; THA = Thailand; VIE = Viet Nam.

Note: Exports, intermediate imports, and output were aggregated to calculate economy-wide import-to-input and export-to-output ratios.

Source: Calculations using the Asian Development Bank Multiregional Input–Output Table. https://mrio.adbx.online/ (accessed July 2021).

Click here for figure data

On a sectoral level, most economies experienced a shrinking in export and import activities relative to output production from 2019 to 2020 (Figures 3.4 and 3.5). Most import-to-input ratios of purchasing sectors were much smaller than the export-to-output ratios of their producing counterparts, indicating that economies were more actively exporting than importing and could sustain local demand via domestic production. With the exception of Bangladesh, Japan, Pakistan, and the Republic of Korea, all economies had producing sectors with export-to-output ratios of 1 or close to 1. This observation is more apparent in Figure 3.4, which shows the export-to-output ratios of all economy-sectors in the region. Four sectors of interest are arbitrarily highlighted: production of refined fuels, electricals manufacturing, hotels and restaurants, and air transport.

Across the 25 economies for 2019 and 2020, the most export-oriented producing sectors were electricals, water transport services, and air transport services. The air transport sector was a close contender in 2019; it was found in the three most export-oriented sectors of Bangladesh; Bhutan; Fiji; India; Japan; Mongolia; the Republic of Korea; Taipei,China; and Thailand. However, due to the closure of

Figure 3.4: Export Orientation Ratios of Select Economies in Asia and the Pacific, by Sector

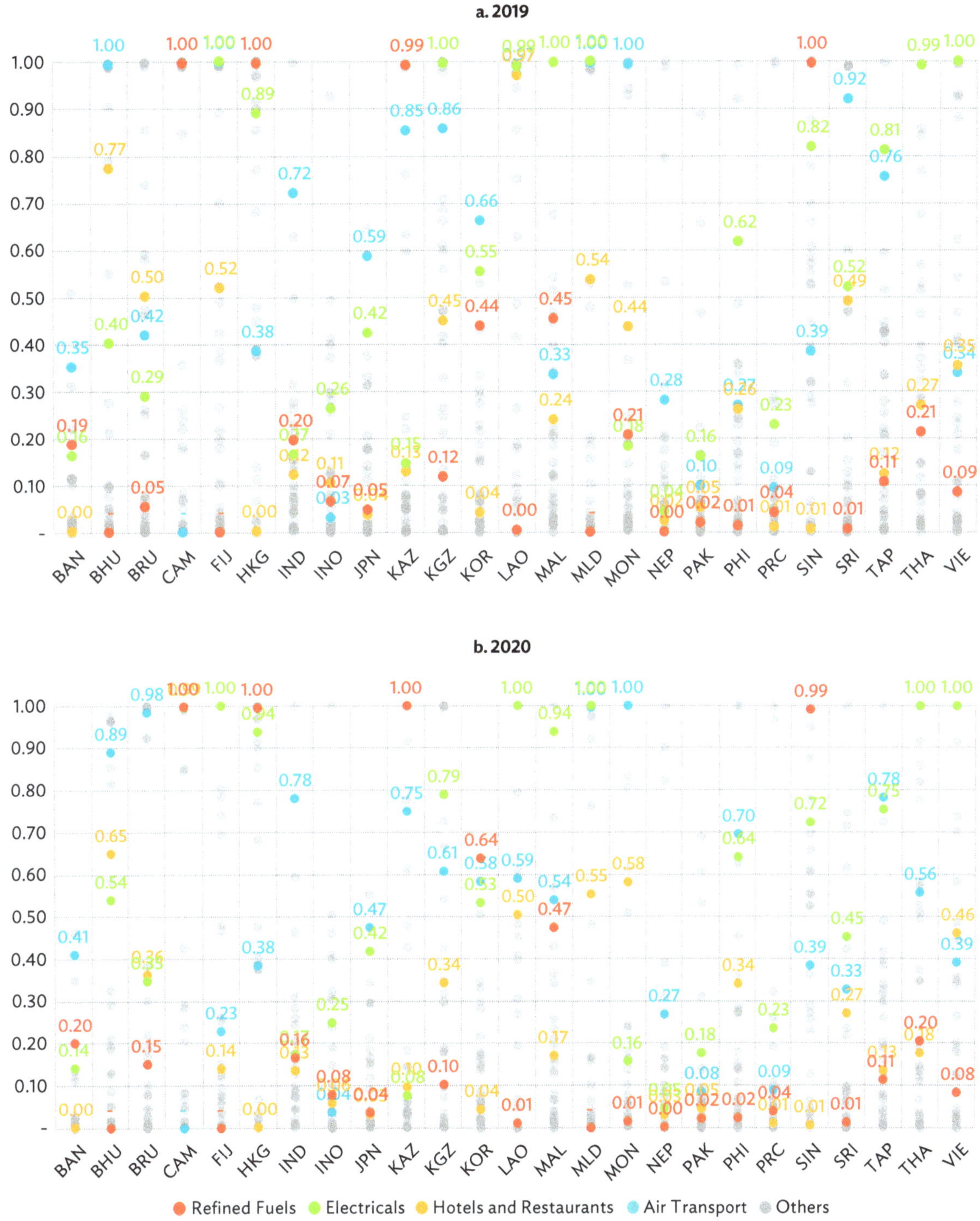

BAN = Bangladesh; BHU = Bhutan; BRU = Brunei Darussalam; CAM = Cambodia; FIJ = Fiji; HKG = Hong Kong, China; IND = India; INO = Indonesia; JPN = Japan; KAZ = Kazakhstan; KGZ = Kyrgyz Republic; KOR = Republic of Korea; LAO = Lao People's Democratic Republic; MAL = Malaysia; MLD = Maldives; MON = Mongolia; NEC = Not elsewhere classified; NEP = Nepal; PAK = Pakistan; PHI = Philippines; PRC = People's Republic of China; SIN = Singapore; SRI = Sri Lanka; TAP = Taipei,China; THA = Thailand; VIE = Viet Nam.

Note: Exports, intermediate imports, and output were aggregated to calculate economy-wide import-to-input and export-to-output ratios.

Source: Calculations using the Asian Development Bank Multiregional Input–Output Table. https://mrio.adbx.online/ (accessed July 2021).

Click here for figure data

Figure 3.5: Import Orientation Ratios of Select Economies in Asia and the Pacific, by Sector

BAN = Bangladesh; BHU = Bhutan; BRU = Brunei Darussalam; CAM = Cambodia; FIJ = Fiji; HKG = Hong Kong, China; IND = India; INO = Indonesia; JPN = Japan; KAZ = Kazakhstan; KGZ = Kyrgyz Republic; KOR = Republic of Korea; LAO = Lao People's Democratic Republic; MAL = Malaysia; MLD = Maldives; MON = Mongolia; NEC = Not elsewhere classified; NEP = Nepal; PAK = Pakistan; PHI = Philippines; PRC = People's Republic of China; SIN = Singapore; SRI = Sri Lanka; TAP = Taipei,China; THA = Thailand; VIE = Viet Nam.

Note: Exports, intermediate imports, and output were aggregated to calculate economy-wide import-to-input and export-to-output ratios.

Source: Calculations using the Asian Development Bank Multiregional Input–Output Table. https://mrio.adbx.online/ (accessed July 2021).

Click here for figure data

borders in 2020, export-to-output ratios in all economies fell, except in Maldives and Mongolia where airport and aviation services may have been dedicated entirely to nonresident passengers and foreign freight, and in Bhutan which experienced a significant decline in output.

With an export-to-output ratio of 1, Fiji, Malaysia, Maldives, and Viet Nam had electricals as their most export-oriented producing sector in 2019 and 2020. Japan; the Kyrgyz Republic; Malaysia; the Philippines; the Republic of Korea; Taipei,China; and Thailand also exhibited strong export-to-output ratios in electricals compared to other sectors. Although the entire Asia and Pacific region saw relatively incremental shifts in export orientation of electricals, Kazakhstan and the Kyrgyz Republic faced a significant drop in the ratio due to increased output and declining exports. Conversely, Bhutan and Brunei Darussalam experienced growth related to elevated export levels in electricals.

Export-to-output ratios in production of refined fuels, in contrast to those in air transport and electricals, sat in the lower segments of the figures, since fewer economies engaged in processing crude oil and petroleum for export. The Lao PDR, Nepal, and the Philippines exported sparse amounts of refined fuels, while Bhutan, Fiji, and Maldives did not export refined fuels at all. Meanwhile, Cambodia; Hong Kong, China; Kazakhstan; and Singapore were the most export-oriented in refined fuels, with ratios close to parity.

The export-to-output ratios in the hotels and restaurants sector varied widely across economies. Generally, East Asian economies, except Mongolia, did not dedicate much of their output to exports: Hong Kong, China;[1] Japan; the PRC, and the Republic of Korea exported less than 5% of their output in this sector. The index was much higher in all Southeast Asian economies, except Singapore. Cambodia and the Lao PDR topped the region in both 2019 and 2020. Tourist hotspots such as Fiji and Maldives boasted greater than average export-to-output shares of 0.52 and 0.54, respectively, in 2019. Maldives maintained its share (0.55) in 2020 despite a sharp decrease in output and export levels (approximately 60%). This is attributable to the Government of Maldives' decision to reopen borders for international travelers early in July 2020. Meanwhile, Fiji dropped to a share of 0.14 in 2020 due to an 80% drop in exports. The economy started welcoming international tourists only on 1 December 2021, almost 2 years after it closed its borders in March 2020.

1 Value for Hong Kong, China excludes direct purchases by nonresidents in the domestic territory.

Looking at Figure 3.5, import-to-input ratios are smaller overall compared to export-to-output ratios. However, there are a few economy-sectors in the region that rely significantly on imported inputs. As observed, only Mongolia's electricals purchasing sector comes the closest in relying completely on imports of inputs, with an import-to-input ratio of 0.84 in 2019 and 0.85 in 2020. Production of refined fuels in Cambodia also features a relatively large import-orientation index of 0.72 in both years. These two purchasing sectors are the most import-oriented sectors across Asia and the Pacific.

In addition, Malaysia, Nepal, Pakistan, the Philippines, the PRC, Sri Lanka, and Viet Nam regard the electricals sector as a significant importing industry. For 2019 and 2020, electricals maintained its position as the most import-oriented sector in Malaysia, Mongolia, Nepal, and Viet Nam, whereas Fiji and Maldives performed rather low on this metric. This is because the majority of the electrical imports in these two economies are for final consumption and, compared to other economies, production of electricals for domestic consumption and exporting is minimal.

Production of refined fuels was in the three most import-oriented sectors in 12 of the 25 participating economies: Cambodia; Hong Kong, China; India; Japan; Pakistan; the Philippines; the PRC; the Republic of Korea; Singapore; Sri Lanka; Taipei,China; and Thailand. This is expected, given not all economies have sufficient petroleum, coal, and oil reserves that can be tapped and processed into usable fuels for domestic consumption. Moreover, each economy has specific input requirements and considerations for power generation. For instance, the PRC is considered a top oil- and coal-producing economy, yet it is also a top importer of the same inputs. India is both a large coal producer and importer. On the other hand, Indonesia has substantial oil reserves and does not import significantly for further processing. Bhutan, Fiji, and Maldives have zero import-to-input ratios, signifying that they only import coal and crude oil as inputs to production minimally.

3.3 Trade Openness

The two sides of trade orientation—exporting and importing activity—can be summarized in a **trade openness** index that considers an economy's gross domestic product (GDP). Also called the trade-to-GDP ratio, trade openness is a measure of the extent to which an economy is integrated in the global economy through trade. It is measured simply by taking the ratio of the economy's total exports and imports to the total GDP. Thus, a value greater than 1 indicates higher reliance on trade, as total trade activity exceeds value-added generation by the domestic economy. A value below 1 may indicate lower dependence on trade, or lower participation in trading which may be due to economic crises, currency fluctuations, supply disruptions, and demand changes, among others.

Figure 3.6 depicts the trade openness indexes mapped and scaled to the GDP (in trillions) of the 25 economies in Asia and the Pacific for 2019 and 2020. Comparing these 2 years, trade openness in all economies, except Brunei Darussalam and Cambodia, fell by an average of 13%. However, not all economies experienced a severe contraction in GDP. For instance, Bangladesh, the PRC, and Viet Nam experienced some economic growth despite the pandemic. Most remarkably, Cambodia's trade activity experienced a rise in both imports and exports, consistent with the findings from the trade orientation ratios.

Evidently, smaller economies are more dependent on trade. Driven by stable levels of exports and imports in electrical and optical equipment, Viet Nam and Singapore led with total trade eclipsing GDP in 2019 and 2020. Generally, trade openness seems to be inversely related to the size of an economy. Trade openness of the five largest economies in Asia and the Pacific (by order of GDP levels)—the PRC, Japan, India, the Republic of Korea, and Indonesia—fell below 1 in both 2019 and 2020.

Most economies with relatively higher degrees of trade openness belong to Southeast Asia and the Pacific, while those with lower degrees of trade openness are found in South and Central Asia.

Figure 3.6: Trade Openness of Select Economies in Asia and the Pacific

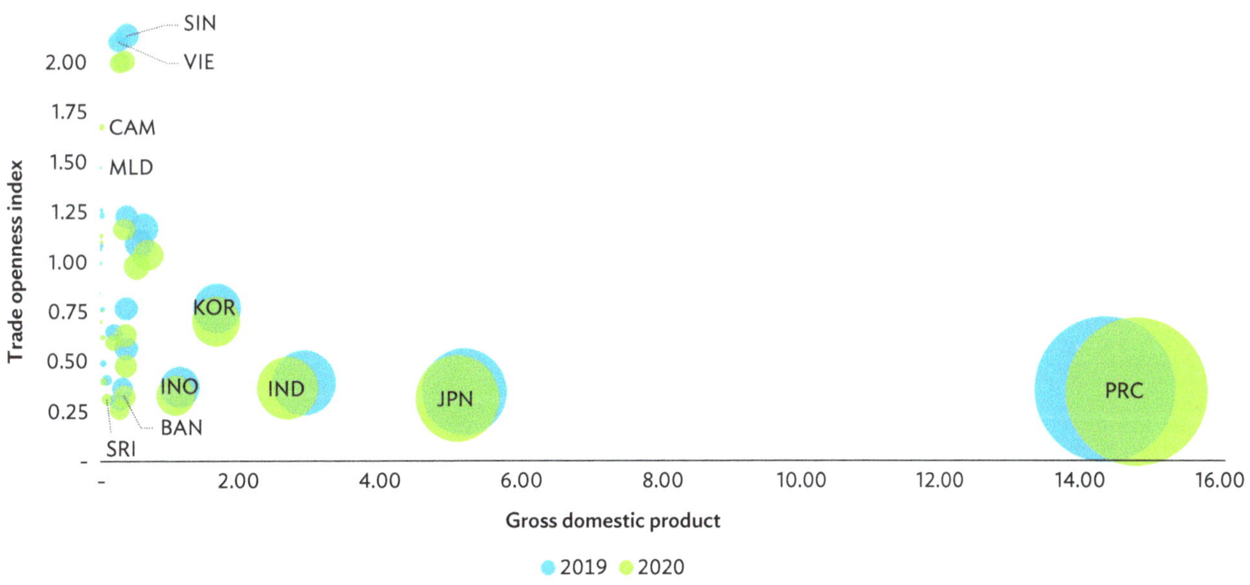

BAN = Bangladesh; CAM = Cambodia; IND = India; INO = Indonesia; JPN = Japan; KOR = Republic of Korea; MLD = Maldives; PRC = People's Republic of China; SIN = Singapore; SRI = Sri Lanka; VIE = Viet Nam.
Note: 25 economies are mapped, but only select economies are labeled.
Source: Calculations using the Asian Development Bank Multiregional Input-Output Table. https://mrio.adbx.online/ (accessed July 2021).

Click here for figure data

In East Asia, the PRC, Japan, and the Republic of Korea boasted the highest trading levels for both 2019 and 2020 (Figure 3.7). The former two economies were the largest producers in all of Asia and the Pacific in 2019 and 2020. However, their immense domestic production bases were irrelevant in the context of trade activities, ranking only 23rd and 24th, respectively, among the 25 participating economies in terms of trade openness in 2019. Meanwhile, Mongolia, albeit the smallest in terms of trade and domestic production, ranked fourth in the entire region and was only one of two economies in East Asia with trade openness indexes above 1.

Figure 3.7: Trade Openness of Select Economies in East Asia

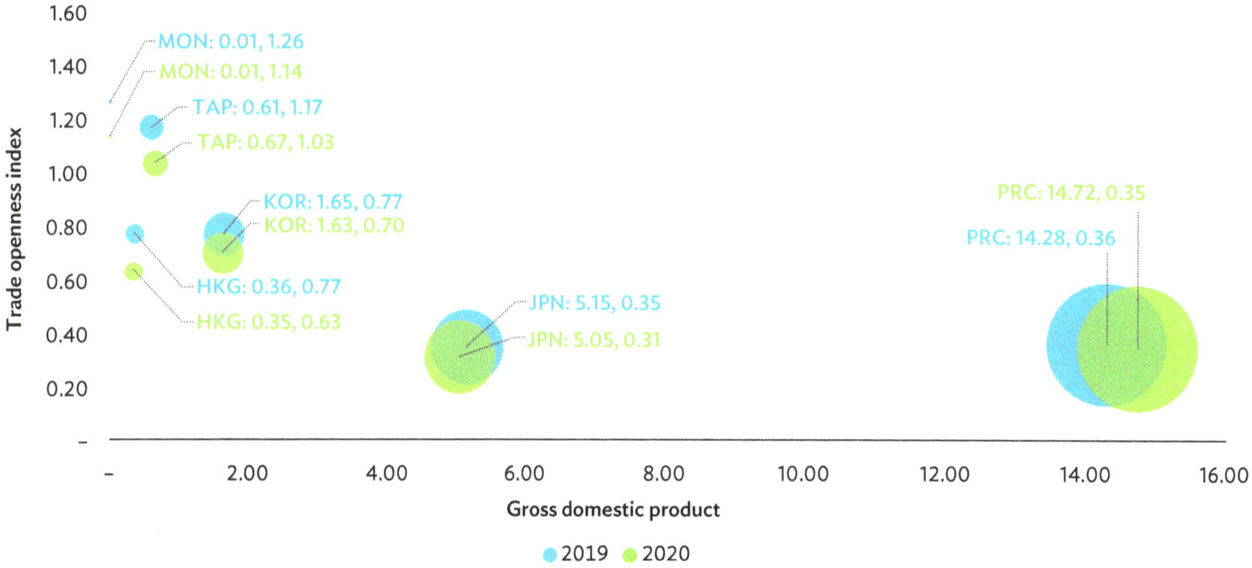

HKG = Hong Kong, China; JPN = Japan; KOR = Republic of Korea; MON = Mongolia; PRC = People's Republic of China; TAP = Taipei,China.
Note: The labels separated by semicolons are ordered as follows: economy abbreviation, gross domestic product in trillions of United States dollars, and trade openness index.
Source: Calculations using the Asian Development Bank Multiregional Input–Output Table. https://mrio.adbx.online/ (accessed July 2021).

Click here for figure data

The observed trend between GDP level and trade openness is most apparent in South and Central Asia, as shown in Figure 3.8. The subregion saw an overall decline in openness to trade 2020, with the effects of falling imports more pronounced than declining exports. All economies, except Maldives, exhibited low indexes for trade openness. With the third-lowest total trade and GDP levels in Asia and the Pacific in 2019, Maldives reported the greatest trade openness in South and Central Asia, being the only economy with an index above 1. In fact, even though its total exports and imports fell by close to 88% in 2020, Maldives remained the most trade-open economy in the subregion. Meanwhile, the Kyrgyz Republic faced the most severe contraction in trade openness among all economies, falling 29% from 2019 to 2020, while Sri Lanka experienced a 25% reduction.

Figure 3.8: Trade Openness of Select Economies in South and Central Asia

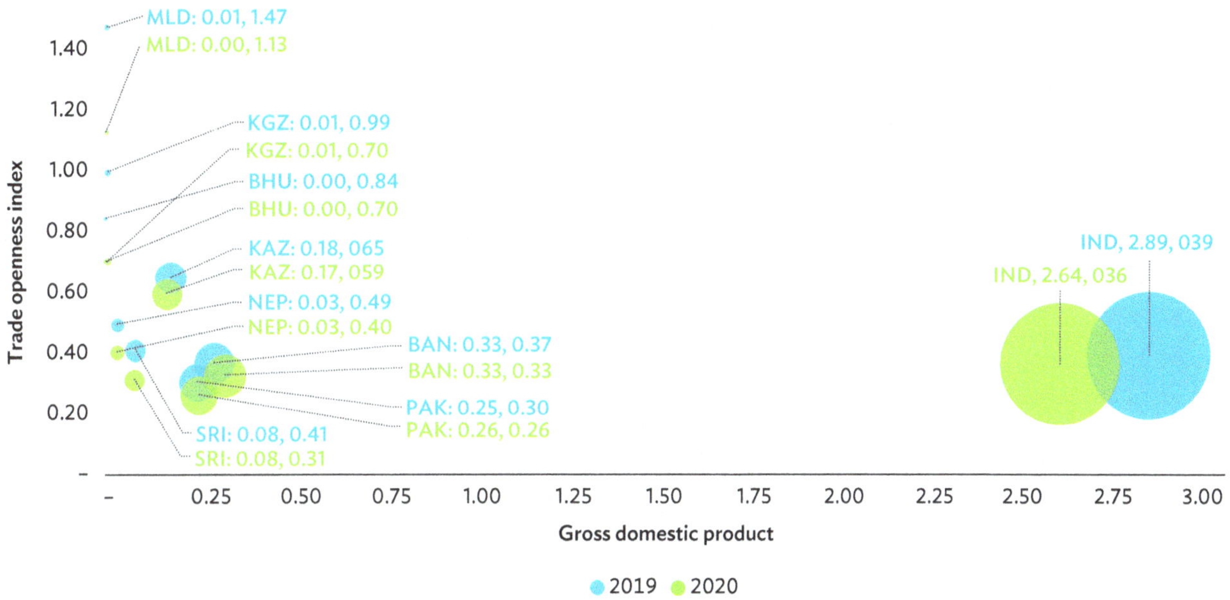

BAN = Bangladesh; BHU = Bhutan; IND = India; KAZ = Kazakhstan; KGZ = Kyrgyz Republic; MLD = Maldives; NEP = Nepal; PAK = Pakistan; SRI = Sri Lanka.

Note: The labels separated by semicolons are ordered as follows: economy abbreviation, gross domestic product in trillions of United States dollars, and trade openness index.

Source: Calculations using the Asian Development Bank Multiregional Input–Output Table. https://mrio.adbx.online/ (accessed July 2021).

Click here for figure data

The subregion of Southeast Asia and the Pacific presents unique perspectives on trade and GDP. Malaysia, Singapore, and Viet Nam—economies with sizable levels of GDP—maintained higher-than-average trade openness indexes in both 2019 and 2020 (Figure 3.9). In fact, after the PRC in East Asia, these three economies felt the smallest contraction in trade openness from 2019 to 2020. Contrary to Maldives in South and Central Asia, the Pacific island economy of Fiji did not post a similar level of trade openness in 2020. Due to a severe contraction in trade of 45%, the economy recorded the second sharpest decline in trade-to-GDP ratio after the Kyrgyz Republic. Nevertheless, Fiji still ranked in the 10 most-open economies in Asia and the Pacific. Finally, Brunei Darussalam and Cambodia were the only economies in the region to experience a rise in their respective trade openness indexes from 2019 to 2020.

Figure 3.9: Trade Openness of Select Economies in Southeast Asia and the Pacific

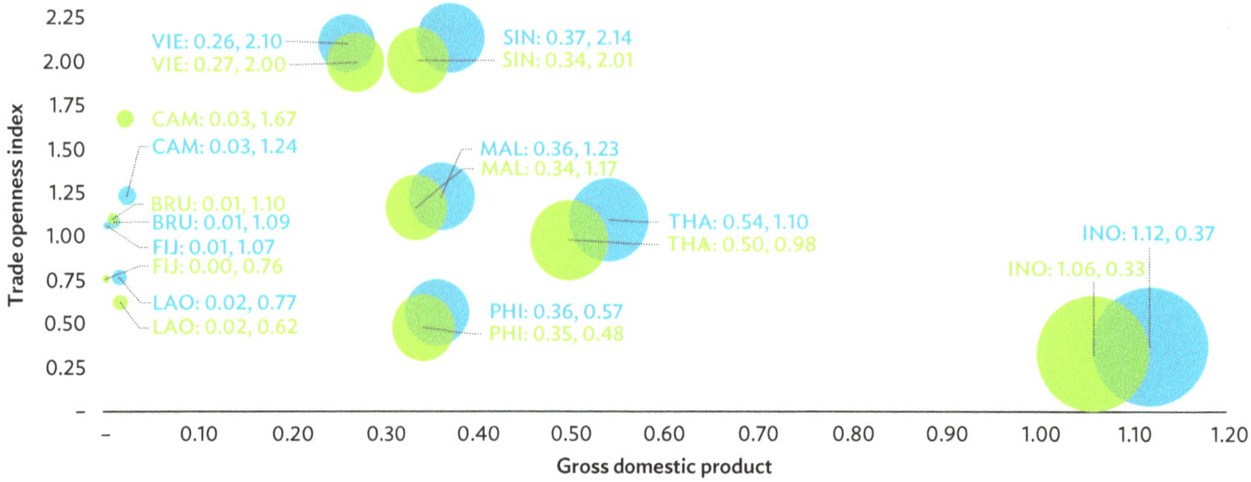

BRU = Brunei Darussalam; CAM = Cambodia; FIJ = Fiji; INO = Indonesia; LAO = Lao People's Democratic Republic; MAL = Malaysia; PHI = Philippines; SIN = Singapore; THA = Thailand; VIE = Viet Nam.

Note: The labels separated by semicolons are ordered as follows: economy abbreviation, gross domestic product in trillions of United States dollars, and trade openness index.

Source: Calculations using the Asian Development Bank Multiregional Input–Output Table. https://mrio.adbx.online/ (accessed July 2021).

Click here for figure data

3.4 Domestic and Foreign Input Shares in Intermediate Inputs

At the height of the COVID-19 pandemic, economies were faced with restricted domestic production capabilities and resources. To fulfill domestic demand, several economies resorted to imports of final goods. Likewise, exporting economies experienced shortages of inputs on account of supply chain disruptions. As a result, the trade orientation of some economies appeared to change direction during the crisis.

Such observations arose from input–output tables that differentiate sources of inputs by the originating economy. Domestic input comprises all intersectoral (intermediate) inputs purchased from domestic sectors, while foreign inputs are purchased from abroad. **Domestic input shares** are obtained by taking the share of total domestic intermediate inputs to total output. By simply replacing the numerator with imported inputs, one obtains the **foreign input shares**, which are the same as import-to-input ratios.

Using these ratios, the multiregional input–output (MRIO) analysis shows that all economies, except Cambodia, experienced a rise in domestic input dependence in 2020. The pandemic was largely responsible for the shrinking of import activity. In fact, the regional average of foreign input share fell by 9.17% from 2019 to 2020, while the domestic input share grew by an average of 2.91%. Figure 3.10 details this by showing the domestic and foreign input shares in the total output of each economy in 2019 and 2020. The results

Figure 3.10: Domestic and Foreign Input Shares of Select Economies in Asia and the Pacific

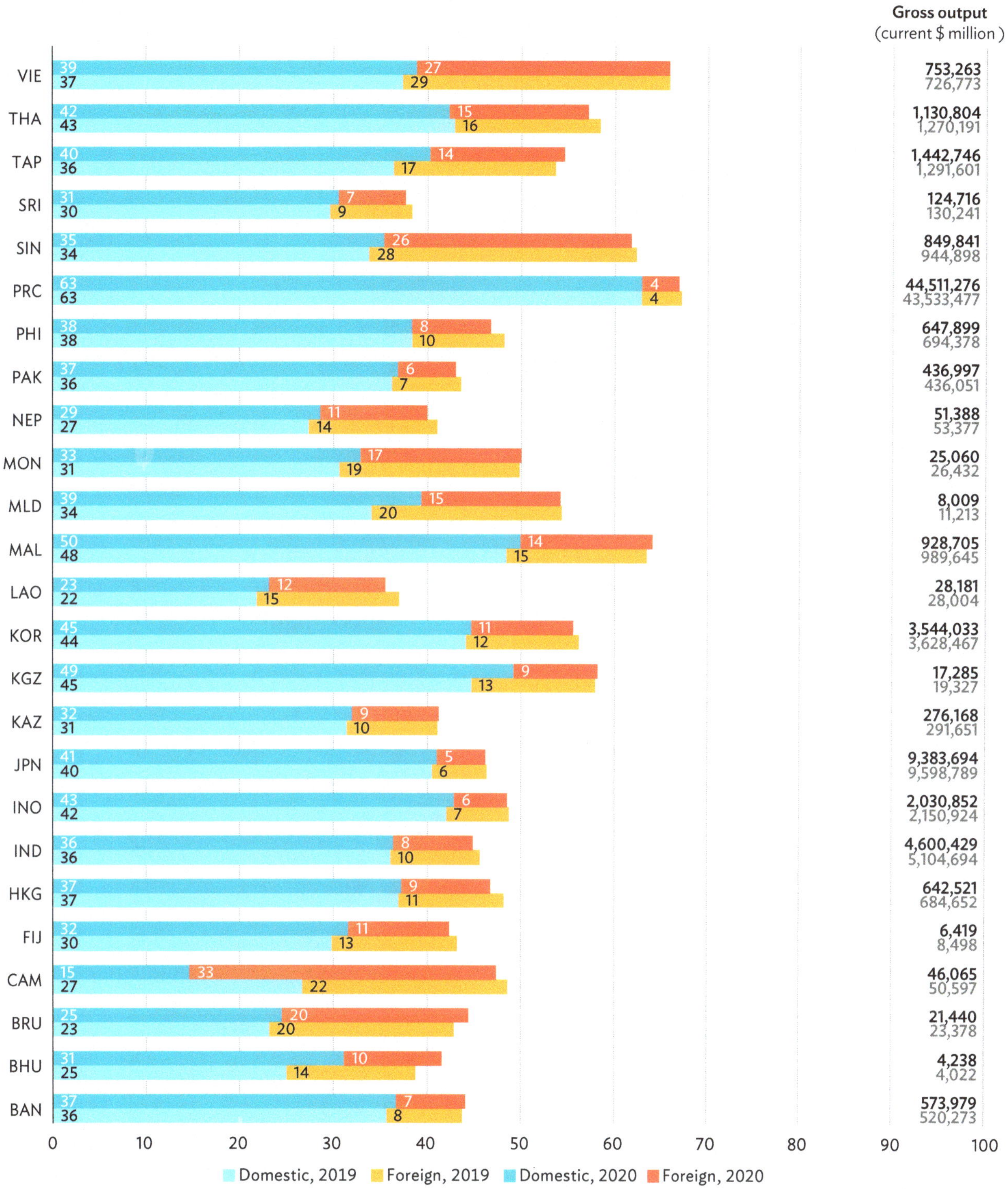

BAN = Bangladesh; BHU = Bhutan; BRU = Brunei Darussalam; CAM = Cambodia; FIJ = Fiji; HKG = Hong Kong, China; IND = India; INO = Indonesia; JPN = Japan; KAZ = Kazakhstan; KGZ = Kyrgyz Republic; KOR = Republic of Korea; LAO = Lao People's Democratic Republic; MAL = Malaysia; MLD = Maldives; MON = Mongolia; NEC = Not elsewhere classified; NEP = Nepal; PAK = Pakistan; PHI = Philippines; PRC = People's Republic of China; SIN = Singapore; SRI = Sri Lanka; TAP = Taipei,China; THA = Thailand; VIE = Viet Nam

Note: Domestic inputs, intermediate imports, and output were aggregated to calculate economy-wide domestic and foreign input shares.

Source: Calculations using the Asian Development Bank Multiregional Input–Output Table. https://mrio.adbx.online/ (accessed July 2021).

Click here for figure data

are the opposite of those found when analyzing import orientation: the PRC reported the highest domestic input share of 63% in both years, followed by Malaysia, the Republic of Korea, and Kazakhstan, with domestic input shares close to 50%. Meanwhile, Cambodia reported one of the lowest domestic input shares in 2019 and the lowest in 2020 at 15%.

3.5 Import Leakage Effects

The shares of foreign inputs discussed in section 3.4 provide first insights into how an economy might be connected to globally integrated production. Many sectors may find importing inputs and resources more affordable than producing them locally. When these industries depend on foreign suppliers, the goods and services they produce at home are then associated with a certain level of production abroad. These dependencies, when modeled in an input–output framework, are called "leakages," alluding to the amount of output that is foregone in domestic production.

Backward linkages indicate how much *domestic* output is generated due to a change in final demand in sector *i*. Meanwhile, forward linkages describe the total *domestic* output resulting from the available primary inputs in sector *j*. This analysis can be extended to capture the output effects in foreign economies (Reis and Rua 2006). **Import leakage effects**, or more formally **import multipliers**, suggest that the gains from production do not accrue entirely to the domestic economy because foreign-sourced inputs are used in production processes, thereby "leaking" into other economies. While leakage may imply a negative effect to the domestic economy, dependence on foreign inputs does not automatically impede an economy's potential output. Recent studies illustrate how some economies can use imports to their advantage, primarily to increase competitiveness of domestic production (World Bank 2020). Analogous to intersectoral linkages, import leakages can also be split into backward and forward leakages.

The backward import multiplier (or backward leakage) indicates the total amount of production that accrues outside the economy due to an exogenous change in final demand of sector *i*. For instance, suppose an economy imports iron ore from a foreign mining sector to produce its own steel. If steel production changes due to changes in demand in, say, increased building construction, the foreign production of iron ore would also be affected through backward leakage effects. Thus, backward leakage identifies the most important sectors in the economy in terms of how those sectors can stimulate productive activities in nondomestic sectors. In other words, sectors that are more dependent on foreign sectors' supply could be interpreted as having high backward leakage effects. Defining A^f as the matrix of imported input coefficients while A^d as the matrix of domestic input coefficients, the backward leakage matrix is expressed as $A^f (I - A^d)^{-1}$. The sum of the elements in the jth column provides the total backward leakage or the value of all imports due to a one-unit increase in the final demand for sector *j*'s output (Dietzenbacher et al. 2005).

The distribution of backward import leakage effects of sectors in the Asia and Pacific region for 2020 are shown in Figure 3.11. Industrial sectors in the region, such as the manufacturing and utilities sectors, generally exhibited high backward leakage effects. Upstream sectors, such as agriculture and mining, were in the median range, given their low dependence on inputs from nondomestic sectors. Meanwhile, the public and private services sector remained at the low end of the distribution, alongside business and financial intermediation services. The utilities sector and financial intermediation services showed the widest range of backward leakage values among the 25 economies in the region. This indicates heterogeneity in production structures and sourcing patterns for their inputs. For example, input–output tables show that Viet Nam's utility sectors have low dependence on foreign supply, while Singapore's financial intermediation services rely on foreign sectors more than the other economies in the region.

Figure 3.11: Sectoral Distribution of Backward Leakages in Select Economies of Asia and the Pacific, 2020

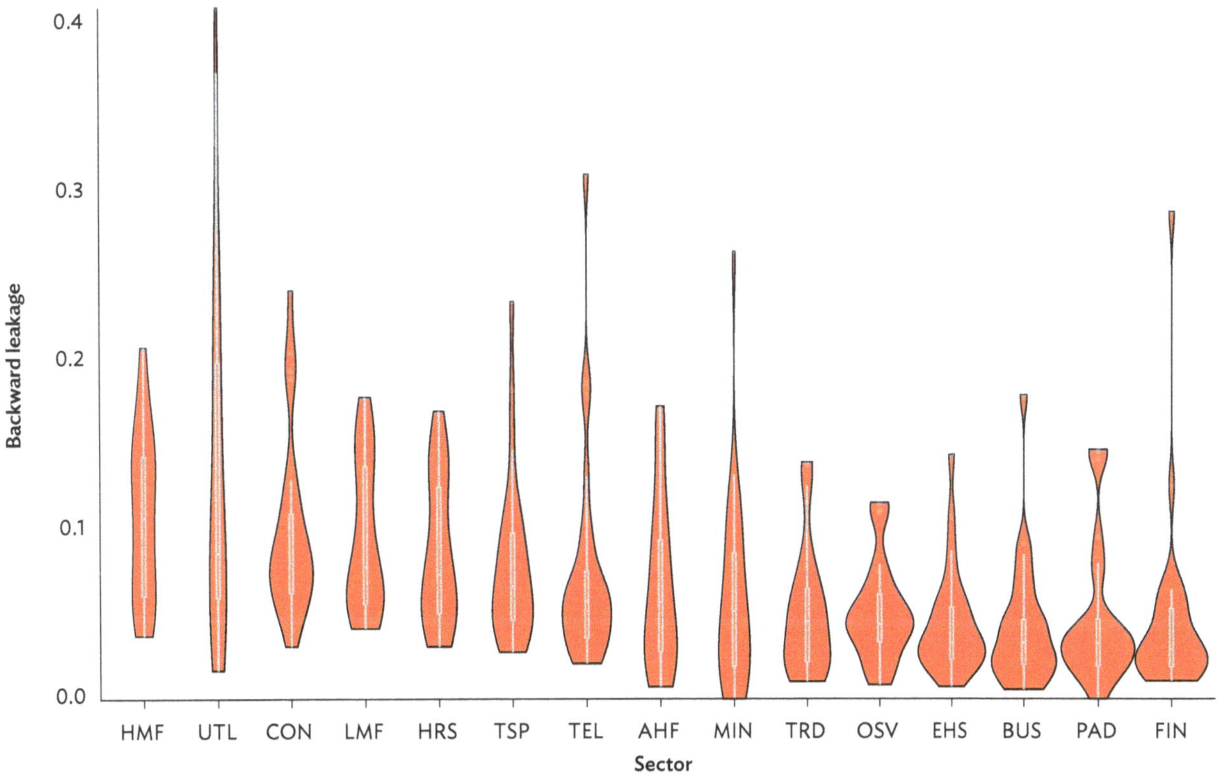

AHF = agriculture, hunting, forestry, and fishing; BUS = business services including real estate; CON = construction; EHS = education and health services; FIN = finance and insurance; HMF = heavy manufacturing; HRS = hotel and restaurant services; LMF = light manufacturing; MIN = mining and quarrying; OSV = other services; PAD = public administration; TEL = post and telecommunications; TRD = wholesale and retail trade; TSP = transport services; UTL = utilities.

Note: The violin plot visualizes the numerical distribution of backward import multipliers, wherein wider sections of the violin plot represent higher probability that sampled economies will exhibit the given value in the vertical axis and vice versa.

Source: Calculations using the Asian Development Bank Multiregional Input–Output Table. https://mrio.adbx.online/ (accessed July 2021).

Click here for figure data

Meanwhile, the **forward import multiplier** (or forward leakage) indicates the total amount of production that accrues outside the economy as a result of an exogenous change in the availability of primary inputs in domestic sector *j*. To take the same example as above, the economy that produces steel may export part of its output to a foreign construction sector, where it will be used to build houses. If the economy's steel output changes, the housing construction abroad would also be affected, resulting in forward leakage. Analysis of forward leakage identifies the most important sectors in the economy in terms of how those sectors can support productive activities in nondomestic sectors. Sectors that provide more inputs to foreign production exhibit high forward leakage effects. If O^f is the matrix of imported output coefficients and O^d is the matrix of domestic output coefficients, the forward leakage matrix can be expressed as $(I - O^d)^{-1} O^f$. The sum of the elements in the ith row of the matrix provides the total forward leakage effect or the total nondomestic output resulting from a unit change in primary inputs in domestic sector *i*.

Figure 3.12 combines the two types of import leakage for aggregated sectors in the 25 participating economies of Asia and the Pacific. Sectors clustered above the 45-degree line, such as business services, have relatively higher forward leakages. That is, these sectors' primary inputs can generate more output abroad than demand for their own products. Conversely, sectors clustered below the 45-degree line, such as low-technology manufacturing and public and welfare services, have relatively higher backward leakages. This implies that final demands for low-technology and public and welfare services could potentially induce more production abroad (i.e., demand-pull), than the mere availability of their primary inputs or value-added and imports for absorption in downstream production (i.e., supply-push). For primary sectors (i.e., agriculture and mining), import leakages are generally dispersed as they are for high- and medium-technology sectors. The range of backward and forward leakage values in Figure 3.12 indicate the various positions that these sectors take in international production chains.

Figure 3.12: Import Leakages by Sectors of Select Economies in Asia and the Pacific, 2020

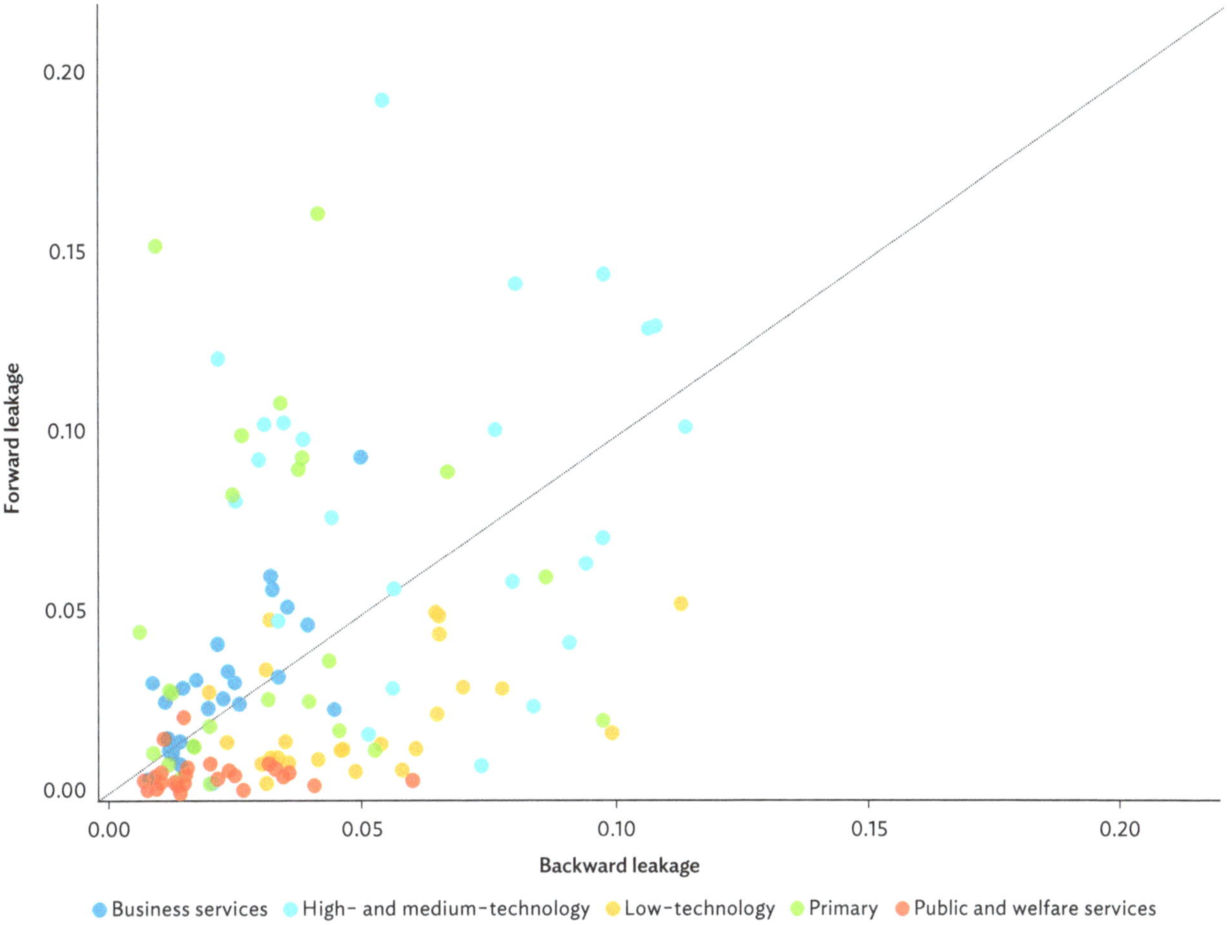

Note: Results are aggregated at the five-sector level.
Source: Calculations using the Asian Development Bank Multiregional Input–Output Table for 2020. https://mrio.adbx.online/ (accessed July 2021).

Click here for figure data

3.6 Intraregional and Interregional Effects

The leakage effects show the direction of impacts from the supply (forward) and demand (backward) of the local economy to foreign counterparts. However, another perspective on international linkage is to determine the reverse: the impact of foreign demand to local production. This can be obtained by first recreating the multiregional input–output table, such that the intersectoral transactions of one region with another are explicitly shown. In the MRIO context, one "region" may be the economy under study, while the other region could represent transactions with the rest of the world.

Using this multiregional input–output table, the output of a sector may be decomposed into four components. First, a sector produces to satisfy final demands (called "direct intraregional" output). Second, it produces to supply domestic sectors with inputs required for their respective final goods and services (known as the "intraregional transfer effect" or "M1"). Third, the sector may supply some inputs to foreign sectors in their own production of final goods and services (referred to as the "interregional spillover effect" or "M2"). Finally, the sector may supply inputs to foreign sectors that also provide inputs to the production of final goods and services within the receiving economy (termed the "interregional feedback effect" or "M3"). The first two terms offer insights on domestic linkages, while the last two describe links with international production chains. Further descriptions of these terms' derivation are available in the technical notes.

To illustrate, consider a metal manufacturer in economy A. Some certain amount of the manufacturer's output will be purchased by sectors inside the economy, such as local car manufacturers and construction firms. These outputs directly and indirectly purchased for domestic production of final goods represent a pure intraregional effect (M1). However, some metals may be purchased by an engine manufacturer in economy B for its own production of foreign cars. The production in A attributable to meeting final demand in B is considered the pure interregional spillover effect.

However, if economy A's manufacture of cars also uses a specialized engine from economy B, which in turn happens to purchase its supply of metal parts from economy A, this results in production in economy A that loops to itself via economy B. The demand for metal parts in economy B's engines, which are ultimately embodied in cars produced by economy A, represents an interregional feedback effect. This effect materializes when economies are involved in vertically integrated production processes.

Results of decomposition of intraregional and interregional effects for the 25 economies of Asia and the Pacific in 2020 are illustrated in Figure 3.13. Bangladesh, Sri Lanka, and Pakistan had larger shares of outputs that were mainly attributable to domestic linkages (M1) rather than external spillover effects (M2 and M3). Meanwhile, Brunei Darussalam, Mongolia, and Singapore posted sizable shares of interregional spillover (M2) and feedback (M3) effects in their gross outputs. Generally, economies that exhibited higher spillover effects tended to be more open to trade, specializing in the export of manufactured goods such as electrical equipment and energy-related products.

Figure 3.13: Intraregional and Interregional Effects of Select Economies in Asia and the Pacific, 2020
(% of total output)

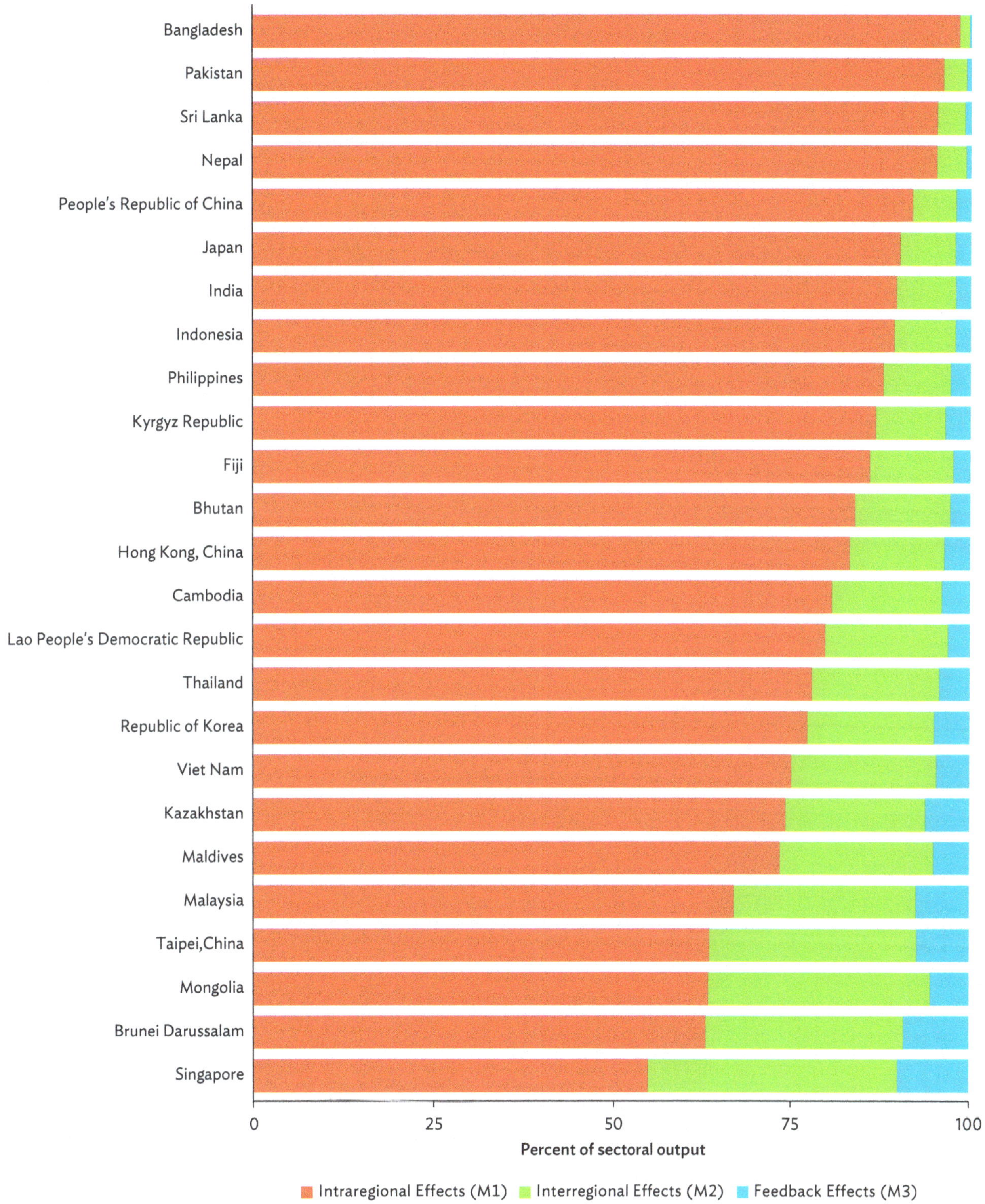

Source: Calculations using the Asian Development Bank Multiregional Input–Output Table for 2020. https://mrio.adbx.online/ (accessed July 2021).

Click here for figure data

3.7 Value-Added Trade Accounting

The decomposition of output described in section 3.6, while providing baseline insights on a sector's engagement in vertically integrated production chains, could be refined by using exports. The familiar measure of gross exports is a composite of several distinct types of trading. A large part of the gross figure consists of direct trading—the classical form of trade that involves value-added crossing one border to be finally consumed. Increasingly, however, trade may be indirect. Taipei,China might receive semiconductor blueprints from Japan, manufacturing them for use in electronics produced in the Republic of Korea, which are then sent to Viet Nam for assembly into appliances that are sold in Singapore's shopping malls. While only adjacent economies along this chain have a direct trading relationship, all participants have an indirect relationship with one another.

The rise of cross-border production-sharing arrangements known as global value chains (GVCs) has made it necessary to develop new indicators that take this phenomenon into account. Several such indicators are derived from a value-added trade accounting framework, which decomposes export flows into their basic value-added components. For example, an export of $100 worth of electronics from Viet Nam to Germany will contain both Vietnamese value-added and value-added that Viet Nam imported from other economies as inputs. Moreover, only some of this $100 will be consumed by Germany; a portion may be reexported and consumed elsewhere. Tracking these portions is the objective of the accounting framework.

As described in ADB's *Key Indicators for Asia and the Pacific* 2021 (ADB 2021), the framework adopted by the ADB GVC research—based primarily on Borin and Mancini (2019)—decomposes export flows from economy *s* to economy *r* into five mutually exclusive value-added categories:

(i) Directly absorbed value-added exports (DAVAX). Value-added solely from economy *s* that is exported to and absorbed solely in economy *r*.
(ii) Reexports (REX). Value-added solely from economy *s* that is exported to and reexported by economy *r*, to be absorbed abroad.
(iii) Reflection (REF). Value-added solely from economy *s* that is exported to and reexported by economy *r*, to eventually be absorbed back home by economy *s*.
(iv) Foreign value-added (FVA). Non-*s* value-added embedded in economy *s* exports to economy *r*.
(v) Pure double-counting (PDC). Any value-added involved in economy *s* exports to economy *r* that cross the same border twice or more.

First on the list is directly absorbed value-added exports (DAVAX), synonymous with direct trading. The other four categories involve indirect trading, defined more precisely as cases where value-added crosses at least two borders before final consumption. This occurs when the direct importer reexports what it imports, passing it along the value chain to be eventually consumed abroad (REX) or back in the original exporter's economy (REF). Indirect trading also occurs when the exporter uses imported inputs, resulting in foreign value-added (FVA) in its exports. Finally, when the same value-added crosses the same border twice or more, it duplicates its own measurement, resulting in pure double-counting (PDC). This component is not actually a value-added category; rather, it accounts for instances where the same value-added is counted more than once. This would be the case if, for example, Vietnamese value-added is exported to Germany, reexported back to Viet Nam, then exported to Germany again. This type of back-and-forth flow represents a particularly intense form of integration.

The five categories of value-added may be decomposed into finer subcategories. One may split FVA, for example, into the portion that is absorbed by economy r and the portion that is reexported. The five listed, however, will suffice for most analyses.

There is no definitive way to bring the accounting framework down to the sectoral level. An intuitive approach would be to divide national values by the sector that exports (or "export-sectors"), but an equally reasonable alternative would be to divide national values by the sector where value-added originates (or "origin-sectors"). Other approaches are possible, but these two are generally the most useful.

Figure 3.14 presents the export makeup of the three subregions of East Asia, South and Central Asia, and Southeast Asia and the Pacific for 2000, 2010, 2019, and 2020. Southeast Asia and the Pacific registered the largest share of FVA in their exports: 36.3% in 2020 compared with 18.3% for East Asia and 17.0% for South and Central Asia. Only East Asia had a significant amount of exported value-added that eventually returned to its borders. In 2020, this was 1.9% of its exports.

Figure 3.14: Components of Gross Exports by Subregion of Asia and the Pacific
(% of exports)

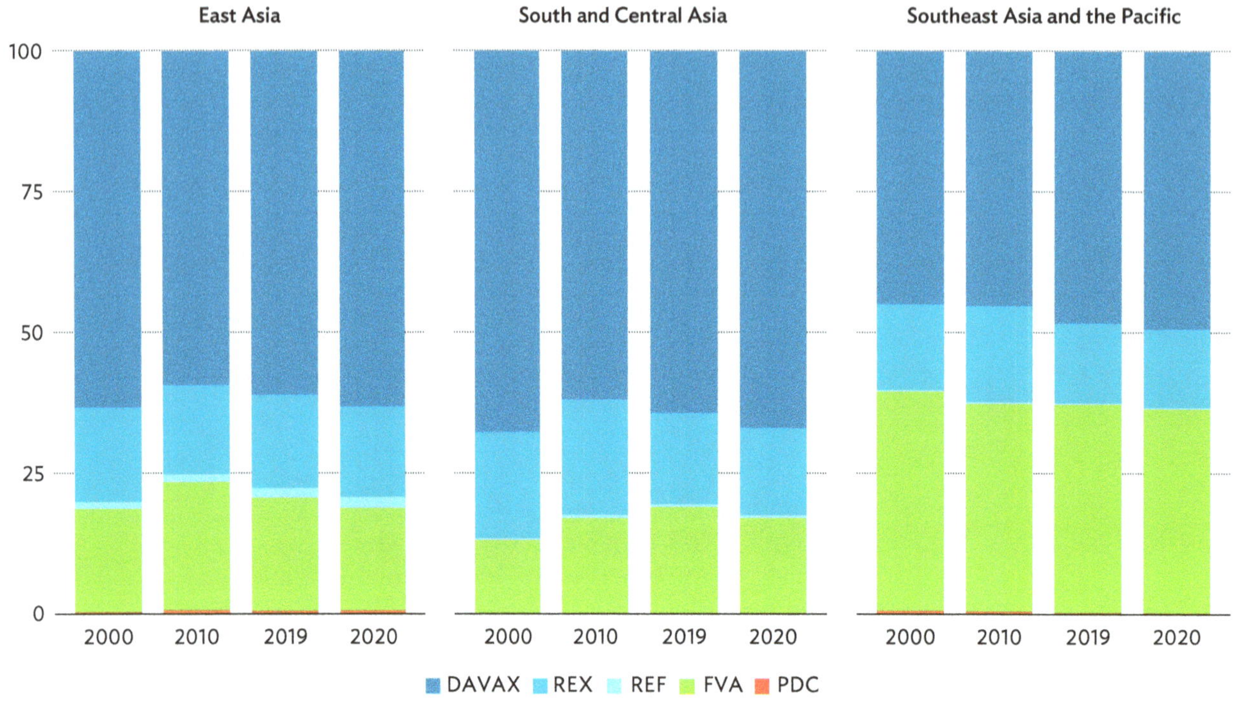

DAVAX = directly absorbed value-added exports, FVA = foreign value-added, PDC = pure double-counting, REF = reflection, REX = reexports.
Notes: Value-added categories derived from the trade accounting framework described in ADB. 2021. *Key Indicators for Asia and the Pacific 2021.* Manila. East Asia is comprised of Hong Kong, China; Japan; Mongolia; the People's Republic of China; the Republic of Korea; and Taipei,China. Southeast Asia and the Pacific is comprised of Brunei Darussalam, Cambodia, Fiji, Indonesia, the Lao People's Democratic Republic, Malaysia, the Philippines, Singapore, Thailand, and Viet Nam. South and Central Asia is comprised of Bangladesh, Bhutan, India, Kazakhstan, the Kyrgyz Republic, Maldives, Nepal, Pakistan, and Sri Lanka.
Source: Calculations using the Asian Development Bank Multiregional Input–Output Table. https://mrio.adbx.online/ (accessed July 2021).

Click here for figure data

Southeast Asia and the Pacific, however, consistently exhibited the highest shares of indirect trading from 2000 to 2020. This was driven by Malaysia, Singapore, and Viet Nam, which count among the most GVC-oriented economies not just in Asia but in the world. In particular, the subregion's niche in the midstream stages of manufacturing was reflected in the high proportion of FVA in its exports. This was exemplified by Viet Nam, where almost half of exports was FVA.

3.8 Global Value Chain Participation

One of the most useful indicators that can be derived from the value-added trade accounting framework is the GVC participation rate. This takes the value of GVC-related trade flows and divides it by some base, thereby measuring the extent to which an economy is participating in GVCs.

Two approaches are possible. Following the strand of literature started by Hummels, Ishii, and Yi (2001), the trade-based approach divides GVC-related flows by total exports. Specifically,

$$\textbf{\textit{Trade-based GVC participation rate}} = \frac{\text{REX} + \text{REF} + \text{FVA} + \text{PDC}}{\text{Exports}}$$

In other words, all categories except DAVAX are considered GVC-related flows. This is because they all involve value-added crossing more than one border, a necessary condition for GVCs.

The second approach, following the work of Wang, Wei, Yu, and Zhu (2017a), is called the production-based approach. This is measured by dividing GVC-related production by GDP:

$$\textbf{\textit{Production-based GVC participation rate}} = \frac{\text{DAVAX2} + \text{REX} + \text{REF}}{\text{GDP}}$$

where DAVAX2 is the portion of DAVAX that is directly absorbed through intermediate exports. The two approaches to the GVC participation rate generally behave in unison, though reporting one or the other may be preferrable given the context.

Figure 3.15 demonstrates one use of the GVC participation rate. The dramatic and simultaneous closure of borders brought about by the COVID-19 pandemic has raised questions about the role trade integration plays in regional and global economic security. On the one hand, trade openness provides access to other markets, mitigating the impact of domestic shocks. On the other hand, such openness exposes economies to shocks from abroad. Which effect dominates will depend on the circumstances prevailing in any given economy. This is confirmed in Figure 3.15, which compares the GVC participation rates of economies in the multiregional input-output table against the size of the pandemic-induced shock to growth these economies experienced in 2020. The U-shaped relationship suggests that GVC participation has a nonlinear correlation with shocks, wherein larger negative shocks are observed in the middle ranges (about 45%), with lower negative shocks observed in the lower and upper ranges of GVC participation. After this point, participation rates become associated with smaller negative shocks. Whereas Pakistan, whose GVC participation rate was 25.4%, performed about 2.8 percentage points lower than its pre-pandemic forecast, India's economy, whose GVC participation was 10 percentage points higher than Pakistan, contracted by about –8%. This is down by around 15 percentage points of India's pre-pandemic forecast of about 7.0% growth. Contrast this to economies with the highest GVC participation rates, namely Singapore and Viet Nam, whose economies experienced less severe contractions at –3.6 and –6.4 percentage points, respectively, below forecast.

Figure 3.15: Global Value Chain Participation Rate and the COVID-19 Shock to Economic Growth

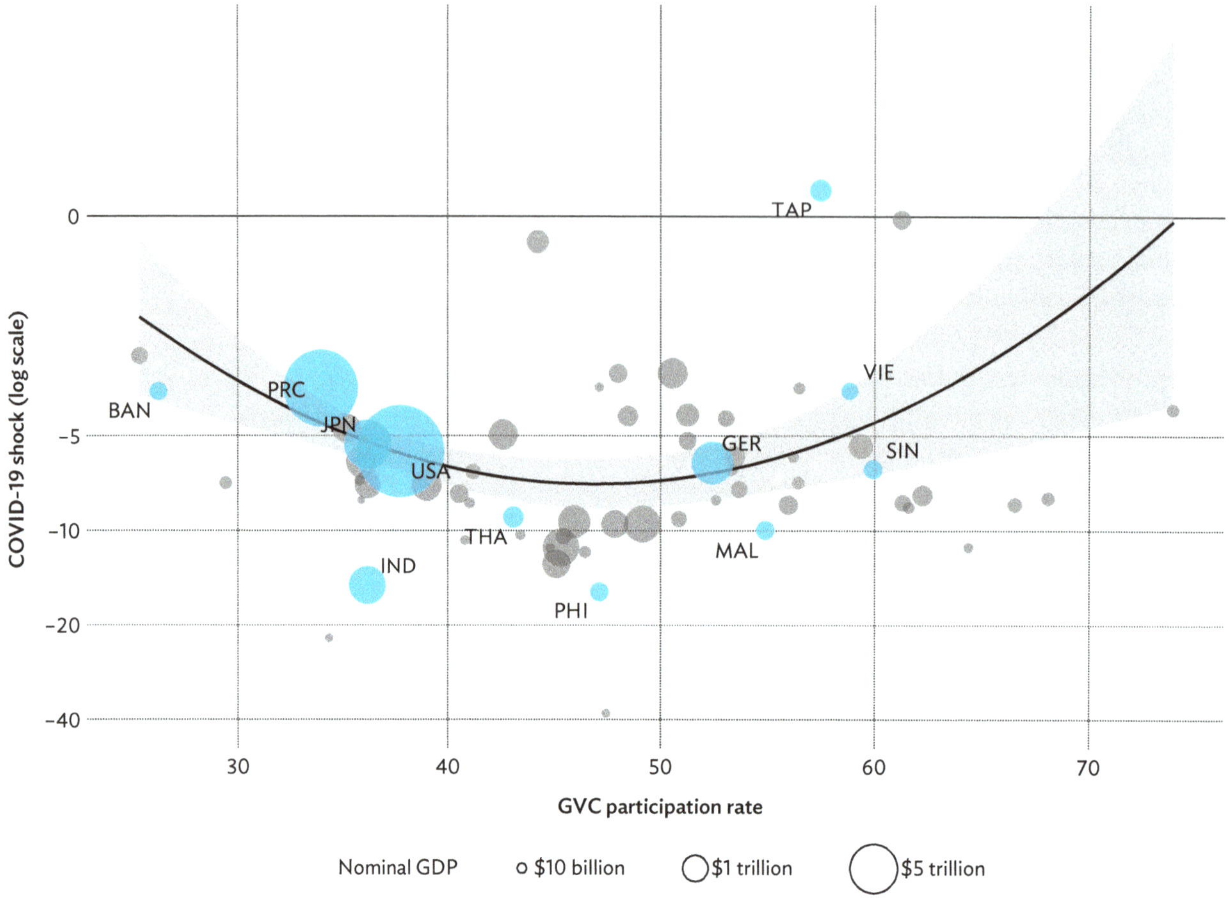

$ = United States dollars; AUS = Australia; BAN = Bangladesh; BRU = Brunei Darussalam; CAM = Cambodia; COVID-19 = coronavirus disease 2019; FIJ = Fiji; GDP = gross domestic product; GVC = global value chain; HKG = Hong Kong, China; IND = India, JPN = Japan; KAZ = Kazakhstan; KGZ = Kyrgyz Republic; KOR = Republic of Korea; LAO = Lao People's Democratic Republic; MAL = Malaysia; PAK = Pakistan; PHI = Philippines; PRC = People's Republic of China; SIN = Singapore; TAP = Taipei,China; THA = Thailand; VIE = Viet Nam.

Notes: Participation rates are trade-based rates calculated using the methodology in Asian Development Bank. 2021. *Key Indicators for Asia and the Pacific 2021*. Manila. The COVID-19 shock is the percentage-point difference between forecasted GDP growth for 2020 and actual growth in 2020. Participation rates and nominal GDP are as of 2019. Point sizes reflect nominal GDP. A quadratic curve is fitted to reveal the estimated relationship, with the shaded band representing the 95% confidence interval.

Sources: Calculations using the Asian Development Bank Multiregional Input–Output Table. https://mrio.adbx.online/ (accessed July 2021); forecasted growth rates from the International Monetary Fund's World Economic Outlook (October 2019); and actual growth rates from the International Monetary Fund's World Economic Outlook (April 2021).

Click here for figure data

It must be noted that the estimated relationship was affected by a confluence of factors. First, impacts were dependent on the type of goods and services that an economy exports. For example, economies trading in services through modes 2 (consumption abroad) and 4 (presence of natural persons) of the General Agreement on Trade in Services were more acutely affected as mobility restrictions took place. The tourism-dependent economies of Fiji and Maldives are two salient examples. Meanwhile, economies engaged in information and communication technology (ICT) goods experienced lower contractions due to increased global demand for these products, as clearly seen in the case of Viet Nam and Taipei,China.

Second, impacts were also dependent on the economy-specific pandemic response. For example, coronavirus resource center data from the Center of Systems Science and Engineering at Johns Hopkins University show that Brunei Darussalam and Taipei,China managed to keep the number of COVID-19 cases low in 2020, whereas India and the Philippines were among the economies with the highest recorded cases in Asia and the Pacific (CSSE 2021). The variance in the economic performance of these two groups are also evident in Figure 3.15. While other factors cannot be ruled out completely, findings on the GVC participation rates, coupled with economy-specific trade structures and pandemic responses, are indicative of the risk exposure of these economies from the pandemic. Taipei,China is a notable example. The economy's participation rates were among the highest, but it still outperformed other economies amid the pandemic due to its position in GVCs as a supplier of ICT goods and its unique data-driven approach to pandemic management (Chiang 2022). More in-depth discussion of this result can be found in ADB's *Key Indicators for Asia and the Pacific 2021* (ADB 2021).

The ***trade-based GVC participation rate*** of an economy can be divided into forward and backward rates as follows:

$$\textit{Trade-based GVC participation rate, forward} = \frac{\text{REX} + \text{REF}}{\text{Exports}}$$

$$\textit{Trade-based GVC participation rate, backward} = \frac{\text{FVA} + \text{PDC}}{\text{Exports}}$$

The share in total exports of domestic value-added (DVA) that is reexported by another importing economy to another foreign economy (REX) or back to the exporting economy (REF) makes up the economy's forward GVC participation rate, or forward supply linkage. For example, Maldives' exports of canned tuna packaged and labeled by Japan and sent to Singapore (REX) or back to Maldives (REF) is forward GVC activity from the perspective of Maldives. The share of Maldives' REX and REF to its total exports represents the economy's trade-based forward GVC participation.

Conversely, exports that embody value-added previously imported from abroad (FVA) and double-counted value-added (PDC) comprise the trade-based backward GVC participation rate. Within Maldives' exports of canned tuna to Japan, its import content in the form of aluminum from India represents the share of trade-based backward GVC activity.

An economy's total trade-based GVC participation combines both trade-based forward and backward participation rates. Figure 3.16 shows the forward and backward GVC participation rates of each subregion in 2000, 2010, 2019, and 2020. Since the GVC participation rates are aggregations of the export decomposition terms, the bars mimic the trends of REX and REF for forward GVC participation rates, and those of FVA and PDC for backward GVC participation rates.

Figure 3.16: Forward and Backward Global Value Chain Participation Rates, by Subregion

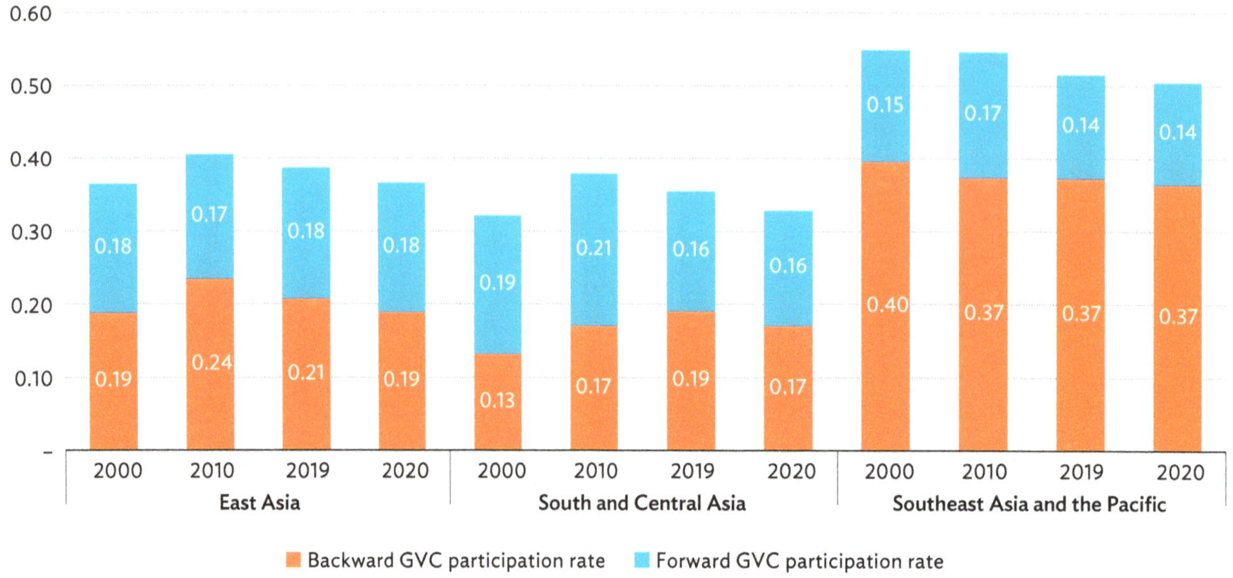

GVC = global value chain.

Note: East Asia is comprised of Hong Kong, China; Japan; Mongolia; the People's Republic of China; the Republic of Korea; and Taipei,China. Southeast Asia and the Pacific is comprised of Brunei Darussalam, Cambodia, Fiji, Indonesia, the Lao People's Democratic Republic, Malaysia, the Philippines, Singapore, Thailand, and Viet Nam. South and Central Asia is comprised of Bangladesh, Bhutan, India, Kazakhstan, the Kyrgyz Republic, Maldives, Nepal, Pakistan, and Sri Lanka.

Source: Calculations using the Asian Development Bank Multiregional Input–Output Table. https://mrio.adbx.online/ (accessed July 2021).

Click here for figure data

In East Asia and South and Central Asia, forward and backward GVC participation rates show synergy, signifying that the domestic and foreign value-added embedded in indirect trading were around the same size. Conversely, in Southeast Asia and the Pacific, a substantial portion of GVC-related trading was attributed to backward GVC linkages. Among the subregion's economies, the Philippines and Singapore took the lead in including FVA.

Figure 3.17 reveals that most economies in 2019 and 2020 embodied more FVA in exports over DVA. It also depicts the waning reliance on FVA from 2019 to 2020. In efforts to limit the spread of COVID-19, economies closed borders, imposed lockdowns, and restricted import activity, thereby hampering markets and GVC activities. This led to declines in both backward and forward GVC engagement: backward GVC participation fell in all economies in Asia and the Pacific, except in Cambodia and Malaysia, and forward GVC activity also slowed.

Looking at the East Asia section of Figure 3.17, Japan exhibited a more forward orientation in GVC activity in 2019 and 2020, despite its East Asian neighbors reexporting the most value-added in the entire Asia and Pacific region. Additionally, economies in the subregion, with the exception of Mongolia, embodied some of the highest levels of FVA in electricals and chemicals. In the South and Central Asian subregion, Kazakhstan and Pakistan exported more DVA intermediates than foreign intermediates. Kazakhstan had considerable forward GVC participation rates in its primary and medium-to-high-technology manufacturing sectors, while Pakistan led in forward participation in business service value-added exports.

Figure 3.17: Backward versus Forward Global Value Chain Participation Rates, by Subregion and Economy

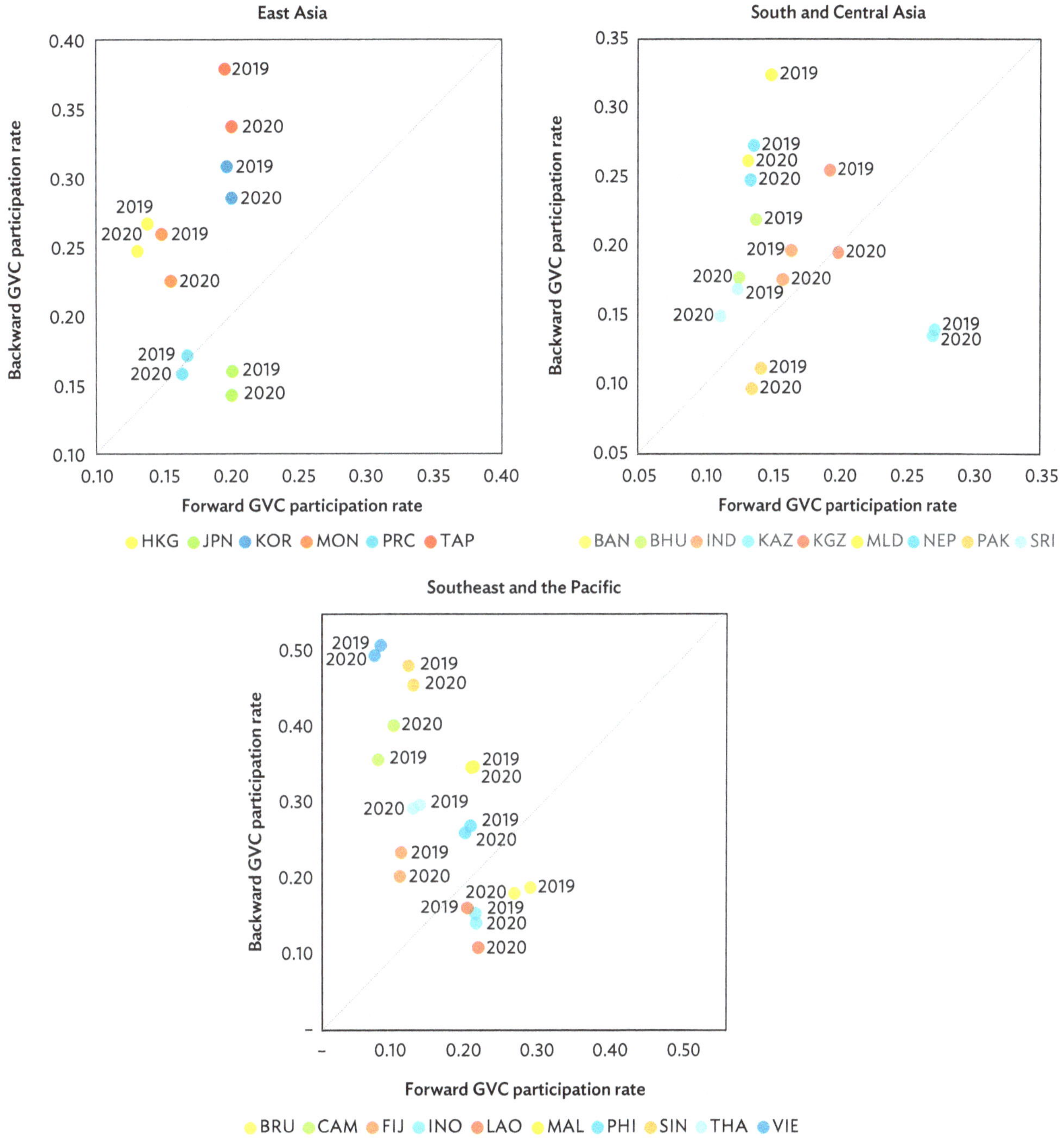

BAN = Bangladesh; BHU = Bhutan; BRU = Brunei Darussalam; CAM = Cambodia; FIJ = Fiji; GVC = global value chain; HKG = Hong Kong, China; IND = India; INO = Indonesia; JPN = Japan; KAZ = Kazakhstan; KGZ = Kyrgyz Republic; KOR = Republic of Korea; LAO = Lao People's Democratic Republic; MAL = Malaysia; MLD = Maldives; MON = Mongolia; NEC = Not elsewhere classified; NEP = Nepal; PAK = Pakistan; PHI = Philippines; PRC = People's Republic of China; SIN = Singapore; SRI = Sri Lanka; TAP = Taipei,China; THA = Thailand; VIE = Viet Nam

Source: Calculations using the Asian Development Bank Multiregional Input–Output Tables for 2019 and 2020. https://mrio.adbx.online/ (accessed July 2021).

Click here for figure data

Meanwhile, Maldives had the highest backward GVC participation rates in the primary and low-technology manufacturing sectors, while Nepal exhibited the greatest ratio of FVA in exports of medium-to-high-technology manufacturing, business services, and personal and public services. In Southeast Asia and the Pacific, the most forward leaning economies were Brunei Darussalam, the Lao PDR, and Indonesia. The GVC participation rates among economies is most diverse in this subregion.

Figures 3.18 to 3.22 rank all trade-based forward and backward GVC participation rates for different sector groupings. By illustrating the gap between each economy-sector's backward participation rate and forward participation rate for 2019 and 2020, the figures provide information on whether an economy-sector grouping is leaning toward a particular role in a value chain, or is balancing its use of domestic value-added and foreign value-added as it exports. The slope of each line connecting the participation rates of each economy also reveals changes in value-added composition or sourcing priorities over the course of two years.

Figure 3.18 presents the participation rates of the primary sector. As observed, Viet Nam's exports embodied the highest FVA content (0.38) among all economies in 2020, paired with one of the smallest reflected and reexported levels of DVA (0.12). Viet Nam also reported the least change in forward and backward GVC participation rates from 2019 to 2020. Further, economies in Southeast Asia and South and Central Asia dominated the export of agricultural DVA intermediates. Throughout 2019 and 2020, Kazakhstan's primary sector continued to have the highest forward GVC participation in its subregion. The economy recorded the highest forward GVC participation rate in all sampled economies for mining.

Within the low-technology manufacturing sector, Cambodia exported the highest foreign (0.56) and lowest domestic (0.01) value-added content in 2020 (Figure 3.19). The growth in its backward GVC participation from 2019 to 2020 can be attributed largely to increased imports in textiles, which are also its top export. Conversely, Pakistan continued to rely least on foreign intermediate inputs (0.09) in 2020, largely on account of its domestic backward linkages in food and beverages, textiles, leather, and wood manufacturing. Pakistan's trade-based forward GVC participation (0.22) was among the highest in South and Central Asia as it was driven significantly by the economy's leather and paper intermediate reexports to third economies (ADB 2022).[2] Bhutan maintained its leadership in forward GVC participation (0.21) within the subregion, driven by the export of utilities.

Despite declining exports and domestic production, Japan maintained its share of reexported and reflected intermediates (0.24), overtaking the Lao PDR (0.22) in 2020. Reexported textiles, rubber, and plastic goods made up the majority of Japan's forward supply linkage.

2 Pakistan's backward linkage measure of trade-based GVC participation rate was much lower than its forward linkage counterpart. This observation implies that Pakistan occupied more upstream stages of GVCs. That is, the economy's inputs were used by other economies to a greater extent than other economies' inputs were used by Pakistan (see the ADB publication *Pakistan's Economy and Trade in the Age of Global Value Chains* for more in-depth discussion).

Figure 3.18: Backward versus Forward Global Value Chain Participation Rates in Primary Sectors

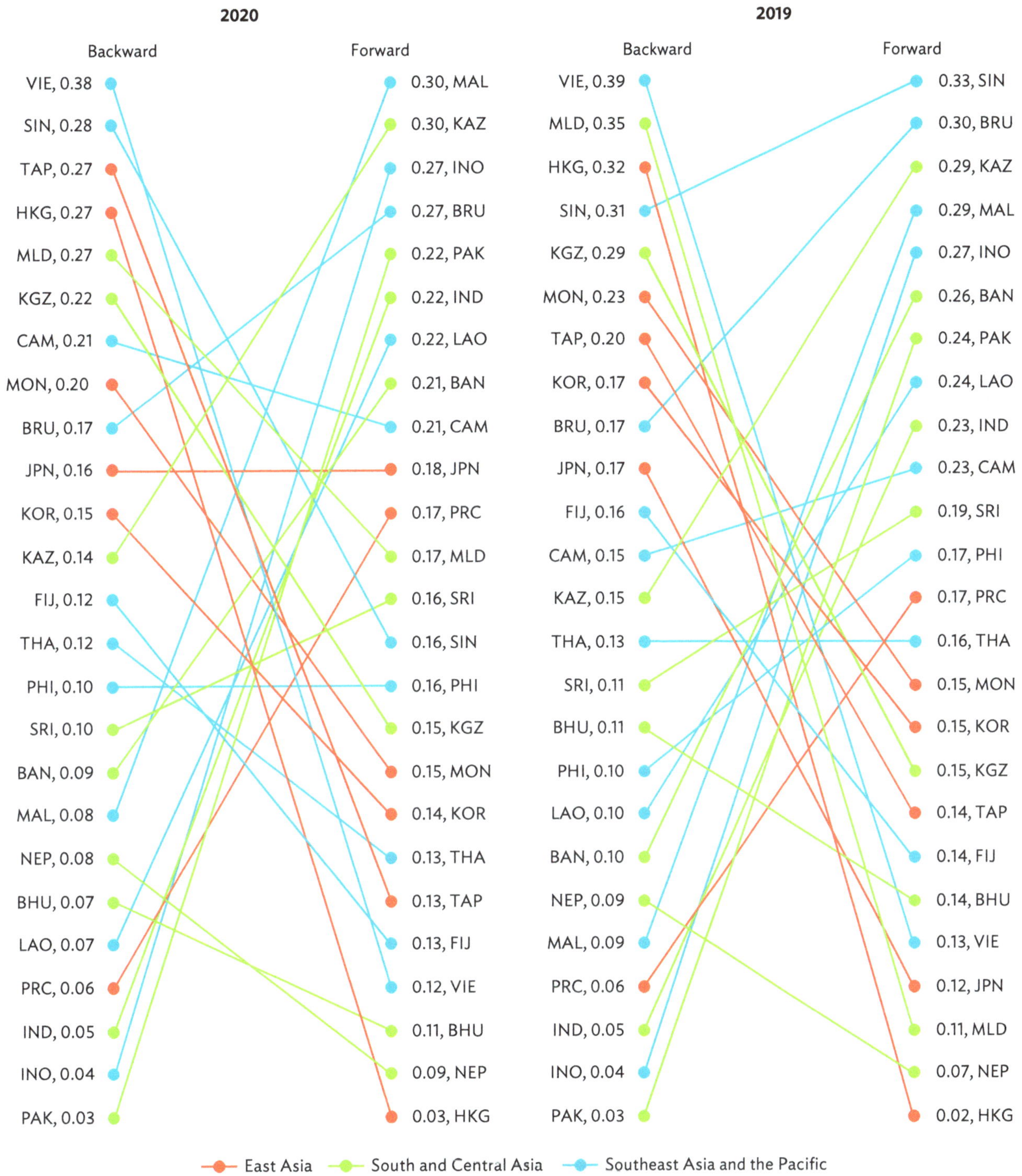

BAN = Bangladesh; BHU = Bhutan; BRU = Brunei Darussalam; CAM = Cambodia; FIJ = Fiji; HKG = Hong Kong, China; IND = India; INO = Indonesia; JPN = Japan; KAZ = Kazakhstan; KGZ = Kyrgyz Republic; KOR = Republic of Korea; LAO = Lao People's Democratic Republic; MAL = Malaysia; MLD = Maldives; MON = Mongolia; NEP = Nepal; PAK = Pakistan; PHI = Philippines; PRC = People's Republic of China; SIN = Singapore; SRI = Sri Lanka; TAP = Taipei,China; THA = Thailand; VIE = Viet Nam

Note: The primary sector comprises the agriculture, hunting, forestry, and fishing, and mining and quarrying sectors.

Source: Calculations using the Asian Development Bank Multiregional Input–Output Tables for 2019 and 2020. https://mrio.adbx.online/ (accessed July 2021).

Click here for figure data

Figure 3.19: Backward versus Forward Global Value Chain Participation Rates in Low-Technology Manufacturing Sectors

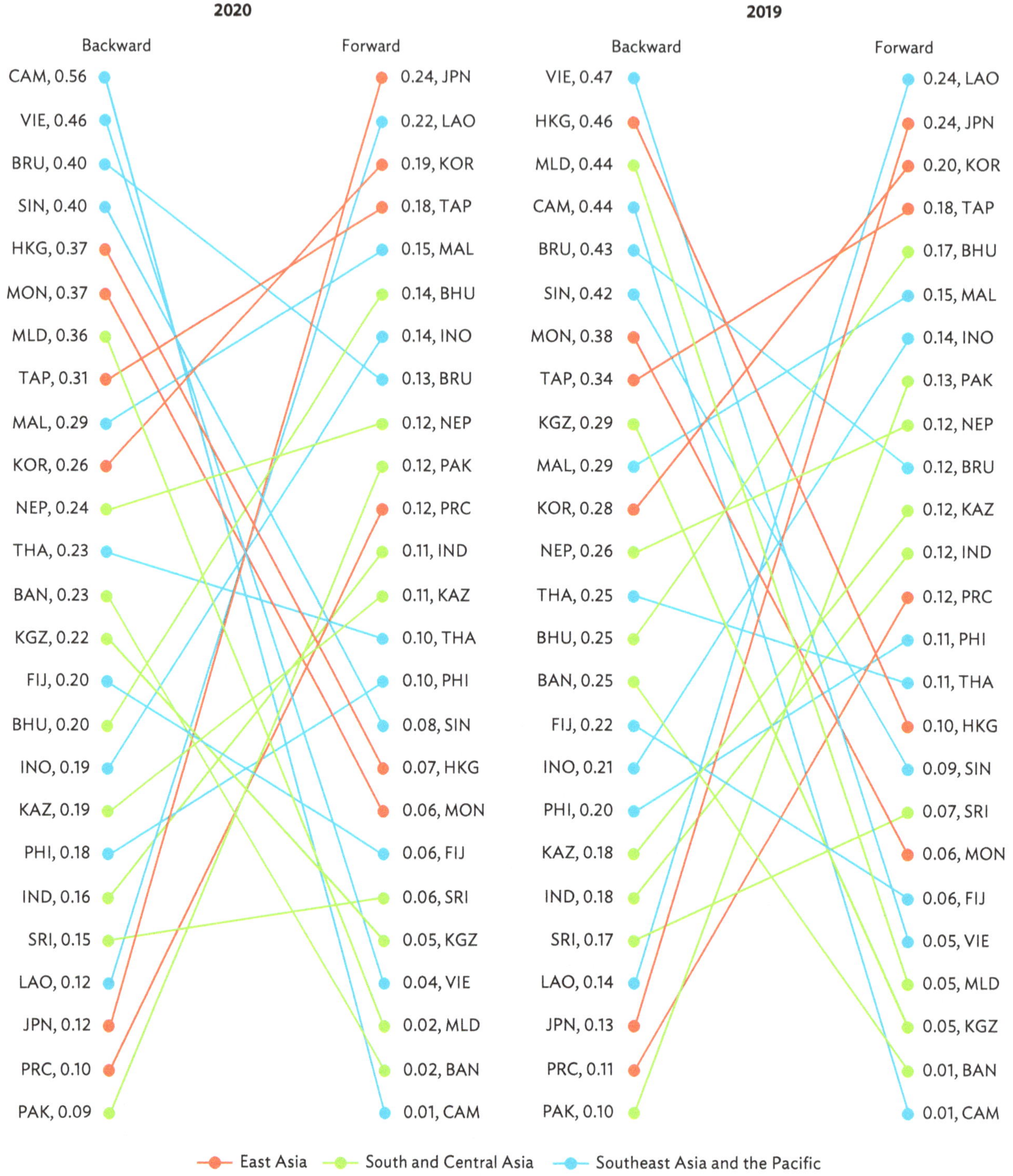

BAN = Bangladesh; BHU = Bhutan; BRU = Brunei Darussalam; CAM = Cambodia; FIJ = Fiji; HKG = Hong Kong, China; IND = India; INO = Indonesia; JPN = Japan; KAZ = Kazakhstan; KGZ = Kyrgyz Republic; KOR = Republic of Korea; LAO = Lao People's Democratic Republic; MAL = Malaysia; MLD = Maldives; MON = Mongolia; NEP = Nepal; PAK = Pakistan; PHI = Philippines; PRC = People's Republic of China; SIN = Singapore; SRI = Sri Lanka; TAP = Taipei,China; THA = Thailand; VIE = Viet Nam

Note: The low-technology manufacturing sector comprises the manufacturing of food and beverages, textiles, leather, wood, paper, rubber and plastics, and products not elsewhere classified as well as the utilities and construction sectors.

Source: Calculations using the Asian Development Bank Multiregional Input–Output Tables for 2019 and 2020. https://mrio.adbx.online/ (accessed July 2021).

Click here for figure data

In medium-to-high-technology manufacturing, Viet Nam exhibited the highest backward GVC participation rates (0.61 and 0.60) for 2019 and 2020 (Figure 3.20). In fact, since 2016, FVA content in exports of metals, electricals, and machinery not elsewhere classified remained greater than 60%. Due to its weak domestic backward linkages in these sectors, Viet Nam relies heavily on foreign metals, machines, and electrical components and then adds its own value-added via subassemblies for exports. Research and development and product design are also mostly performed abroad or by foreign companies based in Viet Nam. Electrical goods were Viet Nam's top export in both 2019 and 2020.

The largest drop in backward GVC participation across all economy-sectors was felt in the refined fuels manufacturing sector of the Philippines, which fell 0.25 percentage points from 2019 to 2020. This may be largely attributed to decreased consumption for electricity by commercial enterprises and manufacturers during the COVID-19 crisis. While a net fossil fuel importer, refined fuels manufacturing was one of the Philippines' weakest importers within the medium-to-high-technology manufacturing sector group. Suppressed by a 0.15-percentage-point rise in chemicals manufacturing, total decline in backward GVC participation for the sector group reached only 0.02 points.

Interestingly, Mongolia exhibited evenness in its backward (0.33) and forward (0.35) GVC participation rates in 2020. Among all economy-sectors, Mongolia's value-added exports of electricals drew the highest foreign intermediate content, at 86% in both 2019 and 2020. The economy's exports of metals to third economies embodied 37% of DVA, the third highest in Asia and the Pacific.

In exporting business services, Mongolia, Singapore, and Viet Nam depended significantly on FVA in 2019 and 2020 (Figure 3.21). Conversely, Indonesia, Japan, Pakistan, the Philippines, and the PRC led the way for DVA. Pakistan's wholesale trade sector was pulled down by 0.28 points in terms of forward value-added contribution, the largest decline in any economy-sector forward GVC participation rate. Influential to this decline was the slowdown in import demand from Pakistan's top three export markets: the PRC, the United States, and the United Kingdom.

Brunei Darussalam and Singapore led in exporting a significant share of FVA in business services in 2019 and 2020. Brunei Darussalam experienced a 4% rise in backward GVC participation in 2020, driven by increased participation in the sale of motor vehicles, wholesale trade, retail trade, hotel and restaurant services, water transport, air transport, other transport support services, and financial services. Conversely, the PRC and the Philippines remained the highest-ranked in forward GVC participation, with water transport and other transport support activities classified as their top export services. Indonesia ranked third on this measure in 2020, driven by sizable reexported DVA in the same sectors. The economy boasted a forward GVC participation rate of 0.43 in water transport services and 0.46 in transport services not elsewhere classified in 2020. It is worth noting though that, in 2020,

Figure 3.20: Backward versus Forward Global Value Chain Participation Rates in Medium-to-High-Technology Manufacturing Sectors

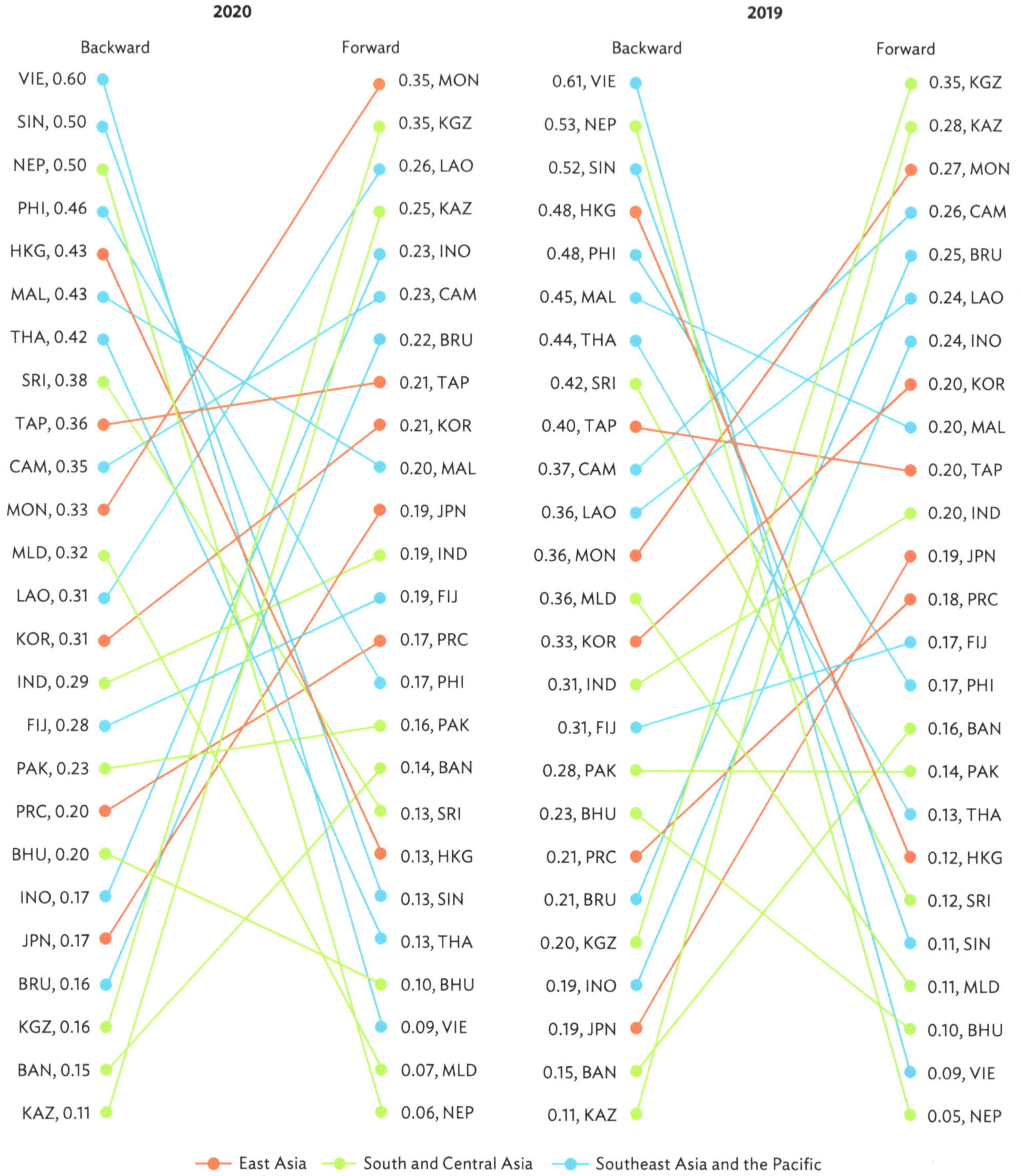

BAN = Bangladesh; BHU = Bhutan; BRU = Brunei Darussalam; CAM = Cambodia; FIJ = Fiji; HKG = Hong Kong, China; IND = India; INO = Indonesia; JPN = Japan; KAZ = Kazakhstan; KGZ = Kyrgyz Republic; KOR = Republic of Korea; LAO = Lao People's Democratic Republic; MAL = Malaysia; MLD = Maldives; MON = Mongolia; NEP = Nepal; PAK = Pakistan; PHI = Philippines; PRC = People's Republic of China; SIN = Singapore; SRI = Sri Lanka; TAP = Taipei,China; THA = Thailand; VIE = Viet Nam

Note: The medium-to-high-technology manufacturing sector comprises the manufacturing of refined fuel, chemicals, minerals not elsewhere classified, metals, machinery not elsewhere classified, electricals, and transport equipment.

Source: Calculations using the Asian Development Bank Multiregional Input–Output Tables for 2019 and 2020. https://mrio.adbx.online/ (accessed July 2021).

Click here for figure data

Figure 3.21: Backward versus Forward Global Value Chain Participation Rates in Business Services

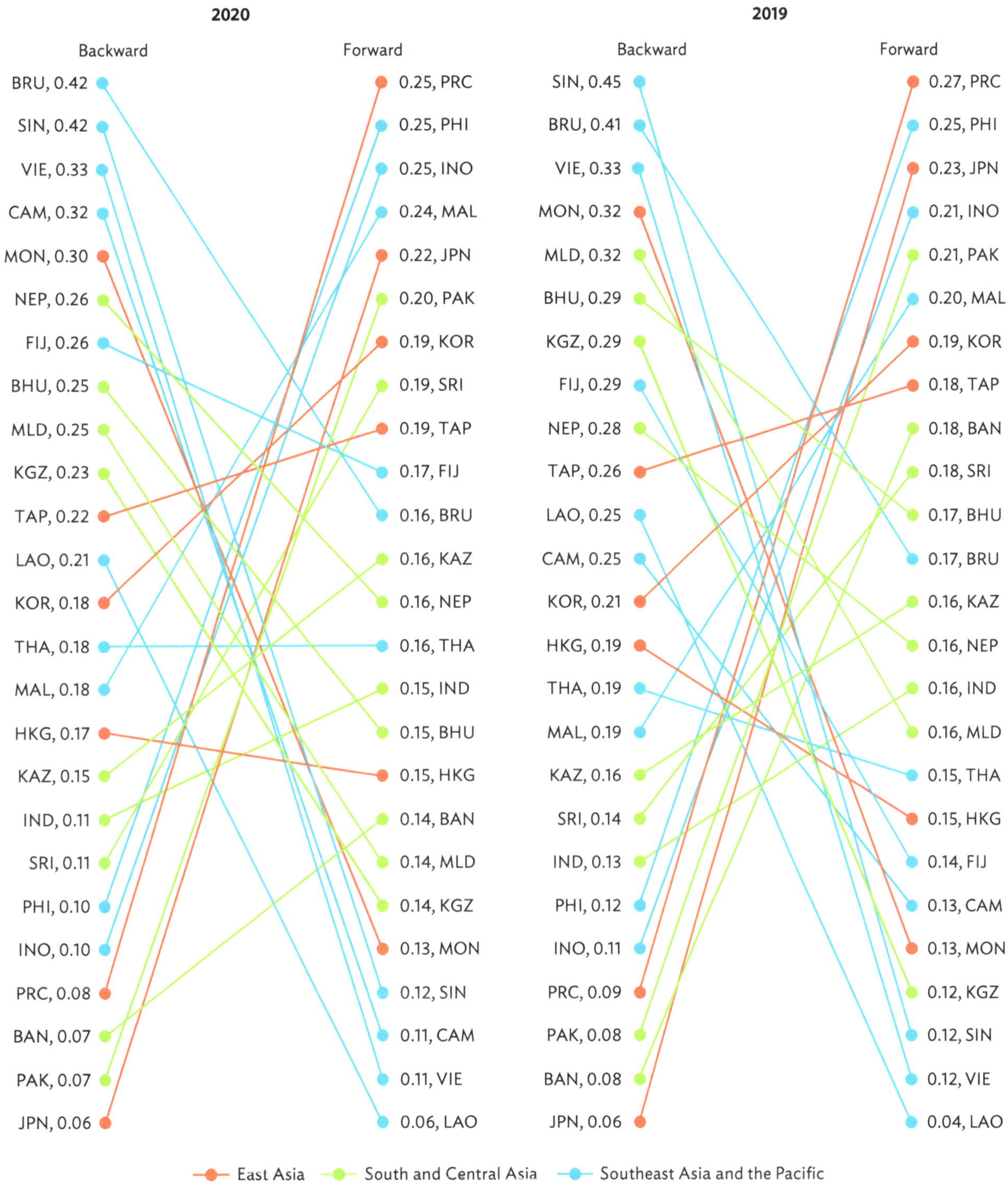

BAN = Bangladesh; BHU = Bhutan; BRU = Brunei Darussalam; CAM = Cambodia; FIJ = Fiji; HKG = Hong Kong, China; IND = India; INO = Indonesia; JPN = Japan; KAZ = Kazakhstan; KGZ = Kyrgyz Republic; KOR = Republic of Korea; LAO = Lao People's Democratic Republic; MAL = Malaysia; MLD = Maldives; MON = Mongolia; NEP = Nepal; PAK = Pakistan; PHI = Philippines; PRC = People's Republic of China; SIN = Singapore; SRI = Sri Lanka; TAP = Taipei,China; THA = Thailand; VIE = Viet Nam

Note: The business services sector comprises the sale of motor vehicles; wholesale and retail trade; hotels and restaurants; inland, water, and air transport; transport activities not elsewhere classified; telecommunications; finance; real estate; and business activities not elsewhere classified.

Source: Calculations using the Asian Development Bank Multiregional Input–Output Tables for 2019 and 2020. https://mrio.adbx.online/ (accessed July 2021).

Click here for figure data

Indonesia suffered a massive decline in REX, REF, and exports. Overall, the sectors of water transport and other transport support activities were generally the most affected in Asia and the Pacific, primarily due to travel restrictions.

Signifying weak activity in exporting transportation services and maintenance thereof, Cambodia has been recording minimal forward GVC participation rates in the sale of motor vehicles and all transport sectors, except inland transport services, since 2000. Hong Kong, China and the PRC also participate minimally in indirect exports of motor vehicle sales, repair, and maintenance services.

As compared to the other sector groupings, the personal and public services sector features the smallest backward GVC participation rates (Figure 3.22). In fact, public administration, education, health and social work, personal services, and services of private households were among the lowest-ranked sectors. This is expected since these services are not commonly imported into other economies.

In terms of forward GVC participation, however, the PRC led in 2019 and 2020, posting 0.25 in both years. The economy was significantly influenced by its forward GVC share in public administration (0.37) and education services (0.28) in 2020. Bhutan's personal service sector had the highest forward GVC participation rate (0.37) among all economy-sectors in this grouping for 2020, overtaking the PRC's public administration sector previously at 0.40.

3.9 Product Specialization

Aside from relative prices, another way to assess an economy's standing in global production is through its revealed comparative advantage (RCA). Comparative advantage is used to explain prevailing patterns of trade: the theory being that economies export goods and services for which they have a comparative advantage and import the rest. Say there are two economies (A and B) and two types of goods (cars and shirts). If A's proficiency in making cars relative to shirts is better than B's proficiency in making cars relative to shirts, then A will export cars to B and B will export shirts to A. Note that B might be absolutely better than A at making both cars and shirts, however, the underlying criterion is B's comparative proficiency between the two types of goods.

Balassa (1965) operationalized this concept through the revealed comparative advantage index. This index is obtained by taking the share of sector i in a given economy's exports and comparing it with the average share of sector i across all economies' exports. If the index is greater than 1, then the economy's export makeup "reveals" it to have a comparative advantage in sector i. If the index is less than 1, it reveals the absence of a comparative advantage in that sector. The traditional use of revealed comparative advantage (TRCA) uses the value of gross exports as the main variable. In this context,

Figure 3.22: Backward versus Forward Global Value Chain Participation Rates in Personal and Public Services

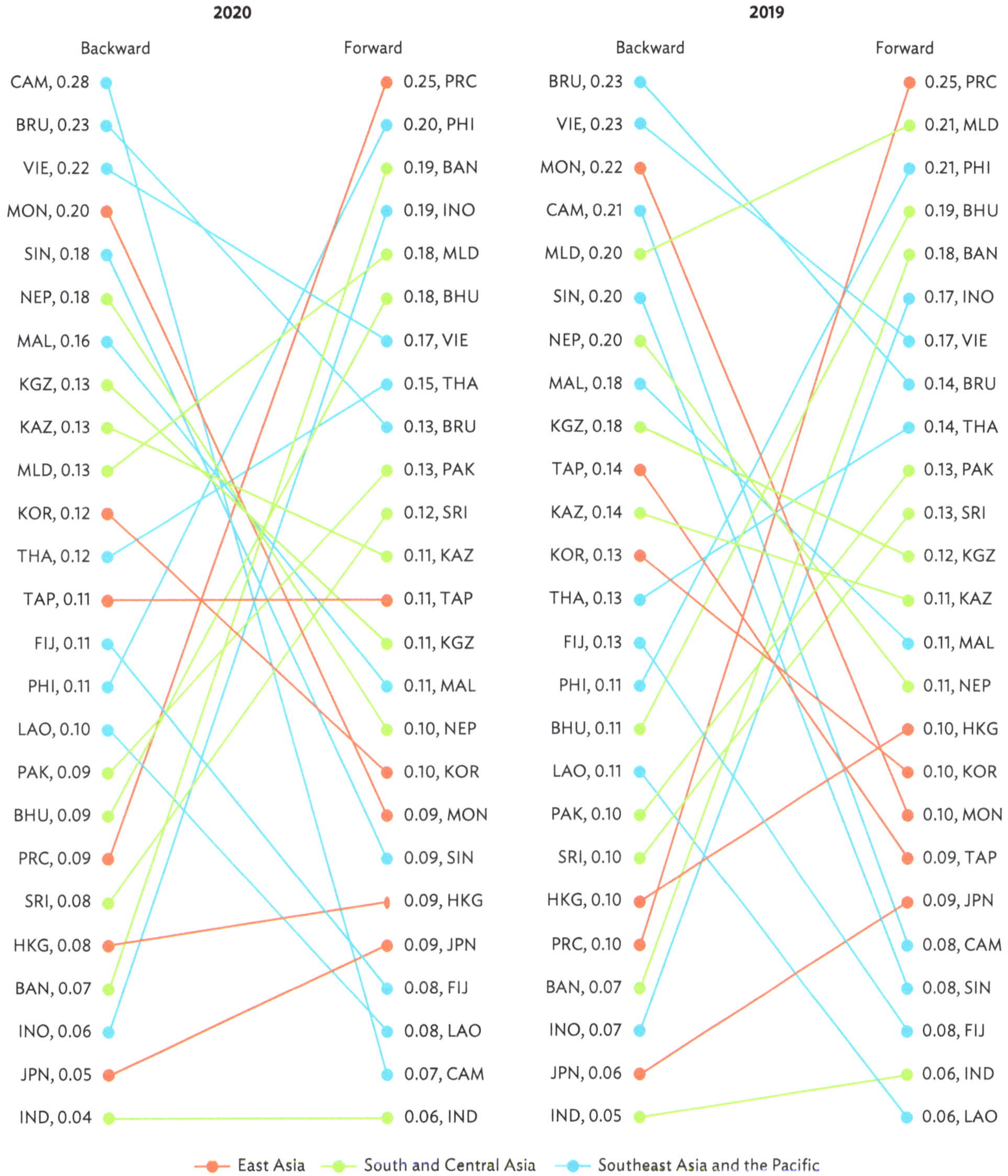

BAN = Bangladesh; BHU = Bhutan; BRU = Brunei Darussalam; CAM = Cambodia; FIJ = Fiji; HKG = Hong Kong, China; IND = India; INO = Indonesia; JPN = Japan; KAZ = Kazakhstan; KGZ = Kyrgyz Republic; KOR = Republic of Korea; LAO = Lao People's Democratic Republic; MAL = Malaysia; MLD = Maldives; MON = Mongolia; NEP = Nepal; PAK = Pakistan; PHI = Philippines; PRC = People's Republic of China; SIN = Singapore; SRI = Sri Lanka; TAP = Taipei,China; THA = Thailand; VIE = Viet Nam

Note: The personal and public services sector comprises public administration, education, health and social work, personal services not elsewhere classified, and services of private households.

Source: Calculations using the Asian Development Bank Multiregional Input–Output Table for 2019 and 2020. https://mrio.adbx.online/ (accessed July 2021).

Click here for figure data

the use of gross exports to characterize an economy's trade activity may be less than ideal, given the double-counting of value-added arising from multiple border crossings that are characteristic of international production-sharing arrangements.

As discussed in ADB's *Key Indicators for Asia and the Pacific 2021* (ADB 2021), the RCA index may be adjusted to account for global value chains by using value-added exports, as calculated from the value-added trade accounting framework. The new revealed comparative advantage (NRCA) index refines TRCA by incorporating the rise of GVCs and considering cross-border production-sharing arrangements. Using the Wang, Wei, and Zhu (2013) decomposition formula, gross exports can be adjusted to arrive at forward-linkage-based DVA in gross exports. This removes FVA and PDC from the economy's exports, resulting in an RCA index that is based on DVA flows that are absorbed abroad.

Figure 3.23 demonstrates the difference between calculating RCA indexes using TRCA and NRCA, using the case of Malaysia for 2020. There is some stability among the sectors where the index is relatively high (refined fuels, electricals) and low (leather, transport equipment), but drastic reordering can also be seen. For example, Malaysia's retail trade services exports exhibited a comparative disadvantage under conventional trade statistics but a comparative advantage when adjusted for exports value-added, suggesting that domestic value-addition from this sector was embodied in the exports actually sent out by the economy. Such "hidden" portions of specialization are useful to uncover for a more comprehensive analysis on the positioning of firms, sectors, or economies within GVCs.

Figure 3.24 illustrates TRCA and NRCA indexes[3] for four sectors that endured significant impacts of the COVID-19 pandemic in 2020: air transport; petroleum and fuel production; manufacture of electrical and optical equipment; and hotels and restaurants. These four sectors were selected simply due to the disproportionate impacts they likely experienced due to lockdowns and imposed mobility restrictions, leading to limited operations in small businesses, factories, air travel, and accommodation. Maldives, a major tourist destination, continued to have a high comparative advantage in the hotels and restaurants sector in 2020. The same can be seen for Brunei Darussalam, whose primary products were in the petroleum and fuel sector, and Taipei,China in the electrical and optical equipment sector. NRCA indexes were generally higher than TRCA indexes for the petroleum and fuel sector, indicating a high DVA content of petroleum exports for most economies in Asia and the Pacific. Meanwhile, mixed results are shown for the other three sectors in some economies in which either higher NRCA indexes or higher TRCA indexes are seen.

3 The cube root transforms indexes to smooth out the values with too high or too low indexes in some economies.

Figure 3.23: Revealed Comparative Advantage Indexes for Economic Sectors of Malaysia, 2020

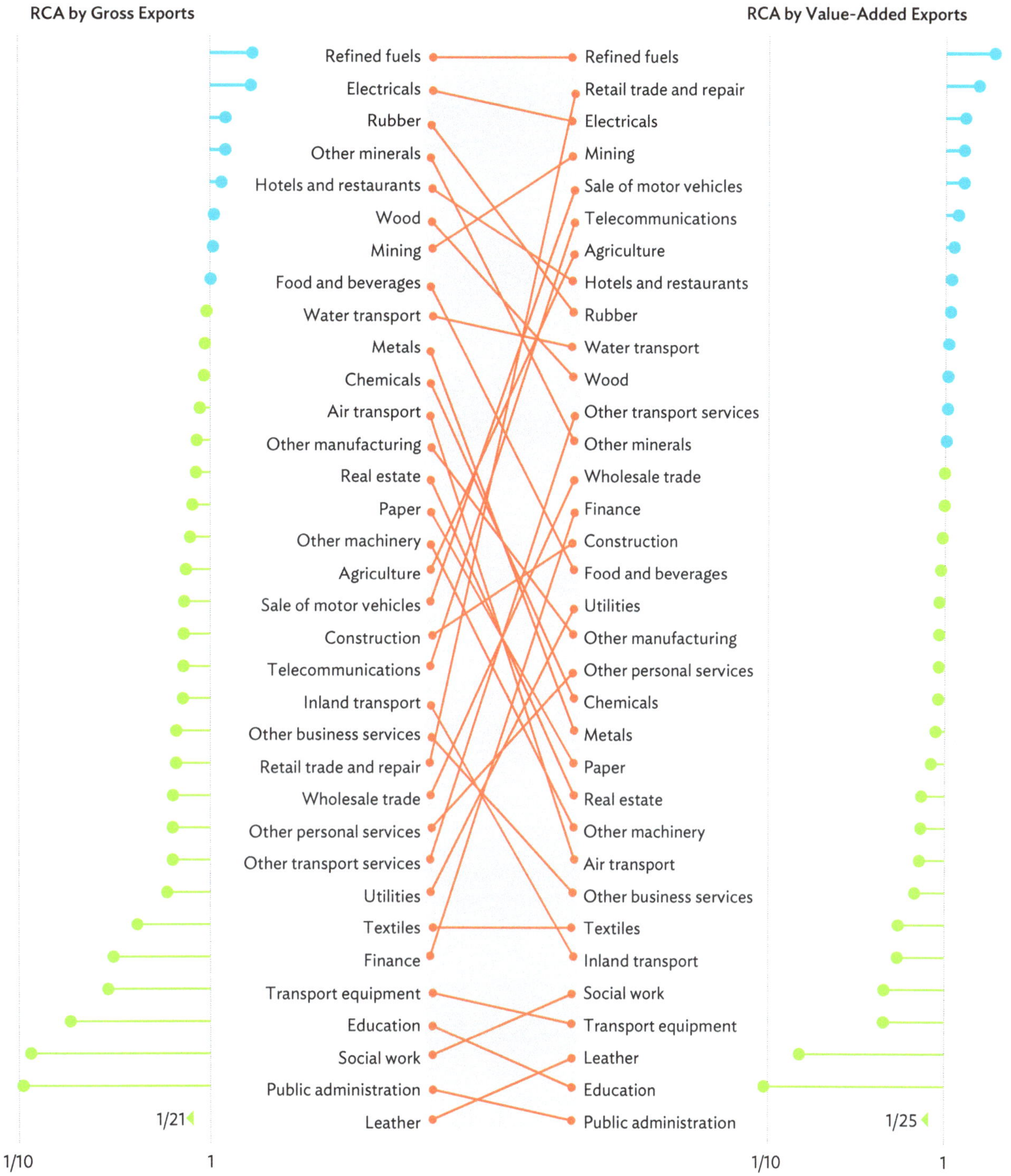

RCA = revealed comparative advantage.

Notes: RCA index calculated according to Balassa's *Trade Liberalisation and "Revealed" Comparative Advantage* (1965) and the Asian Development Bank's *Key Indicators for Asia and the Pacific 2021*. Sectors with RCA indexes of greater than 1 are sectors Malaysia is said to have a RCA over sectors colored in darker blue shade. Sectors with RCA of less than 1 are colored in green. Value-added exports are exports of domestic value-added that are absorbed abroad, disaggregated by origin sectors and calculated following Key Indicators for Asia and the Pacific 2021. Sectors with no value-added exports are omitted.

Sources: Calculations using the Asian Development Bank Multiregional Input–Output Table. https://mrio.adbx.online/ (accessed July 2021); Asian Development Bank. 2021. *Key Indicators for Asia and the Pacific*. Manila; and B. Balassa. 1965. Trade Liberalisation and "Revealed" Comparative Advantage. *The Manchester School*. 33 (2). pp. 99–123.

Click here for figure data

Figure 3.24: Traditional and New Revealed Comparative Advantages in Select Sectors, 2020

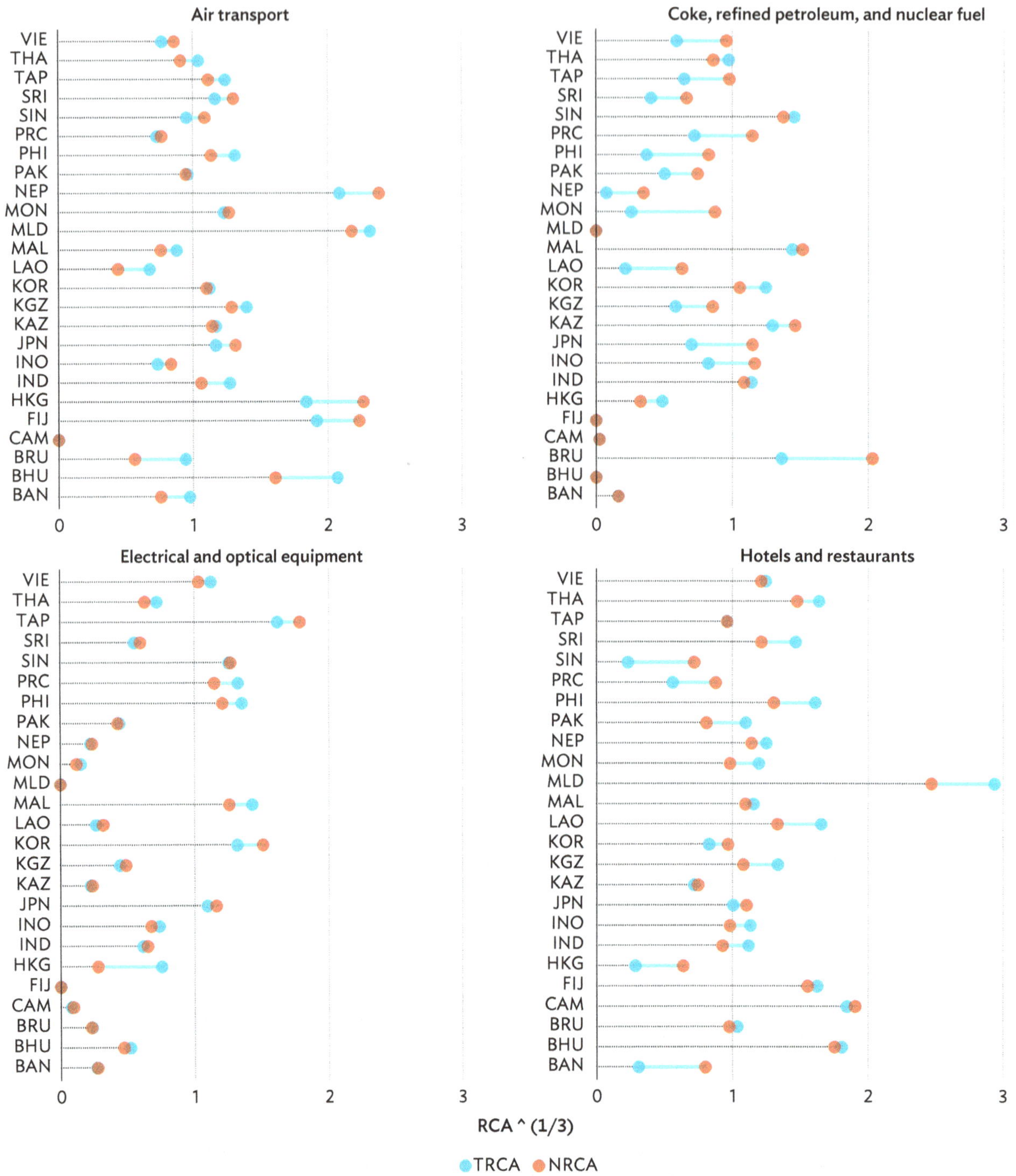

BAN = Bangladesh; BHU = Bhutan; BRU = Brunei Darussalam; CAM = Cambodia; FIJ = Fiji; HKG = Hong Kong, China; IND = India; INO = Indonesia; JPN = Japan; KAZ = Kazakhstan; KGZ = Kyrgyz Republic; KOR = Republic of Korea; LAO = Lao People's Democratic Republic; MAL = Malaysia; MLD = Maldives; MON = Mongolia; NEP = Nepal; NRCA = new (domestic value-added based) revealed comparative advantage; PAK = Pakistan; PHI = Philippines; PRC = People's Republic of China; RCA = revealed comparative advantage; SIN = Singapore; SRI = Sri Lanka; TAP = Taipei,China; THA = Thailand; VIE = Viet Nam; TRCA = traditional (gross exports-based) revealed comparative advantage.

Note: RCA indexes are presented as the cube root of their original values.

Source: Calculations using the Asian Development Bank Multiregional Input–Output Table. https://mrio.adbx.online/ (accessed July 2021).

Click here for figure data

3.10 Production Lengths

Another way to characterize trade participation is to measure production lengths. While production can take many forms, it is useful to conceive of it as a series of sequential stages where each stage adds value until a finished product results. In this context, one can define the position of economy-sectors in a GVC by simply looking at how a sector's output is absorbed in the economy through an input–output table.

A sector is considered to be upstream if its outputs go through multiple stages before being absorbed as final use in the economy. For example, the mining sector produces iron ore for making steel. Steel is then generally used as an input to build houses. Of all the sectors involved, the mining sector is relatively upstream compared to the steel or construction sectors. That is, by supplying a disproportionate amount of its output to other producing sectors, the mining sector has a longer "distance" before its output (iron ore) is absorbed by final users. From this example, **upstreamness** can be simply defined as the average distance of a sector's output to its final use.

Conversely, a sector is considered to be relatively downstream if its production process involves more intermediate inputs from other sectors, relative to its own value-added or primary factors of production (Fally 2012). This measure is referred to as **downstreamness**. In the example above, the construction sector is relatively positioned in the downstream segment, since it uses steel inputs that were previously mined as ores. The remoteness of housing construction from the mining of iron ore signifies the downstream position of the former and the upstreamness of the latter.

A simple way to measure upstreamness is to take the share of gross output of an economy-sector that is sold to final consumers. In this case, a sector with a low ratio between final use and total output is said to be relatively upstream. Similarly, the downstreamness index is given simply by the share of an economy-sector's value-added to the total outlays of a sector. A sector with a low value-added over gross output is considered relatively downstream.

Antràs and Chor (2013) suggested a more complex derivation of the (weighted) average position of an economy-sector's output in GVCs, based on the power series approximation of the Leontief equation. The sequence of terms is taken as a reflection of sector *i*'s different positions in the value chain from its final use. Larger values in this index are associated with relatively higher levels of upstreamness of the output originating from sector *i* in economy *r*. In a similar manner, downstreamness is described as an infinite sequence of terms that reflect the usage of a sector's value-added at different positions in the value chain. In this case, larger values are associated with relatively higher levels of downstreamness of sector *i* in economy *r*.

Upstreamness indexes of select economy-sectors for 2020 are presented in Figure 3.25. These figures are rounded to integers to highlight the index as a measure of the average number of discrete stages it takes for an output of sectors in rows to reach its final consumers. On average, the metals and mining sectors frequently appear as the most upstream. Hence, economies with sizable mining activities and metallurgy also tend to be in upstream stages of the value chain. Contrast this with sectors such as education and health. These sectors generally tend to be located downstream, as these are largely consumed by households and government.

The changes in the economy-level upstreamness indexes for 2000 and 2020 are shown in Figure 3.26. Economies such as the PRC and Taipei,China became more upstream across the 2 decades, meaning their outputs were relatively further from final demand. Meanwhile, economies such as Kazakhstan and Fiji experienced the highest reductions in the upstreamness index, reflecting a reduction in the number of stages before sector outputs were converted into final use.

Wang, Wei, Yu, and Zhu (2017b) refined Antràs and Chor (2013) by defining **average production lengths** (APLs) for both forward and backward perspectives.

The forward length counts the number of stages separating the sector's output from the final consumer. More technically, it measures total gross outputs induced by one unit of value-added at the sector level, which can also be considered as the footprint of each sector's value-added in other products. The more value-added that is counted in the outputs of other sectors in the economy, the longer the production chain and the more upstream the sector. Therefore, this measure is closely related to the upstreamness index defined by Fally (2012) and Antràs and Chor (2013).

Conversely, the backward length counts the number of stages separating a sector's output from primary inputs. It measures the total intermediate inputs embodied in a final product. The more inputs that are counted in the production of a sector's final product, the longer the production chain and the more downstream the sector. This measure is closely related to the downstreamness index defined by Antràs and Chor (2013).

Averaging the two lengths for all the firms in a sector or economy gives average production lengths. Adding both average forward and backward production lengths gives the total length of a particular value chain. Longer production lengths, involving more rounds of value-added contribution, are associated with more complex value chains (Escaith and Inomata 2013). Moreover, Wang, Wei, Yu, and Zhu (2017b) applied the decomposition of production in Wang, Wei, Yu, and Zhu (2017a) to isolate the GVC activity of the sector, defined according to the production-based approach. Thus, it complements the essentially binary approach of the GVC participation rate, which classifies each dollar of exports as either belonging to GVCs or not.

Figure 3.25: Upstreamness Index by Sector in Select Economies of Asia and the Pacific, 2020

Sector	PRC	MAL	KOR	TAP	MON	SIN	JPN	THA	VIE	KGZ	PHI	INO	LAO	BRU	HKG	KAZ	IND	BAN	MLD	BHU	SRI	FIJ	PAK	NEP	CAM
Metals	3	4	3	4	3	3	3	3	3	3	3	3	4	3	3	3	2	2	3	3	2	3	2	2	3
Mining	5	4	4	4	4	0	3	4	4	3	4	4	3	4	0	3	3	3	0	2	2	2	3	2	2
Chemicals	4	4	4	4	3	3	3	4	3	3	3	3	4	4	3	2	3	2	0	3	2	2	2	2	2
Paper	4	3	3	3	3	3	3	3	3	2	3	3	4	1	3	3	2	3	3	2	3	2	2	2	2
Water transport	4	3	3	4	3	4	3	3	3	3	3	2	3	2	3	3	3	2	3	2	3	3	3	0	0
Transport activities, nec	4	3	4	4	3	3	3	3	4	2	2	2	2	3	3	3	2	3	3	2	2	2	3	2	0
Finance	4	4	2	2	4	3	3	3	3	7	2	2	2	2	2	3	2	3	3	2	2	2	2	1	1
Rubber and plastics	4	4	4	4	3	3	3	3	3	3	2	3	2	2	3	2	2	2	0	3	2	2	2	2	2
Utilities	4	3	3	4	4	3	3	3	3	2	3	3	2	3	2	2	3	2	2	2	2	2	2	2	1
Refined fuels	4	3	3	4	3	3	3	2	4	2	3	3	2	3	2	4	2	3	0	0	3	0	2	2	4
Business activities, nec	3	3	3	3	3	3	3	3	3	2	2	3	2	2	3	2	2	2	3	3	3	2	2	2	2
Wood	3	3	3	3	3	3	3	3	3	2	2	2	3	3	2	2	2	2	2	2	2	3	2	2	3
Minerals, nec	3	3	3	3	3	3	3	3	3	3	2	2	2	2	3	2	2	2	2	2	2	2	2	2	2
Agriculture	4	4	3	2	3	3	3	3	3	2	2	2	3	2	1	2	2	2	2	1	2	2	2	2	3
Wholesale trade	3	3	3	3	3	3	2	3	3	2	2	2	2	1	2	3	2	2	3	2	2	2	2	1	2
Air transport	3	3	3	3	3	3	2	2	2	2	2	2	3	3	3	2	2	2	2	3	2	2	1	2	0
Inland transport	3	3	3	3	3	3	2	2	2	2	2	2	2	3	2	2	2	1	2	2	2	2	1	2	2
Telecommunications	3	3	3	2	2	3	2	2	2	2	2	2	1	2	3	2	2	2	3	2	2	2	2	2	2
Machinery, nec	2	2	2	2	3	2	2	2	2	1	2	3	3	2	2	3	2	2	0	1	2	2	1	2	3
Sale of motor vehicles	0	3	3	2	3	3	3	3	2	3	3	2	2	1	0	1	2	1	3	2	2	2	2	1	0
Manufacturing, nec	1	2	3	2	3	2	2	2	1	2	2	1	2	1	2	1	2	2	3	3	2	2	1	2	2
Electricals	3	3	3	3	2	3	3	2	2	1	3	2	2	1	2	1	2	1	0	1	2	0	1	2	2
Textiles	3	2	3	3	1	2	3	2	1	1	2	2	1	2	2	2	2	2	2	1	2	1	1	2	1
Retail trade	3	3	3	2	3	2	1	2	0	2	2	2	2	1	2	1	2	1	2	2	1	1	2	1	2
Hotels and restaurants	3	2	2	2	2	2	2	1	2	2	2	1	1	3	1	1	2	2	2	2	1	2	1	1	2
Leather	3	2	3	2	2	3	3	2	1	3	1	1	1	1	2	2	2	2	0	1	1	2	2	1	0
Personal services, nec	3	2	2	2	2	1	2	2	2	2	2	1	1	2	2	1	2	1	2	2	1	2	1	2	1
Food and beverages	3	3	2	2	1	2	2	2	2	2	2	2	1	2	1	1	1	1	1	1	1	2	1	2	1
Real estate	2	3	2	1	2	3	1	1	2	2	2	2	1	1	2	1	1	1	2	2	1	2	2	1	1
Transport equipment	2	2	2	2	2	2	2	2	2	2	1	2	1	2	1	1	1	1	1	1	1	1	1	2	1
Construction	1	2	1	1	2	2	1	1	1	2	1	1	1	1	2	1	1	1	2	1	1	1	1	1	1
Public administration	1	1	1	1	1	1	1	1	1	1	1	1	1	1	1	1	1	1	2	1	1	1	1	1	1
Education	1	1	1	1	1	1	1	1	1	1	1	1	1	1	1	1	1	1	2	1	1	1	1	1	1
Health and social work	1	1	1	1	1	2	1	1	1	1	1	1	1	1	1	1	1	1	1	1	1	1	1	1	1
Private households	0	0	0	1	1	1	3	0	1	0	0	0	1	0	0	1	1	1	0	0	0	0	0	0	0

BAN = Bangladesh; BHU = Bhutan; BRU = Brunei Darussalam; CAM = Cambodia; FIJ = Fiji; HKG = Hong Kong, China; IND = India; INO = Indonesia; JPN = Japan; KAZ = Kazakhstan; KGZ = Kyrgyz Republic; KOR = Republic of Korea; LAO = Lao People's Democratic Republic; MAL = Malaysia; MLD = Maldives; MON = Mongolia; NEC = Not elsewhere classified; NEP = Nepal; PAK = Pakistan; PHI = Philippines; PRC = People's Republic of China; SIN = Singapore; SRI = Sri Lanka; TAP = Taipei,China; THA = Thailand; VIE = Viet Nam.

Notes: The upstreamness index is measured using Antràs and Chor's *Organizing the Global Value Chain* (2013). Values are rounded to the nearest integer.

Sources: Calculations using the Asian Development Bank Multiregional Input–Output Table. https://mrio.adbx.online/ (accessed July 2021); and P. Antràs and D. Chor. 2013. Organizing the Global Value Chain. *Econometrica*. 81 (6). pp. 2127–2204.

Click here for figure data

Figure 3.26: Changes in Upstreamness Indexes of Select Economies in Asia and the Pacific, 2000 and 2020

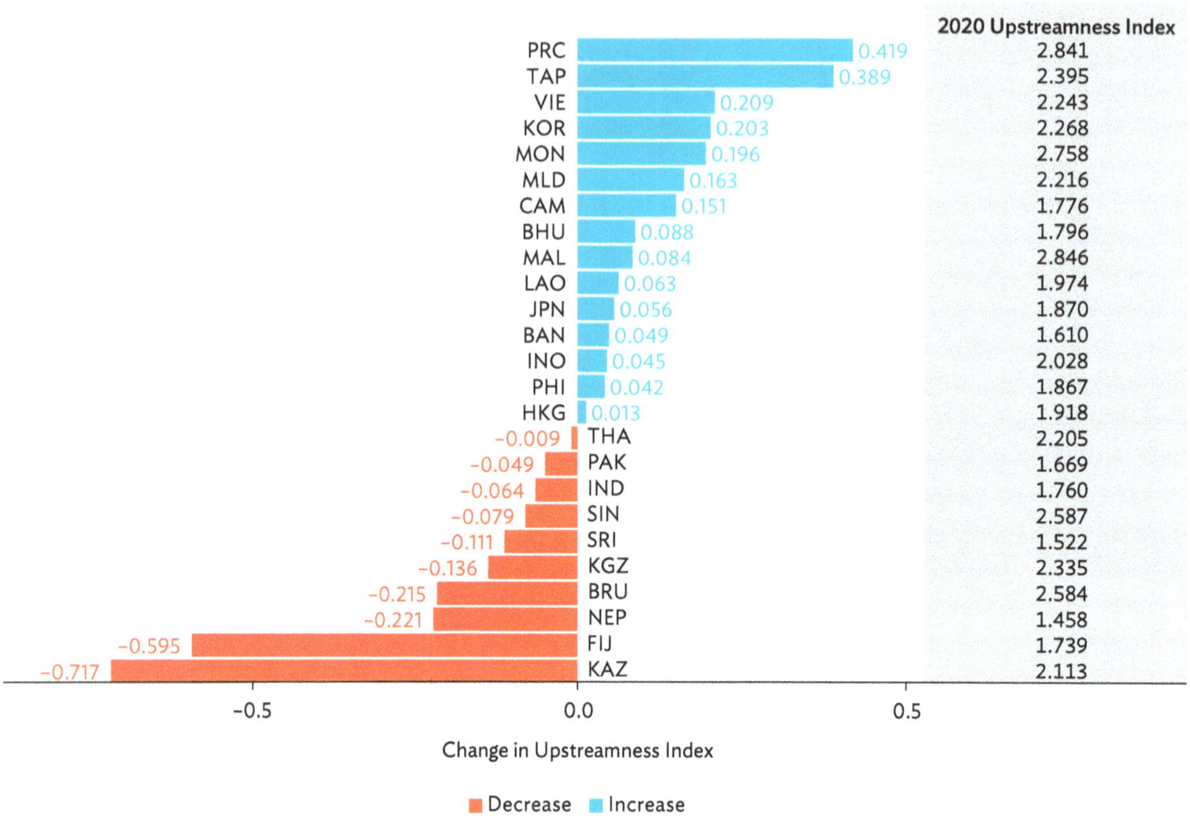

BAN = Bangladesh; BHU = Bhutan; BRU = Brunei Darussalam; CAM = Cambodia; FIJ = Fiji; HKG = Hong Kong, China; IND = India; INO = Indonesia; JPN = Japan; KAZ = Kazakhstan; KGZ = Kyrgyz Republic; KOR = Republic of Korea; LAO = Lao People's Democratic Republic; MAL = Malaysia; MLD = Maldives; MON = Mongolia; NEP = Nepal; PAK = Pakistan; PHI = Philippines; PRC = People's Republic of China; SIN = Singapore; SRI = Sri Lanka; TAP = Taipei,China; THA = Thailand; VIE = Viet Nam.

Notes: The upstreamness index is measured using Antràs and Chor's *Organizing the Global Value Chain* (2013). Sectors are aggregated by value-added origins.

Sources: Calculations using the Asian Development Bank Multiregional Input–Output Table. https://mrio.adbx.online/ (accessed July 2021); and P. Antràs and D. Chor. 2013. Organizing the Global Value Chain. *Econometrica*. 81 (6). pp. 2127–2204.

Click here for figure data

By comparing the forward and backward lengths of an economy, one can derive its relative position along the value chain. Those with longer forward lengths are more upstream, being closer to primary producers and further from final consumers. In the opposite case, sectors are more downstream. In Figure 3.27, the forward and backward GVC lengths of select economies are plotted for the electricals sector, a key sector in GVCs, for 2000 and 2020. The resource-abundant economy of Mongolia tended to be on the upstream end in both years. Reflecting its rapid development over the 2 decades, Viet Nam's electrical and electronics sector shifted from upstream to downstream.

Figure 3.27: Positioning of Select Economies in the Global Value Chain for Electricals

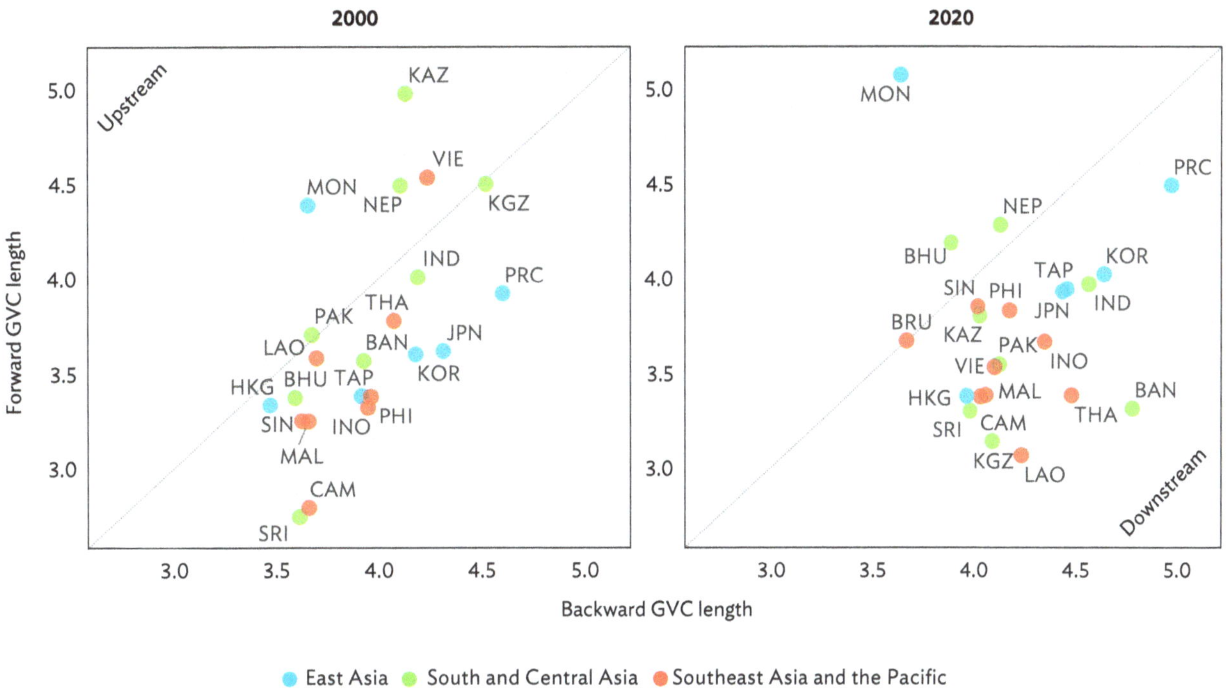

BAN = Bangladesh, BHU = Bhutan; BRU = Brunei Darussalam; CAM = Cambodia; FIJ = Fiji; HKG = Hong Kong, China; IND = India, INO = Indonesia; GVC = global value chain, JPN = Japan, KAZ = Kazakhstan; KGZ = Kyrgyz Republic; LAO = Lao People's Democratic Republic; MAL = Malaysia; MLD = Maldives; MON = Mongolia; NEP = Nepal; PAK = Pakistan; PHI = Philippines; PRC = People's Republic of China; SIN = Singapore; SRI = Sri Lanka; TAP = Taipei,China; THA = Thailand; VIE = Viet Nam.

Notes: Average GVC production lengths are calculated using the methodology of Wang, Wei, Yu, and Zhu's *Characterizing Global Value Chains: Production Length and Upstreamness* (2017). Sectors are disaggregated by value-added origins.

Sources: Z. Wang, S. Wei, X. Yu, and K. Zhu. 2017b. Characterizing Global Value Chains: Production Length and Upstreamness. *NBER Working Paper* No. 23261. Cambridge, MA: National Bureau of Economic Research; and calculations using the Asian Development Bank Multiregional Input–Output Table. https://mrio.adbx.online (accessed 1 August 2021).

Click here for figure data

Figure 3.28 shows the average production length at the aggregate economy-level for 2020. The PRC and Malaysia scored high on both backward and forward measures of APL, suggesting complexity of midstream activities. Viet Nam, meanwhile, displayed a high backward APL, suggesting a relatively strong degree of downstreamness of the economy. Mongolia, on the other hand, exhibited one of the highest forward APLs, indicating that the value-added originating from its sectors underwent several downstream processes before reaching final use. In contrast, Nepal, Sri Lanka, and Pakistan had the lowest number of stages between primary production (value-added) and subsequent final use, both in terms of backward and forward linkages. On average, APL indexes for the economies of Asia and the Pacific indicate that it takes around two production stages before a sector's value-added reaches its final consumer.

Figure 3.28: Average Production Lengths of Select Economies in Asia and the Pacific, 2020

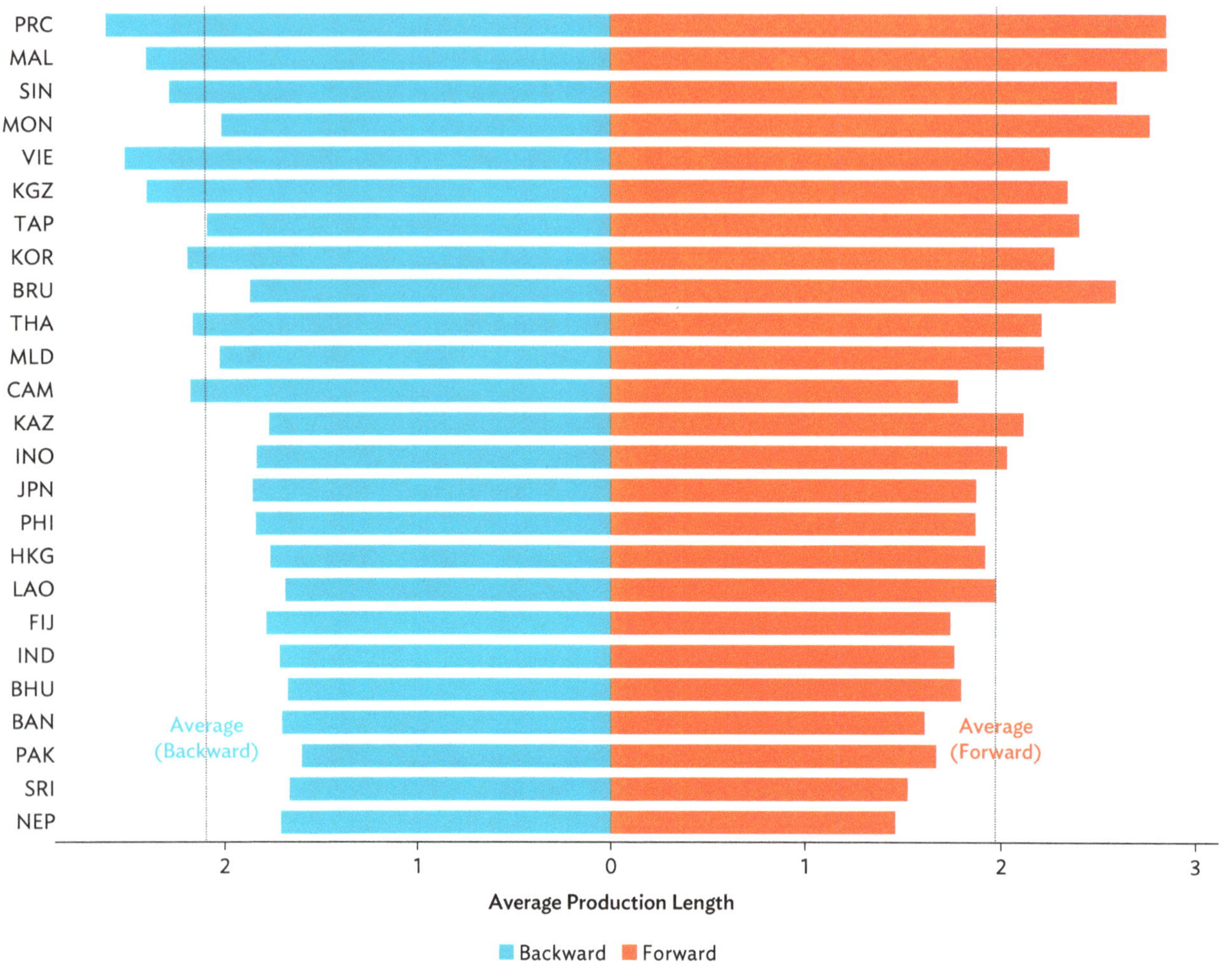

BAN = Bangladesh, BHU = Bhutan; BRU = Brunei Darussalam; CAM = Cambodia; FIJ = Fiji; HKG = Hong Kong, China; IND = India, INO = Indonesia; GVC = global value chain, JPN = Japan, KAZ = Kazakhstan; KGZ = Kyrgyz Republic; LAO = Lao People's Democratic Republic; MAL = Malaysia; MLD = Maldives; MON = Mongolia; NEP = Nepal; PAK = Pakistan; PHI = Philippines; PRC = People's Republic of China; SIN = Singapore; SRI = Sri Lanka; TAP = Taipei,China; THA = Thailand; VIE = Viet Nam.

Notes: Average GVC production lengths are calculated using the methodology of Wang, Wei, Yu, and Zhu's *Characterizing Global Value Chains: Production Length and Upstreamness* (2017). Sectors are disaggregated by value-added origins.

Sources: Z. Wang, S. Wei, X. Yu, and K. Zhu. 2017b. Characterizing Global Value Chains: Production Length and Upstreamness. *NBER Working Paper* No. 23261. Cambridge, MA: National Bureau of Economic Research; and calculations using the Asian Devlopment Bank Multiregional Input-Output Table. https://mrio.adbx.online (accessed July 2021).

Click here for figure data

3.11 Role of Domestic Sectors

An economy's engagement in global production can also be assessed by looking at the sourcing and supplying decisions of individual sectors. While GVCs offer development opportunities for participating economies, there are concerns that the gains in trade differ significantly. For economies wanting to join the GVC trade, the ambition has been to perform and specialize in higher value-added tasks. With this in mind, plans to internationalize have been focused on honing competitive sectors that are engaged in export activities—from skills development to technology transfer and creating a business-friendly environment. However, from a value chain standpoint, exporting sectors are not the only ones engaged in trade. Domestic sectors also indirectly participate and specialize in these production chains by producing intermediate goods that are eventually absorbed in exported products. This implies that successful GVC participation entails extending the focus to domestic sectors and their ability to perform well on value-adding tasks.

The role of domestic sectors is even more emphasized considering the recent "reshoring" phenomenon of global firms. The trend of outsourcing started to wane after the operations of industrial firms were markedly exposed to global shocks and supply chain risks, especially after the severe acute respiratory syndrome (SARS) epidemic of 2003, the 2008 oil price spikes and subsequent global financial crisis, and the 2011 tsunami in Japan and floods in Thailand. More recently, trade conflicts, investment uncertainty, and pandemics have heightened the inherent risks associated with integrated global production chains, and may have increased the pace of localization (Simchi-Levi and Haren 2022). These risks, along with the increasing use of digital technologies, have pushed firms to actively step back from GVC-related activities by reshoring production segments to domestic firms. In effect, reshoring has become a way for international firms to minimize risks from global supply chains.

Therefore, in the context of slower international trade activity, measuring the extent of domestic linkages for global production becomes an important policy tool. Baris et al. (2022) offer an alternative measure called the **domestic agglomeration index**. This index looks at how much value-added is sourced from and/or absorbed in domestic economy-sectors, given the production of final goods in other sectors. It is further calibrated to show how a particular economy-sector fares relative to the world average. Overall, the domestic agglomeration index gives an indication of the sourcing and buying patterns of domestic sectors for the production of final goods and services. If a substantial share of what makes up a final good is accounted for by DVA, then a particular economy-sector tends to be more domestically agglomerated from the backward (user) perspective. Meanwhile, if a substantial share of value-added is generated or driven by domestic consumption, then a particular economy-sector tends to be more domestically agglomerated from the forward (producer) perspective.

More technically, agglomeration indexes are said to be high if the index is greater than 1, and the opposite is true if it is less than 1. A high backward agglomeration signals that DVA embodied in final goods and services consumed domestically is high. Intuitively, this implies that domestic production for domestic consumption is higher than the world average. Meanwhile, a high forward agglomeration indicates that domestic sectors absorb a significant portion of value-added generated by an economy-sector. This means the value-added that goes to domestic production is higher than the world average. A discussion of how the index is constructed is provided in the technical notes for this publication.

Using MRIO data for 2020, Baris et al (2022) saw several economies exhibiting high agglomeration indexes from both forward and backward perspectives. Bangladesh, India, Indonesia, Japan, Nepal, Pakistan, the Philippines, the PRC, and Sri Lanka all showed agglomeration results that were higher than world and regional averages (Figure 3.29). Meanwhile, 15 economies—Bhutan; Brunei Darussalam; Cambodia; Fiji; Hong Kong, China; Kazakhstan; the Kyrgyz Republic; the Lao PDR; Malaysia; Maldives; Mongolia; Singapore; Taipei,China; Thailand; and Viet Nam—all exhibited lower agglomeration measures than world and regional averages from both perspectives. Interestingly, the Republic of Korea scored high on the backward agglomeration index but low on the forward index in 2020.

These domestic linkages in an economy evolve through time and notably differ from one sectoral grouping to another. For example, Baris et al. (2022) also noted upward movements in forward agglomeration in select economies, demonstrating the ability of these domestic sectors to absorb value-added from GVCs. As the index is also closely linked to sourcing and buying patterns of domestic sectors, it consequentially traces whether activities are being reshored to the domestic economy.

Figure 3.29: Domestic Agglomeration Indexes of Select Economies in Asia and the Pacific, 2020

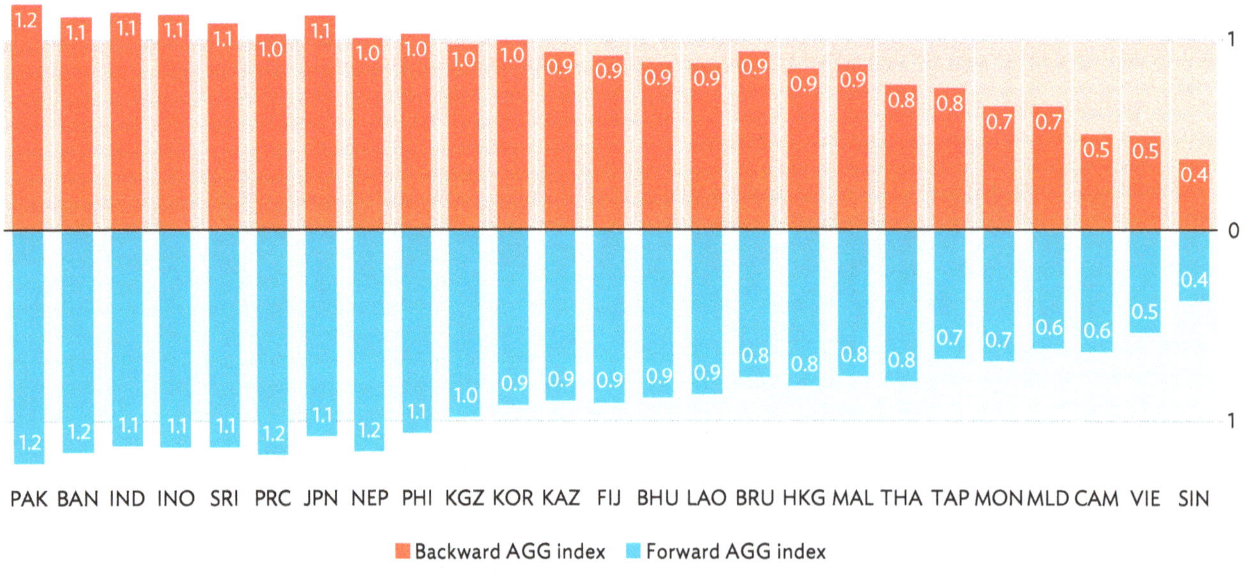

AGG = domestic agglomeration; BAN = Bangladesh; BHU = Bhutan; BRU = Brunei Darussalam; CAM = Cambodia; FIJ = Fiji; HKG = Hong Kong, China; IND = India; INO = Indonesia; JPN = Japan; KAZ = Kazakhstan; KGZ = Kyrgyz Republic; KOR = Republic of Korea; LAO = Lao People's Democratic Republic; MAL = Malaysia; MLD = Maldives; MON = Mongolia; NEP = Nepal; PAK = Pakistan; PHI = Philippines; PRC = People's Republic of China; SIN = Singapore; SRI = Sri Lanka; TAP = Taipei,China; THA = Thailand; VIE = Viet Nam.

Sources: K. Baris, M.C. Crisostomo, K. Garay, C. Jabagat, M. Mariasingham, E. Mores. 2022. Measuring Localization in the Age of Economic Globalization. ADB *Economics Working Paper Series.* No. 647. Manila: Asian Development Bank; and Calculations using the Asian Development Bank Multiregional Input-Output Table. https://mrio.adbx.online/ (accessed July 2021).

Click here for figure data

3.12 Summary

The metrics presented in this chapter examine, from multiple perspectives, the interrelationships of domestic sectors with foreign economies. The analysis begins by assessing how demands in the local economy are complemented by international trade. Whether economies rely on other economies for inputs or demand will depend on the needs and resources of the host economy. The results in the chapter show that, while smaller economies with limited resources tend to exhibit higher openness to trade, the Asia and Pacific region in general is more inclined toward exporting their products than importing materials.

Importing has enabled several economies to participate in internationally fragmented production chains as sectors were able to access cheaper inputs abroad. However, more recent results show a reversal of trend on the domestic and imported sourcing patterns of such sectors. From the demand perspective, the increase in domestically sourced inputs compared to imports reflects a shift in priorities in light of the COVID-19 pandemic. As internal demand puts pressure on domestic supply, attenuated global risks increase the reluctance of firms to source inputs internationally. From the supply perspective, decomposing intraregional versus interregional components of output suggest that the former continue to drive production in several economies.

However, this retreat from global trade, while starkly evident in merchandise statistics even before the pandemic, is not universal. Few economies in Asia and the Pacific are still reliant on global demand, most especially those in Southeast Asia. Participation in GVCs further reveals the two-pronged effects of international trade: that it can provide access to international markets and mitigate shocks in the domestic economy, but can also expose participating economies to global risks. As economies are integrated at different levels of GVCs, revealed comparative advantage signals which sectors and economies could be disproportionately affected by global shocks. For example, economies specializing in trade-reliant tourism sectors suffered significant impacts from the COVID-19 pandemic, as did manufacturing sectors dependent on just-in-time supply chains.

As a result, diversification resurfaced as a strategy for several economies to minimize risks. While some economies were successful in deconcentrating sources of value-added before the COVID-19 pandemic, the growing share of import-dependent sectors in some economies could have contributed to heightening the adverse effects of the 2020 economic recession. Recoiling from weak global demand at the onset of the COVID-19 pandemic, sourcing patterns also increased in favor of domestic suppliers more than foreign counterparts, as evidenced by agglomeration indexes. Domestic demand has also increased in several economies, which may have dulled some of the more severe effects of the pandemic.

Overall, the analytical indicators featured in this chapter are valuable in evaluating trade dependencies, their present economic benefits, and how the nature and behavior of economic actors are evolving in cross-border trade. With the regular compilation of updated multiregional input–output tables, these statistics serve to complement standard analyses of trade and GVCs and their links to economic development.

References

P. Antràs and D. Chor. 2013. Organizing the Global Value Chain. *Econometrica.* 81 (6). pp. 2127–2204.

Asian Development Bank (ADB). 2021. *Key Indicators for Asia and the Pacific 2021.* Manila: Asian Development Bank.

ADB. 2022. *Pakistan's Economy and Trade in the Age of Global Value Chains.* Manila: Asian Development Bank.

B. Balassa. 1965. Trade Liberalisation and "Revealed" Comparative Advantage. *The Manchester School.* 33 (2). pp. 99–123.

K. Baris, M.C. Crisostomo, K. A. Garay, C. R. Jabagat, M. Mariasingham, and E. M. Mores. 2022. Measuring Localization in the Age of Economic Globalization. *ADB Economics Working Papers.* No. 647. Manila: Asian Development Bank.

T. Bohn, S. Brakman, and E. Dietzenbacher. 2021. Who's Afraid of Virginia Wu? US Employment Footprints and Self-Sufficiency. *Economic Systems Research.* https://doi.org/10.1080/09535314.2021.1935219.

A. Borin and M. Mancini. 2019. Measuring What Matters in Global Value Chains and Value-Added Trade. *Policy Research Working Paper.* No. 8804. Washington, DC: World Bank.

P. Byé, M. Fonte, and J. P. Frey. 2021. An Input–Output Approach to the Analysis of Agricultural Policies and Agro-industry Structure. *International Journal of Sociology of Agriculture and Food.* https://doi.org/10.48416/ijsaf.v2i.401.

Center of Systems Science and Engineering (CSSE). 2021. Johns Hopkins Coronavirus Resource Center. https://coronavirus.jhu.edu/map.html (accessed July 2021).

H. Escaith and S. Inomata. 2013. Geometry of Global Value Chains in East Asia: The Role of Industrial Networks and Trade Policies. In D. K. Elms and P. Low, eds. *Global Value Chains in a Changing World.* Geneva: World Trade Organization. pp. 135–157.

T. Fally. 2012. Production Staging: Measurement and Facts. https://www2.gwu.edu/~iiep/assets/docs/fally_productionstaging.pdf.

Food and Agriculture Organization of the United Nations. 1999. *Implications of Economic Policy for Food Security: A Training Manual.* http://www.fao.org/docrep/004/x3936e/x3936e03.htm (1999) (accessed July 2021).

Government of Japan. Ministry of Economy, Trade, and Industry (METI). 2011. White Paper on International Economy and Trade 2011. https://www.meti.go.jp/english/report/data/gWT2011fe.html.

S. Hongsakhone, M. Islam, and M. Ichihashi. 2021. Producing a Village Input–Output Table (VIOT) from Household Survey Data: a Case Study of a VIOT for a Rural Village in Northern Lao PDR. *Journal of Economic Structures*. 10 (1).

D. Hummels, J. Ishii, and K. M. Yi. 2001. The Nature and Growth of Vertical Specialization in World Trade. *Journal of International Economics*. 54. pp. 75–96.

International Monetary Fund (IMF). 2019. *World Economic Outlook (October 2019): Global Manufacturing Downturn, Rising Trade Barriers*. Washington, DC: International Monetary Fund.

IMF. 2021. *World Economic Outlook (April 2021): Managing Divergent Recoveries*. Washington, DC: International Monetary Fund.

Y. Ishikawa. 2019. An Interregional Input–Output Model for Estimating the Effects of Regional Revitalization Policy (Japanese). RIETI Discussion Papers. No. 19062. Research Institute of Economy, Trade, and Industry (RIETI).

R. W. Jackson. 2020. *Input–Output Analysis: A Primer*. Second Edition. WVU Research Repository.

Philippine Statistics Authority (PSA). 2006. *The 2000 Input–Output Accounts of the Philippines*. Makati City.

N. Pourrostami. 2018. An Analysis of Trade Interdependency among East Asian Countries Using Asian International Input–Output Table. *Quarterly Journal of New Economy and Trade*. 13 (2). pp. 1–27.

B. Sim, F. Secretario, and E. Suan. 2007. Developing an Interregional Input–Output Table for Cross-Border Economies: An Application to the Lao People's Democratic Republic and Thailand. *ERD Occasional Statistical Paper Series*. No. 1. Asian Development Bank.

D. Simchi-Levi and P. Haren. 2022. How the War in Ukraine is Further Disrupting Global Supply Chains. *Harvard Business Review*. March 17.

H. Reis and A. Rua. 2006. An Input–Output Analysis: Linkages vs Leakages. *ERD Working Papers*. No. 17. Banco de Portugal Economics Research Department.

Z. Wang, S. Wei, and K. Zhu. 2013. Quantifying International Production Sharing at the Bilateral and Sector Levels. *NBER Working Paper*. No. 19677. Cambridge, MA: National Bureau of Economic Research.

Z. Wang, S. J. Wei, X. Yu, and K. Zhu. 2017a. Measures of Participation in Global Value Chains and Global Business Cycles. *NBER Working Paper*. No. 23222. Cambridge, MA: National Bureau of Economic Research.

Z. Wang, S. Wei, X. Yu, and K. Zhu. 2017b. Characterizing Global Value Chains: Production Length and Upstreamness. *NBER Working Paper*. No. 23261. Cambridge, MA: National Bureau of Economic Research.

World Bank. 2020. World Development Report: Trading for Development in the Age of Global Value Chains. Washington, DC: World Bank.

Estimating the Effects of COVID-19 Using Counterfactual National Input–Output Tables

4

Using input–output analysis, this special chapter presents a methodology to measure the economic effects of the COVID-19 pandemic. The usual assumption is to measure only the observed effects of the pandemic, which renders an incomplete picture since this does not yet account for the missed growth potential (expected losses) in the economy's pre-pandemic trajectory. Thus, the pre-pandemic forecasted growth (decline) should also be considered. In measuring the full impact of the pandemic to the economy, a distinction between observed growth (decline) and unrealized gains (losses) based on pre-pandemic forecasted growth (decline) is made. The key contribution of this methodology is the construction of a counterfactual input–output table for 2020 using the Leontief Quantity Model, which benchmarks the size and composition of economic growth had there been no pandemic in 2020. Applying this methodology to select economies in ADB's Multiregional Input–Output Tables, the chapter presents estimates on the sectoral and economy-wide effects of the COVID-19 pandemic in terms of output, value-added, and employment.

4.1 Introduction

The novel coronavirus disease 2019 (COVID-19) is a respiratory illness that results from the infection of the SARS-CoV-2 virus. The first case of the disease was identified in Wuhan in the People's Republic of China (PRC) during December 2019. Subsequently, this disease has resulted in a global pandemic affecting 190 countries, with 289 million confirmed cases in 2 years.[1] Initial research showed that the disease primarily spreads through droplets of saliva or discharge from the nose of an infected person, but there is growing evidence that airborne transmission in the form of aerosols can also transport the virus (WHO 2020).[2] The symptoms of the disease range from mild to severe and, at worst, the disease has been lethal to the infected, associated with about 5.88 million reported deaths worldwide as of February 2022 (footnote 1).

The rate of contagion, patterns of transmission, and severity of symptoms of COVID-19 have threatened the safety and livelihoods of people and put unprecedented pressure on health care systems globally. It became critical for governments to put in place safety measures to contain the disease, mainly by restricting the movements of people within and outside their national and internal borders. Some of the measures adopted on a global

1 Figures were originally published by WHO on 9 July 2020 and are updated in real time through the interactive dashboard created by E. Dong, H. Du, and L. Gardner.

2 Airborne transmission is the spread of the disease that is due to the suspension of infectious droplets in the air for long periods or distances.

scale were the implementation of social distancing, hygiene protocols in public places, and lockdowns. Generally, lockdowns involved travel bans, the closure of public spaces (such as schools and nonessential businesses), stay-at-home orders, and quarantining. Despite the social and economic losses that were anticipated to arise from these restrictions, they were implemented in 185 countries (as of September 2020) at varying levels of stringency according to rates of infection (Hale et al. 2021).

As expected, the restrictions implemented by governments, while necessary, have had detrimental effects on economic growth. At the macro level, the world's gross domestic product (GDP) contracted by 3.31%, from an estimated $84.61 trillion in 2019 to $81.83 trillion in 2020.[3] Figure 4.1 shows how most of the world's regional and subregional economies experienced economic recession. A year after the onset of the COVID-19 pandemic, the combined GDP of economies in Europe and Central America decreased by $1.25 trillion compared to the 2019 level. The same declining trend was experienced by North American economies, with their combined GDP for 2019 reduced by $770 billion in 2020. South American and South Asian economies contracted the most, with decreases of over 5% in GDP from 2019 levels (World Bank 2020). Further, the problem of unemployment grew in many economies, with the tourism and travel businesses facing extensive losses from the pandemic due to restrictions in mobility and social distancing measures. Overall, the COVID-19 pandemic has changed the world as we know it and these changes can be viewed in various ways.

Figure 4.1: Growth of Real Gross Domestic Product, by Subregion
(%)

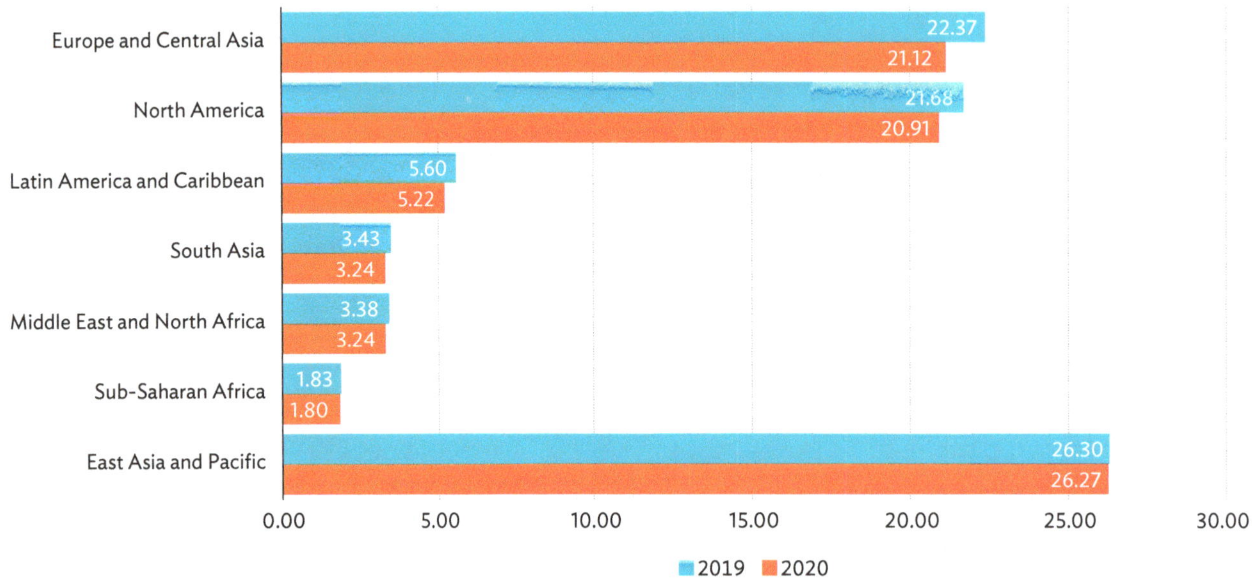

Note: Gross domestic product is in trillions of constant 2015 United States dollars.
Sources: World Bank Development Indicators. https://data.worldbank.org/ (accessed March 2022); and Organisation for Economic Co-operation and Development. National Accounts. https://www.oecd.org/sdd/na/ (accessed March 2022).

Click here for figure data

3 In constant 2015 United States dollars.

4.2 Counterfactual 2020 Methodology

In analyzing the macroeconomic impacts of the COVID-19 pandemic, It is often assumed that observed changes from 2019 to 2020 will contain the impact of the COVID-19 pandemic to output, value-added, and employment. However, this change does not yet account for the missed growth potential (or expected losses) in the economy's pre-pandemic trajectory. Thus, two perspectives should be given consideration: (i) the observed effects during the crisis, and (ii) the counterfactual scenario had there been no crisis. On the one hand, the realized impact observed during the pandemic is estimated by directly comparing 2019 and 2020 levels of output, value-added, and employment. This is a straightforward approach in measuring one portion of the actual impact with the assumption that these observed effects were all related to the pandemic. Multiple events transpired over the year affecting the global market and this is attributed to the confluence of factors brought by the pandemic. On the other hand, a counterfactual scenario without pandemic provides the unobserved portion of the impact, by showing the unrealized gains or losses in an economy based on the pre-pandemic forecasted growth (decline). Hence, in modeling the counterfactual scenario, a key assumption is that the counterfactual basis matches the actual scenario in all aspects, except for the effects of the pandemic. This ensures that the difference between the actual and counterfactual models reveals the unobserved effects of COVID-19 only. The observed and the unobserved effects provide a fuller picture and, combined, give us the actual impact of the pandemic.

In this input–output analysis, three pieces of information are crucial to study each national economy. First is the 2019 national input–output table (NIOT); second is the 2020 NIOT; and third is the counterfactual 2020 NIOT. The main contribution of this chapter is the estimation of a counterfactual input–output table for 2020, which benchmarks the size and composition of economic growth had there been no pandemic in 2020. The methodology in constructing a counterfactual 2020 table uses forecast data and an input- output- based model to project how the economy might have fared in 2020 had there been no pandemic. The information present in these tables allows the calculation of impact of the pandemic on output and value-added. Information on sector-level employment also provides additional insights on the economic effects of the pandemic.

4.2.1 Data Requirements

Aside from the 2019 and 2020 NIOTs, the information needed to form a counterfactual 2020 table must be compiled. Forecast data for 2020, published prior to the pandemic, should be used to produce counterfactual estimates in line with published data on GDP and its expenditures components.[4] Thus, the following forecast data for 2020 are required:[5]

4 If forecasted HFCE and NPISH are lumped as private final consumption expenditure, 2019 information on HFCE and NPISH can be used to disaggregate it. If forecasted CII is not available, forecasted gross capital formation (GCF) can be used to calculate CII by deducting GCF to GFCF.

5 Possible data sources are the OECD's Economic Outlook, the International Monetary Fund's World Economic Outlook, or forecasts by national statistics offices.

(i) Household Final Consumption Expenditure (HFCE),
(ii) Nonprofit Institutions Serving Households Final Consumption Expenditure (NPISH),
(iii) Government Final Consumption Expenditure (GFCE),
(iv) Gross Fixed Capital Formation (GFCF),
(v) Changes in Inventories (CII),
(vi) Exports of Goods and Services (X), and
(vii) Imports of Goods and Services (M).

To avoid the effects of exchange rate fluctuation, all data requirements, including the NIOTs, are expressed in local currency units.

4.2.2 Construction of Final Demand

Given the forecasts for the components of GDP by expenditure approach, the final demand matrix Y in the counterfactual NIOT is first estimated. The consumption patterns across sectors are assumed to remain fixed in the short run. This allows us to use the structure of the 2019 final demand matrix to the counterfactual 2020. Suppose one has the component[6] Y under the $\boldsymbol{Y}$ matrix, then each Y component is derived as follows:

$$Y_{total}^{2020f} = \sum_{i=1}^{n} Y_i^{2020} = \hat{Y}_{total}^{2020f} \left(\frac{\sum_{i=1}^{n} Y_i^{2019}}{Y_{total}^{2019}} \right)$$

where i is the producing sector, and n is the total number of sectors in the economy. This equation indicates that the total final demand component controlled by the pre-pandemic forecast $\hat{Y}_{total}^{2020f}$ is spread out among the domestic final consumption of goods and services acquired within borders following the 2019 $\boldsymbol{Y}$ matrix structure.

With the estimated final demand components, the total final demand per sector can be calculated simply as the sum of HFCE, NPISH, GFCE, GFCF, CII, and Exports for each sector i. This will form a summation vector of dimension $n \times 1$:

$$\boldsymbol{Y}_{2020f}^{iQ} = \sum_{q \in Q} Y_{2020f}^{iQ}$$

where Q is the set of final demand components Y. This summation vector would be used to estimate the gross output of each sector i using the Leontief quantity model (LQM).

4.2.3 Leontief Quantity Model

Note that the other portion of the NIOT comprises of intermediate inputs consumption by sector and the value-added generated through their production process, i.e., gross output = intermediate consumption + value-added. Since the final demand vector is now

6 Final demand Y components include HFCE, NPISH, GFCE, GFCF, CII, and X.

constructed, an input–output-based model can be used to estimate gross outputs, which will be used as a control total for the remaining matrixes of the table.

The LQM uses exogenous information to estimate the gross output per sector. Given that the final consumption of different economic agents is not dependent on the technological interrelation of the productive sectors, the final demand matrix $\boldsymbol{Y}$ is treated as exogenous. The LQM uses information on the interlinkages between sectors to map the output produced by these sectors to satisfy that level of final demand. The model is as follows:

$$\boldsymbol{x}_{2020f} = (\boldsymbol{I} - \boldsymbol{A}_{2019})^{-1}\, \boldsymbol{Y}^{iQ}_{2020f}$$

where $\boldsymbol{x}$ is the gross output vector, $(\boldsymbol{I} - \boldsymbol{A}_{2019})^{-1}$ is the Leontief inverse matrix $\boldsymbol{B}$, in which $\boldsymbol{A}$ is the technical coefficients matrix of the 2019 IOT. The technical coefficients matrix $\boldsymbol{A}$ is given by the ratio of the intermediate input to the gross output. The matrix provides information on the proportion of inputs needed from each sector to produce a sector's output. The underlying assumption is that the technology of production within a year does not change drastically, hence the technical coefficients for the counterfactual 2020 scenario should be the same as that of the 2019 scenario, i.e., $\boldsymbol{A}_{2020f} = \boldsymbol{A}_{2019}$. The resulting gross output for the counterfactual 2020 is an $n \times 1$ vector and will be used to control the intermediate consumption and value-added matrixes, further elaborated in the next subsection.

4.2.4 Fixed Technology Assumption

The intermediate consumption is divided between the domestically sourced inputs and the imported inputs. In deriving these components, a fixed technology assumption is adopted, since changes in production structure due to technological changes can only be reasonably expected in the long run. This fixed technology assumption entails the use of $\boldsymbol{A}$ matrix to derive the intermediate inputs. For the domestically sourced inputs, the interindustrial transactions matrix $\boldsymbol{Z}$ is estimated by multiplying the technical coefficients in 2019 with the resulting counterfactual 2020 gross output from the LQM, i.e.,

$$\boldsymbol{Z}_{2020f} = \boldsymbol{A}_{2019}\, \hat{\boldsymbol{x}}_{2020f}$$

where $\hat{\boldsymbol{x}}_{2020f}$ is the diagonalized gross output matrix estimated using the LQM. For the imported inputs, this has a control from the forecasted data. In a NIOT, the imports are shown as a row vector below the domestic sectors. Note that the total imports m_{total} are composed of both the intermediate m_Z and final consumption m_Y of goods and services from foreign sectors and is defined as $m_{total} = m_Z + m_Y$. Hence, the forecasted total imports $\widehat{m}^{2020f}_{total}$ will be allocated among the sectors and final demand components row-wise to estimate total imports for the counterfactual 2020, i.e.,

$$m^{2020f}_{total} = m^{2020}_{Z,j} + m^{2020}_{Y} = \widehat{m}^{2020f}_{total} \left(\frac{m^{2019}_{Z,j} + m^{2019}_{Y}}{m^{2019}_{total}} \right)$$

where j is the purchasing sector. To ensure that the fixed technology assumption is followed and the imports-to-output ratios of 2019 and the counterfactual 2020 only have small and tolerable differences, manual rebalancing of imports is recommended by reallocating large discrepancies between sectors.

The only component left from the counterfactual 2020 is the value-added matrix $\boldsymbol{V}$ with a $v \times n$ dimension where v is the number of primary units included in the value-added matrix. Since the gross output vector $\boldsymbol{x}$ and the intermediate consumption matrix $\boldsymbol{Z}$ are available, the value-added matrix $\boldsymbol{V}$ can be derived as the residual of the two. To maintain the fixed technology assumption, the $\boldsymbol{V}$ structure of the 2019 table is used for the counterfactual 2020. The residual value is split using the sector-specific shares of gross value-added and of net taxes on products to the sum of these two components. Suppose one has the component V under the $\boldsymbol{V}$ matrix, where V are gross value-added and taxes less subsidies on products, then each V component per purchasing sector j is derived as follows:

$$V_j^{2020f} = \left(x_j^{2020f} - \sum_{i=1}^{n} Z_{i,j}^{2020f} - m_{Z,j}^{2020f} \right) \left(\frac{V_j^{2019}}{V_{total,j}^{2019}} \right)$$

where the first term is the difference between gross output x_j^{2020f} and the intermediate consumption of domestically sourced inputs $\sum_{i=1}^{n} Z_{i,j}^{2020f}$ and imported inputs $m_{Z,j}^{2020f}$ for sector j. This allows for similar gross value-added-to-output ratios (GVAr) for both the 2019 and counterfactual 2020 tables.

To be consistent with the market-clearing condition, the gross output derived by summing intermediate consumption and value-added and the gross output calculated as a sum of intermediate and final consumptions should be equal. Further, the GDP obtained through the expenditures approach, production approach, and income approach (if applicable) should also be equal. If the macroeconomic accounting identities are satisfied, then we have arrived with a balanced counterfactual 2020 table. This counterfactual 2020 table allows us to estimate the impacts of the pandemic in terms of output and value-added. The methodology can then be extended to accommodate further analysis on the impact of the COVID-19 crisis in terms of employment. This extension will be explored in the next subsection.

4.2.5 Employment

The information from the counterfactual 2020 table can be used to generate a counterfactual 2020 employment data by sector. The additional data requirements for this analysis would be the sector-level employment and sector-level gross output (from the NIOT) in 2019. To estimate the counterfactual 2020 employment data, the EBY model is applied, i.e.,

$$emp_j^{2020f} = \left[\sum_{i=1}^{n}\left(\frac{emp_j^{2019}}{x_j^{2019}}\right)b_{ij}\right]\sum_{q\in Q} Y_{2020f}^{iQ}$$

where emp_j^{2019} is the total employment of sector j in 2019, x_j^{2019} is the gross output of sector j in 2019, b_{ij} is the Leontief inverse matrix coefficient, and $\sum_{q\in Q} Y_{2020f}^{iQ}$ is the total final demand per sector i. In compact matrix form, the model is as follows:

$$\boldsymbol{emp}^{2020f} = \hat{\boldsymbol{e}}_{2019}\boldsymbol{B}_{2020f}\boldsymbol{Y}_{2020f}^{iQ}$$

where $\hat{\boldsymbol{e}}_{2019}$ is a diagonalized $n \times n$ matrix with the employment-to-output ratios as diagonals, $\boldsymbol{B}_{2020f}$ is the Leontief inverse matrix, $\boldsymbol{Y}_{2020f}^{iQ}$ is the $n \times 1$ final demand vector, and the resulting $n \times 1$ vector $\boldsymbol{emp}^{2020f}$ is the counterfactual 2020 total employment by sector j.

4.3 Using the Counterfactual National Input-Output Table

The first step in measuring the impact of the COVID-19 pandemic is to compare the 2019 and 2020 NIOTs. From these tables, one can obtain the vector of output x, vector of value-added v, and vector of employment emp levels (if applicable). It is also possible to provide sector-level analysis aside from economy-level analysis. This is one of the advantages of the methodology proposed. This observed growth (decline) is estimated for the following levels:

$$\Delta x_{observed} = x_{2020} - x_{2019}$$

$$\Delta v_{observed} = v_{2020} - v_{2019}$$

$$\Delta emp_{observed} = emp_{2020} - emp_{2019}$$

The second step compares the counterfactual 2020 table to the 2019 NIOT. The difference gives the supposed growth or losses in each sector had there been no pandemic. However, these changes are unrealized because of the demand- and supply-side disruptions present during the crisis. This is important in the analysis of the impact because the comparison of the effects should start from the forecasted 2020 data and not only from the actual 2020 levels. This impact, defined as the unrealized economic impact, is estimated as the negative of the pre-pandemic forecasted growth (decline):

$$\Delta x_{unrealized} = -(x_{2020f} - x_{2019})$$

$$\Delta v_{unrealized} = -(v_{2020f} - v_{2019})$$

$$\Delta emp_{unrealized} = -(emp_{2020f} - emp_{2019})$$

This, along with the observed economic impact, completes the estimation of the actual COVID-19 impact on the economy, i.e.,

$$\Delta impact_{actual} = \Delta impact_{observed} + \Delta impact_{unrealized}$$

where *impact* may be in output, value-added, or employment terms.

Note that comparing the counterfactual 2020 table with the 2020 NIOT is a more direct approach of the estimation. The difference gives the actual economic impact of COVID-19 since those were the gains or losses experienced by each sector after comparing it with the supposed growth of each sector for 2020. Thus, the analysis adheres to the following identity:

$$\Delta impact_{actual} = \Delta impact_{observed} + \Delta impact_{unrealized} = impact_{2020} - impact_{2020f}$$

This concludes the methodology of measuring the effects of the COVID-19 pandemic to the economy. The next section demonstrates the application of this methodology using NIOTs for select economies. These NIOTs are extracted from the ADB multiregional input–output (MRIO) database.

4.4 Effect of the COVID-19 Pandemic on Select Economies

ADB's multiregional input–output tables (MRIOTs) for 2019 and 2020 were used to estimate the macroeconomic impacts of the COVID-19 pandemic on select economies.[7] NIOTs for 2019 and 2020 were extracted from the MRIOTs. The methodology is illustrated using data from Canada, Germany, India, Indonesia, Japan, the Republic of Korea, and the United States (US). For each economy, the following forecast data for 2020 as of November 2019 were collected from the Organisation for Economic Co-operation and Development's Economic Outlook Database (OECD 2019):[8]

(i) Private Final Consumption Expenditure,
(ii) Government Final Consumption Expenditure,
(iii) Gross Capital Formation,
(iv) Gross Fixed Capital Formation,
(v) Changes in Inventories,
(vi) Exports of Goods and Services, and
(vii) Imports of Goods and Services.

Additionally, annual average exchange rates from the International Financial Statistics (IFS) were used to convert US dollars to local currency units. Since the MRIOT's private final demand components are divided between the household (HFCE) and the nonprofit

7 The selection of economies in the application of the methodology heavily depended on the availability of reliable forecasted 2020 data.

8 All figures must be in local currency units to avoid the effects of exchange rate fluctuation. Data collected in USD are converted into local currency units.

institutions serving households (NPISHs), the 2019 total HFCE and total NPISH were used to disaggregate the Private Final Consumption Expenditure. Sector-level employment data were collected through published data from national statistics offices and the OECD.[9] These were mapped to the MRIO sectors under International Standard Industrial Classification revision 3.1 (ISIC Rev. 3.1). The discussion on India's COVID-19 impact is separate from the other select economies as available data only allow for 11 sector-level analyses.

4.4.1 Sector-Level Gains and Losses in Output

Results suggests that economy-sectors have experienced either gains or losses during the COVID-19 pandemic. In output terms, as observed in Figure 4.2, most of the sectors for each select economy experienced a decline in their output, which was expected since there had been both demand- and supply-side disruptions. However, there were also sectors that did not severely suffer as acutely as the rest.

The US, for example, had higher output levels in 2020 compared to its pre-pandemic forecast for its supporting transport activities sector, which includes cargo handling, storage, and warehousing, among others. Its forecasted growth prior to the pandemic is 4%. However, this sector's observed growth rate went way above the forecast, with a 29% increase in output from 2019 to 2020. The growth in excess of the forecast may be attributed to the effects of the pandemic, which is about 25%. This amount relates to unforeseen growth due to the sudden and unexpected events affecting production. Similar patterns are observed with producers involved in the manufacture of wood, paper, furniture, sports equipment, and jewelry. A 4% growth in 2020 was expected yet these sectors had an observed growth of 13%, thereby indicating an associated 9% actual impact of the pandemic.

Meanwhile, Japan experienced a positive growth in refined fuels during the pandemic. This is due to an expected output loss in 2020, such that there was an expected 4.2% reduction from the sector's 2019 output. This expected loss did not eventuate, combined with 2.4% in additional output in 2020. Thus, Japan's refined fuels sector experienced an actual impact of 6.6% gain from its 2019 gross output level. This sector, along with six others, had positive impacts during the pandemic. The other sectors were mostly related to transport services, manufacturing of chemicals and chemical products, and mining.

Indonesia, despite having the highest actual output losses in percentage terms among the select economies (excluding India), still experienced gains for two of its sectors: the manufacture of chemicals and chemical products and the social work sector. Notably, the Republic of Korea and Germany had the highest number of sectors that

9 For the employment data of Republic of Korea and Indonesia, the employment numbers for all manufacturing sectors and some services sectors were aggregated hence, the 2019 GVAr were used to redistribute and estimate employment for sectors under an aggregation. As for India, the available sector-level forecast data are at the 11-sector level. Given this, the IOT for India was aggregated to this level to accommodate the available data.

Figure 4.2: Impact of the COVID-19 Pandemic on Gross Output in Select Economies
(%)

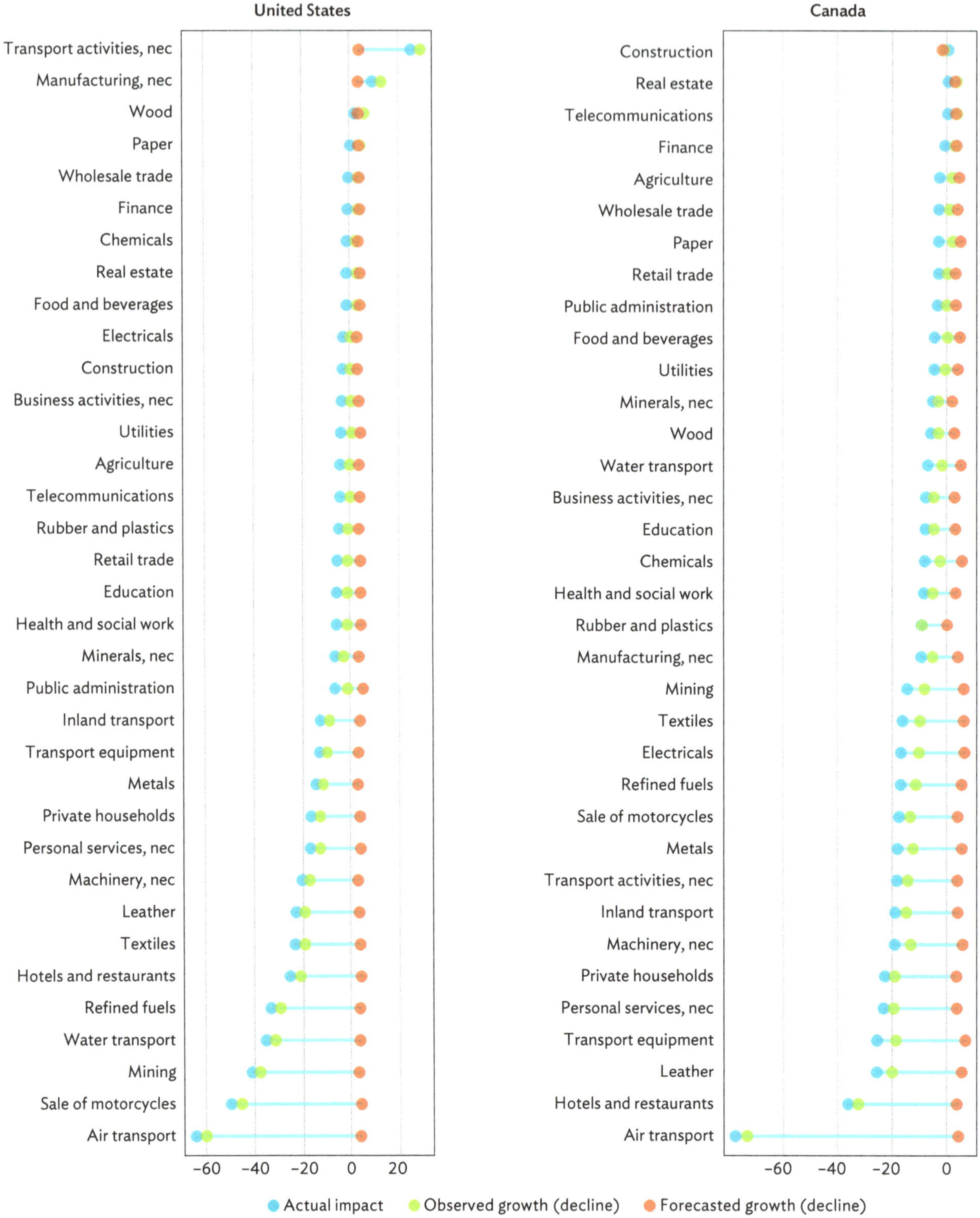

nec = not elsewhere classified.

Note: Percentage impact in terms of 2019 levels. Forecasted growth (decline) refers to the change from 2019 to a pre-pandemic forecasted growth (decline) for 2020.

Source: Calculated using the Asian Development Bank Multiregional Input–Output Tables for 2019 and 2020. https://mrio.adbx.online/ (accessed July 2021).

Click here for figure data

Figure 4.2: Impact of the COVID-19 Pandemic on Gross Output in Select Economies *(continued)*
(%)

nec = not elsewhere classified.
Note: Percentage impact in terms of 2019 levels. Forecasted growth (decline) refers to the change from 2019 to a pre-pandemic forecasted growth (decline) for 2020.
Source: Calculated using the Asian Development Bank Multiregional Input–Output Tables for 2019 and 2020. https://mrio.adbx.online/ (accessed July 2021).

Click here for figure data

Figure 4.2: Impact of the COVID-19 Pandemic on Gross Output in Select Economies *(continued)*
(%)

nec = not elsewhere classified.

Note: Percentage impact in terms of 2019 levels. Forecasted growth (decline) refers to the change from 2019 to a pre-pandemic forecasted growth (decline) for 2020.

Source: Calculated using the Asian Development Bank Multiregional Input–Output Tables for 2019 and 2020. https://mrio.adbx.online/ (accessed July 2021).

Click here for figure data

experienced sector-level gains during the pandemic. On the other side of the spectrum, most of the select economies experienced the highest losses in terms of gross output in their air transport sectors, mainly brought about by the implementation of regional lockdowns and strict no-passenger flight policies. The estimated impact on the air transport sector ranged from 59% to 73% of respective 2019 gross output levels.

4.4.2 Sector-Level Gains and Losses in Value-Added

In value-added terms, the sectors were also observed to have suffered losses or benefited from gains. Again, the actual COVID-19 impact can be separated into two: the pre-pandemic forecasted growth (decline) of the economy that was expected from 2019 to 2020, yet went unrealized; and the observed growth (decline) from 2019 to 2020.

As shown in Figure 4.3, most of the COVID-19 impact on the US's agriculture sector was brought about by unrealized gains for this sector, i.e., $6.8 billion in revenue was unrealized and there was an increase in value-added of about $166 million, hence the actual losses for this sector were $6.6 billion. In percentage levels, with respect to 2019 values, 3.88% of the sector's 2019 gross value-added was unrealized in 2020 due to the demand- and supply-side disruptions during the pandemic. However, there was a 0.09% increase in its 2019 gross value-added during the pandemic. This observed increase lessens the actual impact of the pandemic to 3.79%.

Conversely, the US mining sector's actual losses can be attributed to the observed losses it experienced during the pandemic, as compared to what went unrealized. The sector's unrealized gains were $10.2 billion, but its observed losses climbed to $116.8 billion. Thus, the US mining sector suffered a total of $127 billion in value-added losses as an effect of the COVID-19 pandemic, or 41% of its 2019 gross value-added.

The same trend for losses in value-added was observed with Japan's telecommunication sector. Its supposed gains amounted to ¥185 billion, coupled with losses observed in 2020 of ¥524 billion, thus suffering an actual loss of ¥710 billion. On the other hand, Japan's water transport sector experienced a positive impact because it benefited from gains across 2019 and 2020. Moreover, it was expected that the value-added to be generated for 2020 would be much lower than in 2019 (by ¥11.5 billion). Since this loss was not realized, this has been added to the increase in value-added in 2020 of ¥25.7 billion, resulting in a positive actual impact to the water transport sector of ¥37.2 billion during the pandemic, or 2% of the sector's 2019 gross value-added.

Figure 4.3: Impact of the COVID-19 Pandemic on Value-Added in Select Economies
(%)

nec = not elsewhere classified.

Note: Percentage impact in terms of 2019 levels. Forecasted growth (decline) refers to the change from 2019 to a pre-pandemic forecasted growth (decline) for 2020.

Source: Calculated using the Asian Development Bank Multiregional Input–Output Tables for 2019 and 2020. https://mrio.adbx.online/ (accessed July 2021).

Click here for figure data

Figure 4.3: Impact of the COVID-19 Pandemic on Value-Added in Select Economies *(continued)*
(%)

nec = not elsewhere classified.
Note: Percentage impact in terms of 2019 levels. Forecasted growth (decline) refers to the change from 2019 to a pre-pandemic forecasted growth (decline) for 2020.
Source: Calculated using the Asian Development Bank Multiregional Input–Output Tables for 2019 and 2020. https://mrio.adbx.online/ (accessed July 2021).

Click here for figure data

Figure 4.3: Impact of the COVID-19 Pandemic on Value-Added in Select Economies *(continued)*
(%)

nec = not elsewhere classified.

Note: Percentage impact in terms of 2019 levels. Forecasted growth (decline) refers to the change from 2019 to a pre-pandemic forecasted growth (decline) for 2020.

Source: Calculated using the Asian Development Bank Multiregional Input–Output Tables for 2019 and 2020. https://mrio.adbx.online/ (accessed July 2021).

Click here for figure data

4.4.3 Sectoral Impact on Employment

Results of employment effects brought by the COVID-19 pandemic are given in Figure 4.4. Due to lockdowns and tight constraints, layoffs were expected as businesses tried to minimize their losses. Some people lost their jobs, while some moved to sectors where demand for products and services had increased during the pandemic.

For the US, employment across all sectors in the US contracted by an average of 9% in 2020 from previous year. Most sectors observed losses in employment (in green dots), except for agriculture, manufacture of chemicals, telecommunications, finance, and public administration services—or notably, businesses considered to be essential critical infrastructure sectors at the height of the COVID-19 response. Prior to the pandemic, 2020 was forecast to see employment increases of about 4% across several sectors in the economy (in orange dots). Such employment opportunities however went unrealized, thereby exacerbating the overall impact of the pandemic to an average of 13% in employment losses (in blue dots). Interestingly, the manufacture of chemicals had the most muted impact (-0.5%), with its observed employment increase almost offset by similar loss in employment opportunities in 2020. This is likely attributed to manufacturing firms contending with the surge in demand for pharmaceutical products and disinfectants while retaining workforce on site as mass production of chemicals is difficult to perform remotely.

Meanwhile, Germany and Japan had increased employment during the pandemic in almost half of the 35 sectors assessed, creating numerous job opportunities for their people. The Republic of Korea had nine sectors that experienced positive effects in employment from 2019 to 2020. It can be noted that the inland transportation sector for the Republic of Korea suffered from output and value-added losses in 2020, yet had an increase in employment within that same year. Conversely, the economy's finance and real estate sectors benefited from output and value-added gains, yet had declines in employment. This implies that, during the COVID-19 crisis, work productivity increased in the inland transport sector and decreased in the finance and real estate sectors.

Figure 4.4: Impact of the COVID-19 Pandemic on Employment in Select Economies
(%)

nec = not elsewhere classified.

Note: Percentage impact in terms of 2019 levels. Forecasted growth (decline) refers to the change from 2019 to a pre-pandemic forecasted growth (decline) for 2020.

Source: Calculated using the Asian Development Bank Multiregional Input-Output Tables for 2019 and 2020. https://mrio.adbx.online/ (accessed July 2021).

Click here for figure data

Figure 4.4: Impact of the COVID-19 Pandemic on Employment in Select Economies *(continued)*
(%)

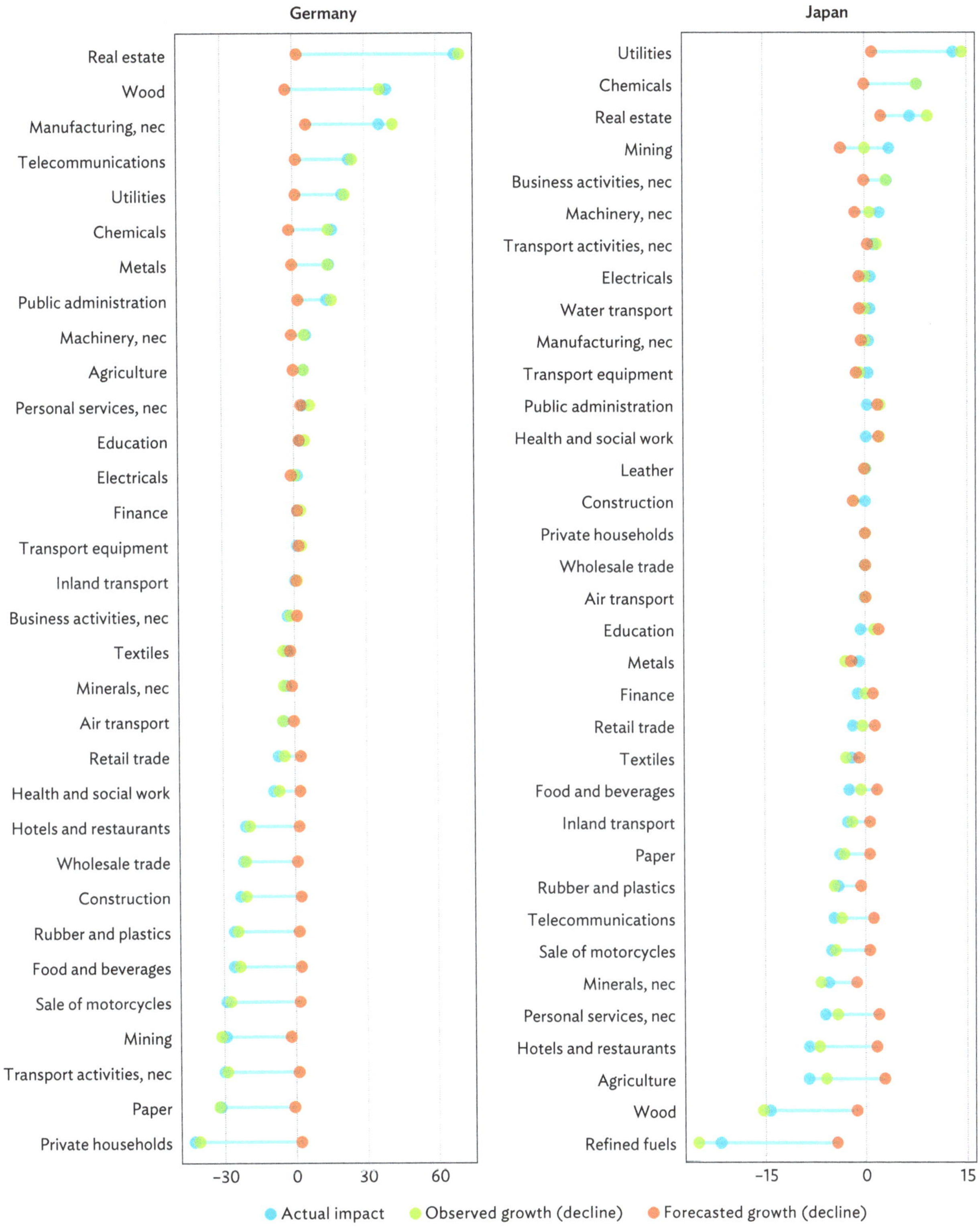

nec = not elsewhere classified.

Note: Percentage impact in terms of 2019 levels. Forecasted growth (decline) refers to the change from 2019 to a pre-pandemic forecasted growth (decline) for 2020.

Source: Calculated using the Asian Development Bank Multiregional Input–Output Tables for 2019 and 2020. https://mrio.adbx.online/ (accessed July 2021).

Click here for figure data

Figure 4.4: Impact of the COVID-19 Pandemic on Employment in Select Economies *(continued)*
(%)

nec = not elsewhere classified.

Note: Percentage impact in terms of 2019 levels. Forecasted growth (decline) refers to the change from 2019 to a pre-pandemic forecasted growth (decline) for 2020.

Source: Calculated using the Asian Development Bank Multiregional Input–Output Tables for 2019 and 2020. https://mrio.adbx.online/ (accessed July 2021).

Click here for figure data

4.4.4 Impact of COVID-19 on India's Economy

As shown in Figure 4.5, all sectors in India experienced actual losses in terms of output, value-added, and employment.

Figure 4.5: Impact of the COVID-19 Pandemic on India
(%)

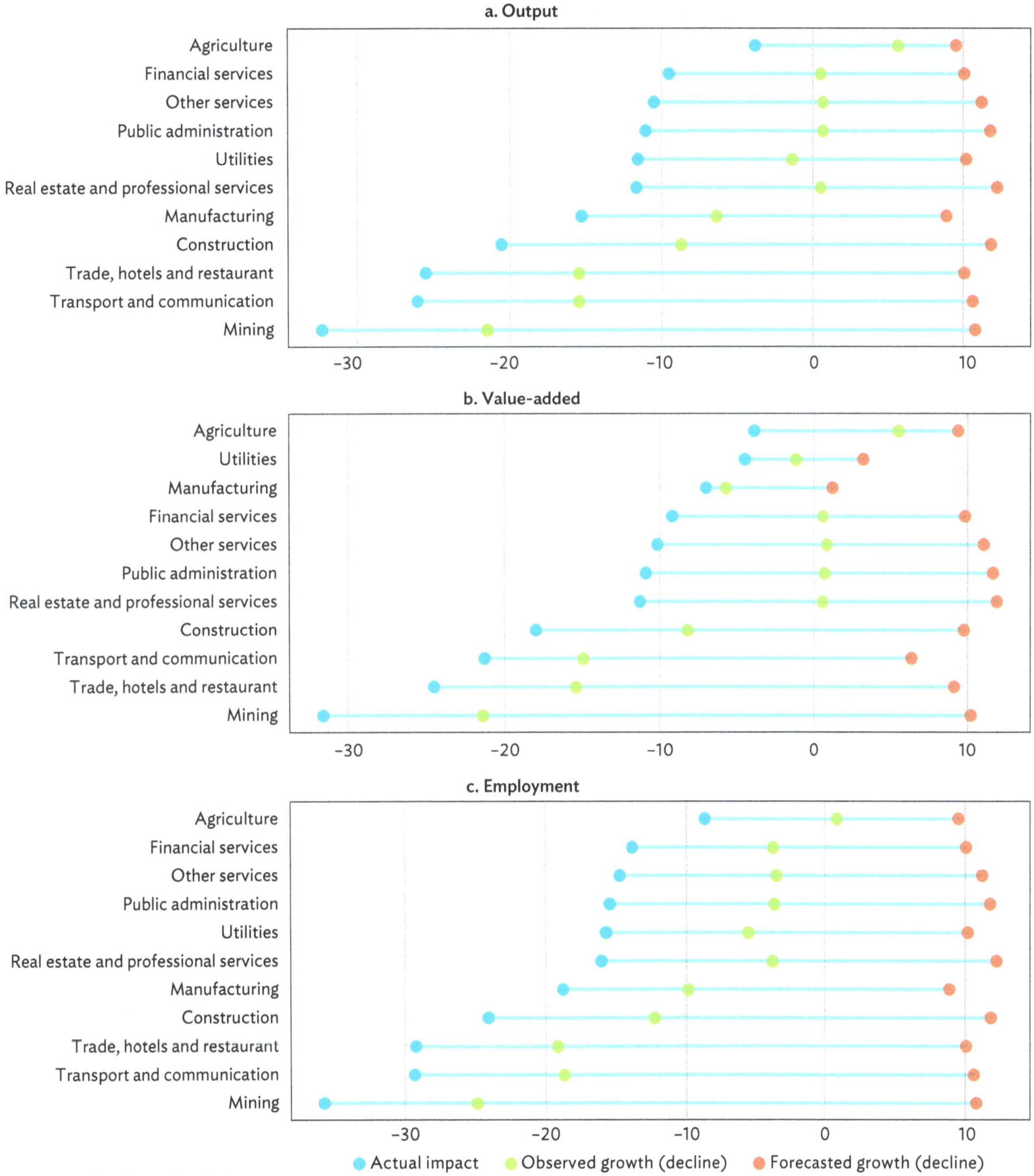

nec = not elsewhere classified.

Note: Percentage impact in terms of 2019 levels. Forecasted growth (decline) refers to the change from 2019 to a pre-pandemic forecasted growth (decline) for 2020.

Source: Calculated using the Asian Development Bank Multiregional Input–Output Tables for 2019 and 2020. https://mrio.adbx.online/ (accessed July 2021).

Click here for figure data

India's agriculture sector experienced higher output in 2020 relative to 2019, by ₹2.4 trillion (or approximately 6%), yet the actual COVID-19 impact was observed to be negative because it was expected that this sector would grow by 10% from 2019 to 2020, or by ₹4 trillion. Not reaching its full capacity in production led to a total unrealized gains of 4%, or a gross output loss of about ₹1.6 trillion due to the pandemic.

India's mining sector, however, took the hardest hit. Expected economy-sector growth levels of 11% for output and 10% for value-added went unrealized, plus the sector had the highest observed losses from 2019 to 2020: 21.5% for output and 21.4% for value-added.

As for employment in India, only the agriculture sector experienced positive gains from 2019 to 2020, yet all sectors suffered employment losses once all the observed and unrealized impacts were taken into consideration.

4.4.5 Overall Impact of the COVID-19 Pandemic

Relative to 2019 GDP, the effect of the COVID-19 pandemic ranged from –3.2% to –12.3% among the seven economies assessed.

In production terms, India experienced the greatest negative impact from the COVID-19 pandemic, as presented in Figure 4.6. The economy's gross output losses were 15.9% of its 2019 output and it forfeited 12.3% of its 2019 GDP. In monetary terms, India lost ₹96.4 trillion of gross output, including both the observed losses and the unrealized gains, and about ₹24.9 trillion of the economy's GDP was forfeited largely due to the loss of potential gains, by about ₹17.3 trillion. Unsurprisingly, employment in India declined by 16.7% from 2019 to 2020, also the highest fall among the seven economies assessed.

Indonesia posted the second-greatest negative impact, with 12.2% and 10.8% in gross output and value-added losses, respectively. Canada had 3.7% of its 9.3% gross output loss attributed to observed losses from 2019 to 2020. Germany's output loss was attributed to unrealized gains, given that the economy had high pre-pandemic projections for output growth from 2019 to 2020.

Strikingly, the Republic of Korea reported positive GDP growth from 2019 to 2020, yet the unrealized gains had such an overwhelming effect that the overall impact of the COVID-19 crisis on the economy was still negative at about –5.2% of 2019 GDP.

In the US, employment in 2020 grew by 1.5% relative to 2019 levels, in contrast to the experience of most economies, which suffered job losses during the same time period. However, prior to the pandemic, the US economy was expecting employment to grow by about 8.1% from 2019 to 2020. This translates to an actual employment loss of 6.6% as a result of the COVID-19 pandemic.

Among the select economies, Japan and the Republic of Korea experienced the lowest overall impact of the pandemic.

Figure 4.6. Impact of the COVID-19 Pandemic on Output, Value-Added, and Employment in Select Economies
(%)

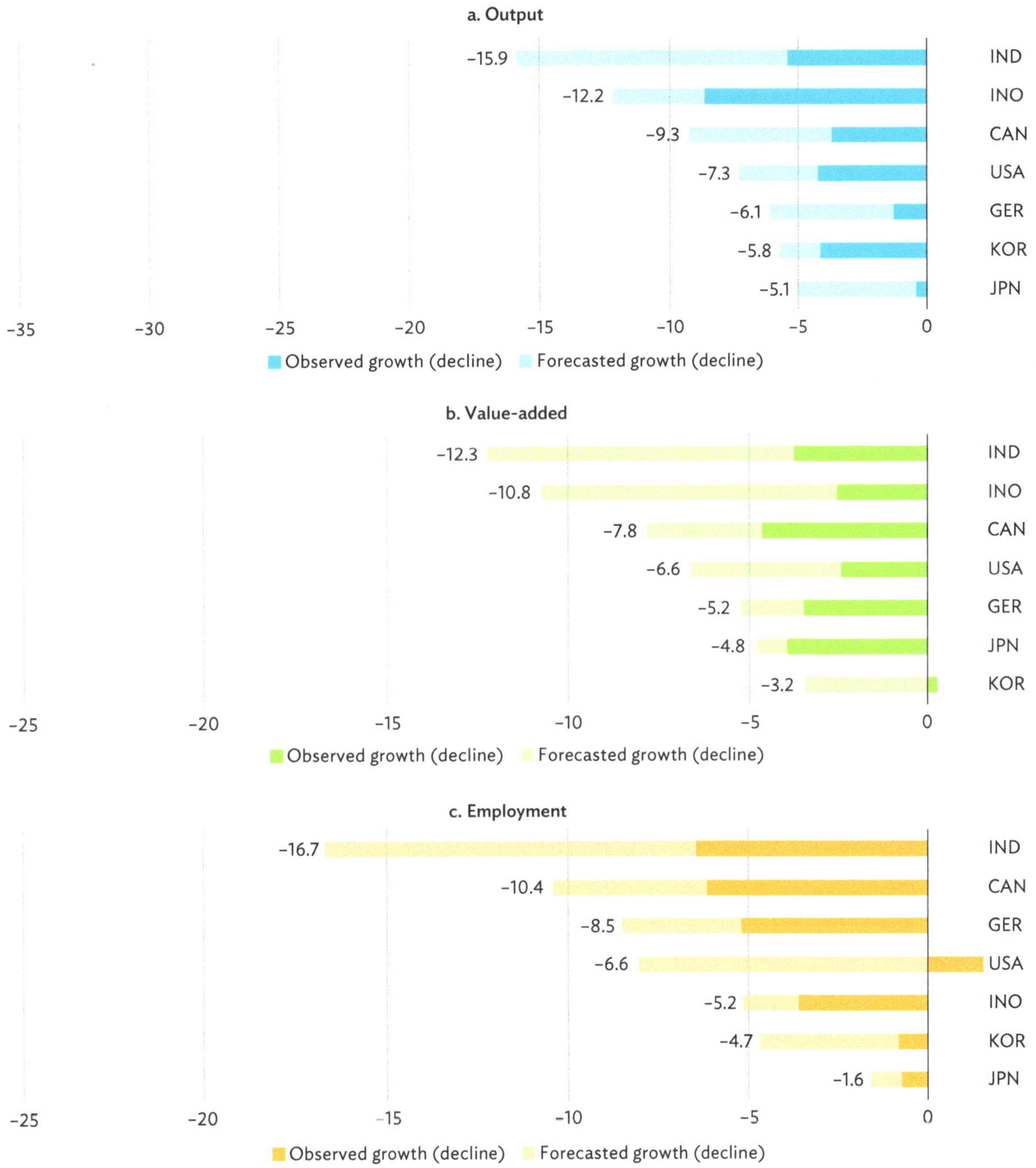

CAN = Canada; GER = Germany; IND = India; INO = Indonesia; JPN = Japan; KOR = Republic of Korea; US = United States.
Note: Percentage impact in terms of 2019 levels. Forecasted growth (decline) refers to the change from 2019 to a pre-pandemic forecasted growth (decline) for 2020.
Source: Calculations using the Asian Development Bank Multiregional Input–Output Tables for 2019 and 2020. https://mrio.adbx.online/ (accessed July 2021).

Click here for figure data

4.5 Conclusion

The COVID-19 pandemic has significantly changed the world in many ways, and it is of interest to measure the impact of these changes from a macroeconomic perspective. The crisis has brought unprecedented disruptions to production and has affected consumption patterns across different sectors.

This chapter highlighted a methodology that provides another perspective in quantifying the effects of the pandemic, particularly on both demand- and supply-side factors. The methodology employs an input–output approach, considering that the use of input–output tables provides both a sector-level and economy-level analysis of different economic indicators, such as output, value-added, and employment.

The usual indicator in pinning down the effects of the pandemic is the observed differences between 2019 and 2020. This is an incomplete picture of the COVID-19 situation since the missed potential growth (expected losses) was not taken into account. The actual pandemic impact can be decomposed into two components: the observed and the forecasted growths. Hence, in measuring the COVID-19 impact, it is important to construct a counterfactual 2020 input–output table as comparison to the 2019 and 2020 tables. The main contribution of this chapter is a detailed methodology of constructing a counterfactual 2020 table, which makes use of the Leontief quantity model which benchmarks the size and composition of economic growth had there been no pandemic in 2020.

As the results imply, there were both gains and losses during the COVID-19 crisis, evidenced through sector-level analyses. Although most sectors suffered declines in output, value-added, and/or employment, some sectors managed to achieve gains. This was the case particularly in transport-related sectors, due to growth in the activities of couriers, logistics businesses, and the like.

The results also show how the actual impact can be divided into two components for more in-depth analysis: (i) the forecasted growth (decline) of the economy that was expected from 2019 to 2020, yet went unrealized, and (ii) the observed growth (decline) from 2019 to 2020.

Finally, the estimates showed the range of the pandemic's effect to be between –3.2% and –12.3%, relative to each economy's 2019 GDP, with Japan and the Republic of Korea having the lowest impacts and India suffering the greatest impact.

Overall, findings from this approach have the potential to inform evidence-based policies aimed at mitigating the economic effects of the COVID-19 pandemic and other potential shocks that may arise in the future.

References

E. Dong, H. Du, and L. Gardner. n.d. An Interactive Web-Based Dashboard to Track COVID-19 in Real Time. *Lancet Inf Dis.* 20(5):533-534. doi: 10.1016/S1473-3099(20)30120-1.

T. Hale, N. Angrist, R. Goldszmidt, B. Kira, A. Petherick, T. Phillips, S. Webster, E. Cameron-Blake, L. Hallas, S. Majumdar, and H. Tatlow. 2021. A Global Panel Database of Pandemic Policies (Oxford COVID-19 Government Response Tracker). *Nature Human Behaviour.* 5 (4). Pp. 529–538. https://doi.org/10.1038/s41562-021-01079-8.

International Monetary Fund. 2019. *World Economic Outlook: Global Manufacturing Downturn, Rising Trade Barriers.* Washington, DC: International Monetary Fund. 15 October.

R. E. Miller and P. D. Blair. 2009. *Input–Output Analysis: Foundations and Extensions.* Second Edition. Cambridge: Cambridge University Press.

Organisation for Economic Co-operation and Development (OECD). 2019. OECD Economic Outlook: Statistics and Projections. https://doi.org/10.1787/eo-data-en (accessed January 2022).

H. Ritchie, E. Mathieu, C. Appel, C. Giattino, L. Rodés-Guirao, E. Ortiz-Ospina, J. Hasell, B. Macdonald, D. Beltekian, and M. Roser. 2020. Coronavirus Pandemic (COVID-19). OurWorldInData.org. https://ourworldindata.org/coronavirus (accessed March 2022).

M. Roser. 2013. Economic Growth. OurWorldInData.org. https://ourworldindata.org/economic-growth (accessed March 2022).

World Bank. 2020. DataBank: World Development Indicators (WDI) [Dataset]. World Bank. https://databank.worldbank.org/Popular-Indicators/id/1ff4a498 (accessed January 2022).

World Health Organization (WHO). 2020. Transmission of SARS-CoV-2: Implications for Infection Prevention Precautions. https://www.who.int/news-room/commentaries/detail/transmission-of-sars-cov-2-implications-for-infection-prevention-precautions.

Establishing a Framework for Measuring the Digital Economy

5

The lack of consensus on an established framework to estimate the digital economy has caused statistical analysis to lag behind the pace of increasing digitalization in many economic activities. This special chapter puts forward the proposed methodology outlined in ADB's Special Supplement to Key Indicators for Asia and the Pacific 2021, which applies the measurement approach to the ADB Multiregional Input–Output Tables. As a continuation of the bank's efforts in 2021, this chapter presents longer-period estimates of the digital economy in 20 select national economies from across Asia and the Pacific.

5.1 Introduction

Digital transformation has become a defining feature of the modern economy. Technologies created through innovation are profoundly reshaping the way economic actors interact and transact with one another. More people communicate online, work remotely, and exchange products through computer networks. This transformation was further accelerated by the COVID-19 pandemic. As economies shifted to a contactless world, digital technologies served as a lifeline for many businesses that otherwise experienced devastating impacts of the pandemic—whether due to supply chain disruptions, containment measures, substantial contractions in consumer spending, or a combination of them all.

While digitalization was underway prior to the pandemic, experts have highlighted that the pace and scale at which it is being deployed in the present day sets it apart from past experience. Many of the largest global companies appear to be predominantly engaged in digital products and digital platform activity. Meanwhile, governments are minting new ministries of information and communication technology, signaling the growing role of digital technologies. Digital infrastructure investments are being rolled out across the globe. Decades-old laws on taxation, privacy, and data-sharing are once again being reopened for debate. In essence, innovating and adapting to changes brought about by digital technologies has progressively become the norm rather than the exception across all parts of the global economy.

As economies progress toward digital transformation, many policies designed for the nondigital world will need to catch up to capture the dynamics, opportunities, and challenges of the new digital economy. Some progress has been made in that regard. For instance, information and communication technologies (ICT) have been instrumental in economic growth and the implementation of the 2030 Agenda for

Sustainable Development (UNCTAD 2020). Impacts of digitalization cut across several areas of economic development, such as the potential for job creation and destruction, skills development, commercial competition, consumer protection, data privacy, taxation, and trade, among many others. As such, considerable attention from governments has been directed toward the designing of ICT policies and strategies, which evidently require sound knowledge of the state of digital sectors and their interactions with the rest of the economy.

Unfortunately, the statistics required to make informed decisions on digital issues are often lacking, especially in developing economies. In many cases, a standard definition of the digital economy and awareness of the international practices for compiling relevant economic statistics are both lacking. This situation makes it difficult for national economies not only to formulate evidence-based policies on the ICT sector but also to institutionalize digital-economy topics into their regular statistical programs (UNCTAD 2020).

5.2 Measurement Challenges

The difficulties in defining the scope of the digital economy are well documented in *A Roadmap Toward a Common Framework for Measuring the Digital Economy*, a report from the Organisation for Economic Co-operation and Development (OECD 2020).

As a starting point, the *Special Supplement to Key Indicators for Asia and the Pacific 2021* (ADB 2021) proposes a narrow definition of the digital economy and provides a simple measurement framework that is already aligned with the System of National Accounts and conventional input–output methodologies. By utilizing existing macroeconomic frameworks, national statistics offices can overcome the costly need to develop new statistical frameworks and collection systems in the short run. Since data requirements are accessible within an economy's own statistical systems, these statistics offices may already be able to provide the much-needed statistics for understanding the size and components of their respective digital economies.

The foremost challenge to a standard measurement approach pertains to definitional issues. As context, the changes brought about by digital products, often used interchangeably with digital technologies, can generally be categorized in three ways representing different degrees of integration: digitization, digitalization, and digital transformation. Digitization refers to the process of converting data into a digital format. Digitalization refers to the incorporation of digitized data into established production processes to achieve higher efficiencies. Digital transformation is a wider application of digitalization in that it involves a more extensive integration of digital products, as might be the case with a large enterprise involving hundreds of employees and tools in its strategic use of digital technologies (ADB 2021).

In the definitional context, two complicating issues arise. First, the process of digitalization pervades almost every activity in the modern economy. Deployment of digital technologies is seen in agriculture, traditional bricks-and-mortar retail activities, hybrid forms of financial services, and increasingly in government services. Second, firms within sectors are in different stages of digital transformation. For example, while there is a huge potential for the food retail sector to undergo digital transformation (say, through use of online ordering platforms), there is a huge disparity in digital adoption within the same sector (World Bank 2021). Hence, measuring the digital economy through the lens of heterogenous digitalization raises a practical issue, especially on deciding whether a type of firm or activity qualifies to be in the scope of the digital economy.

The approach taken by the ADB study was to trace which firms (and therefore sectors) are digital by virtue of what products they produce, how those products are produced, and, ultimately, who the products are sold to. This exercise required clear definitions of digital products, which the authors defined as "goods and services with the main function of generating, processing, and/or storing digitized data" (ADB 2021). While there are other aspects of the digital economy to be considered, defining the "core" digital products was intended to narrow the measurement scope, especially in the case where many sectors in an economy are in the process of digitalizing. The core aspects of the digital economy comprise hardware technologies (e.g., computers and digital communication devices), software and web services (e.g., data processing and hosting), and enabling infrastructure (e.g., internet and telecommunication networks). The product classification of these core digital products is outlined in Appendix 5.1.

As previously alluded, this measurement approach excludes preexisting services and business models that extensively use digital technologies, such as finance, media, tourism, and transportation–remarkably an array of activities that have become the subject of policy interest worldwide. This limitation, however, was put in place under a practical consideration, given the wide differences in levels of digital transformation across sectors and the lack of consensus on which businesses to qualify as being digital. For example, use of digital inputs, intensity of digital investments, number of ICT specialists employed, share of online revenues, or even prevalence of robots are some of the dimensions considered (Calvino et al. 2018). By omitting sectors on the fringes of the digital definition and capturing only the core aspects of the digital economy, the ADB study was better able to determine the lower ranges of the estimates, on which the wider set of digitalizing sectors may be added. This core measure enables analysis to inform policies and investments in the digital economy and to assess potential impacts on enterprises, governments, consumers, and workers (UNCTAD 2019).

Identification of an economy's core digital products entails some effort in obtaining sufficiently detailed data. This remains a challenge in many developing economies whose statistical systems struggle to collect data at disaggregated levels. The issue was overcome by the ADB study by splitting industrial aggregates for digital and nondigital production using appropriate data from manufacturing surveys, information and communication statistics, and enterprise data. These "disaggregators" were obtained from data sources used in national accounts statistics, which are generally preferred over private and industry reports, to maintain coherence with the input-output tables and published national accounts aggregates.

5.3 The Input–Output Approach to Measuring the Core Digital Economy

With core digital products identified, the next objective is to identify which sectors produce these products, the inputs they use, and the respective buyers of their products. This value chain approach in measuring the digital economy systematically considers the span of activities associated with both supply and use of digital products. Such information is useful in determining an economy's overall level of digitalization as well as the potential spillover of core technologies to other sectors.

There are two broad components to the equation in the proposed measurement framework.

First, the framework considers the value-added contribution of suppliers of inputs to the production of final digital goods and services. These technically refer to the backward linkages of the digital sectors to the rest of the economy. For instance, internet service providers may use electrical wires, fiber optics, and other components as inputs to production. The income from producing these intermediate inputs used by the core digital producers is counted as part of the digital economy. Acquisitions of fixed assets by digital industries (for example, construction investments of an information technology services firm) are also considered an extension of its backward linkages, essentially due to their role in enabling the production of digital goods.

The second component refers to the value-added contribution of the digital sectors themselves to all their users. Analogously, this refers to the forward linkages of the digital sectors to the rest of the economy. For example, a software design company may earn revenue by providing services to a foreign car manufacturer. In this case, only the value of the software service embedded in the car is counted, and not the entire value of the manufactured car. Retailers, too, may purchase broadband services to operate their e-commerce businesses. While some argue that the full value of e-commerce sales should be counted as part of the digital economy, the framework first narrows its focus to include only the value of broadband services used in retail activities.

Due to the ability of digital technologies to transform sectors, the forward linkage component seems to garner more attention than the backward linkage. However, focusing on only one side of the value chain could severely undersell the contribution of the digital economy, especially when digital firms can easily occupy both supplier and buyer roles in any given economy. In sum, the **total of exchange or flow of economic value involving core digital products and/or sectors is considered the measure of the digital economy.**

For exposition, the full digital gross domestic product (GDP) equation is specified as

$$\mathrm{GDP}_{\mathrm{digital}} = \underbrace{\boldsymbol{i}^{\mathrm{T}}\hat{\boldsymbol{v}}\boldsymbol{B}\hat{\boldsymbol{y}}\boldsymbol{\varepsilon}_1}_{\textit{Backward linkage}} + \underbrace{\boldsymbol{i}^{\mathrm{T}}(\hat{\boldsymbol{v}}\boldsymbol{B}\hat{\boldsymbol{y}})^{\mathrm{T}}\boldsymbol{\varepsilon}_1}_{\textit{Forward linkage}} - \underbrace{[\mathrm{diag}(\hat{\boldsymbol{v}}\boldsymbol{B}\hat{\boldsymbol{y}})]^{\mathrm{T}}\boldsymbol{\varepsilon}_1}_{\textit{Double counted term}} + \underbrace{(\boldsymbol{i}-\boldsymbol{\varepsilon}_1)^{\mathrm{T}}\hat{\boldsymbol{v}}\boldsymbol{B}\hat{\boldsymbol{y}}\hat{\boldsymbol{r}}\boldsymbol{\varepsilon}_2}_{\substack{\textit{Backward linkage to} \\ \textit{other fixed investments by} \\ \textit{digital sectors}}}$$

where $\boldsymbol{i}$ is a summation vector, $\hat{\boldsymbol{v}}$ is the diagonalized vector of value-added to gross output ratios, $\boldsymbol{B}$ is the Leontief inverse, $\hat{\boldsymbol{y}}$ is the diagonalized vector final demands, $\boldsymbol{\varepsilon}_1$ is the first eliminator vector that excludes transactions related to nondigital industries, and $\boldsymbol{\varepsilon}_2$ is the second eliminator vector that excludes fixed assets in digital products.

The first term in the digital GDP equation indicates the amount of contribution from all sectors to the final demand for digital products (backward linkage). The second term represents the value-added contributions flowing from digital sectors to other sectors in the economy that use digital products as inputs (forward linkage). The third term shows the amount of digital inputs that digital sectors themselves use for their products. Since this amount is both a backward and forward linkage, it is deducted once from the summation to avoid double-counting. The fourth term shows the digital sectors' proportionate shares in the backward linkage of sectors that supply their investment in nondigital assets. Adding all these terms provides the digital GDP, which is the sum of economic production that involves the supply to, or use by, digital sectors. A complete discussion on the methodology is provided in the *Special Supplement to Key Indicators for Asia and the Pacific 2021* (ADB 2021).

5.4 Results for Select Economies

This section presents longer-period estimates of the digital economy for 20 select economies in Asia and the Pacific.[1] These estimates rely on national input–output tables (NIOTS) extracted from the larger multiregional input–output tables (MRIOTs). Given the level of sectoral detail in the NIOTs, further disaggregation of digital sectors was necessary. For example, the NIOT sector of "post and telecommunications"

1 The economies were selected based on the availability of disaggregated sector accounts, with one economy represented from each subregion of Asia and the Pacific. Other economies are prioritized to support internal division analysis. Results will be expanded to include other economies in later publications.

includes postal and courier services that are not considered core digital products. This process required data on gross output, value-added, and intermediate inputs of digital sectors, taken as a share of the aggregate sector containing both nondigital and digital components. Figures used for the compilation of the disaggregators were taken from detailed national accounts statistics, industrial statistics and surveys, and other regularly updated business survey statistics on the information and communications technology sector. For example, establishment surveys include figures on revenues, costs, fixed assets, and number of persons engaged in digital and nondigital sectors within an aggregate MRIO sector. Revenue shares of identified digital sectors are used as proportions for the relevant gross outputs, while operating costs (adjusted for salaries and depreciation) are for disaggregating intermediate consumptions. Once these sectors were properly disaggregated based on the classification in Appendix 5.1, the NIOTs were subjected to the model formulated in the *Special Supplement to Key Indicators for Asia and the Pacific 2021* (ADB 2021) to arrive at nominal estimates of digital sectors' economic contributions.

Additionally, the estimates were translated into local currency units using the average of period exchange rates obtained from the ADB Key Indicators Database. This procedure was undertaken to control the effects of local currency fluctuations against the United States dollar.

The relative sizes of select digital economies for the year 2019 are shown in Figure 5.1. Results for year 2019 is displayed in the chart given the anomalous period of 2020. Among these economies, Taipei,China (17.9% of its GDP) exhibited the highest share of the digital economy to GDP, followed by the Republic of Korea (10.8%), Singapore (8.4%), Malaysia (8.4%), and Viet Nam (7.5%). These economies are known for their active participation in the market for ICT goods and equipment (UNCTAD 2021). Observable too are the dominant shares of term 3 (value-added flow within digital sectors) in the case of Viet Nam and Taipei,China. To an extent, these indicate clustering of digital manufacturing and services. For example, data-related services entail the use of hardware and equipment, such as transmission and storage, across the value chain (UNCTAD 2021). As a result, the delivery of these services has been critically linked to the manufacture of ICT goods inputs, a process that may be likened to the connection between ore and steel. This direct linkage is noticeably stronger in ICT manufacturing hubs such as Viet Nam and Taipei,China.

Figure 5.1: Share and Composition of the Core Digital Economy to Gross Domestic Product, 2019
(% of GDP)

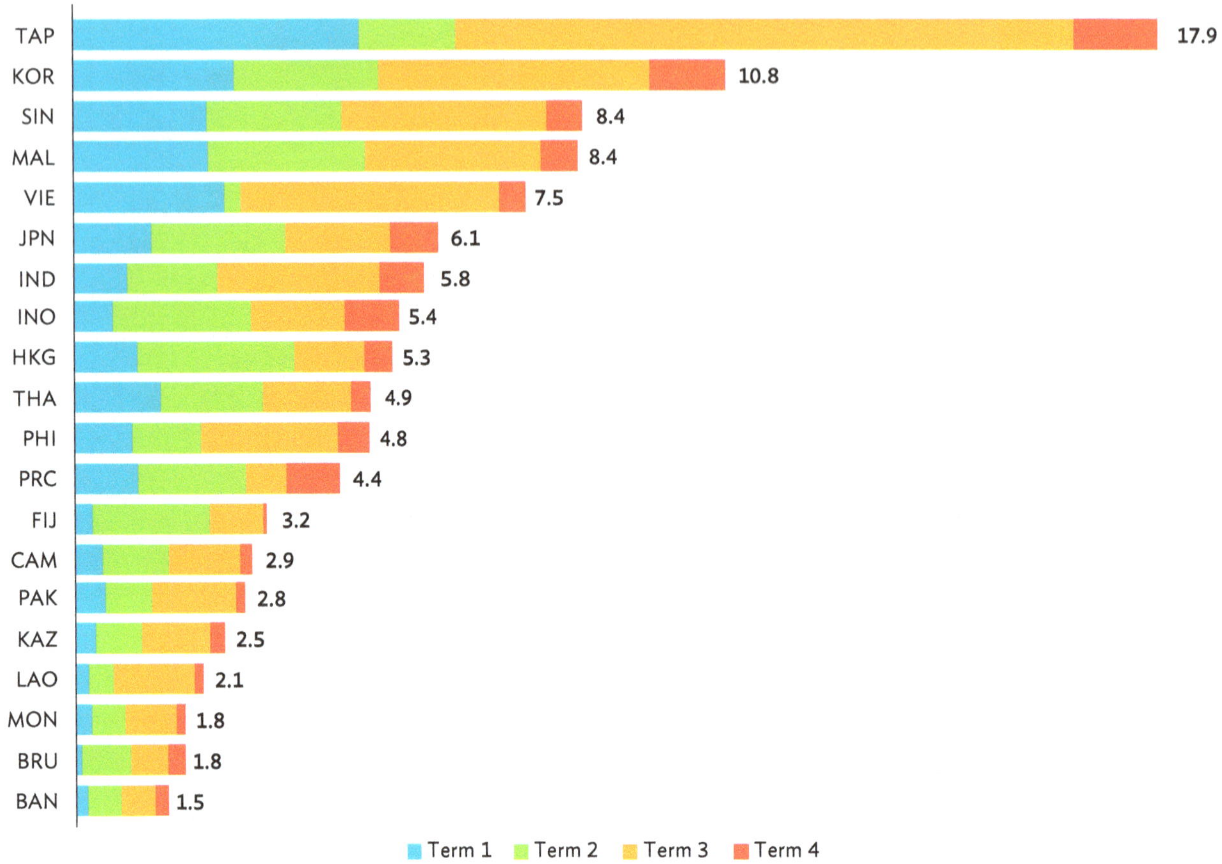

BAN = Bangladesh; BRU = Brunei Darussalam; CAM = Cambodia; FIJ = Fiji; GDP = gross domestic product; HKG = Hong Kong, China; IND = India; INO = Indonesia; JPN = Japan; KAZ = Kazakhstan; KOR = Republic of Korea; LAO = Lao People's Democratic Republic; MAL = Malaysia; MON = Mongolia; PAK = Pakistan; PHI = Philippines; PRC = People's Republic of China; SIN = Singapore; TAP = Taipei,China; THA = Thailand; VIE = Viet Nam.

Notes: Term 1 = economy-wide value-added contribution to digital sectors. Term 2 = value-added contribution from digital sectors. Term 3 = value-added contribution within digital sectors. Term 4 = economy-wide value-added contribution to digital sectors' nondigital assets.

Sources: Calculations using the Asian Development Bank (ADB) Multiregional Input–Output Database. https://mrio.adbx.online/ (accessed July 2021); and ADB. 2021. *Capturing the Digital Economy: A Proposed Measurement Framework and its Applications.* Special Supplement to Key Indicators for Asia and the Pacific 2021. Manila: ADB.

Click here for figure data

Figure 5.2 extends the analysis of Figure 5.1 to multiple years for which the current price MRIOTs are available. While most economies increased their share of the digital economy to GDP from 2000 to 2020, some economies with high involvement in global value chain activity for ICT goods decreased their digital GDP shares over the same period. Prominent examples of this trend are Japan and the Republic of Korea, whose economies occupy sizable shares in the global semiconductors market. As a result, these economies became disproportionately vulnerable to the effects of the COVID-19 pandemic in 2020. For instance, coronavirus containment measures and lack of available workers exacerbated the disruptions in the semiconductors market, which ironically coincided with a surge in demand for consumer electronics (UNCTAD 2021). In addition, the economic slowdown in 2020 affected the

Figure 5.2: Size of the Core Digital Economy in Select Economies of Asia and the Pacific
(% of GDP in local currency units)

	2000	2007	2008	2009	2010	2011	2012	2013	2014	2015	2016	2017	2018	2019	2020
TAP	12.9	15.8	15.9	15.1	16.4	15.8	15.9	15.9	16.6	15.9	15.8	15.8	17.2	17.9	18.6
KOR	10.8	10.4	10.3	11.0	11.2	11.4	11.0	11.0	10.6	10.0	10.0	12.4	12.0	10.8	10.5
SIN	8.3	6.2	6.2	6.9	7.2	8.4	7.8	7.9	8.3	8.9	9.0	8.6	7.8	8.4	8.3
MAL	7.6	7.6	7.1	7.5	7.6	7.4	7.6	7.9	8.2	8.7	8.9	8.5	8.4	8.4	8.8
VIE	6.1	5.7	6.0	6.5	6.1	5.7	6.1	6.5	6.4	6.7	6.7	7.1	6.9	7.5	7.8
JPN	7.8	7.1	7.0	6.6	6.6	6.3	6.2	6.1	6.1	6.1	6.0	6.0	6.2	6.1	6.0
IND	3.9	5.4	5.8	5.8	5.5	5.6	5.5	5.6	5.6	6.0	6.0	5.8	5.9	5.8	5.7
INO	3.9	5.0	5.0	5.1	5.1	4.8	4.8	4.8	4.8	4.8	4.9	4.9	5.3	5.4	5.1
HKG	5.2	4.5	4.3	4.4	4.5	4.8	4.9	4.9	4.9	4.9	4.9	4.8	4.9	5.3	5.3
THA	3.6	4.7	4.8	4.7	4.3	4.0	4.2	4.4	4.6	5.0	4.2	4.2	4.2	4.9	4.8
PHI	4.4	6.8	6.5	6.6	6.2	5.8	5.7	5.5	5.4	5.5	5.3	5.0	4.8	4.8	4.9
PRC	5.8	6.6	5.9	5.4	5.8	5.6	5.7	5.2	5.4	5.6	5.5	5.5	4.3	4.4	4.8
FIJ	4.2	2.9	4.1	5.5	4.9	5.0	4.4	4.4	4.3	4.4	4.3	4.5	3.5	3.2	3.1
CAM	2.8	2.9	3.1	3.1	3.1	3.1	3.1	3.3	3.2	3.0	3.1	3.1	3.0	2.9	2.8
PAK	2.0	2.7	2.4	2.7	2.7	2.4	2.3	2.4	2.2	2.4	2.6	2.7	2.9	2.8	2.8
KAZ	2.3	3.2	3.3	3.5	4.1	3.7	3.6	3.6	3.3	3.7	3.1	3.0	2.3	2.5	2.3
LAO	2.1	2.5	2.6	2.7	2.6	2.2	2.1	1.8	1.8	1.9	1.8	2.0	2.0	2.1	2.3
MON	3.2	4.4	4.4	4.3	2.8	2.4	2.3	2.1	2.0	2.1	2.8	2.2	1.7	1.8	1.8
BRU	0.3	1.8	1.7	2.3	2.0	1.5	1.5	1.7	1.7	1.7	2.1	2.1	1.9	1.8	2.2
BAN	1.0	2.0	2.1	2.1	2.1	2.1	2.1	2.0	2.0	1.9	1.8	1.7	1.6	1.5	1.5

BAN = Bangladesh; BRU = Brunei Darussalam; CAM = Cambodia; FIJ = Fiji; GDP = gross domestic product; HKG = Hong Kong, China; IND = India; INO = Indonesia; JPN = Japan; KAZ = Kazakhstan; KOR = Republic of Korea; LAO = Lao People's Democratic Republic; MAL = Malaysia; MON = Mongolia; PAK = Pakistan; PHI = Philippines; PRC = People's Republic of China; SIN = Singapore; TAP = Taipei,China; THA = Thailand; VIE = Viet Nam.

Note: Cells in shades of red indicate low percentage values, while those in shades of green correspond to higher percentage values.

Sources: Calculations using the Asian Development Bank (ADB) Multiregional Input-Output Database. https://mrio.adbx.online/ (accessed July 2021); and ADB. 2021. *Capturing the Digital Economy: A Proposed Measurement Framework and its Applications.* Special Supplement to Key Indicators for Asia and the Pacific 2021. Manila: ADB.

Click here for figure data

downstream markets of digital sectors. For example, a breakdown of the digital GDP across the select economies showed that backward linkages—generally a measure of demand for digital goods and services—declined by an average of 0.6%, while forward linkages saw a deeper contraction of 2.1%. This meant weaker demand in the market for core digital sectors' goods and services, while the capacity of telecommunications infrastructure was also tested by the surge in transactions online (ADB 2021).

Conversely, some economies—such as Malaysia; the People's Republic of China; Taipei,China; and Viet Nam—experienced some acceleration in their respective digital economies. It must be noted that these estimates were valued at current prices, hence changes in the price levels could affect the trend performance of digital industries. This is an important caveat given the marked decline in the prices of digital goods since the start of the millennium, alongside the increasing productivity of digital industries (ADB 2021).

As a cross-check, the estimates using the MRIOTs are compared with related figures from international organizations in Figure 5.3. These results signal some degree of alignment with comparator estimates. Note that comparator estimates from other organizations generally refer to the 2-digit International Standard Industrial Classification for ICT sectors, which also include wholesale and retail of ICT goods (depending on the availability of the national source).

Figure 5.3: Comparison of Core Digital Economy Estimates by Various International Organizations, 2014–2016
(% of current GDP)

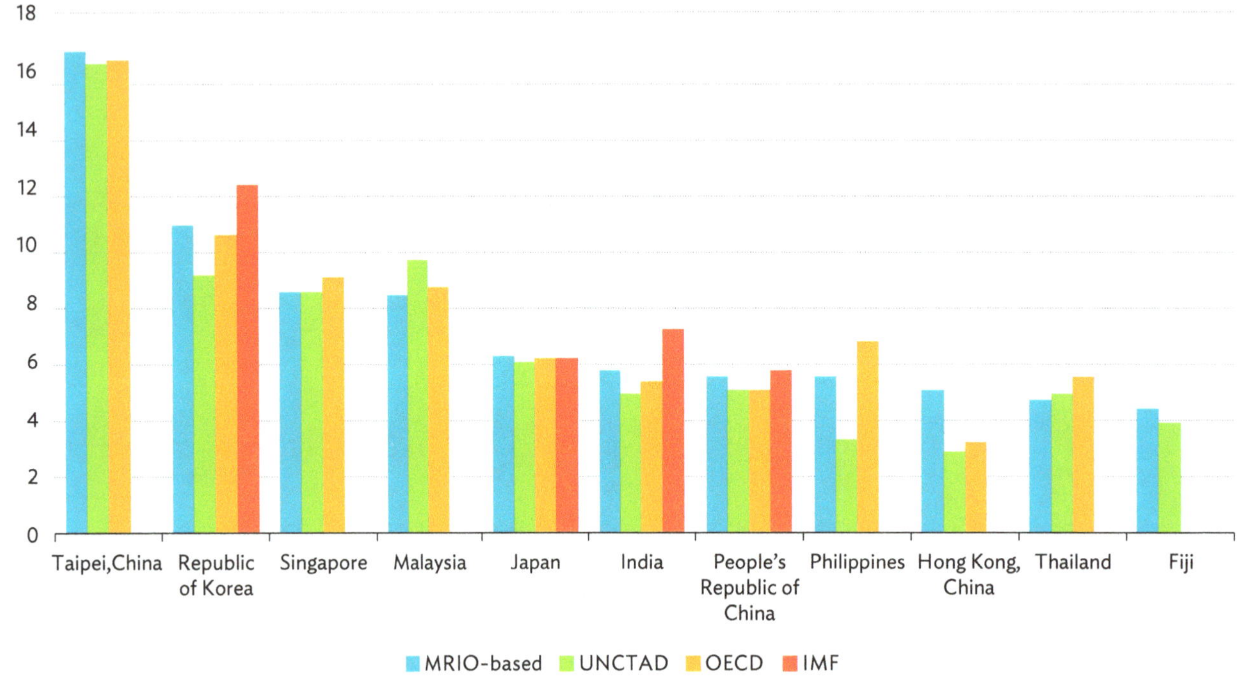

GDP = gross domestic product; IMF = International Monetary Fund; MRIO = multiregional input–output; OECD = Organisation for Economic Co-operation and Development; UNCTAD = United Nations Conference on Trade and Development.

Notes: MRIO-based estimates are for 2014; UNCTAD estimates refer to 2014; OECD estimates refer to 2014, except for the Republic of Korea (2015) and Japan (2015); IMF estimates refer to 2016. Digital economy definitions differ slightly from one international organization to another, but are broadly defined as the economic contribution of the information and communication technology sector.

Sources: Calculations using the Asian Development Bank (ADB) Multiregional Input–Output Database. https://mrio.adbx.online/ (accessed July 2021); ADB. 2021. *Capturing the Digital Economy: A Proposed Measurement Framework and its Applications.* Special Supplement to *Key Indicators for Asia and the Pacific 2021.* Manila: ADB; UNCTAD. 2019. *Digital Economy Report 2019: Value Creation and Capture—Implications for Developing Countries.* New York. https://unctad.org/system/files/official-document/der2019_en.pdf; E. Dabla-Norris, R. de Mooij, A. Hodge, J. Loeprick, D. Prihardini, A. Shah, S. Beer, S. Davidovic, A. M. Modi, and F. Qi. 2021. Digitalization and Taxation in Asia. *IMF Departmental Paper.* No. 17. Washington, DC: IMF; OECD. 2017. Digital Economy Outlook. Paris: OECD Publishing; and OECD. 2021. Input–Output Tables. https://www.oecd.org/sti/ind/input-outputtables.htm (accessed March 2022).

Click here for figure data

The sectoral aggregation of the MRIOTs makes it challenging to produce estimates for the contribution of "digitally disrupted" sectors as listed in the United Nations Advisory Expert Group on National Accounts or AEG (2019). As an alternative, this chapter looks at the forward linkages of core digital sectors to other sectors in the general economy (or term 2 of the digital GDP equation). Such forward linkage may be interpreted as the degree of digitalization among nondigital industries, as it refers to the amount of digital inputs (expressed as value-added) contributing to each sector's respective final products. Higher values indicate that the sector is an intensive user of digital goods and services in the production of its own products.

Figure 5.4 shows the compound annual growth rates (CAGRs) of backward and forward linkages of core digital sectors to their respective economies from 2000 to 2020. While the CAGRs of the digital economy's linkages are observed to be high in Bangladesh, Kazakhstan, the Lao People's Democratic Republic, and Mongolia, these rates were contributed to by low base effects of digital sectors. Viet Nam stands out, given that its digital economy occupied a substantial share of the economy's GDP yet its CAGRs remained in double digits. Growth in Viet Nam's digital economy is more pronounced in terms of backward linkages, which is expected given the economy's active involvement in subassemblies of ICT goods. The same is observed for India, whose growth may be attributed more to services than manufacturing, as is the case for Viet Nam. As specialized information technology and support services tend to be outsourced by various businesses (rather than purchased directly by households), growth in India's digital economy was more evident in terms of forward than backward linkages. This characterizes India's digital economy more strongly as a supplier than a user of digital products.

In contrast, the more mature markets of Japan; the Republic of Korea; Singapore; and Taipei,China, grew at rates lower than the average for the 20 select economies. Japan recorded a negative rate, implying a contracting value-added contribution of core digital sectors to its domestic economy. It should be noted that price effects are also a determinant in these estimates. Using a limited series for constant price tables, Japan showed modest increases in its digital economy (ADB 2021). Nevertheless, the current price tables remain indicative of general observed trends in the economy. For example, Japan has performed rather moderately in competitive rankings on the adoption of digital technologies (EAF 2021; IIMD 2021), while productivity measures have also declined in recent years (ACCJ and McKinsey & Company 2021; ADB 2021).

Figure 5.4: Compound Annual Growth Rates of Core Digital Sectors' Backward and Forward Linkages to the Economy, 2000–2020
(%)

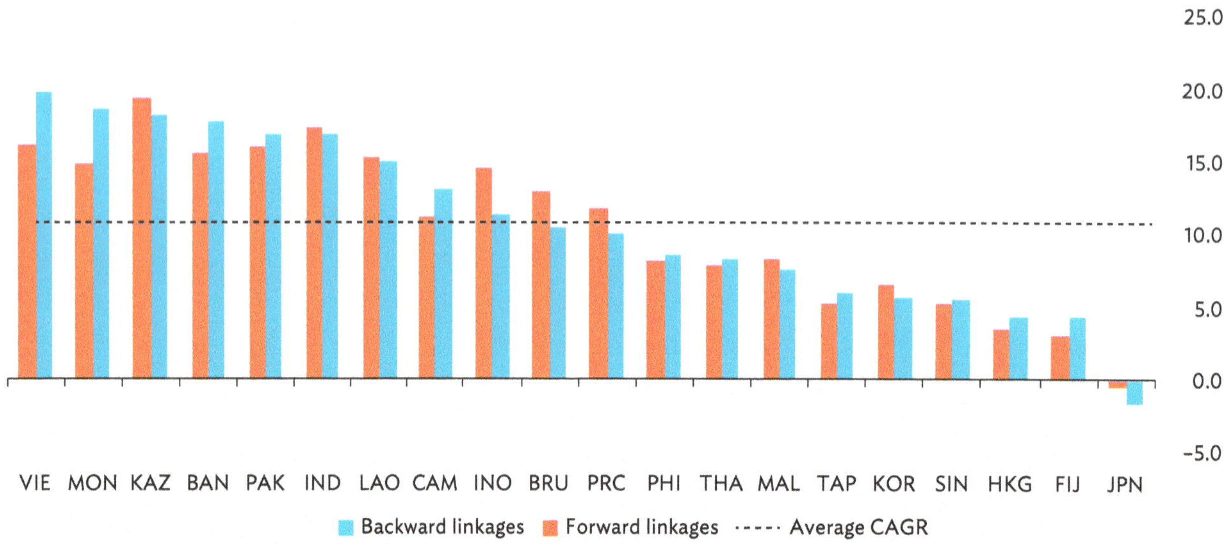

BAN = Bangladesh; BRU = Brunei Darussalam; CAGR = compound annual growth rates; CAM = Cambodia; FIJ = Fiji; HKG = Hong Kong, China; IND = India; INO = Indonesia; JPN = Japan; KAZ = Kazakhstan; KOR = Republic of Korea; LAO = Lao People's Democratic Republic; MAL = Malaysia; MON = Mongolia; PAK = Pakistan; PHI = Philippines; PRC = People's Republic of China; SIN = Singapore; TAP = Taipei,China; THA = Thailand; VIE = Viet Nam.
Note: CAGRs of the backward and forward linkages of core digital sectors are calculated in respect of the total economy from 2000 to 2020.
Sources: Calculations using the Asian Development Bank (ADB) Multiregional Input–Output Database. https://mrio.adbx.online/ (accessed July 2021); and ADB. 2021. *Capturing the Digital Economy: A Proposed Measurement Framework and its Applications*. Special Supplement to *Key Indicators for Asia and the Pacific 2021*. Manila: ADB.

Click here for figure data

Shares of each receiving sector to the forward linkages of digital sectors in 2019 are shown in Figure 5.5. Since a one-to-one relationship cannot be readily established given the sectoral aggregation of the MRIOTs, the sectors shown in Figure 5.5 are proxies for the list of digitally disrupted sectors of the AEG (2019). Highlighted values indicate higher-than-economy's average share of digital sectors' forward linkages. Across sectors, business services (proxy for advertising and market research), finance, hotels and restaurants, and personal services (proxy for motion picture, video and television program production services, sound recording and music publishing, and gambling and betting services) accrued higher-than-economy average shares for value-added from digital sectors. This implies intensive use of digital inputs in the production processes of these sectors. Lower shares, however, were recorded for aggregate sectors of paper and publishing (proxy for publishing services), and transport services not elsewhere classified (proxy for travel agency, tour operation, and other reservation services).

Across the select economies, the economy-wide (excluding digital sectors) average shares of digital sectors' forward linkages did not vary considerably, except for Viet Nam and Taipei,China (Figure 5.5). This may be due to the concentration of digital activities among the core digital sectors themselves. The Peoples Republic of China's high average forward linkage share was attributable to the high receipts of telecommunications services to the construction sector, which was also observed for Indonesia (note that construction is not shown in the set of sectors by the AEG 2019). Generally, wholesale and retail trade activities exhibited high shares for most economies, especially in the economy of Hong Kong, China.

Figure 5.5: Share of Digitally Dependent Sectors in the Core Digital Sectors' Forward Linkages to the Economy, 2019
(%)

	All industries except core digital sectors	Paper and publishing	Hotels and restaurants	Inland transport	Transport, nec	Finance	Business activities, nec	Education	Personal services	Wholesale	Retail
Proxy for:		*CPA 58*	*CPA 55 and 56*	*CPA 49*	*CPA 79*	*CPA K*	*CPA 73*	*CPA P*	*CPA 59 and 92*		
PRC	2.0	0.1	0.6	0.3	0.1	0.9	1.9	4.4	1.6	1.8	0.5
FIJ	2.0	0.1	6.1	0.2	1.6	2.6	5.1	3.6	0.1	0.8	10.3
HKG	2.0	0.2	1.2	1.0	0.1	9.1	1.2	1.0	1.8	26.3	1.9
INO	1.7	0.5	1.0	1.2	0.6	1.9	1.2	2.7	2.4	2.9	1.7
BRU	1.6	0.1	0.9	0.0	0.4	1.6	1.1	1.4	0.4	2.4	2.2
JPN	1.5	0.2	2.0	0.6	0.3	1.6	2.3	0.8	2.1	4.5	4.7
THA	1.5	0.4	11.0	1.7	1.1	1.4	2.9	2.0	1.4	1.6	1.7
BAN	1.4	0.1	0.8	2.1	0.1	0.8	0.3	0.9	1.4	0.3	4.1
CAM	1.3	0.2	5.9	1.2	0.0	0.8	2.6	1.1	1.2	2.8	0.2
MAL	1.3	0.5	2.1	0.4	0.5	1.6	2.3	0.3	4.2	1.2	1.8
MON	1.1	0.0	0.5	0.9	1.0	0.8	2.2	1.1	0.9	3.5	2.7
KAZ	1.1	0.0	0.1	3.4	0.5	0.7	1.9	1.3	1.9	4.0	3.9
SIN	1.0	0.2	0.8	0.4	0.4	1.7	2.7	0.5	1.1	3.5	0.9
PAK	1.0	0.8	2.9	6.1	0.1	1.0	2.0	0.6	1.8	0.3	0.9
IND	1.0	0.3	0.3	0.6	0.8	1.3	2.5	1.0	1.3	0.9	1.4
KOR	1.0	0.1	1.0	0.3	0.2	1.0	2.5	1.1	1.3	1.3	0.6
PHI	0.9	0.1	0.6	0.4	0.4	3.4	4.9	0.6	1.0	1.3	2.6
LAO	0.7	0.0	2.0	0.1	0.0	1.0	0.7	1.2	0.7	0.7	2.8
TAP	0.4	0.1	0.4	0.1	0.0	0.4	0.7	0.3	0.4	0.6	0.5
VIE	0.2	0.0	0.2	0.0	0.0	0.1	0.6	0.1	0.1	0.4	0.0

BAN = Bangladesh; BRU = Brunei Darussalam; CAGR = compound annual growth rate; CAM = Cambodia; CPA = statistical classification of products by activity; FIJ = Fiji; HKG = Hong Kong, China; IND = India; INO = Indonesia; JPN = Japan; KAZ = Kazakhstan; KOR = Republic of Korea; LAO = Lao People's Democratic Republic; MAL = Malaysia; MON = Mongolia; nec = not elsewhere classified; PAK = Pakistan; PHI = Philippines; PRC = People's Republic of China; SIN = Singapore; TAP = Taipei,China; THA = Thailand; VIE = Viet Nam.

Notes: CPA 49 = land transport services and transport services via pipelines; CPA 55 = accommodation services, CPA 56 = food and beverage serving services; CPA 58 = publishing services; CPA 59 = motion picture, video and television program production services, sound recording and music publishing; CPA K = financial and insurance services; CPA 73 = advertising and market research services; CPA 79 = travel agency, tour operator and other reservation services; CPA P = education services; CPA 92 = gambling and betting services. Highlighted cells exhibit higher-than-average shares in the respective national economy shown in the first column from the left.

Sources: Calculations using the Asian Development Bank (ADB) Multiregional Input–Output Database. https://mrio.adbx.online/ (accessed July 2021); ADB. 2021. *Capturing the Digital Economy: A Proposed Measurement Framework and its Applications.* Special Supplement to *Key Indicators for Asia and the Pacific 2021.* Manila: ADB; and United Nations Advisory Expert Group on National Accounts. 2019. 13th Meeting of the Advisory Expert Group on National Accounts: Framework for a Satellite Account on the Digital Economy. Washington, D.C. https://unstats.un.org/unsd/nationalaccount/aeg/2019/M13 (accessed March 2022).

Click here for figure data

5.5 Conclusions and Way Forward

Among the 20 economies assessed, the economy of Taipei,China exhibited the largest share of digital economy to total economy in 2019 and 2020, followed by the Republic of Korea, Singapore, Malaysia, and Viet Nam. Digital economies experienced declines in 2020, particularly due to disrupted supply chains for critical ICT goods and surges in the demand for consumer electronics and internet services. This led backward linkages, generally a measure of demand for digital goods and services, to decline by an average of 0.6% across the select economies. Forward linkages, however, saw a deeper contraction of 2.1% across economies, which is expected given that several sectors that use digital products experienced heavier losses in 2020.

To develop an impression of digitalization, this chapter used digital sectors' forward linkages to the rest of the economy as an indicator of nondigital sectors' absorption of value-added from digital sectors. Forward linkages of the core digital sectors generally increased in several economies whose digital economies are still in their infancy, such as in Bangladesh, Kazakhstan, and the Lao People's Democratic Republic. Meanwhile, steady growth in core digital economy's forward linkages was observed for more mature markets, including Hong Kong, China; the Republic of Korea; Singapore; and Taipei,China. This dependence on digital inputs can also be taken as a sign of digital transformation in traditionally nondigital services such as business services, finance, hotels and restaurants, and wholesale and retail trade.

The statistics presented in this chapter demonstrate the feasibility of estimating the relative sizes of core digital economies in Asia and the Pacific using input–output tables. These estimates are based on the measurement approach in ADB's *Special Supplement to Key Indicators for Asia and the Pacific 2021* (ADB 2021), which narrowly defines the digital economy as the sum of economic activity involving core digital products from both supply and use perspectives.

Extensions to this framework are likewise possible, further revealing not only the structure and dependencies of producing digital goods and services, but also the ability to generate value-added and employment in economies. However, as with any macroeconomic statistics, these monetary estimates are only the first step toward truly understanding the digital economy. Whether considering taxation, productivity, or access to technology, the overall objective is to produce evidence that can support and address new policy challenges in the digital age.

Detailed local currency estimates of the digital economy and its major components are further presented in Appendix 5.2 for the select years 2000, 2007, 2010, 2013, 2016, 2019, and 2020. Note that the objective is not to show point estimates, but rather to highlight the relative magnitudes and trends in economic activities of core digital sectors. Full results are available for download in the publication webpage.

Appendixes

Appendix 5.1: Defining the Core Digital Product Groups

Table A5.1: Main Digital Product Groups Based on Central Product Classification Version 2

Main Activity Group	Code	Product
Hardware	452	Computing machinery and parts and accessories thereof
	475	Disks, tapes, solid-state nonvolatile storage devices and other media, not recorded
Software publishing	38582	Software cartridges for video game consoles
	478	Packaged software
	83143	Software originals
	8434	Software downloads
	84391	Online games
	84392	Online software
Web publishing	83633	Sale of internet advertising space (except on commission)
	843	Online content[a]
Telecommunications services	841	Telephony and other telecommunications services
	842	Internet telecommunications services
Specialized and support services	8313	Information technology (IT) consulting and support services
	83141	IT design and development services for applications
	83142	IT design and development services for networks and systems
	8315	Hosting and IT infrastructure provisioning services
	8316	IT infrastructure and network management services

[a] Excluding items under Central Product Classification Version 2 843 already counted under Software Publishing – 8434, 84391, 84392.
Source: Asian Development Bank. 2021. *Capturing the Digital Economy: A Proposed Measurement Framework and its Applications.* Special Supplement to Key Indicators for Asia and the Pacific 2021. Manila: Asian Development Bank. https://www.adb.org/publications/capturing-digital-economy-measurement-framework.

Appendix 5.2: Contributions of Core Digital Sectors in 20 Economies

Table A5.2: Measures of the Core Digital Economy in Select Economies of Asia and the Pacific
(local currency units, million)

Year	Economy-Wide Value-Added Contribution to Digital Sectors	Value-Added Contribution from Digital Sectors	Value-Added Contribution within Digital Sectors	Economy-Wide Value-Added Contribution to Digital Sectors' Nondigital Assets	Digital Gross Domestic Product
Bangladesh					
2000	9,651.7	19,268.2	7,267.9	2,954.1	24,606.2
2007	63,199.5	80,809.0	46,741.3	13,367.2	110,634.4
2010	97,727.2	125,530.9	74,127.4	20,157.9	169,288.6
2013	136,692.5	183,544.7	105,084.9	28,773.3	243,925.6
2016	175,488.0	230,102.9	131,860.4	42,137.4	315,867.9
2019	194,752.1	283,321.4	145,302.1	53,412.4	386,183.8
2020	214,694.0	301,834.6	158,253.9	58,641.7	416,916.3
Brunei Darussalam					
2000	20.8	28.3	17.4	1.8	33.5
2007	105.2	278.3	79.0	29.2	333.6
2010	91.3	314.6	69.9	47.6	383.6
2013	98.3	288.5	73.3	70.6	384.1
2016	107.4	264.8	89.3	52.6	335.4
2019	128.2	260.1	110.9	55.1	332.4
2020	137.5	287.2	117.5	62.1	369.4
Cambodia					
2000	194,535.0	296,204.2	142,169.4	39,998.0	388,567.7
2007	542,309.1	776,165.8	389,930.1	65,045.1	993,589.9
2010	808,304.4	1,098,076.1	573,368.6	87,000.3	1,420,012.2
2013	1,146,482.2	1,472,297.1	796,731.6	147,482.9	1,969,530.6
2016	1,415,757.0	1,826,672.8	968,055.6	223,905.8	2,498,280.0
2019	1,807,302.9	2,502,483.8	1,308,803.6	230,239.9	3,231,223.0
2020	2,042,784.8	2,231,338.5	1,587,217.6	163,179.4	2,850,085.2
Fiji					
2000	49.3	138.5	39.9	0.7	148.7
2007	31.5	128.6	24.7	7.1	142.5
2010	108.8	247.6	90.2	10.3	276.6
2013	98.3	271.4	81.8	28.9	316.9
2016	204.3	360.5	166.4	21.5	419.8
2019	138.2	339.1	106.0	5.2	376.5
2020	114.1	246.7	93.7	16.7	283.9

continued on next page.

Table A5.2 *continued.*

Year	Economy-Wide Value-Added Contribution to Digital Sectors	Value-Added Contribution from Digital Sectors	Value-Added Contribution within Digital Sectors	Economy-Wide Value-Added Contribution to Digital Sectors' Nondigital Assets	Digital Gross Domestic Product
Hong Kong, China					
2000	26,149.3	51,898.6	17,614.5	9,203.7	69,637.1
2007	29,106.9	57,620.4	19,153.0	6,455.5	74,029.8
2010	30,381.6	61,238.2	19,603.8	7,148.4	79,164.4
2013	40,354.8	80,393.7	26,205.2	9,530.1	104,073.4
2016	46,374.1	94,163.0	29,749.0	12,477.0	123,265.0
2019	61,976.7	105,810.2	32,404.0	13,678.6	149,061.5
2020	59,241.9	100,842.9	30,511.5	13,137.2	142,710.5
India					
2000	532,195.8	629,779.8	398,027.2	87,304.7	851,253.1
2007	1,910,017.6	1,916,159.1	1,454,462.9	356,323.1	2,728,036.9
2010	3,084,186.9	3,038,625.0	2,330,080.4	525,440.7	4,318,172.2
2013	4,409,351.5	5,028,720.0	3,519,181.2	691,513.8	6,610,404.1
2016	5,745,002.1	7,200,260.1	4,420,966.2	1,187,358.2	9,711,654.1
2019	7,229,749.8	8,524,300.9	5,464,117.8	1,519,762.7	11,809,695.7
2020	6,633,755.8	8,270,820.5	5,059,270.5	1,405,215.1	11,250,520.9
Indonesia					
2000	40,048,168.3	34,006,763.5	21,766,570.1	5,615,839.6	57,904,201.3
2007	130,776,356.5	137,391,955.6	86,419,113.2	27,690,097.9	209,439,296.9
2010	212,255,234.0	227,917,964.6	151,046,137.0	51,179,955.4	340,307,017.0
2013	278,190,215.1	305,004,887.4	198,229,868.3	69,268,471.4	454,233,705.6
2016	349,602,353.2	400,335,259.1	249,484,582.4	102,001,183.6	602,454,213.5
2019	347,742,610.8	608,615,569.2	246,531,185.6	140,860,145.7	850,687,140.1
2020	314,187,343.0	561,786,902.3	217,664,459.2	128,517,710.0	786,827,496.1
Japan					
2000	21,184,382.8	23,067,414.8	11,065,295.5	5,698,458.9	38,884,960.9
2007	19,818,161.6	22,612,494.1	10,698,965.5	4,315,641.6	36,047,331.8
2010	16,590,249.7	20,311,871.6	9,242,820.8	3,465,332.1	31,124,632.6
2013	14,805,562.7	19,284,433.2	8,542,228.1	3,254,802.2	28,802,570.0
2016	16,598,944.7	21,353,886.9	9,564,659.4	4,019,088.1	32,407,260.4
2019	16,866,667.6	22,193,632.1	9,722,166.9	4,650,551.8	33,988,684.7
2020	15,828,468.8	21,036,731.8	9,033,877.5	4,482,801.8	32,314,124.9

continued on next page.

Table A5.2 *continued.*

Year	Economy-Wide Value-Added Contribution to Digital Sectors	Value-Added Contribution from Digital Sectors	Value-Added Contribution within Digital Sectors	Economy-Wide Value-Added Contribution to Digital Sectors' Nondigital Assets	Digital Gross Domestic Product
Kazakhstan					
2000	39,598.4	41,692.4	24,616.7	2,446.6	59,120.7
2007	174,051.1	327,477.2	129,695.3	38,698.0	410,531.1
2010	643,566.7	623,163.5	469,520.6	69,827.9	867,037.5
2013	865,276.9	899,892.2	655,627.4	113,966.9	1,223,508.6
2016	974,483.8	1,013,711.8	713,441.8	130,522.5	1,405,276.3
2019	1,032,579.6	1,317,481.3	797,127.3	160,654.5	1,713,588.2
2020	949,542.1	1,197,727.0	715,277.4	154,492.6	1,586,484.3
Republic of Korea					
2000	45,715,347.4	37,594,289.3	24,656,692.5	10,074,349.1	68,727,293.3
2007	69,778,834.8	61,214,764.7	36,851,746.7	14,798,034.2	108,939,887.0
2010	94,814,902.6	79,282,865.2	50,479,461.3	17,655,470.5	141,273,777.1
2013	107,974,057.3	90,860,298.7	60,071,122.6	18,528,743.6	157,291,977.0
2016	109,046,297.0	91,291,498.8	57,981,321.0	21,639,745.6	163,996,220.4
2019	137,192,266.7	131,942,830.7	86,136,423.0	23,979,260.2	206,977,934.6
2020	130,047,070.1	126,500,918.5	80,294,879.3	25,239,454.3	201,492,563.7
Lao People's Democratic Republic					
2000	206,220.7	228,722.3	181,955.0	10,365.3	263,353.3
2007	616,739.7	809,203.3	545,787.2	122,862.7	1,003,018.5
2010	942,500.5	1,144,742.2	823,845.3	164,766.6	1,428,164.0
2013	1,069,366.9	1,419,438.8	917,740.9	121,543.7	1,692,608.5
2016	1,574,492.5	1,982,534.2	1,355,974.3	154,003.9	2,355,056.2
2019	2,550,385.9	2,899,885.7	2,221,702.9	237,690.1	3,466,258.8
2020	2,967,363.9	3,392,487.8	2,541,968.2	341,982.2	4,159,865.7
Malaysia					
2000	18,915.9	18,448.3	13,358.4	1,996.6	26,002.4
2007	38,773.2	35,600.7	26,253.4	2,368.5	50,488.9
2010	39,805.2	45,575.4	26,925.1	3,744.1	62,199.5
2013	50,499.0	52,460.0	27,877.0	5,186.5	80,268.5
2016	67,824.3	69,606.1	35,880.1	7,804.9	109,355.2
2019	78,616.7	83,652.3	44,846.2	8,954.7	126,377.4
2020	73,690.3	83,300.6	40,328.8	8,071.2	124,733.4

continued on next page.

Table A5.2 *continued.*

Year	Economy-Wide Value-Added Contribution to Digital Sectors	Value-Added Contribution from Digital Sectors	Value-Added Contribution within Digital Sectors	Economy-Wide Value-Added Contribution to Digital Sectors' Nondigital Assets	Digital Gross Domestic Product
Mongolia					
2000	15,790.0	34,469.5	15,167.2	3,300.1	38,392.5
2007	98,263.3	169,825.7	76,682.1	24,419.5	215,826.3
2010	115,752.2	210,668.9	86,420.5	29,976.1	269,976.7
2013	188,963.4	309,780.6	148,327.6	51,838.7	402,255.2
2016	348,352.9	541,043.7	266,978.2	63,426.5	685,844.9
2019	411,301.7	521,962.8	316,500.0	59,130.9	675,895.5
2020	408,971.5	483,438.9	296,764.9	58,482.6	654,128.1
Pakistan					
2000	40,216.5	53,906.0	25,073.6	5,474.0	74,523.0
2007	169,297.8	174,037.8	113,136.0	18,539.9	248,739.5
2010	262,989.0	290,440.3	177,735.4	24,112.3	399,806.2
2013	349,834.9	408,993.4	244,217.6	29,813.9	544,424.6
2016	478,098.5	568,685.3	338,058.1	44,875.6	753,601.2
2019	724,980.8	825,091.6	536,844.7	55,534.9	1,068,762.6
2020	791,684.9	916,634.3	588,288.8	65,250.7	1,185,281.0
Philippines					
2000	115,931.4	135,050.5	85,541.1	11,607.7	177,048.5
2007	328,230.6	341,504.3	237,875.5	34,988.1	466,847.5
2010	362,502.4	393,722.5	242,449.2	48,637.5	562,413.2
2013	419,141.2	456,444.3	292,118.5	56,102.4	639,569.4
2016	484,970.7	547,840.1	343,438.0	72,352.4	761,725.1
2019	597,408.3	636,944.9	421,190.4	89,304.8	902,467.6
2020	559,254.0	607,332.4	394,372.1	68,037.4	840,251.6
People's Republic of China					
2000	299,855.8	312,834.0	125,287.1	85,756.2	573,159.0
2007	927,972.6	991,828.3	421,410.2	257,252.6	1,755,643.3
2010	1,121,261.5	1,271,609.6	487,747.7	424,214.1	2,329,337.5
2013	1,400,483.6	1,735,036.8	636,182.0	546,506.6	3,045,845.0
2016	1,783,377.3	2,420,018.9	829,573.4	738,136.6	4,111,959.5
2019	1,703,339.2	2,413,260.3	666,712.0	863,673.4	4,313,560.9
2020	1,862,019.3	2,585,458.4	727,632.4	1,116,104.7	4,835,950.1

continued on next page.

Table A5.2 *continued.*

Year	Economy-Wide Value-Added Contribution to Digital Sectors	Value-Added Contribution from Digital Sectors	Value-Added Contribution within Digital Sectors	Economy-Wide Value-Added Contribution to Digital Sectors' Nondigital Assets	Digital Gross Domestic Product
Singapore					
2000	9,478.5	9,516.3	6,487.6	1,201.4	13,708.5
2007	10,136.1	12,135.4	7,012.8	1,125.5	16,384.1
2010	14,203.8	16,362.1	9,662.5	2,225.7	23,129.1
2013	17,800.4	22,300.5	13,131.0	2,960.9	29,930.8
2016	21,856.7	27,626.6	14,761.8	3,501.6	38,223.1
2019	28,737.7	28,727.1	17,400.8	2,964.7	43,028.9
2020	26,485.1	25,727.0	15,764.2	2,576.2	39,024.1
Taipei,China					
2000	1,002,088.1	878,412.4	684,302.5	141,293.3	1,337,491.2
2007	1,633,482.2	1,467,981.3	1,187,731.0	181,061.8	2,094,794.3
2010	1,821,128.1	1,602,185.4	1,313,006.1	192,167.0	2,302,474.4
2013	1,885,934.6	1,748,908.4	1,440,226.3	213,087.7	2,407,704.3
2016	2,129,709.8	2,007,776.5	1,656,195.3	235,167.9	2,716,458.9
2019	2,809,575.3	2,226,125.0	1,918,623.5	264,023.9	3,381,100.6
2020	2,993,332.0	2,345,891.1	1,977,929.5	309,917.4	3,671,211.0
Thailand					
2000	91,987.7	111,393.1	43,775.0	15,827.3	175,433.0
2007	192,193.4	295,042.7	103,919.3	39,972.5	423,289.3
2010	189,657.9	326,693.0	101,497.0	41,489.3	456,343.2
2013	276,714.7	410,738.7	154,668.5	47,735.2	580,520.0
2016	270,780.5	466,277.0	144,430.3	56,924.6	649,551.8
2019	487,097.8	528,457.7	244,257.3	54,052.9	825,351.0
2020	421,373.5	480,264.1	208,573.9	54,131.9	747,195.6
Viet Nam					
2000	14,241,885.5	16,354,325.6	7,310,881.9	3,465,728.4	26,751,057.6
2007	46,408,085.8	45,300,525.0	30,720,439.2	9,782,182.2	70,770,353.8
2010	91,543,550.0	78,697,681.7	54,916,733.8	15,289,275.5	130,613,773.4
2013	194,542,144.4	139,962,123.6	123,136,702.9	22,779,179.3	234,146,744.3
2016	251,995,497.0	194,418,473.1	169,425,173.1	26,720,409.7	303,709,206.7
2019	409,616,228.7	275,249,079.4	259,014,785.5	26,166,291.2	452,016,813.9
2020	439,154,576.5	285,591,573.7	262,369,760.7	28,800,102.3	491,176,491.8

Sources: Calculations using the Asian Development Bank (ADB) Multiregional Input–Output Database. https://mrio.adbx.online/ (accessed July 2021); and ADB. 2021. *Capturing the Digital Economy: A Proposed Measurement Framework and its Applications.* Special Supplement to Key Indicators for Asia and the Pacific 2021. Manila: ADB. https://www.adb.org/publications/capturing-digital-economy-measurement-framework.

References

American Chamber of Commerce in Japan (ACCJ) and McKinsey & Company. 2021. Japan Digital Agenda 2030. https://www.digitaljapan2030.com/.

Asian Development Bank (ADB). 2021. *Capturing the Digital Economy: A Proposed Measurement Framework and its Applications*. Special Supplement to Key Indicators for Asia and the Pacific 2021. Manila: Asian Development Bank. https://www.adb.org/publications/capturing-digital-economy-measurement-framework.

F. Calvino, C. Criscuolo, L. Marcolin, and M. Squicciarini. 2018. A Taxonomy of Digital Intensive Sectors. *OECD Science, Technology, and Industry Working Papers*. No. 2018/14. https://doi.org/10.1787/f404736a-en.

E. Dabla-Norris, R. de Mooij, A. Hodge, J. Loeprick, D. Prihardini, A. Shah, S. Beer, S. Davidovic, A. M. Modi, and F. Qi. 2021. Digitalization and Taxation in Asia. *IMF Departmental Paper*. No. 17. Washington, DC: International Monetary Fund.

East Asia Forum (EAF) Editorial Board. 2021. *Japan's Digital Drag*. East Asia Forum. https://www.eastasiaforum.org/2021/05/31/japans-digital-drag/. 31 May.

International Institute for Management Development (IIMD). 2021. *World Digital Competitiveness Ranking*. https://www.imd.org/centers/world-competitiveness-center/rankings/world-digital-competitiveness/ (accessed March 2022).

Organisation for Economic Co-operation and Development (OECD). 2017. *Digital Economy Outlook*. Paris: OECD Publishing; OECD. 2021. Input–Output Tables. https://www.oecd.org/sti/ind/input-outputtables.htm (accessed March 2022).

OECD. 2020. *A Roadmap Toward a Common Framework for Measuring the Digital Economy*. Report for the G20 Digital Economy Task Force. Saudi Arabia: OECD. https://www.oecd.org/sti/roadmap-toward-a-common-framework-for-measuring-the-digital-economy.pdf.

United Nations Conference on Trade and Development (UNCTAD). 2019. *Value Creation and Capture - Implications for Developing Countries*. Digital Economy Report. New York. https://unctad.org/system/files/official-document/der2019_en.pdf.

UNCTAD. 2020. *Manual for the Production of Statistics on the Digital Economy*. New York: United Nations.

UNCTAD. 2021. *Cross-Border Data Flows and Development: From Whom the Data Flow*. Digital Economy Report. New York: United Nations.

United Nations Advisory Expert Group on National Accounts (AEG). 2019. *13th Meeting of the Advisory Expert Group on National Accounts: Framework for a Satellite Account on the Digital Economy*. Washington, DC. https://unstats.un.org/unsd/nationalaccount/aeg/2019/M13.asp.

World Bank. 2021. *Beyond Unicorns: Harnessing Digital Technologies for Inclusion in Indonesia*. Washington, DC: World Bank.

Determining the Economic Contribution of Real Estate Activities

6

Using input-output analysis, this special chapter presents a methodology to measure the economic contribution of real estate activities to an economy's gross domestic product. It considers that such activities are undertaken as two primary components: real estate construction and real estate services. Implementing the methodology using ADB's Multiregional Input Output Tables, the chapter presents an estimation of the size of the real estate sector for select economies. As the property sector is prone to market fluctuations, an estimation of its economic significance could aid policy formulation that cushions the impacts of any potential slump in real estate activities.

6.1 Background

The real estate sector is often perceived as a significant contributor to an economy's gross domestic product (GDP) and generally features many interlinkages with other economic sectors. In principle, a sector's linkages can be understood in terms of its relationships with the rest of the economy through its direct and indirect purchases and sales. Understanding such linkages is crucial to understanding the structure of an economy in the form of an interconnected system of sectors that are directly or indirectly integral to one another.

This understanding can aid governments in creating conducive market conditions for the real estate sector, and for the sectors that have direct or indirect linkages with it. Decisions for the real estate sector that are cognizant of such linkages could potentially stimulate higher growth outcomes for crucial economic parameters such as income, production, and employment, while ensuring optimal allocation of resources (Miller and Lahr 2001).

Owing to the myriad of economic linkages of real estate, the sector's related activities have significant impact in terms of demand-side effects. Increased economic activity in the real estate sector has direct repercussions for core industrial sectors, such as cement and steel production, real estate management, and technology, to name a few.

Further, in many economies, the real estate sector itself is not only a major employment driver but also supports employment in other sectors through its backward and forward linkages. For example, the direct share of employment in real estate-related construction and services to total employment in 2018 was about

10.9% in India (RBI 2021), 7.8% in the People's Republic of China (PRC) (NBS 2019), and 6.4% in the Philippines (ADB 2021). Meanwhile, in the United States the share in 2018 was about 4.2% (BLS year) and in Singapore it was 3.3% (ADB 2021).[1]

In terms of their macroeconomic effects, property price fluctuations induced by changes in interest rates theoretically affect private consumption and fixed asset investments through personal wealth and balance sheet effects. Consequently, one must not forget the linkages of the real estate sector with the finance sector. Distress in the real estate sector—and the developers' ability to pay their dues or homeowners' ability to pay their mortgages—could entail grave consequences for the finance sector, as evidenced by the global financial crisis (GFC) of 2008 (Baily et al. 2008; FCIC 2011).

Triggered by unanticipated shocks in the real estate sector, the GFC not only caused cataclysmic economic losses but also underscored the intertwined nature of financial markets and real estate developments. It proved that, while the rapid escalation of the housing market coupled with an enabling monetary policy may stimulate economic growth, such escalation may result in deep financial crisis. Besides the GFC of 2008, similar market conditions have systematically created housing bubbles in numerous other economies, including Japan in the 1980s and Spain in the 1990s, among others. The positive association between real estate valuation appreciation and equity market valuation appreciation, which was at the heart of the GFC, is consistent with the wealth effects from real estate valuation to equity investment, as capital gains in the equity investment spill over to the real estate sector (Aizenman and Jinjarak 2013). To offset the probability of similar future crises, other channels of monetary and fiscal policy that provide households with more liquidity must be explored. Moreover, unconventional measures—such as including owner-occupied housing repayments in consumer price inflation indexes, to better reflect households' comprehensive cost-of-living scenarios in central banks' reaction functions—may also be introduced, in addition to adopting a toolkit of macroprudential instruments (IMF 2011).

Besides the setback from the GFC, the global growth of the real estate sector ushered in varying developmental consequences for different economies, especially since the turn of the millennium. For example, the real estate market in India was still in its infancy, largely unorganized and dominated by numerous small players compared to the other Asian and Western markets, until the beginning of the 21st Century (Planning Commission 2002). However, with an ongoing effort toward institutionalization, including the implementation of the Real Estate (Regulation and Development) Act 2016, the Indian real estate market is ripe for investment and development (PWC and ULI 2018). In Japan, the strength of the real estate sector has been established by strong monetary and fiscal policies, driven by growth-oriented strategies, such as corporate tax reforms and stimulation of financial and capital markets (MLITT 2015).

1 Employment in construction is disaggregated using the same proportions of real estate-related construction. Figures are preliminary and will be revised in future updates to this publication, along with estimates of employment through linkages.

The real estate sector of the PRC has been under scrutiny from both investors and regulators, owing to the intense regulatory pressure on developers' leverage and banks' mortgage exposure, and the consequent contraction in sales and construction activity (Tilton et al. 2021). Estimations for the scale of PRC's real estate sector in (year) ranged from 13% to 30% of the economy's GDP, as reported in the media (*The Economist* 2021). The disparities in these estimations notwithstanding, it cannot be disputed that the real estate sector comprises a significant proportion of GDP, rendering it natural to determine the extent to which a shock in the real estate sector could impact the PRC's economy.

6.2 Defining Real Estate Activities

The estimation process starts by carefully defining what types of activities are considered relevant to real estate. Generally, real estate activities (otherwise known as "the property sector") are undertaken in two primary components: real estate construction and real estate services.

It should be noted that the broader construction sector conducts a vast number of activities; from site preparation to building construction and completion or demolition. For the purposes of estimating real estate activities, the scope of the construction component includes all types of work except for civil engineering. In particular, construction of highways, roads, bridges, waterways, pipelines, power plants, and others belonging to Central Product Classification version 2.1 (CPC 2.1) group 532 (civil engineering works) are not in scope, since these infrastructure-related activities are primarily driven by policy rather than market events. Activities that are in scope include building structures under CPC 2.1 group 531 (buildings). This group includes residential buildings (CPC 2.1 group 531) for private households as well as for communities, such as retirement homes, workers' hostels, fraternity homes, orphanages, homeless shelters, etc. The scope is also extended to nonresidential buildings (CPC 2.1 group 532) including industrial buildings such as factories, plants, and workshops; commercial buildings such as shopping centers, malls, warehouses, exhibition halls, office buildings, and bank buildings; and other nonresidential buildings such as cinemas, hotels, schools, and hospitals. Other construction and installation services (such as the installation of elevators, electricity wiring, plumbing, and decor) are also included, with the condition that these are mostly relevant to residential and nonresidential buildings.

The second component in the property sector is real estate services. In this context, such services refer to (i) the buying, selling, renting, and operating of self-owned or leased property; and (ii) activities of real estate agents and brokers, intermediation of real estate activities, property management services, property appraisals, and escrow services. While construction activities relate more to the flow of (new) buildings, real estate services relate more to the stock of existing structures (Tilton et al. 2021).

Therefore, both components, while behaving differently, are intricately linked to building assets or real estate properties. Taken together, these two components of real estate construction and the associated management and leasing of those buildings complete the scope of economic activities related to real estate.

6.3 Estimating the Contribution of Real Estate Activities

Now that real estate activities are defined, these definitions may be transcribed as sectoral classifications that identify specific products and sectors to be measured. Once distinguished from the rest of the economy, the measurement approach is to take the "relevant amount" and calculate its relative share to all activities. There are two general ways to arrive at the relevant amount of sector activity related to real estate.

At the narrowest level, the real estate sector's contribution to an economy may be measured as the total amount the sector adds to the value of its inputs to produce an output. In national accounts statistics, this refers to the real estate sector's gross value-added, which is also equivalent to the sum of income earned (e.g., wages, profits, and taxes) from engaging in productive activity and returns from the use of fixed assets. Put differently, a value-added measure of the real estate sector is the sum of its output minus all inputs (such as wood and steel) from its upstream suppliers. By excluding these intermediate inputs, the measure narrows down the scope to the production of a single economic activity.

Value-added is, however, a measure of economic production taken from the perspective of the producing sector and not the final product it sells. For example, if one limits the interest to houses, one may argue that the relevant measure should be the value of the dwellings that were sold to households (i.e., the demand perspective). In this perspective, the value of the house includes the value-added not just by the construction component, but also the value-added contributions from all inputs that went into building the house. In effect, the demand for housing is a culmination of all sectors' value-additions involved in the construction of a dwelling. This demand perspective may be considered as the broader measure of the real estate sector, since it includes all sectors in the construction value chain and not just the construction sector itself. That is, it is the sum of all domestic value-added embodied in the final demand for the real estate activities.

Formally, this demand approach is measured through an input–output table (IOT), which provides a disaggregated view of all the sectors in an economy. A standard view of an IOT shows in the rows the amount of a sector 's output that was used as inputs (z) or as final use (f). Table 6.1 illustrates these flows in a simplified three-sector economy. The final use or demand for each sector is the sum of final consumption expenditure by households and nonprofit institutions serving households (c), gross capital formation or investments (i), government final consumption expenditure (g), and exports (e). Meanwhile, the columns of each sector j detail a sector's purchases of inputs from domestic sectors ($z_{\cdot j}$), foreign supplies ($m_{\cdot j}$), and its own value-added (v_j). Each sector's row and column totals (x) are equal, which implies that the total amount of its supply (column outputs, x′) must be equal to total use of its product (row outputs, x).

Table 6.1: Simplified Schematic of an Input–Output Table

		Intermediate Uses (Z)			Final Uses (y)				Gross Output (x′)
		1	2	3					
Sectors	1	z_{11}	z_{12}	z_{13}	c_1	i_1	g_1	e_1	x_1
	2	z_{21}	z_{22}	z_{23}	c_2	i_2	g_2	e_2	x_2
	3	z_{31}	z_{32}	z_{23}	c_3	i_3	g_3	e_3	x_3
Imports (M)		$m_{\cdot 1}$	$m_{\cdot 2}$	$m_{\cdot 3}$	m_c	m_i	m_g	m_3	M_3
Value-added (v)		v_1	v_2	v_3					GDP
Gross output (x′)		x_1'	x_2'	x_3'	C	I	G	E	

C = private consumption expenditure; E = exports; G = government final consumption expenditure; GDP = gross domestic product; I = gross fixed capital formation; X = gross output.

Source: Adapted from R. Miller and P. Blair. 2009. *Input–Output Analysis: Foundations and Extensions* (second edition). Cambridge: Cambridge University Press.

From the row perspective, each sector i's output (x_i)may be expressed as:

$$x_i = \sum_j z_{ij} + \sum_k y_{ik}$$

where k corresponds to categories of final demand.

Establishing the relationship between domestic inputs and outputs, such that

$a_{ij} = \dfrac{z_{ij}}{x_j}$ and therefore, $z_{ij} = a_{ij}x_j$, equation above can be transformed as:

$$x_i = \sum_j a_{ij}x_j + \sum_k y_{ik}$$

Expressed in compact matrix notation, the equation above becomes:

$$x = Ax + y$$

Rearranging to form the usual Leontief equation, output (x) may be evaluated as the function of total productive requirements and demand levels:

$$x = (I - A)^{-1}y$$

Now, taking the amount of value-added per unit output for all sectors j, one arrives at value-added coefficients v_c:

$$v_{(c)j} = \frac{v_j}{x_j}, \text{ which takes the diagonalized vector form of } \hat{\mathbf{v}}_c = \begin{pmatrix} v_{(c)1} & 0 & 0 \\ 0 & \ddots & 0 \\ 0 & 0 & v_{(c)j} \end{pmatrix}$$

Pre-multiplying the Leontief equation $(\mathbf{I} - \mathbf{A})^{-1}\mathbf{y}$ by $\hat{\mathbf{v}}_c$, one yields a $\mathbf{n} \times 1$ vector showing value-added contribution of each sector i embodied in the total final demand f. That is,

$$\mathbf{v} = \hat{\mathbf{v}}_c (\mathbf{I} - \mathbf{A})^{-1}\mathbf{y}$$

For trained readers, since $\mathbf{y}$ includes the final demands for all types of products, the sum of $\mathbf{v}$ would correspond to the total value-added in the economy, or GDP (without the adjustment for taxes less subsidies on products).

Hence, to measure only the total value-added contributions to the final demand for sectors related to real estate, $\mathbf{y}$ in the previous equation is replaced with the subset $\mathbf{y}^p$, which contains only final demands for real estate construction (mostly residential and nonresidential buildings) and real estate services. The final form of the equation used to evaluate the contribution of real estate activities to the economy is expressed as:

$$\mathbf{v}^p = \hat{\mathbf{v}}_c (\mathbf{I} - \mathbf{A})^{-1}\mathbf{y}^p$$

The sum of all elements in $\mathbf{v}^p$ represents all domestic sectors' value-added contribution to the final demand for sectors related to real estate.

There are three advantages to this measure. First, as mentioned, this demand-side measure considers not only the contribution of the main producer (i.e., construction and real estate services) but also the upstream domestic sectors whose outputs were embedded in the final product. In the context of a property downturn, this measure will be indicative of the impacts on the connected sectors in the economy. If, say, the housing construction sector is responsible for an overwhelming market share of domestic wood manufacturers, then a crisis affecting dwelling construction is also expected to affect the income of the wood-manufacturing sector. In contrast, the narrow measure looks only at the effects on the housing construction sector itself.

Second, the use of value-added coefficients ensures that the resulting values are free of double-counting. This is consistent with the national accounting framework, which deducts intermediate inputs that were previously produced by other sectors and which may already be counted elsewhere in the economy.

Third, the overall measure is bounded with the GDP figure of the economy. This affords readers to more easily interpret the figures when expressed as a ratio of GDP.

As an added note, value-added v is mathematically equivalent to gross output x minus domestic intermediate inputs z and imports m. This means that, when taking the value-added coefficients v_c, the intermediate inputs both from domestic and foreign sources are discounted in the final figures. Further, by using noncompetitive IOTs, the final demand y should correspond to domestically produced final products and are hence netted out of imported final products. This implies that the equation to calculate value-added contributions are by construction already net of imports.

6.4 Proportions of Real Estate Construction

The calculations in this chapter were made using the ADB Multiregional Input-Output Table (MRIOT) for 2017. Since the sectoral grouping for construction activities in the MRIOT is aggregated for all types (i.e., residential, nonresidential, civil engineering, and other installation), the estimates rely on the use of proportions of real estate construction taken from national accounts statistics. Ideally, the proportion q indicates the share of all residential and commercial building construction activities, excluding any civil engineering activity. Appendix 6.1 provides the detailed product types included in the final demand.

If real estate construction and real estate services are the bth and r^{th} rows, respectively, in the final demand vector $\boldsymbol{y}$, then for exposition the relevant final demand for the real estate components is equal to $\boldsymbol{y}^p = \mathbf{y}\hat{\mathbf{q}}_b + \mathbf{y}\hat{\mathbf{q}}_r$. $\hat{\mathbf{q}}_b$ is a diagonalized vector of proportions, with the appropriate share of real estate construction demand in the bth element and zeroes for products when $i \neq b$. Similarly, $\mathbf{y}\hat{\mathbf{q}}_r$ is a vector of proportions, with the appropriate share of real estate services demand in the rth element and zeroes for products when $i \neq r$. While proportions of final demand for construction vary by economy, in this study all (or 100%) of real estate services demand is considered in the calculations for all economies. Since the real estate services component is shown separately in the MRIOT, there is no need to apply proportions for this component.

The raw proportions for real estate construction and the sources for their calculations are provided in Table 6.2. The ideal situation for calculating the proportions is when a detailed IOT or supply-use table is available. In such cases, the share of final demand for real estate construction (excluding civil engineering) to the total construction demand is taken. If data are not available, demand is proxied using the data on gross fixed capital formation of dwellings and buildings from the national accounts (Lequiller and Blades 2014). This proxy measure can be generally acceptable, given that most of the construction component is investment in fixed assets. In a few instances, the amount of construction work disaggregated by type of structure is also used to obtain a proxy for the proportions of real estate construction. Given that not all economies in the MRIOT have adequate detail on construction activity, this limits the calculations to a few Asian economies. Also included are estimates for advanced economies, which are accommodated as a comparator for economies with developed property sectors. In total, estimates are done for 18 economies for single period 2017 as most sampled economies would have the required construction data around this year. In future updates, these estimates will be extended to several periods and economies.

Table 6.2: Real Estate Construction as a Proportion of Total Construction Demand in Select Economies

Economy	Proportion	Source
Canada	64.4%	Gross fixed capital formation by type of asset, 2017, Statistics Canada
China, People's Republic of	71.6%	Final demand for construction, excluding civil engineering (149×149 NIOT), 2017, National Bureau of Statistics, People's Republic of China
France	76.3%	Gross fixed capital in dwellings and buildings other than dwellings, 2017, National Institute of Statistics and Economic Studies, France
Germany	86.5%	Gross fixed capital formation in buildings, 2017, Federal Statistical Office of Germany
Hong Kong, China	85.6%	Principal statistics for all establishments in the building, construction and real estate sectors by industry, 2018, Census and Statistics Department, Hong Kong, China
India	59.8%	Output and value-added from Construction, 2017, Ministry of Statistics and Programme Implementation, India
Indonesia	66.9%	Final demand for construction except roads, bridges, and ports (18×85 NIOT), 2016, Badan Pusat Statistik, Indonesia
Italy	71.2%	Gross fixed capital formation by asset and by industry, 2017, National Institute of Statistics, Italy
Japan	64.3%	Final demand for construction excluding public construction and civil engineering (10×07 NIOT), 2015, Statistics Bureau of Japan
Korea, Republic of	73.4%	Gross fixed capital formation in residential and nonresidential buildings, 2017, National Accounts, Bank of Korea
Malaysia	68.8%	Principal Statistics of Construction Sector by sub-sector, 2017, Department of Statistics, Malaysia
Philippines	62.7%	Summary statistics for construction establishments, 2017, Philippine Statistics Authority
Singapore	63.1%	Final demand for construction except for civil engineering works (10×05 NIOT), 2017, Singapore Statistics
Spain	87.4%	Gross fixed capital formation by asset and by industry, 2017, Spanish Statistical Office
Taipei,China	65.1%	Final demand for construction except for public works (16×61 NIOT), 2004, National Statistics, Taipei,China
Thailand	69.9%	Principal Statistics by Category of Construction Industry, 2014, National Statistical Office of Thailand
United Kingdom	71.9%	Gross fixed capital formation by product and industry, 2017, Office for National Statistics, United Kingdom
United States	65.0%	Investment in Private and Government Fixed Assets, 2017, Bureau of Economic Analysis, United States

NIOT = national input–output table.

Note: If disaggregated data on construction final demand are unavailable, the closest available data for detailed types of construction are used as proxy (e.g., gross fixed capital formation, gross output, and construction statistics).

Source: Compiled by the Asian Development Bank Input–Output Study Team using data from national statistics offices.

6.5 Economic Contribution of Real Estate-Related Activities

Results from the application of the described methodology ranged from 5.4% (Thailand) to 21.3% (PRC) of the respective GDP of select economies in 2017 (Figure 6.1).[2] Among the select economies in Asia, Japan and Indonesia followed the PRC with the highest concentration of real estate activities in their overall GDP, at 20.2% and 19.0%, respectively. The contribution of real estate construction was highest in the PRC (16.8%) and Indonesia (16.0%), whereas real estate services were predominant in Japan (13.4%). Thailand had the lowest share of real estate activities to GDP at 5.4%, with around 3% due to construction activities.

Figure 6: Share of Real Estate Activity to Gross Domestic Product in Select Economies, 2017
(%)

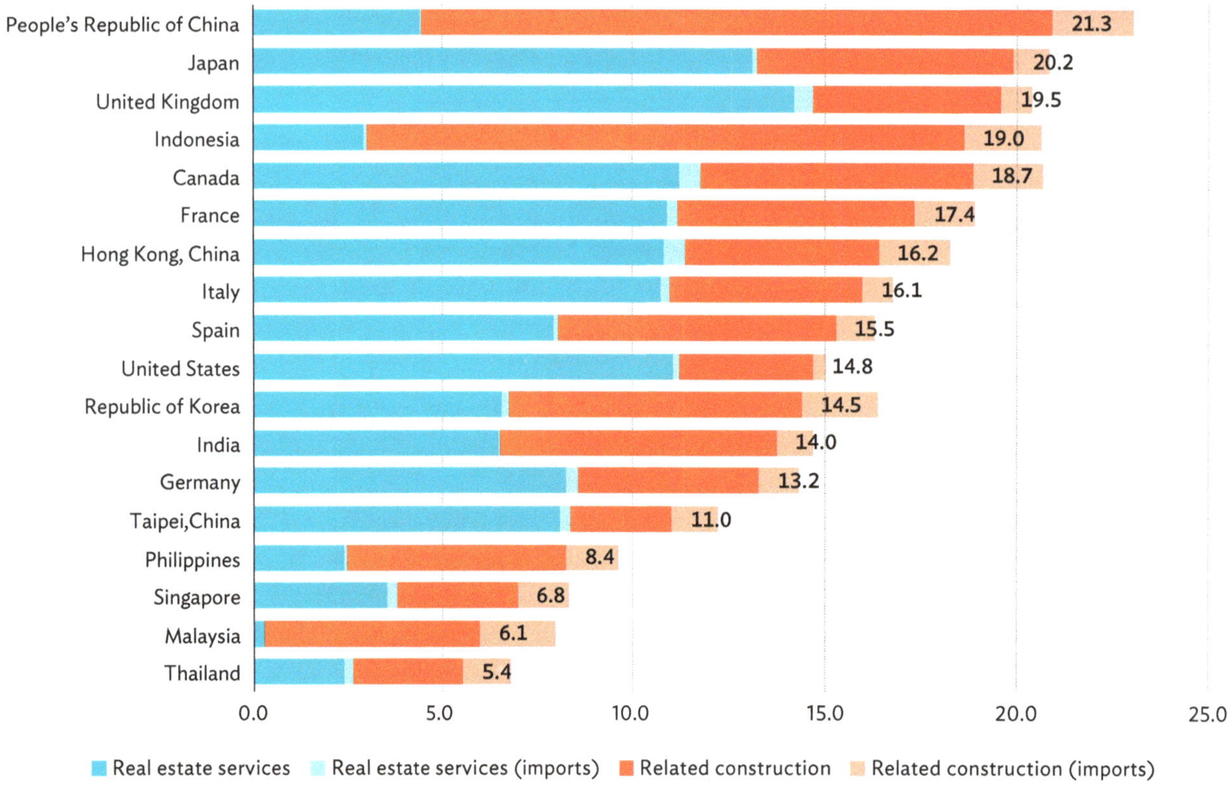

R.E = real estate.

Note: Data labels shown (%) refer to domestic value-added embodied in final demand (i.e., excluding imports). "Real estate activity" refers to the sum of economy-wide value-added embodied in the final demand for real estate construction and real estate services. Values are calculated using current price tables in United States dollars.

Source: Calculated using the Asian Development Bank Multiregional Input–Output Table for 2017. https://mrio.adbx.online/ (accessed July 2021).

Click here for figure data

2 Results in this publication differ from the previous estimates mentioned in *The Economist* (2021). Appendix 6.2 details the differences of these figures from the previous exercise.

Further disaggregation of real estate activities in the PRC and Indonesia suggests that these economies have shares of construction investments of about 79% and 84%, respectively, of all real estate activities, although the highest figure for this measure was posted by Malaysia at about 95%.

In the developed economies of Canada, France, Italy, the United Kingdom, and the United States, much of the share of real estate activities in 2017 was attributable to real estate services, owing to increasing interests in property and facilities management. This is typical of major economies, which have recently embarked on digital transformations in their real estate services, particularly through innovations in new tools and technologies (Baum, Saull, and Braesemann 2020). Additionally, the increasing proliferation of property mortgage services providing competitive interest rates and professional support to real estate investors has also contributed to the bourgeoning of the real estate services component in these economies (Agnello, Castro, and Sousa 2020; Fuster et al. 2018).

6.6 Limitations and Way Forward

The statistics presented in this chapter could potentially complement financial and macroeconomic statistics used to assess the financial and/or economic soundness of the property sector in any given economy, and to flag any potential issues or risks.

While the primary objective was to demonstrate a methodology for calculating the contribution of the real estate sector to total GDP, there is scope to expand this methodology by analyzing the balance sheets of select economies (and their institutional sectors), the structure of liabilities, monetary policies, and the uptake of these buildings, among others. Such analysis might cover the potential fallout from financial dimensions of owning property assets that are not within the purview of conventional input–output frameworks. Future estimations could be further strengthened through a more robust database, enabling the application of comparative time series statistics across economies.

Appendixes

Appendix 6.1: Definitions of Real Estate Activities

Table A6.1: Types of Activity Included in Real Estate Activities

CPC 2.1	Product Description
A. Real Estate Construction	
53111	One- and two-dwelling residential buildings
53112	Multidwelling residential buildings
53121	Industrial buildings
53122	Commercial buildings
53129	Other nonresidential buildings
54111	General construction services of one- and two-dwelling residential buildings
54112	General construction services of multidwelling residential buildings
54121	General construction services of industrial buildings
54122	General construction services of commercial buildings
54129	General construction services of other nonresidential buildings
54400	Assembly and erection of prefabricated constructions
54310	Demolition services
54320	Site formation and clearance services
54330	Excavating and earthmoving services
54611	Electrical wiring and fitting services
54612	Fire alarm installation services
54613	Burglar alarm system installation services
54614	Residential antenna installation services
54619	Other electrical installation services
54621	Water plumbing services
54622	Drain-laying services
54631	Heating equipment installation services
54632	Ventilation and air-conditioning equipment installation services
54640	Gas fitting installation services
54650	Insulation services
54691	Lift and escalator installation services
87157	Maintenance and repair services of elevators and escalators
54699	Other installation services n.e.c.
54710	Glazing services

continued on next page.

Table A6.1 *continued.*

CPC 2.1	Product Description
54720	Plastering services
54730	Painting services
54740	Floor and wall tiling services
54750	Other floor laying, wall covering and wall papering services
54760	Joinery and carpentry services
54770	Fencing and railing services
54790	Other building completion and finishing services
54511	Pile-driving services
54512	Foundation services
54521	Building framing services
54522	Roof framing services
54530	Roofing and waterproofing services
54540	Concrete services
54550	Structural steel erection services
54560	Masonry services
54570	Scaffolding services
54590	Other special trade construction services
B. Real Estate Services	
72111	Rental or leasing services involving own or leased residential property
72112	Rental or leasing services involving own or leased nonresidential property
72121	Trade services of residential buildings
72122	Trade services of nonresidential buildings
72123	Trade services of time-share properties
72130	Trade services of vacant and subdivided land
72211	Residential property management services on a fee or contract basis except of time-share ownership properties
72212	Nonresidential property management services on a fee or contract basis
72213	Time-share property management services on a fee or contract basis
72221	Residential building sales on a fee or contract basis, except of time-share ownership properties
72222	Nonresidential building sales on a fee or contract basis
72223	Sale of time-share properties on a fee or contract basis
72230	Land sales on a fee or contract basis
72240	Real estate appraisal services on a fee or contract basis

CPC = Central Product Classification; n.e.c. = not elsewhere classified.
Source: Compiled by the Asian Development Bank Input–Output Study Team using United Nations Statistical Division. 2015. Central Product Classification (CPC) Version 2.1.

Appendix 6.2: Review of Other Estimates of the Property Sector in the People's Republic of China

This appendix outlines why ADB estimates of the size of People's Republic of China's property sector differ from the widely cited estimates in Rogoff and Yang (2020). The appendix starts by pointing out how the estimation methods in Rogoff and Yang (2020) differ from standard input–output approaches. It then aligns their estimation methods with standard approaches, using the same data they use. Rogoff and Yang have also published an addendum to their paper (Rogoff and Yang 2021), which makes changes to their data and methodology. This appendix documents those changes. It concludes that the methodologies from both sides are now aligned, only differing in the input–output tables used.

The most-cited figure of the property sector in the People's Republic of China (PRC) is from Rogoff and Yang (2020). As with the estimates in this appendix, the Rogoff and Yang (2020) approach used IOTs to measure the size of the property sector relative to the economy's gross domestic product (GDP). The authors calculated that 28.7% of the PRC's economy comprised real estate construction investments and services in 2016. Excluding the amount of imports, the estimate reduced to about 24.8% of GDP for the same year (Rogoff and Yang 2020). The authors used the PRC's official IOTs for the period 2017 published by the National Bureau of Statistics (NBS) of the People's Republic of China (NBS 2019).

In an attempt to replicate the estimates using the same set of data as Rogoff and Yang (2020), the ADB made three observations on the estimations by the two cited authors.

First, the simple output multipliers used by Rogoff and Yang (2020) were deducted by one.[1] In matrix terms, the total input coefficients matrix was subtracted by an identity matrix. Any demand evaluated using this multiplier would exclude the direct demand itself in the calculation. Thus, only indirect production induced by construction investments were counted. This approach therefore could have the effect of underestimating the total domestic contribution of construction activities.

Second, when using the standard specification ($\mathbf{x} = \mathbf{Lf}$) of the Leontief model, the resulting impacts were expressed in gross output terms. This approach overstates the impact of construction as gross outputs include double-counted terms (gross output of one sector is the sum of intermediate inputs and gross value-added). Furthermore, the accounting concept of gross output is not bounded within the value of GDP.

1 This was originally brought to the ADB attention by Simon Cox of *The Economist*.

Third, the contribution of real estate services was not measured in the same way as construction investment. The (a) value-added of real estate services was simply added to the (b) economy-wide contribution of real estate construction (and related purchases of machinery and equipment). Note that the former (a) only refers to the sector's direct contribution to the economy. It does not account for its links to other sectors. Meanwhile the latter includes contributions from linked sectors, such as upstream suppliers. The addition of two different figures derived from two incoherent approaches (one using sector activity, the other using final demand) raises some difficulty in interpreting the final figures.

Due to its unorthodox application of the input–output concepts, the economic contribution of construction investments and real estate as estimated in Rogoff and Yang (2020) may be interpreted as comprising the "indirect" output attributable to construction and installation investments for real estate development, plus the value-added income of the real estate services component. The term "indirect" is used to connote Rogoff and Yang's (2020) deduction of one (1) from the value of the simple output multiplier of construction and machinery sectors.

ADB therefore aligned the approach by Rogoff and Yang (2020) with more conventional input–output methods, used the same data but (i) added back the direct impacts in the total input coefficients, (ii) netted out potential double-counting in gross output via value-added coefficients, and (iii) integrated the final demand for real estate services in the input–output model along with Rogoff and Yang's (2020) demand levels for real estate construction and related equipment purchases.

The ADB implemented the above modifications twice, which resulted in estimates of 15.4% and 13.8% of GDP, with and without imports, respectively. These estimates were cited in *The Economist* (2021). They are lower than the earlier (24.8% to 28.7%) estimates by Rogoff and Yang (2020). The differences between the two estimates are all attributed to the change in methods and not the data. In particular, the ADB study applied the same data series as Rogoff and Yang (2020) for investment in construction and equipment (taken from Table 19–5 of NBS Statistical Yearbook), although the data used was for 2017 not 2016. Therefore, ADB estimates include both residential real estate (i.e., housing) and commercial real estate (i.e., office buildings and the like) to the same extent that Rogoff and Yang (2020) includes them. Modifications to the initial ADB estimates were as follows:

First, the simple output multipliers in the ADB estimates were not deducted by 1 as implemented in Rogoff and Yang (2020). This is to account for both the direct and indirect production associated with the relevant final demands.

Second, the gross outputs were translated into value-added terms by pre-multiplying a diagonalized matrix of value-added coefficients to the Leontief inverse (now corrected for direct and indirect impacts). The resulting $\hat{\mathbf{v}}_c\mathbf{L}$ matrix yielded the total value-added contributed by each sector in rows to a unit of final demand for each sector in columns. The column sum of this matrix provided the total economy-wide value-added contributions to a unit of final demand in the corresponding industry. The ADB study then used this matrix of total value-added coefficients to post-multiply a vector of relevant final demands. In matrix form, the model then became $\hat{\mathbf{v}}_c\mathbf{L}\mathbf{y}$, where $\boldsymbol{v}$ is value-added, $\hat{\mathbf{v}}_c$ is the diagonalized value-added-to-output ratios, $\mathbf{L}$ is the total input coefficients matrix, and $\boldsymbol{y}$ is the final demand of interest.

Lastly, the final demand in the model was modified to include all three products deemed relevant in Rogoff and Yang (2020): purchases of construction-related equipment and instruments, construction investments for real estate development, and final demand for real estate services. This was performed so that the contributions of all relevant sectors are evaluated in the same manner, and that the mixing of value-added and gross output terms in the final figure was avoided. The amount of construction investments given in Rogoff and Yang (2020) was only about 36% of the total final use in construction. This figure was honored to emphasize the effects of methodological change.

In a new paper released by Rogoff and Yang (2021), the authors made considerable changes to their approach, which reduced the PRC figure for 2016 from 24.8% (figure without imports published in August 2020) to 21.9% (published in December 2021). While the 2.9-percentage-point difference between the two estimates seems insignificant, the updated figure is a combined result of changes in both methodology and data, especially for final demand. Rogoff and Yang (2021) explained data-related changes but did not elaborate on the impacts of changing the input–output approach.

Some of Rogoff and Yang's (2021) changes push the estimate down; others increase it. The changes that lowered it include: (i) the use of value-added coefficients, (ii) the movement of real estate services from sector activity (or value-added) perspective to final demand perspective, and (iii) the exclusion of related machinery and equipment purchases in the final demand. Value-added coefficients eliminate double-counted terms as it translates output results into value-added terms. Judging from the value-added coefficients of the PRC for 2017, one would expect that implementing this change would be responsible for most of the decline in the figures. The change in the evaluation of real estate services, however, would explain the second-most notable decline in the figure. This is primarily because the position of real estate services is more upstream (i.e., larger output goes to business demand) than downstream. The elimination of final demand for machinery and equipment previously included by Rogoff and Yang (2020) would also reduce the new result, albeit only by a few percentage points.

The above factors all reduce the measured size of the real estate sector. They are however largely offset by other changes that increase its measured size. First, a larger 42×42 input–output table was used by Rogoff and Yang (2021), which adds back the value of linkages (or, more generally, information) lost in the previous 17×17 table due to aggregation bias. Second, in their addendum, Rogoff and Yang no longer deduct 1 from their output multipliers. That is, the direct impacts were now included in the measurement. Third and most importantly, the value of final demand for construction-related investments for real estate development was doubled. Rogoff and Yang (2021) noted that the previous demand levels used to evaluate construction demand differed from fixed capital formation in that the latter does not include housing appreciation and intangible costs. This previous value for construction demand was taken directly from Table 19–5 of the NBS Statistical Yearbook (NBS 2017). In addition, Xu et al. (2015) noted that "the real estate investment does not include the value added of commercial housing sales, i.e. the difference between the sales value and investment cost of commercial housing, which is however included in the GFCF." Therefore, in the updated calculations, Rogoff and Yang (2021) used the real estate-related proportion of construction in Tilton et al. (2021), which implied an upward revision from the previously derived 36% (as taken from the NBS data) to 72% of construction final demand.

Lastly, the GDP denominator was also changed from the figures in the national accounts series to the figures derived from the NBS input–output table. This did not impact the measured levels, but slightly changed the final ratio presented. Ideally the GDP figures are consistent. In the case of the PRC, the GDP figures from the IOT were higher than the national accounts figures, which therefore enlarged the denominator moderately, thereby producing lower ratios.

The estimates in this special chapter (i.e., 21.3% for the PRC) take a similar approach to Tilton et al. (2021) and to the revised estimates by Rogoff and Yang in their 2021 addendum. The measurement scope in principle is the same. That is, the property sector's size relative to the economy is equal to direct and indirect value-added contributions embodied in the final demand for real estate services, and all construction demand except for civil engineering. To briefly summarize the changes, Table A6.2 compares methods and data between old and new estimates.

Table A6.2: Differences in the Measurement of the Property Sector in the People's Republic of China

	Rogoff and Yang (2020)[1]	Rogoff and Yang (2021)[2]	ADB (as cited in *The Economist* 2021)[3]	ADB (2022)[4]
Property sector share to GDP (Year), without imports (%)	24.8% (2016)	21.9% (2016); 22.5% (2017); 23.3% (2018); 23.4% (2019); 23.6% (2020)	13.8% (2017)	22.5% (2017);[5] 21.3% (2017)[6]
Input-Output Table used	17-sector 2017 IOT from NBS	42-sector 2017 and 2018 IOT from NBS	17-sector 2017 IOT from NBS	42-sector 2018 IOT from NBS
Construction demand	Construction and installation for real estate development, Table 19-5 of NBS Statistical Yearbook	Construction final demand in the input-output table (72% of total), excluding infrastructure-related	Following Rogoff and Yang (2020); Construction and installation for real estate development, Table 19-5 of NBS Statistical Yearbook	Final demand for building construction, construction and installation, and building decoration, renovation, and other construction services
Proportion of construction final demand included (%)	35.9%	72.0%	35.9%; Following Rogoff and Yang (2020)	71.6%
Machinery and equipment demand	Purchases of machinery and instruments for real estate development, Table 19-5 NBS Statistical Yearbook	None	Purchases of machinery and instruments for real estate development, Table 19-5 NBS Statistical Yearbook; Following Rogoff and Yang (2020)	None
Treatment of real estate services	Value-added of real estate services	Final demand for real estate services	Final demand for real estate services	Final demand for real estate services
Methodology	GDP share of real estate related activity $= (v_{rea} + (\mathbf{L} - \mathbf{I})\mathbf{y}_c) / GDP_{NAS}$	GDP share of real estate related activity $= [\hat{\mathbf{v}}_c (\mathbf{I} - \mathbf{A}_d + \mathbf{A}_m)^{-1} (\mathbf{f}_p - \mathbf{A}_m)^{-1} (\mathbf{f}_p - \mathbf{A}_m (\mathbf{I} - \mathbf{A}_d)^{-1} \mathbf{y}_{c+r})] / GDP_{IOT}$	GDP share of real estate related activity $= [\hat{\mathbf{v}}_c (\mathbf{I} - \mathbf{A}_d)^{-1} \mathbf{y}_{c+r}] / GDP_{NAS}$	GDP share of real estate related activity $= [\hat{\mathbf{v}}_c (\mathbf{I} - \mathbf{A}_d)^{-1} \mathbf{y}_p] / GDP_{IOT}$

$\mathbf{A}_d$ = direct input coefficients matrix of domestic inputs; $\mathbf{A}_m$ = direct input coefficients matrix of imported inputs; ADB = Asian Development Bank; GDP = gross domestic product; GDP_{IOT} = derived from input-output tables; GDP_{NAS} = GDP from national accounts statistics; $\mathbf{I}$ = identity matrix; IOT = input-output table; $\mathbf{L}$ = Leontief inverse; NBS = National Bureau of Statistics (People's Republic of China); v_{rea} = value-added of real estate services sector in the national accounts; $\hat{\mathbf{v}}_c$ = diagonalized vector of value-added to output coefficients; $\mathbf{y}_c$ = final demand for construction investments and purchase of machinery and instruments for real estate development obtained from Table 19-5 of NBS Statistical Yearbook; $\mathbf{y}_{c+r}$ = final demand vector containing values for $\mathbf{y}_c$ and real estate services; $\mathbf{y}_p$ = final demand vector containing values for construction (excluding civil engineering) and real estate services.

Notes:

1 K. Rogoff and Y. Yang. 2020. Peak China Housing. NBER Working Paper Series. No. 27697. Cambridge: National Bureau of Economic Research. http://www.nber.org/papers/w27697 (Accessed 11 November 2021).

2 K. Rogoff and Y. Yang. 2021. The Size of China's Real Estate Sector. Scholars at Harvard. 21 December. https://scholar.harvard.edu/files/rogoff/files/the_size_of_chinas_real_estate_sector_december_21_2021.pdf.

3 As cited in *The Economist*. 2021. Measuring the Universe's Most Important Sector. 27 November.

4 Estimates made by the Asian Development Bank Input-Output Study Team.

5 Using NBS 42-sector input-output for 2017.

6 Using ADB Multiregional Input-Output Table for 2017.

Source: Compiled by the Asian Development Bank Input-Output Study Team.

To further illustrate the differences, the previous Rogoff and Yang (2020) estimate for 2016 (which was about 24.8% of the PRC's GDP) was first replicated using the same approach, national input-output table (NIOT), and NBS yearbook data for 2017 (Figure A6.1). This ensured that the NBS data on real estate investments were consistent with the period represented in the NIOT. In 2017, Rogoff and Yang's (2020) methodology and data would result in a ratio of 23.7% (Figure A6.1, second bar).

Thereafter, the same methodology and data were replicated, but using the larger 42×42 input–output matrix of the NBS. The change in result between the 17-sector and 42-sector NIOT is a measure of the aggregation bias in the data. The resulting figure indicates that the use of a larger input–output matrix will revise the estimates upward by 0.5 percentage points from the previous number (Figure A6.1, third bar).

The fourth bar in Figure A6.1 indicates the change in Rogoff and Yang's approach for accounting real estate services. Previously, real estate services' value-added from the NBS yearbook was added to final demand for relevant construction. In the new approach, services are now evaluated as final demand. Note that this is one of three main observations considered in the initial ADB estimate. Since real estate services are relatively positioned upstream, most of their outputs are consumed by other businesses, and less by final consumers. Therefore, when real estate services were moved to the final demand side from value-added, the overall share of real estate-related activity went down by about 3.7 percentage points.

Value-added coefficients were also adopted in the new approach of Rogoff and Yang (2021), which is corollary to the issue of double-counting observed by the ADB study. The effect of this change in methodology is isolated in the fifth bar from the left of Figure A6.1. This was calculated by retaining previously discussed changes, but only changing the model specification so that value-added coefficients were used. This change in method exhibited the largest effect on the results, especially considering the low value-added ratios observed in several sectors of the PRC.

Rogoff and Yang (2021) also seemed to apply the Leontief inverse without deducting 1 from the output multipliers, as originally performed in their 2020 paper. This change increased the results upward by 6.5 percentage points in the sixth bar of Figure A6.1. This considerably high difference corresponds to the returned direct value-added attributed to the final demand for real estate construction and purchases of machinery and equipment.

At this point, all major ADB observations were already accounted for in the results, which netted to about 14.0%. This is slightly higher than the replication of the ADB estimate of 13.8% since the old estimates are using the 17×17 table instead of the 42×42 input–output matrix, in keeping with Rogoff and Yang (2020).

Another information gain from the 42×42 IOT was the availability of a detailed imports matrix. In the previous Rogoff and Yang (2020) paper, the imports were deducted from the results by using the ratio of imports to the total use by product. This approach implicitly assumed that the respective shares of import and domestically sourced products were the same for all users for each type of product. The use of the detailed imports matrix eliminated the need for such an assumption. This imports matrix was not available for the 17×17 table, but was available for the 42×42 table used in the revised estimates. The impact of using this disaggregated information on imports is shown in the seventh bar of Figure A6.1, which slightly changed the results upward by 0.2 percentage points from the previous estimate.

The succeeding eighth to 10th bars of Figure 6A.1 detail the impacts from the change in demand composition and levels. First, purchases of machinery and equipment for real estate development were no longer counted in the final demand in the 2021 paper. This led the final ratio to decrease by 0.2 percentage points from the previous estimate (bar 8). Second, the final demand for real estate construction was revised, citing that the previous figure used was not in congruence with the concept of gross fixed capital formation, as discussed in Xu et al. (2015). Rogoff and Yang (2021) instead used the final demand for construction multiplied by the proportion of 72% to deduct civil engineering construction following Tilton et al. (2021). As previously mentioned, the new amount was double the previous estimate in Table 19-5 of the Statistical Yearbook (NBS 2017). Hence, this change considerably enlarged the final ratio again by 8.5 percentage points (bar 9).

The 10th bar of Figure A6.1 documents the impact of choosing IOT-based estimates of GDP as denominators in lieu of the previously used GDP estimates from national accounts statistics in the NBS yearbook. The difference in those estimates resulted in a marginal difference of 0.1 percentage points in the results (bar 10).

Collectively, these changes in the method, input–output information, and demand levels resulted in the final figure of 22.5% (bar 11), which is exactly the estimate of Rogoff and Yang (2021, pp. 5) for 2017. The new methodology is mathematically aligned with the previous ADB estimate. This exercise, however, revealed that the results are sensitive to the proportions and amount of construction final demand evaluated. Hence, a precise definition of in-scope construction and real estate services demand should be carefully described in the estimation process. In the main, the measurement objective remains the same, and that real estate activity is defined as the total amount of domestic value-added embodied in the demand for real estate services and construction of dwellings and nonresidential buildings.

Figure A6.1: Change in Share of Real Estate Activities to Total Gross Domestic Product for 2017, Comparing 2020 and 2021 Methodologies
(%)

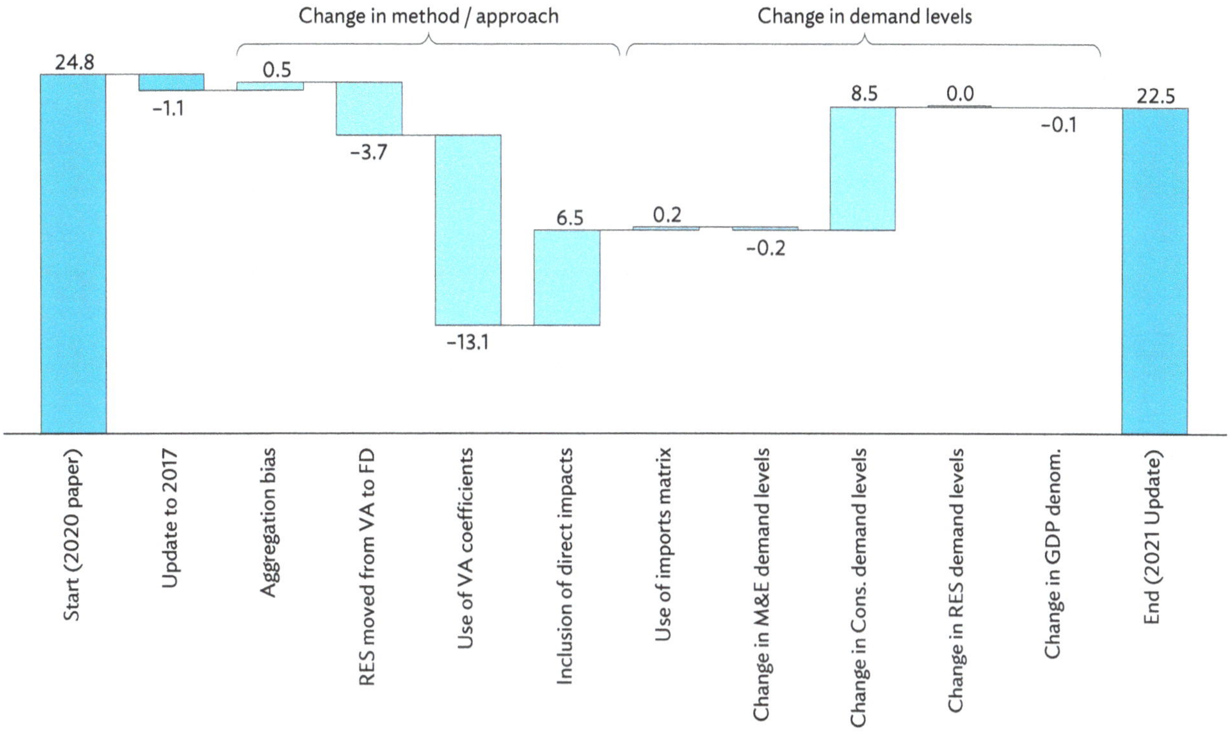

Cons = construction; FD = final demand; GDP = gross domestic product; M&E = machinery and equipment; RES = real estate services; VA = (gross) value-added.

Sources: Calculations by the Asian Development Bank Input–Output Study Team using data from the National Bureau of Statistics, People's Republic of China, and estimation approaches by Rogoff and Yang (2020; 2021); K. Rogoff and Y. Yang. 2021. The Size of China's Real Estate Sector. *Scholars at Harvard*. 21 December. https://scholar.harvard.edu/files/rogoff/files/the_size_of_chinas_real_estate_sector_december_21_2021.pdf; and K. Rogoff and Y. Yang. 2020. Peak China Housing. *NBER Working Paper Series*. No. 27697. Cambridge: National Bureau of Economic Research. http://www.nber.org/papers/w27697.

Click here for figure data

In conclusion, the estimates from Rogoff and Yang (2020; 2021), while showing close results, had substantive differences in terms of methodology and data. Notable among the revisions were the use of value-added coefficients and changes in the demand levels for construction. Meanwhile, the differences in ADB estimates, at least for the PRC, were explained by the change in demand levels for in-scope construction activity. As of writing, these seemingly different estimation processes are now aligned in terms of input–output methodology. For cross-economy comparison, this publication used the ADB Multiregional Input–Output Tables for its estimates of property sector shares to the economy.

References

L. Agnello, V. Castro, and R.M. Sousa. 2020. The Housing Cycle: What Role for Mortgage Market Development and Housing Finance? *Journal of Real Estate Finance and Economics*. No. 61, 607–670. https://doi.org/10.1007/s11146-019-09705-z.

J. Aizenman and Y. Jinjarak. 2013. *Real Estate Valuation, Current Account, and Credit Growth Patterns Before and After the 2008–2009 Crisis*. Tokyo: ADB Institute.

Asian Development Bank (ADB). 2021. Key Indicators Database. https://kidb.adb.org/ (accessed March 2022).

A. Baum, A. Saull, and F. Braesemann. 2020. PropTech 2020: the Future of Real Estate. University of Oxford. https://www.sbs.ox.ac.uk/sites/default/files/2020-02/proptech2020.pdf.

M. N. Baily, R. E. Litan, and M. S. Johnson. 2008. The Origins of a Financial Crisis. Fixing Finance Series – Paper. No. 3. The Brookings Institution.

Construction Industry Development Board (CIDB) Malaysia. 2017. Malaysia Country Report. 22nd AsiaConstruct Conference. Seoul, Republic of Korea. https://www.cidb.gov.my/sites/default/files/2020-04/Malaysia----Country-Report-2017--22nd-Asia-Construct.pdf.

D. K. Das, A. A. Erumban, S. Aggarwal, and P. C. Das. 2020. Measuring Productivity at the Industry Level: The India KLEMS Database Data Manual (version 7). Reserve Bank of India. https://www.rbi.org.in/Scripts/KLEMS.aspx.

The Economist. 2021. Measuring the Universe's Most Important Sector. 27 November.

A. Fuster, M. Plosser, P. Schnabl, and J. Vickery. 2018. The Role of Technology in Mortgage Lending. Federal Reserve Bank of New York Staff Report. No. 836.

Government of India, Planning Commission. 2002. Tenth Five Year Plan 2002-2007. New Delhi.

Government of Japan, Ministry of Land, Infrastructure, Transport and Tourism (MLITT). 2015. Japanese Real Estate Market, Today, Tokyo: Land Economy & Construction Industries Bureau.

Government of the United States, Bureau of Labor Statistics (BLS). 2021. Employment and output by industry. 8 September. https://www.bls.gov/emp/tables/industry-employment-and-output.htm (accessed March 2022).

Government of the United States, Financial Crisis Inquiry Commission (FCIC). 2011. *The Financial Crisis Inquiry Report*.

International Monetary Fund (IMF). 2011. Macroprudential Policy: An Organizing Framework.

F. Lequiller and D. Blades. 2014. Understanding National Accounts (Second Edition). Organisation for Economic Co-operation and Development (OECD) Publishing.

W. Maennig. 2012. Size and Impact of Real Estate Sector and Its Role for Business Cycles and Growth. In T. Just and W. Maennig, eds. *Understanding German Real Estate Markets. Management for Professionals.* Berlin, Heidelberg: Springer. https://doi.org/10.1007/978-3-642-23611-2_2.

R. Miller and P. Blair. 2009. *Input–Output Analysis: Foundations and Extensions* (second edition). Cambridge: Cambridge University Press.

R. Miller and M. Lahr. 2001. A Taxonomy of Extractions. In *Regional Science Perspectives in Economic Analysis: A Festschrift in Memory of Benjamin H. Stevens.* Amsterdam: Elsevier Science. pp. 407–441.

National Bureau of Statistics (NBS) of the People's Republic of China. 2017. Statistical Yearbook. http://www.stats.gov.cn/tjsj/ndsj/2017/indexeh.htm.

NBS. 2018. Statistical Yearbook. http://www.stats.gov.cn/tjsj/ndsj/2018/indexeh.htm.

NBS. 2019. Statistical Yearbook. http://www.stats.gov.cn/tjsj/ndsj/2019/indexeh.htm.

PricewaterhouseCoopers (PWC) and the Urban Land Institute (ULI). 2018. Emerging Trends in Real Estate Asia Pacific 2019. Washington, D.C.

Reserve Bank of India (RBI). 2021. Measuring Productivity at the Industry Level – The India KLEMS Database. https://www.rbi.org.in/Scripts/KLEMS.aspx (accessed March 2022).

K. Rogoff and Y. Yang. 2020. Peak China Housing. NBER Working Paper Series. No. 27697. Cambridge: National Bureau of Economic Research. http://www.nber.org/papers/w27697 (Accessed 11 November 2021).

K. Rogoff and Y. Yang. 2021. The Size of China's Real Estate Sector. *Scholars at Harvard.* 21 December. https://scholar.harvard.edu/files/rogoff/files/the_size_of_chinas_real_estate_sector_december_21_2021.pdf.

A. Tilton, J. Sequeira, H. Shan, G. Kwon, H. Hu, M. Wei, and X. Chen. 2021. China Data Insights: How Big is China's Property Sector? *Goldman Sachs.* 11 October.

M. P. Timmer, E. Dietzenbacher, B. Los, R. Stehrer, and G. J. de Vries. 2015. An Illustrated User Guide to the World Input–Output Database: the Case of Global Automotive Production. *Review of International Economics.* 23. pp. 575–605.

X. Xu, H. Jia, and J. Li. 2015. On the Role Played by Real Estate in the Growth of China's National Economy. *Social Sciences in China.* 1. pp. 84–101.

Economy Profiles

7

This chapter presents a high-level overview of economic indicators for each of the 25 economies of Asia and the Pacific covered in the ADB Multiregional Input–Output database. The profiles are intended to provide users with easily accessible information on the trends, structure, and linkages of domestic and international trade-related activities of each economy. The full dataset for these analyses can be downloaded from the publication's web page.

7.1 How to Read the Economy Profiles

1 Bangladesh
South Asia

2 Basic Economic Indicators

3

Economic Aggregates ($ million)	2000	2007	2010	2013	2016	2019	2020
Value-added at basic price	43,871	75,987	106,116	142,066	203,914	279,759	307,217
Gross output	73,355	130,220	184,902	254,976	364,245	513,497	566,584
Total intermediate inputs	28,840	52,654	76,647	109,875	155,860	227,428	252,824
Taxes less subsidies on products	645	1,578	2,139	3,035	4,472	6,310	6,544
International transport margins	0	0	0	0	0	0	0
CIF/FOB adjustment	0	0	0	0	0	0	0
Direct purchases abroad by residents	0	0	0	0	0	0	0
Purchases by nonresidents on the domestic territory	0	0	0	0	0	0	0
Household final consumption expenditure	31,712	50,719	70,226	91,443	125,714	182,379	200,711
Final consumption expenditure by NPISHs	0	0	0	0	0	0	0
Government final consumption expenditure	2,076	4,163	5,607	7,644	12,619	18,392	20,069
Gross fixed capital formation	8,770	17,237	24,811	34,228	54,098	81,235	90,699
Changes in inventories	0	0	0	0	0	0	0
Total final demand	42,558	72,120	100,644	133,316	192,431	282,006	311,478
Exports	5,436	13,623	18,349	29,992	36,682	46,131	44,090
Imports	7,851	18,360	24,929	40,939	46,647	64,310	63,652

4 South Asia

2 Domestic Linkages

Indicator and Top 3 Sectors, 2020	2000	2007	2010	2013	2016	2019	2020
Simple value-added multiplier							
Real estate	0.99	0.99	0.99	0.99	0.99	0.98	0.98
Retail trade	0.98	0.98	0.99	0.98	0.98	0.98	0.98
Sale of motor vehicles	0.99	0.97	0.97	0.97	0.98	0.97	0.97
Type I value-added multiplier							
Refined fuels	3.17	4.00	4.10	3.99	3.88	4.18	4.27
Air transport	2.87	3.76	3.83	3.67	3.93	3.74	3.88
Food and beverages	3.28	3.39	3.38	3.32	3.32	3.34	3.57
Direct backward linkage							
Refined fuels	0.64	0.68	0.69	0.67	0.63	0.67	0.68
Food and beverages	0.65	0.65	0.66	0.64	0.66	0.63	0.66
Hotels and restaurants	0.60	0.61	0.65	0.61	0.63	0.61	0.62
Complete hypothetical extraction (backward)							
Refined fuels	1.92	1.96	1.99	1.93	1.91	1.98	2.02
Air transport	1.84	1.82	1.85	1.81	1.90	1.89	1.94
Hotels and restaurants	1.86	1.86	1.93	1.85	1.91	1.89	1.92

5 South Asia

2 International Linkages

Indicator and Top 3 Sectors, 2020	2000	2007	2010	2013	2016	2019	2020
Self-sufficiency ratio							
Textiles	1.71	1.94	1.96	1.84	1.86	1.64	1.53
Business activities, NEC	0.98	1.11	1.12	1.11	1.10	1.44	1.53
Leather	1.09	1.53	1.22	1.68	1.88	1.23	1.21
Import-to-input ratio							
Metals	0.14	0.17	0.16	0.19	0.14	0.26	0.24
Paper	0.12	0.14	0.14	0.16	0.15	0.24	0.21
Air transport	0.17	0.22	0.23	0.23	0.19	0.23	0.21
Export-to-output ratio							
Textiles	0.49	0.55	0.57	0.55	0.57	0.51	0.46
Air transport	0.02	0.00	0.04	0.00	0.00	0.35	0.41
Business activities, NEC	0.00	0.10	0.12	0.11	0.10	0.31	0.35
Domestic inputs share to output							
Refined fuels	0.64	0.68	0.69	0.67	0.63	0.67	0.68
Food and beverages	0.65	0.65	0.66	0.64	0.66	0.63	0.66
Hotels and restaurants	0.60	0.61	0.65	0.61	0.63	0.61	0.62

1 The **name of the economy** and its **subregional grouping** are indicated in this section of each profile. The profiles are presented in alphabetical order and cover the following ADB member economies: Bangladesh; Bhutan; Brunei Darussalam; Cambodia; Fiji; Hong Kong, China; India; Indonesia; Japan; Kazakhstan; the Republic of Korea; the Kyrgyz Republic; the Lao People's Democratic Republic; Malaysia, Maldives; Mongolia; Nepal; Pakistan; the People's Republic of China; the Philippines; Singapore; Sri Lanka; Taipei,China; Thailand; and Viet Nam.

2 The **major indicators** presented in tabular form are indicated in the top right corner of each table. These tables cover basic economic indicators, domestic multipliers and linkages, and international linkages for each economy.

3 The **Basic Economic Indicators** table contains main aggregates commonly compiled in national accounts statistics, valued in current million United States (US) dollars. While based on official national accounts statistics, note that these values may deviate from published data due to rebasing, levels of sectoral aggregation and classification, data confrontation, and rebalancing, among other factors.

4 The **Domestic Linkages** table shows the various indexes of linkages and multipliers among domestic sectors and their corresponding multipliers derived from national input–output tables. The sectors shown refer to the top three sectors with the highest values based on the corresponding indices for 2020. The complete description of each sector can be found in Table 7.1.

5 The **International Linkages** table consists of the analytical indicators relevant to each economy's international trade activity. This section shows the top three sectors with the largest value based on the respective indicator for 2020. The complete description of each sector can be found in Table 7.1.

Each economy profile also provides a visual representation of select input–output indicators, dividing these into three sections that correspond to the tabular format.

7.2 Economy Rankings

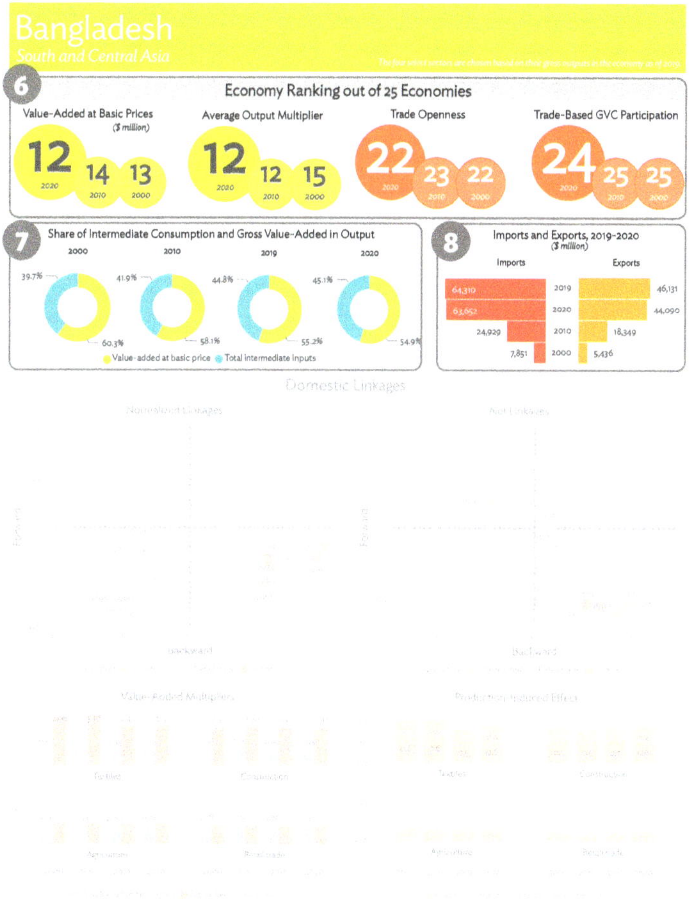

6 This subsection shows the rankings of each economy for 2019 and 2020, in the context of the other 24 economies from across Asia and the Pacific. Five core economic indicators are presented: gross domestic product, average output multiplier, trade openness, trade-based global value chain (GVC) participation rate, and export diversification. The average output multipliers are calculated as the arithmetic average across all 35 sectors' output multipliers.

7 This subsection visualizes key economic aggregates derived from the input-output tables. Specifically, these are the respective economy-wide shares of intermediate consumption at purchasers' prices and gross value-added at basic prices to the gross output for 2019 and 2020 in the production account.

8 This subsection summarizes the economy's trade levels as reported in the input–output tables under the expenditure account. Both imports and exports are shown in gross terms at current million US dollars.

7.3 Domestic Linkages

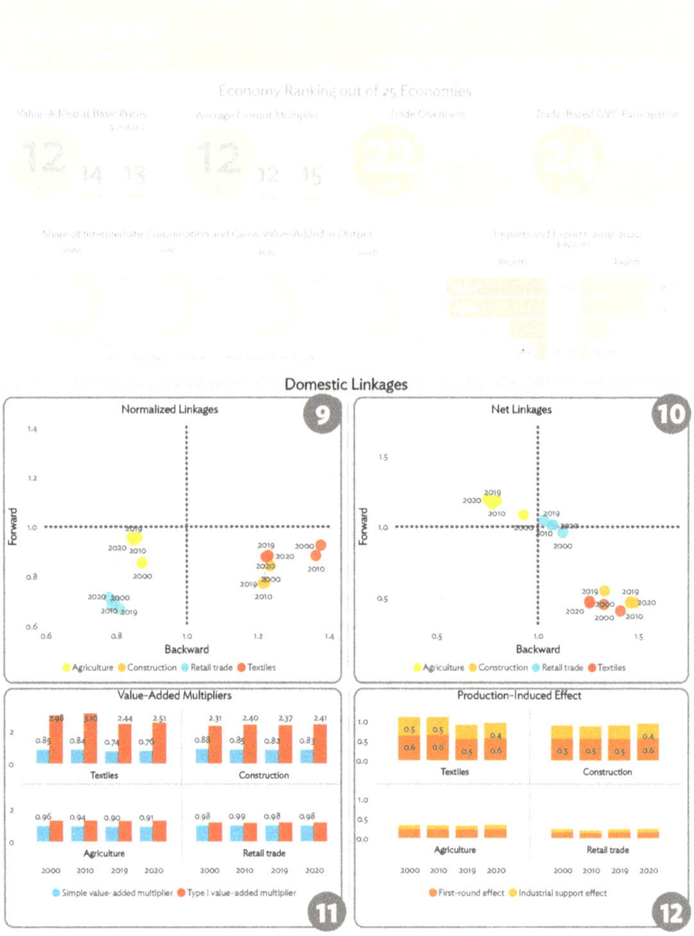

9 This subsection visualizes the normalized forward and backward linkages of four select sectors, based on the key sector analysis described in Miller and Blair (2009). For each economy, the linkages are only shown for sectors with the highest gross outputs in 2019. Sectors that exhibit normalized linkages higher than 1 are considered as having "strong" or higher-than-average dependencies on other domestic sectors.

10 This subsection outlines the net forward and backward linkages of four select sectors, based on the key sector analysis described in Oosterhaven (2019). For each economy, the linkages are only shown for sectors with the highest gross outputs in 2019. Compared to normalized linkages, net linkages are adjusted for the sector's relative size in the economy.

11 This subsection shows the simple and type I value-added multipliers of select sectors for 2000, 2010, 2019, and 2020. Simple value-added multipliers quantify the total value-added (or income) accrued in the economy resulting from the sector's unit increase in final demand. Type I value-added multipliers refer to the ratio of total value-added accrued to the initial value-added effect of a unit change in the sector's final demand.

12 This subsection displays the production-induced effects, a subset of simple output multipliers, for select sectors for 2000, 2010, 2019, and 2020. Each bar represents the extra output required (that is, the output required other than the value of demand itself) for every unit change in the demand for the corresponding sector's product. Production-induced effects can be further presented as a sum of first-round and industrial support effects. First-round effects refer to the direct inputs required by the sector to produce each one-dollar unit of its output. Industrial support effects sum the round-by-round production effects to fulfill these direct inputs from the rest of the economy.

7.4 International Linkages

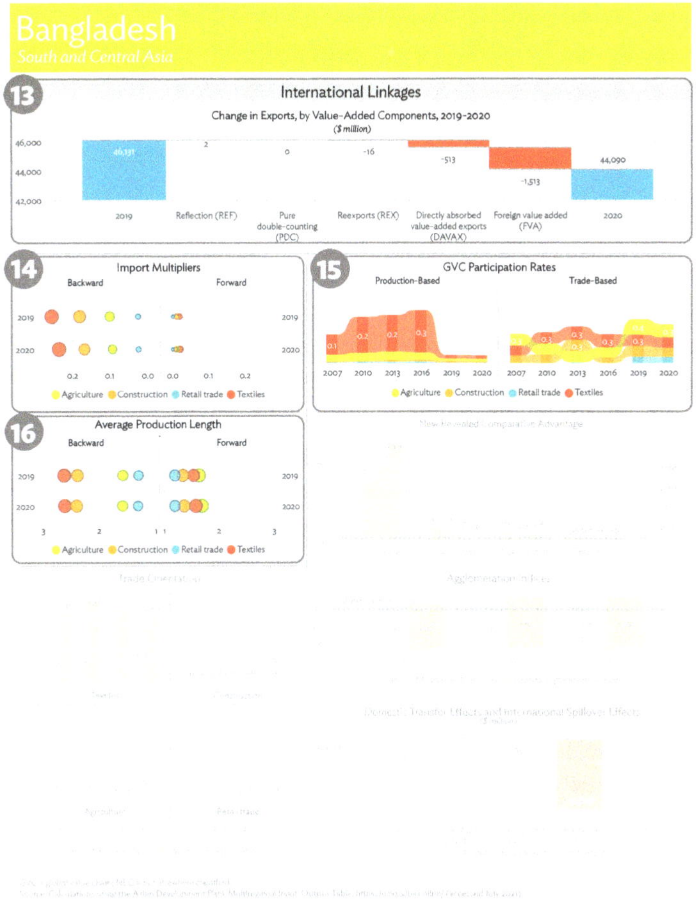

13 The subsection presents the indicators related to international linkages for 2019 and 2020. This subsection analyzes the change in the economy's exports from 2019 to 2020 by showing changes in the economy's individual components. Exports are decomposed based on the method by Borin and Mancini (2019). Values are shown in current million US dollars.

14 This subsection presents import multipliers or leakages. For backward import multipliers, sectors farthest to the left exhibit larger dependence on foreign sectors for inputs. For forward import multipliers, sectors farthest to the right depict larger dependence on foreign sectors for demand for its products. The size of each dot reflects the values of import multipliers.

15 This subsection depicts movements in the GVC participation rates of select sectors. Sectors that rate higher are stacked on top of sectors with lower participation rates. Taller data points represent larger participation rates. Trade-based participation rates are based on the terminology by Borin and Mancini (2019), while production-based participation rates are adapted from Wang et al. (2017a).

16 This subsection visualizes average production lengths (APLs) of select sectors for 2019 and 2020. The APLs are calculated using the method of Wang et al. (2017b). For backward APL, final products of sectors farthest to the left undergo longer upstream production stages compared to other sectors in the chart. For forward APL, rightmost sectors produce goods and services that undergo longer production stages before reaching their final use.

17 This subsection presents new revealed comparative advantages based on value-added exports for select sectors for 2000, 2010, 2019, and 2020. Sectors whose index for new revealed comparative advantage exceeds 1 are said to have specialization in this export activity (that is, those sectors exhibit comparative advantage compared to the world average).

18 This subsection shows the trade orientation of the economy's four select sectors for 2000, 2010, 2019, and 2020. Two types of trade are distinguished. Export-to-output ratios suggest a sector's degree of sales dependence to international markets. Import-to-input ratios indicate a sector's degree of supply dependence from foreign producers.

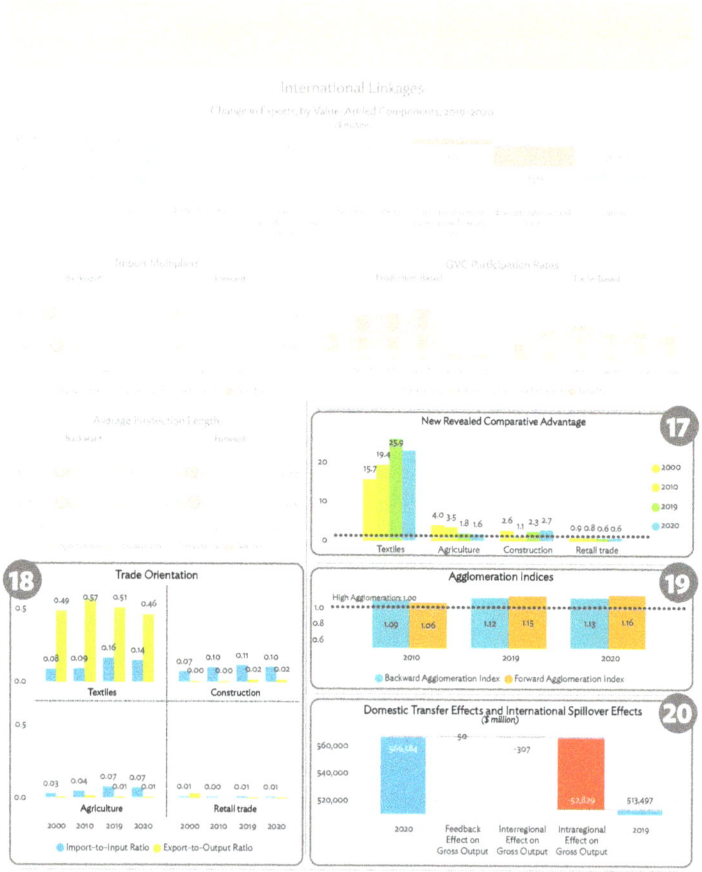

GVC = global value chain; NEC = not elsewhere classified.
Source: Calculations using the Asian Development Bank Multiregional Input-Output Table. https://mrio.adbx.online/ (accessed July 2021).

19 This subsection visualizes the domestic agglomeration indices at the aggregate economy-level for 2010, 2019, and 2020. These indices reflect the sourcing (backward) and supply (forward) decisions of sectors in the economy. Values larger than 1 indicate that domestic sectors transact more with other domestic sectors than foreign counterparts.

20 This subsection decomposes the changes in output from 2019 to 2020, based on intraregional (or domestic) transfer effects (M1), interregional effects (M2), and feedback effects (M3). The values are presented in current million US dollars.

Table 7.1: Sector Title Abbreviations

Sector Description	Short title
Agriculture, hunting, forestry, and fishing	Agriculture
Mining and quarrying	Mining
Food, beverages, and tobacco	Food and beverages
Textiles and textile products	Textiles
Leather, leather products, and footwear	Leather
Wood and products of wood and cork	Wood
Pulp, paper, paper products, printing, and publishing	Paper
Coke, refined petroleum, and nuclear fuel	Refined fuels
Chemicals and chemical products	Chemicals
Rubber and plastics	Rubber and plastics
Other nonmetallic minerals	Minerals, nec
Basic metals and fabricated metal	Metals
Machinery, nec	Machinery, nec
Electrical and optical equipment	Electricals
Transport equipment	Transport equipment
Manufacturing, nec; recycling	Manufacturing, nec
Electricity, gas, and water supply	Utilities
Construction	Construction
Sale, maintenance, and repair of motor vehicles and motorcycles; retail sale of fuel	Sale of motor vehicles
Wholesale trade and commission trade, except of motor vehicles and motorcycles	Wholesale trade
Retail trade, except of motor vehicles and motorcycles; repair of household goods	Retail trade
Hotels and restaurants	Hotels and restaurants
Inland transport	Inland transport
Water transport	Water transport
Air transport	Air transport
Other supporting and auxiliary transport activities; activities of travel agencies	Transport activities, nec
Post and telecommunications	Telecommunications
Financial intermediation	Finance
Real estate activities	Real estate
Renting of M&Eq and other business activities	Business activities, nec
Public administration and defense; compulsory social security	Public administration
Education	Education
Health and social work	Health and social work
Other community, social, and personal services	Personal services, nec
Private households with employed persons	Private households

M&Eq = machinery and equipment, nec = not elsewhere classified.
Source: Asian Development Bank Multiregional Input–Output Database Team.

Bangladesh

South and Central Asia

Basic Economic Indicators

Economic Aggregates ($ million)	2000	2007	2010	2013	2016	2019	2020
Value-added at basic price	43,871	75,987	109,305	146,122	209,439	286,535	314,611
Gross output	73,355	130,220	188,091	259,032	369,771	520,273	573,979
Total intermediate inputs	28,840	52,654	76,647	109,875	155,860	227,428	252,824
Taxes less subsidies on products	645	1,578	2,139	3,035	4,472	6,310	6,544
International transport margins	0	0	0	0	0	0	0
CIF/FOB adjustment	0	0	0	0	0	0	0
Direct purchases abroad by residents	0	0	0	0	0	0	0
Purchases by nonresidents on the domestic territory	0	0	0	0	0	0	0
Household final consumption expenditure	31,712	50,719	73,415	95,499	131,239	189,155	208,105
Final consumption expenditure by NPISHs	0	0	0	0	0	0	0
Government final consumption expenditure	2,076	4,163	5,607	7,644	12,619	18,392	20,069
Gross fixed capital formation	8,770	17,237	24,811	34,228	54,098	81,235	90,699
Changes in inventories	0	0	0	0	0	0	0
Total final demand	42,558	72,120	103,833	137,372	197,956	288,782	318,873
Exports	5,436	13,623	18,349	29,992	36,682	46,131	44,090
Imports	7,851	18,374	25,030	41,076	46,937	64,533	63,863

Economic Aggregates, Top 3 Sectors ($ million)	2000	2007	2010	2013	2016	2019	2020
Value-added at basic price							
Agriculture	11,195	14,214	19,468	23,783	30,945	38,174	41,013
Retail trade	2,500	7,319	11,425	14,735	20,267	28,431	31,624
Construction	3,379	4,866	7,103	10,554	16,065	23,256	26,446
Gross output							
Construction	9,185	13,997	20,433	30,360	46,210	68,459	78,025
Textiles	9,487	17,582	24,997	43,040	53,527	72,313	71,944
Agriculture	15,089	19,397	27,042	33,514	43,514	54,702	58,885
Total intermediate inputs							
Construction	5,681	9,027	13,186	19,580	29,793	44,710	51,056
Textiles	6,773	12,798	18,193	31,132	38,523	50,212	50,026
Food and beverages	2,036	4,199	5,843	8,915	13,724	19,519	22,983
Total final demand							
Construction	6,500	10,777	16,189	23,399	34,525	51,825	57,738
Retail trade	2,630	7,495	11,556	14,549	19,889	29,807	33,245
Agriculture	10,378	11,687	15,821	18,782	23,745	31,759	32,722
Exports							
Textiles	4,609	9,745	14,138	23,605	30,266	36,763	33,257
Business activities, NEC	1	192	362	430	599	2,583	3,279
Construction	6	35	8	44	127	1,124	1,351
Imports							
Metals	754	2,877	2,717	3,854	4,906	9,262	9,653
Transport equipment	1,147	1,735	3,268	6,895	7,568	8,361	8,262
Textiles	671	1,223	1,910	3,952	5,553	8,646	8,196

Domestic Linkages

Indicator and Top 3 Sectors, 2020	2000	2007	2010	2013	2016	2019	2020
First-round effect							
Refined fuels	0.64	0.68	0.69	0.67	0.63	0.67	0.68
Food and beverages	0.65	0.65	0.66	0.64	0.66	0.63	0.66
Hotels and restaurants	0.60	0.61	0.65	0.61	0.63	0.61	0.62
Industrial support effect							
Metals	0.40	0.37	0.43	0.36	0.44	0.36	0.41
Textiles	0.47	0.39	0.45	0.45	0.44	0.36	0.39
Leather	0.33	0.29	0.32	0.29	0.29	0.35	0.38
Production-induced effect							
Refined fuels	0.92	0.97	0.99	0.93	0.91	0.98	1.02
Metals	1.03	1.00	1.08	0.97	1.11	0.91	0.99
Leather	0.90	0.86	0.89	0.83	0.84	0.95	0.98

continued on next page.

continued.

Bangladesh

South and Central Asia

Domestic Linkages

Indicator and Top 3 Sectors, 2020	2000	2007	2010	2013	2016	2019	2020
Simple value-added multiplier							
Real estate	0.99	0.99	0.99	0.99	0.99	0.98	0.98
Retail trade	0.98	0.98	0.99	0.98	0.98	0.98	0.98
Sale of motor vehicles	0.99	0.97	0.97	0.97	0.98	0.97	0.97
Type I value-added multiplier							
Refined fuels	3.17	4.00	4.10	3.99	3.88	4.18	4.27
Air transport	2.87	3.76	3.83	3.67	3.93	3.74	3.88
Food and beverages	3.28	3.39	3.38	3.32	3.32	3.34	3.57
Direct backward linkage							
Refined fuels	0.64	0.68	0.69	0.67	0.63	0.67	0.68
Food and beverages	0.65	0.65	0.66	0.64	0.66	0.63	0.66
Hotels and restaurants	0.60	0.61	0.65	0.61	0.63	0.61	0.62
Complete hypothetical extraction (backward)							
Refined fuels	1.92	1.96	1.99	1.93	1.91	1.98	2.02
Air transport	1.84	1.82	1.85	1.81	1.90	1.89	1.94
Hotels and restaurants	1.86	1.86	1.93	1.85	1.91	1.89	1.92
Partial hypothetical extraction (backward)							
Refined fuels	0.92	0.97	0.99	0.93	0.91	0.98	1.02
Air transport	0.87	0.86	0.88	0.83	0.92	0.90	0.95
Hotels and restaurants	0.87	0.87	0.94	0.86	0.92	0.90	0.93
Total backward linkage							
Refined fuels	1.92	1.97	1.99	1.93	1.91	1.98	2.02
Metals	2.03	2.00	2.08	1.97	2.11	1.91	1.99
Leather	1.90	1.86	1.89	1.83	1.84	1.95	1.98
Direct forward linkage							
Mining	0.93	0.96	0.92	0.97	0.99	0.99	0.99
Minerals, NEC	0.85	0.86	0.83	0.85	0.93	0.94	0.94
Paper	0.84	0.82	0.85	0.86	0.91	0.93	0.93
Complete hypothetical extraction (forward)							
Mining	2.57	2.61	2.51	2.55	2.68	2.69	2.74
Paper	2.37	2.27	2.34	2.41	2.53	2.58	2.60
Transport activities, NEC	2.40	2.37	2.29	2.31	2.43	2.25	2.41
Partial hypothetical extraction (forward)							
Mining	1.58	1.63	1.52	1.56	1.69	1.71	1.76
Paper	1.43	1.33	1.41	1.46	1.58	1.62	1.64
Finance	1.34	1.42	1.38	1.32	1.37	1.40	1.43
Total forward linkage							
Mining	2.60	2.65	2.54	2.58	2.71	2.73	2.78
Paper	2.52	2.42	2.52	2.54	2.66	2.68	2.70
Finance	2.37	2.45	2.43	2.37	2.43	2.47	2.50
Normalized backward linkage							
Refined fuels	1.26	1.30	1.30	1.28	1.23	1.28	1.28
Metals	1.33	1.32	1.35	1.31	1.35	1.23	1.26
Leather	1.25	1.23	1.23	1.21	1.18	1.26	1.25
Normalized forward linkage							
Mining	1.52	1.60	1.50	1.54	1.56	1.59	1.58
Paper	1.48	1.46	1.49	1.52	1.53	1.56	1.54
Finance	1.39	1.48	1.44	1.41	1.40	1.43	1.42
Net backward linkage							
Air transport	1.41	1.33	1.38	1.33	1.38	1.57	1.60
Electricals	1.30	1.53	1.43	1.47	1.49	1.58	1.58
Food and beverages	1.51	1.49	1.50	1.49	1.49	1.53	1.57
Net forward linkage							
Mining	2.28	2.37	2.26	2.29	2.43	2.40	2.44
Finance	1.68	1.93	1.75	1.70	1.75	1.75	1.77
Wholesale trade	1.90	1.68	1.72	1.75	1.79	1.73	1.77

continued on next page.

continued.

Bangladesh

South and Central Asia

International Linkages

Indicator and Top 3 Sectors, 2020	2000	2007	2010	2013	2016	2019	2020
Self-sufficiency ratio							
Textiles	1.71	1.94	1.96	1.84	1.86	1.64	1.53
Business activities, NEC	0.98	1.11	1.12	1.11	1.10	1.44	1.53
Leather	1.09	1.53	1.22	1.68	1.88	1.23	1.21
Import-to-input ratio							
Metals	0.14	0.17	0.16	0.19	0.14	0.26	0.24
Paper	0.12	0.14	0.14	0.16	0.15	0.24	0.21
Air transport	0.17	0.22	0.23	0.23	0.19	0.23	0.21
Export-to-output ratio							
Textiles	0.49	0.55	0.57	0.55	0.57	0.51	0.46
Air transport	0.02	0.00	0.04	0.00	0.00	0.35	0.41
Business activities, NEC	0.00	0.10	0.12	0.11	0.10	0.31	0.35
Domestic inputs share to output							
Refined fuels	0.64	0.68	0.69	0.67	0.63	0.67	0.68
Food and beverages	0.65	0.65	0.66	0.64	0.66	0.63	0.66
Hotels and restaurants	0.60	0.61	0.65	0.61	0.63	0.61	0.62
Foreign inputs share to output							
Metals	0.14	0.17	0.16	0.19	0.14	0.26	0.24
Paper	0.12	0.14	0.14	0.16	0.15	0.24	0.21
Air transport	0.17	0.22	0.23	0.23	0.19	0.23	0.21
Backward import multipliers							
Metals	0.21	0.25	0.25	0.27	0.21	0.37	0.35
Air transport	0.22	0.28	0.29	0.29	0.24	0.30	0.27
Paper	0.16	0.20	0.19	0.21	0.19	0.29	0.26
Forward import multipliers							
Air transport	0.03	0.02	0.06	0.04	0.03	0.23	0.25
Refined fuels	0.24	0.17	0.21	0.22	0.18	0.15	0.15
Transport activities, NEC	0.03	0.05	0.05	0.06	0.05	0.12	0.13
Intraregional transfer multiplier							
Refined fuels	1.92	1.97	1.99	1.93	1.91	1.98	2.02
Metals	2.03	2.00	2.08	1.97	2.11	1.91	1.99
Leather	1.90	1.86	1.89	1.83	1.84	1.95	1.98
Interregional spillover multiplier							
Metals	1.27	1.31	1.32	1.37	1.29	1.57	1.54
Paper	1.22	1.27	1.27	1.30	1.31	1.50	1.47
Air transport	1.31	1.37	1.45	1.41	1.38	1.45	1.42
Interregional feedback multiplier							
Metals	1.08	1.10	1.10	1.14	1.10	1.15	1.13
Air transport	1.08	1.15	1.14	1.17	1.12	1.13	1.12
Paper	1.06	1.08	1.08	1.09	1.08	1.12	1.10
Intraregional effect on gross output ($ million)							
Construction	9,125.97	13,904.80	20,282.41	30,052.29	45,750.17	67,604.50	77,291.84
Textiles	8,313.72	15,381.13	19,397.40	33,254.17	39,519.67	70,773.63	70,281.12
Agriculture	14,882.18	18,631.92	25,788.88	31,830.14	41,572.30	54,008.95	58,137.57
Interregional effect on gross output ($ million)							
Textiles	981.96	1,762.78	4,772.67	8,176.59	11,795.75	1,253.39	1,376.98
Business activities, NEC	15.23	177.08	80.81	158.34	193.61	1,143.74	950.81
Agriculture	174.94	637.74	1,072.85	1,414.70	1,636.40	592.69	655.93
Feedback effect on gross output ($ million)							
Textiles	191.55	438.01	827.07	1,609.15	2,211.53	286.46	286.39
Business activities, NEC	3.41	46.21	16.13	43.55	42.14	260.37	209.63
Transport activities, NEC	1.20	5.11	6.12	12.33	12.79	86.62	104.79
Directly absorbed value-added exports (DAVAX) ($ million)							
Textiles	3,601.07	7,490.54	10,373.81	16,389.64	21,170.68	27,037.74	25,059.53
Business activities, NEC	1.01	128.49	348.21	386.18	575.10	2,097.42	2,848.12
Construction	4.47	29.17	6.30	32.33	110.03	846.06	1,073.60
Reflection (REF) ($ million)							
Transport activities, NEC	0.00	0.00	0.00	0.00	0.00	0.79	1.64
Business activities, NEC	0.00	0.08	0.01	0.29	0.04	1.50	1.47
Textiles	0.31	0.91	3.70	6.54	25.17	1.26	1.47

continued on next page.

continued.

Bangladesh

South and Central Asia — *International Linkages*

Indicator and Top 3 Sectors, 2020	2000	2007	2010	2013	2016	2019	2020
Reexports (REX) ($ million)							
Textiles	328.38	633.53	1,533.82	2,631.50	3,497.67	346.03	372.67
Business activities, NEC	0.41	56.80	0.91	24.83	3.80	366.53	290.55
Transport activities, NEC	0.30	0.00	0.06	0.00	0.00	105.21	132.55
Foreign value added (FVA) ($ million)							
Textiles	678.59	1,619.04	2,224.60	4,567.32	5,539.95	9,375.33	7,821.01
Construction	0.65	6.00	1.18	7.38	16.20	201.77	225.25
Leather	8.82	42.82	45.06	125.26	118.88	150.42	141.46
Pure double-counting (PDC) ($ million)							
Textiles	0.27	0.91	2.54	10.31	32.63	2.59	2.39
Leather	0.00	0.01	0.02	0.07	0.27	0.03	0.04
Construction	0.00	0.00	0.00	0.00	0.00	0.03	0.03
Trade-based GVC participation rate							
Refined fuels	0.31	0.36	0.50	0.37	0.28	0.70	0.64
Transport activities, NEC	0.40	0.22	0.07			0.60	0.59
Metals	0.29	0.44	0.31	0.31	0.25	0.59	0.55
Production-based GVC participation rate							
Air transport	0.03	0.02	0.06	0.04	0.03	0.23	0.25
Refined fuels	0.24	0.17	0.21	0.22	0.18	0.15	0.15
Transport activities, NEC	0.03	0.05	0.05	0.06	0.05	0.12	0.13
Trade-based backward GVC participation rate							
Metals	0.21	0.25	0.25	0.27	0.21	0.37	0.35
Air transport	0.22	0.28	0.29	0.29	0.24	0.30	0.27
Paper	0.16	0.20	0.19	0.21	0.19	0.29	0.26
Trade-based forward GVC participation rate							
Transport activities, NEC	0.35	0.16	0.01			0.52	0.53
Refined fuels	0.17	0.19	0.34	0.19	0.08	0.50	0.45
Water transport	0.37	0.22	0.26	0.28	0.40	0.41	0.31
Traditional revealed comparative advantage							
Textiles	18.78	20.59	24.15	23.90	24.93	26.01	22.06
Construction	0.23	0.74	0.10	0.27	0.55	4.24	5.62
Leather	1.91	3.60	3.32	4.55	4.05	3.30	3.35
New revealed comparative advantage							
Textiles	15.74	15.51	19.44	20.59	20.05	25.94	22.92
Leather	2.33	4.04	4.06	5.54	4.72	4.75	4.76
Construction	2.56	1.59	1.14	1.38	1.70	2.34	2.69
Backward production length							
Metals	2.57	2.64	2.75	2.74	2.72	2.97	3.00
Air transport	2.40	2.61	2.68	2.63	2.60	2.69	2.69
Textiles	2.46	2.44	2.52	2.59	2.56	2.62	2.61
Forward production length							
Mining	2.64	2.72	2.62	2.69	2.80	2.77	2.81
Transport activities, NEC	2.45	2.47	2.39	2.44	2.54	2.58	2.78
Paper	2.62	2.67	2.68	2.77	2.83	2.76	2.78
Backward production length of GVC segment							
Real estate	4.59	4.65	4.67	4.63	4.75	4.83	4.93
Retail trade	4.34	4.56	4.78	4.65	4.71	4.80	4.88
Electricals	3.93	4.02	4.23	4.13	4.64	4.69	4.78
Forward production length of GVC segment							
Mining	4.71	5.01	4.90	4.81	5.06	4.95	5.09
Utilities	4.53	4.64	4.57	4.74	4.70	4.85	4.90
Retail trade	3.35	4.72	4.63	4.84	4.77	4.76	4.86
Backward agglomeration index							
Electricals	-	1.10	2.43	1.59	2.33	3.01	3.07
Manufacturing, NEC	-	1.95	2.02	2.09	2.10	2.53	2.30
Transport equipment	-	2.29	1.91	1.86	1.86	2.24	2.07
Forward agglomeration index							
Manufacturing, NEC	-	1.68	1.74	1.80	1.77	2.27	2.23
Mining	-	2.10	1.96	1.98	1.79	2.29	2.15
Electricals	-	1.11	2.13	1.35	1.83	2.04	2.00

CIF = cost, insurance, and freight; FOB = free on board; GVC = global value chain; NEC = not elsewhere classified; NPISHs = nonprofit institutions serving households.
Source: Calculations using the Asian Development Bank Multiregional Input-Output Table. https://mrio.adbx.online/ (accessed July 2021).

continued on next page.

continued.

Bangladesh

South and Central Asia

The four select sectors are chosen based on their gross outputs in the economy as of 2019.

Economy Ranking out of 25 Economies

	2020	2010	2000
Value-Added at Basic Prices ($ million)	12	14	13
Average Output Multiplier	12	12	15
Trade Openness	22	23	22
Trade-Based GVC Participation	24	25	25

Share of Intermediate Consumption and Gross Value-Added in Output

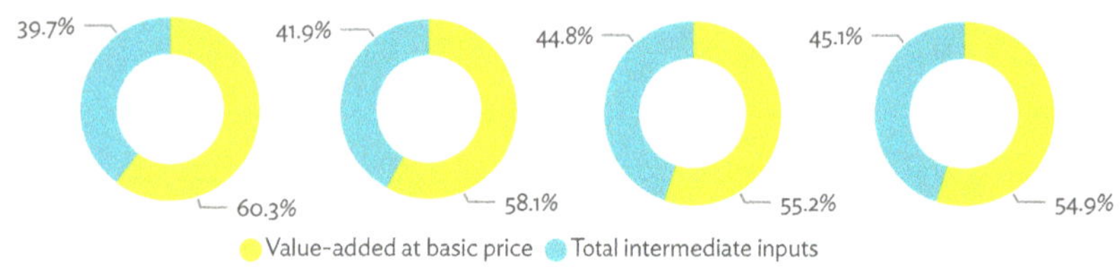

Imports and Exports, 2019-2020

($ million)

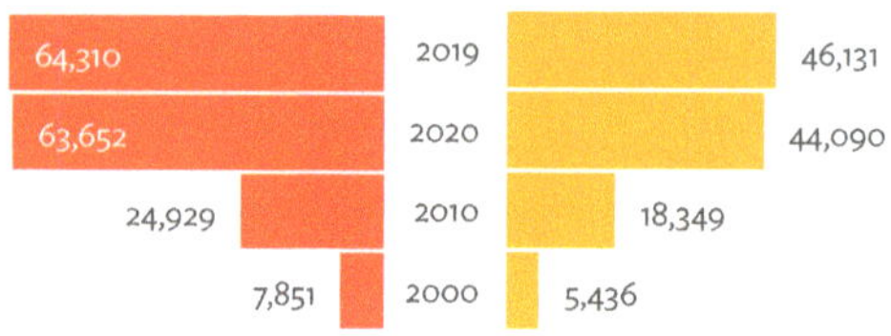

Domestic Linkages

Normalized Linkages

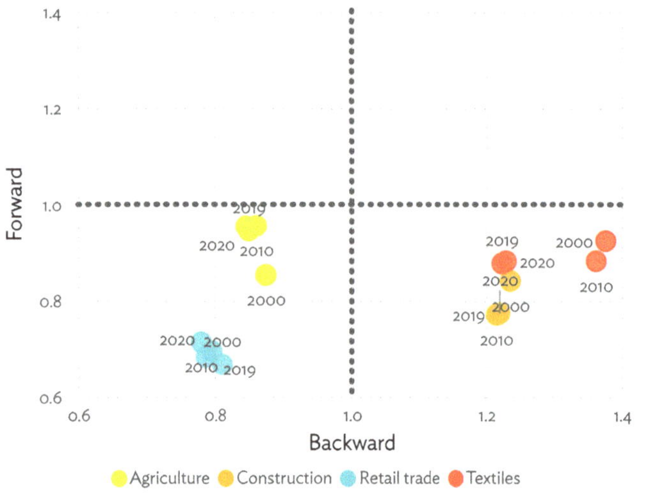

Net Linkages

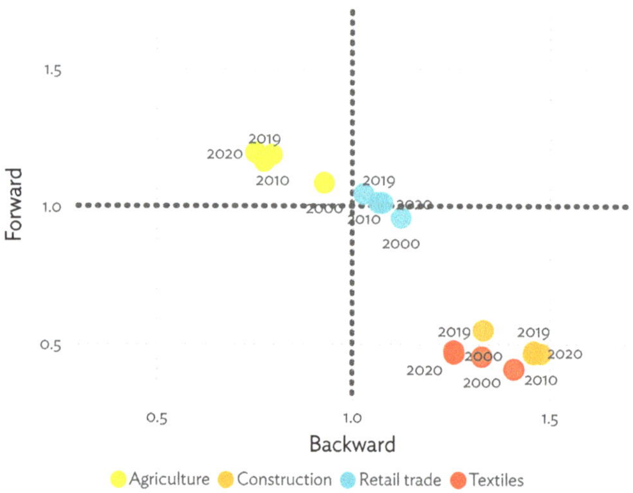

Value-Added Multipliers

Production-Induced Effect

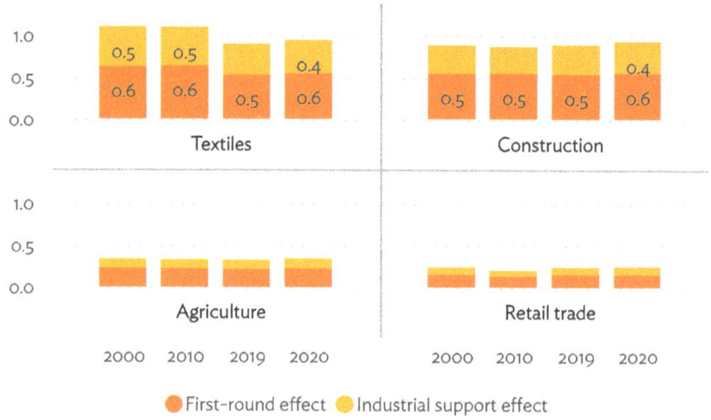

continued on next page.

Click here for figure data

continued.

Bangladesh

South and Central Asia

International Linkages

Change in Exports, by Value-Added Components, 2019-2020

($ million)

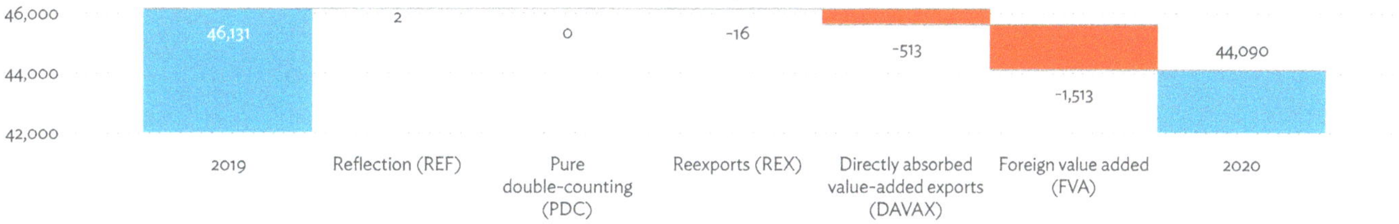

Import Multipliers

GVC Participation Rates

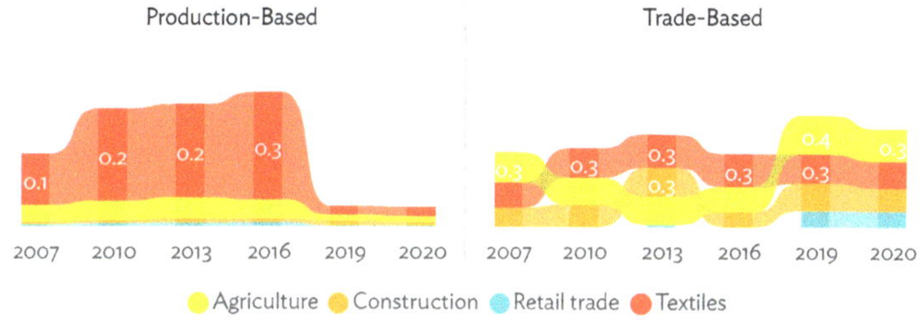

Average Production Length

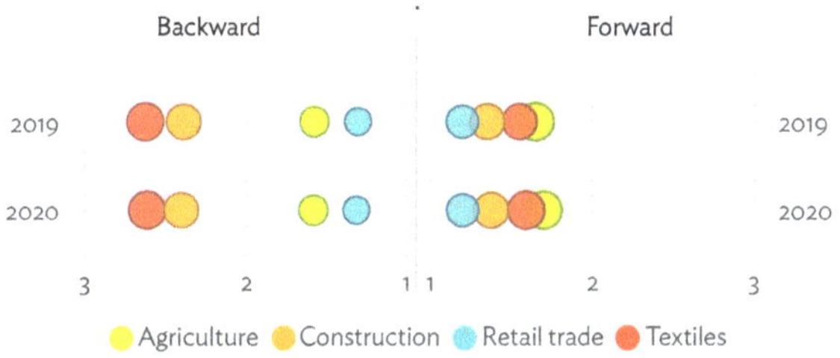

New Revealed Comparative Advantage

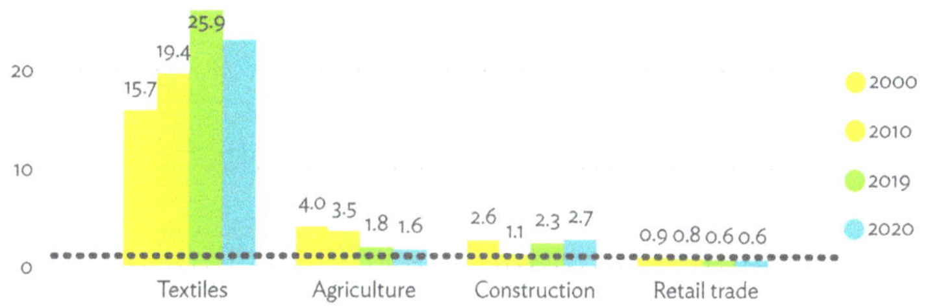

Trade Orientation

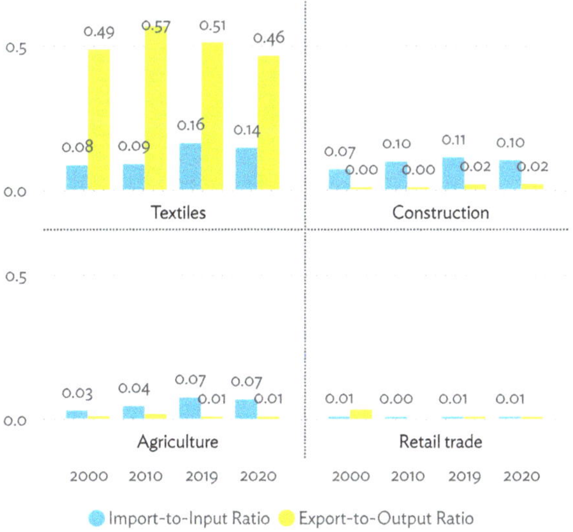

Agglomeration Indices

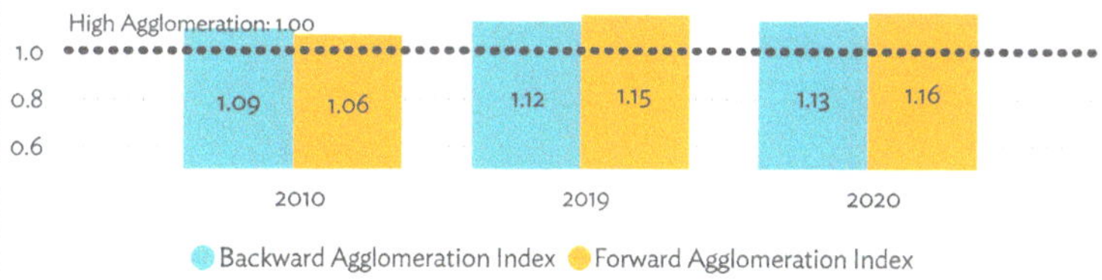

Domestic Transfer Effects and International Spillover Effects

($ million)

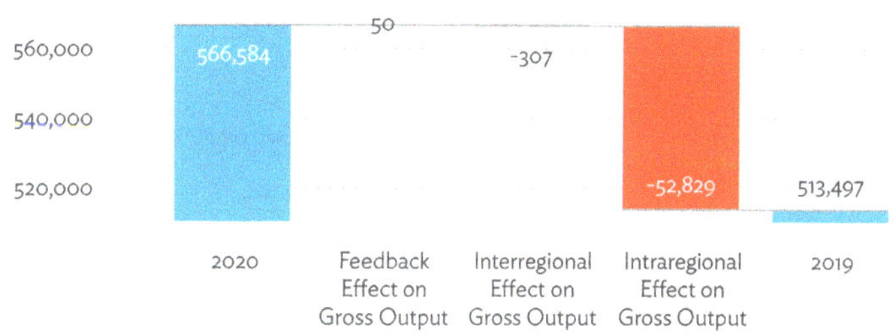

GVC = global value chain; NEC = not elsewhere classified.

Source: Calculations using the Asian Development Bank Multiregional Input-Output Table. https://mrio.adbx.online/ (accessed July 2021).

Click here for figure data

Bhutan

South and Central Asia

Basic Economic Indicators

Economic Aggregates ($ million)	2000	2007	2010	2013	2016	2019	2020
Value-added at basic price	430	1,161	1,522	1,705	2,022	2,412	2,430
Gross output	679	1,943	2,691	3,026	3,256	4,022	4,238
Total intermediate inputs	246	770	1,146	1,288	1,191	1,560	1,760
Taxes less subsidies on products	3	12	23	33	43	51	47
International transport margins	0	0	0	0	0	0	0
CIF/FOB adjustment	0	0	0	0	0	0	0
Direct purchases abroad by residents	0	0	0	0	0	0	0
Purchases by nonresidents on the domestic territory	0	0	0	0	0	0	0
Household final consumption expenditure	177	366	479	651	750	1,011	1,023
Final consumption expenditure by NPISHs	0	0	0	0	0	0	0
Government final consumption expenditure	92	203	271	268	308	429	506
Gross fixed capital formation	180	373	639	521	796	724	811
Changes in inventories	-8	48	17	-57	5	-6	-215
Total final demand	441	990	1,406	1,383	1,859	2,158	2,125
Exports	74	447	521	757	665	861	791
Imports	158	589	981	1,028	1,210	1,274	992

Economic Aggregates, Top 3 Sectors ($ million)	2000	2007	2010	2013	2016	2019	2020
Value-added at basic price							
Agriculture	118	223	266	298	352	400	399
Utilities	50	244	279	245	303	322	313
Construction	61	164	225	300	330	291	302
Gross output							
Construction	164	389	584	845	823	697	802
Utilities	51	309	340	272	331	552	537
Agriculture	131	248	297	326	379	446	445
Total intermediate inputs							
Construction	101	219	348	528	472	386	484
Utilities	0	65	60	26	27	227	214
Inland transport	19	59	81	103	106	171	214
Total final demand							
Construction	149	328	517	471	718	596	652
Public administration	61	130	171	182	204	275	341
Agriculture	103	137	193	193	271	361	263
Exports							
Mining	2	10	24	27	46	180	141
Utilities	27	207	196	156	220	116	105
Minerals, NEC	4	41	63	22	34	122	78
Imports							
Manufacturing, NEC	40	192	207	214	197	278	221
Agriculture	6	37	115	137	118	191	177
Electricals	9	22	78	70	59	68	63

Domestic Linkages

Indicator and Top 3 Sectors, 2020	2000	2007	2010	2013	2016	2019	2020
First-round effect							
Chemicals	0.49	0.53	0.54	0.63	0.60	0.61	0.63
Wood	0.44	0.56	0.57	0.62	0.55	0.58	0.61
Manufacturing, NEC	0.49	0.53	0.54	0.60	0.55	0.56	0.59
Industrial support effect							
Chemicals	0.09	0.13	0.15	0.18	0.13	0.18	0.24
Rubber and plastics	0.11	0.17	0.19	0.28	0.20	0.15	0.24
Manufacturing, NEC	0.09	0.13	0.15	0.17	0.12	0.17	0.23
Production-induced effect							
Chemicals	0.58	0.66	0.70	0.81	0.73	0.79	0.87
Manufacturing, NEC	0.58	0.66	0.70	0.78	0.67	0.73	0.82
Wood	0.50	0.65	0.68	0.71	0.61	0.70	0.76

continued on next page.

continued.

Bhutan

South and Central Asia

Domestic Linkages

Indicator and Top 3 Sectors, 2020	2000	2007	2010	2013	2016	2019	2020
Simple value-added multiplier							
Real estate	0.99	0.82	0.78	0.97	0.98	0.99	0.99
Agriculture	0.96	0.96	0.96	0.97	0.97	0.96	0.97
Transport activities, NEC	0.88	0.87	0.87	0.95	0.95	0.96	0.96
Type I value-added multiplier							
Wood	1.95	2.55	2.70	3.22	2.74	2.80	2.97
Food and beverages	1.98	2.34	2.46	2.87	2.47	2.41	2.89
Chemicals	2.04	2.36	2.49	3.11	2.79	2.63	2.84
Direct backward linkage							
Chemicals	0.49	0.53	0.54	0.63	0.60	0.61	0.63
Wood	0.44	0.56	0.57	0.62	0.55	0.58	0.61
Manufacturing, NEC	0.49	0.53	0.54	0.60	0.55	0.56	0.59
Complete hypothetical extraction (backward)							
Chemicals	1.56	1.64	1.66	1.76	1.69	1.79	1.87
Manufacturing, NEC	1.57	1.64	1.66	1.73	1.63	1.69	1.79
Wood	1.50	1.65	1.68	1.71	1.61	1.70	1.76
Partial hypothetical extraction (backward)							
Chemicals	0.58	0.65	0.68	0.79	0.71	0.79	0.87
Manufacturing, NEC	0.58	0.65	0.68	0.76	0.65	0.71	0.80
Wood	0.50	0.65	0.68	0.71	0.61	0.70	0.76
Total backward linkage							
Chemicals	1.58	1.66	1.70	1.81	1.73	1.79	1.87
Manufacturing, NEC	1.58	1.66	1.70	1.78	1.67	1.73	1.82
Wood	1.50	1.65	1.68	1.71	1.61	1.70	1.76
Direct forward linkage							
Business activities, NEC	0.00	0.59	0.74	0.68	0.59	0.77	0.80
Manufacturing, NEC	0.64	0.70	0.74	0.75	0.67	0.86	0.79
Real estate	0.51	0.26	0.49	0.63	0.50	0.62	0.72
Complete hypothetical extraction (forward)							
Real estate	1.69	1.38	1.72	1.95	1.67	1.91	2.18
Business activities, NEC	1.00	1.77	1.99	1.91	1.74	2.00	2.11
Finance	1.95	1.81	1.98	1.92	1.65	1.79	2.09
Partial hypothetical extraction (forward)							
Real estate	0.69	0.38	0.73	0.95	0.67	0.91	1.19
Business activities, NEC	0.00	0.77	1.00	0.92	0.75	1.00	1.11
Finance	0.95	0.81	0.98	0.92	0.65	0.79	1.10
Total forward linkage							
Real estate	1.69	1.38	1.73	1.95	1.67	1.91	2.19
Finance	1.96	1.81	1.98	1.93	1.66	1.79	2.12
Business activities, NEC	1.00	1.78	2.01	1.93	1.75	2.00	2.12
Normalized backward linkage							
Chemicals	1.19	1.18	1.18	1.28	1.30	1.32	1.28
Manufacturing, NEC	1.19	1.18	1.18	1.25	1.25	1.27	1.24
Wood	1.13	1.18	1.17	1.21	1.21	1.25	1.21
Normalized forward linkage							
Real estate	1.20	0.97	1.17	1.32	1.24	1.52	1.63
Finance	1.39	1.27	1.35	1.31	1.23	1.43	1.59
Business activities, NEC	0.71	1.25	1.36	1.31	1.30	1.59	1.58
Net backward linkage							
Chemicals	0.50	0.55	0.46	0.45	0.60	1.63	1.84
Food and beverages	1.33	1.46	1.49	1.55	1.50	1.58	1.72
Metals	1.22	1.12	1.23	1.28	1.25	1.56	1.71
Net forward linkage							
Real estate	1.64	0.91	1.00	1.86	1.62	1.88	2.09
Finance	1.75	1.75	1.82	1.71	1.50	1.58	1.70
Retail trade	1.18	1.19	0.88	1.03	1.05	1.18	1.31

continued on next page.

continued.

Bhutan

South and Central Asia — *International Linkages*

Indicator and Top 3 Sectors, 2020	2000	2007	2010	2013	2016	2019	2020
Self-sufficiency ratio							
Air transport	1.23	1.35	1.72	1.82	1.82	20.91	7.66
Transport activities, NEC	0.84	1.03	1.01	0.92	0.60	3.74	5.59
Mining	1.19	1.31	1.67	1.54	1.76	20.08	4.29
Import-to-input ratio							
Air transport	0.20	0.47	0.47	0.42	0.48	0.48	0.36
Rubber and plastics	0.29	0.30	0.31	0.28	0.32	0.33	0.25
Paper	0.20	0.26	0.27	0.24	0.27	0.28	0.23
Export-to-output ratio							
Chemicals	0.25	0.33	0.21	0.19	0.24	0.90	0.98
Water transport	1.00	0.00	0.60	0.67	0.65	1.00	0.96
Transport activities, NEC	0.39	0.18	0.21	0.17	0.15	0.99	0.96
Domestic inputs share to output							
Chemicals	0.49	0.53	0.54	0.63	0.60	0.61	0.63
Wood	0.44	0.56	0.57	0.62	0.55	0.58	0.61
Manufacturing, NEC	0.49	0.53	0.54	0.60	0.55	0.56	0.59
Foreign inputs share to output							
Air transport	0.20	0.47	0.47	0.42	0.48	0.48	0.36
Rubber and plastics	0.29	0.30	0.31	0.28	0.32	0.33	0.25
Paper	0.20	0.26	0.27	0.24	0.27	0.28	0.23
Backward import multipliers							
Air transport	0.23	0.55	0.54	0.50	0.55	0.55	0.44
Rubber and plastics	0.32	0.37	0.38	0.36	0.39	0.40	0.32
Paper	0.23	0.32	0.33	0.29	0.32	0.36	0.30
Forward import multipliers							
Metals	0.19	0.62	0.47	0.49	0.43	0.99	0.97
Rubber and plastics	0.18	0.49	0.33	0.45	0.37	0.99	0.91
Chemicals	0.20	0.46	0.27	0.37	0.28	0.71	0.77
Intraregional transfer multiplier							
Chemicals	1.58	1.66	1.70	1.81	1.73	1.79	1.87
Manufacturing, NEC	1.58	1.66	1.70	1.78	1.67	1.73	1.82
Wood	1.50	1.65	1.68	1.71	1.61	1.70	1.76
Interregional spillover multiplier							
Air transport	1.37	1.91	1.93	1.84	2.00	1.95	1.72
Rubber and plastics	1.54	1.59	1.64	1.59	1.69	1.64	1.49
Paper	1.36	1.46	1.50	1.45	1.51	1.52	1.44
Interregional feedback multiplier							
Air transport	1.08	1.23	1.28	1.22	1.21	1.24	1.16
Rubber and plastics	1.14	1.16	1.19	1.17	1.17	1.15	1.11
Transport equipment	1.07	1.12	1.15	1.12	1.12	1.13	1.10
Intraregional effect on gross output ($ million)							
Construction	161.72	382.80	578.78	552.58	800.40	685.58	789.40
Agriculture	128.03	195.18	263.52	277.45	343.56	435.81	421.94
Utilities	25.28	89.74	131.94	91.00	96.90	368.75	370.00
Interregional effect on gross output ($ million)							
Utilities	20.35	169.73	164.16	141.88	181.38	147.05	137.29
Mining	1.84	11.84	24.51	34.10	47.60	82.05	72.26
Inland transport	4.14	13.44	30.18	54.52	42.03	50.00	54.56
Feedback effect on gross output ($ million)							
Utilities	5.03	49.59	43.44	39.51	52.95	36.09	30.17
Mining	0.16	1.03	1.75	3.44	3.65	20.17	15.86
Inland transport	0.75	2.92	6.13	11.13	10.46	12.69	12.17
Directly absorbed value-added exports (DAVAX) ($ million)							
Mining	1.97	8.47	20.17	21.42	38.89	134.19	109.01
Minerals, NEC	3.74	33.15	52.19	19.57	30.96	100.65	65.69
Utilities	18.29	113.53	113.72	94.73	136.92	63.06	63.28
Reflection (REF) ($ million)							
Metals	0.00	0.01	0.01	0.01	0.01	0.02	0.01
Mining	0.00	0.00	0.01	0.01	0.01	0.01	0.01
Minerals, NEC	0.00	0.01	0.00	0.00	0.00	0.01	0.00

continued on next page.

continued.

Bhutan

South and Central Asia *International Linkages*

Indicator and Top 3 Sectors, 2020	2000	2007	2010	2013	2016	2019	2020
Reexports (REX) ($ million)							
Utilities	8.46	66.88	61.16	52.66	72.64	26.30	22.40
Mining	0.16	0.74	1.69	2.27	3.44	25.36	18.69
Hotels and restaurants	0.21	0.92	2.15	4.70	9.55	15.37	11.37
Foreign value added (FVA) ($ million)							
Air transport	0.37	4.74	10.25	11.11	15.18	41.67	33.68
Utilities	0.11	26.70	21.30	8.67	10.49	27.07	19.51
Metals	0.48	6.57	10.70	12.82	13.26	25.67	14.85
Pure double-counting (PDC) ($ million)							
Air transport	0.00	0.00	0.00	0.00	0.00	0.00	0.00
Utilities	0.00	0.00	0.00	0.00	0.00	0.00	0.00
Metals	0.00	0.00	0.00	0.00	0.00	0.00	0.00
Trade-based GVC participation rate							
Air transport	0.43	0.61	0.62	0.60	0.66	0.66	0.54
Personal services, NEC	0.34	0.33	0.32	0.33	0.45	0.54	0.50
Rubber and plastics	0.39	0.43	0.45	0.50	0.53	0.56	0.47
Production-based GVC participation rate							
Metals	0.19	0.62	0.47	0.49	0.43	0.99	0.97
Rubber and plastics	0.18	0.49	0.33	0.45	0.37	0.99	0.91
Chemicals	0.20	0.46	0.27	0.37	0.28	0.71	0.77
Trade-based backward GVC participation rate							
Air transport	0.23	0.55	0.54	0.50	0.55	0.55	0.44
Rubber and plastics	0.32	0.37	0.38	0.36	0.39	0.40	0.32
Paper	0.23	0.32	0.33	0.29	0.32	0.36	0.30
Trade-based forward GVC participation rate							
Personal services, NEC	0.18	0.14	0.13	0.18	0.28	0.38	0.37
Finance	0.33	0.36	0.35	0.35	0.34	0.36	0.31
Retail trade	0.18	0.30	0.24	0.29	0.28	0.28	0.28
Traditional revealed comparative advantage							
Utilities	67.94	74.22	82.11	46.84	59.92	22.39	20.35
Minerals, NEC	5.16	9.79	13.75	3.19	5.41	15.43	10.73
Air transport	1.60	1.55	2.93	2.53	3.18	6.45	8.90
New revealed comparative advantage							
Utilities	18.37	17.80	17.90	11.18	15.72	9.24	8.40
Minerals, NEC	3.06	4.08	5.59	4.94	4.31	11.21	6.61
Hotels and restaurants	0.95	0.84	1.44	2.44	4.31	4.63	5.34
Backward production length							
Air transport	1.76	2.80	2.91	2.81	2.79	2.78	2.73
Rubber and plastics	2.15	2.48	2.62	2.73	2.66	2.53	2.54
Metals	1.96	2.31	2.42	2.42	2.35	2.43	2.42
Forward production length							
Chemicals	2.24	2.84	2.55	2.76	2.41	2.89	3.06
Metals	1.56	2.56	2.22	2.26	2.04	2.94	2.91
Rubber and plastics	2.44	2.93	2.82	3.21	2.91	3.01	2.87
Backward production length of GVC segment							
Sale of motor vehicles	3.68	4.03	4.16	4.00	3.94	4.17	4.38
Wholesale trade	3.48	3.99	4.13	3.97	3.85	4.09	4.36
Minerals, NEC	3.87	4.18	4.25	4.25	4.18	4.22	4.35
Forward production length of GVC segment							
Real estate	3.78	4.50	4.38	4.70	4.34	4.74	5.04
Telecommunications	3.69	4.32	4.43	4.14	3.74	4.65	4.92
Finance	3.91	4.22	4.04	4.52	4.12	4.62	4.92
Backward agglomeration index							
Leather	-	1.87	1.57	1.87	1.81	2.24	2.23
Textiles	-	1.41	1.59	2.06	1.88	2.30	1.75
Metals	-	0.96	0.60	0.46	0.55	1.48	1.59
Forward agglomeration index							
Leather	-	2.27	2.07	1.84	1.90	1.99	1.93
Transport equipment	-	2.12	1.83	1.73	1.73	1.54	1.56
Textiles	-	1.69	1.99	1.97	1.85	1.88	1.47

CIF = cost, insurance, and freight; FOB = free on board; GVC = global value chain; NEC = not elsewhere classified; NPISHs = nonprofit institutions serving households.
Source: Calculations using the Asian Development Bank Multiregional Input-Output Table. https://mrio.adbx.online/ (accessed July 2021).

continued on next page.

continued.

Bhutan

South and Central Asia

The four select sectors are chosen based on their gross outputs in the economy as of 2019.

Economy Ranking out of 25 Economies

Share of Intermediate Consumption and Gross Value-Added in Output

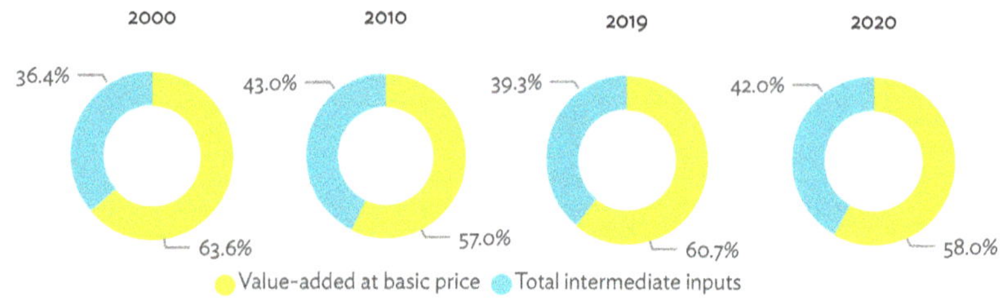

Imports and Exports, 2019-2020

($ million)

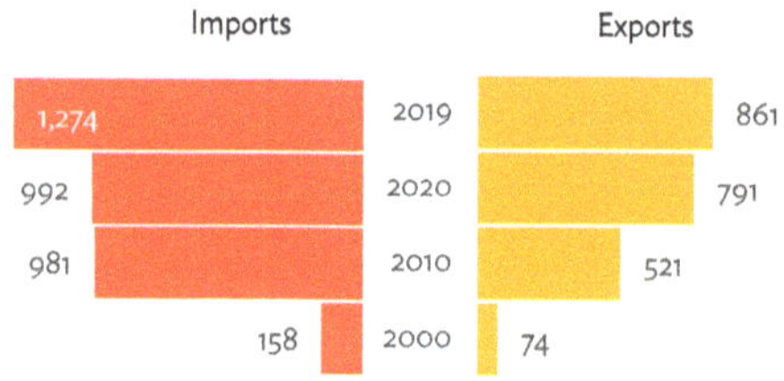

Domestic Linkages

Normalized Linkages

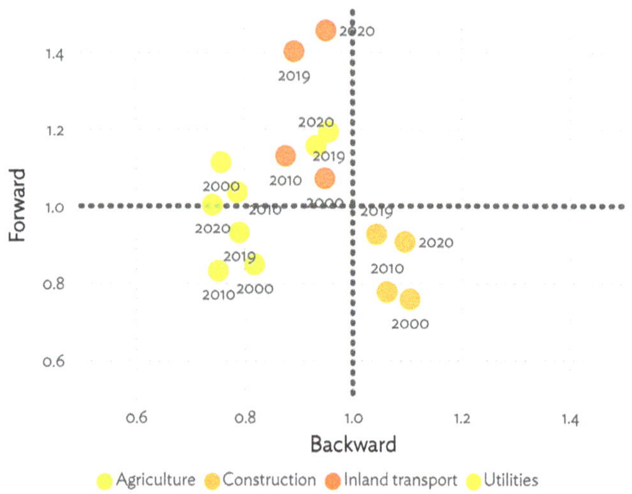

Net Linkages

Value-Added Multipliers

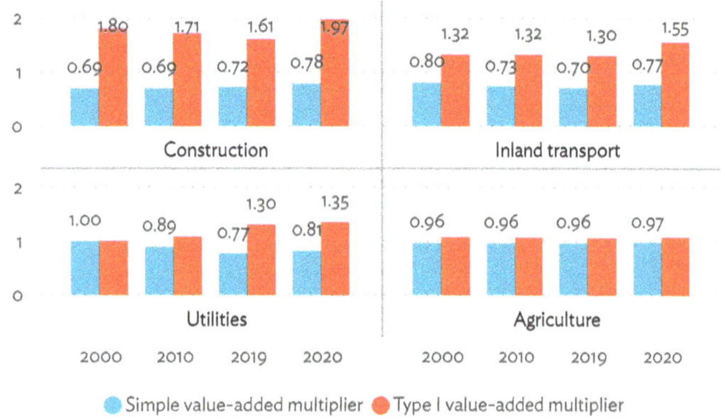

Production-Induced Effect

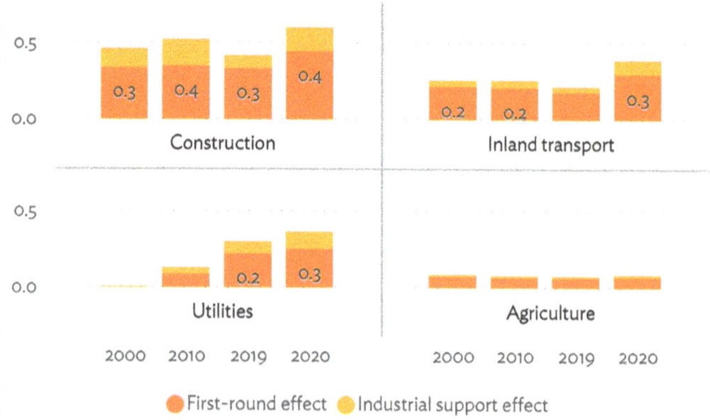

continued on next page.

Click here for figure data

continued.

Bhutan

South and Central Asia

International Linkages

Change in Exports, by Value-Added Components, 2019-2020

($ million)

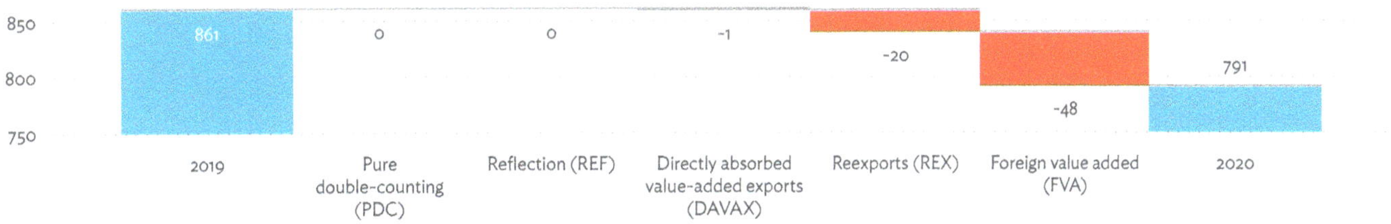

Import Multipliers

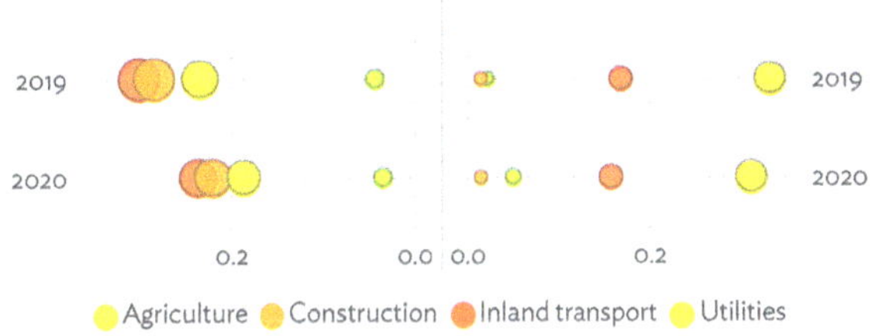

GVC Participation Rates

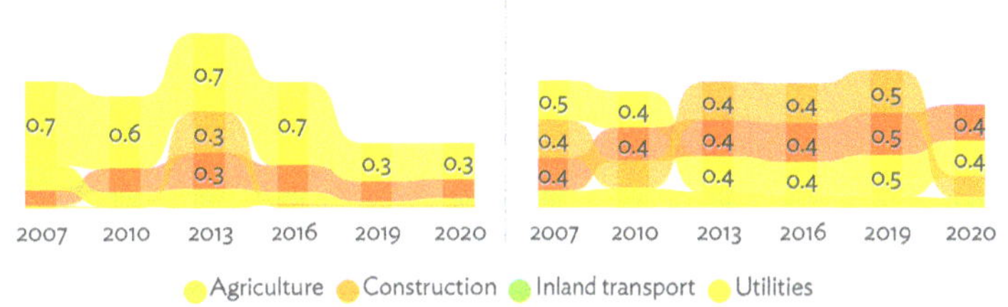

Average Production Length

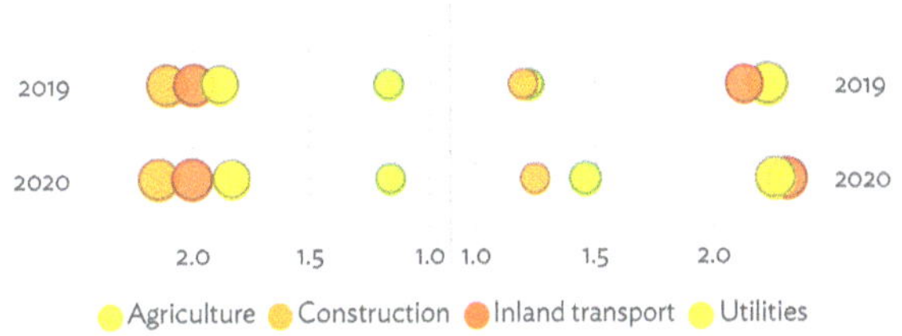

New Revealed Comparative Advantage

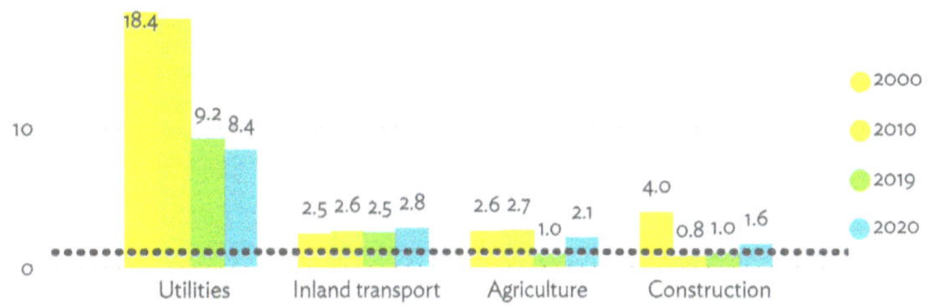

Trade Orientation

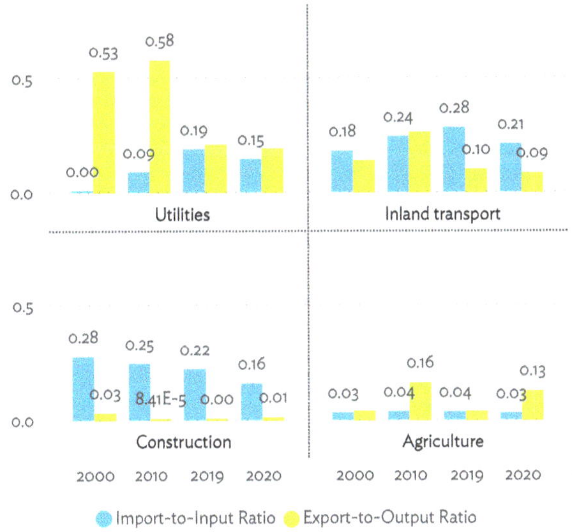

Agglomeration Indices

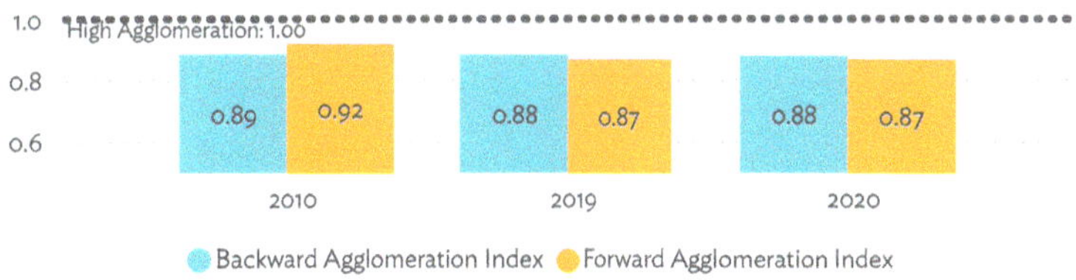

Domestic Transfer Effects and International Spillover Effects

($ million)

GVC = global value chain; NEC = not elsewhere classified.

Source: Calculations using the Asian Development Bank Multiregional Input-Output Table. https://mrio.adbx.online/ (accessed July 2021).

Click here for figure data

Brunei Darussalam

Southeast Asia and the Pacific

Basic Economic Indicators

Economic Aggregates ($ million)	2000	2007	2010	2013	2016	2019	2020
Value-added at basic price	6,581	12,248	13,966	18,447	11,571	13,695	12,232
Gross output	8,880	20,694	23,344	31,708	19,701	23,378	21,440
Total intermediate inputs	2,299	8,447	9,460	13,372	8,189	10,020	9,513
Taxes less subsidies on products	0	0	-82	-112	-59	-338	-305
International transport margins	0	0	0	0	0	0	0
CIF/FOB adjustment	0	0	0	0	0	0	0
Direct purchases abroad by residents	0	0	0	0	0	0	0
Purchases by nonresidents on the domestic territory	0	0	0	0	0	0	0
Household final consumption expenditure	1,104	1,873	1,586	1,965	1,976	1,795	1,821
Final consumption expenditure by NPISHs	1,884	0	2,971	0	0	0	0
Government final consumption expenditure	20	2,609	0	3,528	2,990	3,373	3,053
Gross fixed capital formation	546	1,378	2,450	5,199	2,873	3,832	3,730
Changes in inventories	-29	831	26	192	737	1,165	692
Total final demand	3,525	6,692	7,032	10,884	8,577	10,165	9,296
Exports	3,476	7,849	9,000	11,057	5,654	7,805	6,886
Imports	1,385	2,854	3,400	6,271	4,304	6,811	6,355

Economic Aggregates, Top 3 Sectors ($ million)	2000	2007	2010	2013	2016	2019	2020
Value-added at basic price							
Mining	2,208	7,036	7,022	9,130	4,829	6,116	4,722
Refined fuels	903	1,143	1,837	2,684	1,170	1,685	1,742
Public administration	936	1,087	1,462	1,739	1,489	1,602	1,539
Gross output							
Mining	2,771	9,175	9,157	11,907	6,298	7,976	6,158
Refined fuels	1,133	2,963	4,252	6,212	2,708	3,899	4,033
Public administration	1,512	2,149	2,430	2,890	2,475	2,663	2,558
Total intermediate inputs							
Refined fuels	230	1,820	2,423	3,539	1,544	2,250	2,326
Construction	185	1,577	1,177	2,106	1,350	1,575	1,652
Mining	563	2,139	2,143	2,787	1,474	1,898	1,464
Total final demand							
Public administration	1,430	2,068	2,304	2,777	2,457	2,646	2,502
Construction	215	1,552	1,207	2,211	1,332	1,864	1,972
Refined fuels	158	233	58	202	75	992	718
Exports							
Mining	2,167	5,049	4,843	5,578	2,881	6,821	5,689
Refined fuels	739	2,173	3,396	4,862	2,054	213	610
Hotels and restaurants	21	7	12	28	49	155	102
Imports							
Food and beverages	110	204	284	499	448	987	964
Mining	4	175	525	550	186	567	593
Metals	30	211	321	813	243	606	571

Domestic Linkages

Indicator and Top 3 Sectors, 2020	2000	2007	2010	2013	2016	2019	2020
First-round effect							
Refined fuels	0.19	0.48	0.56	0.48	0.54	0.57	0.57
Transport activities, NEC	0.44	0.58	0.59	0.60	0.62	0.40	0.38
Air transport	0.10	0.70	0.70	0.69	0.55	0.38	0.35
Industrial support effect							
Refined fuels	0.04	0.13	0.15	0.13	0.11	0.25	0.32
Air transport	0.04	0.34	0.40	0.36	0.27	0.29	0.29
Water transport	0.13	0.29	0.36	0.33	0.29	0.27	0.26
Production-induced effect							
Refined fuels	0.23	0.61	0.71	0.60	0.65	0.82	0.89
Air transport	0.14	1.04	1.10	1.05	0.82	0.67	0.64
Transport activities, NEC	0.52	0.90	0.98	0.99	0.98	0.63	0.60

continued on next page.

continued.

Brunei Darussalam

Southeast Asia and the Pacific *Domestic Linkages*

Indicator and Top 3 Sectors, 2020	2000	2007	2010	2013	2016	2019	2020
Simple value-added multiplier							
Real estate	0.97	0.97	0.97	0.96	0.96	0.94	0.95
Personal services, NEC	0.95	0.96	0.93	0.92	0.93	0.89	0.89
Refined fuels	0.98	0.83	0.94	0.86	0.91	0.89	0.89
Type I value-added multiplier							
Air transport	1.11	4.51	5.64	5.31	4.55	4.57	4.19
Construction	3.22	3.76	3.12	3.25	2.87	2.45	2.48
Transport activities, NEC	1.82	2.47	2.80	2.76	2.71	2.52	2.42
Direct backward linkage							
Refined fuels	0.19	0.48	0.56	0.48	0.54	0.57	0.57
Transport activities, NEC	0.44	0.58	0.59	0.60	0.62	0.40	0.38
Air transport	0.10	0.70	0.70	0.69	0.55	0.38	0.35
Complete hypothetical extraction (backward)							
Air transport	1.13	2.02	2.08	2.02	1.81	1.67	1.64
Water transport	1.43	1.75	1.82	1.77	1.81	1.62	1.56
Construction	1.56	1.68	1.62	1.66	1.52	1.51	1.54
Partial hypothetical extraction (backward)							
Air transport	0.14	1.03	1.09	1.04	0.82	0.67	0.64
Refined fuels	0.22	0.60	0.69	0.59	0.64	0.61	0.62
Water transport	0.43	0.79	0.88	0.84	0.83	0.63	0.57
Total backward linkage							
Refined fuels	1.23	1.61	1.71	1.60	1.65	1.82	1.89
Air transport	1.14	2.04	2.10	2.05	1.82	1.67	1.64
Transport activities, NEC	1.52	1.90	1.98	1.99	1.98	1.63	1.60
Direct forward linkage							
Utilities	0.61	0.55	0.64	0.68	0.47	0.71	0.71
Refined fuels	0.21	0.19	0.19	0.18	0.21	0.69	0.67
Business activities, NEC	0.44	0.86	0.83	0.86	0.91	0.65	0.67
Complete hypothetical extraction (forward)							
Utilities	1.62	1.77	1.88	1.93	1.60	2.20	2.29
Finance	1.86	2.35	1.73	1.74	1.48	1.81	1.93
Hotels and restaurants	1.02	1.65	2.04	1.96	1.70	1.64	1.89
Partial hypothetical extraction (forward)							
Utilities	0.65	0.77	0.88	0.94	0.61	1.21	1.30
Finance	0.91	1.37	0.77	0.77	0.52	0.84	0.96
Hotels and restaurants	0.02	0.65	1.05	0.96	0.70	0.64	0.90
Total forward linkage							
Utilities	1.67	1.78	1.89	1.95	1.61	2.22	2.32
Refined fuels	1.27	1.26	1.28	1.28	1.28	2.00	2.04
Telecommunications	1.28	2.20	2.37	2.23	2.03	1.92	2.02
Normalized backward linkage							
Refined fuels	0.93	1.08	1.14	1.08	1.23	1.34	1.38
Air transport	0.87	1.37	1.40	1.38	1.35	1.23	1.19
Transport activities, NEC	1.15	1.27	1.32	1.34	1.47	1.20	1.16
Normalized forward linkage							
Utilities	1.30	1.02	1.17	1.18	1.10	1.72	1.74
Refined fuels	0.99	0.73	0.79	0.77	0.87	1.54	1.54
Telecommunications	1.00	1.27	1.47	1.35	1.38	1.49	1.52
Net backward linkage							
Air transport	0.83	1.52	1.45	1.28	1.59	1.62	1.62
Construction	1.54	1.51	1.47	1.54	1.36	1.50	1.53
Wood	0.80	0.36	0.65	0.82	0.75	1.40	1.50
Net forward linkage							
Finance	1.71	1.89	1.42	1.42	1.22	1.45	1.54
Personal services, NEC	0.95	1.81	1.20	1.25	1.11	1.19	1.27
Textiles	0.28	1.24	1.21	1.41	1.01	1.10	1.15

continued on next page.

continued.

Brunei Darussalam

Southeast Asia and the Pacific *International Linkages*

Indicator and Top 3 Sectors, 2020	2000	2007	2010	2013	2016	2019	2020
Self-sufficiency ratio							
Mining	4.56	2.13	1.89	1.73	1.75	4.63	5.80
Air transport	3.17	1.98	2.49	1.00	0.98	1.52	4.23
Chemicals	0.00	2.63	2.87	3.14	2.23	1.49	1.64
Import-to-input ratio							
Air transport	0.05	0.13	0.17	0.17	0.32	0.53	0.55
Construction	0.28	0.22	0.35	0.32	0.38	0.48	0.47
Transport activities, NEC	0.05	0.10	0.15	0.14	0.10	0.40	0.42
Export-to-output ratio							
Leather	0.95	0.20	0.99	0.12	0.93	1.00	1.00
Chemicals	0.00	0.80	0.80	0.81	0.76	1.00	1.00
Inland transport	1.00	0.39	0.41	0.45	0.50	1.00	1.00
Domestic inputs share to output							
Refined fuels	0.19	0.48	0.56	0.48	0.54	0.57	0.57
Transport activities, NEC	0.44	0.58	0.59	0.60	0.62	0.40	0.38
Air transport	0.10	0.70	0.70	0.69	0.55	0.38	0.35
Foreign inputs share to output							
Air transport	0.05	0.13	0.17	0.17	0.32	0.53	0.55
Construction	0.28	0.22	0.35	0.32	0.38	0.48	0.47
Transport activities, NEC	0.05	0.10	0.15	0.14	0.10	0.40	0.42
Backward import multipliers							
Air transport	0.05	0.24	0.24	0.28	0.40	0.57	0.60
Construction	0.32	0.31	0.45	0.43	0.50	0.55	0.55
Transport activities, NEC	0.07	0.21	0.27	0.27	0.24	0.51	0.52
Forward import multipliers							
Chemicals	0.00	0.84	0.82	0.79	0.74	1.00	1.00
Wood	0.06	0.31	0.17	0.13	0.15	0.56	0.99
Metals	0.73	0.44	0.21	0.16	0.17	0.96	0.97
Intraregional transfer multiplier							
Refined fuels	1.23	1.61	1.71	1.60	1.65	1.82	1.89
Air transport	1.14	2.04	2.10	2.05	1.82	1.67	1.64
Transport activities, NEC	1.52	1.90	1.98	1.99	1.98	1.63	1.60
Interregional spillover multiplier							
Air transport	1.08	1.23	1.28	1.32	1.60	2.03	2.14
Construction	1.54	1.40	1.62	1.60	1.69	1.91	1.92
Transport activities, NEC	1.09	1.17	1.25	1.24	1.17	1.80	1.86
Interregional feedback multiplier							
Air transport	1.02	1.06	1.06	1.08	1.14	1.25	1.26
Construction	1.14	1.11	1.15	1.17	1.18	1.22	1.23
Sale of motor vehicles	1.02	1.07	1.11	1.11	1.13	1.20	1.21
Intraregional effect on gross output ($ million)							
Refined fuels	280.99	684.63	857.73	1,512.54	671.68	2,962.24	2,732.82
Public administration	1,511.41	2,126.27	2,393.29	2,865.99	2,468.83	2,657.55	2,544.71
Construction	230.50	1,846.46	1,389.55	2,504.81	1,594.71	1,896.92	2,001.46
Interregional effect on gross output ($ million)							
Mining	1,910.54	5,171.98	5,519.26	6,213.37	3,066.22	5,024.32	4,350.55
Refined fuels	685.70	1,775.91	2,510.77	3,447.72	1,561.09	682.76	972.37
Finance	16.48	63.22	111.79	110.20	75.53	85.86	99.59
Feedback effect on gross output ($ million)							
Mining	672.65	1,694.63	1,827.68	2,287.26	1,191.81	1,912.20	1,419.22
Refined fuels	166.47	502.39	883.41	1,251.64	475.72	253.74	327.68
Finance	4.94	20.03	37.27	40.77	28.45	31.27	33.10
Directly absorbed value-added exports (DAVAX) ($ million)							
Mining	1,385.32	3,154.86	3,056.35	3,341.56	1,592.19	3,654.22	3,177.68
Refined fuels	552.72	1,272.99	2,146.94	2,794.83	1,298.14	133.94	412.33
Hotels and restaurants	15.51	4.38	7.75	18.31	31.80	95.23	59.83
Reflection (REF) ($ million)							
Mining	0.13	0.37	0.28	0.52	0.14	0.77	1.00
Refined fuels	0.04	0.17	0.24	0.56	0.13	0.04	0.09
Metals	0.00	0.00	0.00	0.00	0.00	0.01	0.03

continued on next page.

continued.

Brunei Darussalam

Southeast Asia and the Pacific

International Linkages

Indicator and Top 3 Sectors, 2020	2000	2007	2010	2013	2016	2019	2020
Reexports (REX) ($ million)							
Mining	731.57	1,584.60	1,449.11	1,777.73	967.28	2,012.01	1,552.43
Refined fuels	169.49	540.15	1,054.16	1,409.40	564.71	56.50	131.59
Water transport	2.97	35.51	46.64	32.05	26.20	31.12	20.30
Foreign value added (FVA) ($ million)							
Mining	50.46	309.54	336.94	458.11	321.45	1,153.97	957.86
Refined fuels	17.22	359.74	194.64	657.12	191.31	22.58	65.98
Air transport	7.46	36.57	54.77	6.01	9.05	62.62	37.50
Pure double-counting (PDC) ($ million)							
Mining	0.01	0.10	0.07	0.11	0.03	0.20	0.22
Refined fuels	0.00	0.08	0.04	0.15	0.02	0.00	0.02
Air transport	0.00	0.02	0.01	0.00	0.00	0.01	0.01
Trade-based GVC participation rate							
Transport activities, NEC	0.21	0.41	0.46	0.47	0.49	0.77	0.76
Water transport	0.30	0.50	0.49	0.48	0.50	0.72	0.74
Metals	0.45	0.46	0.56	0.57	0.68	0.66	0.72
Production-based GVC participation rate							
Chemicals	-	0.84	0.82	0.79	0.74	1.00	1.00
Wood	0.06	0.31	0.17	0.13	0.15	0.56	0.99
Metals	0.73	0.44	0.21	0.16	0.17	0.96	0.97
Trade-based backward GVC participation rate							
Air transport	0.05	0.24	0.24	0.28	0.40	0.57	0.60
Construction	0.32	0.31	0.45	0.43	0.50	0.55	0.55
Transport activities, NEC	0.07	0.21	0.27	0.27	0.24	0.51	0.52
Trade-based forward GVC participation rate							
Metals	0.20	0.20	0.29	0.28	0.18	0.26	0.33
Water transport	0.15	0.34	0.33	0.30	0.31	0.33	0.31
Utilities	0.19	0.19	0.27	0.22	0.23	0.27	0.29
Traditional revealed comparative advantage							
Mining	10.34	8.12	6.38	5.38	7.59	12.96	12.67
Refined fuels	8.87	7.20	9.37	9.21	9.24	0.79	2.52
Water transport	0.31	0.68	0.87	0.62	1.00	1.52	1.23
New revealed comparative advantage							
Mining	8.67	8.21	6.30	5.89	7.88	9.92	10.81
Refined fuels	20.93	8.13	12.67	14.06	14.05	4.94	8.40
Hotels and restaurants	0.20	0.16	0.38	0.37	0.60	0.84	0.92
Backward production length							
Air transport	1.27	2.59	2.63	2.73	2.77	3.12	3.21
Transport activities, NEC	1.68	2.38	2.57	2.64	2.54	2.95	2.98
Construction	2.40	2.62	2.77	2.85	2.80	2.89	2.95
Forward production length							
Chemicals	-	3.33	3.28	3.21	3.08	4.21	4.35
Mining	3.96	3.51	3.79	3.53	3.43	3.58	3.69
Metals	3.12	3.08	2.14	1.94	1.89	3.22	3.22
Backward production length of GVC segment							
Refined fuels	3.65	3.44	4.33	3.82	4.12	4.75	5.03
Agriculture	3.36	3.72	3.83	3.88	3.83	3.89	3.99
Food and beverages	3.62	3.74	3.85	3.91	3.74	3.85	3.95
Forward production length of GVC segment							
Real estate	3.16	5.22	5.03	5.03	4.40	5.40	5.54
Finance	4.90	5.02	5.11	5.14	4.80	5.27	5.43
Sale of motor vehicles	4.36	4.73	4.83	4.72	4.27	5.16	5.34
Backward agglomeration index							
Rubber and plastics	-	0.00	1.29	0.00	0.63	2.57	2.35
Electricals	-	0.00	2.42	2.21	1.18	1.94	1.66
Refined fuels	-	1.11	0.27	0.52	0.61	1.91	1.63
Forward agglomeration index							
Manufacturing, NEC	-	0.51	1.38	1.41	1.47	1.22	1.86
Rubber and plastics	-	1.34	1.46	1.35	1.36	1.57	1.54
Electricals	-	0.75	2.06	1.87	1.44	1.73	1.52

CIF = cost, insurance, and freight; FOB = free on board; GVC = global value chain; NEC = not elsewhere classified; NPISHs = nonprofit institutions serving households.
Source: Calculations using the Asian Development Bank Multiregional Input-Output Table. https://mrio.adbx.online/ (accessed July 2021).

continued on next page.

continued.

Brunei Darussalam

Southeast Asia and the Pacific

The four select sectors are chosen based on their gross outputs in the economy as of 2019.

Economy Ranking out of 25 Economies

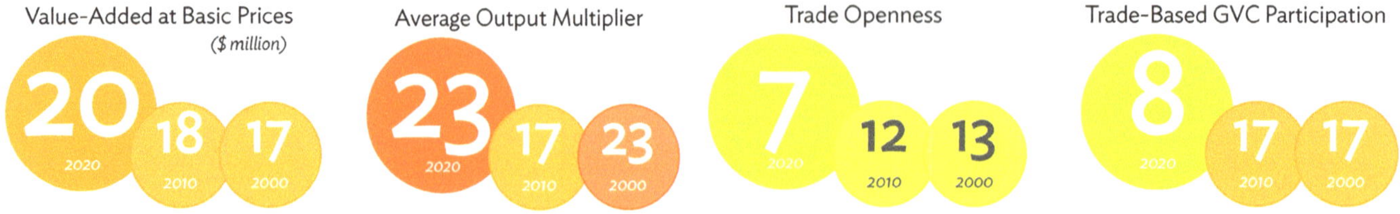

Share of Intermediate Consumption and Gross Value-Added in Output

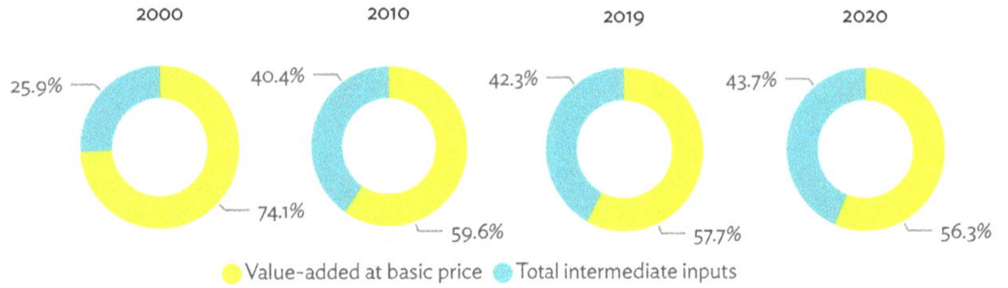

Imports and Exports, 2019-2020

($ million)

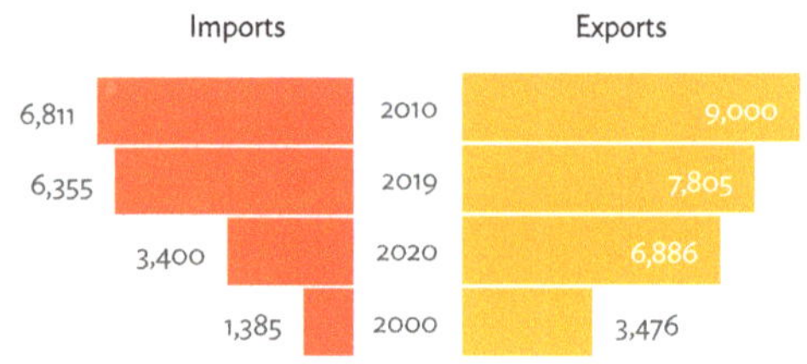

Domestic Linkages

Normalized Linkages

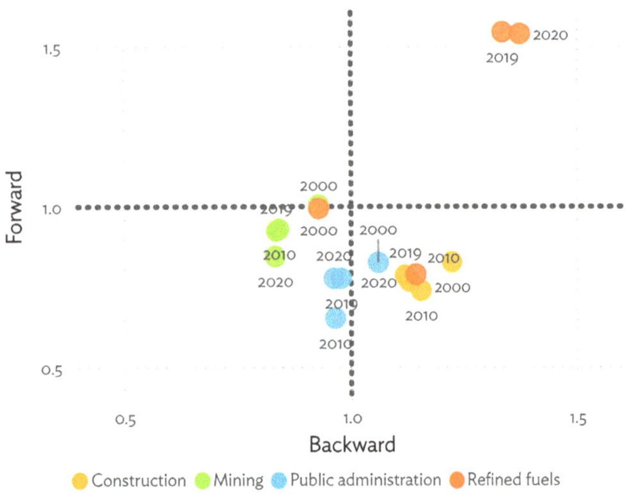

Net Linkages

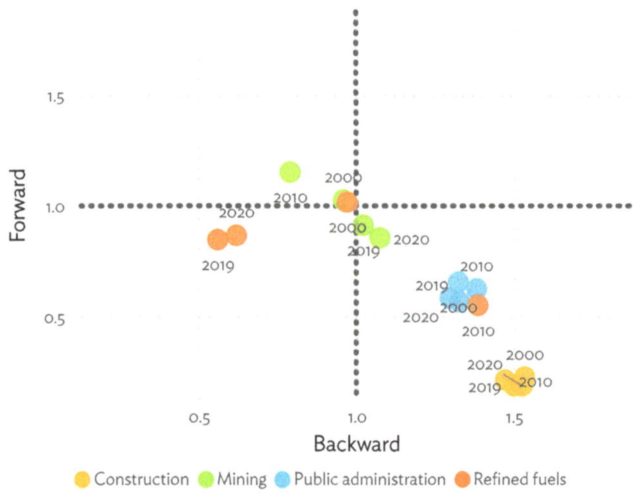

Value-Added Multipliers

Production-Induced Effect

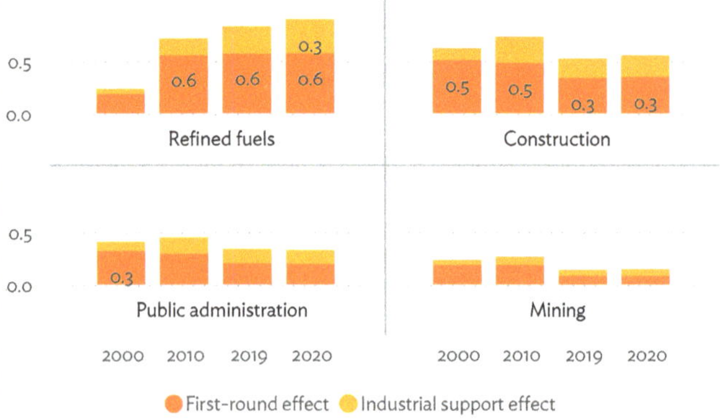

continued on next page.

Click here for figure data

continued.

Brunei Darussalam

Southeast Asia and the Pacific

International Linkages

Change in Exports, by Value-Added Components, 2019-2020

($ million)

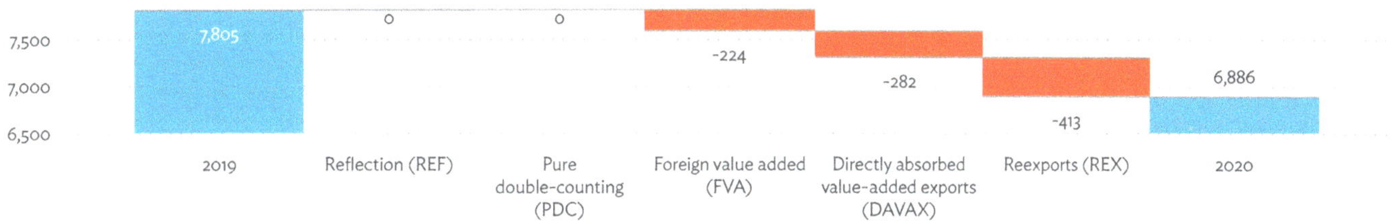

Import Multipliers

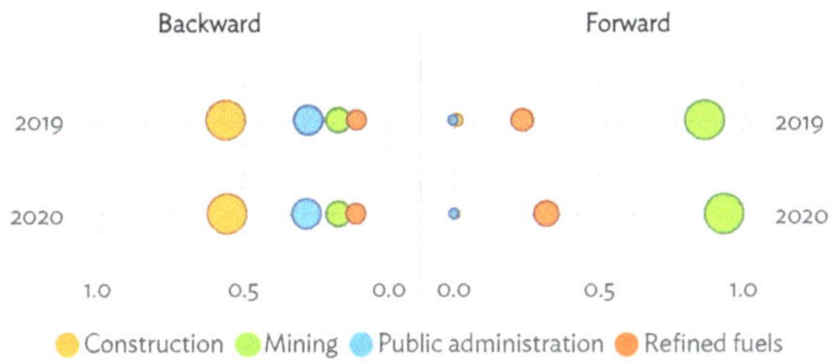

GVC Participation Rates

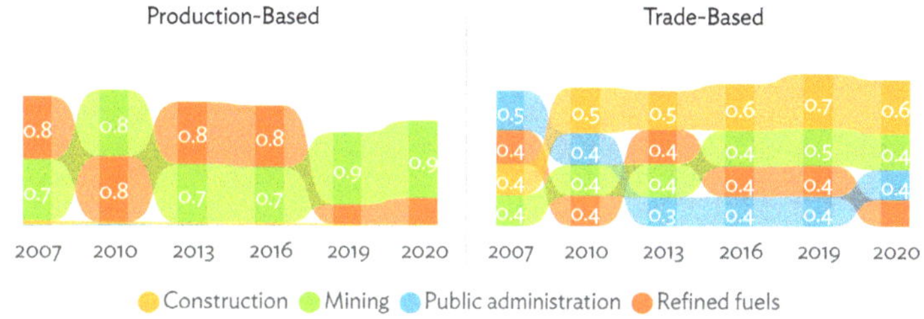

Average Production Length

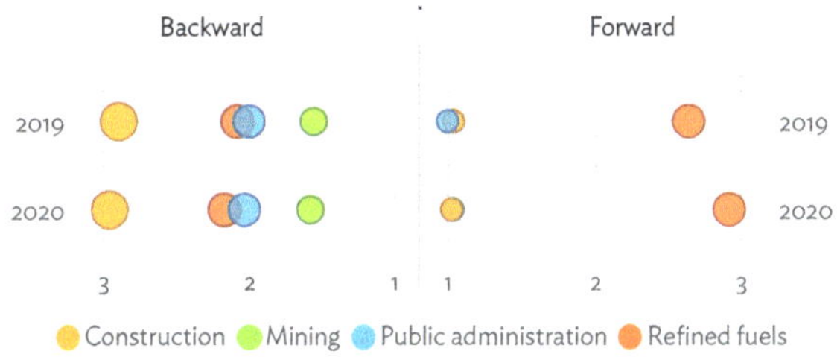

New Revealed Comparative Advantage

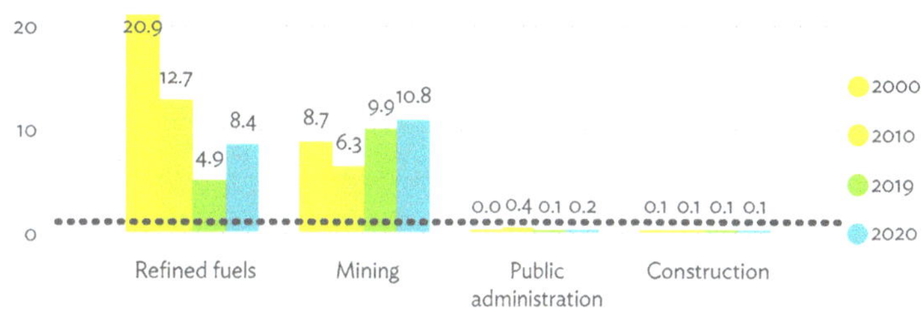

Trade Orientation

Agglomeration Indices

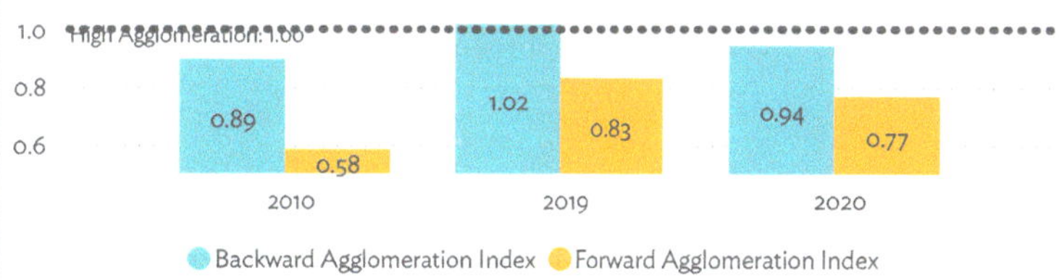

Domestic Transfer Effects and International Spillover Effects

($ million)

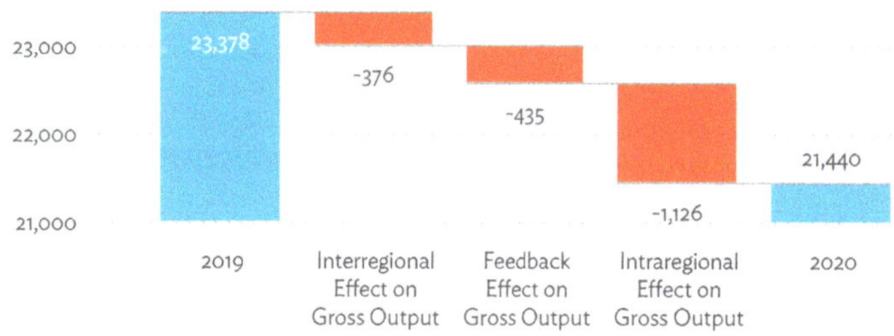

GVC = global value chain; NEC = not elsewhere classified.

Source: Calculations using the Asian Development Bank Multiregional Input-Output Table. https://mrio.adbx.online/ (accessed July 2021).

Click here for figure data

Cambodia

Southeast Asia and the Pacific

Basic Economic Indicators

Economic Aggregates ($ million)	2000	2007	2010	2013	2016	2019	2020
Value-added at basic price	3,442	7,930	10,434	14,175	18,489	25,064	23,410
Gross output	6,570	15,694	19,801	27,623	36,850	50,597	46,065
Total intermediate inputs	3,050	7,529	9,087	13,067	17,807	24,566	21,810
Taxes less subsidies on products	78	235	280	381	554	968	846
International transport margins	0	0	0	0	0	0	0
CIF/FOB adjustment	0	0	0	0	0	0	0
Direct purchases abroad by residents	0	0	0	0	0	0	0
Purchases by nonresidents on the domestic territory	0	0	0	0	0	0	0
Household final consumption expenditure	2,414	5,134	7,270	9,149	11,414	15,047	14,938
Final consumption expenditure by NPISHs	78	173	221	271	309	343	341
Government final consumption expenditure	182	460	671	771	934	1,140	1,184
Gross fixed capital formation	623	1,000	1,180	1,957	3,125	3,485	3,074
Changes in inventories	-68	243	130	280	153	543	440
Total final demand	3,229	7,010	9,472	12,427	15,935	20,558	19,978
Exports	1,258	3,645	4,041	6,142	8,586	16,549	19,340
Imports	1,750	4,477	4,860	7,223	9,850	16,921	23,035

Economic Aggregates, Top 3 Sectors ($ million)	2000	2007	2010	2013	2016	2019	2020
Value-added at basic price							
Agriculture	1,303	2,530	3,763	4,669	4,905	5,535	5,170
Construction	188	568	672	1,142	2,255	4,094	3,823
Textiles	381	1,053	1,064	1,510	2,094	2,854	2,665
Gross output							
Textiles	1,161	3,314	3,247	4,613	6,428	8,758	8,180
Construction	398	1,140	1,339	2,205	4,272	7,754	7,242
Agriculture	1,750	3,411	5,043	6,325	6,664	7,520	7,024
Total intermediate inputs							
Textiles	758	2,196	2,107	2,997	4,180	5,641	5,284
Construction	204	553	645	1,033	1,973	3,567	3,337
Food and beverages	266	544	749	1,093	1,521	2,120	1,984
Total final demand							
Construction	341	947	1,142	1,830	3,394	6,171	6,841
Wholesale trade	271	456	759	881	1,147	1,196	2,366
Real estate	181	424	479	576	790	1,280	1,504
Exports							
Textiles	646	1,990	1,950	2,945	4,326	8,731	8,155
Agriculture	47	251	221	608	937	1,375	5,992
Hotels and restaurants	193	572	880	948	1,163	3,016	1,615
Imports							
Textiles	294	609	830	1,345	1,920	3,354	4,815
Metals	175	414	425	555	939	1,897	2,893
Refined fuels	234	302	644	1,071	1,198	1,994	2,841

Domestic Linkages

Indicator and Top 3 Sectors, 2020	2000	2007	2010	2013	2016	2019	2020
First-round effect							
Rubber and plastics	0.42	0.42	0.42	0.40	0.41	0.22	0.43
Food and beverages	0.62	0.57	0.61	0.60	0.59	0.51	0.41
Business activities, NEC	0.46	0.41	0.44	0.45	0.45	0.42	0.39
Industrial support effect							
Food and beverages	0.30	0.23	0.25	0.28	0.29	0.18	0.12
Rubber and plastics	0.21	0.22	0.22	0.21	0.22	0.07	0.11
Wood	0.19	0.18	0.19	0.20	0.21	0.14	0.10
Production-induced effect							
Rubber and plastics	0.63	0.64	0.64	0.61	0.63	0.29	0.55
Food and beverages	0.92	0.80	0.86	0.88	0.88	0.69	0.53
Business activities, NEC	0.71	0.63	0.69	0.72	0.72	0.60	0.49

continued on next page.

continued.

Cambodia

Southeast Asia and the Pacific

Domestic Linkages

Indicator and Top 3 Sectors, 2020	2000	2007	2010	2013	2016	2019	2020
Simple value-added multiplier							
Finance	0.95	0.94	0.94	0.95	0.95	0.94	0.93
Real estate	0.87	0.86	0.86	0.88	0.88	0.86	0.83
Education	0.91	0.91	0.92	0.89	0.89	0.86	0.82
Type I value-added multiplier							
Rubber and plastics	2.23	2.38	2.18	2.20	2.24	1.58	2.06
Food and beverages	2.96	2.78	3.00	2.95	2.92	2.47	1.97
Utilities	3.33	3.52	3.55	3.74	3.77	2.72	1.67
Direct backward linkage							
Rubber and plastics	0.42	0.42	0.42	0.40	0.41	0.22	0.43
Food and beverages	0.62	0.57	0.61	0.60	0.59	0.51	0.41
Business activities, NEC	0.46	0.41	0.44	0.45	0.45	0.42	0.39
Complete hypothetical extraction (backward)							
Wood	1.58	1.57	1.59	1.60	1.60	1.57	1.47
Rubber and plastics	1.49	1.46	1.45	1.47	1.48	1.22	1.39
Business activities, NEC	1.56	1.53	1.59	1.53	1.53	1.42	1.36
Partial hypothetical extraction (backward)							
Rubber and plastics	0.58	0.57	0.57	0.56	0.57	0.28	0.49
Wood	0.64	0.61	0.64	0.66	0.66	0.57	0.47
Food and beverages	0.76	0.71	0.77	0.76	0.76	0.61	0.46
Total backward linkage							
Rubber and plastics	1.63	1.64	1.64	1.61	1.63	1.29	1.55
Food and beverages	1.92	1.80	1.86	1.88	1.88	1.69	1.53
Business activities, NEC	1.71	1.63	1.69	1.72	1.72	1.60	1.49
Direct forward linkage							
Inland transport	0.65	0.62	0.56	0.63	0.65	0.65	0.53
Chemicals	0.60	0.66	0.66	0.66	0.64	0.48	0.42
Minerals, NEC	0.70	0.61	0.67	0.57	0.59	0.54	0.39
Complete hypothetical extraction (forward)							
Inland transport	1.84	1.82	1.72	1.83	1.86	1.82	1.65
Chemicals	1.78	1.87	1.88	1.90	1.89	1.60	1.50
Minerals, NEC	2.02	1.89	1.98	1.81	1.86	1.75	1.50
Partial hypothetical extraction (forward)							
Inland transport	0.91	0.88	0.79	0.90	0.94	0.87	0.66
Chemicals	0.82	0.90	0.91	0.94	0.92	0.62	0.52
Minerals, NEC	1.04	0.90	0.99	0.82	0.87	0.75	0.50
Total forward linkage							
Inland transport	1.98	1.95	1.85	1.98	2.01	1.91	1.67
Chemicals	1.84	1.93	1.94	1.98	1.96	1.63	1.52
Minerals, NEC	2.05	1.92	2.00	1.83	1.88	1.76	1.50
Normalized backward linkage							
Rubber and plastics	1.20	1.22	1.21	1.17	1.19	1.02	1.31
Food and beverages	1.41	1.33	1.37	1.37	1.37	1.34	1.30
Business activities, NEC	1.26	1.21	1.24	1.26	1.25	1.27	1.26
Normalized forward linkage							
Inland transport	1.39	1.34	1.27	1.37	1.38	1.49	1.44
Chemicals	1.29	1.33	1.33	1.37	1.34	1.27	1.30
Minerals, NEC	1.44	1.32	1.37	1.27	1.29	1.37	1.29
Net backward linkage							
Wood	0.79	0.90	0.71	0.99	1.01	1.57	1.47
Public administration	1.56	1.40	1.46	1.52	1.52	1.37	1.30
Food and beverages	1.36	1.35	1.39	1.35	1.34	1.28	1.27
Net forward linkage							
Finance	1.32	1.27	1.24	1.37	1.40	1.38	1.13
Mining	1.41	1.33	1.45	1.37	1.34	1.23	1.01
Inland transport	1.04	1.05	1.01	1.05	1.08	1.03	0.90

continued on next page.

continued.

Cambodia

Southeast Asia and the Pacific — *International Linkages*

Indicator and Top 3 Sectors, 2020	2000	2007	2010	2013	2016	2019	2020
Export-to-output ratio							
Leather	1.00	1.00	1.00	1.00	1.00	1.00	1.00
Sale of motor vehicles	1.00	1.00	1.00	1.00	1.00	1.00	1.00
Transport activities, NEC	1.00	1.00	1.00	1.00	1.00	1.00	1.00
Water transport	1.00	1.00	1.00	1.00	1.00	1.00	1.00
Self-sufficiency ratio							
Retail trade	0.88	1.16	1.21	1.31	1.27	4.72	6.54
Agriculture	1.00	1.01	1.01	1.04	1.09	1.09	3.62
Wood	0.84	0.85	0.85	1.28	1.27	4.77	3.13
Import-to-input ratio							
Refined fuels	0.66	0.34	0.82	0.96	0.85	0.72	0.72
Utilities	0.41	0.32	0.32	0.31	0.31	0.47	0.67
Textiles	0.23	0.22	0.22	0.24	0.23	0.35	0.53
Domestic inputs share to output							
Rubber and plastics	0.42	0.42	0.42	0.40	0.41	0.22	0.43
Food and beverages	0.62	0.57	0.61	0.60	0.59	0.51	0.41
Business activities, NEC	0.46	0.41	0.44	0.45	0.45	0.42	0.39
Foreign inputs share to output							
Refined fuels	0.66	0.34	0.82	0.96	0.85	0.72	0.72
Utilities	0.41	0.32	0.32	0.31	0.31	0.47	0.67
Textiles	0.23	0.22	0.22	0.24	0.23	0.35	0.53
Backward import multipliers							
Utilities	0.54	0.47	0.45	0.44	0.43	0.57	0.74
Refined fuels	0.68	0.34	0.83	0.96	0.86	0.73	0.73
Textiles	0.37	0.37	0.36	0.37	0.36	0.44	0.58
Forward import multipliers							
Metals	0.03	0.04	0.06	0.07	0.07	0.99	0.98
Wood	0.11	0.13	0.11	0.33	0.39	0.97	0.97
Refined fuels	0.94	0.30	0.45	0.62	0.92	0.95	0.96
Intraregional transfer multiplier							
Rubber and plastics	1.63	1.64	1.64	1.61	1.63	1.29	1.55
Food and beverages	1.92	1.80	1.86	1.88	1.88	1.69	1.53
Business activities, NEC	1.71	1.63	1.69	1.72	1.72	1.60	1.49
Interregional spillover multiplier							
Utilities	1.73	1.59	1.66	1.68	1.68	1.97	2.43
Textiles	1.42	1.46	1.51	1.56	1.53	1.92	2.42
Refined fuels	2.09	1.58	2.61	2.50	2.83	2.29	2.32
Interregional feedback multiplier							
Refined fuels	1.48	1.19	1.52	1.29	1.49	1.54	1.57
Utilities	1.24	1.22	1.22	1.23	1.20	1.33	1.49
Inland transport	1.15	1.13	1.14	1.14	1.12	1.20	1.31
Intraregional effect on gross output ($ million)							
Textiles	1,091.62	3,008.28	2,830.76	4,280.01	5,322.52	8,493.24	7,943.15
Construction	387.15	1,119.09	1,306.58	2,105.39	4,215.65	7,666.59	7,220.22
Wholesale trade	570.77	1,065.52	1,458.84	1,929.79	2,585.96	3,985.37	3,717.06
Interregional effect on gross output ($ million)							
Agriculture	66.70	211.82	274.40	470.45	683.08	941.05	3,592.17
Inland transport	52.15	127.15	191.38	281.02	407.11	683.59	664.56
Hotels and restaurants	68.86	191.74	314.76	382.49	471.95	1,122.31	601.57
Feedback effect on gross output ($ million)							
Agriculture	22.81	82.82	91.28	156.16	300.41	230.66	1,058.52
Hotels and restaurants	15.56	50.33	82.94	106.83	139.37	285.03	135.65
Inland transport	9.57	27.20	38.95	59.43	88.76	154.62	134.87
Directly absorbed value-added exports (DAVAX) ($ million)							
Agriculture	25.01	135.07	128.60	391.23	500.23	853.59	3,516.79
Textiles	393.94	1,185.29	1,167.45	1,792.01	2,568.98	4,821.39	3,422.21
Hotels and restaurants	142.39	403.25	640.04	673.86	816.51	1,976.25	1,028.76
Reflection (REF) ($ million)							
Agriculture	0.06	0.28	0.41	1.10	1.93	1.29	2.67
Metals	0.00	0.00	0.00	0.00	0.00	0.87	1.15
Hotels and restaurants	0.00	0.01	0.02	0.03	0.07	0.29	0.20

continued on next page.

continued.

Cambodia

Southeast Asia and the Pacific — *International Linkages*

Indicator and Top 3 Sectors, 2020	2000	2007	2010	2013	2016	2019	2020
Reexports (REX) ($ million)							
Agriculture	17.19	86.73	70.03	156.87	336.21	310.85	1,239.14
Hotels and restaurants	19.52	58.28	107.10	116.23	144.24	358.62	158.10
Metals	0.09	0.58	1.03	1.60	2.73	188.75	157.92
Foreign value added (FVA) ($ million)							
Textiles	235.62	738.23	710.42	1,091.24	1,567.77	3,850.86	4,693.08
Agriculture	4.87	28.58	21.90	58.74	98.39	209.51	1,232.65
Hotels and restaurants	30.90	110.93	133.07	157.75	202.55	680.70	428.14
Pure double-counting (PDC) ($ million)							
Textiles	0.02	0.08	0.11	0.13	0.37	0.86	1.23
Agriculture	0.00	0.00	0.00	0.01	0.02	0.05	0.46
Hotels and restaurants	0.00	0.01	0.01	0.04	0.09	0.23	0.23
Trade-based GVC participation rate							
Utilities	0.63	0.73	0.74	0.64	0.71	0.76	0.87
Refined fuels	0.81	0.62	0.89	0.98	0.95	0.91	0.85
Machinery, NEC	0.54	0.56	0.54	0.65	0.67	0.79	0.68
Production-based GVC participation rate							
Metals	0.03	0.04	0.06	0.07	0.07	0.99	0.98
Wood	0.11	0.13	0.11	0.33	0.39	0.97	0.97
Refined fuels	0.94	0.30	0.45	0.62	0.92	0.95	0.96
Trade-based backward GVC participation rate							
Utilities	0.54	0.47	0.45	0.44	0.43	0.57	0.74
Refined fuels	0.68	0.34	0.83	0.96	0.86	0.73	0.73
Textiles	0.37	0.37	0.36	0.37	0.36	0.44	0.58
Trade-based forward GVC participation rate							
Finance	0.32	0.38	0.36	0.38	0.38	0.32	0.29
Metals	0.05	0.09	0.18	0.10	0.11	0.32	0.29
Real estate	0.12	0.09		0.28	0.28	0.25	0.22
Traditional revealed comparative advantage							
Textiles	11.37	15.71	15.12	14.56	15.23	17.22	12.33
Agriculture	1.74	3.39	2.42	4.21	4.66	2.88	10.05
Hotels and restaurants	12.43	15.97	20.14	15.02	10.78	10.98	6.26
New revealed comparative advantage							
Textiles	13.84	20.13	19.62	17.16	17.26	17.22	14.00
Agriculture	3.78	4.07	4.11	4.38	4.17	3.40	7.13
Hotels and restaurants	7.41	8.69	10.77	8.80	6.88	6.55	6.86
Backward production length							
Utilities	3.00	2.98	3.03	3.09	3.08	3.18	3.43
Refined fuels	2.82	1.85	3.34	2.85	3.47	2.98	3.06
Rubber and plastics	2.84	2.97	2.99	3.00	3.00	3.06	2.99
Forward production length							
Refined fuels	3.13	2.80	3.06	2.72	4.25	3.63	3.78
Metals	1.72	1.76	1.90	1.92	2.01	3.47	3.44
Agriculture	1.52	1.62	1.62	1.72	1.85	1.65	2.87
Backward production length of GVC segment							
Real estate	4.68	4.36	4.61	4.64	4.66	4.55	4.62
Business activities, NEC	4.51	4.23	4.56	4.62	4.63	4.46	4.48
Metals	3.80	4.09	4.18	4.43	4.48	4.33	4.42
Forward production length of GVC segment							
Construction	3.51	3.96	3.72	3.73	4.73	4.93	4.78
Finance	3.43	3.81	3.75	4.27	4.32	4.82	4.76
Personal services, NEC	4.32	4.53	4.62	4.69	4.69	4.54	4.71
Backward agglomeration index							
Chemicals	-	1.50	1.55	1.49	1.39	1.52	1.25
Minerals, NEC	-	1.20	1.32	1.52	1.44	1.37	1.17
Mining	-	1.23	1.20	1.20	1.18	1.17	1.07
Forward agglomeration index							
Mining	-	2.23	2.07	2.12	1.84	1.99	1.93
Utilities	-	1.25	1.17	1.21	1.17	1.17	1.24
Finance	-	1.01	1.00	1.09	1.07	1.08	1.17

CIF = cost, insurance, and freight; FOB = free on board; GVC = global value chain; NEC = not elsewhere classified; NPISHs = nonprofit institutions serving households.
Source: Calculations using the Asian Development Bank Multiregional Input-Output Table. https://mrio.adbx.online/ (accessed July 2021).

continued on next page.

continued.

Cambodia

Southeast Asia and the Pacific

The four select sectors are chosen based on their gross outputs in the economy as of 2019.

Economy Ranking out of 25 Economies

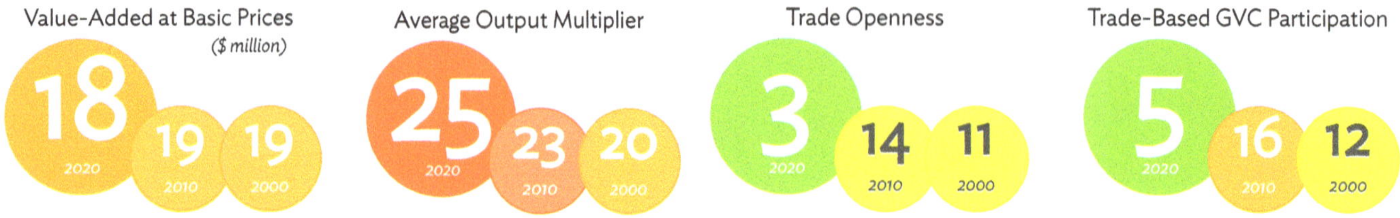

Share of Intermediate Consumption and Gross Value-Added in Output

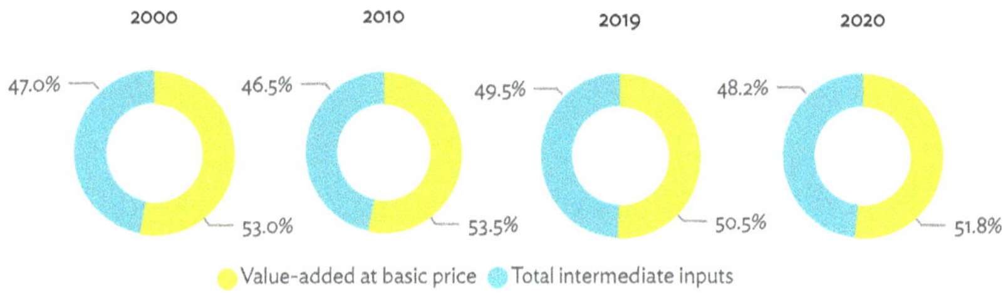

Imports and Exports, 2019-2020

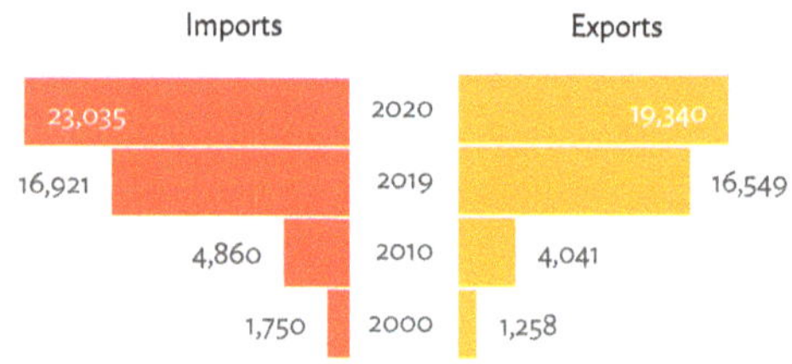

Domestic Linkages

Normalized Linkages

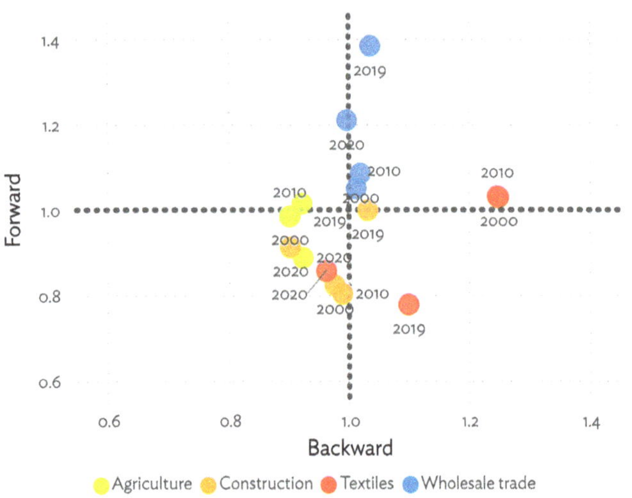

Net Linkages

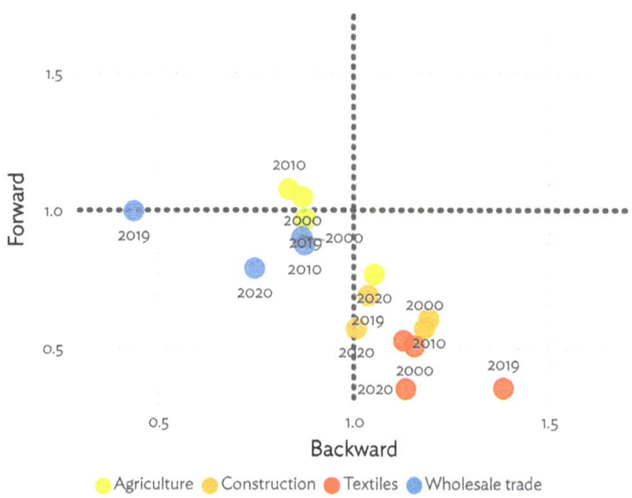

Value-Added Multipliers

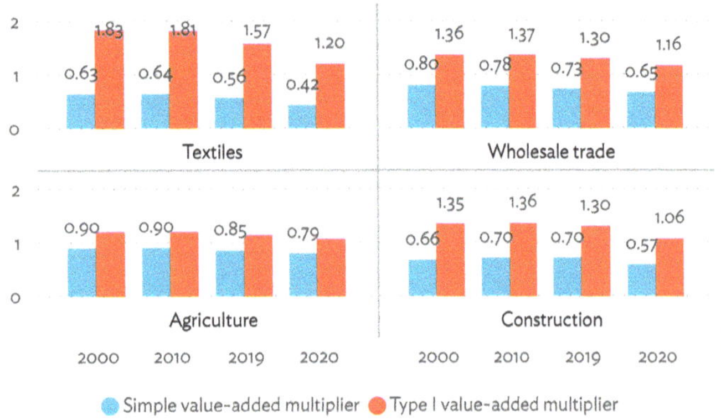

Production-Induced Effect

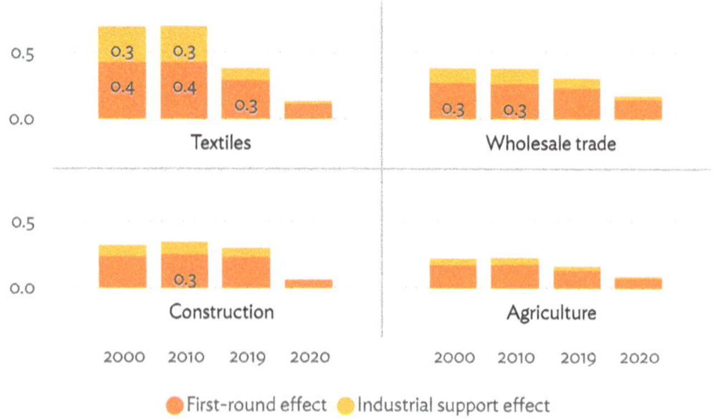

continued on next page.

Click here for figure data

continued.

Cambodia

Southeast Asia and the Pacific

International Linkages

Change in Exports, by Value-Added Components, 2019-2020

($ million)

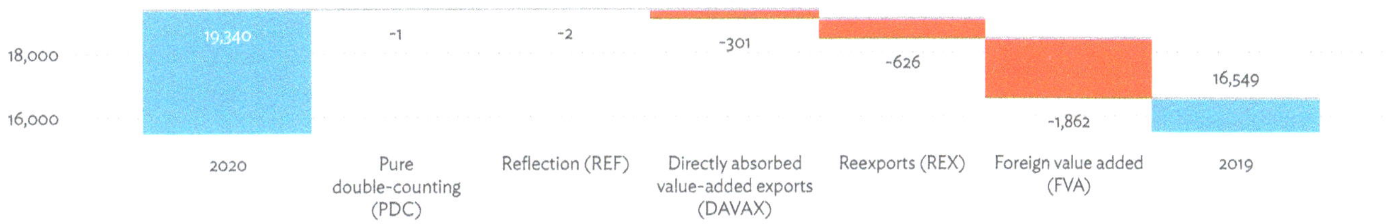

Import Multipliers

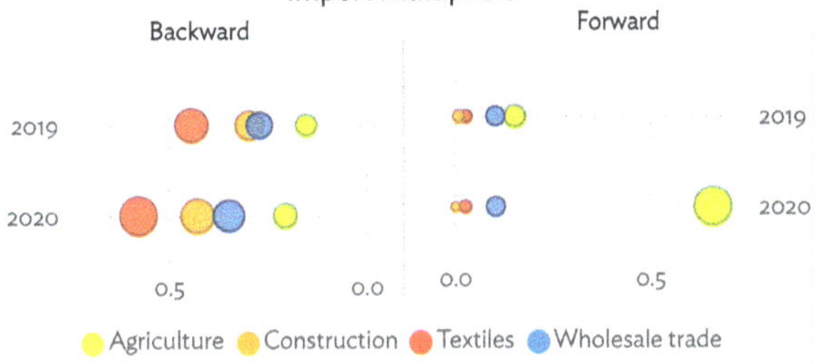

GVC Participation Rates

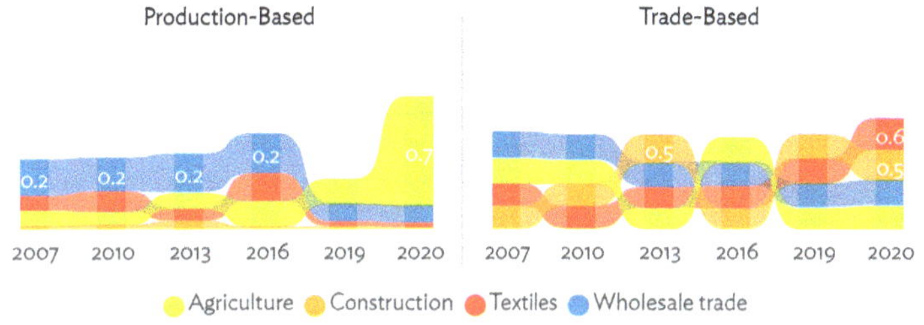

Average Production Length

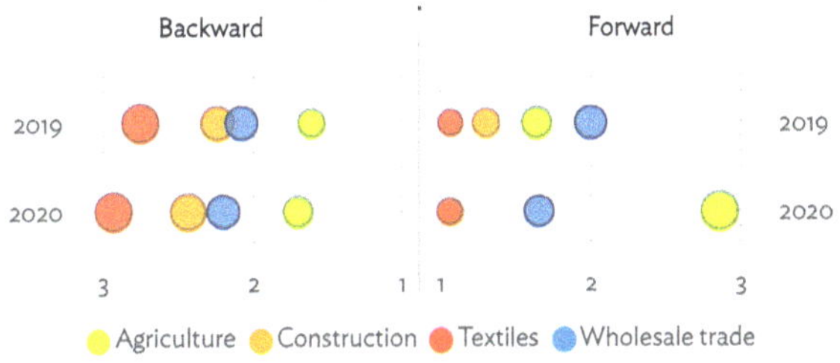

New Revealed Comparative Advantage

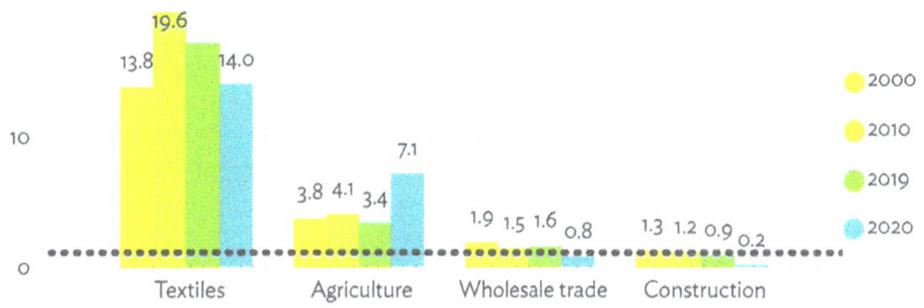

Trade Orientation

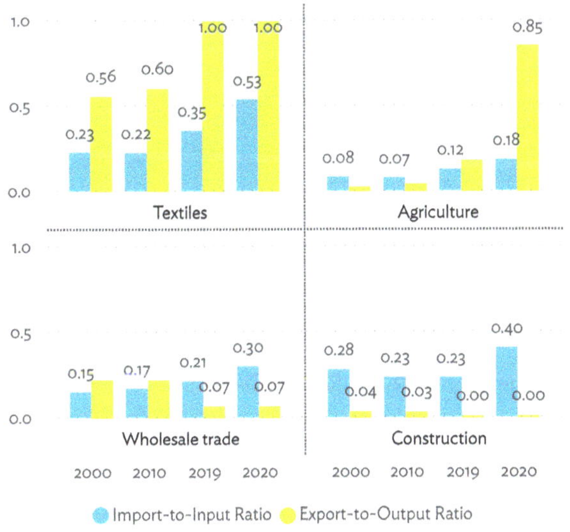

Agglomeration Indices

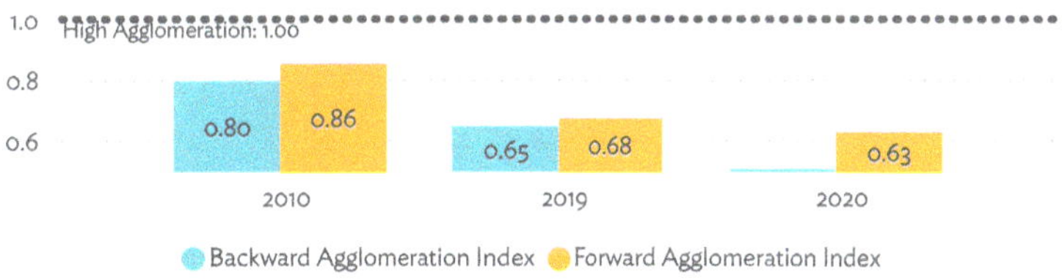

Domestic Transfer Effects and International Spillover Effects

($ million)

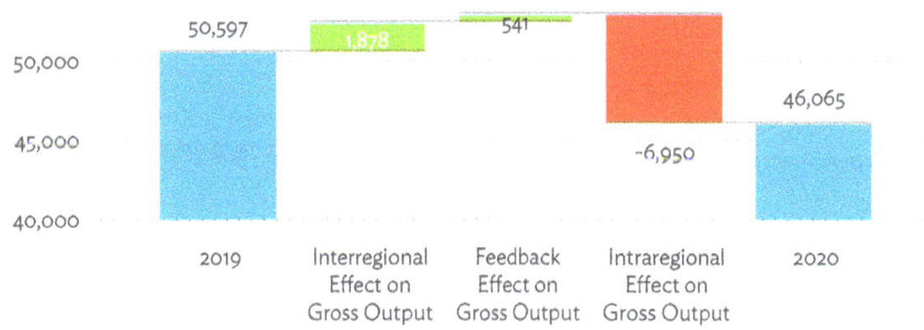

GVC = global value chain; NEC = not elsewhere classified.

Source: Calculations using the Asian Development Bank Multiregional Input-Output Table. https://mrio.adbx.online/ (accessed July 2021).

Click here for figure data

People's Republic of China

East Asia

Basic Economic Indicators

Economic Aggregates ($ million)	2000	2007	2010	2013	2016	2019	2020
Value-added at basic price	1,198,452	3,495,060	5,931,147	9,380,359	11,191,026	14,276,634	14,724,439
Gross output	3,253,016	10,654,372	18,053,714	29,232,642	33,583,226	43,533,477	44,511,276
Total intermediate inputs	2,042,182	7,094,831	12,041,273	19,750,806	22,392,200	29,256,843	29,786,837
Taxes less subsidies on products	0	0	0	0	0	0	0
International transport margins	12,381	64,481	81,294	101,478	0	0	0
CIF/FOB adjustment	0	0	0	0	0	0	0
Direct purchases abroad by residents	0	0	0	0	0	0	0
Purchases by nonresidents on the domestic territory	0	0	0	0	0	0	0
Household final consumption expenditure	541,040	1,198,104	1,937,722	3,207,960	4,041,375	5,328,471	5,222,258
Final consumption expenditure by NPISHs	0	0	0	0	0	0	0
Government final consumption expenditure	189,483	460,831	772,580	1,286,635	1,601,919	2,361,528	2,438,848
Gross fixed capital formation	366,845	1,235,105	2,482,132	3,953,503	4,497,722	5,822,197	7,265,049
Changes in inventories	10,520	82,584	131,957	164,255	76,137	-348	-1,145,000
Total final demand	1,107,888	2,976,624	5,324,391	8,612,353	10,217,154	13,511,848	13,781,155
Exports	262,018	1,304,802	1,697,752	2,293,014	2,164,513	2,664,103	2,732,326
Imports	220,613	924,476	1,358,259	1,863,449	1,601,470	2,499,153	2,362,586

Economic Aggregates, Top 3 Sectors ($ million)	2000	2007	2010	2013	2016	2019	2020
Value-added at basic price							
Finance	49,365	162,223	309,926	542,716	775,588	1,103,482	1,218,407
Agriculture	181,870	376,408	598,762	919,771	1,008,065	1,064,789	1,175,419
Wholesale trade	81,658	228,114	437,527	746,178	900,468	1,146,961	1,149,046
Gross output							
Construction	248,694	869,204	1,702,013	2,745,012	3,233,231	4,229,942	4,376,834
Electricals	216,840	926,154	1,622,230	2,493,839	2,716,257	3,470,097	3,498,871
Chemicals	167,779	544,418	884,556	1,573,618	1,713,965	2,793,140	2,816,321
Total intermediate inputs							
Construction	181,102	664,777	1,303,215	2,104,850	2,509,012	3,207,538	3,318,925
Electricals	169,076	752,987	1,331,900	2,072,349	2,270,842	2,933,146	2,957,464
Chemicals	124,992	425,796	693,845	1,280,852	1,400,314	2,310,819	2,329,998
Total final demand							
Construction	231,450	833,709	1,584,925	2,513,001	2,937,095	3,820,227	4,116,648
Health and social work	43,438	134,420	239,482	459,128	593,638	2,043,229	2,087,912
Public administration	94,970	255,736	415,813	636,706	903,486	1,379,184	1,408,489
Exports							
Electricals	65,374	426,450	561,086	733,621	691,327	790,466	820,531
Textiles	41,381	155,531	177,812	232,740	214,248	261,741	308,474
Machinery, NEC	8,791	99,189	136,754	176,968	166,806	274,864	279,975
Imports							
Electricals	62,143	274,459	345,617	462,080	364,202	561,097	549,618
Mining	14,291	104,463	208,657	346,355	241,088	324,240	318,865
Chemicals	25,967	90,410	118,854	147,823	128,899	241,451	241,642

Domestic Linkages

Indicator and Top 3 Sectors, 2020	2000	2007	2010	2013	2016	2019	2020
First-round effect							
Leather	0.64	0.75	0.74	0.80	0.82	0.82	0.82
Transport equipment	0.71	0.73	0.75	0.77	0.78	0.78	0.78
Textiles	0.66	0.73	0.76	0.76	0.77	0.78	0.78
Industrial support effect							
Rubber and plastics	1.05	1.19	1.26	1.43	1.51	1.54	1.51
Transport equipment	1.19	1.32	1.43	1.56	1.67	1.56	1.51
Electricals	1.03	0.99	1.20	1.37	1.52	1.43	1.43
Production-induced effect							
Transport equipment	1.90	2.05	2.18	2.33	2.45	2.34	2.29
Rubber and plastics	1.74	1.90	1.99	2.18	2.28	2.30	2.28
Leather	1.52	1.99	1.94	2.27	2.35	2.29	2.24

continued on next page.

continued.

People's Republic of China

East Asia *Domestic Linkages*

Indicator and Top 3 Sectors, 2020	2000	2007	2010	2013	2016	2019	2020
Simple value-added multiplier							
Real estate	0.96	0.96	0.98	0.98	0.99	0.97	0.98
Finance	0.96	0.95	0.96	0.96	0.97	0.96	0.96
Wholesale trade	0.91	0.92	0.94	0.95	0.96	0.95	0.95
Type I value-added multiplier							
Leather	3.57	4.78	4.21	5.50	5.84	6.18	6.27
Metals	4.13	3.81	3.81	4.60	5.08	5.64	5.75
Electricals	3.41	3.49	4.00	4.37	4.86	4.83	4.93
Direct backward linkage							
Leather	0.64	0.75	0.74	0.80	0.82	0.82	0.82
Transport equipment	0.71	0.73	0.75	0.77	0.78	0.78	0.78
Textiles	0.66	0.73	0.76	0.76	0.77	0.78	0.78
Complete hypothetical extraction (backward)							
Construction	2.68	2.84	2.82	2.91	3.00	2.79	2.83
Health and social work	2.50	2.61	2.64	2.76	2.73	2.81	2.78
Machinery, NEC	2.26	2.29	2.33	2.46	2.54	2.55	2.64
Partial hypothetical extraction (backward)							
Construction	1.68	1.85	1.85	1.96	2.05	1.84	1.86
Health and social work	1.51	1.62	1.65	1.77	1.74	1.86	1.84
Machinery, NEC	1.43	1.49	1.53	1.67	1.75	1.75	1.80
Total backward linkage							
Transport equipment	2.90	3.05	3.18	3.33	3.45	3.34	3.29
Rubber and plastics	2.74	2.90	2.99	3.18	3.28	3.30	3.28
Leather	2.52	2.99	2.94	3.27	3.35	3.29	3.24
Direct forward linkage							
Mining	0.89	0.97	0.97	0.98	0.98	0.99	0.99
Refined fuels	0.94	0.96	0.93	0.92	0.93	0.93	0.95
Rubber and plastics	0.82	0.79	0.86	0.87	0.89	0.95	0.95
Complete hypothetical extraction (forward)							
Mining	3.50	3.80	3.73	3.84	3.92	4.15	4.11
Transport activities, NEC	2.72	2.54	3.10	3.48	3.58	3.58	3.55
Refined fuels	3.44	3.43	3.32	3.40	3.45	3.42	3.41
Partial hypothetical extraction (forward)							
Mining	2.57	2.92	2.89	3.00	3.08	3.22	3.18
Transport activities, NEC	1.82	1.56	2.13	2.52	2.62	2.62	2.58
Refined fuels	2.49	2.52	2.44	2.53	2.59	2.54	2.54
Total forward linkage							
Mining	3.77	4.30	4.40	4.57	4.68	4.48	4.43
Utilities	3.38	4.26	4.08	4.17	4.24	4.00	3.97
Refined fuels	3.60	3.75	3.77	3.91	4.00	3.88	3.90
Normalized backward linkage							
Transport equipment	1.28	1.31	1.34	1.34	1.37	1.34	1.33
Rubber and plastics	1.21	1.24	1.26	1.28	1.30	1.32	1.32
Leather	1.11	1.28	1.24	1.32	1.32	1.32	1.31
Normalized forward linkage							
Mining	1.58	1.79	1.77	1.75	1.74	1.66	1.66
Utilities	1.42	1.77	1.64	1.60	1.57	1.49	1.48
Refined fuels	1.51	1.56	1.52	1.50	1.48	1.44	1.46
Net backward linkage							
Construction	2.51	2.78	2.74	2.81	2.89	2.67	2.76
Health and social work	2.32	2.31	2.49	2.67	2.63	2.67	2.62
Manufacturing, NEC	1.21	1.62	1.58	1.68	1.55	2.14	2.08
Net forward linkage							
Mining	2.27	2.06	2.05	2.12	2.18	2.34	2.32
Agriculture	1.23	1.52	1.63	1.75	1.78	1.92	2.23
Finance	2.32	2.11	2.17	2.25	2.29	2.18	2.18

continued on next page.

continued.

People's Republic of China

East Asia *International Linkages*

Indicator and Top 3 Sectors, 2020	2000	2007	2010	2013	2016	2019	2020
Self-sufficiency ratio							
Manufacturing, NEC	1.32	1.55	1.24	1.32	1.33	3.27	2.96
Textiles	1.27	1.54	1.34	1.28	1.23	1.33	1.41
Leather	1.08	1.37	1.31	1.21	1.18	1.31	1.26
Import-to-input ratio							
Refined fuels	0.09	0.16	0.17	0.17	0.12	0.14	0.13
Electricals	0.13	0.20	0.13	0.11	0.08	0.11	0.11
Metals	0.06	0.08	0.08	0.09	0.06	0.08	0.08
Export-to-output ratio							
Sale of motor vehicles	1.00	1.00	1.00	1.00	1.00	1.00	1.00
Manufacturing, NEC	0.28	0.54	0.51	0.52	0.46	0.99	0.97
Textiles	0.28	0.38	0.28	0.24	0.21	0.27	0.32
Domestic inputs share to output							
Leather	0.64	0.75	0.74	0.80	0.82	0.82	0.82
Transport equipment	0.71	0.73	0.75	0.77	0.78	0.78	0.78
Textiles	0.66	0.73	0.76	0.76	0.77	0.78	0.78
Foreign inputs share to output							
Refined fuels	0.09	0.16	0.17	0.17	0.12	0.14	0.13
Electricals	0.13	0.20	0.13	0.11	0.08	0.11	0.11
Metals	0.06	0.08	0.08	0.09	0.06	0.08	0.08
Backward import multipliers							
Electricals	0.25	0.35	0.28	0.26	0.20	0.25	0.24
Refined fuels	0.15	0.26	0.27	0.27	0.20	0.22	0.20
Metals	0.16	0.21	0.21	0.22	0.17	0.20	0.19
Forward import multipliers							
Metals	0.16	0.23	0.17	0.16	0.15	0.18	0.17
Electricals	0.16	0.23	0.23	0.23	0.21	0.16	0.17
Textiles	0.10	0.15	0.14	0.13	0.12	0.15	0.17
Intraregional transfer multiplier							
Transport equipment	2.90	3.05	3.18	3.33	3.45	3.34	3.29
Rubber and plastics	2.74	2.90	2.99	3.18	3.28	3.30	3.28
Leather	2.52	2.99	2.94	3.27	3.35	3.29	3.24
Interregional spillover multiplier							
Refined fuels	1.13	1.26	1.28	1.29	1.22	1.24	1.24
Electricals	1.24	1.36	1.24	1.20	1.15	1.19	1.19
Metals	1.10	1.14	1.16	1.17	1.12	1.15	1.15
Interregional feedback multiplier							
Electricals	1.10	1.16	1.12	1.11	1.07	1.08	1.07
Refined fuels	1.03	1.06	1.05	1.06	1.04	1.04	1.04
Air transport	1.02	1.04	1.04	1.04	1.03	1.04	1.03
Intraregional effect on gross output ($ million)							
Construction	246,959.42	862,807.03	1,688,897.53	2,719,370.35	3,209,696.38	4,209,658.02	4,361,984.96
Electricals	181,094.66	714,133.23	1,244,902.86	1,928,934.02	2,147,350.11	2,902,569.76	2,914,267.93
Chemicals	144,128.57	418,806.60	709,347.62	1,302,079.16	1,454,238.77	2,466,977.80	2,484,274.70
Interregional effect on gross output ($ million)							
Electricals	26,234.84	145,573.16	265,645.33	387,707.26	394,951.64	397,406.75	409,530.91
Metals	27,299.60	157,612.28	180,750.23	275,577.49	276,100.73	270,520.03	260,006.72
Chemicals	17,955.62	92,299.55	128,220.52	196,691.87	187,845.14	236,392.87	243,416.71
Feedback effect on gross output ($ million)							
Electricals	9,510.21	66,447.58	111,681.83	177,197.36	173,955.47	170,120.72	175,072.44
Metals	8,418.36	57,940.53	62,644.54	103,613.32	102,606.77	106,601.95	97,771.69
Chemicals	5,695.00	33,311.79	46,988.03	74,847.20	71,880.96	89,768.98	88,629.99
Directly absorbed value-added exports (DAVAX) ($ million)							
Electricals	40,903.58	227,353.32	319,502.45	425,051.90	431,279.93	476,995.31	506,937.88
Textiles	32,068.58	118,118.29	141,618.49	187,120.16	177,383.38	201,749.15	240,706.67
Machinery, NEC	6,489.82	67,623.48	93,398.72	120,201.36	119,445.62	191,841.73	201,243.23
Reflection (REF) ($ million)							
Electricals	563.88	5,476.96	12,454.47	22,860.72	21,127.18	21,227.03	26,168.41
Metals	290.86	2,369.00	3,151.46	5,612.65	5,523.21	10,106.05	10,824.81
Chemicals	181.54	1,589.72	2,950.06	4,163.14	4,378.50	6,566.35	7,536.35

continued on next page.

continued.

People's Republic of China

East Asia

International Linkages

Indicator and Top 3 Sectors, 2020	2000	2007	2010	2013	2016	2019	2020
Reexports (REX) ($ million)							
Electricals	7,691.24	45,080.57	69,476.11	94,075.55	98,404.21	92,911.14	93,410.89
Metals	4,039.22	23,088.98	21,185.92	30,655.81	33,294.40	54,602.07	49,354.57
Textiles	3,430.10	12,428.98	13,522.86	19,297.78	18,186.76	30,421.77	36,196.30
Foreign value added (FVA) ($ million)							
Electricals	15,882.08	140,420.16	148,767.59	175,560.67	129,617.93	187,454.63	180,201.13
Machinery, NEC	1,328.99	21,176.89	26,414.74	31,498.44	22,526.85	46,655.29	43,470.49
Metals	2,455.94	19,421.34	21,448.43	33,244.59	24,528.15	45,710.55	40,108.26
Pure double-counting (PDC) ($ million)							
Electricals	333.59	8,118.76	10,885.42	16,072.38	10,897.70	11,877.51	13,812.21
Machinery, NEC	21.13	828.49	1,258.52	1,949.11	1,321.94	2,200.71	2,437.03
Metals	35.54	589.65	683.75	1,288.14	1,003.10	1,447.67	1,541.87
Trade-based GVC participation rate							
Refined fuels	0.40	0.53	0.54	0.55	0.49	0.49	0.48
Water transport	0.32	0.39	0.38	0.37	0.34	0.57	0.47
Metals	0.43	0.48	0.45	0.45	0.42	0.48	0.46
Production-based GVC participation rate							
Metals	0.16	0.23	0.17	0.16	0.15	0.18	0.17
Electricals	0.16	0.23	0.23	0.23	0.21	0.16	0.17
Textiles	0.10	0.15	0.14	0.13	0.12	0.15	0.17
Trade-based backward GVC participation rate							
Electricals	0.25	0.35	0.28	0.26	0.20	0.25	0.24
Refined fuels	0.15	0.26	0.27	0.27	0.20	0.22	0.20
Metals	0.16	0.21	0.21	0.22	0.17	0.20	0.19
Trade-based forward GVC participation rate							
Water transport	0.22	0.26	0.25	0.26	0.27	0.47	0.39
Public administration	0.24	0.20	0.20	0.20	0.19	0.40	0.37
Transport activities, NEC	0.33	0.28	0.37	0.31	0.33	0.42	0.34
Traditional revealed comparative advantage							
Textiles	3.50	3.43	3.28	3.08	2.99	3.21	3.30
Leather	3.81	3.56	3.24	3.09	2.92	3.37	2.87
Manufacturing, NEC	2.26	2.02	1.30	1.73	1.71	2.76	2.54
New revealed comparative advantage							
Manufacturing, NEC	2.33	2.19	1.39	1.63	1.54	2.99	2.76
Textiles	3.49	3.19	3.19	2.96	2.69	2.50	2.52
Rubber and plastics	1.59	1.40	1.35	1.37	1.28	2.71	2.48
Backward production length							
Electricals	3.31	3.57	3.69	3.83	3.84	3.81	3.78
Transport equipment	3.28	3.64	3.68	3.79	3.81	3.75	3.67
Rubber and plastics	3.17	3.53	3.52	3.64	3.63	3.71	3.67
Forward production length							
Mining	4.15	4.77	4.78	4.93	4.99	4.79	4.76
Refined fuels	3.96	4.20	4.16	4.28	4.32	4.18	4.21
Utilities	3.59	4.61	4.37	4.45	4.48	4.23	4.20
Backward production length of GVC segment							
Health and social work	5.37	5.54	5.67	5.97	6.01	5.70	5.71
Transport equipment	5.17	5.46	5.72	5.93	5.97	5.61	5.57
Textiles	4.88	5.50	5.72	5.95	5.97	5.64	5.56
Forward production length of GVC segment							
Real estate	5.52	5.77	5.76	6.02	6.16	6.56	6.59
Utilities	5.66	6.55	6.46	6.62	6.72	6.21	6.24
Agriculture	4.93	5.50	5.82	6.19	6.30	6.03	6.18
Backward agglomeration index							
Transport equipment	-	1.61	1.52	1.59	1.60	1.89	1.80
Water transport	-	1.08	1.00	1.37	1.33	1.73	1.50
Machinery, NEC	-	1.16	1.22	1.34	1.39	1.36	1.50
Forward agglomeration index							
Mining	-	1.57	1.64	1.75	1.60	1.96	1.83
Transport equipment	-	1.50	1.45	1.48	1.47	1.75	1.67
Air transport	-	0.61	0.76	0.97	1.11	1.41	1.44

CIF = cost, insurance, and freight; FOB = free on board; GVC = global value chain; NEC = not elsewhere classified; NPISHs = nonprofit institutions serving households.
Source: Calculations using the Asian Development Bank Multiregional Input-Output Table. https://mrio.adbx.online/ (accessed July 2021).

continued on next page.

continued.

People's Republic of China

East Asia

The four select sectors are chosen based on their gross outputs in the economy as of 2019.

Economy Ranking out of 25 Economies

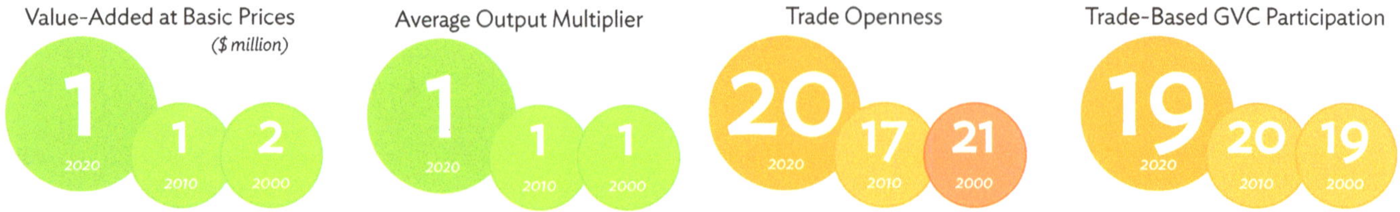

Share of Intermediate Consumption and Gross Value-Added in Output

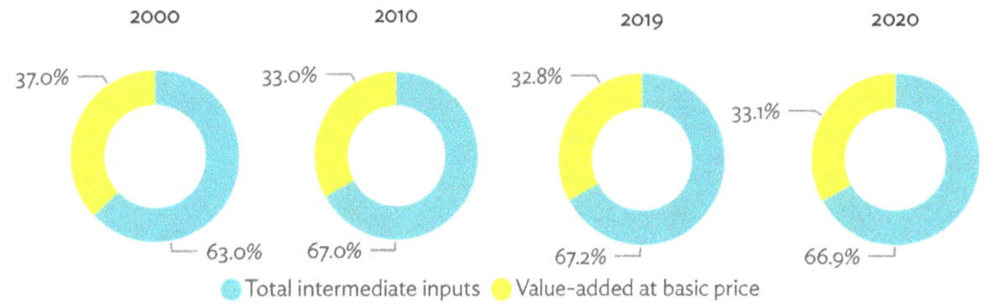

Imports and Exports, 2019-2020

($ million)

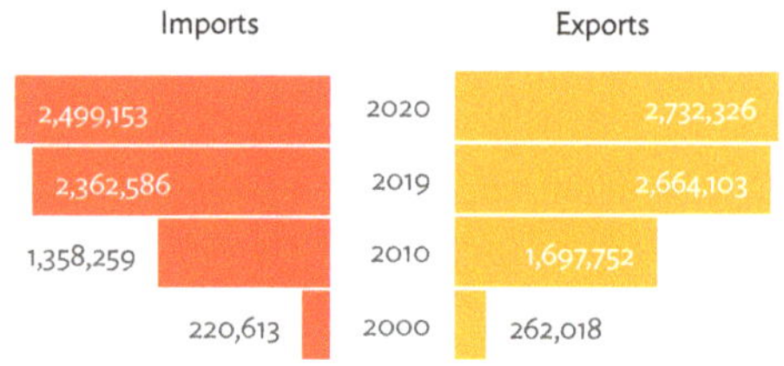

Domestic Linkages

Normalized Linkages

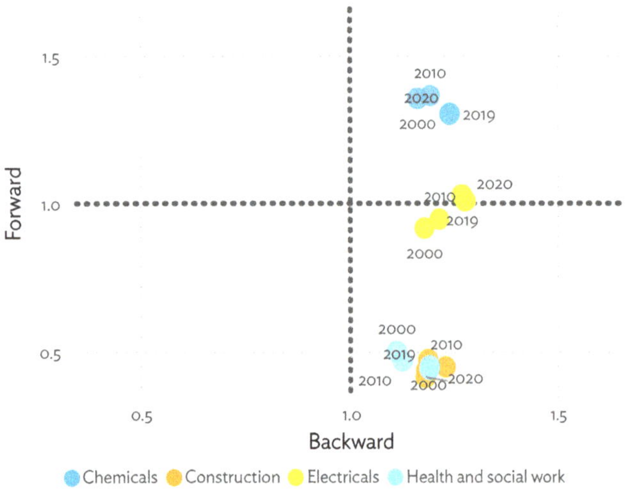

Net Linkages

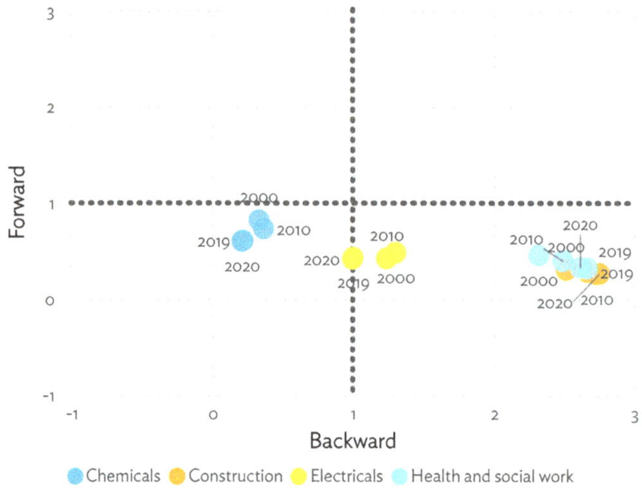

Value-Added Multipliers

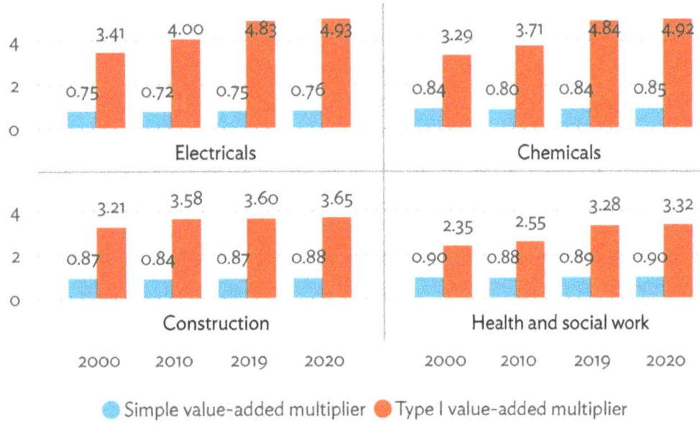

Production-Induced Effect

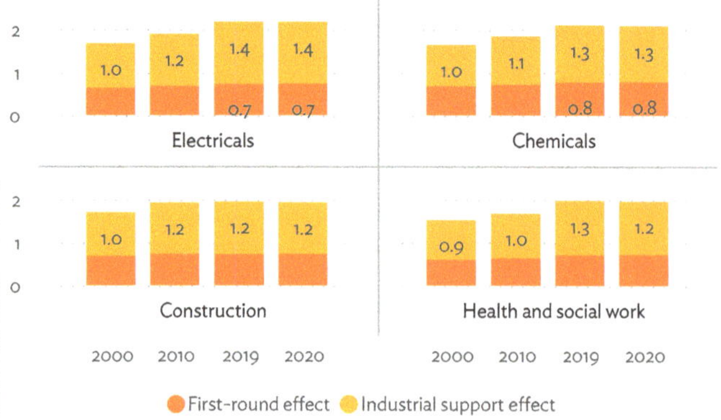

continued on next page.

Click here for figure data

continued.

People's Republic of China

East Asia

International Linkages

Change in Exports, by Value-Added Components, 2019-2020

($ million)

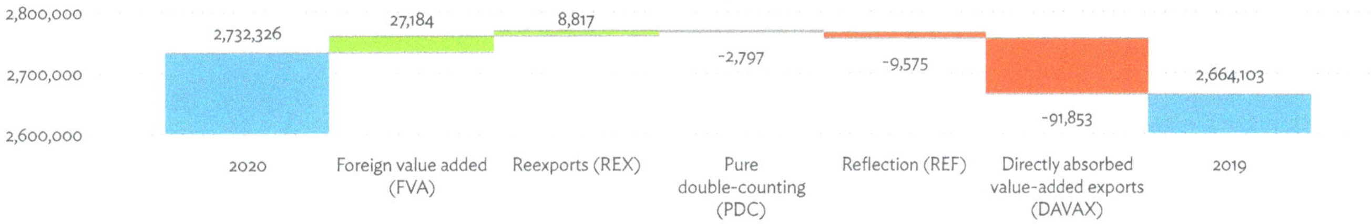

Import Multipliers

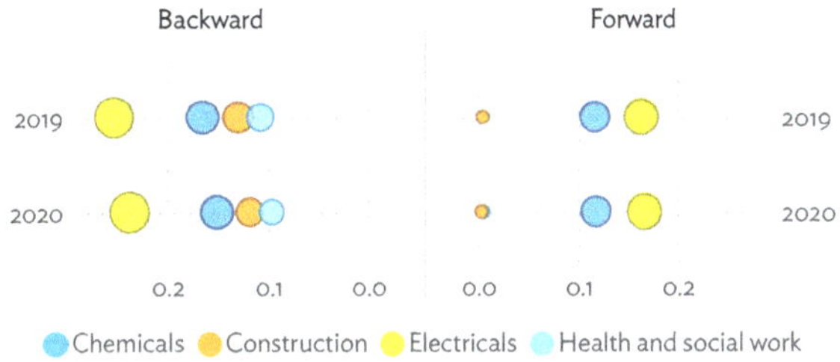

GVC Participation Rates

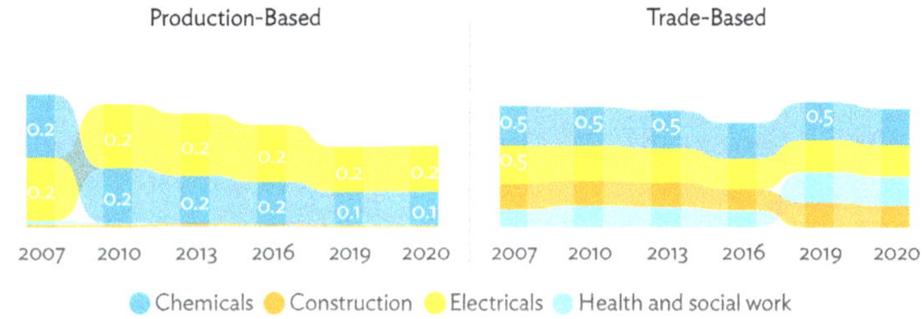

Average Production Length

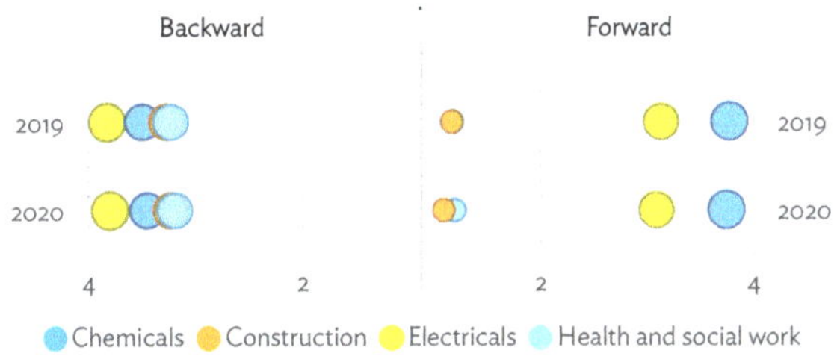

New Revealed Comparative Advantage

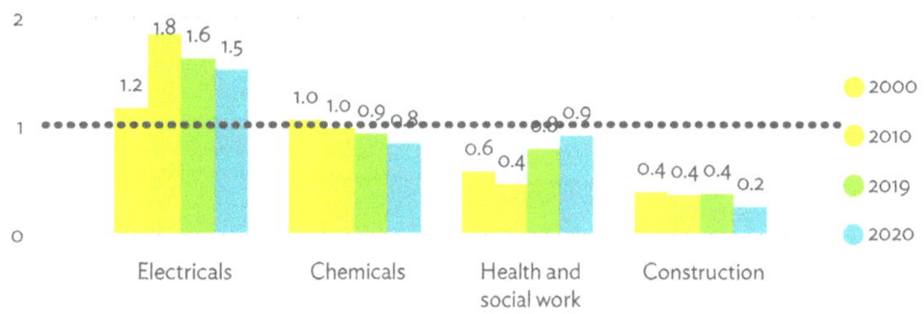

Trade Orientation

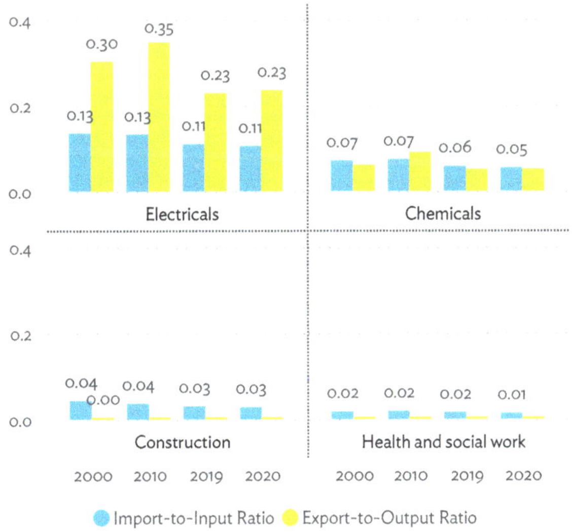

Agglomeration Indices

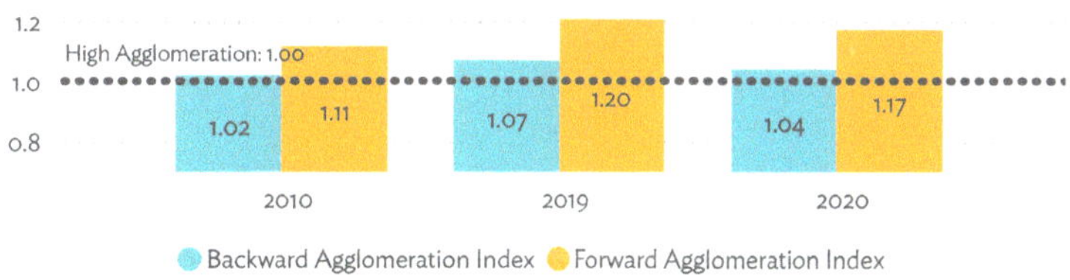

Domestic Transfer Effects and International Spillover Effects

($ million)

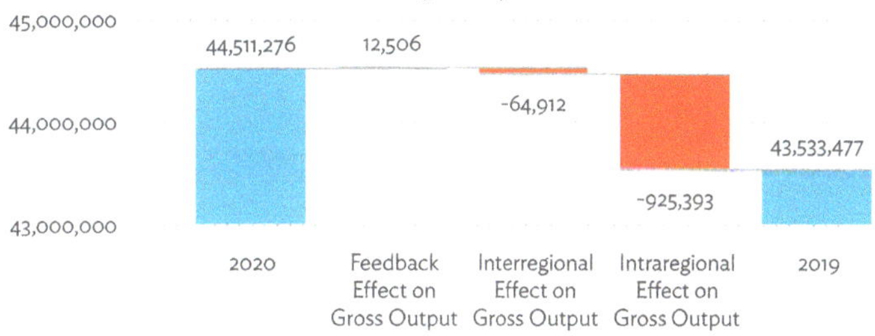

GVC = global value chain; NEC = not elsewhere classified.

Source: Calculations using the Asian Development Bank Multiregional Input-Output Table. https://mrio.adbx.online/ (accessed July 2021).

Click here for figure data

Fiji

Southeast Asia and the Pacific

Basic Economic Indicators

Economic Aggregates ($ million)	2000	2007	2010	2013	2016	2019	2020
Value-added at basic price	1,480	2,771	2,633	3,420	3,717	4,475	3,308
Gross output	3,401	6,074	5,314	7,131	7,146	8,498	6,419
Total intermediate inputs	1,866	3,158	2,535	3,480	3,024	3,669	2,719
Taxes less subsidies on products	56	146	146	231	405	353	392
International transport margins	0	0	0	0	0	0	0
CIF/FOB adjustment	0	0	0	0	0	0	0
Direct purchases abroad by residents	0	0	0	0	0	0	0
Purchases by nonresidents on the domestic territory	0	0	0	0	0	0	0
Household final consumption expenditure	792	2,043	1,677	1,850	1,985	1,710	1,703
Final consumption expenditure by NPISHs	0	0	57	139	154	169	153
Government final consumption expenditure	316	767	459	789	923	1,063	893
Gross fixed capital formation	17	263	191	651	379	103	373
Changes in inventories	1	-25	34	-25	-60	272	34
Total final demand	1,126	3,047	2,418	3,404	3,381	3,317	3,156
Exports	640	844	1,160	1,425	1,724	2,645	1,233
Imports	1,053	1,868	1,532	2,257	2,018	3,212	1,969

Economic Aggregates, Top 3 Sectors ($ million)	2000	2007	2010	2013	2016	2019	2020
Value-added at basic price							
Agriculture	244	362	290	426	419	651	432
Public administration	86	221	157	192	330	400	308
Finance	83	229	299	364	318	383	289
Gross output							
Agriculture	538	617	481	707	679	1,144	696
Food and beverages	150	600	578	764	686	831	605
Hotels and restaurants	277	479	398	582	557	653	510
Total intermediate inputs							
Food and beverages	112	425	395	525	443	542	385
Hotels and restaurants	212	269	215	313	275	299	248
Air transport	197	403	243	363	215	243	244
Total final demand							
Public administration	125	333	234	296	447	490	375
Education	104	274	160	200	351	346	340
Hotels and restaurants	88	140	39	151	80	209	331
Exports							
Food and beverages	77	96	153	225	228	405	283
Utilities	1	0	0	0	2	242	221
Air transport	2	175	217	262	246	383	94
Imports							
Transport equipment	185	387	325	513	479	875	523
Refined fuels	212	452	392	608	437	522	346
Food and beverages	82	242	151	217	227	363	216

Domestic Linkages

Indicator and Top 3 Sectors, 2020	2000	2007	2010	2013	2016	2019	2020
First-round effect							
Food and beverages	0.65	0.55	0.55	0.54	0.50	0.53	0.54
Wood	0.69	0.56	0.54	0.55	0.51	0.52	0.53
Minerals, NEC	0.56	0.53	0.53	0.52	0.48	0.50	0.52
Industrial support effect							
Manufacturing, NEC	0.41	0.32	0.28	0.27	0.20	0.26	0.26
Minerals, NEC	0.49	0.25	0.24	0.22	0.24	0.24	0.25
Construction	0.52	0.27	0.20	0.19	0.21	0.30	0.24
Production-induced effect							
Minerals, NEC	1.05	0.78	0.77	0.74	0.72	0.74	0.77
Food and beverages	1.29	0.84	0.79	0.77	0.68	0.75	0.76
Wood	1.38	0.84	0.78	0.79	0.71	0.75	0.76

continued on next page.

continued.

Fiji

Southeast Asia and the Pacific — *Domestic Linkages*

Indicator and Top 3 Sectors, 2020	2000	2007	2010	2013	2016	2019	2020
Simple value-added multiplier							
Real estate	0.97	0.88	0.92	0.91	0.91	0.92	0.92
Public administration	0.92	0.83	0.84	0.82	0.90	0.86	0.91
Retail trade	0.91	0.82	0.85	0.83	0.89	0.88	0.91
Type I value-added multiplier							
Food and beverages	3.27	2.43	2.37	2.34	2.15	2.25	2.26
Wood	3.34	2.35	2.31	2.29	2.13	2.14	2.15
Minerals, NEC	2.64	1.75	2.08	2.02	1.87	2.08	2.11
Direct backward linkage							
Food and beverages	0.65	0.55	0.55	0.54	0.50	0.53	0.54
Wood	0.69	0.56	0.54	0.55	0.51	0.52	0.53
Minerals, NEC	0.56	0.53	0.53	0.52	0.48	0.50	0.52
Complete hypothetical extraction (backward)							
Minerals, NEC	1.95	1.67	1.67	1.64	1.65	1.67	1.71
Food and beverages	2.01	1.76	1.72	1.70	1.62	1.69	1.70
Construction	1.91	1.56	1.58	1.57	1.64	1.26	1.70
Partial hypothetical extraction (backward)							
Minerals, NEC	1.00	0.73	0.72	0.69	0.69	0.71	0.75
Food and beverages	1.13	0.81	0.76	0.74	0.66	0.73	0.74
Construction	0.95	0.65	0.60	0.58	0.66	0.54	0.71
Total backward linkage							
Minerals, NEC	2.05	1.78	1.77	1.74	1.72	1.74	1.77
Food and beverages	2.29	1.84	1.79	1.77	1.68	1.75	1.76
Wood	2.38	1.84	1.78	1.79	1.71	1.75	1.76
Direct forward linkage							
Minerals, NEC	0.18	0.93	0.92	0.91	0.85	0.91	0.89
Rubber and plastics	0.23	0.88	0.87	0.83	0.78	0.84	0.83
Personal services, NEC	0.87	0.28	0.19	0.22	0.87	0.62	0.75
Complete hypothetical extraction (forward)							
Minerals, NEC	1.25	2.23	2.13	2.11	2.00	2.23	2.08
Personal services, NEC	2.39	1.36	1.21	1.25	2.10	1.80	2.00
Chemicals	1.31	1.93	1.94	1.90	1.98	1.86	1.96
Partial hypothetical extraction (forward)							
Minerals, NEC	0.30	1.30	1.18	1.17	1.05	1.27	1.12
Personal services, NEC	1.50	0.37	0.22	0.26	1.11	0.82	1.05
Chemicals	0.32	0.97	1.00	0.96	1.04	0.99	1.04
Total forward linkage							
Rubber and plastics	1.41	2.43	2.32	2.24	2.08	2.40	2.20
Minerals, NEC	1.31	2.38	2.26	2.24	2.09	2.32	2.16
Chemicals	1.32	2.02	2.07	2.02	2.09	2.13	2.13
Normalized backward linkage							
Minerals, NEC	1.16	1.18	1.22	1.21	1.28	1.26	1.25
Food and beverages	1.30	1.22	1.24	1.23	1.25	1.27	1.25
Wood	1.35	1.22	1.23	1.25	1.27	1.27	1.25
Normalized forward linkage							
Rubber and plastics	0.82	1.48	1.54	1.49	1.42	1.62	1.49
Minerals, NEC	0.76	1.45	1.50	1.49	1.42	1.56	1.46
Chemicals	0.77	1.23	1.37	1.34	1.43	1.43	1.44
Net backward linkage							
Construction	1.34	1.54	1.58	1.56	1.63	0.93	1.70
Food and beverages	1.22	1.48	1.54	1.51	1.44	1.48	1.53
Textiles	1.58	0.79	0.97	0.97	0.95	1.38	1.38
Net forward linkage							
Telecommunications	1.94	1.35	1.35	1.38	1.30	1.30	1.46
Transport activities, NEC	1.25	0.81	0.70	0.67	1.07	1.04	1.37
Wholesale trade	1.17	1.10	1.01	1.01	1.08	1.29	1.29

continued on next page.

continued.

Fiji

Southeast Asia and the Pacific *International Linkages*

Indicator and Top 3 Sectors, 2020	2000	2007	2010	2013	2016	2019	2020
Self-sufficiency ratio							
Utilities	0.99	1.00	1.00	1.00	1.01	83.48	5.09
Textiles	2.32	0.88	0.94	0.93	0.97	1.81	2.26
Inland transport	1.08	1.02	1.15	1.11	1.21	3.39	2.09
Import-to-input ratio							
Air transport	0.08	0.34	0.46	0.45	0.42	0.41	0.29
Water transport	0.18	0.27	0.37	0.36	0.34	0.39	0.28
Inland transport	0.03	0.21	0.29	0.29	0.34	0.37	0.27
Export-to-output ratio							
Electricals	1.00	1.00	1.00	1.00	1.00	1.00	1.00
Transport equipment	0.83	0.02	0.11	0.03	0.05	0.99	1.00
Textiles	0.80	0.10	0.18	0.16	0.23	0.99	1.00
Domestic inputs share to output							
Food and beverages	0.65	0.55	0.55	0.54	0.50	0.53	0.54
Wood	0.69	0.56	0.54	0.55	0.51	0.52	0.53
Minerals, NEC	0.56	0.53	0.53	0.52	0.48	0.50	0.52
Foreign inputs share to output							
Air transport	0.08	0.34	0.46	0.45	0.42	0.41	0.29
Water transport	0.18	0.27	0.37	0.36	0.34	0.39	0.28
Inland transport	0.03	0.21	0.29	0.29	0.34	0.37	0.27
Backward import multipliers							
Rubber and plastics	0.49	0.54	0.50	0.53	0.49	0.45	0.36
Air transport	0.18	0.45	0.52	0.51	0.45	0.45	0.34
Water transport	0.22	0.38	0.43	0.43	0.37	0.42	0.32
Forward import multipliers							
Metals	0.26	0.07	0.10	0.08	0.12	0.62	0.72
Water transport	0.46	0.03	0.16	0.16	0.16	0.88	0.69
Wood	0.52	0.21	0.33	0.27	0.35	0.43	0.53
Intraregional transfer multiplier							
Minerals, NEC	2.05	1.78	1.77	1.74	1.72	1.74	1.77
Food and beverages	2.29	1.84	1.79	1.77	1.68	1.75	1.76
Wood	2.38	1.84	1.78	1.79	1.71	1.75	1.76
Interregional spillover multiplier							
Rubber and plastics	1.76	1.81	1.82	1.89	1.87	1.76	1.59
Air transport	1.15	1.64	1.89	1.89	1.85	1.72	1.53
Water transport	1.38	1.51	1.70	1.69	1.68	1.72	1.52
Interregional feedback multiplier							
Water transport	1.10	1.17	1.24	1.27	1.24	1.25	1.18
Air transport	1.03	1.21	1.27	1.31	1.28	1.26	1.17
Inland transport	1.01	1.13	1.16	1.19	1.21	1.20	1.14
Intraregional effect on gross output ($ million)							
Agriculture	423.91	566.72	416.33	617.23	574.18	985.53	592.96
Food and beverages	82.10	515.46	467.14	628.03	544.96	677.21	492.16
Hotels and restaurants	239.23	352.43	254.37	407.41	346.29	433.91	448.21
Interregional effect on gross output ($ million)							
Food and beverages	61.66	75.22	96.62	116.97	119.82	128.05	98.04
Air transport	36.89	124.91	158.31	165.20	169.98	255.93	92.18
Agriculture	104.24	43.98	56.17	77.13	89.32	134.62	90.41
Feedback effect on gross output ($ million)							
Metals	3.24	1.46	1.89	2.23	3.25	19.00	16.55
Air transport	12.03	21.01	27.08	29.64	32.50	35.89	16.45
Water transport	3.45	0.42	1.81	2.86	2.63	20.24	15.56
Directly absorbed value-added exports (DAVAX) ($ million)							
Food and beverages	54.66	58.43	98.28	143.89	150.08	285.47	207.89
Utilities	0.35	0.15	0.14	0.19	1.21	172.43	153.80
Textiles	119.39	9.71	16.66	19.65	26.20	83.21	67.38
Reflection (REF) ($ million)							
Metals	0.02	0.00	0.00	0.00	0.00	0.01	0.01
Hotels and restaurants	0.00	0.03	0.02	0.03	0.04	0.03	0.01
Water transport	0.00	0.00	0.00	0.00	0.00	0.01	0.01

continued on next page.

continued.

Fiji

Southeast Asia and the Pacific *International Linkages*

Indicator and Top 3 Sectors, 2020	2000	2007	2010	2013	2016	2019	2020
Reexports (REX) ($ million)							
Food and beverages	8.66	9.38	16.36	21.08	23.88	32.04	25.66
Water transport	3.71	0.15	1.36	2.15	2.24	17.35	15.85
Metals	2.34	0.61	0.84	0.97	1.36	14.34	11.99
Foreign value added (FVA) ($ million)							
Utilities	0.07	0.12	0.16	0.19	0.86	63.91	60.17
Food and beverages	13.41	27.99	38.35	60.39	53.75	87.80	49.60
Air transport	0.33	79.31	112.07	134.86	110.62	171.50	32.20
Pure double-counting (PDC) ($ million)							
Utilities	0.00	0.00	0.00	0.00	0.00	0.01	0.00
Food and beverages	0.00	0.00	0.00	0.00	0.01	0.01	0.00
Air transport	0.00	0.00	0.00	0.00	0.01	0.02	0.00
Trade-based GVC participation rate							
Water transport	0.51	0.41	0.55	0.59	0.51	0.73	0.66
Mining	0.44	0.85	0.40	0.51	0.46	0.44	0.56
Metals	0.52	0.56	0.49	0.51	0.47	0.49	0.50
Production-based GVC participation rate							
Metals	0.26	0.07	0.10	0.08	0.12	0.62	0.72
Water transport	0.46	0.03	0.16	0.16	0.16	0.88	0.69
Wood	0.52	0.21	0.33	0.27	0.35	0.43	0.53
Trade-based backward GVC participation rate							
Rubber and plastics	0.49	0.54	0.50	0.53	0.49	0.45	0.36
Air transport	0.18	0.45	0.52	0.51	0.45	0.45	0.34
Water transport	0.22	0.38	0.43	0.43	0.37	0.42	0.32
Trade-based forward GVC participation rate							
Water transport	0.29	0.02	0.13	0.16	0.14	0.31	0.34
Mining	0.28	0.05	0.06	0.12	0.09	0.13	0.32
Transport activities, NEC	0.31	0.18	0.19	0.17	0.21	0.35	0.31
Traditional revealed comparative advantage							
Utilities	0.15	0.06	0.06	0.07	0.24	15.15	27.49
Health and social work	0.32	4.63	2.98	2.84	3.90	18.82	9.19
Education	0.06	3.28	2.31	2.12	3.41	15.72	7.87
New revealed comparative advantage							
Air transport	3.44	10.44	9.85	9.96	10.78	9.08	11.14
Health and social work	1.01	2.59	2.29	2.28	3.01	11.81	5.71
Wood	2.13	1.42	2.01	1.84	1.74	3.14	5.59
Backward production length							
Rubber and plastics	3.03	3.03	2.79	2.89	2.69	2.73	2.61
Metals	2.87	3.09	2.91	3.03	2.82	2.49	2.51
Chemicals	2.72	2.76	2.58	2.64	2.40	2.34	2.31
Forward production length							
Metals	1.82	2.26	2.11	2.04	2.12	2.82	3.33
Water transport	2.81	1.30	1.60	1.55	1.56	3.46	2.97
Wood	2.74	2.22	2.42	2.21	2.29	2.32	2.57
Backward production length of GVC segment							
Manufacturing, NEC	4.02	4.58	4.57	4.68	4.61	4.36	4.48
Business activities, NEC	4.94	4.15	4.15	4.25	4.54	4.25	4.41
Metals	3.89	4.38	4.43	4.57	4.53	4.18	4.41
Forward production length of GVC segment							
Telecommunications	5.46	4.34	4.48	4.43	4.13	4.63	4.84
Real estate	5.41	4.73	4.68	4.71	4.58	4.53	4.77
Retail trade	4.33	4.03	4.10	4.06	3.75	4.59	4.76
Backward agglomeration index							
Rubber and plastics	-	0.66	1.05	1.17	1.20	2.52	2.58
Leather	-	1.91	1.72	1.67	1.59	1.87	2.33
Machinery, NEC	-	1.34	1.30	1.26	1.18	1.36	1.79
Forward agglomeration index							
Mining	-	1.50	0.46	1.01	0.43	2.03	2.00
Leather	-	2.26	1.95	1.91	1.77	1.62	1.97
Machinery, NEC	-	1.57	1.38	1.43	1.33	1.05	1.47

CIF = cost, insurance, and freight; FOB = free on board; GVC = global value chain; NEC = not elsewhere classified; NPISHs = nonprofit institutions serving households.
Source: Calculations using the Asian Development Bank Multiregional Input-Output Table. https://mrio.adbx.online/ (accessed July 2021).

continued on next page.

continued.

Fiji

Southeast Asia and the Pacific

The four select sectors are chosen based on their gross outputs in the economy as of 2019.

Economy Ranking out of 25 Economies

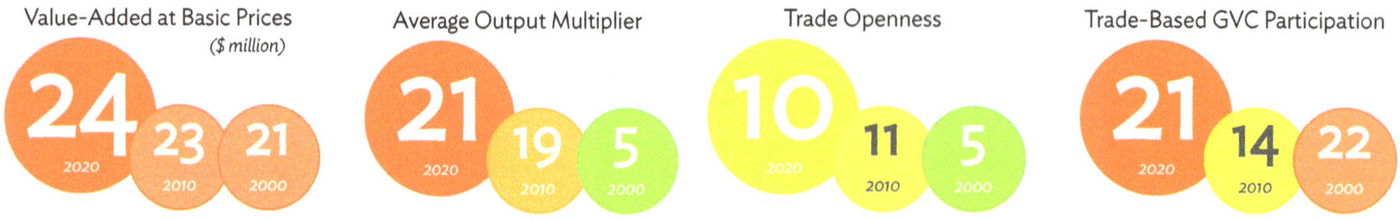

Share of Intermediate Consumption and Gross Value-Added in Output

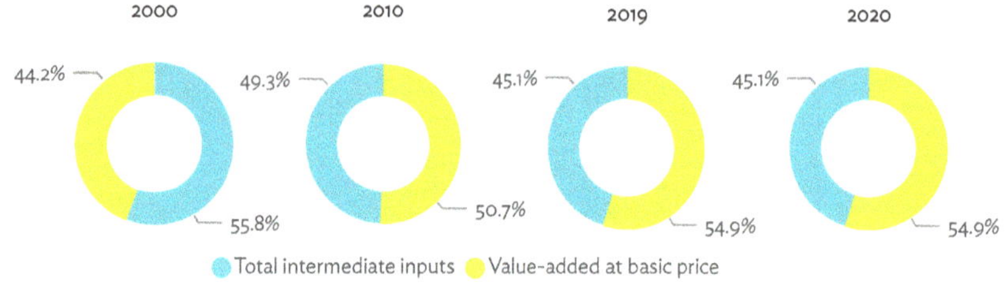

Imports and Exports, 2019-2020

($ million)

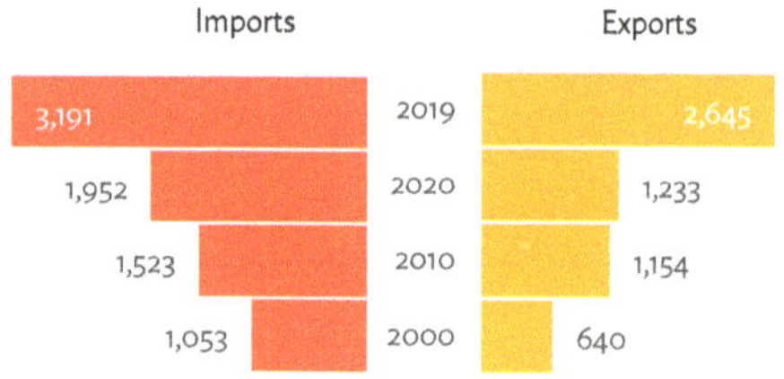

Domestic Linkages

Normalized Linkages

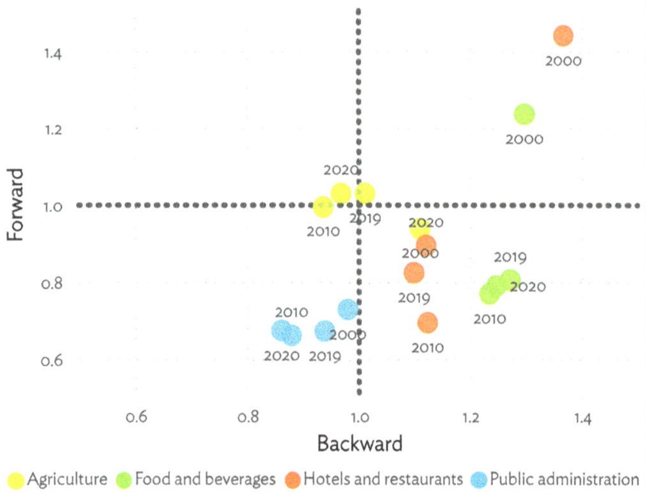

Net Linkages

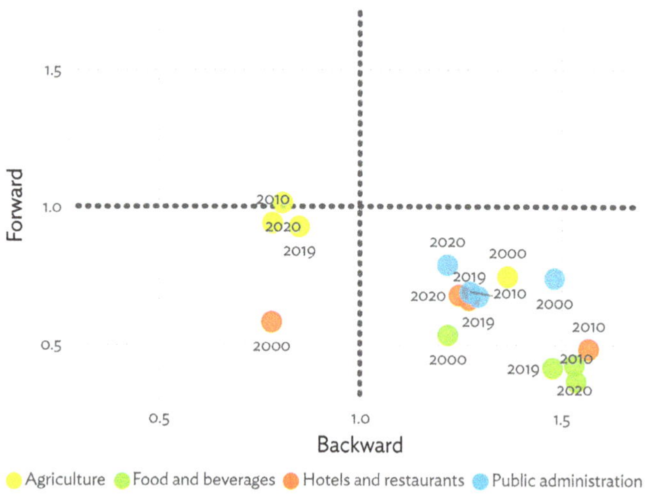

Value-Added Multipliers

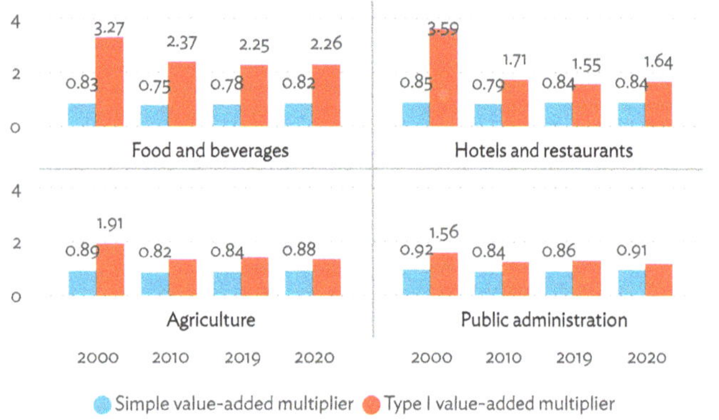

Production-Induced Effect

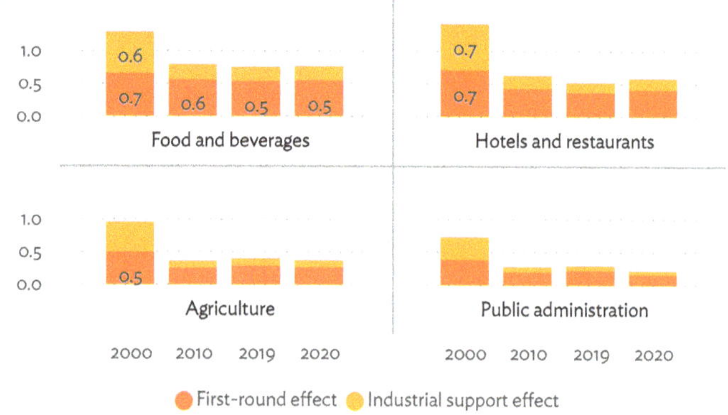

continued on next page.

Click here for figure data

continued.

Fiji

Southeast Asia and the Pacific

International Linkages

Change in Exports, by Value-Added Components, 2019-2020

($ million)

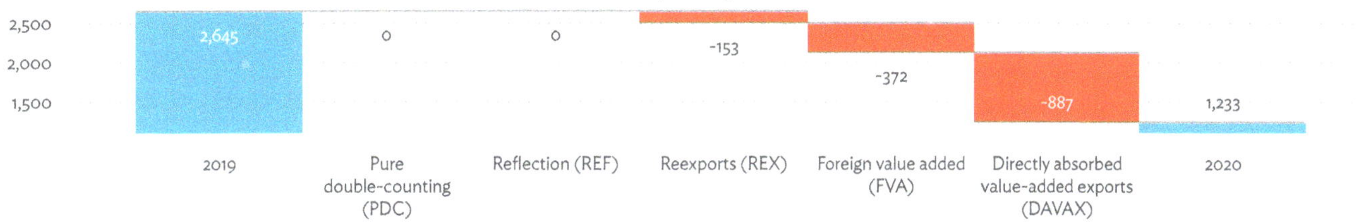

Import Multipliers

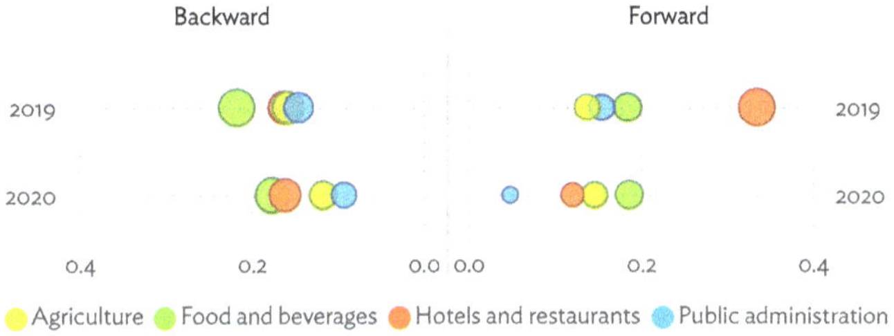

GVC Participation Rates

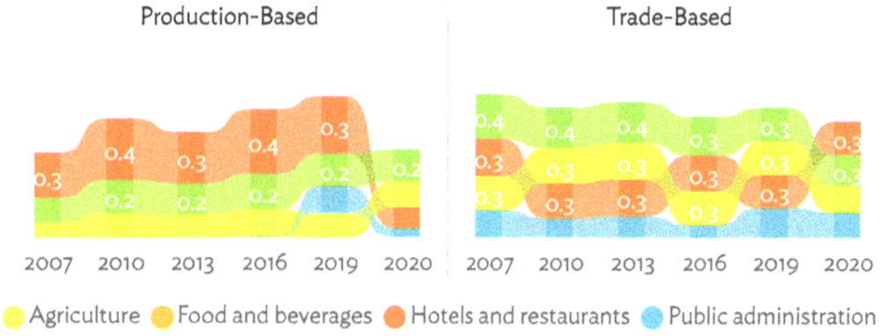

Average Production Length

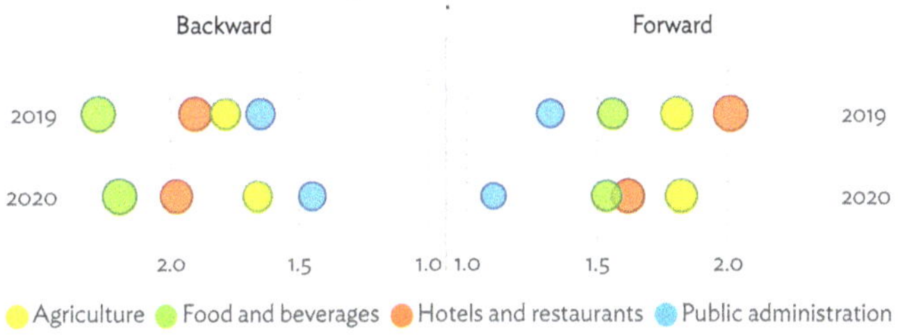

New Revealed Comparative Advantage

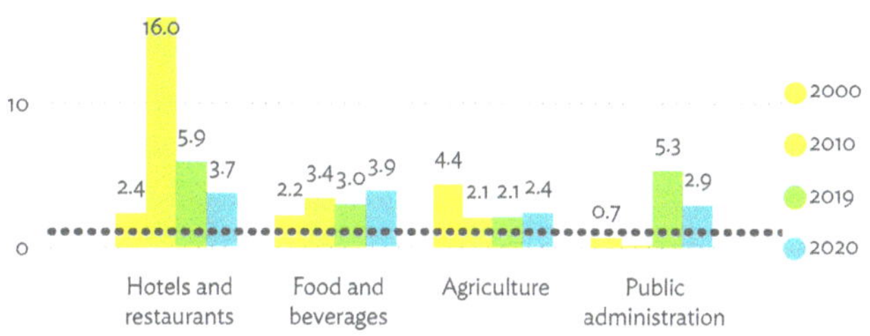

Trade Orientation

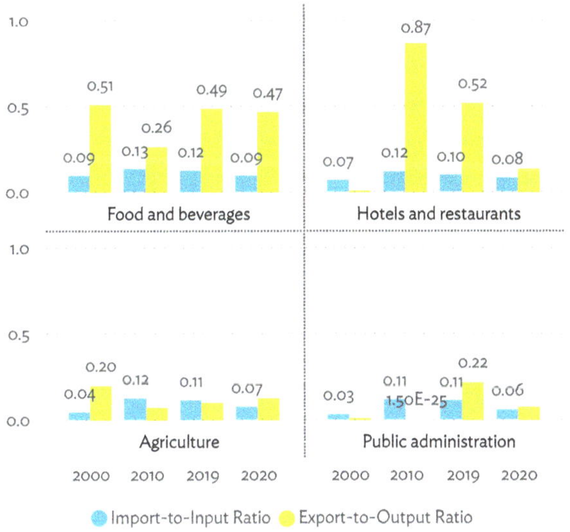

Agglomeration Indices

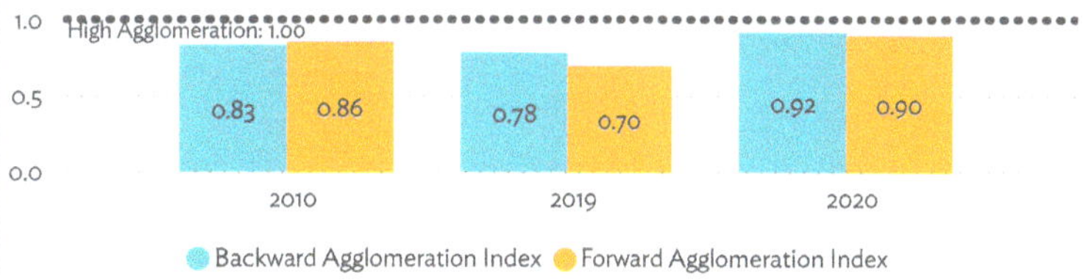

Domestic Transfer Effects and International Spillover Effects

($ million)

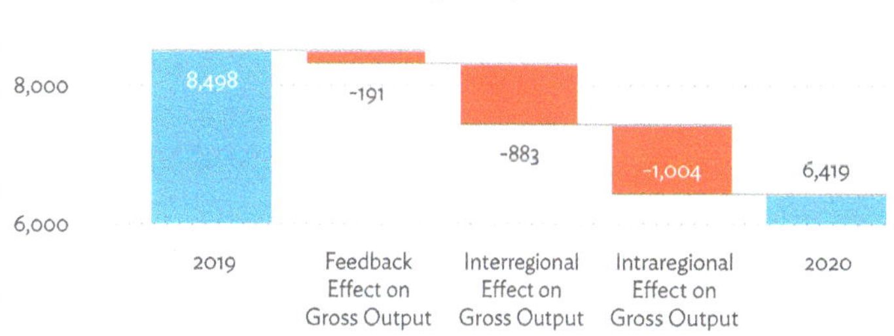

GVC = global value chain; NEC = not elsewhere classified.
Source: Calculations using the Asian Development Bank Multiregional Input-Output Table. https://mrio.adbx.online/ (accessed July 2021).

Click here for figure data

Hong Kong, China

East Asia

Basic Economic Indicators

Economic Aggregates ($ million)	2000	2007	2010	2013	2016	2019	2020
Value-added at basic price	167,660	203,312	219,795	265,986	310,394	349,585	334,038
Gross output	312,246	388,587	438,835	537,316	611,933	684,652	642,521
Total intermediate inputs	141,051	179,179	211,680	262,763	292,265	329,726	300,305
Taxes less subsidies on products	1,357	2,976	3,528	4,017	4,384	5,342	8,179
International transport margins	0	0	0	0	0	0	0
CIF/FOB adjustment	0	0	0	0	0	0	0
Direct purchases abroad by residents	2,178	3,120	3,831	4,549	4,890	0	0
Purchases by nonresidents on the domestic territory	0	0	0	0	0	0	0
Household final consumption expenditure	70,067	87,099	92,975	119,858	133,433	188,142	175,405
Final consumption expenditure by NPISHs	6,126	7,770	8,888	11,545	13,125	16,563	15,136
Government final consumption expenditure	15,969	17,640	20,088	25,426	31,546	39,136	43,824
Gross fixed capital formation	31,307	25,231	30,247	38,952	50,009	50,466	47,230
Changes in inventories	871	203	571	-21	-2	-4,803	7,773
Total final demand	124,340	137,944	152,768	195,760	228,110	289,504	289,369
Exports	86,578	127,881	143,434	162,861	177,849	142,328	113,829
Imports	72,921	105,280	136,149	180,277	181,457	136,113	107,089

Economic Aggregates, Top 3 Sectors ($ million)	2000	2007	2010	2013	2016	2019	2020
Value-added at basic price							
Finance	21,456	40,864	35,899	43,334	55,092	74,030	70,738
Wholesale trade	29,487	39,155	42,600	53,569	55,100	58,777	56,163
Real estate	26,068	29,179	34,980	42,342	49,158	55,037	52,589
Gross output							
Wholesale trade	62,202	86,598	100,748	127,930	132,076	141,142	131,446
Finance	30,983	62,987	59,599	73,932	90,594	121,521	108,817
Real estate	32,541	37,453	45,486	54,915	63,671	72,030	68,881
Total intermediate inputs							
Wholesale trade	31,862	46,092	56,746	72,727	75,212	81,467	73,909
Finance	9,098	21,222	22,373	29,059	33,845	46,083	35,924
Construction	18,068	12,769	17,320	25,460	38,815	35,669	34,030
Total final demand							
Finance	11,533	19,664	16,360	20,476	27,480	47,114	49,445
Real estate	22,520	23,903	26,742	31,947	38,567	47,551	45,596
Wholesale trade	9,451	12,030	15,420	24,582	20,303	37,177	44,206
Exports							
Wholesale trade	43,697	64,577	71,290	84,795	96,004	63,445	49,271
Air transport	5,598	9,989	11,740	12,588	12,370	8,032	7,674
Food and beverages	5,198	3,534	3,480	3,003	3,177	7,816	7,469
Imports							
Wholesale trade	19,172	41,697	63,703	91,526	87,903	56,511	36,203
Food and beverages	16,044	14,794	20,867	27,937	30,389	26,193	26,060
Electricals	2,605	2,548	4,080	5,170	5,058	6,571	6,380

Domestic Linkages

Indicator and Top 3 Sectors, 2020	2000	2007	2010	2013	2016	2019	2020
First-round effect							
Rubber and plastics	0.35	0.24	0.24	0.23	0.26	0.71	0.76
Water transport	0.52	0.58	0.54	0.56	0.54	0.71	0.75
Machinery, NEC	0.36	0.26	0.24	0.23	0.26	0.67	0.71
Industrial support effect							
Construction	0.54	0.48	0.50	0.48	0.58	0.60	0.65
Water transport	0.30	0.36	0.32	0.34	0.33	0.57	0.64
Rubber and plastics	0.16	0.11	0.12	0.12	0.14	0.48	0.51
Production-induced effect							
Water transport	0.82	0.94	0.87	0.90	0.87	1.28	1.39
Rubber and plastics	0.51	0.35	0.35	0.34	0.40	1.19	1.27
Construction	1.11	1.02	1.04	1.01	1.14	1.18	1.24

continued on next page.

continued.

Hong Kong, China

East Asia *Domestic Linkages*

Indicator and Top 3 Sectors, 2020	2000	2007	2010	2013	2016	2019	2020
Simple value-added multiplier							
Real estate	0.95	0.95	0.95	0.96	0.95	0.97	0.97
Public administration	0.92	0.91	0.92	0.93	0.94	0.96	0.96
Finance	0.92	0.89	0.90	0.89	0.91	0.94	0.96
Type I value-added multiplier							
Rubber and plastics	2.65	2.63	4.46	4.52	6.20	36.20	39.12
Chemicals	3.29	3.00	3.99	3.88	5.19	29.96	32.93
Transport equipment	2.67	3.30	4.78	4.67	6.43	32.22	31.37
Direct backward linkage							
Rubber and plastics	0.35	0.24	0.24	0.23	0.26	0.71	0.76
Water transport	0.52	0.58	0.54	0.56	0.54	0.71	0.75
Machinery, NEC	0.36	0.26	0.24	0.23	0.26	0.67	0.71
Complete hypothetical extraction (backward)							
Rubber and plastics	1.48	1.34	1.34	1.33	1.39	2.18	2.26
Machinery, NEC	1.51	1.37	1.34	1.33	1.38	2.11	2.18
Transport equipment	1.48	1.36	1.34	1.33	1.38	2.11	2.16
Partial hypothetical extraction (backward)							
Rubber and plastics	0.50	0.35	0.35	0.34	0.39	1.18	1.26
Machinery, NEC	0.53	0.38	0.35	0.34	0.39	1.11	1.19
Transport equipment	0.50	0.37	0.35	0.34	0.39	1.13	1.18
Total backward linkage							
Water transport	1.82	1.94	1.87	1.90	1.87	2.28	2.39
Rubber and plastics	1.51	1.35	1.35	1.34	1.40	2.19	2.27
Construction	2.11	2.02	2.04	2.01	2.14	2.18	2.24
Direct forward linkage							
Business activities, NEC	0.83	0.80	0.78	0.80	0.80	0.80	0.80
Telecommunications	0.71	0.70	0.70	0.69	0.70	0.71	0.72
Air transport	0.39	0.35	0.31	0.32	0.34	0.55	0.55
Complete hypothetical extraction (forward)							
Business activities, NEC	2.08	2.03	1.98	2.02	2.02	2.12	2.11
Transport activities, NEC	1.59	1.53	1.46	1.47	1.50	1.92	1.94
Telecommunications	1.62	1.67	1.75	1.75	1.76	1.88	1.87
Partial hypothetical extraction (forward)							
Business activities, NEC	1.14	1.09	1.05	1.09	1.09	1.20	1.20
Telecommunications	0.90	0.89	0.93	0.92	0.93	1.06	1.06
Transport activities, NEC	0.59	0.54	0.46	0.47	0.50	0.93	0.95
Total forward linkage							
Business activities, NEC	2.22	2.15	2.12	2.18	2.19	2.31	2.31
Telecommunications	2.24	2.16	2.13	2.12	2.13	2.29	2.30
Air transport	1.59	1.53	1.46	1.47	1.51	1.99	2.00
Normalized backward linkage							
Water transport	1.25	1.37	1.33	1.35	1.31	1.41	1.43
Rubber and plastics	1.04	0.96	0.96	0.95	0.98	1.35	1.36
Construction	1.46	1.43	1.45	1.42	1.50	1.34	1.34
Normalized forward linkage							
Business activities, NEC	1.64	1.63	1.59	1.62	1.61	1.71	1.72
Telecommunications	1.65	1.63	1.59	1.57	1.57	1.70	1.71
Air transport	1.17	1.15	1.09	1.09	1.11	1.47	1.49
Net backward linkage							
Rubber and plastics	1.30	1.21	1.24	1.22	1.29	2.13	2.21
Machinery, NEC	1.39	1.32	1.30	1.30	1.35	2.08	2.15
Chemicals	1.39	1.26	1.26	1.26	1.31	2.06	2.13
Net forward linkage							
Business activities, NEC	1.37	1.33	1.32	1.36	1.39	1.45	1.46
Finance	1.24	1.14	1.12	1.11	1.11	1.14	1.28
Real estate	1.17	1.19	1.25	1.26	1.24	1.20	1.20

continued on next page.

continued.

Hong Kong, China

East Asia

International Linkages

Indicator and Top 3 Sectors, 2020	2000	2007	2010	2013	2016	2019	2020
Export-to-output ratio							
Mining	1.00	1.00	1.00	1.00	1.00	1.00	1.00
Sale of motor vehicles	1.00	1.00	1.00	1.00	1.00	1.00	1.00
Minerals, NEC	0.99	0.96	0.96	0.96	0.96	1.00	1.00
Self-sufficiency ratio							
Wood	3.11	2.75	2.92	2.11	1.82	138.53	141.05
Chemicals	1.74	1.11	1.23	1.05	1.17	3.81	3.66
Minerals, NEC	6.14	2.90	2.74	2.53	2.22	2.52	2.46
Import-to-input ratio							
Minerals, NEC	0.45	0.62	0.70	0.71	0.69	0.67	0.58
Refined fuels	0.36	0.59	0.66	0.68	0.67	0.62	0.53
Metals	0.47	0.63	0.71	0.71	0.70	0.60	0.50
Domestic inputs share to output							
Rubber and plastics	0.35	0.24	0.24	0.23	0.26	0.71	0.76
Water transport	0.52	0.58	0.54	0.56	0.54	0.71	0.75
Machinery, NEC	0.36	0.26	0.24	0.23	0.26	0.67	0.71
Foreign inputs share to output							
Minerals, NEC	0.45	0.62	0.70	0.71	0.69	0.67	0.58
Refined fuels	0.36	0.59	0.66	0.68	0.67	0.62	0.53
Metals	0.47	0.63	0.71	0.71	0.70	0.60	0.50
Backward import multipliers							
Minerals, NEC	0.53	0.69	0.78	0.78	0.77	0.73	0.65
Refined fuels	0.44	0.65	0.73	0.74	0.73	0.68	0.60
Metals	0.56	0.70	0.78	0.78	0.77	0.67	0.57
Forward import multipliers							
Metals	0.83	0.84	0.84	0.83	0.86	0.96	0.97
Minerals, NEC	0.93	0.87	0.89	0.89	0.88	0.97	0.91
Chemicals	0.79	0.80	0.81	0.79	0.80	0.86	0.81
Intraregional transfer multiplier							
Water transport	1.82	1.94	1.87	1.90	1.87	2.28	2.39
Rubber and plastics	1.51	1.35	1.35	1.34	1.40	2.19	2.27
Construction	2.11	2.02	2.04	2.01	2.14	2.18	2.24
Interregional spillover multiplier							
Minerals, NEC	1.79	2.05	2.26	2.29	2.23	2.33	2.20
Refined fuels	1.62	1.99	2.09	2.15	2.14	2.22	2.09
Metals	1.88	2.14	2.31	2.29	2.14	2.15	2.01
Interregional feedback multiplier							
Metals	1.15	1.25	1.31	1.32	1.30	1.21	1.20
Refined fuels	1.11	1.23	1.26	1.27	1.24	1.21	1.19
Minerals, NEC	1.13	1.22	1.24	1.25	1.23	1.21	1.19
Intraregional effect on gross output ($ million)							
Finance	24,385.22	45,477.53	41,000.28	52,569.77	64,867.48	97,857.70	98,772.66
Wholesale trade	39,790.17	57,258.62	64,095.63	84,196.36	83,570.18	97,540.66	95,520.44
Real estate	30,332.03	34,295.95	40,771.66	49,770.53	58,069.80	67,561.45	65,097.48
Interregional effect on gross output ($ million)							
Wholesale trade	17,851.41	23,381.69	28,833.10	34,771.89	37,320.97	34,397.34	28,383.63
Air transport	5,049.34	8,453.10	9,904.95	9,870.76	9,302.55	9,119.21	8,742.20
Finance	5,301.19	14,116.60	14,736.95	17,024.54	20,387.76	18,021.40	7,862.73
Feedback effect on gross output ($ million)							
Wholesale trade	4,560.33	5,957.94	7,819.27	8,961.91	11,184.76	9,203.77	7,541.80
Water transport	1,122.67	2,403.63	2,991.21	3,297.93	3,052.62	3,083.73	2,834.01
Finance	1,296.43	3,392.94	3,862.02	4,337.77	5,338.39	5,641.89	2,181.41
Directly absorbed value-added exports (DAVAX) ($ million)							
Wholesale trade	29,592.70	42,487.91	44,475.87	53,123.60	61,497.84	42,652.03	34,239.80
Retail trade	7,067.71	10,626.39	11,582.62	13,993.32	13,961.55	6,516.09	6,014.56
Air transport	2,941.88	4,241.28	5,144.25	5,294.04	5,809.46	5,059.17	5,227.36
Reflection (REF) ($ million)							
Water transport	14.26	20.14	27.70	36.32	36.33	23.25	26.87
Wholesale trade	75.42	79.15	75.44	94.94	138.17	24.83	16.89
Air transport	19.02	23.10	26.66	29.20	32.46	8.85	7.46

continued on next page.

continued.

Hong Kong, China

East Asia

International Linkages

Indicator and Top 3 Sectors, 2020	2000	2007	2010	2013	2016	2019	2020
Reexports (REX) ($ million)							
Wholesale trade	4,821.69	5,607.74	6,838.88	7,413.20	9,669.67	6,669.67	5,830.47
Water transport	941.69	1,773.40	2,136.02	2,053.60	1,984.02	2,241.47	2,330.20
Electricals	172.17	161.82	191.82	149.39	193.29	1,137.58	1,014.50
Foreign value added (FVA) ($ million)							
Wholesale trade	9,135.89	16,293.23	19,740.39	24,011.82	24,538.62	14,070.50	9,170.31
Food and beverages	2,047.87	1,579.24	1,753.10	1,532.82	1,721.06	4,243.33	3,636.84
Electricals	692.65	1,174.92	2,171.66	1,819.27	2,114.15	3,102.61	2,503.32
Pure double-counting (PDC) ($ million)							
Wholesale trade	70.82	109.21	159.45	151.43	159.79	27.51	13.58
Food and beverages	11.08	6.17	5.82	4.17	6.43	5.63	4.19
Electricals	3.17	3.15	7.59	4.51	8.00	5.15	3.75
Trade-based GVC participation rate							
Metals	0.73	0.83	0.86	0.85	0.85	0.80	0.77
Minerals, NEC	0.61	0.76	0.82	0.82	0.80	0.76	0.72
Refined fuels	0.63	0.75	0.85	0.82	0.80	0.76	0.66
Production-based GVC participation rate							
Metals	0.83	0.84	0.84	0.83	0.86	0.96	0.97
Minerals, NEC	0.93	0.87	0.89	0.89	0.88	0.97	0.91
Chemicals	0.79	0.80	0.81	0.79	0.80	0.86	0.81
Trade-based backward GVC participation rate							
Minerals, NEC	0.53	0.69	0.78	0.78	0.77	0.73	0.65
Refined fuels	0.44	0.65	0.73	0.74	0.73	0.68	0.60
Metals	0.56	0.70	0.78	0.78	0.77	0.67	0.57
Trade-based forward GVC participation rate							
Transport activities, NEC	0.46	0.25	0.48	0.45	0.47	0.38	0.38
Water transport	0.22	0.21	0.22	0.19	0.20	0.30	0.33
Finance	0.20	0.20	0.22	0.19	0.19	0.30	0.30
Traditional revealed comparative advantage							
Wholesale trade	9.18	9.88	7.80	8.13	8.16	10.25	10.99
Retail trade	11.43	11.47	9.38	10.07	8.67	7.14	9.47
Water transport	2.58	3.48	3.84	4.44	3.86	6.60	8.30
New revealed comparative advantage							
Air transport	7.43	8.03	9.59	7.68	6.72	8.01	11.61
Wholesale trade	4.34	4.42	3.85	3.94	3.69	4.43	4.60
Telecommunications	2.16	2.42	3.05	3.48	3.17	3.63	4.06
Backward production length							
Minerals, NEC	2.73	2.89	3.09	3.09	3.07	3.21	3.21
Chemicals	2.97	3.05	3.19	3.17	3.13	3.24	3.21
Machinery, NEC	2.82	3.00	3.14	3.13	3.09	3.23	3.20
Forward production length							
Chemicals	3.18	3.41	3.51	3.52	3.55	3.29	3.40
Metals	3.05	3.27	3.28	3.28	3.45	3.38	3.39
Water transport	3.04	3.10	3.16	2.96	2.89	3.24	3.27
Backward production length of GVC segment							
Construction	4.25	4.11	4.12	4.18	4.19	4.45	4.55
Transport activities, NEC	3.63	3.73	3.86	3.99	3.90	4.25	4.35
Water transport	3.75	3.84	3.74	3.79	3.71	4.11	4.23
Forward production length of GVC segment							
Construction	4.79	5.06	5.39	5.37	5.55	5.44	5.29
Real estate	4.54	4.59	4.66	4.71	4.69	5.06	5.17
Finance	3.99	3.96	4.05	4.08	4.01	4.35	5.13
Backward agglomeration index							
Inland transport	-	1.04	1.00	1.01	1.06	1.13	1.12
Business activities, NEC	-	1.00	0.98	1.04	1.07	1.11	1.11
Finance	-	0.87	0.87	0.87	0.90	1.04	1.08
Forward agglomeration index							
Hotels and restaurants	-	1.07	1.06	1.07	1.06	1.12	1.12
Inland transport	-	1.08	1.00	1.01	1.02	1.15	1.12
Construction	-	1.00	1.01	1.01	1.02	1.03	1.03

CIF = cost, insurance, and freight; FOB = free on board; GVC = global value chain; NEC = not elsewhere classified; NPISHs = nonprofit institutions serving households.
Source: Calculations using the Asian Development Bank Multiregional Input-Output Table. https://mrio.adbx.online/ (accessed July 2021).

continued on next page.

continued.

Hong Kong, China

East Asia

The four select sectors are chosen based on their gross outputs in the economy as of 2019.

Economy Ranking out of 25 Economies

	2020	2010	2000
Value-Added at Basic Prices ($ million)	9	10	7
Average Output Multiplier	9	21	19
Trade Openness	14	7	9
Trade-Based GVC Participation	15	11	11

Share of Intermediate Consumption and Gross Value-Added in Output

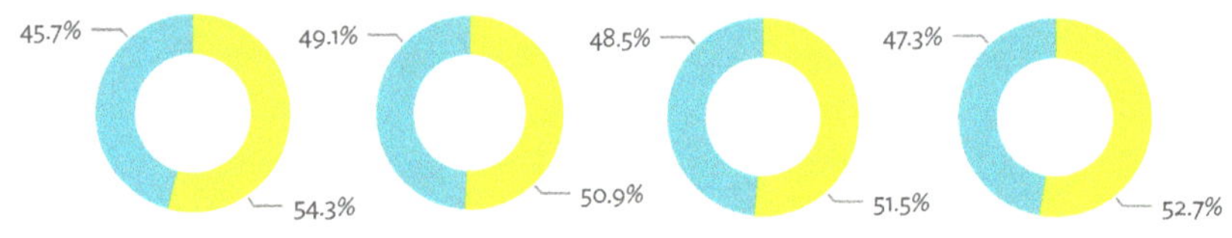

Imports and Exports, 2019-2020

($ million)

Imports	Year	Exports
136,149	2010	143,434
136,113	2019	142,328
107,089	2020	113,829
72,921	2000	86,578

Domestic Linkages

Normalized Linkages

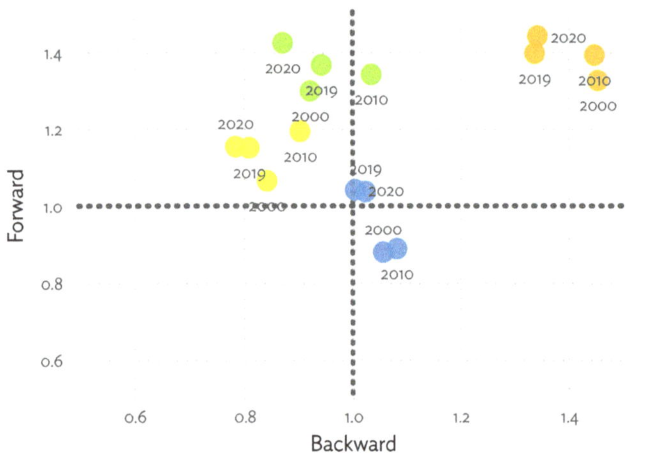

Net Linkages

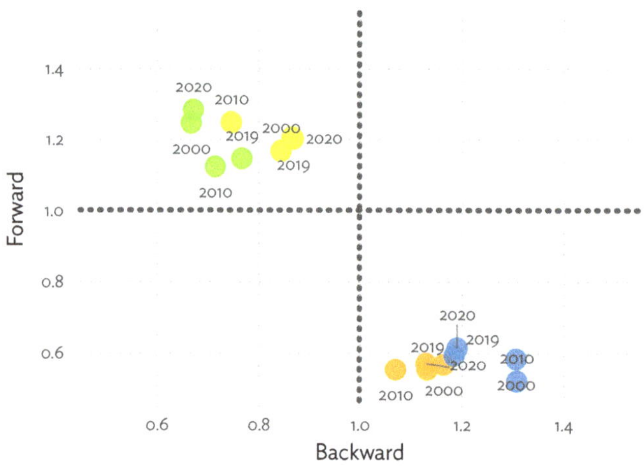

Value-Added Multipliers

Production-Induced Effect

continued on next page.

Click here for figure data

continued.

Hong Kong, China

East Asia

International Linkages

Change in Exports, by Value-Added Components, 2019-2020

($ million)

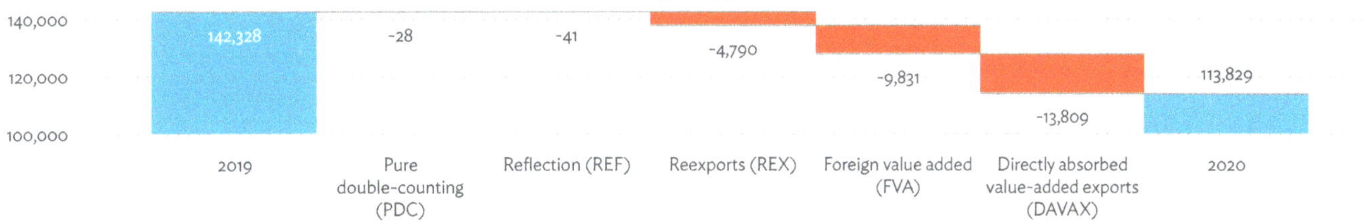

Import Multipliers

GVC Participation Rates

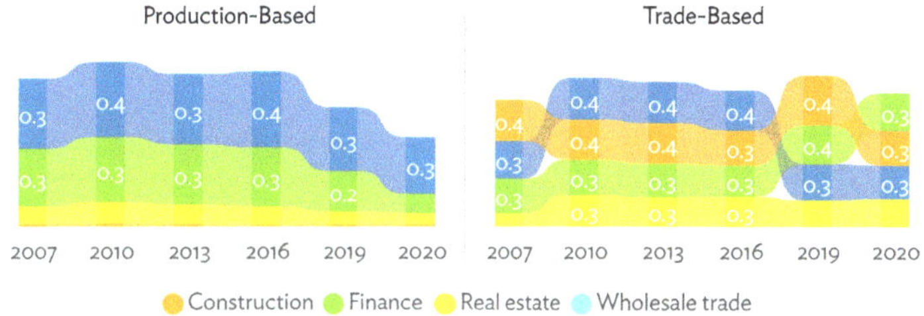

Average Production Length

New Revealed Comparative Advantage

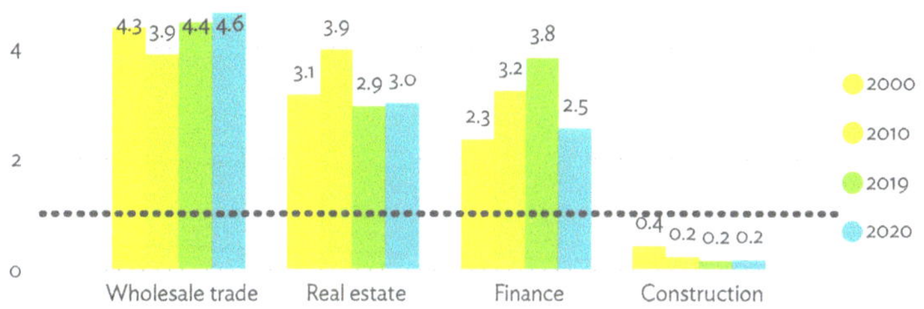

Trade Orientation

Agglomeration Indices

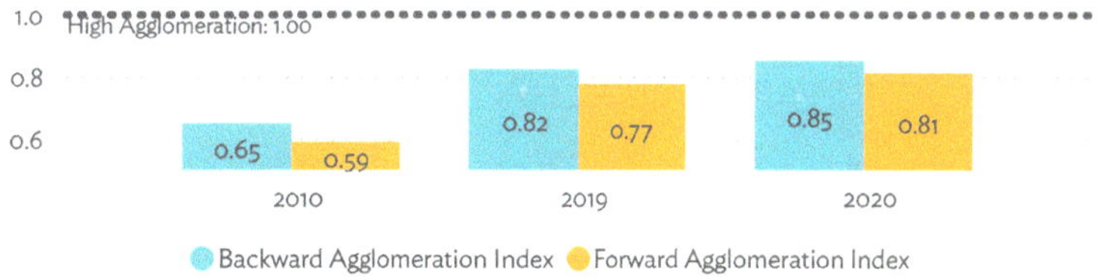

Domestic Transfer Effects and International Spillover Effects

($ million)

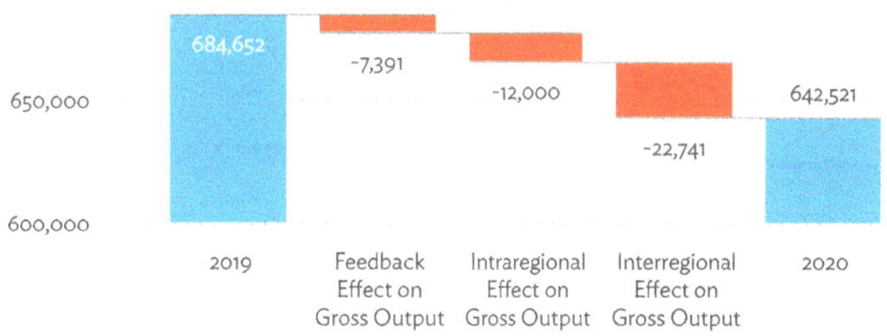

GVC = global value chain; NEC = not elsewhere classified.
Source: Calculations using the Asian Development Bank Multiregional Input-Output Table. https://mrio.adbx.online/ (accessed July 2021).

Click here for figure data

India

South and Central Asia

Basic Economic Indicators

Economic Aggregates ($ million)	2000	2007	2010	2013	2016	2019	2020
Value-added at basic price	457,035	1,135,324	1,618,577	1,886,274	2,185,884	2,621,592	2,399,625
Gross output	889,777	2,351,577	3,338,038	3,780,995	4,367,450	5,104,694	4,600,429
Total intermediate inputs	409,427	1,154,211	1,633,622	1,787,997	2,055,553	2,329,534	2,063,533
Taxes less subsidies on products	19,783	45,080	61,958	75,850	126,013	153,567	137,271
International transport margins	3,532	16,961	23,880	30,875	0	0	0
CIF/FOB adjustment	0	0	0	0	0	0	0
Direct purchases abroad by residents	0	0	0	0	0	0	0
Purchases by nonresidents on the domestic territory	0	0	0	0	0	0	0
Household final consumption expenditure	309,547	642,147	946,220	1,177,584	1,338,269	1,671,511	1,492,924
Final consumption expenditure by NPISHs	0	0	0	0	0	0	0
Government final consumption expenditure	59,679	118,249	192,702	232,502	237,157	283,920	293,099
Gross fixed capital formation	94,670	353,183	458,663	459,262	600,526	722,748	615,647
Changes in inventories	4,156	49,598	61,112	53,021	71,232	52,452	46,581
Total final demand	468,053	1,163,178	1,658,697	1,922,368	2,247,183	2,730,631	2,448,251
Exports	62,071	236,097	315,328	381,501	346,535	532,597	477,804
Imports	67,123	275,069	363,223	386,927	336,438	605,655	486,176

Economic Aggregates, Top 3 Sectors ($ million)	2000	2007	2010	2013	2016	2019	2020
Value-added at basic price							
Agriculture	102,570	202,675	288,693	320,803	345,244	481,968	484,212
Business activities, NEC	10,540	45,569	73,723	99,397	121,542	227,651	217,524
Real estate	27,728	60,442	91,527	117,521	144,995	178,911	170,952
Gross output							
Agriculture	135,173	264,133	372,988	415,905	444,965	599,235	602,025
Construction	77,004	270,882	363,915	384,384	374,792	536,585	465,335
Business activities, NEC	16,333	66,482	107,545	131,743	161,094	333,272	318,446
Total intermediate inputs							
Construction	46,553	166,674	225,750	235,956	223,703	310,557	268,152
Food and beverages	35,630	104,352	151,732	163,933	179,999	222,170	197,795
Metals	28,177	120,922	171,331	167,159	141,872	179,861	158,785
Total final demand							
Construction	59,176	219,488	287,829	297,971	315,086	448,282	385,745
Agriculture	78,236	139,180	199,952	231,296	246,575	361,467	363,686
Real estate	28,886	64,493	98,200	126,027	154,501	191,852	183,873
Exports							
Business activities, NEC	9,561	59,017	81,860	70,610	63,158	104,983	98,770
Chemicals	4,753	13,602	18,049	30,998	26,751	52,196	47,336
Textiles	12,010	16,693	20,292	29,832	28,827	41,404	34,171
Imports							
Mining	12,407	71,491	94,929	141,576	72,884	164,707	131,450
Metals	8,067	33,149	45,984	39,390	30,682	57,551	45,868
Transport equipment	3,134	20,160	24,839	24,111	40,375	45,217	33,979

Domestic Linkages

Indicator and Top 3 Sectors, 2020	2000	2007	2010	2013	2016	2019	2020
First-round effect							
Wood	0.48	0.55	0.59	0.53	0.57	0.83	0.83
Food and beverages	0.79	0.83	0.84	0.83	0.85	0.78	0.79
Manufacturing, NEC	0.56	0.65	0.55	0.61	0.68	0.71	0.71
Industrial support effect							
Rubber and plastics	0.65	0.61	0.62	0.60	0.71	0.43	0.44
Manufacturing, NEC	0.45	0.55	0.44	0.50	0.59	0.41	0.44
Air transport	0.36	0.31	0.30	0.21	0.26	0.41	0.43
Production-induced effect							
Food and beverages	1.25	1.31	1.32	1.27	1.31	1.18	1.19
Wood	0.73	0.81	0.87	0.78	0.83	1.16	1.17
Manufacturing, NEC	1.02	1.20	0.99	1.10	1.27	1.12	1.15

continued on next page.

continued.

India

South and Central Asia

Domestic Linkages

Indicator and Top 3 Sectors, 2020	2000	2007	2010	2013	2016	2019	2020
Simple value-added multiplier							
Public administration	1.00	1.00	1.00	1.00	1.00	1.00	1.00
Real estate	0.99	0.99	0.99	0.99	0.99	0.99	0.99
Agriculture	0.97	0.97	0.97	0.97	0.98	0.97	0.97
Type I value-added multiplier							
Wood	1.96	2.27	2.52	2.16	2.26	6.51	6.55
Food and beverages	5.43	6.54	6.98	6.78	7.29	5.52	5.62
Manufacturing, NEC	2.43	3.34	2.90	2.89	3.24	4.18	4.26
Direct backward linkage							
Wood	0.48	0.55	0.59	0.53	0.57	0.83	0.83
Food and beverages	0.79	0.83	0.84	0.83	0.85	0.78	0.79
Manufacturing, NEC	0.56	0.65	0.55	0.61	0.68	0.71	0.71
Complete hypothetical extraction (backward)							
Wood	1.70	1.78	1.85	1.74	1.79	2.13	2.14
Air transport	1.79	1.71	1.68	1.50	1.60	2.10	2.12
Manufacturing, NEC	1.80	1.78	1.69	1.63	1.68	1.97	1.99
Partial hypothetical extraction (backward)							
Wood	0.72	0.80	0.86	0.76	0.81	1.14	1.15
Air transport	0.79	0.71	0.68	0.50	0.60	1.10	1.12
Manufacturing, NEC	0.91	0.97	0.84	0.86	0.94	1.04	1.06
Total backward linkage							
Food and beverages	2.25	2.31	2.32	2.27	2.31	2.18	2.19
Wood	1.73	1.81	1.87	1.78	1.83	2.16	2.17
Manufacturing, NEC	2.02	2.20	1.99	2.10	2.27	2.12	2.15
Direct forward linkage							
Mining	0.95	0.68	0.75	0.81	0.88	0.92	0.86
Minerals, NEC	0.80	0.81	0.82	0.80	0.79	0.75	0.74
Utilities	0.81	0.83	0.82	0.77	0.84	0.75	0.74
Complete hypothetical extraction (forward)							
Mining	3.06	2.36	2.51	2.50	2.64	2.59	2.53
Utilities	1.97	2.15	2.17	2.08	2.18	1.98	1.95
Finance	2.08	2.14	2.15	2.05	2.21	1.95	1.92
Partial hypothetical extraction (forward)							
Mining	2.08	1.37	1.51	1.51	1.66	1.61	1.55
Utilities	1.24	1.32	1.33	1.23	1.37	1.13	1.12
Finance	1.14	1.18	1.19	1.09	1.25	1.02	1.01
Total forward linkage							
Mining	3.10	2.38	2.53	2.52	2.68	2.64	2.57
Utilities	2.70	2.59	2.59	2.44	2.67	2.34	2.35
Finance	2.21	2.24	2.25	2.14	2.30	2.09	2.10
Normalized backward linkage							
Food and beverages	1.31	1.38	1.38	1.39	1.35	1.34	1.33
Wood	1.01	1.08	1.11	1.09	1.07	1.33	1.32
Manufacturing, NEC	1.18	1.32	1.18	1.28	1.33	1.30	1.31
Normalized forward linkage							
Mining	1.79	1.42	1.48	1.52	1.56	1.70	1.64
Utilities	1.56	1.55	1.52	1.47	1.55	1.50	1.50
Finance	1.28	1.34	1.32	1.29	1.33	1.34	1.34
Net backward linkage							
Air transport	1.44	1.65	1.56	1.25	1.53	2.07	2.09
Manufacturing, NEC	1.44	1.42	1.30	1.23	1.27	1.75	1.75
Food and beverages	1.76	1.61	1.65	1.72	1.72	1.74	1.74
Net forward linkage							
Mining	2.47	1.84	2.02	1.96	1.64	1.71	1.67
Finance	1.75	1.86	1.87	1.80	1.94	1.55	1.56
Retail trade	1.58	1.63	1.65	1.59	1.65	1.32	1.38

continued on next page.

continued.

India

South and Central Asia *International Linkages*

Indicator and Top 3 Sectors, 2020	2000	2007	2010	2013	2016	2019	2020
Self-sufficiency ratio							
Manufacturing, NEC	1.01	0.93	0.80	0.98	1.04	1.71	1.73
Air transport	0.76	0.67	0.77	0.92	1.13	1.51	1.72
Leather	1.39	1.16	1.16	1.24	1.16	1.68	1.63
Import-to-input ratio							
Refined fuels	0.34	0.47	0.46	0.55	0.23	0.39	0.36
Metals	0.14	0.20	0.19	0.25	0.19	0.37	0.34
Hotels and restaurants	0.04	0.03	0.04	0.04	0.18	0.32	0.29
Export-to-output ratio							
Water transport	0.87	1.00	1.00	0.95	0.72	1.00	1.00
Air transport	0.44	0.92	0.82	0.52	0.39	0.72	0.78
Manufacturing, NEC	0.22	0.13	0.18	0.15	0.11	0.63	0.59
Domestic inputs share to output							
Wood	0.48	0.55	0.59	0.53	0.57	0.83	0.83
Food and beverages	0.79	0.83	0.84	0.83	0.85	0.78	0.79
Manufacturing, NEC	0.56	0.65	0.55	0.61	0.68	0.71	0.71
Foreign inputs share to output							
Refined fuels	0.34	0.47	0.46	0.55	0.23	0.39	0.36
Metals	0.14	0.20	0.19	0.25	0.19	0.37	0.34
Hotels and restaurants	0.04	0.03	0.04	0.04	0.18	0.32	0.29
Backward import multipliers							
Refined fuels	0.39	0.52	0.51	0.58	0.32	0.45	0.43
Metals	0.23	0.33	0.32	0.37	0.28	0.46	0.43
Hotels and restaurants	0.08	0.08	0.09	0.09	0.22	0.35	0.32
Forward import multipliers							
Water transport	0.58	0.62	0.71	0.79	0.56	0.75	0.74
Air transport	0.31	0.78	0.71	0.43	0.31	0.61	0.66
Chemicals	0.20	0.24	0.23	0.31	0.25	0.34	0.35
Intraregional transfer multiplier							
Food and beverages	2.25	2.31	2.32	2.27	2.31	2.18	2.19
Wood	1.73	1.81	1.87	1.78	1.83	2.16	2.17
Manufacturing, NEC	2.02	2.20	1.99	2.10	2.27	2.12	2.15
Interregional spillover multiplier							
Refined fuels	1.49	1.76	1.79	2.02	1.44	1.71	1.67
Metals	1.25	1.37	1.37	1.49	1.37	1.71	1.67
Hotels and restaurants	1.07	1.05	1.07	1.07	1.34	1.61	1.57
Interregional feedback multiplier							
Metals	1.06	1.10	1.08	1.11	1.09	1.14	1.13
Inland transport	1.01	1.04	1.03	1.03	1.14	1.13	1.11
Refined fuels	1.09	1.18	1.14	1.20	1.09	1.10	1.10
Intraregional effect on gross output ($ million)							
Agriculture	131,431.96	254,417.68	358,944.49	394,597.09	428,647.55	578,776.47	581,187.66
Construction	75,701.30	266,622.72	358,323.96	379,498.04	371,715.43	529,180.11	458,575.45
Business activities, NEC	7,760.82	24,647.33	43,469.73	91,743.23	123,517.03	255,338.12	242,166.52
Interregional effect on gross output ($ million)							
Business activities, NEC	6,768.77	30,980.45	48,968.48	29,798.78	27,732.55	61,783.09	61,411.98
Chemicals	5,727.55	14,934.94	20,364.06	31,823.90	31,725.18	47,563.63	44,005.42
Metals	4,217.41	17,031.47	26,022.40	30,365.87	21,373.81	31,203.33	31,231.12
Feedback effect on gross output ($ million)							
Business activities, NEC	1,803.53	10,854.13	15,106.87	10,200.76	9,844.06	16,150.47	14,867.30
Chemicals	1,861.67	5,289.38	7,513.63	12,631.38	12,137.61	16,979.01	14,213.15
Metals	1,272.39	6,948.92	9,168.76	11,480.51	7,533.35	11,906.97	10,131.94
Directly absorbed value-added exports (DAVAX) ($ million)							
Business activities, NEC	6,032.68	38,163.62	54,143.38	54,689.28	50,162.37	80,881.70	77,776.51
Chemicals	2,420.67	6,372.85	8,520.06	14,102.13	14,250.71	27,913.23	26,622.87
Textiles	9,168.66	12,150.13	14,832.28	21,454.41	21,744.06	29,980.45	25,530.07
Reflection (REF) ($ million)							
Business activities, NEC	42.93	438.93	706.02	355.61	277.38	589.53	535.29
Chemicals	17.89	70.22	123.14	179.10	175.62	410.19	313.10
Metals	15.87	133.12	220.40	185.90	128.75	265.67	218.96

continued on next page.

continued.

India

South and Central Asia *International Linkages*

Indicator and Top 3 Sectors, 2020	2000	2007	2010	2013	2016	2019	2020
Reexports (REX) ($ million)							
Business activities, NEC	2,242.03	12,706.49	17,564.03	11,494.69	10,241.22	15,226.86	13,372.45
Chemicals	1,298.18	3,420.97	4,682.90	8,166.93	7,837.32	13,865.35	12,152.08
Metals	922.98	4,163.54	5,306.35	6,582.76	5,046.59	6,835.99	6,156.51
Foreign value added (FVA) ($ million)							
Metals	892.40	5,260.56	7,072.94	10,494.06	5,652.06	15,688.33	13,360.57
Refined fuels	66.90	9,272.77	13,928.13	26,977.76	14,144.82	15,065.92	10,714.42
Chemicals	1,011.98	3,706.12	4,679.74	8,473.04	4,452.96	9,927.05	8,183.10
Pure double-counting (PDC) ($ million)							
Metals	3.18	43.08	52.80	71.33	35.81	117.74	108.87
Refined fuels	0.21	77.53	101.63	170.86	92.54	96.59	77.65
Chemicals	4.49	31.59	43.08	77.11	34.08	80.03	64.37
Trade-based GVC participation rate							
Metals	0.48	0.59	0.56	0.60	0.54	0.67	0.63
Refined fuels	0.56	0.72	0.69	0.75	0.54	0.61	0.58
Water transport	0.36	0.46	0.56	0.74	0.60	0.53	0.50
Production-based GVC participation rate							
Water transport	0.58	0.62	0.71	0.79	0.56	0.75	0.74
Air transport	0.31	0.78	0.71	0.43	0.31	0.61	0.66
Chemicals	0.20	0.24	0.23	0.31	0.25	0.34	0.35
Trade-based backward GVC participation rate							
Refined fuels	0.39	0.52	0.51	0.58	0.32	0.45	0.43
Metals	0.23	0.33	0.32	0.37	0.28	0.46	0.43
Hotels and restaurants	0.08	0.08		0.09	0.22	0.35	0.32
Trade-based forward GVC participation rate							
Water transport	0.26	0.32	0.41	0.58	0.52	0.33	0.32
Rubber and plastics	0.25	0.27	0.26	0.26	0.28	0.29	0.28
Chemicals	0.28	0.26	0.27	0.27	0.30	0.27	0.26
Traditional revealed comparative advantage							
Telecommunications	1.52	1.68	1.43	0.95	0.90	6.33	6.78
Real estate	0.04	0.00	0.04	0.00	0.00	3.20	3.62
Business activities, NEC	2.80	4.34	4.05	2.78	2.45	2.47	2.64
New revealed comparative advantage							
Telecommunications	1.24	1.24	1.13	1.01	1.04	2.65	2.58
Private households	0.00	0.00	0.00	0.00	0.00	2.16	2.42
Business activities, NEC	1.11	1.87	2.03	1.73	1.59	1.74	1.87
Backward production length							
Manufacturing, NEC	2.39	2.80	2.86	2.74	2.72	2.72	2.72
Refined fuels	2.37	2.47	2.53	2.64	2.78	2.63	2.71
Electricals	2.67	2.81	2.85	2.80	2.68	2.66	2.65
Forward production length							
Mining	3.58	3.81	3.76	3.52	3.55	3.27	3.33
Water transport	2.51	2.74	3.11	3.46	2.93	3.05	3.07
Chemicals	2.80	2.78	2.82	2.86	2.97	2.77	2.81
Backward production length of GVC segment							
Real estate	4.76	5.10	5.27	5.46	5.48	5.21	5.29
Education	4.01	4.30	4.47	4.83	4.85	4.88	4.95
Sale of motor vehicles	4.10	4.34	4.44	4.68	4.96	4.81	4.91
Forward production length of GVC segment							
Utilities	5.14	5.16	5.16	5.22	5.37	5.00	5.12
Mining	4.41	4.75	4.84	4.76	4.82	4.70	4.79
Retail trade	4.09	4.10	4.19	4.40	4.55	4.67	4.71
Backward agglomeration index							
Rubber and plastics	-	1.58	1.72	1.87	2.04	3.74	3.37
Electricals	-	2.30	2.32	2.32	2.44	2.24	2.28
Textiles	-	1.80	1.77	1.73	1.72	1.92	1.97
Forward agglomeration index							
Electricals	-	2.43	2.15	1.97	1.91	1.76	1.66
Transport equipment	-	1.78	1.44	1.31	1.30	1.74	1.63
Mining	-	1.25	1.29	1.33	1.22	1.73	1.56

CIF = cost, insurance, and freight; FOB = free on board; GVC = global value chain; NEC = not elsewhere classified; NPISHs = nonprofit institutions serving households.
Source: Calculations using the Asian Development Bank Multiregional Input-Output Table. https://mrio.adbx.online/ (accessed July 2021).

continued on next page.

continued.

India

South and Central Asia

The four select sectors are chosen based on their gross outputs in the economy as of 2019.

Economy Ranking out of 25 Economies

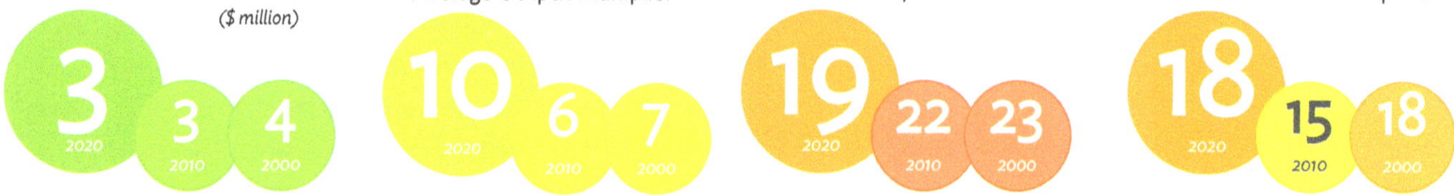

Share of Intermediate Consumption and Gross Value-Added in Output

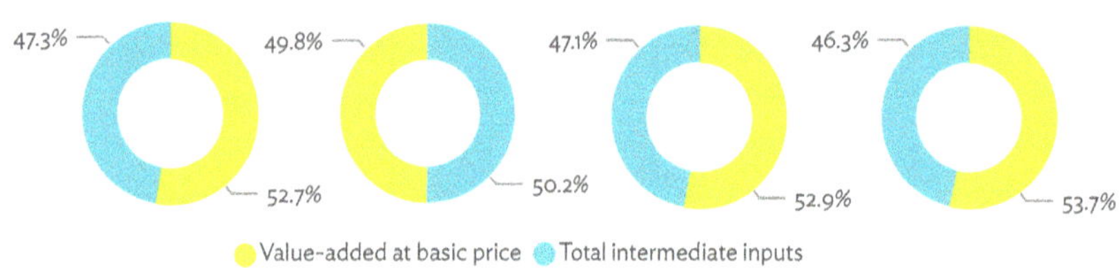

Imports and Exports, 2019-2020

($ million)

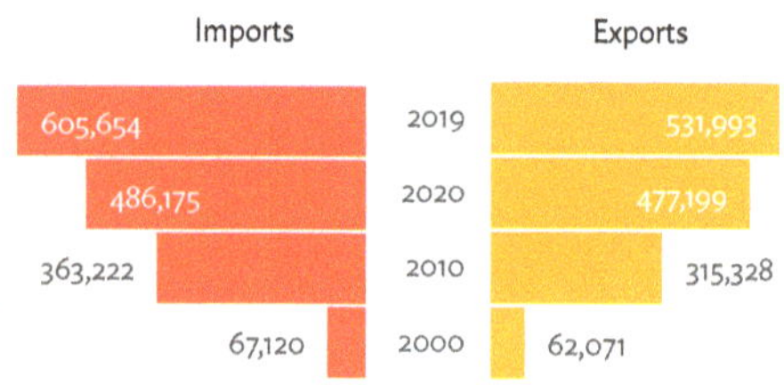

Domestic Linkages

Normalized Linkages

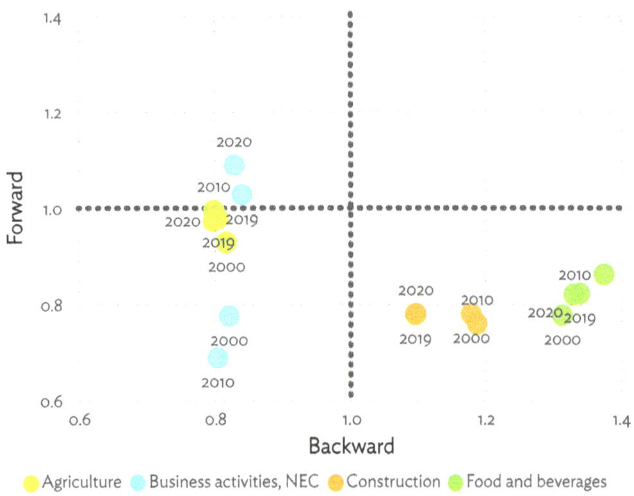

Net Linkages

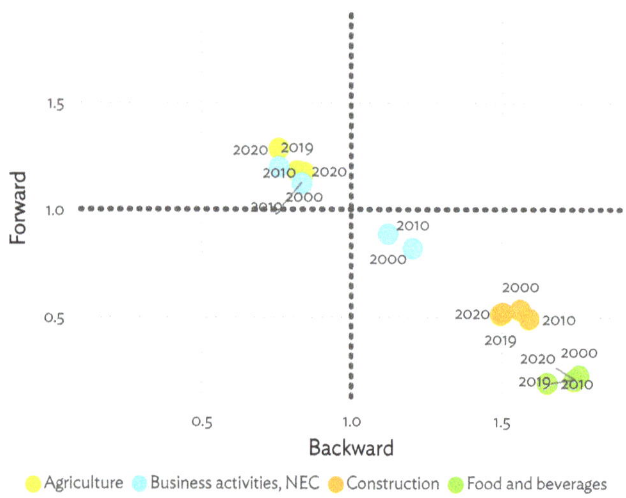

Value-Added Multipliers

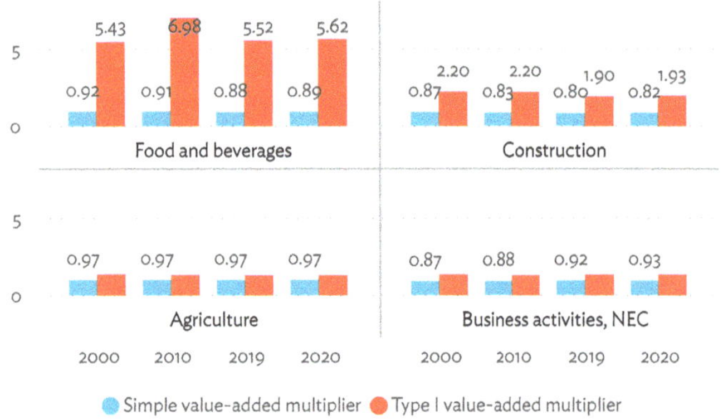

Production-Induced Effect

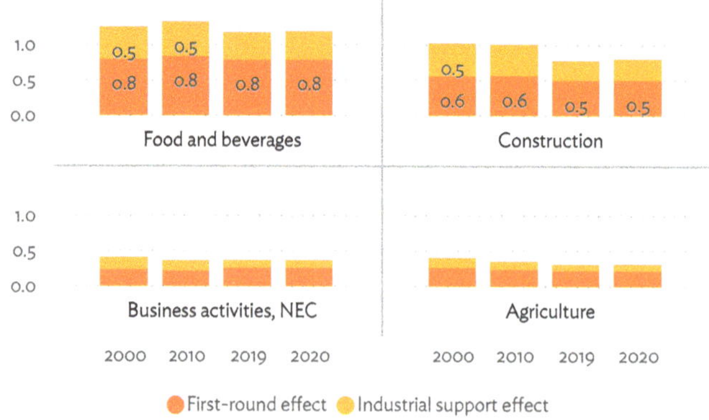

continued on next page.

Click here for figure data

continued.

India

South and Central Asia

International Linkages

Change in Exports, by Value-Added Components, 2019-2020

($ million)

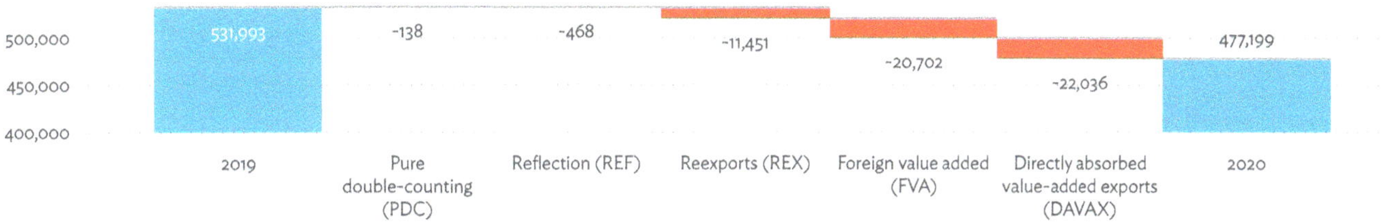

Import Multipliers

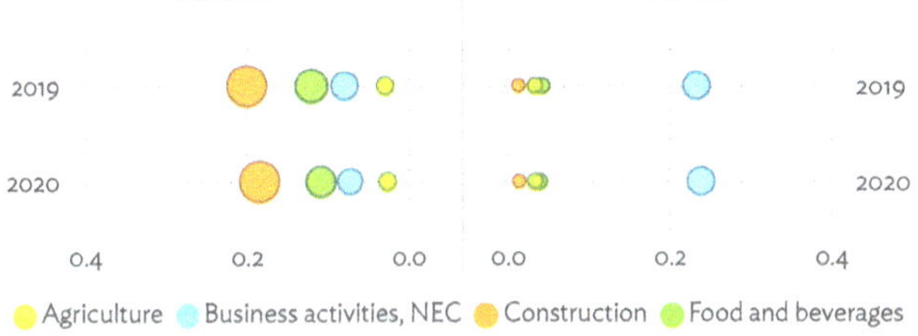

GVC Participation Rates

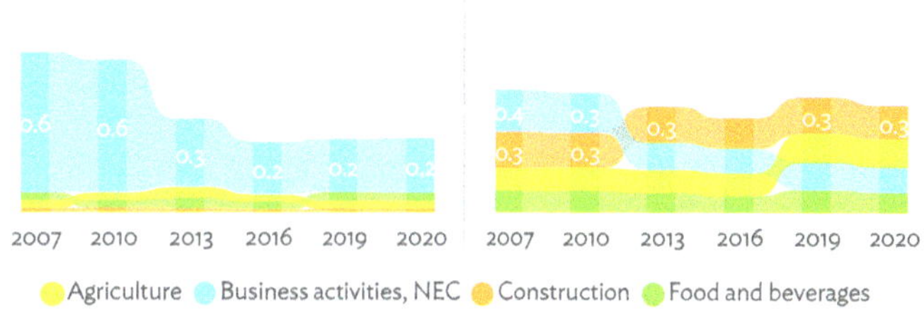

Average Production Length

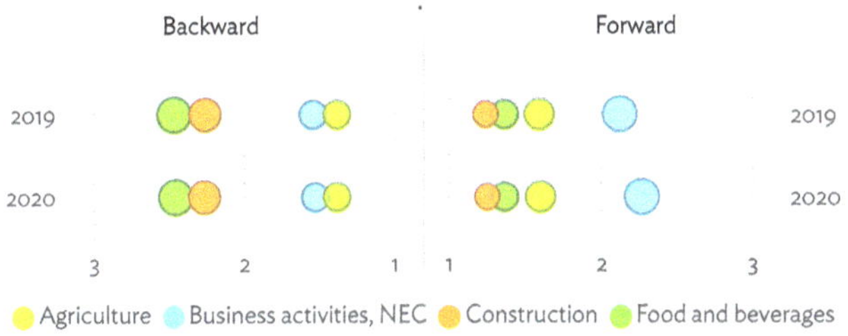

New Revealed Comparative Advantage

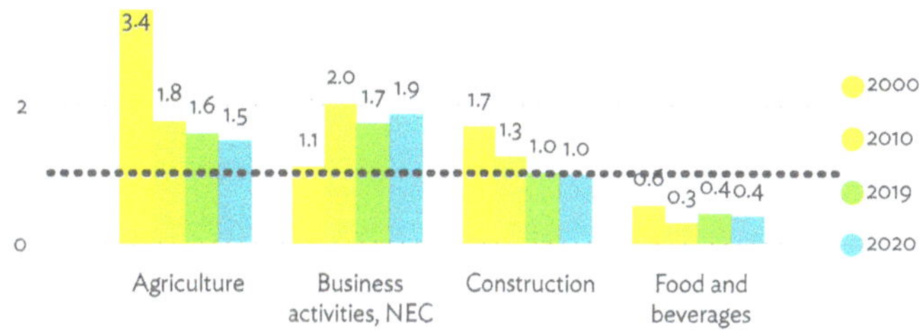

Trade Orientation

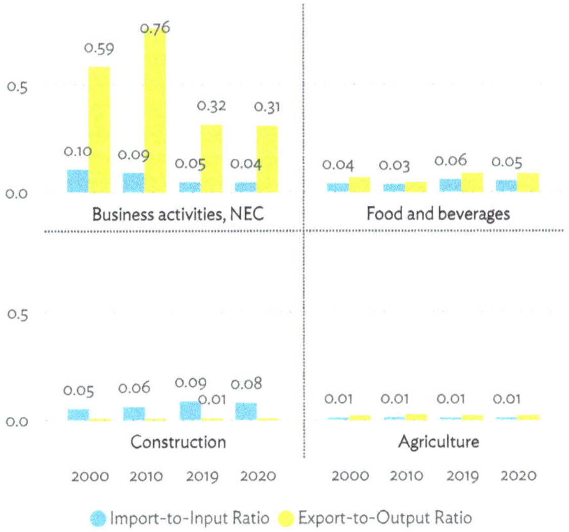

Agglomeration Indices

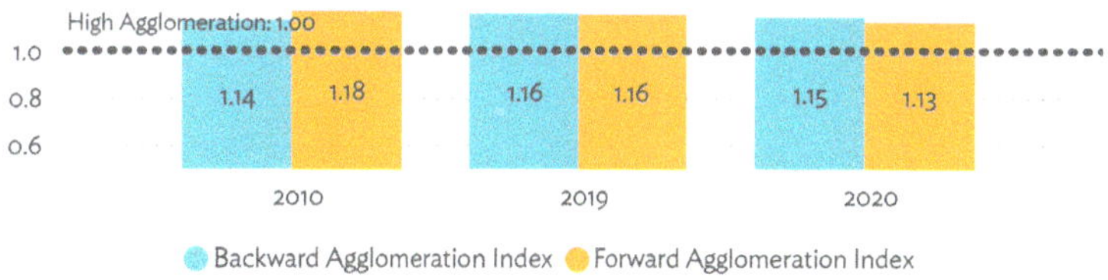

Domestic Transfer Effects and International Spillover Effects

($ million)

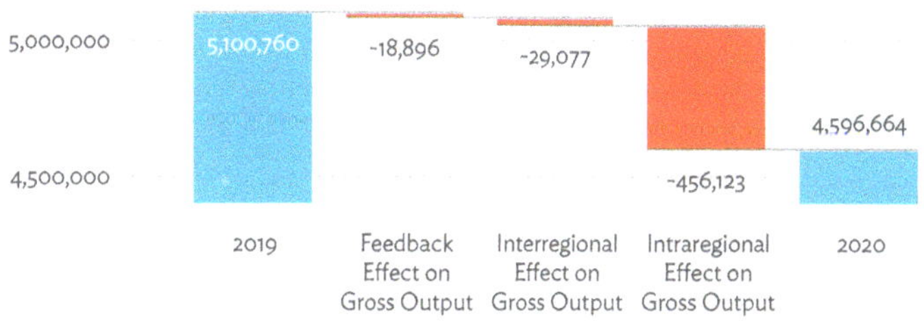

GVC = global value chain; NEC = not elsewhere classified.

Source: Calculations using the Asian Development Bank Multiregional Input-Output Table. https://mrio.adbx.online/ (accessed July 2021).

Click here for figure data

Indonesia

Southeast Asia and the Pacific

Basic Economic Indicators

Economic Aggregates ($ million)	2000	2007	2010	2013	2016	2019	2020
Value-added at basic price	177,730	455,190	735,405	895,520	901,557	1,073,069	1,019,942
Gross output	352,660	898,557	1,443,519	1,752,939	1,797,971	2,150,924	2,030,852
Total intermediate inputs	172,331	438,261	699,822	845,727	879,586	1,047,640	985,513
Taxes less subsidies on products	0	0	0	0	16,828	30,215	25,397
International transport margins	2,599	5,106	8,292	11,692	0	0	0
CIF/FOB adjustment	0	0	0	0	0	0	0
Direct purchases abroad by residents	0	0	0	0	0	0	0
Purchases by nonresidents on the domestic territory	0	0	0	0	0	0	0
Household final consumption expenditure	94,466	248,458	378,614	470,522	500,940	602,402	575,552
Final consumption expenditure by NPISHs	0	0	0	0	0	0	0
Government final consumption expenditure	11,817	38,239	64,932	84,550	84,020	96,751	95,054
Gross fixed capital formation	34,677	118,995	216,186	272,128	290,682	328,373	302,548
Changes in inventories	5,485	-1,622	12,657	15,344	-9,199	13,116	5,397
Total final demand	146,445	404,070	672,388	842,544	866,442	1,040,642	978,552
Exports	70,239	132,631	183,521	219,867	181,313	206,431	181,714
Imports	49,759	109,956	157,932	211,678	170,192	212,655	169,583

Economic Aggregates, Top 3 Sectors ($ million)	2000	2007	2010	2013	2016	2019	2020
Value-added at basic price							
Agriculture	25,786	58,123	105,202	122,668	125,527	142,267	145,046
Construction	8,692	31,659	68,978	87,162	96,779	120,284	113,334
Food and beverages	12,325	26,561	47,059	55,206	56,781	81,563	81,808
Gross output							
Construction	25,844	89,912	200,420	253,253	281,213	349,511	329,315
Food and beverages	36,219	78,093	144,837	170,033	174,885	251,214	251,968
Agriculture	33,352	73,778	127,768	148,816	153,293	173,736	177,130
Total intermediate inputs							
Construction	16,878	57,518	129,527	163,308	181,801	224,317	211,863
Food and beverages	23,690	51,137	97,273	114,073	116,467	166,123	167,009
Utilities	4,304	15,513	26,071	30,935	34,729	41,782	39,625
Total final demand							
Construction	24,888	85,146	182,761	231,943	252,654	304,532	283,330
Food and beverages	20,094	40,470	81,179	94,944	101,128	147,704	149,911
Public administration	9,467	24,335	41,430	52,506	52,052	59,531	58,694
Exports							
Mining	9,793	26,678	44,315	55,341	21,967	32,690	30,025
Food and beverages	4,844	15,308	21,957	29,530	27,304	31,494	26,242
Metals	2,696	9,855	11,350	11,194	9,291	17,869	21,108
Imports							
Electricals	2,391	12,176	20,452	28,635	22,150	25,726	22,539
Refined fuels	3,544	11,731	20,713	30,487	27,531	27,644	21,117
Chemicals	6,128	10,797	15,546	22,236	20,079	21,830	18,554

Domestic Linkages

Indicator and Top 3 Sectors, 2020	2000	2007	2010	2013	2016	2019	2020
First-round effect							
Utilities	0.60	0.63	0.69	0.67	0.59	0.63	0.64
Food and beverages	0.59	0.59	0.63	0.61	0.62	0.61	0.62
Construction	0.52	0.52	0.53	0.51	0.60	0.60	0.61
Industrial support effect							
Utilities	0.24	0.53	0.77	0.70	0.53	0.56	0.61
Construction	0.32	0.33	0.34	0.30	0.39	0.39	0.42
Chemicals	0.18	0.25	0.29	0.25	0.33	0.36	0.41
Production-induced effect							
Utilities	0.84	1.16	1.46	1.37	1.13	1.18	1.25
Construction	0.84	0.85	0.87	0.81	0.98	0.99	1.02
Rubber and plastics	0.66	0.83	0.90	0.81	0.90	0.94	0.99

continued on next page.

continued.

Indonesia

Southeast Asia and the Pacific — *Domestic Linkages*

Indicator and Top 3 Sectors, 2020	2000	2007	2010	2013	2016	2019	2020
Simple value-added multiplier							
Agriculture	0.94	0.95	0.97	0.96	0.97	0.97	0.98
Real estate	0.95	0.91	0.96	0.96	0.97	0.97	0.98
Finance	0.93	0.95	0.95	0.95	0.94	0.95	0.96
Type I value-added multiplier							
Utilities	2.95	2.91	3.39	3.28	2.85	3.05	3.14
Rubber and plastics	2.14	2.63	2.86	2.70	2.91	2.77	2.88
Machinery, NEC	1.79	2.35	2.02	1.90	2.52	2.66	2.80
Direct backward linkage							
Utilities	0.60	0.63	0.69	0.67	0.59	0.63	0.64
Food and beverages	0.59	0.59	0.63	0.61	0.62	0.61	0.62
Construction	0.52	0.52	0.53	0.51	0.60	0.60	0.61
Complete hypothetical extraction (backward)							
Water transport	1.72	1.74	1.87	1.82	1.87	1.87	1.92
Minerals, NEC	1.61	1.64	1.78	1.74	1.77	1.84	1.88
Air transport	1.69	1.64	1.75	1.73	1.70	1.82	1.88
Partial hypothetical extraction (backward)							
Construction	0.84	0.85	0.85	0.80	0.95	0.92	0.94
Water transport	0.75	0.77	0.88	0.83	0.89	0.88	0.93
Rubber and plastics	0.63	0.77	0.82	0.76	0.85	0.86	0.91
Total backward linkage							
Utilities	1.84	2.16	2.46	2.37	2.13	2.18	2.25
Construction	1.84	1.85	1.87	1.81	1.98	1.99	2.02
Rubber and plastics	1.66	1.83	1.90	1.81	1.90	1.94	1.99
Direct forward linkage							
Minerals, NEC	0.65	0.76	0.83	0.84	0.89	0.83	0.87
Business activities, NEC	0.88	0.47	0.70	0.72	0.81	0.80	0.87
Utilities	0.77	0.69	0.69	0.66	0.67	0.81	0.82
Complete hypothetical extraction (forward)							
Business activities, NEC	2.33	1.75	2.10	2.11	2.27	2.20	2.30
Mining	1.79	1.86	1.86	1.84	2.12	2.17	2.15
Minerals, NEC	1.69	1.82	1.93	1.93	2.03	1.99	2.05
Partial hypothetical extraction (forward)							
Business activities, NEC	1.36	0.78	1.16	1.16	1.33	1.24	1.35
Mining	0.85	0.94	0.96	0.95	1.21	1.23	1.20
Refined fuels	0.43	0.92	0.91	0.88	0.64	1.13	1.12
Total forward linkage							
Utilities	2.35	2.42	2.57	2.43	2.46	2.78	2.85
Business activities, NEC	2.40	1.81	2.23	2.23	2.40	2.29	2.41
Mining	1.91	2.03	2.07	2.07	2.33	2.32	2.28
Normalized backward linkage							
Utilities	1.16	1.31	1.48	1.46	1.29	1.33	1.34
Construction	1.16	1.12	1.12	1.12	1.21	1.21	1.21
Rubber and plastics	1.04	1.11	1.14	1.12	1.16	1.18	1.18
Normalized forward linkage							
Utilities	1.52	1.50	1.54	1.48	1.43	1.61	1.64
Business activities, NEC	1.55	1.12	1.33	1.36	1.40	1.33	1.39
Mining	1.23	1.25	1.24	1.26	1.36	1.35	1.31
Net backward linkage							
Construction	1.78	1.75	1.71	1.66	1.78	1.74	1.74
Health and social work	1.51	1.47	1.60	1.57	1.58	1.61	1.66
Manufacturing, NEC	1.77	1.55	1.44	1.41	1.43	1.62	1.65
Net forward linkage							
Agriculture	1.43	1.45	1.55	1.51	1.55	1.75	1.79
Mining	1.63	1.59	1.52	1.52	1.73	1.73	1.70
Finance	1.50	1.53	1.56	1.53	1.57	1.53	1.56

continued on next page.

continued.

Indonesia

Southeast Asia and the Pacific *International Linkages*

Indicator and Top 3 Sectors, 2020	2000	2007	2010	2013	2016	2019	2020
Self-sufficiency ratio							
Manufacturing, NEC	2.36	1.52	1.40	1.37	1.61	1.55	1.65
Leather	5.23	1.71	1.47	2.68	1.03	1.29	1.56
Paper	1.24	1.11	1.10	1.11	1.09	1.34	1.38
Import-to-input ratio							
Leather	0.19	0.13	0.28	0.25	0.44	0.44	0.39
Textiles	0.18	0.12	0.16	0.21	0.39	0.39	0.35
Machinery, NEC	0.35	0.27	0.35	0.39	0.24	0.24	0.21
Export-to-output ratio							
Leather	1.00	0.56	0.63	0.99	0.77	0.93	1.00
Manufacturing, NEC	0.64	0.43	0.38	0.41	0.48	0.49	0.50
Metals	0.18	0.30	0.32	0.26	0.22	0.37	0.46
Domestic inputs share to output							
Utilities	0.60	0.63	0.69	0.67	0.59	0.63	0.64
Food and beverages	0.59	0.59	0.63	0.61	0.62	0.61	0.62
Construction	0.52	0.52	0.53	0.51	0.60	0.60	0.61
Foreign inputs share to output							
Leather	0.19	0.13	0.28	0.25	0.44	0.44	0.39
Textiles	0.18	0.12	0.16	0.21	0.39	0.39	0.35
Machinery, NEC	0.35	0.27	0.35	0.39	0.24	0.24	0.21
Backward import multipliers							
Textiles	0.26	0.19	0.22	0.27	0.43	0.45	0.42
Leather	0.25	0.19	0.33	0.29	0.46	0.46	0.41
Machinery, NEC	0.41	0.37	0.45	0.48	0.36	0.31	0.28
Forward import multipliers							
Paper	0.54	0.37	0.33	0.34	0.30	0.50	0.51
Metals	0.25	0.36	0.34	0.28	0.24	0.39	0.48
Mining	0.63	0.60	0.56	0.54	0.46	0.41	0.45
Intraregional transfer multiplier							
Utilities	1.84	2.16	2.46	2.37	2.13	2.18	2.25
Construction	1.84	1.85	1.87	1.81	1.98	1.99	2.02
Rubber and plastics	1.66	1.83	1.90	1.81	1.90	1.94	1.99
Interregional spillover multiplier							
Leather	1.36	1.25	1.56	1.53	1.94	1.95	1.85
Textiles	1.35	1.24	1.38	1.50	1.91	1.85	1.77
Machinery, NEC	1.69	1.53	1.75	1.86	1.54	1.52	1.46
Interregional feedback multiplier							
Leather	1.11	1.07	1.18	1.16	1.28	1.23	1.20
Textiles	1.09	1.06	1.08	1.11	1.23	1.21	1.18
Electricals	1.08	1.13	1.20	1.21	1.17	1.12	1.11
Intraregional effect on gross output ($ million)							
Construction	25,666.39	89,204.60	197,334.69	249,893.67	277,808.26	346,601.99	326,939.53
Food and beverages	32,734.71	64,734.60	122,405.70	142,550.82	149,835.43	218,242.60	224,752.16
Agriculture	29,141.45	63,977.19	111,544.89	130,070.73	136,339.42	147,698.94	152,920.80
Feedback effect on gross output ($ million)							
Mining	3,528.31	10,880.60	19,925.29	26,719.68	13,126.91	10,450.61	9,662.05
Metals	911.95	3,092.74	3,191.47	3,315.99	2,745.00	5,028.97	4,752.10
Chemicals	984.56	2,576.00	3,498.13	4,206.90	4,319.45	3,983.83	3,632.05
Directly absorbed value-added exports (DAVAX) ($ million)							
Food and beverages	3,771.89	10,793.89	15,959.35	21,407.65	20,996.27	23,844.90	20,010.89
Mining	6,294.69	15,087.91	23,139.43	27,691.75	12,072.55	21,552.46	19,616.31
Metals	1,360.38	4,466.09	5,602.01	5,287.11	4,796.39	8,677.31	11,603.50
Reflection (REF) ($ million)							
Mining	67.79	191.59	531.66	719.43	241.02	252.70	191.96
Metals	7.42	51.97	74.96	82.91	50.03	125.95	109.99
Paper	6.20	15.54	28.60	29.63	21.19	56.99	48.52
Interregional effect on gross output ($ million)							
Food and beverages	3,049.82	11,438.65	19,369.41	23,658.53	22,146.14	28,810.32	23,600.60
Mining	11,288.61	26,213.65	40,068.69	47,371.48	29,483.42	34,810.24	32,058.77
Agriculture	3,641.80	8,247.27	13,695.49	15,792.08	14,491.74	22,386.37	20,893.88

continued on next page.

continued.

Indonesia

Southeast Asia and the Pacific

International Linkages

Indicator and Top 3 Sectors, 2020	2000	2007	2010	2013	2016	2019	2020
Reexports (REX) ($ million)							
Mining	2,995.48	9,691.47	17,570.98	22,883.24	8,635.28	9,209.04	8,867.38
Metals	671.68	2,931.59	3,321.91	3,301.76	3,070.54	6,039.35	6,197.69
Food and beverages	483.51	2,730.36	4,090.75	5,005.81	3,820.50	4,989.76	4,305.78
Foreign value added (FVA) ($ million)							
Textiles	2,107.89	2,015.47	2,593.27	3,485.94	4,850.88	6,523.63	5,275.89
Metals	652.28	2,389.10	2,330.72	2,499.86	1,364.89	3,008.38	3,179.34
Leather	572.14	396.60	1,035.17	1,705.52	2,028.15	2,907.04	2,522.86
Pure double-counting (PDC) ($ million)							
Textiles	18.24	14.49	23.38	29.13	31.84	37.57	27.55
Metals	4.27	16.20	20.71	22.00	8.76	17.65	17.78
Electricals	13.86	19.50	41.15	43.89	22.04	15.37	13.10
Trade-based GVC participation rate							
Water transport	0.48	0.54	0.52	0.56	0.58	0.51	0.59
Transport activities, NEC	0.46	0.58	0.49	0.52	0.59	0.44	0.53
Utilities	0.29	0.49	0.19	0.23	0.32	0.51	0.52
Production-based GVC participation rate							
Paper	0.54	0.37	0.33	0.34	0.30	0.50	0.51
Metals	0.25	0.36	0.34	0.28	0.24	0.39	0.48
Mining	0.63	0.60	0.56	0.54	0.46	0.41	0.45
Trade-based backward GVC participation rate							
Textiles	0.26	0.19	0.22	0.27	0.43	0.45	0.42
Leather	0.25	0.19	0.33	0.29	0.46	0.46	0.41
Machinery, NEC	0.41	0.37	0.45	0.48	0.36	0.31	0.28
Trade-based forward GVC participation rate							
Transport activities, NEC	0.33	0.51	0.40	0.43	0.51	0.36	0.46
Water transport	0.21	0.32	0.34	0.36	0.41	0.33	0.43
Utilities	0.10	0.31	0.05	0.06	0.04	0.30	0.33
Traditional revealed comparative advantage							
Leather	3.38	1.97	2.34	3.52	3.05	3.80	3.97
Wood	7.12	3.80	3.29	3.61	4.05	2.93	2.88
Paper	1.73	1.71	1.78	1.85	1.85	2.56	2.82
New revealed comparative advantage							
Leather	3.81	2.56	2.35	4.39	3.60	4.74	4.81
Agriculture	2.62	2.47	2.59	2.39	2.58	3.32	3.11
Mining	3.36	3.02	2.67	2.70	2.49	2.41	2.91
Backward production length							
Utilities	2.24	2.59	2.85	2.86	2.92	2.72	2.77
Machinery, NEC	2.48	2.83	2.91	2.94	2.97	2.72	2.70
Electricals	2.45	2.58	2.79	2.84	2.84	2.70	2.68
Forward production length							
Mining	3.57	3.81	3.80	3.80	3.74	3.44	3.54
Paper	3.24	3.09	3.18	3.09	3.15	3.29	3.35
Utilities	2.66	2.65	2.76	2.60	2.64	2.98	3.07
Backward production length of GVC segment							
Personal services, NEC	3.77	4.46	4.64	4.80	5.06	4.94	5.04
Public administration	3.82	4.15	4.17	4.41	4.75	4.83	4.95
Transport activities, NEC	4.20	4.23	4.52	4.78	5.00	4.74	4.89
Forward production length of GVC segment							
Utilities	4.89	5.48	5.80	5.76	5.68	5.61	5.68
Telecommunications	4.80	4.82	4.60	4.67	3.94	5.03	5.32
Real estate	5.20	4.53	4.75	4.80	5.15	5.05	5.31
Backward agglomeration index							
Rubber and plastics	-	1.36	1.47	1.57	1.35	3.31	2.76
Refined fuels	-	1.19	1.38	1.51	1.06	1.98	1.95
Electricals	-	1.38	1.06	1.23	1.34	1.71	1.82
Forward agglomeration index							
Air transport	-	1.31	1.46	1.53	1.60	1.65	1.67
Electricals	-	1.35	1.14	1.24	1.31	1.70	1.66
Water transport	-	2.76	2.39	2.32	2.06	1.60	1.50

CIF = cost, insurance, and freight; FOB = free on board; GVC = global value chain; NEC = not elsewhere classified; NPISHs = nonprofit institutions serving households.
Source: Calculations using the Asian Development Bank Multiregional Input-Output Table. https://mrio.adbx.online/ (accessed July 2021).

continued on next page.

continued.

Indonesia

Southeast Asia and the Pacific

The four select sectors are chosen based on their gross outputs in the economy as of 2019.

Economy Ranking out of 25 Economies

Share of Intermediate Consumption and Gross Value-Added in Output

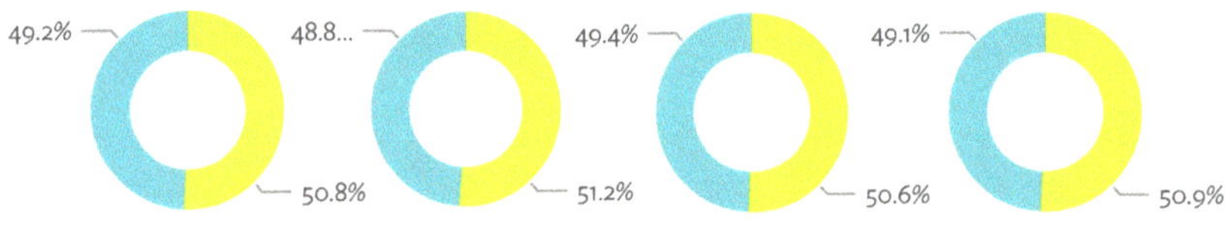

Imports and Exports, 2019-2020

($ million)

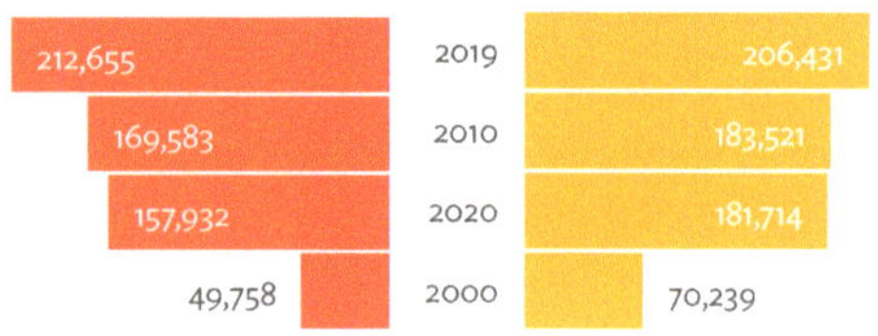

Domestic Linkages

Normalized Linkages

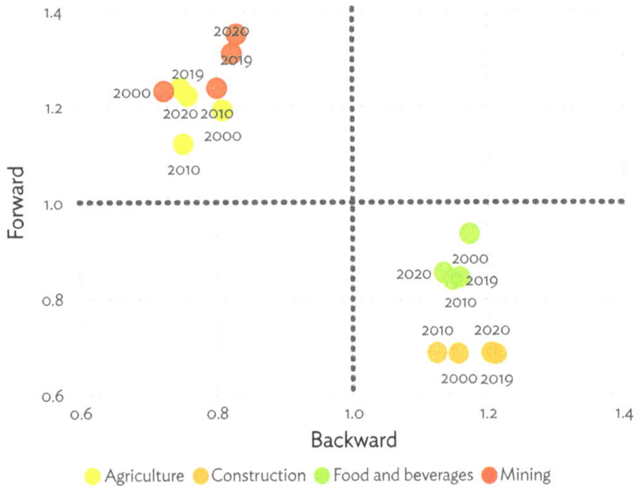

Net Linkages

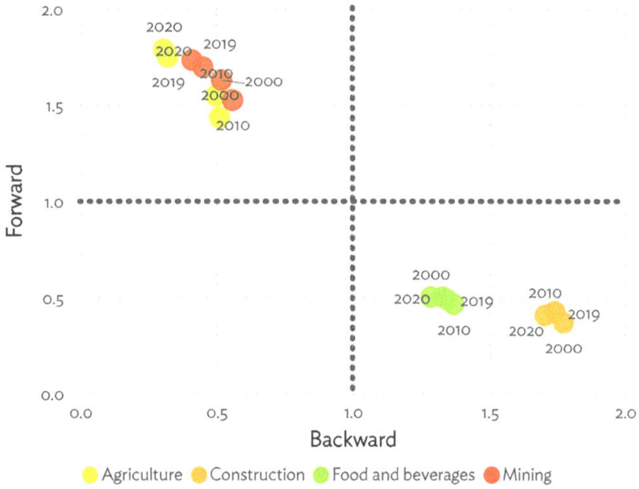

Value-Added Multipliers

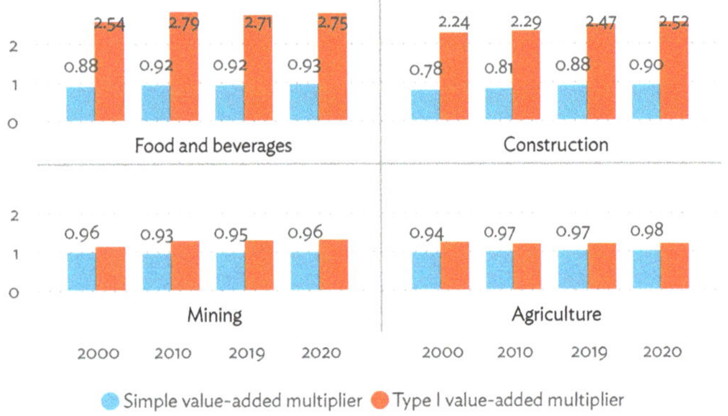

Production-Induced Effect

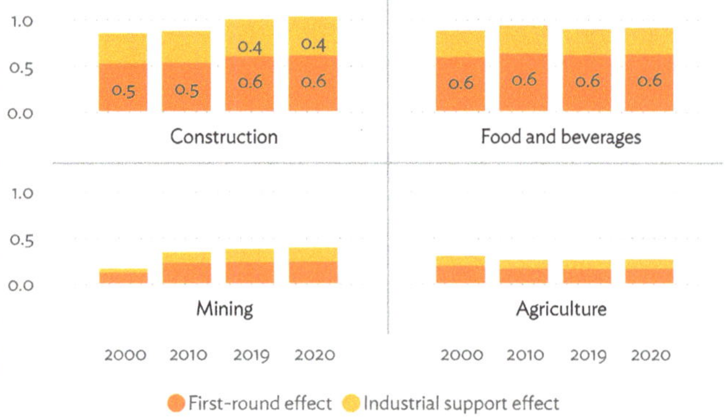

continued on next page.

Click here for figure data

continued.

Indonesia

Southeast Asia and the Pacific

International Linkages

Change in Exports, by Value-Added Components, 2019-2020

($ million)

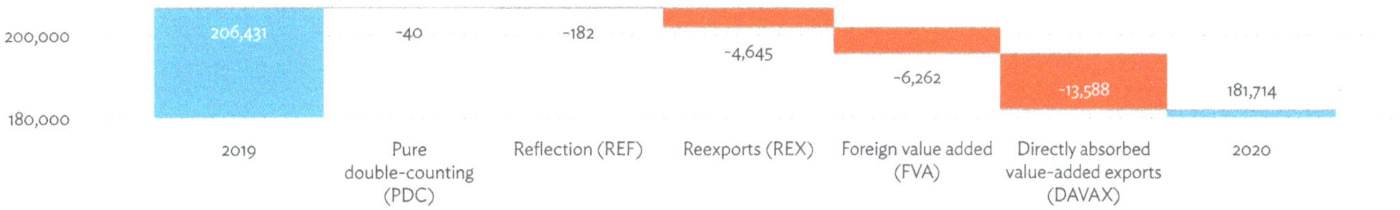

Import Multipliers

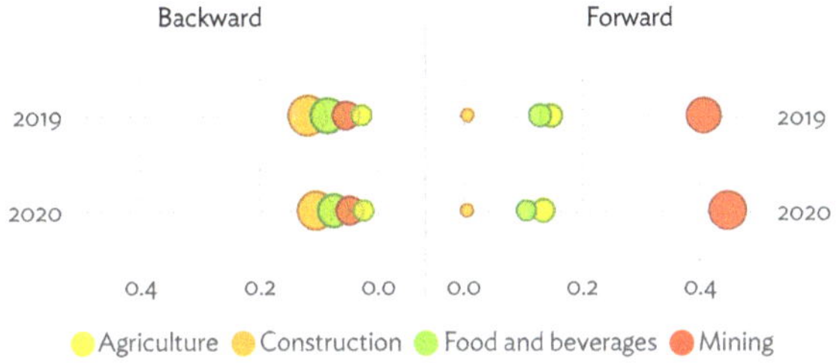

GVC Participation Rates

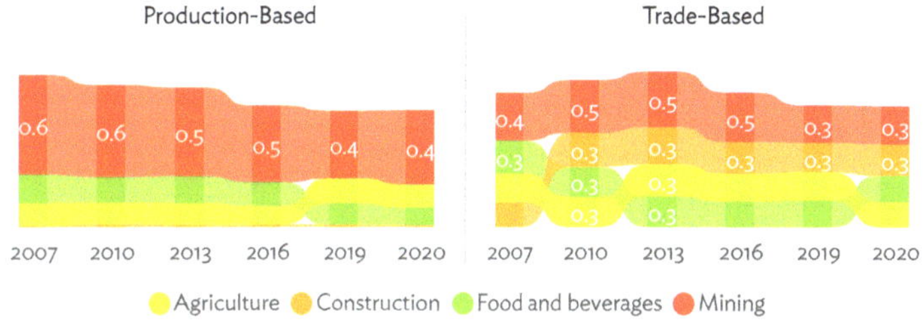

Average Production Length

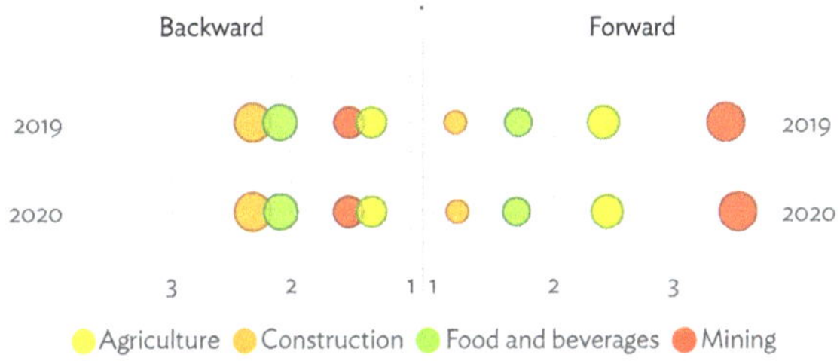

New Revealed Comparative Advantage

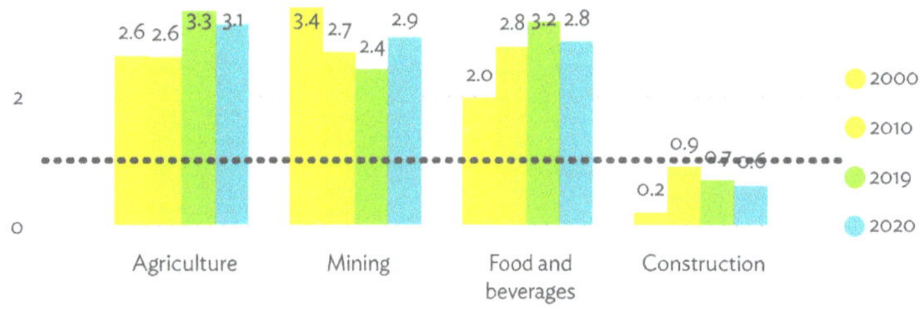

Trade Orientation

Agglomeration Indices

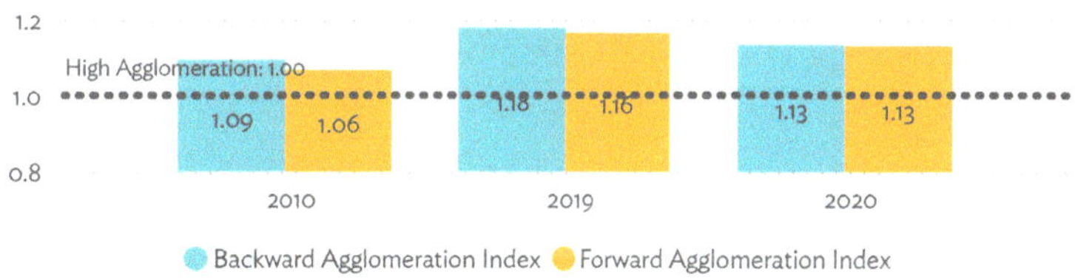

Domestic Transfer Effects and International Spillover Effects

($ million)

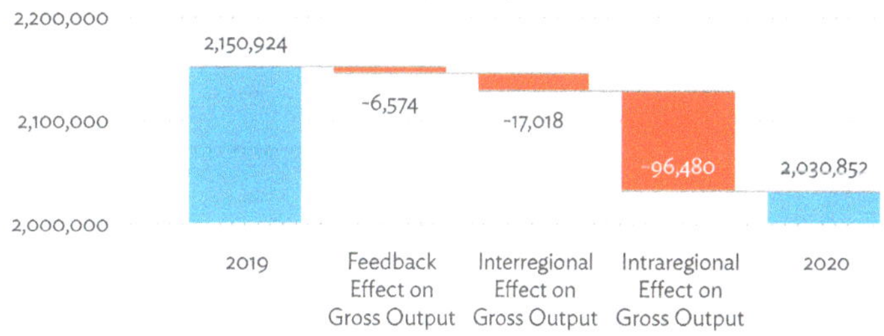

GVC = global value chain; NEC = not elsewhere classified.
Source: Calculations using the Asian Development Bank Multiregional Input-Output Table. https://mrio.adbx.online/ (accessed July 2021).

Click here for figure data

Japan

East Asia

Basic Economic Indicators

Economic Aggregates ($ million)	2000	2007	2010	2013	2016	2019	2020
Value-added at basic price	4,637,896	4,310,742	5,411,385	4,820,354	4,949,274	5,148,782	5,048,688
Gross output	8,691,189	8,489,256	10,317,384	9,378,219	9,348,505	9,598,789	9,383,694
Total intermediate inputs	4,034,603	4,149,457	4,864,502	4,504,497	4,399,231	4,450,007	4,335,006
Taxes less subsidies on products	0	0	0	0	0	0	0
International transport margins	18,689	29,056	41,498	53,367	0	0	0
CIF/FOB adjustment	0	0	0	0	0	0	0
Direct purchases abroad by residents	0	0	0	0	0	0	0
Purchases by nonresidents on the domestic territory	0	0	0	0	0	0	0
Household final consumption expenditure	2,427,270	2,265,354	2,960,045	2,671,756	2,545,291	2,516,499	2,425,316
Final consumption expenditure by NPISHs	48,779	48,904	67,593	73,104	72,745	66,143	70,307
Government final consumption expenditure	784,515	781,072	1,066,855	990,343	977,820	1,019,150	1,065,466
Gross fixed capital formation	1,139,837	918,285	1,029,034	970,297	1,079,057	1,197,150	1,179,141
Changes in inventories	-5,057	12,768	-9,043	-28,903	847	19,450	9,278
Total final demand	4,395,344	4,026,384	5,114,483	4,676,598	4,675,759	4,818,391	4,749,508
Exports	515,442	773,812	835,356	796,145	797,781	894,082	781,054
Imports	417,075	656,572	712,370	862,842	749,688	895,685	790,988

Economic Aggregates, Top 3 Sectors ($ million)	2000	2007	2010	2013	2016	2019	2020
Value-added at basic price							
Real estate	509,120	499,356	689,962	612,787	618,846	639,249	628,524
Business activities, NEC	337,542	358,889	443,855	396,944	413,977	443,442	439,871
Public administration	301,505	327,848	453,394	411,705	412,446	436,675	433,034
Gross output							
Real estate	597,809	578,158	789,349	721,682	717,500	782,426	769,293
Construction	723,757	596,402	673,695	691,890	674,520	759,616	745,984
Business activities, NEC	563,286	580,034	710,393	647,692	648,502	674,387	668,952
Total intermediate inputs							
Construction	384,041	332,925	348,165	380,153	354,967	419,341	411,813
Transport equipment	292,124	350,637	404,626	323,611	342,468	416,106	390,238
Metals	277,390	400,523	468,512	423,985	408,290	321,724	305,245
Total final demand							
Real estate	557,663	546,935	745,418	681,840	676,384	725,805	713,498
Construction	635,719	505,051	569,627	578,139	586,815	664,489	653,534
Public administration	420,385	435,535	621,978	572,446	553,304	597,128	598,569
Exports							
Transport equipment	101,921	174,915	173,959	175,458	182,720	171,212	150,627
Electricals	152,813	176,991	170,482	161,506	155,799	147,024	132,551
Machinery, NEC	49,308	61,578	65,031	62,961	67,084	132,105	107,267
Imports							
Mining	57,781	163,779	172,330	238,895	199,271	193,586	168,879
Electricals	72,403	96,885	109,505	133,678	118,712	126,645	114,102
Food and beverages	32,995	43,430	50,142	58,817	49,962	75,009	68,724

Domestic Linkages

Indicator and Top 3 Sectors, 2020	2000	2007	2010	2013	2016	2019	2020
First-round effect							
Transport equipment	0.71	0.67	0.68	0.65	0.66	0.69	0.70
Paper	0.56	0.58	0.56	0.55	0.56	0.58	0.59
Manufacturing, NEC	0.59	0.63	0.59	0.59	0.60	0.58	0.59
Industrial support effect							
Transport equipment	1.00	0.89	0.92	0.80	0.83	0.88	0.93
Metals	0.61	0.71	0.77	0.65	0.67	0.51	0.55
Food and beverages	0.46	0.48	0.48	0.45	0.48	0.51	0.53
Production-induced effect							
Transport equipment	1.71	1.56	1.60	1.46	1.49	1.57	1.63
Metals	1.21	1.33	1.42	1.25	1.29	1.07	1.13
Paper	1.08	1.14	1.08	1.04	1.06	1.09	1.12

continued on next page.

continued.

Japan

East Asia *Domestic Linkages*

Indicator and Top 3 Sectors, 2020	2000	2007	2010	2013	2016	2019	2020
Simple value-added multiplier							
Real estate	0.99	0.99	0.99	0.98	0.99	0.98	0.98
Education	0.99	0.98	0.97	0.96	0.97	0.97	0.97
Finance	0.98	0.97	0.97	0.96	0.97	0.96	0.97
Type I value-added multiplier							
Transport equipment	3.54	3.06	3.09	2.89	3.01	3.39	3.48
Metals	2.55	2.91	3.22	2.85	2.94	2.50	2.59
Manufacturing, NEC	2.47	2.76	2.47	2.44	2.54	2.43	2.48
Direct backward linkage							
Transport equipment	0.71	0.67	0.68	0.65	0.66	0.69	0.70
Paper	0.56	0.58	0.56	0.55	0.56	0.58	0.59
Manufacturing, NEC	0.59	0.63	0.59	0.59	0.60	0.58	0.59
Complete hypothetical extraction (backward)							
Hotels and restaurants	1.92	1.91	1.91	1.90	1.87	1.95	1.97
Manufacturing, NEC	2.02	2.11	2.07	2.03	2.05	1.94	1.96
Construction	1.92	1.95	1.89	1.86	1.84	1.82	1.85
Partial hypothetical extraction (backward)							
Manufacturing, NEC	1.08	1.17	1.11	1.08	1.10	0.99	1.01
Hotels and restaurants	0.94	0.94	0.94	0.92	0.90	0.97	0.99
Transport equipment	1.00	0.95	0.96	0.94	0.95	0.90	0.92
Total backward linkage							
Transport equipment	2.71	2.56	2.60	2.46	2.49	2.57	2.63
Metals	2.21	2.33	2.42	2.25	2.29	2.07	2.13
Paper	2.08	2.14	2.08	2.04	2.06	2.09	2.12
Direct forward linkage							
Wood	1.03	0.95	0.98	0.99	0.97	0.97	0.97
Paper	0.90	0.91	0.90	0.90	0.90	0.91	0.92
Mining	0.98	0.97	0.98	0.95	0.92	0.91	0.92
Complete hypothetical extraction (forward)							
Mining	3.06	3.08	3.08	2.95	2.98	2.89	2.98
Sale of motor vehicles	2.42	2.49	2.47	2.40	2.46	2.40	2.43
Wood	2.45	2.36	2.43	2.45	2.38	2.36	2.37
Partial hypothetical extraction (forward)							
Mining	2.11	2.13	2.15	2.01	2.02	1.90	2.00
Wood	1.55	1.48	1.53	1.53	1.46	1.42	1.44
Sale of motor vehicles	1.44	1.51	1.48	1.42	1.47	1.41	1.44
Total forward linkage							
Mining	3.25	3.25	3.32	3.13	3.10	2.93	3.03
Paper	3.02	3.05	2.99	2.96	2.97	2.94	2.99
Wood	2.73	2.69	2.71	2.66	2.59	2.52	2.54
Normalized backward linkage							
Transport equipment							
Metals							
Paper							
Normalized forward linkage							
Mining							
Paper							
Wood							
Net backward linkage							
Machinery, NEC							
Construction							
Public administration							
Net forward linkage							
Sale of motor vehicles							
Business activities, NEC							
Finance							

continued on next page.

continued.

Japan

East Asia *International Linkages*

Indicator and Top 3 Sectors, 2020	2000	2007	2010	2013	2016	2019	2020
Self-sufficiency ratio							
Machinery, NEC	1.26	1.29	1.35	1.30	1.33	2.25	1.89
Transport equipment	1.28	1.44	1.36	1.45	1.46	1.31	1.29
Chemicals	1.05	1.07	1.04	1.04	1.07	1.28	1.28
Import-to-input ratio							
Refined fuels	0.29	0.49	0.45	0.51	0.43	0.47	0.40
Mining	0.13	0.31	0.31	0.43	0.35	0.29	0.25
Utilities	0.07	0.16	0.14	0.29	0.23	0.21	0.18
Export-to-output ratio							
Machinery, NEC	0.28	0.31	0.34	0.33	0.33	0.64	0.55
Air transport	0.27	0.30	0.18	0.13	0.13	0.59	0.47
Electricals	0.29	0.40	0.35	0.39	0.40	0.42	0.42
Domestic inputs share to output							
Transport equipment	0.71	0.67	0.68	0.65	0.66	0.69	0.70
Paper	0.56	0.58	0.56	0.55	0.56	0.58	0.59
Manufacturing, NEC	0.59	0.63	0.59	0.59	0.60	0.58	0.59
Foreign inputs share to output							
Refined fuels	0.29	0.49	0.45	0.51	0.43	0.47	0.40
Mining	0.13	0.31	0.31	0.43	0.35	0.29	0.25
Utilities	0.07	0.16	0.14	0.29	0.23	0.21	0.18
Backward import multipliers							
Refined fuels	0.33	0.55	0.52	0.55	0.51	0.53	0.48
Mining	0.18	0.41	0.41	0.51	0.43	0.34	0.31
Utilities	0.10	0.24	0.21	0.37	0.31	0.26	0.23
Forward import multipliers							
Rubber and plastics	0.17	0.30	0.31	0.34	0.34	0.43	0.40
Air transport	0.21	0.23	0.16	0.13	0.13	0.47	0.39
Chemicals	0.20	0.30	0.28	0.32	0.32	0.43	0.39
Intraregional transfer multiplier							
Transport equipment	2.71	2.56	2.60	2.46	2.49	2.57	2.63
Metals	2.21	2.33	2.42	2.25	2.29	2.07	2.13
Paper	2.08	2.14	2.08	2.04	2.06	2.09	2.12
Interregional spillover multiplier							
Refined fuels	1.41	1.77	1.75	1.90	1.78	1.82	1.73
Mining	1.18	1.49	1.52	1.77	1.64	1.51	1.45
Utilities	1.10	1.25	1.23	1.52	1.42	1.36	1.32
Interregional feedback multiplier							
Refined fuels	1.07	1.17	1.12	1.17	1.14	1.11	1.11
Water transport	1.06	1.10	1.11	1.11	1.07	1.07	1.07
Mining	1.04	1.11	1.09	1.15	1.12	1.07	1.07
Intraregional effect on gross output ($ million)							
Real estate	594,847.34	574,713.20	784,529.34	717,373.74	713,129.90	776,652.98	764,056.43
Construction	719,768.66	589,434.09	666,459.15	684,338.85	668,309.12	752,529.08	739,917.38
Public administration	447,887.17	463,873.12	658,585.95	602,637.73	582,909.53	634,042.94	629,961.49
Interregional effect on gross output ($ million)							
Metals	58,720.88	118,015.74	148,319.60	145,497.55	139,656.16	110,414.94	103,130.81
Electricals	87,007.58	104,197.23	106,832.50	100,679.92	99,596.14	89,495.12	85,560.80
Business activities, NEC	26,464.15	39,367.68	45,636.80	41,774.98	40,313.07	90,444.48	82,447.95
Feedback effect on gross output ($ million)							
Metals	18,601.99	45,154.55	50,657.15	51,325.99	50,036.02	38,245.21	32,285.38
Electricals	35,358.42	45,010.46	45,349.57	43,843.10	42,152.17	32,424.99	28,596.31
Chemicals	13,328.19	24,605.04	28,987.72	29,161.22	33,243.97	25,662.66	22,865.65
Directly absorbed value-added exports (DAVAX) ($ million)							
Transport equipment	86,231.51	135,831.01	134,581.20	126,114.86	136,977.97	120,446.69	110,415.00
Machinery, NEC	38,549.04	44,459.84	47,564.19	42,850.87	47,062.25	96,655.06	80,441.16
Electricals	95,642.15	95,204.50	94,185.22	86,553.08	85,983.35	84,835.60	78,183.46
Reflection (REF) ($ million)							
Electricals	3,788.48	2,960.21	2,747.04	2,334.18	2,157.42	1,726.87	1,631.74
Metals	1,281.07	1,760.63	1,865.15	1,514.81	1,496.84	1,192.45	1,061.43
Chemicals	1,060.28	1,053.74	1,178.74	1,051.65	1,144.22	1,080.18	926.59

continued on next page.

continued.

Japan

East Asia

International Linkages

Indicator and Top 3 Sectors, 2020	2000	2007	2010	2013	2016	2019	2020
Reexports (REX) ($ million)							
Electricals	37,199.66	48,777.60	45,525.18	40,089.12	39,345.76	35,842.08	33,162.97
Chemicals	9,880.96	15,527.36	18,117.19	17,333.76	19,774.15	22,611.92	21,244.66
Metals	11,496.28	23,455.52	26,620.00	24,046.03	25,223.39	22,659.44	19,995.31
Foreign value added (FVA) ($ million)							
Transport equipment	8,591.54	26,083.54	24,329.39	32,707.65	31,022.73	32,408.74	25,353.69
Electricals	15,240.63	28,802.44	26,907.93	31,555.04	27,428.25	24,107.70	19,187.90
Metals	4,729.04	18,901.31	24,448.53	31,790.99	27,605.75	20,964.39	16,428.15
Pure double-counting (PDC) ($ million)							
Transport equipment	327.43	789.91	702.66	756.83	733.12	672.04	485.34
Electricals	941.79	1,246.10	1,116.84	974.40	883.96	511.77	385.43
Machinery, NEC	168.19	280.72	270.67	249.78	247.04	341.27	227.28
Trade-based GVC participation rate							
Refined fuels	0.49	0.68	0.71	0.71	0.69	0.66	0.62
Mining	0.43	0.64	0.63	0.69	0.63	0.58	0.59
Water transport	0.40	0.52	0.50	0.54	0.53	0.60	0.55
Production-based GVC participation rate							
Rubber and plastics	0.17	0.30	0.31	0.34	0.34	0.43	0.40
Air transport	0.21	0.23	0.16	0.13	0.13	0.47	0.39
Chemicals	0.20	0.30	0.28	0.32	0.32	0.43	0.39
Trade-based backward GVC participation rate							
Refined fuels	0.33	0.55	0.52	0.55	0.51	0.53	0.48
Mining	0.18	0.41	0.41	0.51	0.43	0.34	0.31
Utilities	0.10	0.24	0.21	0.37	0.31	0.26	0.23
Trade-based forward GVC participation rate							
Water transport	0.21	0.24	0.23	0.26	0.30	0.43	0.40
Transport activities, NEC	0.40	0.48	0.52	0.45	0.43	0.43	0.40
Textiles	0.40	0.40	0.35	0.34	0.33	0.36	0.37
Traditional revealed comparative advantage							
Machinery, NEC	1.62	1.28	1.35	1.43	1.51	2.29	2.12
Transport equipment	1.98	2.37	2.42	2.58	2.47	1.90	1.97
Water transport	2.06	2.40	2.20	1.93	1.69	1.50	1.66
New revealed comparative advantage							
Water transport	1.88	2.48	2.28	2.33	2.22	2.43	2.61
Transport equipment	2.01	2.71	2.71	2.92	2.83	2.22	2.31
Air transport	1.09	1.08	0.84	0.69	0.58	1.86	2.25
Backward production length							
Transport equipment	2.92	2.96	2.98	2.99	2.98	3.08	3.08
Metals	2.46	2.88	3.01	3.04	2.99	2.67	2.68
Refined fuels	2.06	2.41	2.38	2.37	2.56	2.37	2.42
Forward production length							
Mining	3.46	3.75	3.87	3.73	3.71	3.34	3.42
Rubber and plastics	3.15	3.35	3.37	3.42	3.44	3.41	3.35
Paper	3.19	3.34	3.29	3.27	3.30	3.32	3.32
Backward production length of GVC segment							
Transport equipment	4.99	5.18	5.30	5.24	5.26	5.01	5.07
Real estate	4.67	5.05	5.01	5.21	5.18	4.69	4.75
Sale of motor vehicles	4.62	4.90	4.98	5.01	5.01	4.64	4.69
Forward production length of GVC segment							
Mining	5.35	5.45	5.49	5.28	5.37	5.48	5.53
Telecommunications	5.38	5.65	5.51	5.57	5.68	5.41	5.45
Agriculture	5.51	5.64	5.80	5.77	5.69	5.58	5.42
Backward agglomeration index							
Textiles	-	2.15	2.03	1.83	1.80	2.14	2.17
Electricals	-	1.82	2.01	1.79	1.66	1.77	1.93
Manufacturing, NEC	-	1.33	1.40	1.52	1.36	1.74	1.67
Forward agglomeration index							
Mining	-	1.81	1.66	1.65	1.46	2.03	1.91
Manufacturing, NEC	-	1.35	1.39	1.49	1.42	1.69	1.72
Textiles	-	1.63	1.50	1.46	1.35	1.42	1.50

CIF = cost, insurance, and freight; FOB = free on board; GVC = global value chain; NEC = not elsewhere classified; NPISHs = nonprofit institutions serving households.
Source: Calculations using the Asian Development Bank Multiregional Input-Output Table. https://mrio.adbx.online/ (accessed July 2021).

continued on next page.

continued.

Japan

East Asia

The four select sectors are chosen based on their gross outputs in the economy as of 2019.

Economy Ranking out of 25 Economies

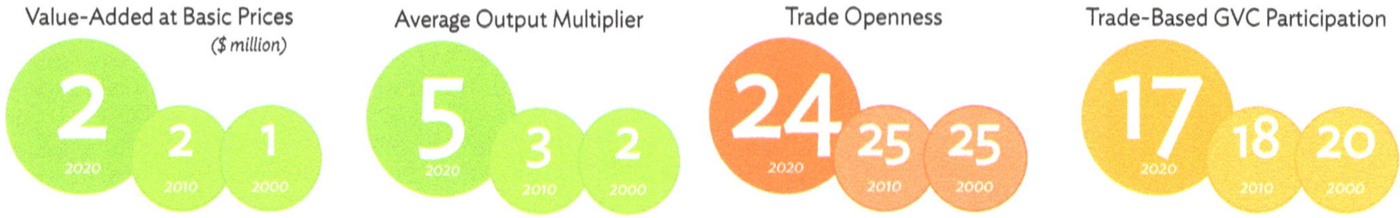

Share of Intermediate Consumption and Gross Value-Added in Output

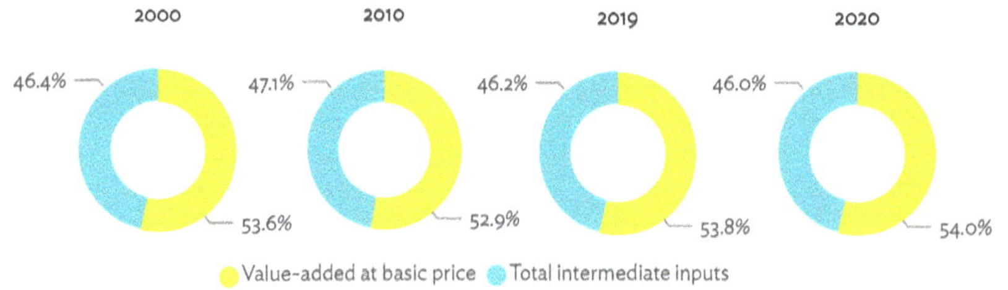

Imports and Exports, 2019-2020

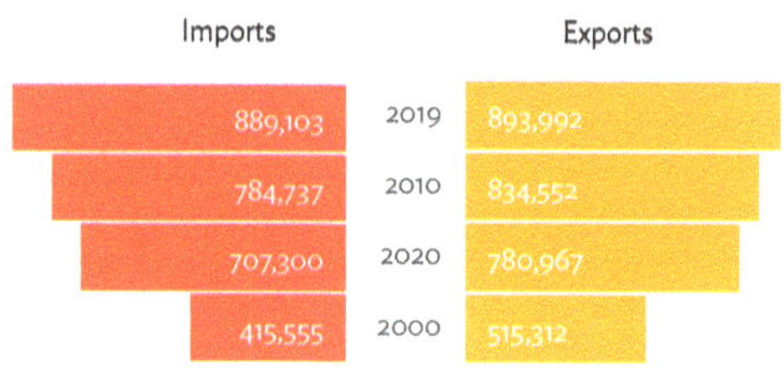

Domestic Linkages

Normalized Linkages

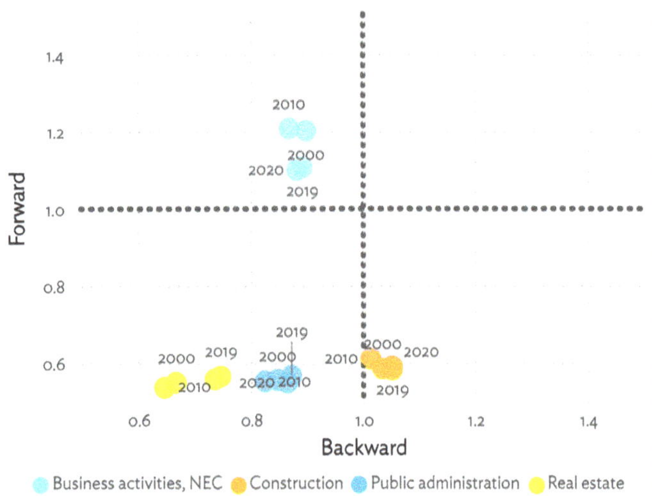

Net Linkages

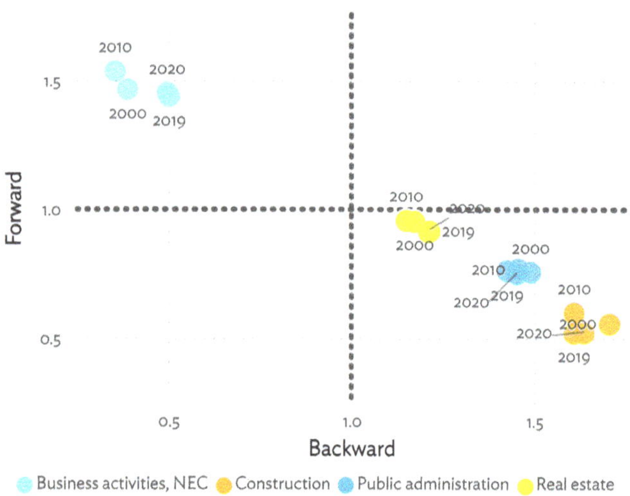

Value-Added Multipliers

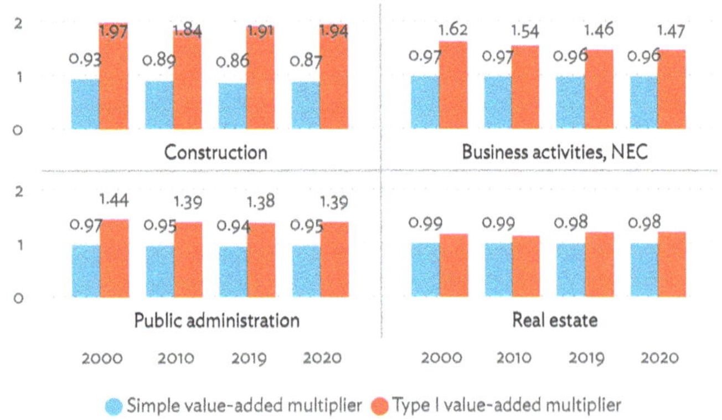

Production-Induced Effect

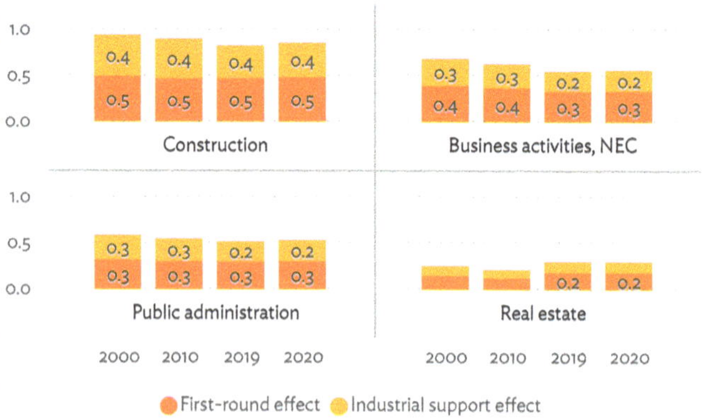

continued on next page.

Click here for figure data

continued.

Japan

East Asia

International Linkages

Change in Exports, by Value-Added Components, 2019-2020

($ million)

Import Multipliers

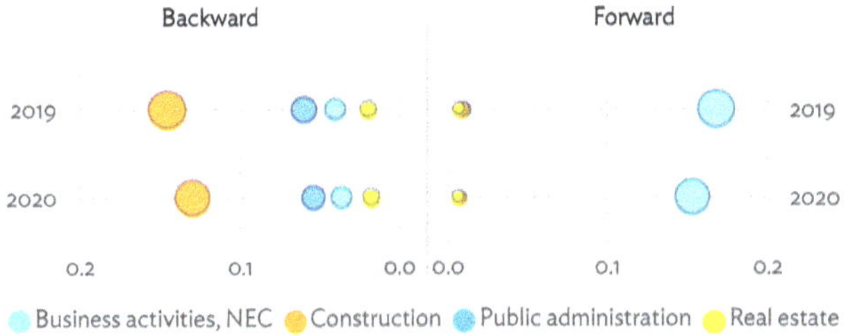

GVC Participation Rates

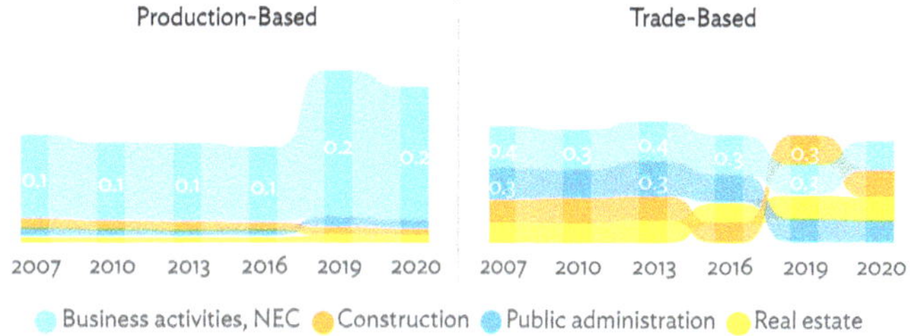

Average Production Length

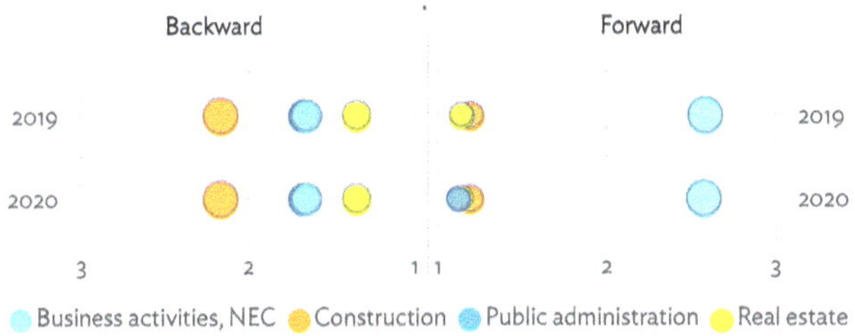

New Revealed Comparative Advantage

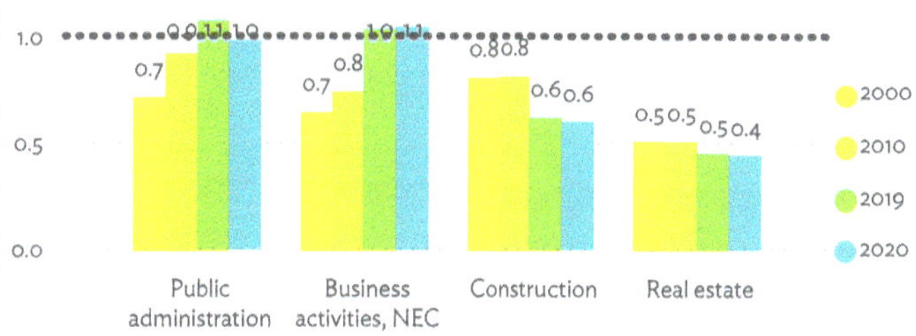

Trade Orientation

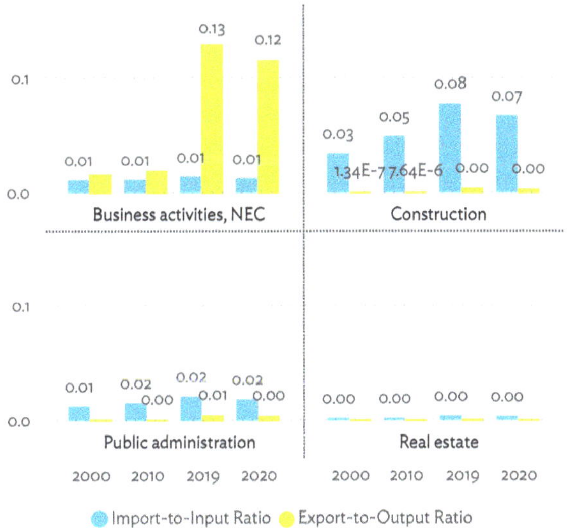

Agglomeration Indices

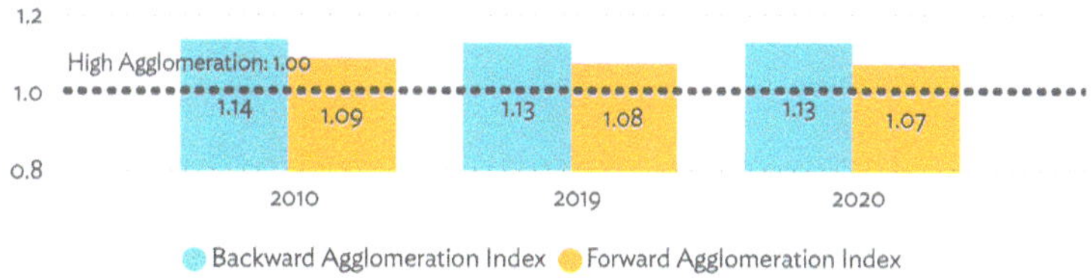

Domestic Transfer Effects and International Spillover Effects

($ million)

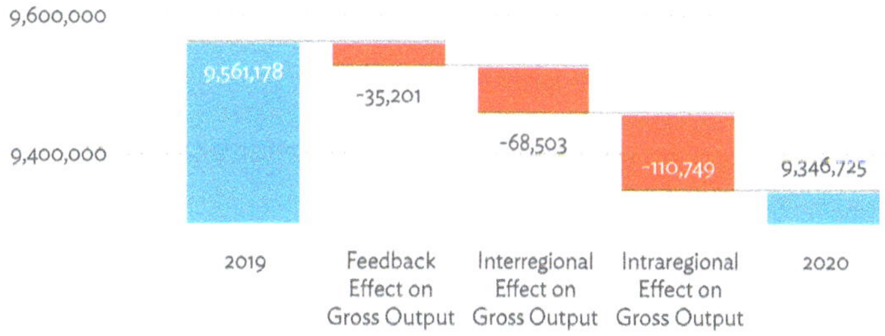

GVC = global value chain; NEC = not elsewhere classified.

Source: Calculations using the Asian Development Bank Multiregional Input-Output Table. https://mrio.adbx.online/ (accessed July 2021).

Click here for figure data

Kazakhstan

South and Central Asia

Basic Economic Indicators

Economic Aggregates ($ million)	2000	2007	2010	2013	2016	2019	2020
Value-added at basic price	17,264	97,348	135,500	208,137	125,967	168,993	159,982
Gross output	40,786	197,889	246,553	357,549	211,520	291,651	276,168
Total intermediate inputs	23,005	96,696	106,450	145,536	84,465	119,791	113,899
Taxes less subsidies on products	518	3,845	4,603	3,876	1,087	2,867	2,287
International transport margins	0	0	0	0	0	0	0
CIF/FOB adjustment	0	0	0	0	0	0	0
Direct purchases abroad by residents	0	0	0	0	0	0	0
Purchases by nonresidents on the domestic territory	0	0	0	0	0	0	0
Household final consumption expenditure	8,794	35,643	55,309	87,868	60,185	80,471	75,872
Final consumption expenditure by NPISHs	104	1,212	1,214	2,272	1,556	2,105	1,963
Government final consumption expenditure	2,085	11,167	15,240	23,890	15,966	17,138	21,832
Gross fixed capital formation	1,586	17,684	21,182	34,637	20,528	28,481	27,780
Changes in inventories	355	5,638	1,815	3,847	4,706	5,675	6,884
Total final demand	12,925	71,344	94,760	152,515	102,941	133,870	134,330
Exports	9,065	50,998	62,624	86,728	39,751	66,198	53,391
Imports	8,161	44,472	42,032	60,341	37,425	51,629	47,622

Economic Aggregates, Top 3 Sectors ($ million)	2000	2007	2010	2013	2016	2019	2020
Value-added at basic price							
Mining	1,855	16,867	30,161	44,575	18,594	26,211	21,318
Wholesale trade	1,184	9,695	15,284	22,827	16,717	20,154	18,638
Gross output							
Mining	5,128	37,793	55,155	77,894	32,500	50,047	40,704
Wholesale trade	2,006	14,723	23,881	32,609	23,142	30,380	28,078
Business activities, NEC	1,319	9,958	11,136	16,050	11,991	20,381	19,016
Total intermediate inputs							
Mining	3,169	20,316	24,120	32,037	13,768	23,445	19,123
Wholesale trade	734	4,728	7,627	9,746	6,413	10,196	9,417
Construction	788	11,589	9,771	15,607	7,898	7,938	8,242
Total final demand							
Real estate	1,333	10,993	14,242	19,115	14,306	16,372	16,030
Construction	914	14,404	14,516	23,243	11,425	13,973	14,770
Agriculture	1,062	4,826	6,524	10,349	7,046	10,109	11,632
Exports							
Mining	1,829	23,277	34,362	51,339	17,724	38,097	31,639
Metals	4,527	6,205	9,479	9,066	5,853	10,082	7,660
Refined fuels	1,069	3,091	2,201	3,943	1,012	4,438	4,061
Imports							
Machinery, NEC	870	7,059	4,963	8,318	5,214	7,698	7,531
Electricals	442	3,911	3,672	6,732	3,931	4,722	4,609
Metals	446	4,067	4,262	5,808	2,789	4,731	4,540

Domestic Linkages

Indicator and Top 3 Sectors, 2020	2000	2007	2010	2013	2016	2019	2020
First-round effect							
Public administration	0.42	0.41	0.44	0.38	0.48	0.50	0.52
Refined fuels	0.61	0.69	0.56	0.48	0.59	0.48	0.49
Water transport	0.38	0.47	0.37	0.28	0.44	0.46	0.46
Industrial support effect							
Refined fuels	0.57	0.44	0.32	0.23	0.28	0.22	0.23
Public administration	0.31	0.21	0.24	0.17	0.21	0.19	0.21
Electricals	0.54	0.20	0.29	0.30	0.29	0.19	0.20
Production-induced effect							
Public administration	0.73	0.62	0.68	0.55	0.70	0.69	0.73
Refined fuels	1.18	1.13	0.88	0.70	0.86	0.70	0.72
Water transport	0.74	0.72	0.57	0.44	0.67	0.64	0.66

continued on next page.

continued.

Kazakhstan

South and Central Asia

Domestic Linkages

Indicator and Top 3 Sectors, 2020	2000	2007	2010	2013	2016	2019	2020
Simple value-added multiplier							
Real estate	0.75	0.84	0.93	0.93	0.95	0.92	0.93
Refined fuels	0.75	0.75	0.84	0.85	0.92	0.92	0.92
Metals	0.84	0.83	0.92	0.90	0.91	0.90	0.90
Type I value-added multiplier							
Public administration	1.71	1.74	1.85	1.63	1.99	2.11	2.18
Water transport	1.61	1.79	1.69	1.51	1.89	2.01	2.05
Refined fuels	2.81	4.23	2.46	2.00	2.32	1.82	1.86
Direct backward linkage							
Public administration	0.42	0.41	0.44	0.38	0.48	0.50	0.52
Refined fuels	0.61	0.69	0.56	0.48	0.59	0.48	0.49
Water transport	0.38	0.47	0.37	0.28	0.44	0.46	0.46
Complete hypothetical extraction (backward)							
Public administration	1.73	1.62	1.68	1.55	1.70	1.69	1.73
Refined fuels	1.88	2.11	1.79	1.69	1.84	1.70	1.72
Water transport	1.73	1.71	1.49	1.43	1.66	1.64	1.66
Partial hypothetical extraction (backward)							
Public administration	0.73	0.62	0.68	0.55	0.70	0.69	0.73
Refined fuels	1.02	1.12	0.84	0.70	0.85	0.70	0.72
Water transport	0.73	0.71	0.55	0.43	0.67	0.64	0.66
Total backward linkage							
Public administration	1.73	1.62	1.68	1.55	1.70	1.69	1.73
Refined fuels	2.18	2.13	1.88	1.70	1.86	1.70	1.72
Water transport	1.74	1.72	1.57	1.44	1.67	1.64	1.66
Direct forward linkage							
Finance	0.75	0.86	0.91	0.81	0.78	0.81	0.86
Paper	0.68	0.60	0.85	0.83	0.93	0.77	0.83
Minerals, NEC	0.41	0.51	0.75	0.82	0.85	0.78	0.79
Complete hypothetical extraction (forward)							
Paper	1.82	1.88	2.25	2.17	2.34	2.20	2.29
Finance	2.30	1.44	2.22	2.01	1.93	1.99	2.02
Machinery, NEC	1.91	1.67	2.32	2.28	2.29	2.12	2.00
Partial hypothetical extraction (forward)							
Paper	0.98	0.91	1.28	1.20	1.34	1.20	1.30
Finance	1.35	1.02	1.31	1.12	1.03	1.11	1.16
Minerals, NEC	0.55	0.77	1.00	1.12	1.11	1.01	1.02
Total forward linkage							
Finance	2.41	3.43	2.45	2.27	2.15	2.27	2.36
Paper	2.16	1.94	2.33	2.23	2.35	2.21	2.31
Minerals, NEC	1.66	1.82	2.06	2.19	2.18	2.07	2.09
Normalized backward linkage							
Public administration	1.01	1.04	1.10	1.05	1.13	1.21	1.22
Refined fuels	1.28	1.37	1.24	1.15	1.24	1.21	1.22
Water transport	1.02	1.11	1.03	0.97	1.11	1.17	1.18
Normalized forward linkage							
Finance	1.47	2.04	1.57	1.48	1.39	1.58	1.65
Paper	1.31	1.15	1.50	1.45	1.52	1.54	1.61
Minerals, NEC	1.01	1.08	1.32	1.43	1.41	1.45	1.46
Net backward linkage							
Public administration	1.73	1.62	1.68	1.55	1.69	1.68	1.72
Refined fuels	1.18	1.65	1.19	0.99	0.63	1.69	1.72
Water transport	1.45	0.96	0.45	0.25	0.34	1.62	1.66
Net forward linkage							
Finance	1.61	0.46	1.69	1.63	1.58	1.52	1.55
Rubber and plastics	0.66	1.04	0.80	0.82	0.81	1.60	1.54
Paper	0.82	1.18	1.16	1.13	1.18	1.25	1.32

continued on next page.

continued.

Kazakhstan

South and Central Asia *International Linkages*

Indicator and Top 3 Sectors, 2020	2000	2007	2010	2013	2016	2019	2020
Self-sufficiency ratio							
Mining	1.23	2.09	2.34	2.63	2.04	3.65	3.77
Refined fuels	1.37	1.90	1.24	1.33	1.13	2.95	3.00
Air transport	0.38	1.27	1.05	0.96	0.82	2.28	2.00
Import-to-input ratio							
Manufacturing, NEC	0.34	0.17	0.30	0.33	0.26	0.33	0.34
Leather	0.21	0.12	0.19	0.25	0.25	0.28	0.28
Transport equipment	0.12	0.13	0.20	0.13	0.20	0.26	0.26
Export-to-output ratio							
Refined fuels	0.35	0.64	0.49	0.51	0.32	0.99	1.00
Water transport	0.75	0.43	0.18	0.03	0.03	0.99	1.00
Transport equipment	0.12	0.14	0.35	0.17	0.26	0.99	0.92
Domestic inputs share to output							
Public administration	0.42	0.41	0.44	0.38	0.48	0.50	0.52
Refined fuels	0.61	0.69	0.56	0.48	0.59	0.48	0.49
Water transport	0.38	0.47	0.37	0.28	0.44	0.46	0.46
Foreign inputs share to output							
Manufacturing, NEC	0.34	0.17	0.30	0.33	0.26	0.33	0.34
Leather	0.21	0.12	0.19	0.25	0.25	0.28	0.28
Transport equipment	0.12	0.13	0.20	0.13	0.20	0.26	0.26
Backward import multipliers							
Manufacturing, NEC	0.41	0.26	0.33	0.36	0.28	0.35	0.35
Leather	0.28	0.16	0.23	0.28	0.28	0.29	0.29
Transport equipment	0.20	0.20	0.23	0.17	0.23	0.29	0.29
Forward import multipliers							
Refined fuels	0.48	0.58	0.53	0.52	0.36	0.94	0.95
Mining	0.70	0.83	0.83	0.82	0.63	0.74	0.81
Water transport	0.81	0.61	0.58	0.42	0.29	0.73	0.73
Intraregional transfer multiplier							
Public administration	1.73	1.62	1.68	1.55	1.70	1.69	1.73
Refined fuels	2.18	2.13	1.88	1.70	1.86	1.70	1.72
Water transport	1.74	1.72	1.57	1.44	1.67	1.64	1.66
Interregional spillover multiplier							
Manufacturing, NEC	1.63	1.35	1.64	1.69	1.53	1.68	1.70
Leather	1.41	1.24	1.44	1.62	1.59	1.69	1.70
Transport equipment	1.24	1.25	1.41	1.28	1.42	1.55	1.56
Interregional feedback multiplier							
Transport equipment	1.05	1.07	1.11	1.08	1.12	1.14	1.14
Manufacturing, NEC	1.10	1.07	1.12	1.12	1.10	1.13	1.13
Paper	1.06	1.06	1.10	1.06	1.10	1.12	1.11
Intraregional effect on gross output ($ million)							
Wholesale trade	950.09	6,790.62	12,457.41	16,203.64	12,577.72	21,767.73	20,756.13
Construction	1,273.80	20,929.05	18,277.46	30,436.89	14,292.68	17,405.32	18,147.45
Real estate	1,585.52	13,795.65	15,390.85	20,741.02	15,436.23	18,423.89	17,990.65
Interregional effect on gross output ($ million)							
Mining	2,474.48	23,011.77	32,361.26	44,532.55	14,032.28	26,204.36	23,976.43
Metals	5,448.59	5,669.18	8,719.50	6,995.34	4,466.37	8,646.78	7,225.07
Wholesale trade	738.36	6,007.44	8,669.83	12,442.86	7,914.32	6,383.27	5,581.23
Feedback effect on gross output ($ million)							
Mining	1,113.14	8,279.17	13,203.88	19,414.51	6,567.50	11,022.41	8,975.95
Metals	2,552.58	2,932.85	3,971.91	3,665.72	2,469.32	2,638.95	1,809.28
Wholesale trade	317.64	1,924.77	2,753.60	3,962.50	2,649.60	2,228.75	1,740.32
Directly absorbed value-added exports (DAVAX) ($ million)							
Mining	857.52	12,234.92	18,905.52	27,422.54	9,739.06	21,351.10	17,686.35
Metals	2,089.84	2,492.85	4,545.22	4,044.35	2,665.50	5,834.14	4,716.30
Refined fuels	538.62	1,653.71	1,327.65	2,640.54	747.65	2,944.39	2,738.50
Reflection (REF) ($ million)							
Mining	1.75	25.22	36.64	67.78	13.93	31.33	30.86
Metals	12.46	17.13	18.11	24.73	9.61	21.79	20.46
Refined fuels	2.50	6.47	4.70	9.69	3.22	10.93	8.63

continued on next page.

continued.

Kazakhstan

South and Central Asia

International Linkages

Indicator and Top 3 Sectors, 2020	2000	2007	2010	2013	2016	2019	2020
Reexports (REX) ($ million)							
Mining	587.85	6,626.07	11,785.05	18,375.59	6,110.32	11,217.95	9,538.77
Metals	1,714.27	2,659.84	4,115.59	4,125.41	2,677.45	3,228.48	2,191.31
Refined fuels	261.42	654.69	524.03	720.21	184.77	1,110.09	983.45
Foreign value added (FVA) ($ million)							
Mining	379.84	4,369.74	3,618.38	5,439.78	1,855.38	5,478.46	4,369.29
Metals	704.80	1,029.86	796.09	865.29	499.11	992.87	728.70
Refined fuels	265.58	772.94	343.09	570.83	75.87	371.30	329.32
Pure double-counting (PDC) ($ million)							
Mining	1.98	21.49	16.27	33.35	5.55	18.44	13.98
Metals	5.39	5.77	4.39	6.46	1.55	4.44	2.88
Refined fuels	1.26	2.72	1.11	1.76	0.20	1.40	1.12
Trade-based GVC participation rate							
Chemicals	0.53	0.43	0.50	0.39	0.26	0.54	0.53
Leather	0.33		0.35	0.39	0.34	0.55	0.50
Water transport	0.56	0.54	0.52	0.55	0.53	0.49	0.48
Production-based GVC participation rate							
Refined fuels	0.48	0.58	0.53	0.52	0.36	0.94	0.95
Mining	0.70	0.83	0.83	0.82	0.63	0.74	0.81
Water transport	0.81	0.61	0.58	0.42	0.29	0.73	0.73
Trade-based backward GVC participation rate							
Manufacturing, NEC	0.41	0.26	0.33	0.36	0.28	0.35	0.35
Leather	0.28		0.23	0.28	0.28	0.29	0.29
Transport equipment	0.20	0.20	0.23	0.17	0.23	0.29	0.29
Trade-based forward GVC participation rate							
Chemicals	0.23	0.26	0.25	0.18	0.13	0.34	0.33
Mining	0.32	0.29	0.34	0.36	0.35	0.30	0.30
Metals	0.38	0.43	0.44	0.46	0.46	0.32	0.29
Traditional revealed comparative advantage							
Mining	3.35	5.76	6.50	6.31	6.65	8.54	9.09
Metals	8.38	1.62	2.24	1.62	2.31	2.31	2.21
Refined fuels	4.92	1.58	0.87	0.95	0.65	1.93	2.17
New revealed comparative advantage							
Mining	2.74	3.98	4.29	4.39	4.24	5.07	5.99
Refined fuels	5.89	0.91	1.17	1.74	1.33	2.77	3.13
Metals	8.24	1.38	2.11	1.42	2.19	2.66	2.61
Backward production length							
Water transport	2.19	2.14	2.10	2.14	2.07	2.20	2.21
Transport equipment	2.28	2.20	2.20	2.15	2.23	2.13	2.14
Public administration	2.13	2.09	1.95	1.83	2.04	2.12	2.12
Forward production length							
Refined fuels	3.02	2.85	3.01	3.10	2.98	3.58	3.74
Mining	4.04	3.73	3.87	3.89	3.33	3.30	3.49
Water transport	3.39	3.34	3.89	3.43	3.12	3.06	3.02
Backward production length of GVC segment							
Refined fuels	3.92	3.90	3.74	3.83	4.74	4.48	4.52
Education	3.85	4.09	4.10	4.05	4.19	4.04	4.12
Metals	4.30	4.39	4.29	4.18	4.36	4.09	4.12
Forward production length of GVC segment							
Real estate	5.97	5.31	5.54	5.05	5.19	5.48	5.63
Finance	5.52	6.30	5.36	5.35	5.14	5.27	5.38
Paper	5.49	4.66	4.94	4.90	4.94	4.89	5.23
Backward agglomeration index							
Rubber and plastics	-	1.20	1.28	1.90	1.83	4.18	3.74
Electricals	-	1.88	2.30	1.28	1.62	2.70	2.89
Metals	-	1.50	0.97	1.47	1.35	1.80	2.03
Forward agglomeration index							
Electricals	-	1.87	2.04	1.13	1.47	2.08	2.16
Manufacturing, NEC	-	0.85	1.77	1.74	1.61	2.06	1.82
Rubber and plastics	-	1.23	1.50	1.60	1.53	1.37	1.43

CIF = cost, insurance, and freight; FOB = free on board; GVC = global value chain; NEC = not elsewhere classified; NPISHs = nonprofit institutions serving households.
Source: Calculations using the Asian Development Bank Multiregional Input-Output Table. https://mrio.adbx.online/ (accessed July 2021).

continued on next page.

continued.

Kazakhstan

South and Central Asia

The four select sectors are chosen based on their gross outputs in the economy as of 2019.

Economy Ranking out of 25 Economies

Share of Intermediate Consumption and Gross Value-Added in Output

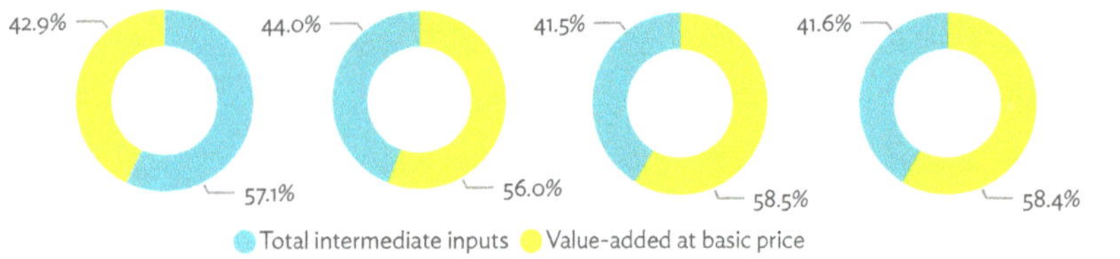

Imports and Exports, 2019-2020

($ million)

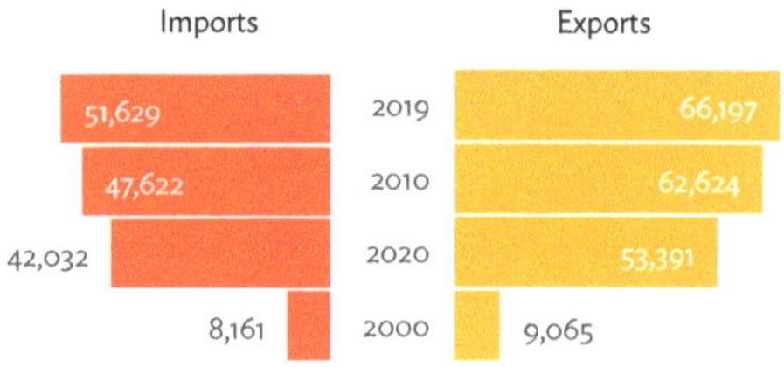

Domestic Linkages

Normalized Linkages

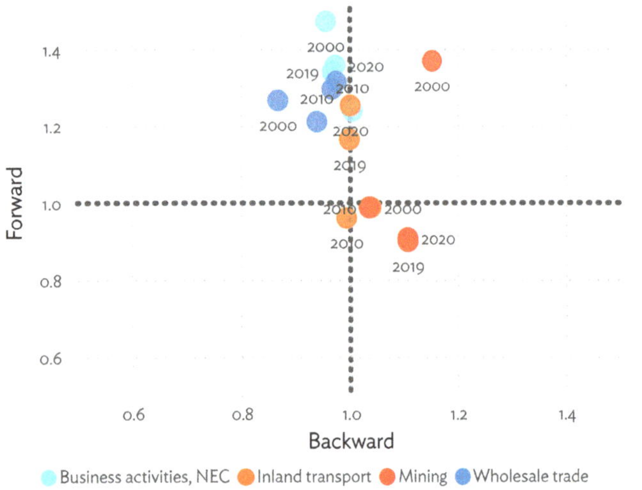

Net Linkages

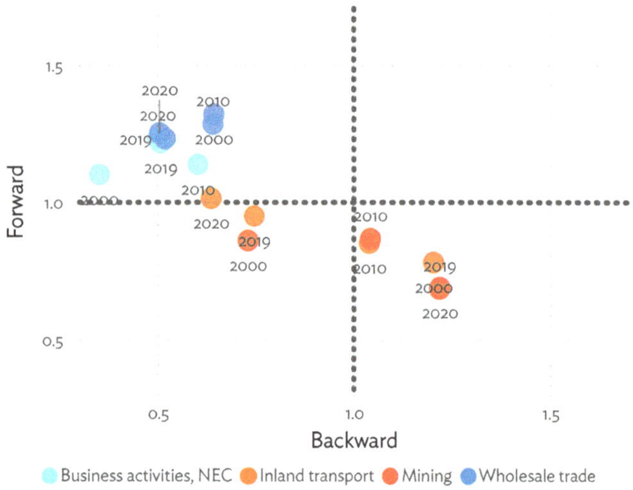

Value-Added Multipliers

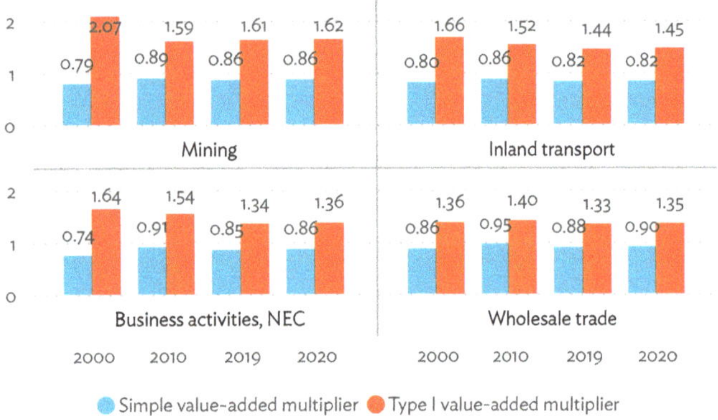

Production-Induced Effect

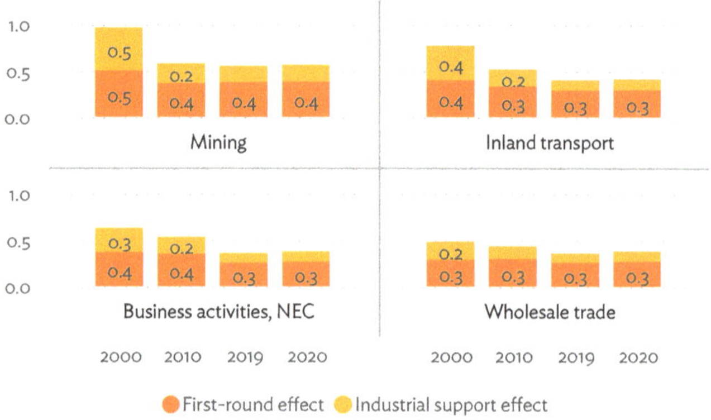

continued on next page.

Click here for figure data

continued.

Kazakhstan

South and Central Asia

International Linkages

Change in Exports, by Value-Added Components, 2019-2020

($ million)

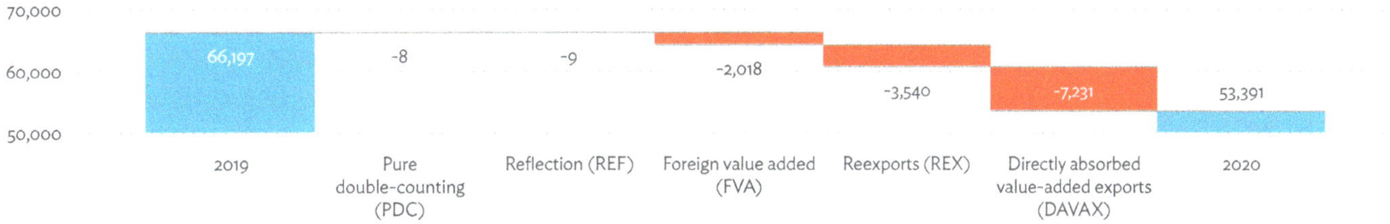

Import Multipliers

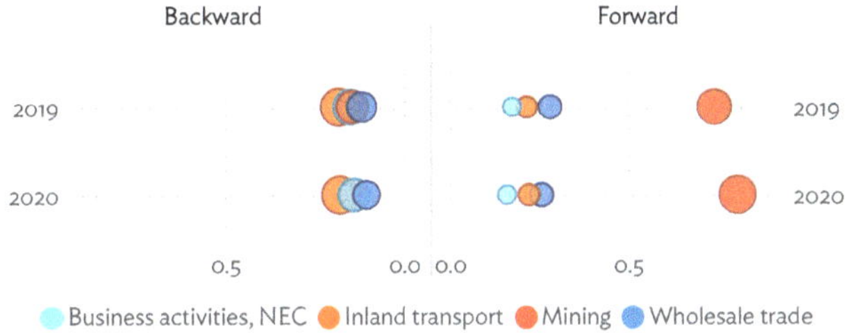

GVC Participation Rates

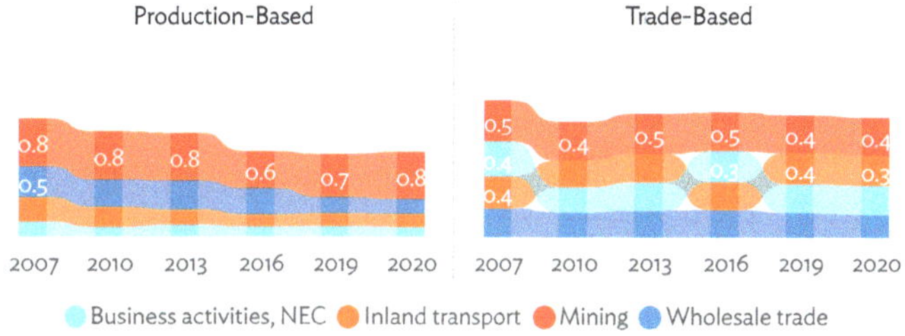

Average Production Length

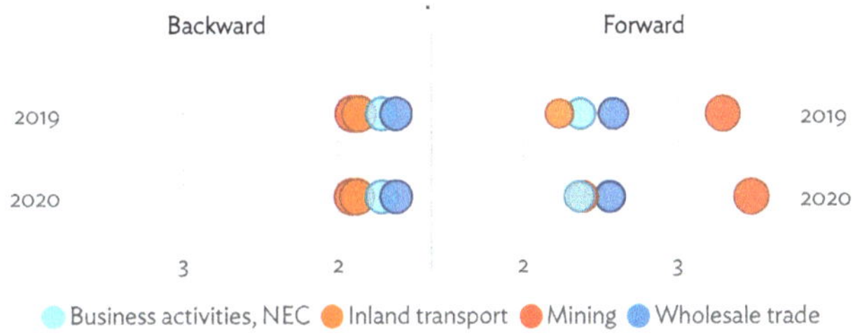

New Revealed Comparative Advantage

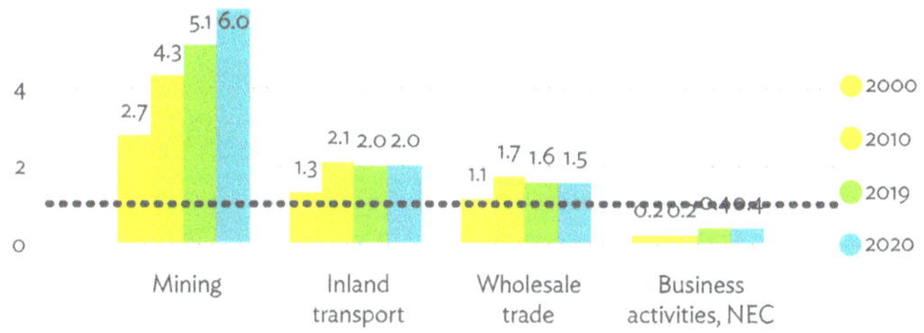

Trade Orientation

Agglomeration Indices

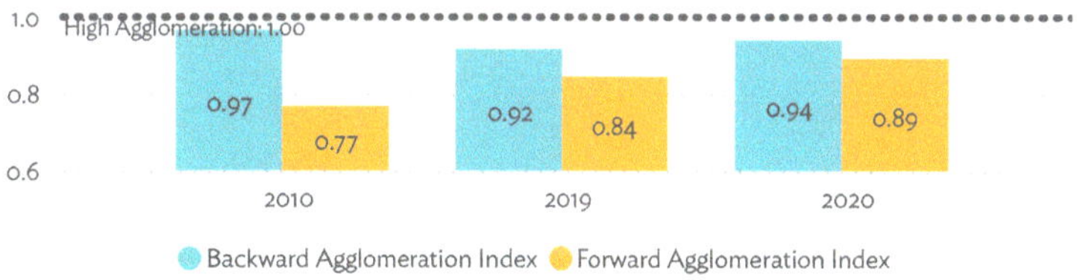

Domestic Transfer Effects and International Spillover Effects

($ million)

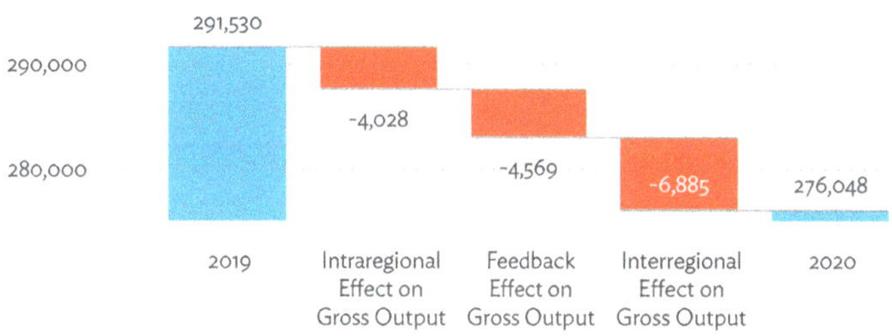

GVC = global value chain; NEC = not elsewhere classified.
Source: Calculations using the Asian Development Bank Multiregional Input-Output Table. https://mrio.adbx.online/ (accessed July 2021).

Click here for figure data

Republic of Korea

East Asia

Basic Economic Indicators

Economic Aggregates ($ million)	2000	2007	2010	2013	2016	2019	2020
Value-added at basic price	504,457	1,013,652	991,192	1,191,048	1,282,768	1,507,364	1,493,186
Gross output	1,175,976	2,516,482	2,638,334	3,201,879	3,350,901	3,628,467	3,544,033
Total intermediate inputs	645,799	1,448,265	1,582,801	1,931,477	2,024,205	2,038,584	1,970,058
Taxes less subsidies on products	15,544	32,510	34,280	39,256	43,928	82,519	80,789
International transport margins	10,177	22,054	30,062	40,099	0	0	0
CIF/FOB adjustment	0	0	0	0	0	0	0
Direct purchases abroad by residents	0	0	0	0	0	0	0
Purchases by nonresidents on the domestic territory	0	0	0	0	0	0	0
Household final consumption expenditure	257,273	494,774	457,643	543,270	538,207	679,743	650,838
Final consumption expenditure by NPISHs	0	0	0	0	0	0	0
Government final consumption expenditure	62,103	158,179	158,885	195,106	207,090	271,168	284,341
Gross fixed capital formation	138,611	265,576	256,646	299,697	338,926	392,793	413,656
Changes in inventories	5,201	17,670	13,152	-2,476	7,390	26,982	10,908
Total final demand	463,188	936,199	886,327	1,035,596	1,091,613	1,370,686	1,359,742
Exports	191,713	408,206	518,902	686,573	643,588	657,824	601,615
Imports	162,976	363,673	440,528	562,228	509,489	610,103	541,017

Economic Aggregates, Top 3 Sectors ($ million)	2000	2007	2010	2013	2016	2019	2020
Value-added at basic price							
Business activities, NEC	33,502	79,163	78,111	98,169	103,901	178,120	180,361
Electricals	38,493	77,808	85,181	105,400	105,118	134,154	132,917
Real estate	45,988	83,813	76,513	91,864	102,001	122,482	124,324
Gross output							
Electricals	143,595	292,054	328,037	382,512	377,304	336,136	333,037
Business activities, NEC	56,989	137,319	137,184	171,727	179,369	318,287	322,292
Construction	81,214	173,201	157,671	177,017	191,861	225,545	224,841
Total intermediate inputs							
Electricals	102,569	210,026	236,949	270,090	270,957	195,291	193,427
Transport equipment	45,132	136,305	144,183	177,945	185,709	175,257	163,069
Metals	41,865	128,380	148,105	169,359	166,574	147,844	138,186
Total final demand							
Construction	77,922	163,593	149,144	167,113	183,182	207,702	208,686
Public administration	43,155	97,305	96,932	119,861	128,663	136,441	143,473
Health and social work	23,012	63,895	67,263	87,167	96,160	132,009	136,027
Exports							
Electricals	67,423	127,990	164,945	206,103	184,143	186,240	177,571
Chemicals	13,606	34,990	49,484	69,730	70,706	82,431	84,486
Transport equipment	22,477	72,069	102,406	129,491	114,927	76,459	70,616
Imports							
Electricals	39,061	54,802	68,945	85,890	76,207	77,038	78,727
Mining	27,042	67,950	90,493	128,173	104,532	88,780	72,374
Metals	16,750	46,708	50,332	54,494	48,712	55,756	50,152

Domestic Linkages

Indicator and Top 3 Sectors, 2020	2000	2007	2010	2013	2016	2019	2020
First-round effect							
Food and beverages	0.71	0.71	0.70	0.71	0.74	0.68	0.68
Textiles	0.57	0.61	0.62	0.62	0.64	0.61	0.62
Hotels and restaurants	0.39	0.42	0.44	0.45	0.43	0.60	0.61
Industrial support effect							
Textiles	0.51	0.62	0.66	0.66	0.75	0.63	0.65
Food and beverages	0.55	0.63	0.67	0.68	0.80	0.60	0.63
Leather	0.60	0.72	0.73	0.76	0.84	0.59	0.62
Production-induced effect							
Food and beverages	1.26	1.34	1.37	1.39	1.54	1.28	1.31
Textiles	1.08	1.23	1.28	1.27	1.39	1.24	1.27
Leather	1.19	1.36	1.38	1.41	1.50	1.17	1.21

continued on next page.

continued.

Republic of Korea

East Asia — *Domestic Linkages*

Indicator and Top 3 Sectors, 2020	2000	2007	2010	2013	2016	2019	2020
Simple value-added multiplier							
Real estate	0.97	0.96	0.96	0.96	0.96	0.94	0.95
Public administration	0.92	0.92	0.91	0.91	0.92	0.93	0.94
Education	0.93	0.92	0.91	0.90	0.90	0.90	0.91
Type I value-added multiplier							
Water transport	1.66	1.75	1.86	1.78	1.87	3.38	3.77
Food and beverages	3.91	3.84	3.96	4.05	4.39	3.47	3.54
Refined fuels	1.73	1.71	1.68	1.67	3.25	2.94	3.28
Direct backward linkage							
Food and beverages	0.71	0.71	0.70	0.71	0.74	0.68	0.68
Textiles	0.57	0.61	0.62	0.62	0.64	0.61	0.62
Hotels and restaurants	0.39	0.42	0.44	0.45	0.43	0.60	0.61
Complete hypothetical extraction (backward)							
Hotels and restaurants	1.75	1.82	1.86	1.89	1.90	2.12	2.15
Manufacturing, NEC	1.70	1.94	2.11	2.09	2.15	2.03	2.05
Water transport	1.71	1.80	1.84	1.80	1.90	1.90	1.95
Partial hypothetical extraction (backward)							
Hotels and restaurants	0.75	0.83	0.87	0.90	0.91	1.14	1.17
Manufacturing, NEC	0.72	0.97	1.15	1.14	1.20	1.07	1.10
Leather	1.02	1.13	1.10	1.14	1.19	1.02	1.05
Total backward linkage							
Food and beverages	2.26	2.34	2.37	2.39	2.54	2.28	2.31
Textiles	2.08	2.23	2.28	2.27	2.39	2.24	2.27
Leather	2.19	2.36	2.38	2.41	2.50	2.17	2.21
Direct forward linkage							
Wood	0.96	0.97	0.96	0.95	0.90	0.75	0.88
Minerals, NEC	0.83	0.85	0.86	0.82	0.85	0.83	0.84
Transport activities, NEC	0.87	0.88	0.90	0.88	0.90	0.82	0.83
Complete hypothetical extraction (forward)							
Transport activities, NEC	2.42	2.61	2.71	2.68	2.80	2.56	2.60
Mining	3.87	3.55	3.40	3.11	3.15	2.31	2.43
Water transport	1.00	1.00	1.00	1.00	1.11	2.33	2.38
Partial hypothetical extraction (forward)							
Transport activities, NEC	1.52	1.67	1.76	1.72	1.84	1.60	1.64
Agriculture	1.02	1.12	1.24	1.33	1.51	1.47	1.46
Mining	2.87	2.56	2.40	2.11	2.15	1.31	1.43
Total forward linkage							
Wood	2.48	2.78	2.91	2.86	2.81	2.41	2.73
Transport activities, NEC	2.68	2.79	2.86	2.81	2.93	2.65	2.69
Agriculture	2.15	2.26	2.40	2.50	2.72	2.63	2.65
Normalized backward linkage							
Food and beverages	1.29	1.27	1.28	1.29	1.32	1.26	1.26
Textiles	1.19	1.21	1.22	1.23	1.24	1.24	1.24
Leather	1.25	1.29	1.28	1.30	1.30	1.20	1.20
Normalized forward linkage							
Wood	1.34	1.43	1.45	1.45	1.36	1.24	1.38
Transport activities, NEC	1.45	1.43	1.43	1.42	1.42	1.36	1.36
Agriculture	1.16	1.16	1.20	1.27	1.32	1.35	1.34
Net backward linkage							
Construction	1.82	1.88	1.89	1.85	1.90	1.75	1.77
Health and social work	1.70	1.70	1.63	1.64	1.61	1.62	1.63
Education	1.36	1.39	1.40	1.39	1.45	1.42	1.42
Net forward linkage							
Agriculture	1.39	1.32	1.30	1.36	1.45	1.44	1.45
Sale of motor vehicles	1.12	1.18	1.23	1.17	1.24	1.27	1.31
Paper	1.07	1.01	0.95	0.96	0.96	1.27	1.30

continued on next page.

continued.

Republic of Korea

East Asia *International Linkages*

Indicator and Top 3 Sectors, 2020	2000	2007	2010	2013	2016	2019	2020
Self-sufficiency ratio							
Air transport	1.38	2.40	1.95	1.86	1.81	1.56	1.47
Electricals	1.25	1.33	1.41	1.46	1.40	1.48	1.42
Chemicals	1.01	1.05	1.10	1.14	1.12	1.37	1.37
Import-to-input ratio							
Refined fuels	0.63	0.64	0.68	0.67	0.64	0.47	0.44
Utilities	0.22	0.26	0.31	0.31	0.25	0.39	0.37
Water transport	0.10	0.11	0.13	0.13	0.12	0.27	0.24
Export-to-output ratio							
Refined fuels	0.28	0.31	0.39	0.43	0.40	0.44	0.64
Air transport	0.47	0.85	0.70	0.70	0.63	0.66	0.58
Electricals	0.47	0.44	0.50	0.54	0.49	0.55	0.53
Domestic inputs share to output							
Food and beverages	0.71	0.71	0.70	0.71	0.74	0.68	0.68
Textiles	0.57	0.61	0.62	0.62	0.64	0.61	0.62
Hotels and restaurants	0.39	0.42	0.44	0.45	0.43	0.60	0.61
Foreign inputs share to output							
Refined fuels	0.63	0.64	0.68	0.67	0.64	0.47	0.44
Utilities	0.22	0.26	0.31	0.31	0.25	0.39	0.37
Water transport	0.10	0.11	0.13	0.13	0.12	0.27	0.24
Backward import multipliers							
Refined fuels	0.68	0.70	0.74	0.75	0.75	0.60	0.55
Utilities	0.30	0.36	0.42	0.45	0.41	0.50	0.48
Metals	0.31	0.36	0.41	0.40	0.38	0.40	0.38
Forward import multipliers							
Refined fuels	0.38	0.43	0.50	0.56	0.55	0.56	0.61
Chemicals	0.46	0.45	0.51	0.55	0.53	0.61	0.58
Electricals	0.39	0.40	0.40	0.47	0.48	0.58	0.57
Intraregional transfer multiplier							
Food and beverages	2.26	2.34	2.37	2.39	2.54	2.28	2.31
Textiles	2.08	2.23	2.28	2.27	2.39	2.24	2.27
Leather	2.19	2.36	2.38	2.41	2.50	2.17	2.21
Interregional spillover multiplier							
Refined fuels	1.90	2.03	2.15	2.23	2.20	1.84	1.81
Utilities	1.31	1.43	1.53	1.58	1.48	1.70	1.68
Metals	1.34	1.41	1.48	1.47	1.44	1.50	1.49
Interregional feedback multiplier							
Refined fuels	1.16	1.21	1.19	1.23	1.23	1.12	1.12
Water transport	1.04	1.05	1.07	1.08	1.07	1.12	1.11
Air transport	1.02	1.05	1.07	1.08	1.06	1.12	1.11
Intraregional effect on gross output ($ million)							
Business activities, NEC	44,576.34	108,368.69	111,665.42	133,852.30	136,783.85	259,660.93	266,188.36
Construction	81,007.19	172,328.23	156,528.80	175,651.83	190,550.86	219,638.26	220,484.19
Transport equipment	61,210.88	155,605.12	166,951.37	191,951.95	196,566.04	177,520.19	169,098.56
Interregional effect on gross output ($ million)							
Electricals	41,341.83	83,201.74	95,062.32	127,810.41	130,998.97	146,941.49	143,740.23
Chemicals	25,901.26	52,630.70	67,951.98	95,078.83	104,077.72	73,832.99	74,866.99
Metals	16,817.54	45,664.78	59,889.86	72,184.93	66,578.88	74,355.62	67,907.62
Feedback effect on gross output ($ million)							
Electricals	15,137.66	33,995.05	37,789.22	52,174.74	48,564.96	48,100.07	45,447.15
Chemicals	7,174.26	17,687.04	21,832.61	30,875.61	34,596.21	21,067.64	21,579.25
Metals	4,653.15	16,001.45	19,150.36	24,110.06	23,262.38	24,439.24	21,566.98
Directly absorbed value-added exports (DAVAX) ($ million)							
Electricals	31,981.54	58,007.80	74,697.80	92,221.15	84,326.11	86,753.46	85,168.33
Chemicals	5,964.46	13,632.18	19,093.86	25,976.16	27,402.10	37,882.25	42,228.09
Transport equipment	16,156.86	47,606.04	65,764.19	79,426.23	72,477.73	40,619.98	39,547.38
Reflection (REF) ($ million)							
Electricals	320.65	746.07	692.49	869.16	859.96	1,427.75	1,564.15
Chemicals	70.45	246.17	275.98	349.19	382.15	458.79	476.02
Metals	72.07	202.98	240.69	277.91	305.28	382.75	415.97

continued on next page.

continued.

Republic of Korea

East Asia

International Linkages

Indicator and Top 3 Sectors, 2020	2000	2007	2010	2013	2016	2019	2020
Reexports (REX) ($ million)							
Electricals	12,862.61	30,305.57	31,756.70	39,694.33	37,041.32	53,125.33	50,117.44
Chemicals	3,097.96	8,693.04	10,461.66	13,632.23	14,737.63	16,735.53	17,580.48
Metals	2,603.49	7,443.57	8,861.59	10,204.21	10,522.33	13,691.44	12,417.47
Foreign value added (FVA) ($ million)							
Electricals	21,929.40	38,180.92	56,620.64	71,649.58	60,348.22	43,997.87	39,756.68
Transport equipment	5,664.30	20,181.16	31,956.75	41,974.09	35,056.30	27,682.77	24,366.56
Chemicals	4,446.30	12,309.36	19,480.72	29,451.86	27,862.46	27,126.78	23,981.12
Pure double-counting (PDC) ($ million)							
Electricals	329.18	749.79	1,177.28	1,668.71	1,567.43	935.48	964.55
Transport equipment	51.33	250.07	411.06	631.82	585.33	412.74	390.85
Chemicals	27.15	109.37	171.58	320.79	321.85	227.61	220.23
Trade-based GVC participation rate							
Refined fuels	0.74	0.77	0.81	0.83	0.82	0.70	0.67
Water transport	0.42	0.50	0.52	0.54	0.52	0.70	0.64
Metals	0.51	0.61	0.62	0.62	0.61	0.63	0.61
Production-based GVC participation rate							
Refined fuels	0.38	0.43	0.50	0.56	0.55	0.56	0.61
Chemicals	0.46	0.45	0.51	0.55	0.53	0.61	0.58
Electricals	0.39	0.40	0.40	0.47	0.48	0.58	0.57
Trade-based backward GVC participation rate							
Refined fuels	0.68	0.70	0.74	0.75	0.75	0.60	0.55
Utilities	0.30	0.36	0.42	0.45	0.41	0.50	0.48
Metals	0.31	0.36	0.41	0.40	0.38	0.40	0.38
Trade-based forward GVC participation rate							
Transport activities, NEC	0.30	0.31	0.32	0.29	0.29	0.38	0.36
Textiles	0.24	0.28	0.25	0.26	0.27	0.31	0.30
Electricals	0.20	0.24	0.20	0.20	0.21	0.29	0.29
Traditional revealed comparative advantage							
Electricals	2.16	2.31	2.38	2.39	2.30	2.31	2.27
Refined fuels	2.11	1.57	1.71	1.88	2.04	2.08	1.93
Chemicals	1.04	1.18	1.25	1.39	1.49	1.56	1.63
New revealed comparative advantage							
Electricals	2.41	3.00	3.08	3.22	2.93	3.51	3.43
Metals	1.45	1.57	1.92	1.89	1.78	1.90	1.83
Rubber and plastics	0.93	0.74	0.83	0.75	0.78	1.96	1.79
Backward production length							
Leather	2.88	3.09	3.23	3.30	3.35	3.15	3.15
Transport equipment	2.75	3.11	3.09	3.15	3.27	3.11	3.11
Textiles	2.65	2.89	2.99	3.05	3.09	3.06	3.05
Forward production length							
Mining	4.87	4.65	4.63	4.41	4.50	3.95	3.98
Transport activities, NEC	3.14	3.40	3.53	3.61	3.79	3.53	3.54
Rubber and plastics	2.93	3.17	3.26	3.32	3.47	3.53	3.53
Backward production length of GVC segment							
Real estate	4.52	4.85	4.96	5.13	5.16	4.68	4.77
Personal services, NEC	4.49	4.81	4.88	5.02	5.12	4.69	4.76
Machinery, NEC	4.32	4.83	4.82	4.88	5.02	4.66	4.71
Forward production length of GVC segment							
Real estate	5.26	4.77	5.21	5.50	5.61	5.75	5.83
Agriculture	5.19	5.82	5.84	5.96	6.30	5.76	5.83
Telecommunications	4.96	5.27	5.39	5.38	5.52	5.53	5.64
Backward agglomeration index							
Textiles	-	1.59	1.42	1.15	1.13	1.78	1.77
Rubber and plastics	-	0.80	0.60	0.33	0.00	1.79	1.72
Electricals	-	0.87	0.62	0.61	0.71	1.38	1.51
Forward agglomeration index							
Textiles	-	1.17	0.98	0.73	0.74	1.22	1.27
Manufacturing, NEC	-	1.02	0.84	0.81	0.81	1.13	1.14
Leather	-	1.65	1.11	0.94	0.91	1.17	1.12

CIF = cost, insurance, and freight; FOB = free on board; GVC = global value chain; NEC = not elsewhere classified; NPISHs = nonprofit institutions serving households.
Source: Calculations using the Asian Development Bank Multiregional Input-Output Table. https://mrio.adbx.online/ (accessed July 2021).

continued on next page.

continued.

Republic of Korea

East Asia

The four select sectors are chosen based on their gross outputs in the economy as of 2019.

Economy Ranking out of 25 Economies

Share of Intermediate Consumption and Gross Value-Added in Output

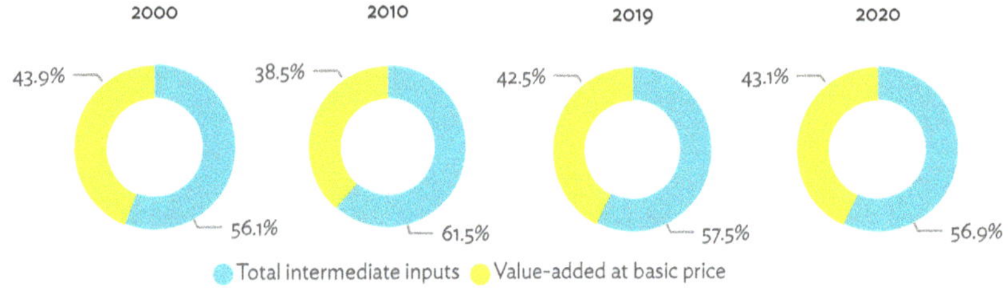

Imports and Exports, 2019-2020

($ million)

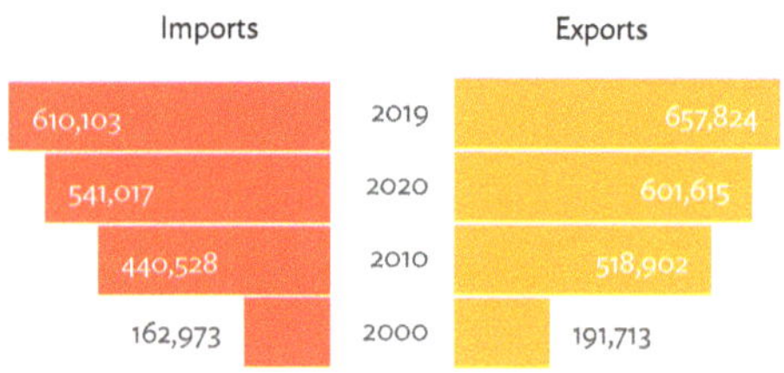

Domestic Linkages

Normalized Linkages

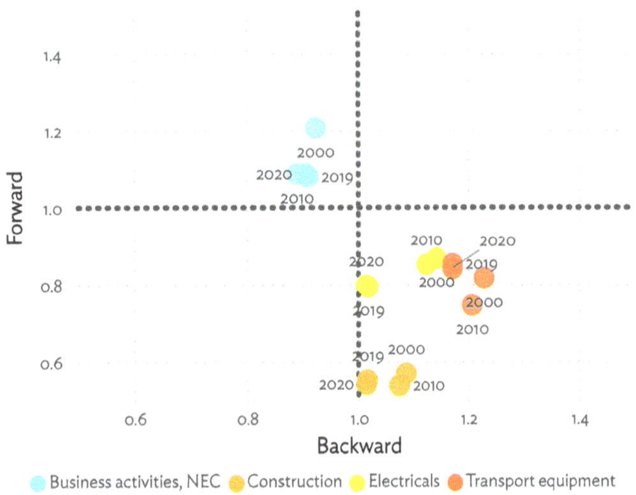

Net Linkages

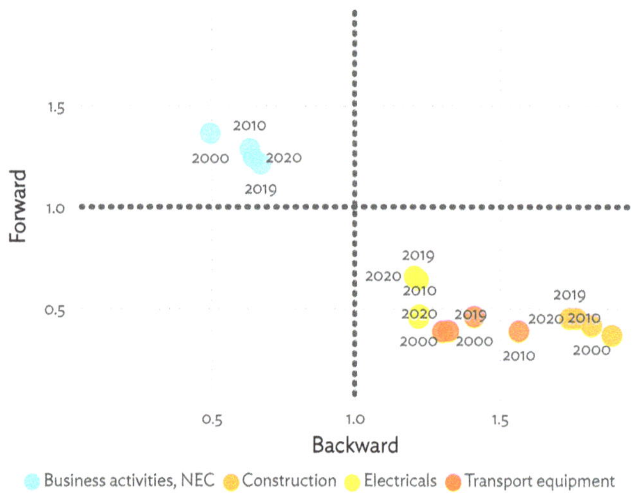

Value-Added Multipliers

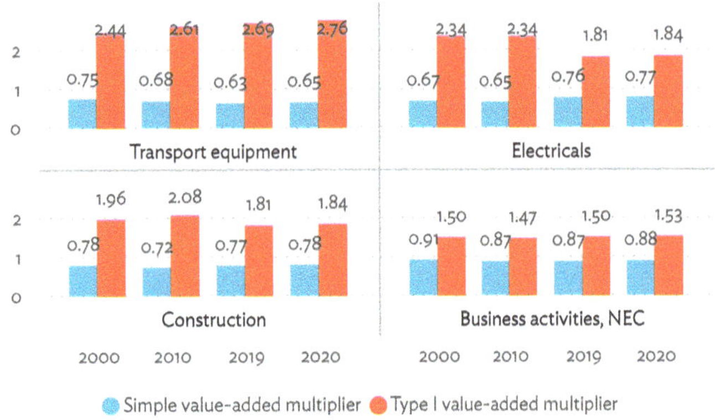

Production-Induced Effect

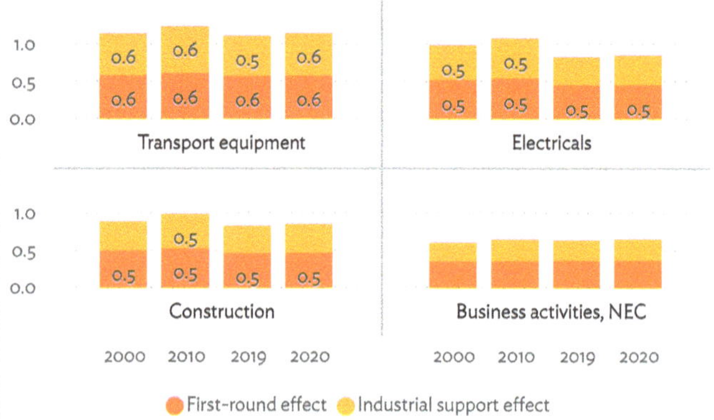

continued on next page.

Click here for figure data

continued.

Republic of Korea

East Asia

International Linkages

Change in Exports, by Value-Added Components, 2019-2020

($ million)

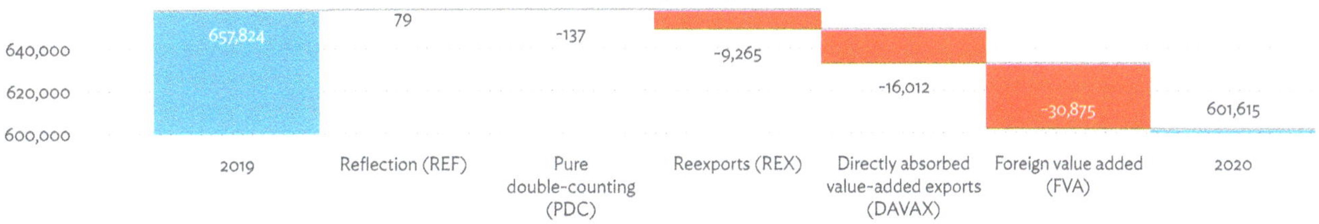

Import Multipliers

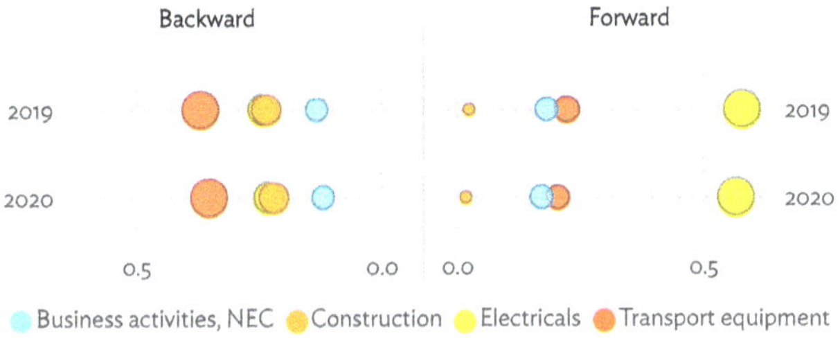

GVC Participation Rates

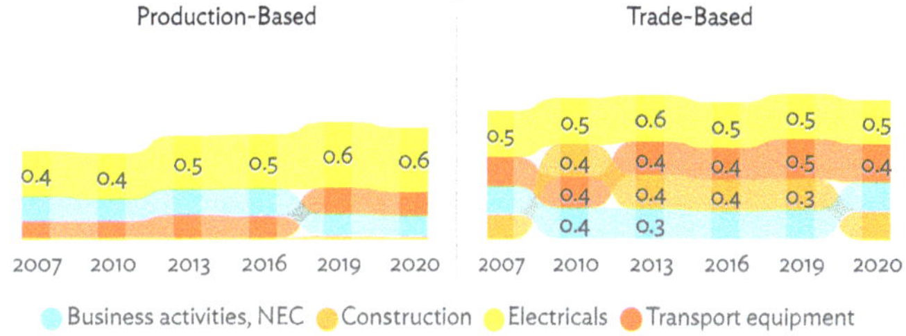

Average Production Length

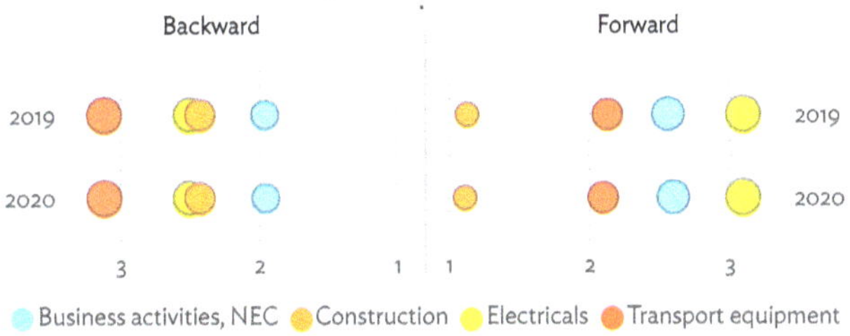

New Revealed Comparative Advantage

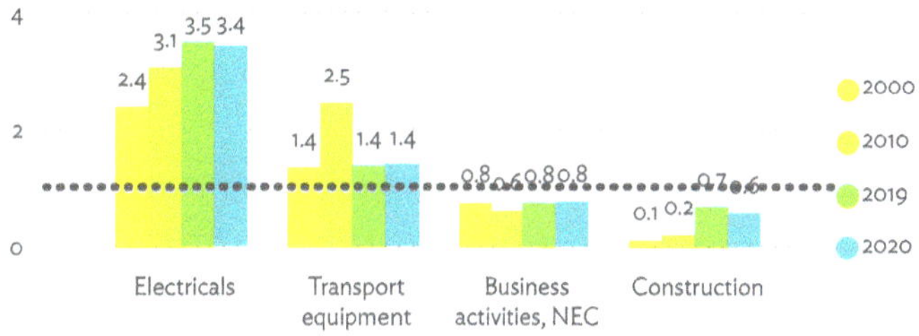

Trade Orientation

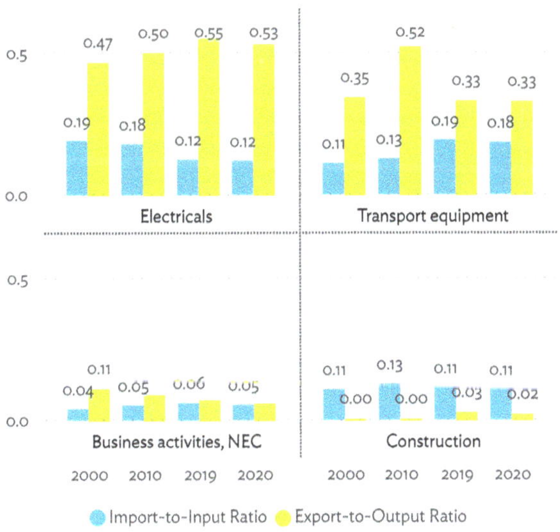

Agglomeration Indices

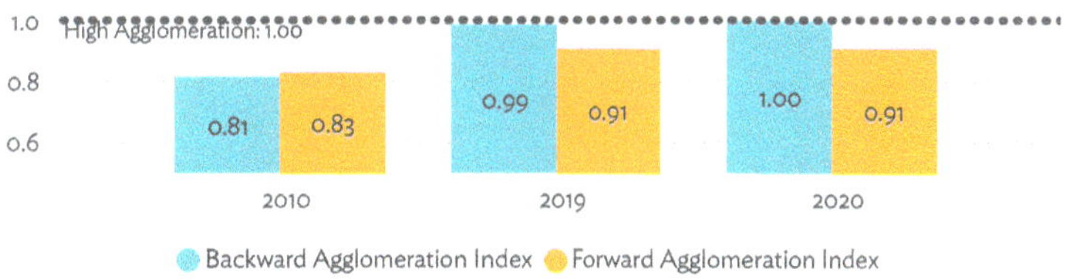

Domestic Transfer Effects and International Spillover Effects

($ million)

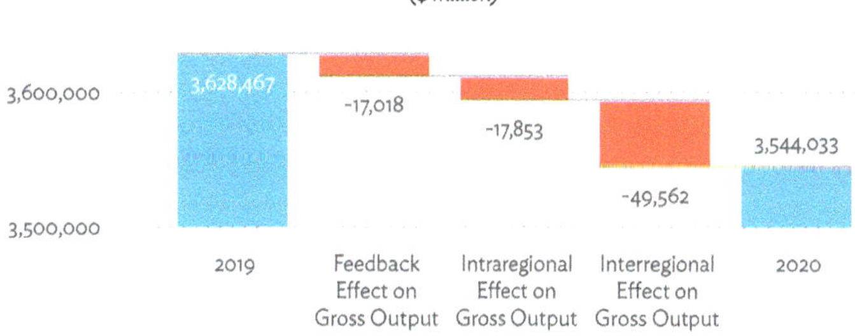

GVC = global value chain; NEC = not elsewhere classified.
Source: Calculations using the Asian Development Bank Multiregional Input-Output Table. https://mrio.adbx.online/ (accessed July 2021).

Click here for figure data

Kyrgyz Republic

South and Central Asia

Basic Economic Indicators

Economic Aggregates ($ million)	2000	2007	2010	2013	2016	2019	2020
Value-added at basic price	1,275	3,290	4,219	6,315	5,412	7,691	6,900
Gross output	3,382	8,303	10,277	14,821	12,582	19,327	17,285
Total intermediate inputs	2,068	4,801	5,879	8,273	6,965	11,194	10,055
Taxes less subsidies on products	39	212	179	233	205	442	330
International transport margins	0	0	0	0	0	0	0
CIF/FOB adjustment	0	0	0	0	0	0	0
Direct purchases abroad by residents	0	0	0	0	0	0	0
Purchases by nonresidents on the domestic territory	0	0	0	0	0	0	0
Household final consumption expenditure	632	2,225	2,449	3,855	2,745	4,225	3,827
Final consumption expenditure by NPISHs	33	80	60	55	43	82	70
Government final consumption expenditure	242	555	748	1,087	895	1,293	1,071
Gross fixed capital formation	171	596	1,056	1,615	1,627	1,761	1,606
Changes in inventories	22	53	-19	222	-92	205	202
Total final demand	1,099	3,509	4,293	6,834	5,219	7,567	6,774
Exports	509	1,399	2,289	2,801	2,245	3,126	2,010
Imports	594	2,623	3,826	6,696	4,518	5,690	3,422

Economic Aggregates, Top 3 Sectors ($ million)	2000	2007	2010	2013	2016	2019	2020
Value-added at basic price							
Agriculture	467	992	817	1,142	863	997	1,007
Retail trade	143	573	592	977	916	1,239	993
Metals	117	173	550	571	447	853	860
Gross output							
Agriculture	1,198	2,547	2,503	3,795	2,862	3,219	3,250
Finance	39	782	251	348	323	2,962	2,685
Construction	197	428	830	1,687	1,686	2,639	2,017
Total intermediate inputs							
Finance	32	652	222	283	266	2,483	2,271
Agriculture	726	1,528	1,657	2,642	1,989	2,208	2,232
Construction	134	264	550	1,125	1,132	1,758	1,352
Total final demand							
Agriculture	227	827	513	1,360	976	1,404	1,274
Construction	109	313	655	1,263	1,169	1,664	1,250
Retail trade	48	416	416	775	592	1,040	768
Exports							
Metals	238	343	692	812	721	829	533
Mining	4	10	9	27	126	353	319
Agriculture	107	194	960	624	275	229	240
Imports							
Refined fuels	112	462	801	1,288	618	975	578
Machinery, NEC	79	382	253	599	549	701	426
Food and beverages	43	169	346	650	438	586	361

Domestic Linkages

Indicator and Top 3 Sectors, 2020	2000	2007	2010	2013	2016	2019	2020
First-round effect							
Finance	0.63	0.79	0.81	0.72	0.80	0.82	0.83
Agriculture	0.59	0.56	0.48	0.54	0.62	0.62	0.64
Food and beverages	0.76	0.62	0.49	0.48	0.57	0.55	0.59
Industrial support effect							
Finance	0.82	1.68	3.04	1.69	2.72	3.67	4.07
Agriculture	0.71	0.55	0.32	0.44	0.68	0.61	0.74
Food and beverages	0.97	0.63	0.28	0.32	0.50	0.55	0.71
Production-induced effect							
Finance	1.44	2.48	3.85	2.42	3.52	4.48	4.91
Agriculture	1.29	1.11	0.80	0.98	1.31	1.23	1.38
Food and beverages	1.73	1.25	0.77	0.80	1.07	1.11	1.31

continued on next page.

continued.

Kyrgyz Republic

South and Central Asia

Domestic Linkages

Indicator and Top 3 Sectors, 2020	2000	2007	2010	2013	2016	2019	2020
Simple value-added multiplier							
Education	0.89	0.85	0.84	0.87	0.90	0.91	0.94
Finance	0.65	0.75	0.60	0.67	0.86	0.89	0.92
Health and social work	0.87	0.81	0.79	0.84	0.88	0.87	0.90
Type I value-added multiplier							
Finance	3.52	4.53	5.30	3.58	4.78	5.51	5.94
Agriculture	2.36	2.21	1.96	2.22	2.62	2.59	2.73
Food and beverages	4.66	3.41	2.45	2.08	2.50	2.34	2.56
Direct backward linkage							
Finance	0.63	0.79	0.81	0.72	0.80	0.82	0.83
Agriculture	0.59	0.56	0.48	0.54	0.62	0.62	0.64
Food and beverages	0.76	0.62	0.49	0.48	0.57	0.55	0.59
Complete hypothetical extraction (backward)							
Food and beverages	2.35	2.10	1.63	1.68	1.92	1.97	2.12
Hotels and restaurants	1.94	1.74	1.57	1.55	1.68	1.78	1.97
Air transport	1.18	1.11	1.23	1.17	1.37	1.68	1.94
Partial hypothetical extraction (backward)							
Food and beverages	1.49	1.17	0.71	0.75	0.99	1.04	1.20
Hotels and restaurants	0.97	0.78	0.60	0.57	0.70	0.79	0.98
Air transport	0.18	0.11	0.23	0.17	0.38	0.68	0.95
Total backward linkage							
Finance	2.44	3.48	4.85	3.42	4.52	5.48	5.91
Agriculture	2.29	2.11	1.80	1.98	2.31	2.23	2.38
Food and beverages	2.73	2.25	1.77	1.80	2.07	2.11	2.31
Direct forward linkage							
Finance	0.55	0.71	0.82	0.79	0.87	0.86	0.88
Sale of motor vehicles	0.89	0.65	0.65	0.76	0.78	0.76	0.83
Wood	0.91	0.86	0.36	0.31	0.10	0.62	0.69
Complete hypothetical extraction (forward)							
Sale of motor vehicles	2.36	1.56	1.98	2.19	2.35	2.21	2.40
Wood	2.17	2.37	1.52	1.43	1.15	1.88	2.03
Wholesale trade	2.74	2.03	1.67	1.73	2.01	1.64	1.93
Partial hypothetical extraction (forward)							
Sale of motor vehicles	1.61	0.89	0.98	1.19	1.35	1.23	1.42
Wood	1.56	1.52	0.54	0.43	0.15	0.91	1.08
Utilities	0.72	0.52	0.55	0.48	0.84	0.87	0.97
Total forward linkage							
Finance	2.13	3.12	4.90	3.77	5.04	5.83	6.39
Sale of motor vehicles	3.17	2.32	1.99	2.20	2.36	2.25	2.45
Metals	1.64	1.56	1.97	1.68	1.60	1.97	2.15
Normalized backward linkage							
Finance	1.34	2.40	3.24	2.39	2.86	3.31	3.23
Agriculture	1.26	1.46	1.20	1.39	1.46	1.34	1.30
Food and beverages	1.49	1.55	1.18	1.26	1.31	1.27	1.26
Normalized forward linkage							
Finance	1.14	2.09	3.15	2.54	3.08	3.80	3.87
Sale of motor vehicles	1.69	1.56	1.28	1.48	1.44	1.47	1.48
Metals	0.88	1.05	1.27	1.13	0.98	1.28	1.30
Net backward linkage							
Textiles	1.63	1.63	1.58	1.61	1.81	1.74	1.92
Leather	1.42	1.87	1.57	1.59	1.71	1.72	1.90
Chemicals	0.68	1.03	0.98	1.32	1.32	1.56	1.76
Net forward linkage							
Sale of motor vehicles	0.14	0.10	1.23	1.56	1.76	1.42	1.54
Wholesale trade	1.86	1.39	1.04	1.17	1.38	1.10	1.29
Retail trade	1.89	1.34	1.06	1.08	1.18	1.15	1.24

continued on next page.

continued.

Kyrgyz Republic

South and Central Asia *International Linkages*

Indicator and Top 3 Sectors, 2020	2000	2007	2010	2013	2016	2019	2020
Self-sufficiency ratio							
Mining	0.31	0.20	0.39	0.61	1.93	1.84	2.50
Air transport	0.68	0.38	0.70	0.48	0.62	3.53	1.94
Hotels and restaurants	1.03	0.99	1.00	1.01	1.02	1.79	1.50
Import-to-input ratio							
Wood	0.18	0.64	0.33	0.58	0.35	0.41	0.30
Air transport	0.01	0.01	0.36	0.39	0.33	0.36	0.27
Manufacturing, NEC	0.15	0.50	0.29	0.40	0.34	0.35	0.25
Export-to-output ratio							
Transport equipment	0.15	0.91	0.69	0.76	0.98	1.00	1.00
Textiles	0.31	0.58	0.63	0.71	0.89	1.00	1.00
Leather	0.25	0.76	0.63	0.71	0.53	1.00	1.00
Domestic inputs share to output							
Finance	0.63	0.79	0.81	0.72	0.80	0.82	0.83
Agriculture	0.59	0.56	0.48	0.54	0.62	0.62	0.64
Food and beverages	0.76	0.62	0.49	0.48	0.57	0.55	0.59
Foreign inputs share to output							
Wood	0.18	0.64	0.33	0.58	0.35	0.41	0.30
Air transport	0.01	0.01	0.36	0.39	0.33	0.36	0.27
Manufacturing, NEC	0.15	0.50	0.29	0.40	0.34	0.35	0.25
Backward import multipliers							
Wood	0.50	0.83	0.43	0.62	0.41	0.49	0.39
Air transport	0.03	0.03	0.41	0.43	0.39	0.44	0.34
Manufacturing, NEC	0.24	0.55	0.39	0.49	0.42	0.44	0.34
Forward import multipliers							
Chemicals	0.53	0.23	0.10	0.12	0.14	0.95	0.94
Water transport	0.98	0.12	0.22	0.28	0.37	0.56	0.74
Leather	0.21	0.53	0.51	0.54	0.30	0.63	0.67
Intraregional transfer multiplier							
Finance	2.44	3.48	4.85	3.42	4.52	5.48	5.91
Agriculture	2.29	2.11	1.80	1.98	2.31	2.23	2.38
Food and beverages	2.73	2.25	1.77	1.80	2.07	2.11	2.31
Interregional spillover multiplier							
Wood	1.34	2.23	1.66	2.17	1.71	1.80	1.57
Air transport	1.02	1.03	1.71	1.84	1.67	1.75	1.56
Manufacturing, NEC	1.27	1.99	1.58	1.86	1.72	1.71	1.51
Interregional feedback multiplier							
Wood	1.09	1.37	1.16	1.29	1.15	1.15	1.11
Air transport	1.01	1.01	1.13	1.14	1.11	1.13	1.10
Manufacturing, NEC	1.06	1.21	1.10	1.16	1.14	1.13	1.09
Intraregional effect on gross output ($ million)							
Agriculture	890.25	2,203.79	1,766.13	3,148.35	2,531.97	3,053.81	3,093.82
Finance	30.34	746.85	247.73	302.52	296.42	2,753.78	2,530.38
Construction	176.07	412.56	814.38	1,606.03	1,602.14	2,560.84	1,970.84
Interregional effect on gross output ($ million)							
Metals	191.66	201.02	586.15	659.67	595.27	818.19	577.09
Mining	4.62	5.70	7.48	18.98	42.09	193.96	166.08
Agriculture	239.59	283.69	590.12	532.89	267.86	141.74	135.85
Feedback effect on gross output ($ million)							
Metals	97.53	85.86	209.02	253.93	227.33	444.95	305.75
Mining	2.68	2.22	2.32	6.53	13.25	102.21	83.53
Finance	2.14	7.33	0.62	10.09	6.65	41.52	32.64
Directly absorbed value-added exports (DAVAX) ($ million)							
Metals	102.10	126.88	384.74	382.40	421.10	349.70	239.38
Agriculture	80.42	142.62	523.48	339.67	176.57	168.43	188.79
Mining	1.36	5.16	4.71	13.86	68.86	154.22	162.95
Reflection (REF) ($ million)							
Mining	0.01	0.01	0.00	0.01	0.02	0.36	0.27
Minerals, NEC	0.00	0.01	0.00	0.01	0.01	0.11	0.08
Metals	0.01	0.02	0.04	0.07	0.07	0.10	0.06

continued on next page.

continued.

Kyrgyz Republic

South and Central Asia

International Linkages

Indicator and Top 3 Sectors, 2020	2000	2007	2010	2013	2016	2019	2020
Reexports (REX) ($ million)							
Metals	87.02	55.71	128.85	153.44	179.98	333.87	222.76
Mining	1.52	1.52	1.20	4.02	12.75	69.43	68.31
Agriculture	19.22	28.36	112.40	81.61	43.01	17.65	16.52
Foreign value added (FVA) ($ million)							
Mining	0.79	3.80	2.63	9.01	44.27	128.56	87.13
Metals	49.06	160.58	178.69	276.44	119.80	144.88	70.78
Agriculture	7.37	22.51	324.32	202.44	54.81	42.98	34.30
Pure double-counting (PDC) ($ million)							
Mining	0.00	0.00	0.00	0.00	0.00	0.04	0.03
Metals	0.01	0.03	0.02	0.03	0.01	0.06	0.03
Minerals, NEC	0.00	0.00	0.00	0.00	0.00	0.02	0.01
Trade-based GVC participation rate							
Metals	0.57	0.63	0.44	0.53	0.42	0.58	0.55
Mining	0.63	0.51	0.45	0.48	0.45	0.56	0.49
Chemicals	0.43	0.48	0.62	0.47	0.38	0.57	0.48
Production-based GVC participation rate							
Chemicals	0.53	0.23	0.10	0.12	0.14	0.95	0.94
Water transport	0.98	0.12	0.22	0.28	0.37	0.56	0.74
Leather	0.21	0.53	0.51	0.54	0.30	0.63	0.67
Trade-based backward GVC participation rate							
Wood	0.50	0.83	0.43	0.62	0.41	0.49	0.39
Air transport	0.03	0.03	0.41	0.43	0.39	0.44	0.34
Manufacturing, NEC	0.24	0.55	0.39	0.49	0.42	0.44	0.34
Trade-based forward GVC participation rate							
Metals	0.37	0.16	0.19	0.19	0.25	0.40	0.42
Water transport	0.43	0.35	0.24	0.25	0.21	0.41	0.27
Transport activities, NEC	0.35	0.10	0.14	0.18	0.16	0.18	0.23
Traditional revealed comparative advantage							
Minerals, NEC	2.21	2.59	0.32	1.53	1.51	3.42	4.83
Metals	7.84	3.26	4.48	4.48	5.04	4.02	4.08
Agriculture	9.75	6.82	18.60	9.46	5.22	2.54	3.87
New revealed comparative advantage							
Metals	4.55	3.08	6.59	5.64	5.78	7.04	7.20
Retail trade	3.39	3.36	4.84	4.53	5.60	2.83	2.96
Minerals, NEC	2.16	2.76	0.36	1.62	1.56	2.17	2.76
Backward production length							
Finance	3.28	4.12	5.69	4.07	4.81	5.70	6.07
Air transport	1.24	1.19	2.23	2.28	2.35	2.79	2.81
Food and beverages	3.05	2.89	2.84	2.68	2.72	2.69	2.76
Forward production length							
Finance	2.64	3.22	4.92	4.07	5.24	5.99	6.52
Metals	3.52	2.84	3.31	3.28	3.40	3.74	3.43
Chemicals	3.43	1.70	1.64	1.47	1.61	3.37	3.22
Backward production length of GVC segment							
Finance	4.31	6.18	6.95	5.40	6.68	7.51	7.95
Agriculture	5.11	4.86	3.81	4.41	4.99	4.77	4.93
Metals	4.32	3.91	4.49	4.43	4.93	4.45	4.46
Forward production length of GVC segment							
Finance	4.64	5.98	8.67	6.11	8.21	8.74	9.53
Retail trade	5.53	4.51	4.17	4.22	4.42	4.66	4.93
Utilities	5.21	4.33	3.75	4.39	5.11	4.75	4.91
Backward agglomeration index							
Metals	-	0.21	0.11	0.26	0.00	0.43	1.68
Refined fuels	-	0.30	0.44	0.34	1.07	1.34	1.50
Finance	-	0.87	0.70	0.70	0.97	1.02	1.04
Forward agglomeration index							
Refined fuels	-	0.84	0.68	0.29	1.10	1.24	1.24
Agriculture	-	1.05	0.50	0.90	0.98	1.16	1.12
Finance	-	1.19	1.22	0.99	1.08	1.10	1.10

CIF = cost, insurance, and freight; FOB = free on board; GVC = global value chain; NEC = not elsewhere classified; NPISHs = nonprofit institutions serving households.
Source: Calculations using the Asian Development Bank Multiregional Input-Output Table. https://mrio.adbx.online/ (accessed July 2021).

continued on next page.

continued.

Kyrgyz Republic

South and Central Asia

The four select sectors are chosen based on their gross outputs in the economy as of 2019.

Economy Ranking out of 25 Economies

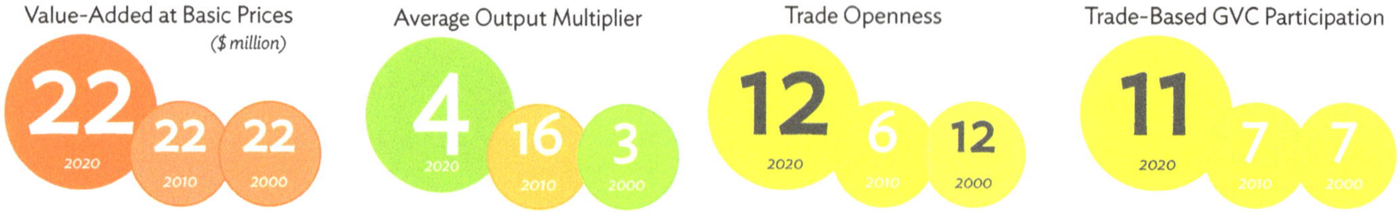

Share of Intermediate Consumption and Gross Value-Added in Output

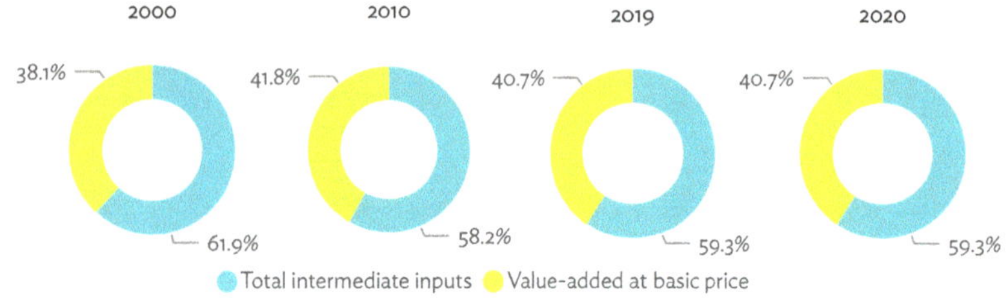

Imports and Exports, 2019-2020

($ million)

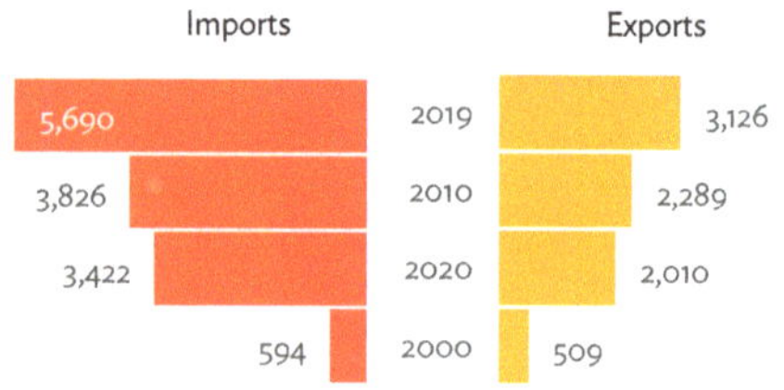

Domestic Linkages

Normalized Linkages

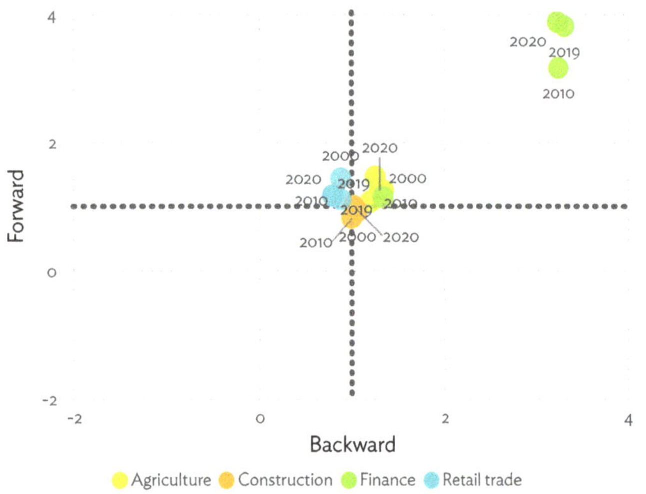

Net Linkages

Value-Added Multipliers

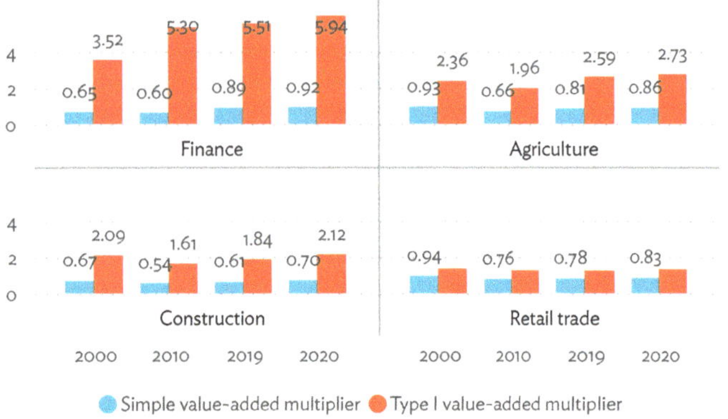

Production-Induced Effect

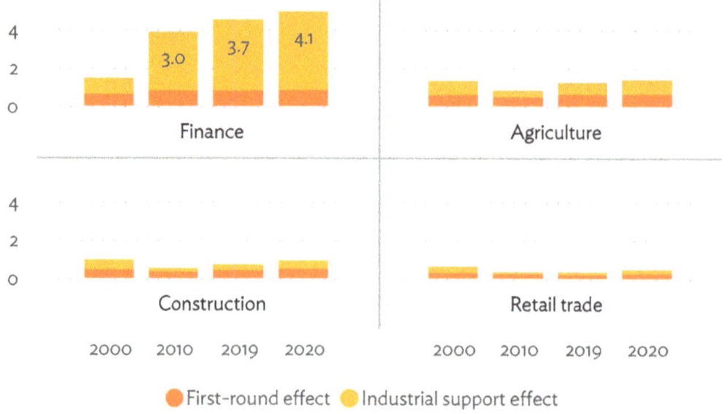

continued on next page.

Click here for figure data

continued.

Kyrgyz Republic
South and Central Asia

International Linkages

Change in Exports, by Value-Added Components, 2019-2020
($ million)

Import Multipliers

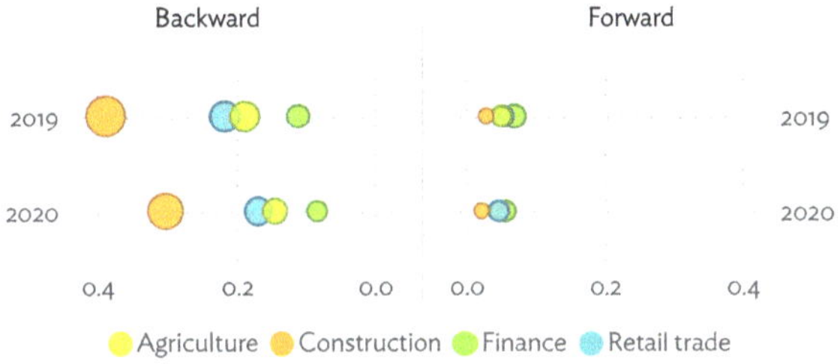

GVC Participation Rates

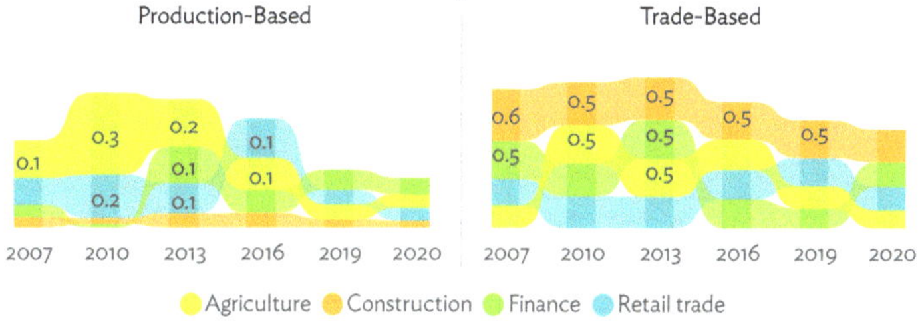

Average Production Length

New Revealed Comparative Advantage

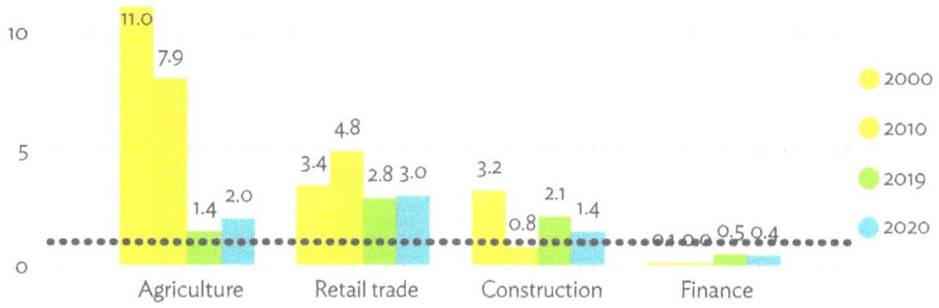

Trade Orientation

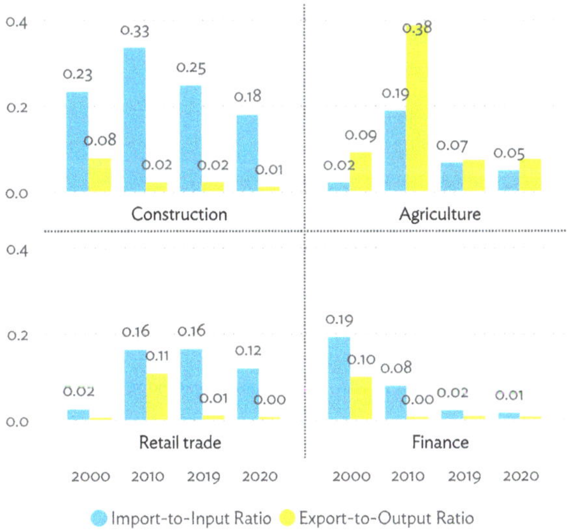

Agglomeration Indices

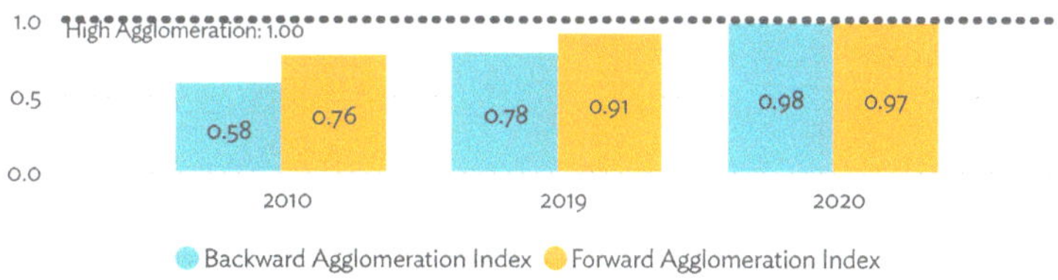

Domestic Transfer Effects and International Spillover Effects
($ million)

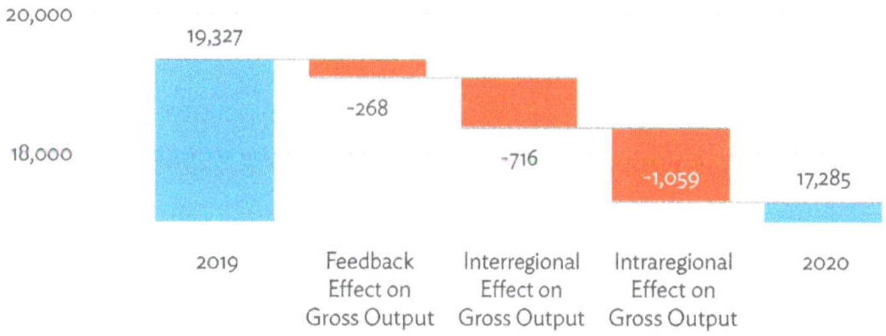

GVC = global value chain; NEC = not elsewhere classified.
Source: Calculations using the Asian Development Bank Multiregional Input-Output Table. https://mrio.adbx.online/ (accessed July 2021).

Click here for figure data

Lao People's Democratic Republic

Southeast Asia and the Pacific

Basic Economic Indicators

Economic Aggregates ($ million)	2000	2007	2010	2013	2016	2019	2020
Value-added at basic price	1,546	3,940	6,347	11,466	13,983	16,803	17,166
Gross output	2,360	6,300	10,364	18,935	23,013	28,004	28,181
Total intermediate inputs	768	2,195	3,798	7,153	8,352	10,362	10,012
Taxes less subsidies on products	46	166	219	316	678	840	1,003
International transport margins	0	0	0	0	0	0	0
CIF/FOB adjustment	0	0	0	0	0	0	0
Direct purchases abroad by residents	0	0	0	0	0	0	0
Purchases by nonresidents on the domestic territory	0	0	0	0	0	0	0
Household final consumption expenditure	1,159	2,386	3,838	6,727	7,238	9,374	9,256
Final consumption expenditure by NPISHs	0	0	0	0	0	0	0
Government final consumption expenditure	106	522	840	1,789	1,950	2,427	2,382
Gross fixed capital formation	131	958	1,520	1,905	1,858	3,113	3,519
Changes in inventories	0	0	-2E-16	0	0	0	0
Total final demand	1,395	3,866	6,198	10,421	11,047	14,914	15,157
Exports	452	924	1,548	3,680	5,646	6,985	6,489
Imports	693	959	1,640	5,560	5,768	7,518	5,819

Economic Aggregates, Top 3 Sectors ($ million)	2000	2007	2010	2013	2016	2019	2020
Value-added at basic price							
Agriculture	751	1,292	1,832	2,065	2,520	2,866	3,010
Utilities	72	107	244	670	1,069	1,915	2,539
Public administration	48	231	470	1,145	1,432	1,699	1,783
Gross output							
Construction	258	650	1,029	2,528	3,580	4,689	4,836
Agriculture	866	1,491	2,115	2,383	2,858	3,251	3,414
Utilities	93	139	317	871	1,341	2,404	3,186
Total intermediate inputs							
Construction	170	425	678	1,641	2,246	2,904	2,923
Food and beverages	131	328	592	840	959	1,188	1,216
Public administration	26	125	263	635	895	1,067	1,108
Total final demand							
Construction	162	622	997	1,966	1,884	3,263	3,522
Public administration	65	367	733	1,625	2,201	2,750	2,870
Retail trade	119	488	797	762	528	1,395	1,384
Exports							
Agriculture	110	75	102	75	557	1,578	2,717
Utilities	75	65	175	400	1,240	1,805	1,441
Mining	5	573	806	2,603	1,857	670	550
Imports							
Metals	292	276	562	1,915	1,541	2,401	2,029
Refined fuels	174	267	525	1,234	1,082	1,587	1,322
Electricals	35	49	89	537	811	614	457

Domestic Linkages

Indicator and Top 3 Sectors, 2020	2000	2007	2010	2013	2016	2019	2020
First-round effect							
Food and beverages	0.61	0.61	0.61	0.62	0.57	0.52	0.54
Wood	0.50	0.50	0.50	0.49	0.47	0.45	0.45
Hotels and restaurants	0.00	0.46	0.49	0.47	0.46	0.43	0.43
Industrial support effect							
Wood	0.07	0.09	0.12	0.13	0.09	0.14	0.17
Food and beverages	0.10	0.11	0.13	0.15	0.13	0.13	0.16
Paper	0.07	0.09	0.11	0.13	0.09	0.12	0.15
Production-induced effect							
Food and beverages	0.70	0.72	0.74	0.76	0.71	0.65	0.70
Wood	0.57	0.59	0.62	0.63	0.56	0.59	0.62
Hotels and restaurants	0.00	0.65	0.71	0.67	0.65	0.57	0.57

continued on next page.

continued.

Lao People's Democratic Republic

Southeast Asia and the Pacific *Domestic Linkages*

Indicator and Top 3 Sectors, 2020	2000	2007	2010	2013	2016	2019	2020
Simple value-added multiplier							
Finance	0.89	0.89	0.92	0.91	0.96	0.94	0.96
Real estate	0.00	0.97	0.97	0.96	0.97	0.96	0.96
Agriculture	0.96	0.96	0.96	0.95	0.97	0.95	0.96
Type I value-added multiplier							
Food and beverages	2.82	2.78	2.79	2.85	2.67	2.44	2.48
Air transport	1.49	1.62	1.51	1.54	1.10	1.36	2.46
Water transport	1.40	1.51	1.41	1.43	1.00	1.12	2.09
Direct backward linkage							
Food and beverages	0.61	0.61	0.61	0.62	0.57	0.52	0.54
Wood	0.50	0.50	0.50	0.49	0.47	0.45	0.45
Hotels and restaurants	0.00	0.46	0.49	0.47	0.46	0.43	0.43
Complete hypothetical extraction (backward)							
Food and beverages	1.63	1.64	1.61	1.62	1.60	1.55	1.58
Hotels and restaurants	1.00	1.65	1.71	1.67	1.65	1.57	1.57
Paper	1.57	1.58	1.60	1.60	1.51	1.52	1.55
Partial hypothetical extraction (backward)							
Food and beverages	0.67	0.69	0.68	0.70	0.66	0.61	0.65
Hotels and restaurants	0.00	0.65	0.71	0.67	0.65	0.57	0.57
Paper	0.57	0.58	0.60	0.61	0.51	0.52	0.55
Total backward linkage							
Food and beverages	1.70	1.72	1.74	1.76	1.71	1.65	1.70
Wood	1.57	1.59	1.62	1.63	1.56	1.59	1.62
Hotels and restaurants	1.00	1.65	1.71	1.67	1.65	1.57	1.57
Direct forward linkage							
Inland transport	0.64	0.87	0.82	0.85	0.59	0.61	0.69
Minerals, NEC	0.95	0.97	0.97	0.98	0.83	0.57	0.66
Refined fuels	0.57	0.69	0.64	0.66	0.72	0.55	0.59
Complete hypothetical extraction (forward)							
Inland transport	1.78	2.05	1.97	2.10	1.80	1.77	1.89
Minerals, NEC	2.06	1.98	1.93	2.18	2.22	1.71	1.81
Refined fuels	1.79	1.95	1.86	1.91	1.99	1.68	1.73
Partial hypothetical extraction (forward)							
Inland transport	0.83	1.10	1.02	1.13	0.83	0.79	0.91
Minerals, NEC	1.21	1.03	1.01	1.22	1.26	0.75	0.86
Refined fuels	0.81	0.97	0.88	0.92	1.01	0.70	0.76
Total forward linkage							
Inland transport	1.88	2.16	2.08	2.18	1.84	1.80	1.92
Minerals, NEC	2.43	2.08	2.10	2.27	2.30	1.79	1.91
Refined fuels	1.83	1.98	1.89	1.94	2.03	1.71	1.78
Normalized backward linkage							
Food and beverages	1.33	1.30	1.31	1.34	1.30	1.31	1.31
Wood	1.23	1.21	1.22	1.24	1.19	1.26	1.24
Hotels and restaurants	0.78	1.25	1.29	1.27	1.26	1.25	1.21
Normalized forward linkage							
Inland transport	1.40	1.48	1.44	1.40	1.19	1.45	1.47
Minerals, NEC	1.81	1.43	1.46	1.46	1.48	1.44	1.47
Refined fuels	1.36	1.36	1.31	1.25	1.30	1.38	1.37
Net backward linkage							
Paper	1.51	0.93	0.98	0.86	1.21	1.52	1.55
Hotels and restaurants	0.00	1.55	1.63	1.58	1.57	1.57	1.55
Food and beverages	1.59	1.56	1.54	1.41	1.41	1.43	1.50
Net forward linkage							
Business activities, NEC	0.00	1.41	1.44	1.45	1.40	1.19	1.24
Inland transport	0.98	1.15	1.09	1.24	1.16	1.10	1.23
Wholesale trade	1.01	1.08	1.00	1.12	1.27	1.12	1.19

continued on next page.

continued.

Lao People's Democratic Republic

Southeast Asia and the Pacific *International Linkages*

Indicator and Top 3 Sectors, 2020	2000	2007	2010	2013	2016	2019	2020
Self-sufficiency ratio							
Chemicals	0.99	0.89	0.97	0.98	1.10	23.07	35.77
Leather	1.44	1.17	1.38	1.12	2.34	5.62	7.08
Paper	4.33	1.59	1.73	1.38	2.59	5.58	6.66
Import-to-input ratio							
Air transport	0.81	0.78	0.81	0.81	0.87	0.83	0.66
Water transport	0.79	0.76	0.79	0.79	0.86	0.83	0.65
Transport activities, NEC	0.69	0.61	0.69	0.69	0.74	0.71	0.60
Export-to-output ratio							
Paper	0.95	0.48	0.52	0.44	0.75	1.00	1.00
Leather	0.60	0.32	0.38	0.33	0.73	1.00	1.00
Chemicals	0.10	0.03	0.04	0.03	0.13	0.99	1.00
Domestic inputs share to output							
Food and beverages	0.61	0.61	0.61	0.62	0.57	0.52	0.54
Wood	0.50	0.50	0.50	0.49	0.47	0.45	0.45
Hotels and restaurants	0.00	0.46	0.49	0.47	0.46	0.43	0.43
Foreign inputs share to output							
Air transport	0.81	0.78	0.81	0.81	0.87	0.83	0.66
Water transport	0.79	0.76	0.79	0.79	0.86	0.83	0.65
Transport activities, NEC	0.69	0.61	0.69	0.69	0.74	0.71	0.60
Backward import multipliers							
Air transport	0.83	0.80	0.82	0.83	0.87	0.84	0.69
Water transport	0.81	0.78	0.80	0.80	0.86	0.84	0.68
Transport activities, NEC	0.71	0.64	0.70	0.70	0.74	0.72	0.62
Forward import multipliers							
Metals	0.12	0.03	0.03	0.08	0.20	0.97	0.98
Chemicals	0.22	0.15	0.18	0.18	0.30	0.98	0.96
Paper	0.57	0.48	0.53	0.47	0.70	0.95	0.96
Intraregional transfer multiplier							
Food and beverages	1.70	1.72	1.74	1.76	1.71	1.65	1.70
Wood	1.57	1.59	1.62	1.63	1.56	1.59	1.62
Hotels and restaurants	1.00	1.65	1.71	1.67	1.65	1.57	1.57
Interregional spillover multiplier							
Water transport	2.33	2.28	2.47	2.51	2.84	2.39	2.09
Air transport	2.37	2.32	2.50	2.54	2.90	2.35	2.08
Metals	1.80	1.68	1.88	1.87	1.86	2.21	2.02
Interregional feedback multiplier							
Air transport	1.48	1.52	1.53	1.61	1.54	1.96	1.86
Water transport	1.54	1.50	1.55	1.65	1.63	1.97	1.86
Transport activities, NEC	1.48	1.45	1.50	1.56	1.51	1.89	1.81
Intraregional effect on gross output ($ million)							
Construction	231.83	646.36	1,024.74	2,465.58	3,232.27	4,632.35	4,792.50
Public administration	69.76	367.70	742.89	1,743.17	2,310.26	2,806.62	2,945.61
Retail trade	177.36	696.16	1,075.06	1,211.33	1,262.14	2,206.83	2,243.35
Interregional effect on gross output ($ million)							
Agriculture	90.83	85.13	120.87	108.16	466.18	1,164.72	2,173.00
Utilities	56.31	52.73	154.24	370.48	838.18	1,177.07	1,070.32
Mining	3.66	379.68	645.42	1,747.26	1,644.25	610.17	475.35
Feedback effect on gross output ($ million)							
Agriculture	18.98	17.97	26.23	26.55	184.76	208.70	283.83
Utilities	15.12	16.37	40.35	110.64	223.37	330.13	260.58
Mining	0.94	109.92	112.04	462.35	419.72	128.12	90.28
Directly absorbed value-added exports (DAVAX) ($ million)							
Agriculture	78.16	44.36	66.67	42.79	270.06	1,084.79	1,983.39
Utilities	44.99	42.32	107.53	244.81	837.20	1,067.53	898.18
Mining	2.78	349.29	498.41	1,595.30	1,229.14	411.35	354.01
Reflection (REF) ($ million)							
Utilities	0.00	0.00	0.00	0.05	0.13	1.77	1.62
Mining	0.00	0.02	0.07	0.98	0.79	0.50	0.65
Agriculture	0.03	0.01	0.02	0.05	0.49	0.42	0.52

continued on next page.

continued.

Lao People's Democratic Republic

Southeast Asia and the Pacific *International Linkages*

Indicator and Top 3 Sectors, 2020	2000	2007	2010	2013	2016	2019	2020
Reexports (REX) ($ million)							
Agriculture	27.11	27.49	30.75	28.24	267.33	412.23	613.92
Utilities	21.80	17.82	50.83	115.72	309.11	559.39	425.84
Mining	1.23	132.53	168.23	542.89	442.88	117.97	99.94
Foreign value added (FVA) ($ million)							
Agriculture	4.47	2.67	4.13	3.54	18.85	80.91	119.25
Utilities	7.82	5.10	16.22	39.15	93.79	175.81	114.85
Mining	0.93	90.84	139.09	463.29	184.55	139.85	95.70
Pure double-counting (PDC) ($ million)							
Agriculture	0.00	0.00	0.00	0.00	0.00	0.06	0.11
Utilities	0.00	0.00	0.00	0.01	0.03	0.13	0.10
Mining	0.00	0.00	0.01	0.07	0.04	0.10	0.08
Trade-based GVC participation rate							
Water transport	0.88	0.86	0.87	0.88	0.91	0.88	0.78
Transport activities, NEC	0.79	0.75	0.79	0.81	0.83	0.81	0.75
Air transport	0.88	0.85	0.87	0.88	0.92	0.87	0.75
Production-based GVC participation rate							
Metals	0.12	0.03	0.03	0.08	0.20	0.97	0.98
Chemicals	0.22	0.15	0.18	0.18	0.30	0.98	0.96
Paper	0.57	0.48	0.53	0.47	0.70	0.95	0.96
Trade-based backward GVC participation rate							
Air transport	0.83	0.80	0.82	0.83	0.87	0.84	0.69
Water transport	0.81	0.78	0.80	0.80	0.86	0.84	0.68
Transport activities, NEC	0.71	0.64	0.70	0.70	0.74	0.72	0.62
Trade-based forward GVC participation rate							
Chemicals	0.32	0.32	0.30	0.36	0.35	0.33	0.36
Utilities	0.29	0.27	0.29	0.29	0.25	0.31	0.30
Wood	0.11	0.17	0.14	0.16	0.11	0.23	0.25
Traditional revealed comparative advantage							
Utilities	30.70	11.31	24.58	24.67	39.76	42.76	33.98
Agriculture	11.27	3.98	2.91	0.86	4.21	7.83	13.59
Hotels and restaurants	0.00	0.10	0.04	0.00	0.49	10.75	4.52
New revealed comparative advantage							
Utilities	6.82	3.35	5.38	5.69	8.25	10.51	9.12
Agriculture	9.99	3.48	2.92	0.99	3.04	5.49	7.80
Wood	5.72	5.02	7.06	3.66	4.05	2.54	2.63
Backward production length							
Air transport	3.08	3.14	3.28	3.42	3.58	3.56	3.47
Water transport	3.11	3.08	3.28	3.44	3.62	3.57	3.44
Transport activities, NEC	2.88	2.83	3.03	3.17	3.28	3.27	3.18
Forward production length							
Paper	2.07	2.52	2.61	2.66	2.70	4.25	4.23
Chemicals	2.31	2.28	2.33	2.41	2.75	3.85	3.70
Metals	1.77	1.27	1.28	1.73	2.52	3.50	3.53
Backward production length of GVC segment							
Real estate	-	4.27	4.47	4.98	5.20	4.96	5.12
Education	4.20	4.06	4.25	4.20	4.98	5.02	5.10
Public administration	4.09	3.92	4.13	4.48	4.88	4.82	4.97
Forward production length of GVC segment							
Real estate	-	4.72	4.55	5.26	4.90	5.01	5.48
Finance	4.44	4.88	5.06	5.08	4.62	4.95	5.33
Construction	3.60	4.16	3.91	4.41	4.05	4.82	5.23
Backward agglomeration index							
Rubber and plastics	-	1.41	1.40	1.66	1.76	3.15	1.81
Refined fuels	-	1.46	1.42	1.51	1.43	1.59	1.66
Minerals, NEC	-	1.37	1.40	1.54	1.52	1.52	1.60
Forward agglomeration index							
Refined fuels	-	1.26	1.26	1.29	1.12	1.38	1.31
Business activities, NEC	-	1.24	1.19	1.25	1.15	1.24	1.27
Wholesale trade	-	1.27	1.27	1.27	0.96	1.12	1.20

CIF = cost, insurance, and freight; FOB = free on board; GVC = global value chain; NEC = not elsewhere classified; NPISHs = nonprofit institutions serving households.
Source: Calculations using the Asian Development Bank Multiregional Input-Output Table. https://mrio.adbx.online/ (accessed July 2021).

continued on next page.

continued.

Lao People's Democratic Republic

Southeast Asia and the Pacific

The four select sectors are chosen based on their gross outputs in the economy as of 2019.

Economy Ranking out of 25 Economies

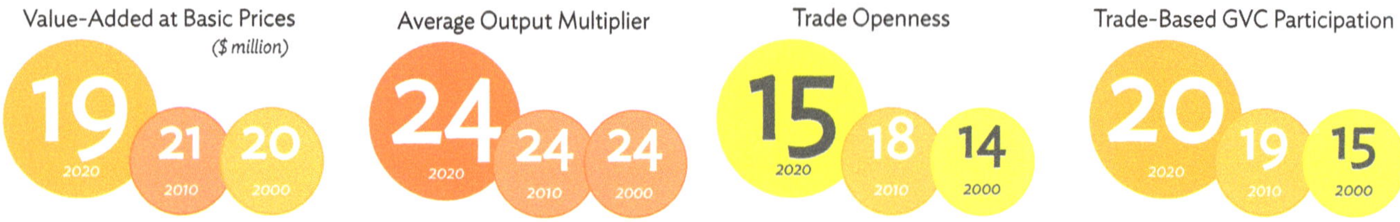

Share of Intermediate Consumption and Gross Value-Added in Output

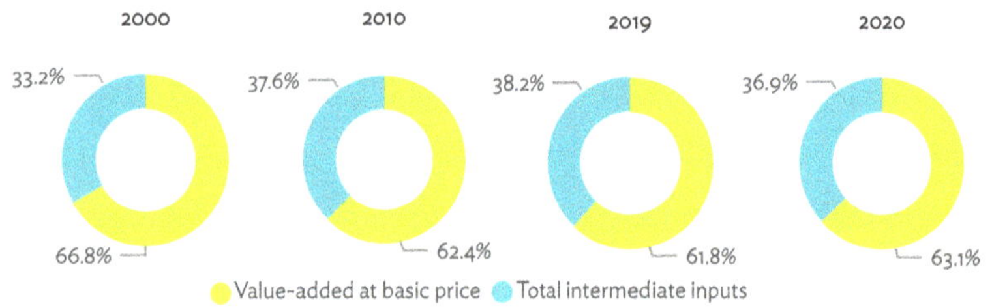

Imports and Exports, 2019-2020

($ million)

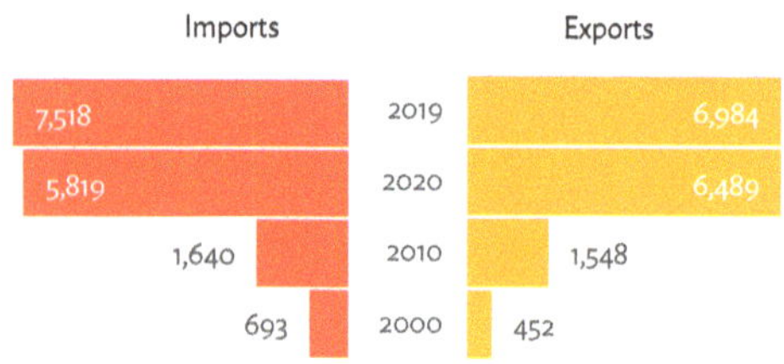

Domestic Linkages

Normalized Linkages

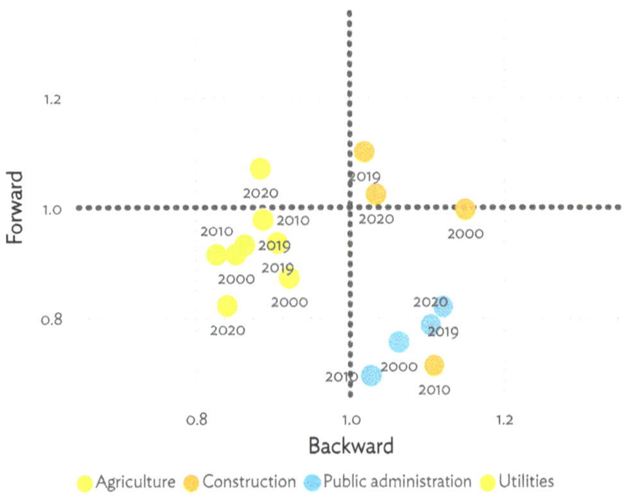

Net Linkages

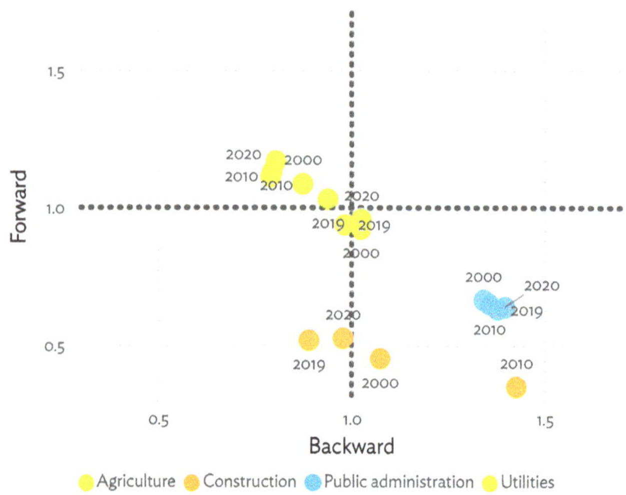

Value-Added Multipliers

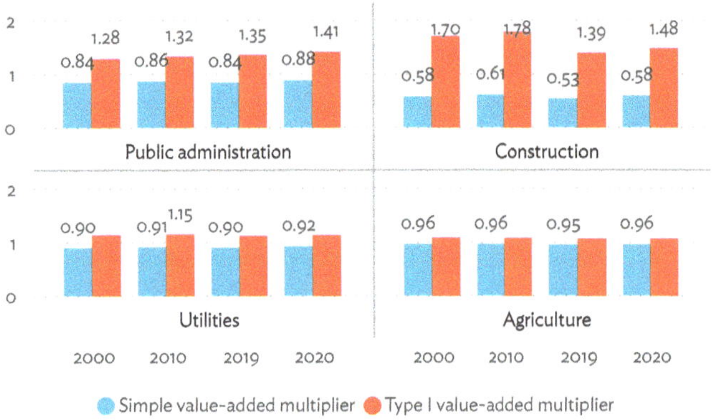

Production-Induced Effect

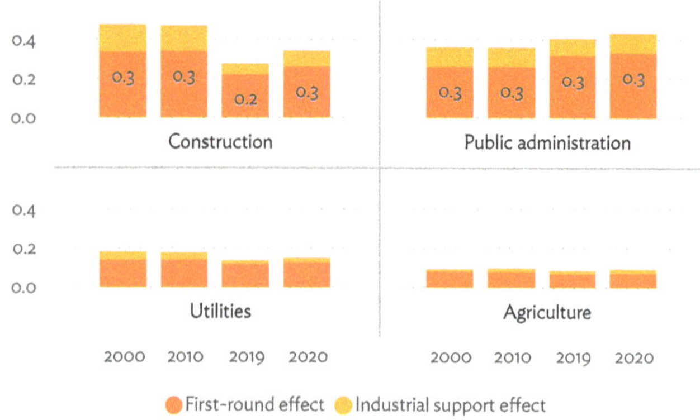

continued on next page.

Click here for figure data

continued.

Lao People's Democratic Republic

Southeast Asia and the Pacific

International Linkages

Change in Exports, by Value-Added Components, 2019-2020

($ million)

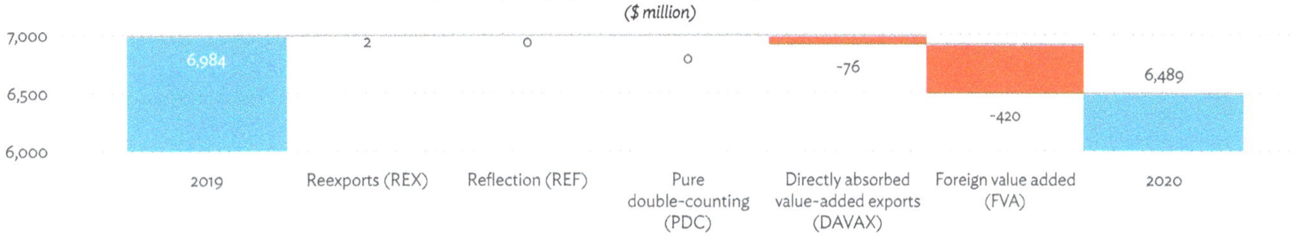

Import Multipliers

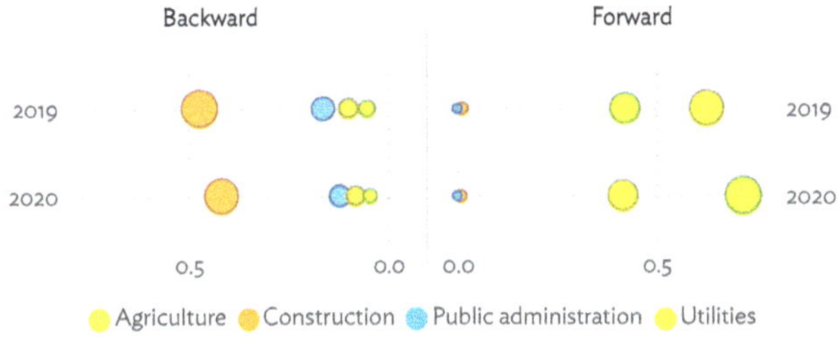

GVC Participation Rates

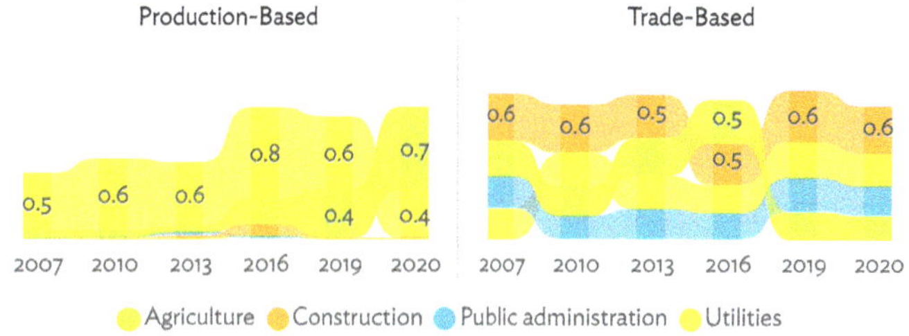

Average Production Length

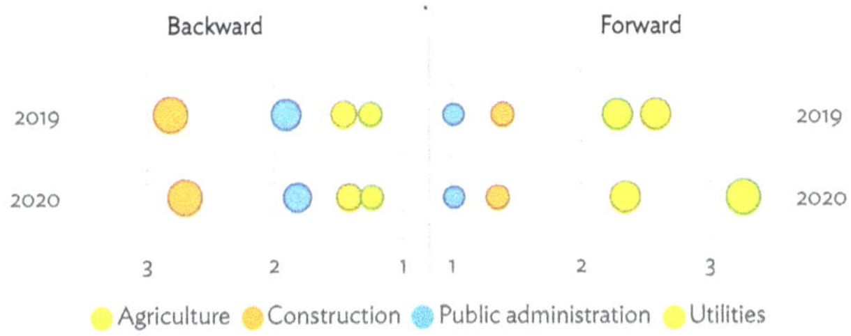

New Revealed Comparative Advantage

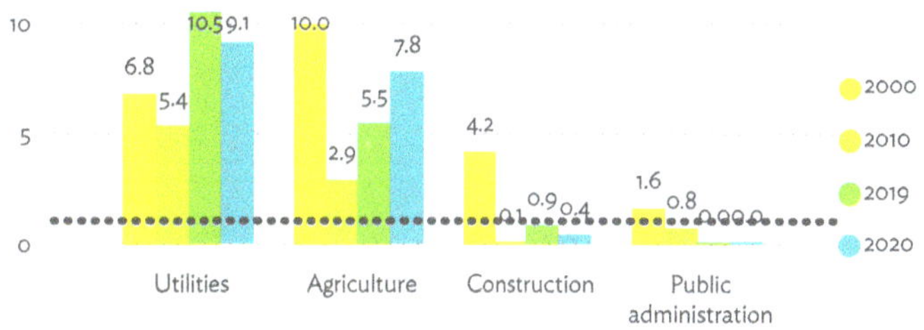

Trade Orientation

Agglomeration Indices

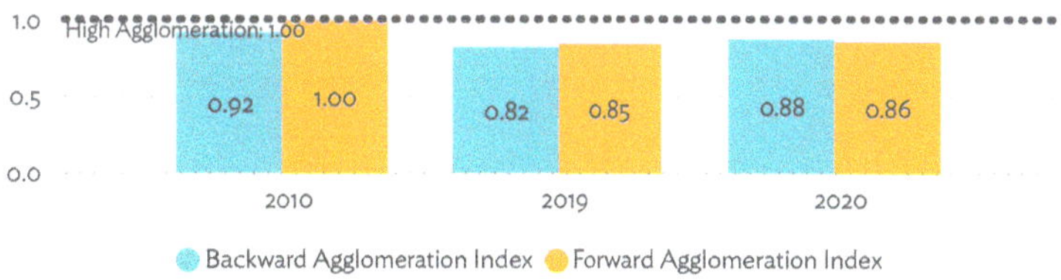

Domestic Transfer Effects and International Spillover Effects

($ million)

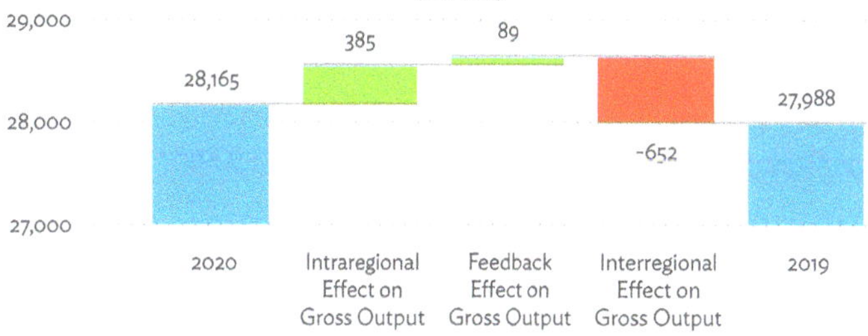

GVC = global value chain; NEC = not elsewhere classified.
Source: Calculations using the Asian Development Bank Multiregional Input-Output Table. https://mrio.adbx.online/ (accessed July 2021).

Click here for figure data

Malaysia

Southeast Asia and the Pacific

Basic Economic Indicators

Economic Aggregates ($ million)	2000	2007	2010	2013	2016	2019	2020
Value-added at basic price	85,165	188,861	248,516	314,939	288,264	360,781	333,231
Gross output	236,007	492,771	640,777	821,441	756,295	989,645	928,705
Total intermediate inputs	148,630	303,049	391,105	504,969	466,471	627,857	594,380
Taxes less subsidies on products	2,212	862	1,156	1,532	1,560	1,007	1,094
International transport margins	0	0	0	0	0	0	0
CIF/FOB adjustment	0	0	0	0	0	0	0
Direct purchases abroad by residents	0	0	0	0	0	0	0
Purchases by nonresidents on the domestic territory	0	0	0	0	0	0	0
Household final consumption expenditure	27,540	68,362	98,321	137,669	136,464	179,661	171,777
Final consumption expenditure by NPISHs	3,036	36	40	55	54	134	151
Government final consumption expenditure	9,115	21,772	31,292	43,758	37,103	40,925	42,366
Gross fixed capital formation	13,454	19,966	29,693	49,393	47,158	58,520	48,143
Changes in inventories	404	444	1,805	-3,945	-2,179	-6,503	-4,107
Total final demand	53,550	110,581	161,151	226,929	218,601	272,737	258,330
Exports	105,312	203,883	219,918	242,488	199,506	237,991	207,126
Imports	90,493	164,089	179,362	213,074	177,937	210,838	185,425

Economic Aggregates, Top 3 Sectors ($ million)	2000	2007	2010	2013	2016	2019	2020
Value-added at basic price							
Public administration	2,789	8,192	12,930	18,315	16,604	29,545	30,431
Retail trade	6,941	9,276	14,391	19,396	20,698	31,242	29,102
Agriculture	7,861	17,695	23,917	27,399	23,799	26,477	27,650
Gross output							
Electricals	60,084	76,839	73,463	88,024	92,458	80,462	83,405
Food and beverages	13,177	40,206	57,751	70,530	65,319	76,486	79,531
Public administration	5,377	15,401	24,310	34,434	31,216	55,547	57,213
Total intermediate inputs							
Food and beverages	11,210	35,429	50,869	62,156	57,601	67,104	69,790
Electricals	49,746	56,860	54,327	67,357	70,755	61,677	63,928
Rubber and plastics	4,043	11,114	15,257	21,938	16,951	38,927	48,253
Total final demand							
Public administration	5,027	15,307	20,905	34,323	31,121	55,393	57,110
Construction	10,253	11,413	19,247	29,993	31,688	38,558	29,631
Food and beverages	2,595	8,426	13,868	18,693	19,693	19,287	26,575
Exports							
Electricals	54,818	71,272	68,804	69,483	75,297	80,340	78,172
Refined fuels	2,352	10,981	15,911	27,949	11,007	23,699	21,704
Mining	7,101	20,255	16,176	19,675	8,994	17,601	15,453
Imports							
Electricals	39,229	55,369	40,459	51,058	47,996	44,934	45,490
Metals	6,284	17,867	18,637	25,741	20,067	23,327	19,440
Chemicals	6,006	10,753	15,306	17,860	15,798	18,425	17,328

Domestic Linkages

Indicator and Top 3 Sectors, 2020	2000	2007	2010	2013	2016	2019	2020
First-round effect							
Food and beverages	0.70	0.76	0.77	0.77	0.79	0.80	0.80
Wood	0.59	0.72	0.73	0.71	0.74	0.77	0.77
Rubber and plastics	0.38	0.55	0.59	0.62	0.65	0.67	0.69
Industrial support effect							
Rubber and plastics	0.20	0.40	0.43	0.59	0.63	0.81	0.91
Food and beverages	0.61	0.60	0.63	0.70	0.74	0.86	0.90
Wood	0.32	0.44	0.48	0.54	0.60	0.76	0.77
Production-induced effect							
Food and beverages	1.31	1.36	1.40	1.47	1.54	1.66	1.70
Rubber and plastics	0.58	0.95	1.02	1.20	1.27	1.49	1.59
Wood	0.91	1.16	1.21	1.25	1.34	1.53	1.54

continued on next page.

continued.

Malaysia

Southeast Asia and the Pacific *Domestic Linkages*

Indicator and Top 3 Sectors, 2020	2000	2007	2010	2013	2016	2019	2020
Simple value-added multiplier							
Real estate	0.97	0.92	0.93	0.94	0.95	0.94	0.94
Mining	0.87	0.90	0.91	0.91	0.92	0.92	0.93
Finance	0.69	0.89	0.90	0.92	0.92	0.91	0.92
Type I value-added multiplier							
Food and beverages	4.38	5.79	6.00	6.17	6.45	6.23	6.35
Rubber and plastics	1.83	4.13	4.71	4.65	5.15	5.12	5.20
Wood	2.74	4.32	4.31	4.25	4.49	4.98	5.07
Direct backward linkage							
Food and beverages	0.70	0.76	0.77	0.77	0.79	0.80	0.80
Wood	0.59	0.72	0.73	0.71	0.74	0.77	0.77
Rubber and plastics	0.38	0.55	0.59	0.62	0.65	0.67	0.69
Complete hypothetical extraction (backward)							
Air transport	1.84	1.84	1.90	2.02	2.07	2.17	2.29
Minerals, NEC	1.44	1.69	1.77	1.80	1.86	1.90	2.02
Inland transport	1.36	1.70	1.77	1.80	1.83	1.93	2.01
Partial hypothetical extraction (backward)							
Air transport	0.84	0.86	0.94	1.04	1.10	1.19	1.29
Wood	0.83	1.08	1.12	1.10	1.15	1.17	1.21
Minerals, NEC	0.59	0.85	0.90	0.97	1.00	1.09	1.17
Total backward linkage							
Food and beverages	2.31	2.36	2.40	2.47	2.54	2.66	2.70
Rubber and plastics	1.58	1.95	2.02	2.20	2.27	2.49	2.59
Wood	1.91	2.16	2.21	2.25	2.34	2.53	2.54
Direct forward linkage							
Real estate	0.28	0.45	0.48	0.93	0.93	0.91	0.92
Agriculture	0.57	0.69	0.73	0.79	0.85	0.89	0.87
Wood	0.22	0.20	0.30	0.55	0.68	0.87	0.84
Complete hypothetical extraction (forward)							
Agriculture	1.79	1.96	1.99	2.18	2.31	2.67	2.63
Real estate	1.41	1.49	1.61	2.32	2.33	2.46	2.55
Sale of motor vehicles	1.86	1.69	1.84	1.75	1.73	2.25	2.40
Partial hypothetical extraction (forward)							
Agriculture	0.87	1.04	1.07	1.26	1.40	1.76	1.72
Real estate	0.48	0.63	0.72	1.48	1.50	1.58	1.66
Utilities	1.21	0.93	1.22	1.19	1.20	1.34	1.47
Total forward linkage							
Finance	3.12	2.32	2.38	2.70	2.77	2.89	2.99
Agriculture	1.95	2.13	2.16	2.38	2.54	2.94	2.91
Real estate	1.52	1.73	1.81	2.77	2.78	2.80	2.87
Normalized backward linkage							
Food and beverages	1.46	1.44	1.41	1.40	1.41	1.39	1.38
Rubber and plastics	1.00	1.19	1.19	1.25	1.26	1.30	1.32
Wood	1.20	1.32	1.30	1.28	1.30	1.32	1.30
Normalized forward linkage							
Finance	1.94	1.45	1.43	1.53	1.52	1.48	1.49
Agriculture	1.22	1.33	1.29	1.35	1.39	1.50	1.45
Real estate	0.94	1.08	1.08	1.57	1.52	1.43	1.43
Net backward linkage							
Machinery, NEC	0.94	1.30	1.41	1.38	1.47	1.82	1.88
Public administration	1.37	1.56	1.38	1.64	1.68	1.75	1.79
Electricals	1.18	1.10	1.23	1.20	1.31	1.69	1.76
Net forward linkage							
Real estate	1.29	1.11	1.16	1.77	1.78	1.79	1.83
Agriculture	1.29	1.29	1.31	1.45	1.54	1.79	1.77
Finance	0.43	1.18	1.22	1.38	1.42	1.47	1.52

continued on next page.

continued.

Malaysia

Southeast Asia and the Pacific *International Linkages*

Indicator and Top 3 Sectors, 2020	2000	2007	2010	2013	2016	2019	2020
Self-sufficiency ratio							
Electricals	1.35	1.26	1.63	1.26	1.42	1.79	1.64
Mining	1.82	1.83	1.49	1.33	1.12	1.27	1.40
Refined fuels	1.05	1.36	1.14	1.56	1.05	1.34	1.37
Import-to-input ratio							
Electricals	0.62	0.64	0.56	0.53	0.47	0.42	0.40
Transport equipment	0.36	0.48	0.42	0.38	0.34	0.32	0.29
Metals	0.46	0.46	0.40	0.37	0.33	0.29	0.27
Export-to-output ratio							
Machinery, NEC	0.69	0.84	0.86	0.72	0.76	1.00	1.00
Electricals	0.91	0.93	0.94	0.79	0.81	1.00	0.94
Manufacturing, NEC	0.50	0.42	0.41	0.38	0.34	0.67	0.73
Domestic inputs share to output							
Food and beverages	0.70	0.76	0.77	0.77	0.79	0.80	0.80
Wood	0.59	0.72	0.73	0.71	0.74	0.77	0.77
Rubber and plastics	0.38	0.55	0.59	0.62	0.65	0.67	0.69
Foreign inputs share to output							
Electricals	0.62	0.64	0.56	0.53	0.47	0.42	0.40
Transport equipment	0.36	0.48	0.42	0.38	0.34	0.32	0.29
Metals	0.46	0.46	0.40	0.37	0.33	0.29	0.27
Backward import multipliers							
Transport equipment	0.53	0.65	0.59	0.58	0.52	0.55	0.52
Electricals	0.70	0.69	0.63	0.63	0.58	0.52	0.49
Rubber and plastics	0.42	0.56	0.50	0.50	0.45	0.46	0.45
Forward import multipliers							
Mining	0.70	0.79	0.71	0.81	0.52	0.76	0.80
Electricals	0.65	0.58	0.63	0.58	0.61	0.79	0.73
Metals	0.57	0.55	0.38	0.39	0.37	0.58	0.60
Intraregional transfer multiplier							
Food and beverages	2.31	2.36	2.40	2.47	2.54	2.66	2.70
Rubber and plastics	1.58	1.95	2.02	2.20	2.27	2.49	2.59
Wood	1.91	2.16	2.21	2.25	2.34	2.53	2.54
Interregional spillover multiplier							
Electricals	2.14	2.17	2.04	2.01	1.89	1.82	1.78
Metals	1.87	1.91	1.86	1.80	1.72	1.59	1.57
Transport equipment	1.72	1.96	1.92	1.75	1.68	1.59	1.57
Interregional feedback multiplier							
Electricals	1.34	1.57	1.51	1.44	1.41	1.25	1.23
Metals	1.20	1.28	1.24	1.23	1.20	1.17	1.16
Transport equipment	1.14	1.27	1.24	1.23	1.20	1.16	1.14
Intraregional effect on gross output ($ million)							
Food and beverages	9,488.03	29,232.16	45,460.52	55,925.15	52,839.77	51,471.10	59,752.65
Public administration	5,316.06	15,379.60	23,503.64	34,409.14	31,189.73	55,466.51	57,153.02
Construction	11,079.91	15,748.29	25,500.97	38,706.53	41,136.85	51,744.13	41,304.35
Interregional effect on gross output ($ million)							
Electricals	26,067.70	25,208.37	25,522.03	27,861.54	33,539.21	48,276.96	47,161.83
Refined fuels	2,611.62	5,407.66	9,833.59	20,065.15	6,233.56	20,692.66	17,848.32
Rubber and plastics	2,910.88	5,748.55	7,303.61	9,034.45	7,224.59	13,342.03	17,202.68
Feedback effect on gross output ($ million)							
Electricals	12,741.89	19,480.58	20,687.34	23,514.46	22,896.52	14,996.54	13,886.77
Refined fuels	948.62	3,141.78	5,638.90	8,891.28	3,518.54	8,404.61	7,408.40
Mining	2,311.66	11,363.19	11,607.51	13,954.10	6,453.05	7,403.31	5,939.14
Directly absorbed value-added exports (DAVAX) ($ million)							
Electricals	9,863.19	13,044.62	14,329.19	14,316.06	19,120.43	23,980.33	25,292.22
Refined fuels	944.18	5,243.42	6,921.77	12,976.05	5,897.37	10,260.64	9,599.71
Mining	4,027.63	7,326.97	4,690.57	6,524.77	3,842.30	10,776.61	9,269.23
Reflection (REF) ($ million)							
Refined fuels	6.49	18.40	42.28	120.45	31.27	242.33	165.96
Electricals	92.81	133.92	121.97	198.17	225.16	129.44	132.72
Mining	20.11	127.19	253.46	306.22	113.70	100.06	97.78

continued on next page.

continued.

Malaysia

Southeast Asia and the Pacific

International Linkages

Indicator and Top 3 Sectors, 2020	2000	2007	2010	2013	2016	2019	2020
Reexports (REX) ($ million)							
Electricals	6,292.50	9,152.27	10,825.44	11,088.99	12,341.18	14,587.49	14,136.83
Refined fuels	555.06	2,147.99	4,163.49	7,210.43	2,512.55	7,464.55	6,653.41
Mining	2,142.33	10,680.06	9,717.24	11,074.28	4,322.62	5,354.70	4,958.91
Foreign value added (FVA) ($ million)							
Electricals	37,570.33	46,823.85	41,848.66	42,831.43	42,319.57	41,192.93	38,207.40
Refined fuels	839.27	3,551.63	4,707.92	7,594.28	2,554.35	5,702.05	5,257.29
Chemicals	1,461.36	5,908.77	5,529.20	5,750.17	4,709.25	5,093.01	4,729.20
Pure double-counting (PDC) ($ million)							
Electricals	999.46	2,116.93	1,678.28	1,048.08	1,290.72	450.10	403.07
Metals	13.63	36.54	28.14	27.97	18.47	43.01	34.60
Chemicals	13.67	78.20	63.99	91.14	36.12	41.74	33.88
Trade-based GVC participation rate							
Electricals	0.82	0.82	0.79	0.79	0.75	0.70	0.68
Transport activities, NEC	0.54	0.49	0.49	0.47	0.45	0.61	0.65
Metals	0.73	0.76	0.66	0.68	0.61	0.66	0.63
Production-based GVC participation rate							
Mining	0.70	0.79	0.71	0.81	0.52	0.76	0.80
Electricals	0.65	0.58	0.63	0.58	0.61	0.79	0.73
Metals	0.57	0.55	0.38	0.39	0.37	0.58	0.60
Trade-based backward GVC participation rate							
Transport equipment	0.53	0.65	0.59	0.58	0.52	0.55	0.52
Electricals	0.70	0.69	0.63	0.63	0.58	0.52	0.49
Rubber and plastics	0.42	0.56	0.50	0.50	0.45	0.46	0.45
Trade-based forward GVC participation rate							
Transport activities, NEC	0.14	0.14	0.17	0.18	0.18	0.33	0.40
Water transport	0.11	0.16	0.05	0.11	0.14	0.28	0.39
Business activities, NEC	0.22	0.26	0.24	0.29	0.30	0.25	0.33
Traditional revealed comparative advantage							
Refined fuels	0.93	1.40	1.80	2.41	1.40	2.87	2.98
Electricals	3.20	2.57	2.34	2.29	3.04	2.76	2.90
Rubber and plastics	1.78	1.57	2.14	2.01	1.80	1.36	1.73
New revealed comparative advantage							
Refined fuels	2.09	1.90	2.57	3.06	2.26	3.31	3.48
Retail trade	3.59	1.43	3.14	2.25	2.35	2.43	2.68
Electricals	2.36	2.59	2.15	1.93	2.54	1.85	1.99
Backward production length							
Rubber and plastics	2.57	3.28	3.31	3.56	3.46	3.63	3.74
Transport equipment	2.87	3.31	3.35	3.40	3.33	3.49	3.55
Metals	2.96	3.27	3.31	3.41	3.33	3.31	3.30
Forward production length							
Mining	3.52	3.70	3.89	4.03	3.82	4.13	4.14
Chemicals	3.44	3.39	3.54	3.82	3.18	3.79	3.80
Rubber and plastics	2.90	3.35	3.08	3.54	3.54	3.53	3.80
Backward production length of GVC segment							
Real estate	4.51	4.58	4.64	4.73	4.72	4.90	5.04
Finance	5.19	4.59	4.73	4.74	4.76	4.90	5.03
Food and beverages	4.36	4.45	4.56	4.58	4.64	4.73	4.82
Forward production length of GVC segment							
Health and social work	3.93	5.78	5.97	6.56	6.35	5.73	5.99
Telecommunications	4.29	4.00	4.88	4.21	4.31	5.40	5.77
Finance	5.53	4.83	4.97	5.61	5.65	5.61	5.73
Backward agglomeration index							
Leather	-	0.01	0.08	0.78	0.97	1.61	1.72
Rubber and plastics	-	0.63	0.65	0.59	0.82	1.97	1.61
Wood	-	0.02	0.40	0.01	0.03	0.67	1.23
Forward agglomeration index							
Transport equipment	-	1.14	0.80	1.07	1.07	1.64	1.54
Leather	-	0.01	0.10	0.88	1.10	1.45	1.48
Public administration	-	1.02	0.97	1.02	1.02	1.03	1.02

CIF = cost, insurance, and freight; FOB = free on board; GVC = global value chain; NEC = not elsewhere classified; NPISHs = nonprofit institutions serving households.
Source: Calculations using the Asian Development Bank Multiregional Input-Output Table. https://mrio.adbx.online/ (accessed July 2021).

continued on next page.

continued.

Malaysia

Southeast Asia and the Pacific

The four select sectors are chosen based on their gross outputs in the economy as of 2019.

Economy Ranking out of 25 Economies

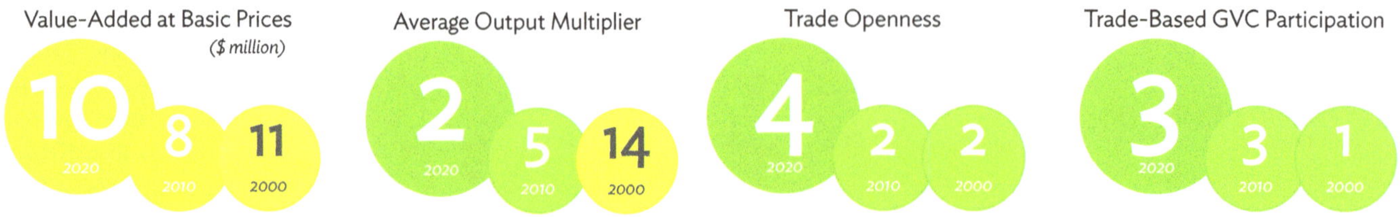

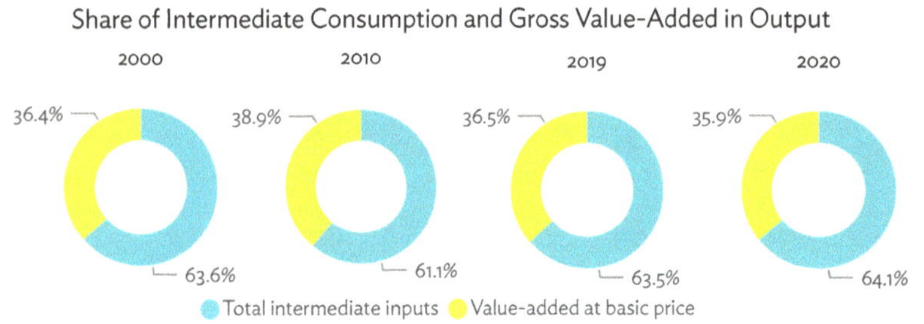

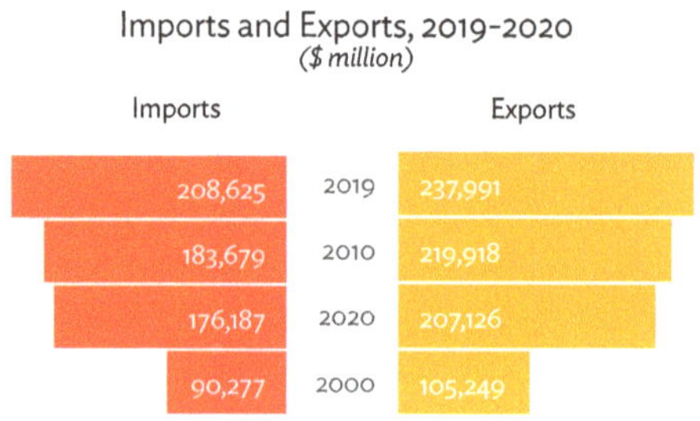

Domestic Linkages

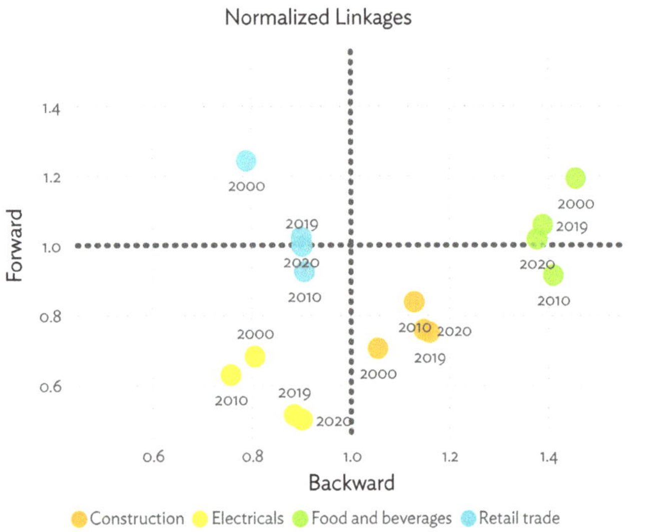

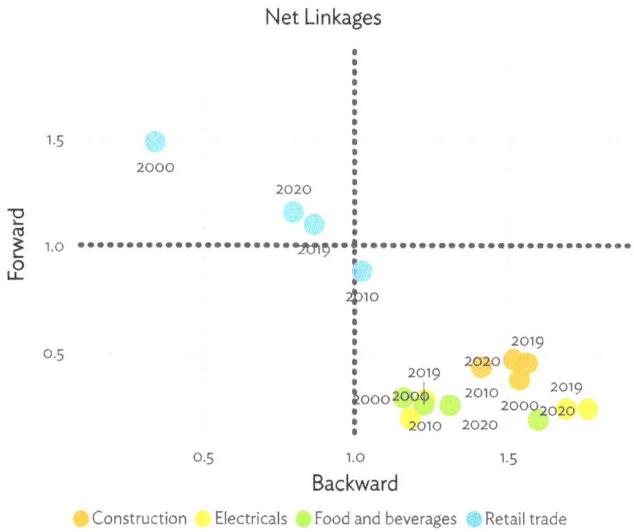

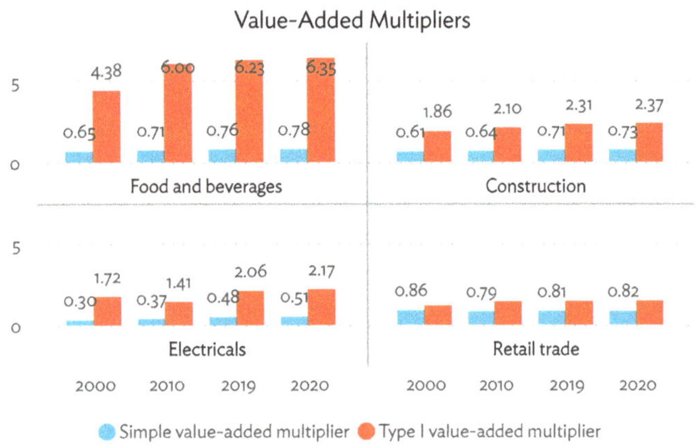

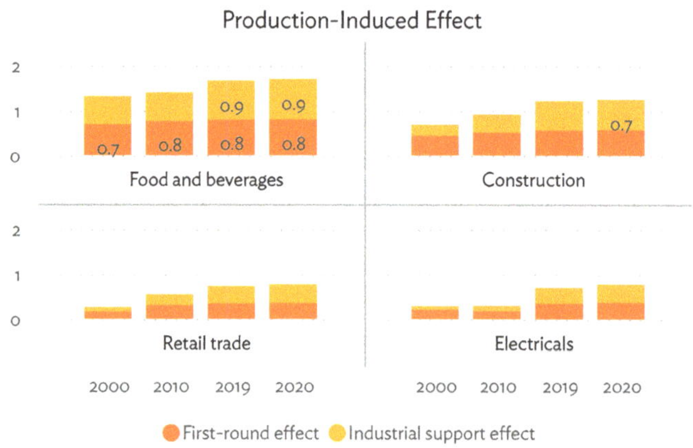

continued on next page.

Click here for figure data

continued.

Malaysia

Southeast Asia and the Pacific

International Linkages

Change in Exports, by Value-Added Components, 2019-2020

($ million)

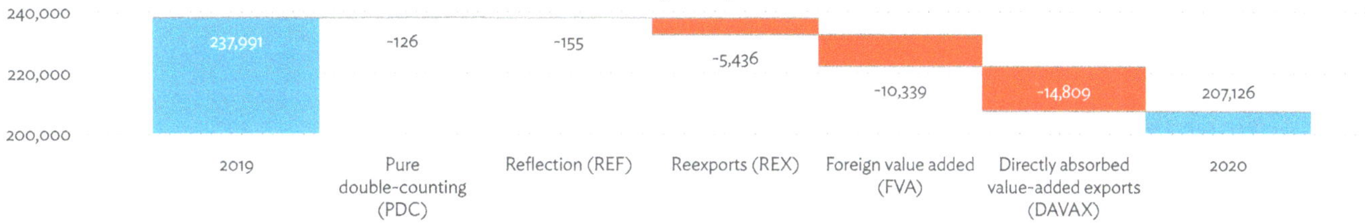

Import Multipliers

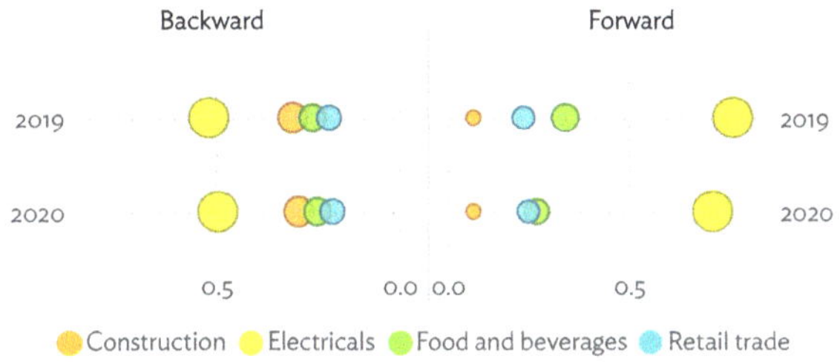

GVC Participation Rates

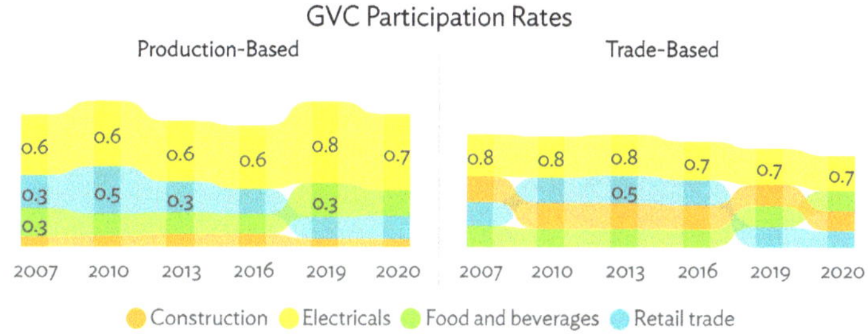

Average Production Length

New Revealed Comparative Advantage

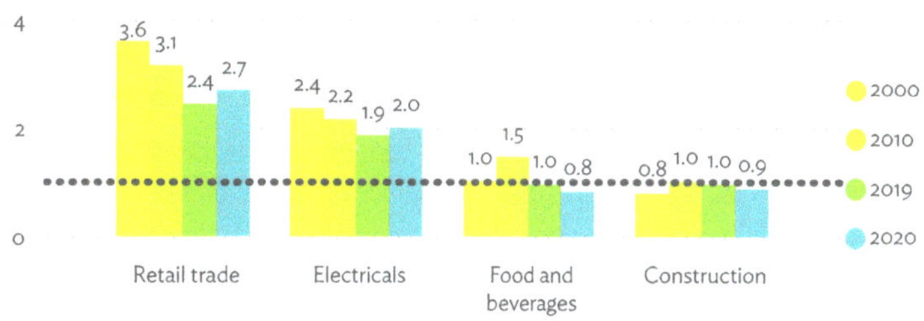

Trade Orientation

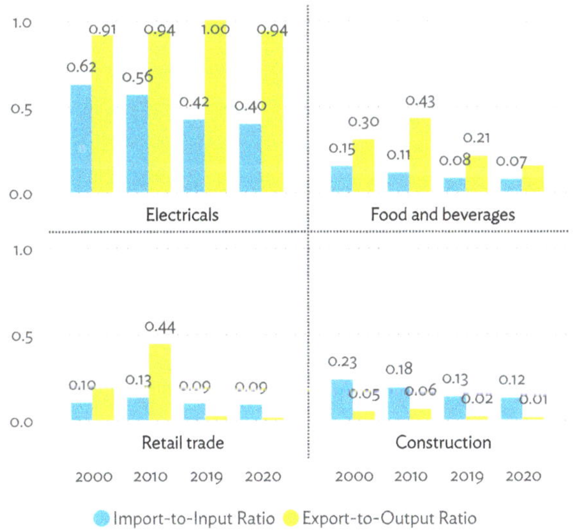

Agglomeration Indices

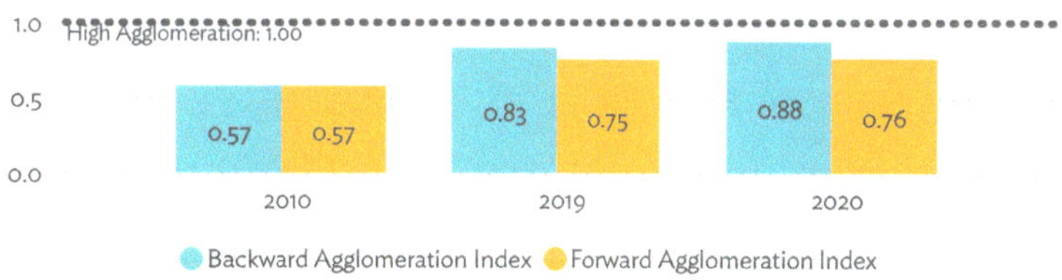

Domestic Transfer Effects and International Spillover Effects

($ million)

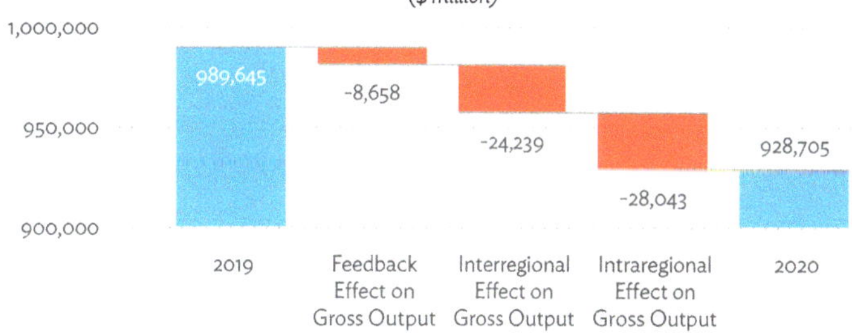

GVC = global value chain; NEC = not elsewhere classified.
Source: Calculations using the Asian Development Bank Multiregional Input-Output Table. https://mrio.adbx.online/ (accessed July 2021).

Click here for figure data

Maldives

South and Central Asia

Basic Economic Indicators

Economic Aggregates ($ million)	2000	2007	2010	2013	2016	2019	2020
Value-added at basic price	523	1,663	2,401	2,915	3,443	4,906	3,607
Gross output	1,010	4,021	5,159	6,605	7,854	11,213	8,009
Total intermediate inputs	466	2,269	2,723	3,622	4,306	6,095	4,340
Taxes less subsidies on products	21	89	34	68	104	212	62
International transport margins	0	0	0	0	0	0	0
CIF/FOB adjustment	0	0	0	0	0	0	0
Direct purchases abroad by residents	0	0	0	0	0	0	0
Purchases by nonresidents on the domestic territory	0	0	0	0	0	0	0
Household final consumption expenditure	97	399	687	770	901	1,446	1,445
Final consumption expenditure by NPISHs	0	0	467	0	0	0	0
Government final consumption expenditure	117	364	0	532	720	798	521
Gross fixed capital formation	36	253	418	206	422	1,173	640
Changes in inventories	1	59	70	-1	10	87	139
Total final demand	251	1,075	1,642	1,507	2,054	3,504	2,745
Exports	473	1,465	1,790	2,716	3,165	3,894	2,113
Imports	377	1,644	1,644	1,923	2,403	4,399	2,321

Economic Aggregates, Top 3 Sectors ($ million)	2000	2007	2010	2013	2016	2019	2020
Value-added at basic price							
Public administration	45	136	236	330	567	461	491
Hotels and restaurants	165	551	677	774	844	1,214	449
Real estate	68	155	209	213	182	399	408
Gross output							
Hotels and restaurants	336	1,668	1,580	2,244	2,508	3,622	1,291
Agriculture	38	291	489	308	273	750	800
Construction	85	210	444	704	1,422	1,107	794
Total intermediate inputs							
Hotels and restaurants	160	1,064	883	1,410	1,571	2,231	794
Utilities	12	131	131	159	165	479	502
Agriculture	7	167	340	159	161	441	474
Total final demand							
Construction	59	114	253	217	625	971	605
Public administration	68	194	266	406	614	532	418
Hotels and restaurants	9	188	140	61	10	738	304
Exports							
Hotels and restaurants	319	1,155	1,398	2,123	2,488	1,939	713
Air transport	22	19	36	63	119	327	288
Food and beverages	20	116	13	62	88	284	224
Imports							
Transport equipment	38	217	138	185	199	705	376
Food and beverages	29	195	44	163	216	541	246
Manufacturing, NEC	102	215	165	58	116	316	208

Domestic Linkages

Indicator and Top 3 Sectors, 2020	2000	2007	2010	2013	2016	2019	2020
First-round effect							
Sale of motor vehicles	0.45	0.72	0.48	0.67	0.72	0.77	0.81
Wholesale trade	0.00	0.44	0.48	0.50	0.53	0.52	0.69
Food and beverages	0.26	0.39	0.24	0.70	0.61	0.56	0.62
Industrial support effect							
Food and beverages	0.08	0.21	0.12	0.43	0.25	0.28	0.44
Sale of motor vehicles	0.11	0.28	0.17	0.25	0.29	0.34	0.44
Utilities	0.11	0.19	0.15	0.15	0.16	0.19	0.36
Production-induced effect							
Sale of motor vehicles	0.55	1.00	0.65	0.92	1.02	1.10	1.24
Food and beverages	0.34	0.61	0.36	1.13	0.86	0.84	1.05
Wholesale trade	0.00	0.61	0.65	0.69	0.72	0.72	0.99

continued on next page.

continued.

Maldives

South and Central Asia — *Domestic Linkages*

Indicator and Top 3 Sectors, 2020	2000	2007	2010	2013	2016	2019	2020
Simple value-added multiplier							
Finance	0.87	0.91	0.91	0.91	0.90	0.91	0.93
Education	0.91	0.90	0.91	0.91	0.91	0.90	0.92
Real estate	0.94	0.86	0.87	0.88	0.87	0.88	0.90
Type I value-added multiplier							
Sale of motor vehicles	2.05	7.38	1.89	5.31	6.48	7.03	7.93
Food and beverages	1.45	2.24	1.30	3.29	2.87	2.83	3.42
Utilities	1.29	2.12	1.68	1.89	2.18	2.23	2.92
Direct backward linkage							
Sale of motor vehicles	0.45	0.72	0.48	0.67	0.72	0.77	0.81
Wholesale trade	0.00	0.44	0.48	0.50	0.53	0.52	0.69
Food and beverages	0.26	0.39	0.24	0.70	0.61	0.56	0.62
Complete hypothetical extraction (backward)							
Sale of motor vehicles	1.55	1.99	1.65	1.87	1.99	2.06	2.20
Food and beverages	1.33	1.60	1.36	1.65	1.82	1.84	2.05
Wholesale trade	1.00	1.58	1.61	1.62	1.69	1.70	1.92
Partial hypothetical extraction (backward)							
Sale of motor vehicles	0.55	1.00	0.65	0.90	1.00	1.08	1.22
Food and beverages	0.34	0.60	0.36	0.88	0.84	0.84	1.05
Wholesale trade	0.00	0.60	0.64	0.66	0.71	0.72	0.95
Total backward linkage							
Sale of motor vehicles	1.55	2.00	1.65	1.92	2.02	2.10	2.24
Food and beverages	1.34	1.61	1.36	2.13	1.86	1.84	2.05
Wholesale trade	1.00	1.61	1.65	1.69	1.72	1.72	1.99
Direct forward linkage							
Finance	0.94	0.78	0.80	0.92	0.92	0.98	0.96
Paper	0.81	0.72	1.00	0.89	0.90	0.89	0.83
Sale of motor vehicles	0.49	0.62	0.70	0.83	0.79	0.71	0.77
Complete hypothetical extraction (forward)							
Finance	1.44	2.04	2.03	2.20	2.17	2.34	2.36
Paper	2.05	2.08	2.43	2.11	2.14	2.32	2.31
Business activities, NEC	2.29	2.29	2.20	2.20	2.13	2.07	2.07
Partial hypothetical extraction (forward)							
Finance	1.02	1.11	1.08	1.27	1.23	1.41	1.47
Paper	1.05	1.10	1.46	1.17	1.21	1.36	1.36
Business activities, NEC	1.30	1.32	1.25	1.23	1.14	1.09	1.09
Total forward linkage							
Finance	3.46	2.19	2.14	2.37	2.30	2.51	2.63
Paper	2.06	2.12	2.51	2.25	2.31	2.40	2.43
Business activities, NEC	2.31	2.35	2.31	2.28	2.16	2.10	2.11
Normalized backward linkage							
Sale of motor vehicles							
Food and beverages							
Wholesale trade							
Normalized forward linkage							
Finance							
Paper							
Business activities, NEC							
Net backward linkage							
Food and beverages							
Air transport							
Water transport							
Net forward linkage							
Finance							
Real estate							
Education							

continued on next page.

continued.

Maldives

South and Central Asia — *International Linkages*

Indicator and Top 3 Sectors, 2020	2000	2007	2010	2013	2016	2019	2020
Export-to-output ratio							
Electricals	1.00	1.00	1.00	1.00	0.00	1.00	1.00
Leather	0.98	1.00	1.00	1.00	0.00	1.00	1.00
Mining	0.16	1.00	1.00	1.00	1.00	1.00	1.00
Rubber and plastics	1.00	1.00	1.00	1.00	1.00	1.00	1.00
Self-sufficiency ratio							
Air transport	1.83	0.95	0.99	1.03	1.20	4.65	8.82
Inland transport	1.12	0.93	1.28	1.08	1.42	5.39	8.31
Water transport	1.85	0.98	1.07	0.86	1.04	4.52	5.63
Import-to-input ratio							
Utilities	0.34	0.47	0.44	0.52	0.54	0.50	0.40
Minerals, NEC	0.00	0.21	0.30	0.24	0.26	0.36	0.32
Metals	0.00	0.28	0.36	0.30	0.31	0.36	0.32
Domestic inputs share to output							
Sale of motor vehicles	0.45	0.72	0.48	0.67	0.72	0.77	0.81
Wholesale trade	0.00	0.44	0.48	0.50	0.53	0.52	0.69
Food and beverages	0.26	0.39	0.24	0.70	0.61	0.56	0.62
Foreign inputs share to output							
Utilities	0.34	0.47	0.44	0.52	0.54	0.50	0.40
Minerals, NEC	0.00	0.21	0.30	0.24	0.26	0.36	0.32
Metals	0.00	0.28	0.36	0.30	0.31	0.36	0.32
Backward import multipliers							
Utilities	0.38	0.58	0.53	0.59	0.63	0.62	0.51
Food and beverages	0.31	0.53	0.35	0.35	0.43	0.44	0.37
Minerals, NEC	0.00	0.28	0.38	0.31	0.32	0.38	0.35
Forward import multipliers							
Metals	0.00	0.09	0.11	0.29	0.28	0.79	0.83
Water transport	0.75	0.30	0.19	0.36	0.43	0.74	0.72
Telecommunications	0.48	0.26	0.35	0.47	0.48	0.82	0.71
Intraregional transfer multiplier							
Sale of motor vehicles	1.55	2.00	1.65	1.92	2.02	2.10	2.24
Food and beverages	1.34	1.61	1.36	2.13	1.86	1.84	2.05
Wholesale trade	1.00	1.61	1.65	1.69	1.72	1.72	1.99
Interregional spillover multiplier							
Utilities	1.50	1.82	1.72	1.82	1.91	1.92	1.76
Metals	1.00	1.45	1.57	1.48	1.55	1.77	1.69
Minerals, NEC	1.00	1.38	1.62	1.49	1.56	1.67	1.61
Interregional feedback multiplier							
Metals	1.00	1.30	1.40	1.33	1.28	1.23	1.21
Utilities	1.35	1.33	1.22	1.28	1.27	1.20	1.16
Transport equipment	1.10	1.18	1.20	1.14	1.14	1.15	1.13
Intraregional effect on gross output ($ million)							
Hotels and restaurants	160.03	932.06	738.71	1,278.65	1,047.77	2,149.62	808.48
Construction	80.22	184.70	386.65	475.61	1,105.88	1,072.90	756.27
Agriculture	30.26	184.42	311.18	205.87	157.86	514.09	611.58
Interregional effect on gross output ($ million)							
Hotels and restaurants	137.25	559.10	662.23	730.55	1,097.50	1,143.17	391.48
Air transport	15.94	31.59	49.89	78.18	108.15	188.24	167.00
Telecommunications	16.04	31.13	69.41	92.61	117.80	247.42	165.67
Feedback effect on gross output ($ million)							
Hotels and restaurants	39.14	177.18	179.16	235.17	363.06	328.98	91.13
Water transport	3.14	5.30	8.13	13.58	19.43	50.70	39.46
Telecommunications	3.70	8.27	17.82	25.92	33.73	67.35	38.30
Directly absorbed value-added exports (DAVAX) ($ million)							
Hotels and restaurants	182.81	610.31	807.88	1,160.45	1,231.06	978.34	409.08
Air transport	12.48	10.38	17.52	36.17	66.28	184.92	187.19
Wholesale trade	0.00	7.38	9.35	16.17	9.49	191.47	142.68
Reflection (REF) ($ million)							
Telecommunications	0.00	0.00	0.00	0.00	0.00	0.03	0.01
Water transport	0.00	0.00	0.00	0.00	0.00	0.03	0.01
Hotels and restaurants							

continued on next page.

continued.

Maldives

South and Central Asia *International Linkages*

Indicator and Top 3 Sectors, 2020	2000	2007	2010	2013	2016	2019	2020
Reexports (REX) ($ million)							
Hotels and restaurants	45.70	162.29	215.11	239.12	349.41	263.58	82.16
Telecommunications	2.35	3.12	10.68	17.22	17.22	86.24	46.01
Water transport	2.66	0.85	1.57	3.87	7.28	46.05	42.75
Foreign value added (FVA) ($ million)							
Hotels and restaurants	90.21	382.44	375.04	723.50	907.51	697.19	222.21
Food and beverages	6.39	61.54	4.56	21.62	37.45	126.34	81.92
Air transport	8.50	6.81	15.25	23.40	46.03	108.77	69.57
Pure double-counting (PDC) ($ million)							
Hotels and restaurants	0.01	0.02	0.02	0.04	0.12	0.07	0.01
Air transport	0.00	0.00	0.00	0.00	0.01	0.01	0.00
Water transport	0.00	0.00	0.01	0.00	0.01	0.01	0.00
Trade-based GVC participation rate							
Water transport	0.54	0.47	0.69	0.63	0.62	0.61	0.53
Utilities	0.50	0.70	0.68	0.72	0.76	0.62	0.51
Metals	-	0.32	0.54	0.36	0.36	0.48	0.47
Production-based GVC participation rate							
Metals	-	0.09	0.11	0.29	0.28	0.79	0.83
Water transport	0.75	0.30	0.19	0.36	0.43	0.74	0.72
Telecommunications	0.48	0.26	0.35	0.47	0.48	0.82	0.71
Trade-based backward GVC participation rate							
Utilities	0.38	0.58	0.53	0.59	0.63	0.62	0.51
Food and beverages	0.31	0.53	0.35	0.35	0.43	0.44	0.37
Minerals, NEC	-	0.28	0.38	0.31	0.32	0.38	0.35
Trade-based forward GVC participation rate							
Finance	0.27	-	0.30	0.31	0.30	0.25	0.26
Transport activities, NEC	0.19	0.17	0.18	0.16	0.20	0.22	0.25
Personal services, NEC	0.07	0.18	0.21	0.20	0.21	0.23	0.22
Traditional revealed comparative advantage							
Hotels and restaurants	54.66	80.15	72.19	76.05	62.54	29.99	25.32
Telecommunications	3.13	1.53	4.45	4.01	3.34	14.39	16.01
Air transport	3.31	1.02	1.64	2.00	2.86	6.18	12.48
New revealed comparative advantage							
Hotels and restaurants	38.13	44.49	41.71	37.14	33.24	20.64	14.82
Air transport	2.06	3.25	4.00	4.97	4.26	5.60	10.31
Public administration	0.56	0.95	0.88	3.28	5.36	3.13	9.23
Backward production length							
Utilities	2.32	3.00	2.67	2.76	2.92	2.96	2.99
Sale of motor vehicles	2.24	2.87	2.19	2.82	2.96	2.86	2.84
Food and beverages	2.02	2.82	2.21	2.88	2.74	2.74	2.80
Forward production length							
Finance	4.45	2.79	2.86	3.27	3.35	3.24	3.23
Business activities, NEC	3.20	3.04	3.15	3.11	3.21	3.16	3.08
Paper	2.78	2.57	3.13	2.97	3.15	3.04	2.98
Backward production length of GVC segment							
Wholesale trade	-	4.09	4.09	4.39	4.52	4.52	4.82
Telecommunications	3.56	3.83	3.41	4.05	3.86	4.15	4.54
Retail trade	4.19	4.30	4.37	4.24	4.35	4.29	4.52
Forward production length of GVC segment							
Wood	4.24	4.93	4.71	4.96	5.20	4.98	5.44
Construction	4.11	5.02	4.88	4.11	4.65	5.13	5.31
Utilities	4.70	3.93	4.52	5.10	4.95	4.84	5.08
Backward agglomeration index							
Textiles	-	2.08	1.76	2.03	1.77	1.91	2.13
Manufacturing, NEC	-	0.47	1.70	2.04	1.77	1.97	2.03
Wood	-	1.10	0.00	0.92	0.85	1.35	1.22
Forward agglomeration index							
Textiles	-	0.85	0.59	0.76	0.76	0.88	1.36
Manufacturing, NEC	-	0.56	0.86	1.03	0.70	1.18	1.25
Wood	-	0.84	0.64	0.59	0.74	1.21	1.24

CIF = cost, insurance, and freight; FOB = free on board; GVC = global value chain; NEC = not elsewhere classified; NPISHs = nonprofit institutions serving households.
Source: Calculations using the Asian Development Bank Multiregional Input-Output Table. https://mrio.adbx.online/ (accessed July 2021).

continued on next page.

continued.

Maldives

South and Central Asia

The four select sectors are chosen based on their gross outputs in the economy as of 2019.

Economy Ranking out of 25 Economies

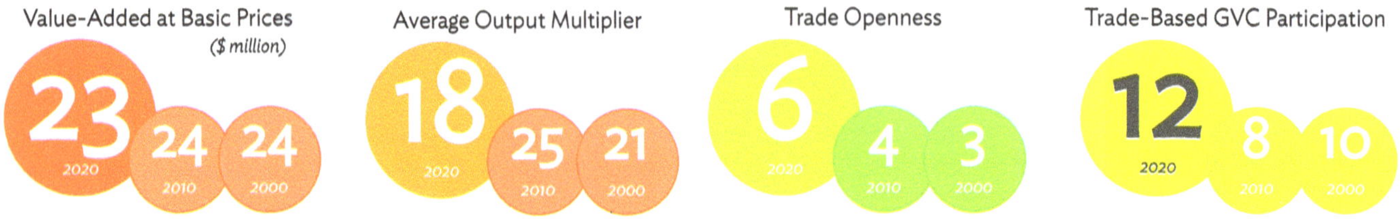

Share of Intermediate Consumption and Gross Value-Added in Output

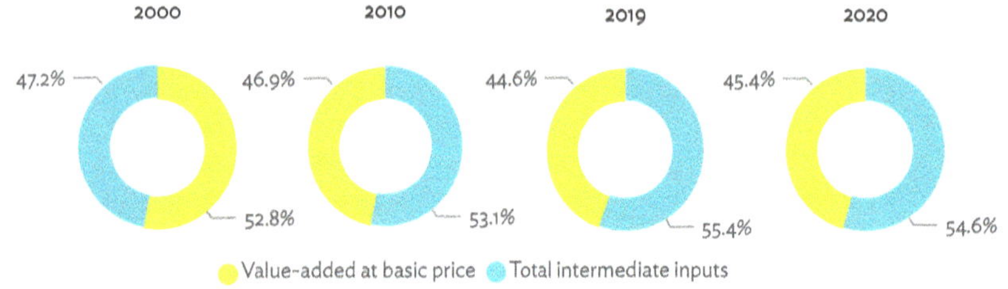

Imports and Exports, 2019-2020

($ million)

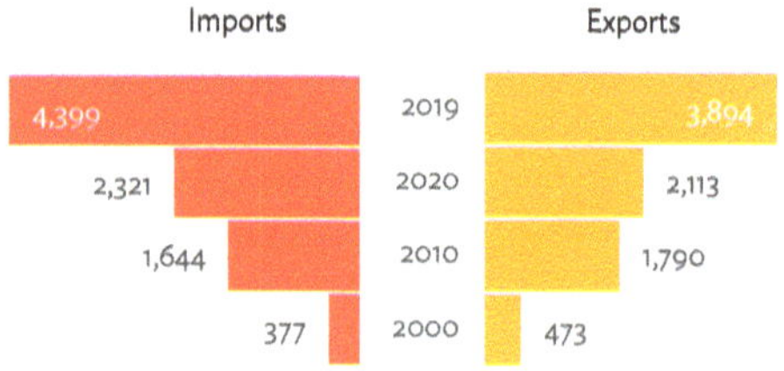

Domestic Linkages

Normalized Linkages

Net Linkages

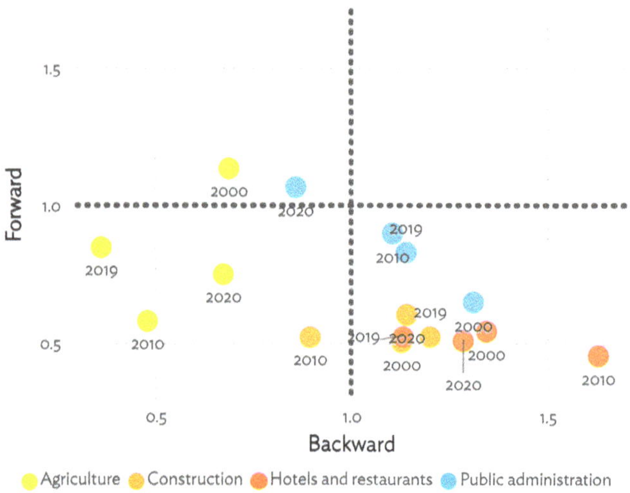

Value-Added Multipliers

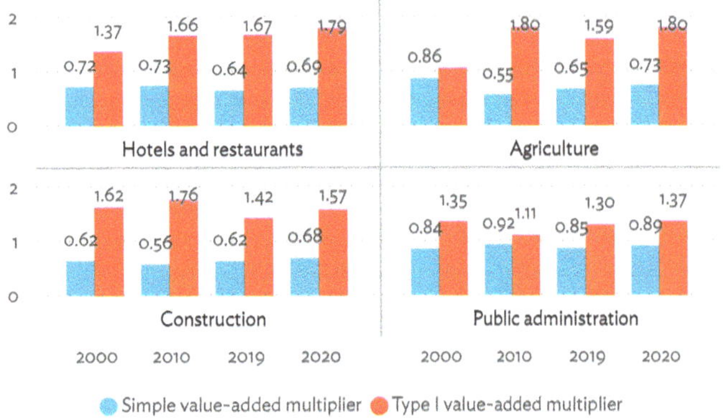

Production-Induced Effect

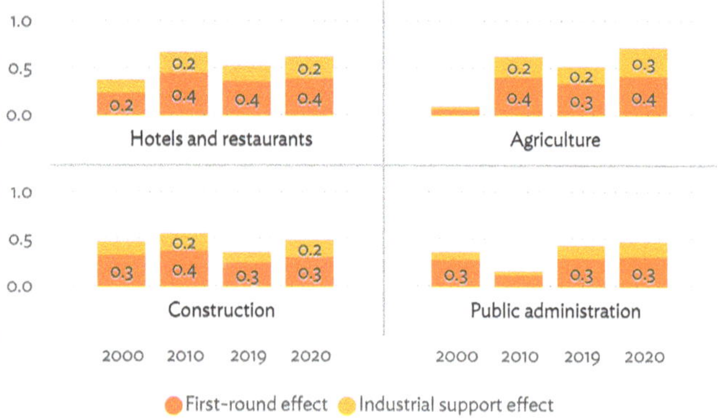

continued on next page.

Click here for figure data

continued.

Maldives

South and Central Asia

International Linkages

Change in Exports, by Value-Added Components, 2019-2020

($ million)

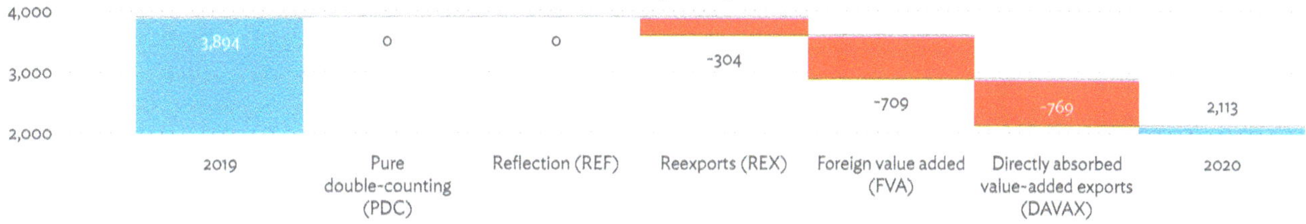

Import Multipliers

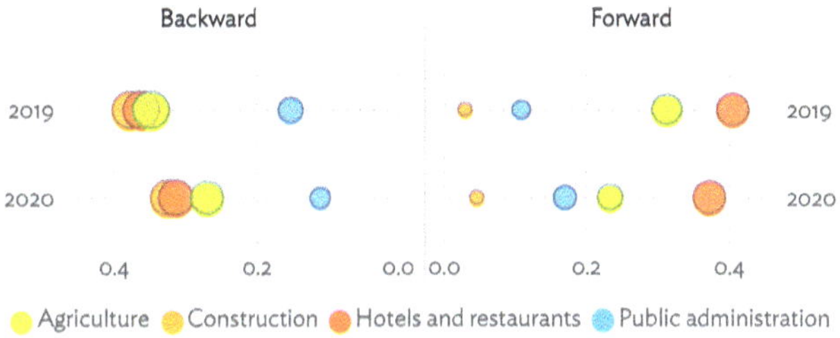

GVC Participation Rates

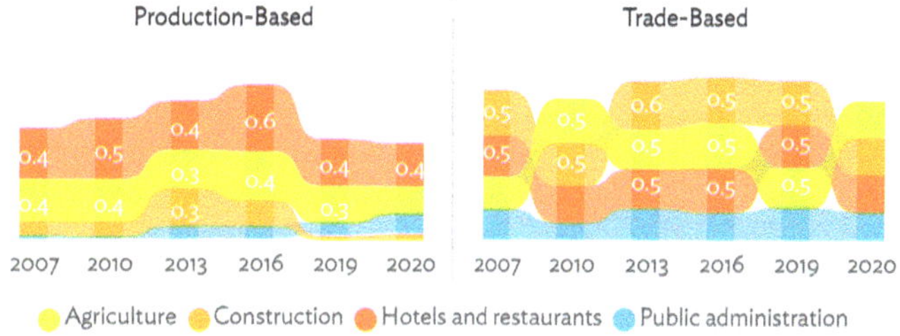

Average Production Length

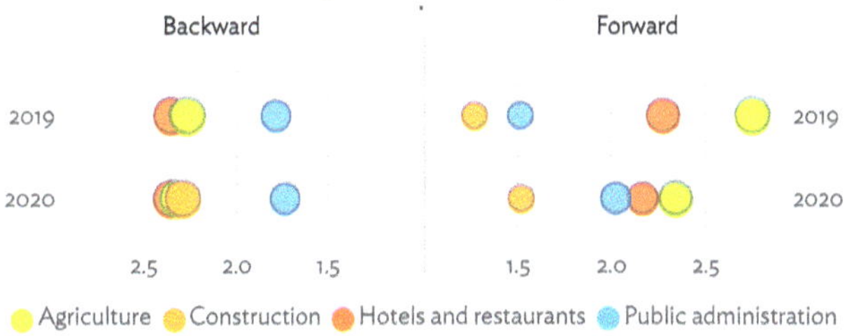

New Revealed Comparative Advantage

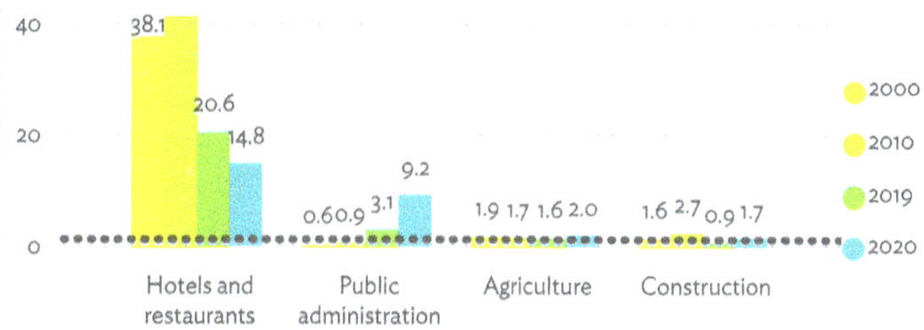

Trade Orientation

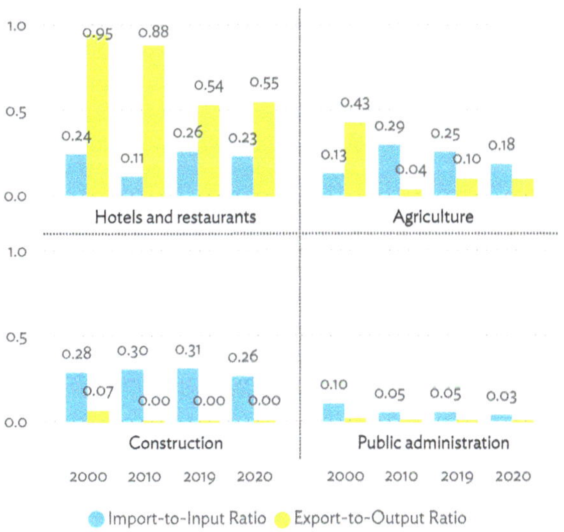

Agglomeration Indices

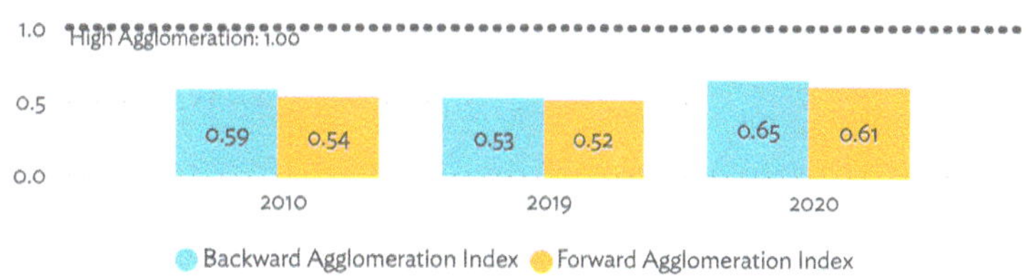

Domestic Transfer Effects and International Spillover Effects

($ million)

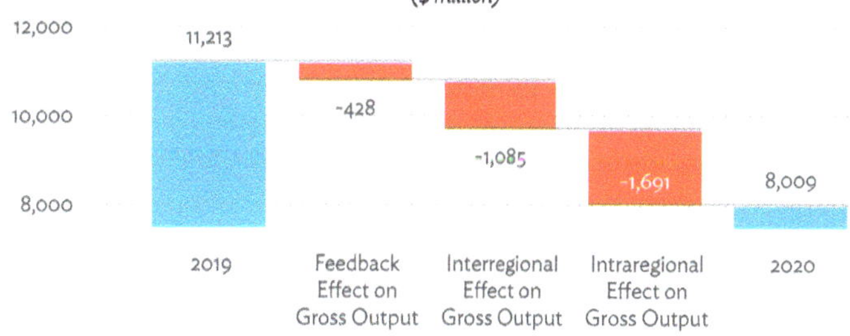

GVC = global value chain; NEC = not elsewhere classified.

Source: Calculations using the Asian Development Bank Multiregional Input-Output Table. https://mrio.adbx.online/ (accessed July 2021).

Click here for figure data

Mongolia

East Asia

Basic Economic Indicators

Economic Aggregates ($ million)	2000	2007	2010	2013	2016	2019	2020
Value-added at basic price	1,010	3,815	6,454	11,153	10,440	12,490	11,873
Gross output	2,106	7,737	13,205	22,269	20,315	26,432	25,060
Total intermediate inputs	1,068	3,734	6,422	10,543	9,389	13,165	12,525
Taxes less subsidies on products	27	188	329	573	486	777	662
International transport margins	0	0	0	0	0	0	0
CIF/FOB adjustment	0	0	0	0	0	0	0
Direct purchases abroad by residents	0	0	0	0	0	0	0
Purchases by nonresidents on the domestic territory	0	0	0	0	0	0	0
Household final consumption expenditure	614	1,543	3,001	4,988	4,422	5,248	5,293
Final consumption expenditure by NPISHs	10	15	43	55	40	65	66
Government final consumption expenditure	168	490	875	1,625	1,569	1,606	1,855
Gross fixed capital formation	182	883	1,532	3,205	1,811	2,271	2,213
Changes in inventories	-16	44	302	1,141	654	732	-349
Total final demand	958	2,975	5,752	11,014	8,496	9,923	9,077
Exports	441	2,115	2,955	4,048	4,937	8,413	7,746
Imports	621	2,079	3,675	6,813	4,412	9,254	7,168

Economic Aggregates, Top 3 Sectors ($ million)	2000	2007	2010	2013	2016	2019	2020
Value-added at basic price							
Mining	110	1,146	1,549	1,870	2,287	3,245	2,842
Agriculture	312	780	844	1,688	1,330	1,512	1,585
Food and beverages	28	156	292	548	447	660	703
Gross output							
Mining	170	2,229	3,036	4,003	4,700	6,450	5,649
Agriculture	400	1,183	1,287	2,287	1,890	2,281	2,391
Construction	94	483	972	2,580	1,827	2,471	2,256
Total intermediate inputs							
Mining	58	1,029	1,392	2,018	2,311	3,012	2,650
Construction	65	363	737	1,804	1,304	1,805	1,657
Food and beverages	46	356	666	900	1,021	1,220	1,305
Total final demand							
Construction	62	317	663	2,063	1,125	1,615	1,684
Food and beverages	53	414	796	1,316	1,286	1,426	1,527
Public administration	91	173	418	777	729	779	907
Exports							
Mining	155	1,457	1,994	2,767	3,738	5,988	4,553
Agriculture	32	164	104	151	200	436	1,466
Metals	27	33	50	30	69	232	351
Imports							
Machinery, NEC	6	284	453	898	514	1,219	895
Construction	56	30	26	254	161	658	602
Electricals	2	151	234	390	384	820	597

Domestic Linkages

Indicator and Top 3 Sectors, 2020	2000	2007	2010	2013	2016	2019	2020
First-round effect							
Transport equipment	0.26	0.28	0.00	0.34	0.56	0.97	0.90
Leather	0.59	0.65	0.64	0.64	0.67	0.59	0.62
Refined fuels	0.05	0.22	0.24	0.40	0.72	0.61	0.62
Industrial support effect							
Transport equipment	0.13	0.15	0.00	0.17	0.28	0.43	0.46
Utilities	0.16	0.45	0.59	0.57	0.34	0.30	0.34
Refined fuels	0.02	0.08	0.09	0.19	0.38	0.28	0.33
Production-induced effect							
Transport equipment	0.39	0.44	0.00	0.51	0.83	1.40	1.37
Refined fuels	0.06	0.30	0.34	0.59	1.10	0.90	0.95
Leather	0.75	0.92	0.92	0.89	0.92	0.80	0.87

continued on next page.

continued.

Mongolia

East Asia *Domestic Linkages*

Indicator and Top 3 Sectors, 2020	2000	2007	2010	2013	2016	2019	2020
Simple value-added multiplier							
Real estate	0.86	0.92	0.93	0.93	0.93	0.91	0.92
Finance	0.84	0.88	0.88	0.91	0.92	0.89	0.90
Education	0.90	0.88	0.88	0.89	0.90	0.87	0.88
Type I value-added multiplier							
Transport equipment	1.43	2.22	0.00	1.52	2.39	448.14	136.05
Leather	2.54	3.06	2.95	3.01	3.60	3.74	3.90
Metals	2.40	2.03	1.86	1.72	1.57	1.51	2.43
Direct backward linkage							
Transport equipment	0.26	0.28	0.00	0.34	0.56	0.97	0.90
Leather	0.59	0.65	0.64	0.64	0.67	0.59	0.62
Refined fuels	0.05	0.22	0.24	0.40	0.72	0.61	0.62
Complete hypothetical extraction (backward)							
Transport equipment	1.39	1.44	1.00	1.51	1.83	2.40	2.37
Refined fuels	1.06	1.29	1.32	1.56	2.09	1.88	1.92
Leather	1.71	1.87	1.84	1.80	1.86	1.76	1.81
Partial hypothetical extraction (backward)							
Transport equipment	0.39	0.44	0.00	0.51	0.83	1.40	1.37
Refined fuels	0.06	0.30	0.33	0.58	1.09	0.89	0.93
Leather	0.73	0.90	0.88	0.85	0.89	0.78	0.84
Total backward linkage							
Transport equipment	1.39	1.44	1.00	1.51	1.83	2.40	2.37
Refined fuels	1.06	1.30	1.34	1.59	2.10	1.90	1.95
Leather	1.75	1.92	1.92	1.89	1.92	1.80	1.87
Direct forward linkage							
Minerals, NEC	0.80	0.89	0.90	0.79	0.85	0.81	0.88
Rubber and plastics	0.54	0.88	0.76	0.67	0.87	0.84	0.88
Finance	0.83	0.77	0.76	0.82	0.81	0.81	0.82
Complete hypothetical extraction (forward)							
Refined fuels	1.03	2.21	2.22	1.91	2.35	1.85	2.21
Rubber and plastics	1.71	2.21	2.08	1.88	2.23	2.07	2.16
Finance	1.92	2.06	2.11	2.16	2.15	2.05	2.12
Partial hypothetical extraction (forward)							
Rubber and plastics	0.76	1.26	1.11	0.92	1.26	1.14	1.23
Refined fuels	0.03	1.22	1.23	0.92	1.35	0.86	1.22
Minerals, NEC	1.18	1.26	1.27	1.00	1.22	1.12	1.17
Total forward linkage							
Utilities	2.08	1.96	2.41	2.49	2.37	2.37	2.40
Rubber and plastics	1.80	2.32	2.15	1.95	2.28	2.22	2.32
Minerals, NEC	2.21	2.36	2.36	2.10	2.33	2.20	2.27
Normalized backward linkage							
Transport equipment							
Refined fuels							
Leather							
Normalized forward linkage							
Utilities							
Rubber and plastics							
Minerals, NEC							
Net backward linkage							
Transport equipment							
Metals							
Leather							
Net forward linkage							
Finance							
Chemicals							
Real estate							

continued on next page.

continued.

Mongolia

East Asia — *International Linkages*

Indicator and Top 3 Sectors, 2020	2000	2007	2010	2013	2016	2019	2020
Self-sufficiency ratio							
Air transport	0.94	3.12	2.74	1.90	1.24	7.61	8.35
Mining	7.93	2.61	2.50	2.50	4.52	10.61	4.69
Metals	1.24	0.80	0.87	0.56	0.89	1.42	3.00
Import-to-input ratio							
Electricals	0.36	0.42	0.45	0.38	0.28	0.85	0.84
Machinery, NEC	0.44	0.23	0.24	0.30	0.28	0.66	0.62
Paper	0.33	0.25	0.26	0.25	0.22	0.50	0.45
Export-to-output ratio							
Air transport	0.27	0.76	0.69	0.51	0.24	1.00	1.00
Water transport	0.94	0.43	0.10	0.00	0.00	0.99	1.00
Metals	0.58	0.48	0.39	0.25	0.38	1.00	1.00
Domestic inputs share to output							
Transport equipment	0.26	0.28	0.00	0.34	0.56	0.97	0.90
Leather	0.59	0.65	0.64	0.64	0.67	0.59	0.62
Refined fuels	0.05	0.22	0.24	0.40	0.72	0.61	0.62
Foreign inputs share to output							
Electricals	0.36	0.42	0.45	0.38	0.28	0.85	0.84
Machinery, NEC	0.44	0.23	0.24	0.30	0.28	0.66	0.62
Paper	0.33	0.25	0.26	0.25	0.22	0.50	0.45
Backward import multipliers							
Electricals	0.51	0.49	0.51	0.43	0.33	0.86	0.86
Machinery, NEC	0.57	0.31	0.32	0.38	0.35	0.68	0.64
Paper	0.41	0.36	0.35	0.32	0.30	0.53	0.49
Forward import multipliers							
Metals	0.70	0.64	0.52	0.42	0.56	0.99	0.92
Air transport	0.29	0.87	0.81	0.66	0.39	0.88	0.88
Water transport	0.94	0.46	0.21	0.34	0.34	0.79	0.78
Intraregional transfer multiplier							
Transport equipment	1.39	1.44	1.00	1.51	1.83	2.40	2.37
Refined fuels	1.06	1.30	1.34	1.59	2.10	1.90	1.95
Leather	1.75	1.92	1.92	1.89	1.92	1.80	1.87
Interregional spillover multiplier							
Electricals	1.61	1.94	2.08	1.87	1.67	2.80	2.81
Machinery, NEC	1.74	1.50	1.55	1.69	1.68	2.42	2.33
Paper	1.58	1.53	1.59	1.56	1.55	2.06	1.94
Interregional feedback multiplier							
Electricals	1.17	1.20	1.20	1.18	1.12	1.33	1.31
Machinery, NEC	1.22	1.11	1.10	1.14	1.12	1.25	1.23
Paper	1.09	1.11	1.10	1.10	1.08	1.17	1.15
Intraregional effect on gross output ($ million)							
Construction	83.93	384.13	819.15	2,411.63	1,545.68	2,110.10	2,010.83
Food and beverages	59.84	487.18	943.70	1,468.67	1,462.52	1,805.64	1,953.69
Mining	12.42	597.00	997.93	1,081.15	806.91	1,829.90	1,433.52
Interregional effect on gross output ($ million)							
Mining	132.14	1,282.70	1,699.41	2,436.00	3,292.67	3,843.21	3,576.40
Agriculture	34.12	202.89	113.88	148.48	149.09	329.10	1,101.68
Utilities	10.71	41.96	83.13	150.56	263.04	320.39	324.89
Feedback effect on gross output ($ million)							
Mining	24.97	349.63	338.71	485.51	599.93	777.21	638.73
Metals	3.61	7.76	9.67	7.79	13.81	82.47	108.39
Agriculture	3.89	30.52	15.95	21.31	19.66	35.24	104.58
Directly absorbed value-added exports (DAVAX) ($ million)							
Mining	85.32	663.08	1,063.71	1,416.98	2,175.36	3,633.18	2,855.61
Agriculture	24.08	117.81	71.60	109.04	148.91	304.57	1,043.77
Wholesale trade	12.29	45.42	132.13	112.74	115.47	135.01	120.63
Reflection (REF) ($ million)							
Mining	0.01	0.12	0.24	0.52	0.37	0.63	0.44
Agriculture	0.00	0.00	0.01	0.01	0.01	0.04	0.12
Metals	0.00	0.00	0.00	0.00	0.01	0.02	0.02

continued on next page.

continued.

Mongolia

East Asia

International Linkages

Indicator and Top 3 Sectors, 2020	2000	2007	2010	2013	2016	2019	2020
Reexports (REX) ($ million)							
Mining	31.55	424.90	420.73	592.74	751.82	918.25	718.78
Agriculture	2.99	30.67	18.78	30.42	31.95	58.55	195.94
Metals	2.94	8.09	8.88	5.27	12.70	84.21	129.13
Foreign value added (FVA) ($ million)							
Mining	38.20	368.70	509.22	756.76	810.06	1,435.93	977.56
Agriculture	4.50	15.75	13.83	11.77	19.33	73.18	226.58
Metals	11.92	9.61	17.60	10.85	14.86	91.13	112.00
Pure double-counting (PDC) ($ million)							
Mining	0.00	0.06	0.09	0.24	0.23	0.22	0.14
Agriculture	0.00	0.00	0.00	0.00	0.00	0.01	0.02
Metals	0.00	0.00	0.00	0.00	0.01	0.02	0.02
Trade-based GVC participation rate							
Electricals	0.65	0.58	0.57	0.51	0.44	0.90	0.88
Machinery, NEC	0.59	0.44	0.45	0.50	0.52	0.70	0.69
Metals	0.56	0.54	0.53	0.53	0.40	0.76	0.69
Production-based GVC participation rate							
Metals	0.70	0.64	0.52	0.42	0.56	0.99	0.92
Air transport	0.29	0.87	0.81	0.66	0.39	0.88	0.88
Water transport	0.94	0.46	0.21	0.34	0.34	0.79	0.78
Trade-based backward GVC participation rate							
Electricals	0.51	0.49	0.51	0.43	0.33	0.86	0.86
Machinery, NEC	0.57	0.31	0.32	0.38	0.35	0.68	0.64
Paper	0.41	0.36	0.35	0.32	0.30	0.53	0.49
Trade-based forward GVC participation rate							
Metals	0.11	0.24	0.18	0.17	0.18	0.36	0.37
Water transport	0.31	0.25	0.19	0.15	0.17	0.33	0.25
Leather	0.24	0.24	0.16	0.36	0.47	0.19	0.24
Traditional revealed comparative advantage							
Mining	5.83	8.70	8.00	7.29	11.28	10.56	9.01
Agriculture	3.32	3.83	1.56	1.59	1.73	1.80	6.14
Air transport	2.15	1.59	1.90	1.92	0.61	1.79	1.85
New revealed comparative advantage							
Mining	4.62	6.01	4.78	4.11	5.94	6.17	6.21
Agriculture	4.83	3.39	1.38	1.15	1.03	1.28	3.18
Air transport	1.03	1.48	2.02	1.49	1.16	2.05	2.02
Backward production length							
Electricals	2.78	2.82	2.88	2.53	2.32	3.35	3.33
Transport equipment	2.27	2.89		2.08	2.42	3.16	3.12
Construction	2.53	2.73	2.80	2.74	2.74	2.83	2.79
Forward production length							
Mining	4.26	3.86	3.63	3.93	4.32	3.70	4.01
Utilities	2.61	2.46	2.98	3.29	3.89	3.73	3.71
Finance	3.27	3.48	3.16	3.14	3.55	3.38	3.64
Backward production length of GVC segment							
Refined fuels	3.37	3.71	3.68	4.75	4.86	4.65	4.72
Personal services, NEC	3.88	4.18	4.27	4.36	4.37	4.42	4.45
Transport equipment	3.61	3.59		4.02	4.20	4.68	4.44
Forward production length of GVC segment							
Utilities	5.12	5.84	5.95	5.84	6.12	6.16	6.21
Minerals, NEC	4.96	5.93	5.79	5.48	6.17	6.09	6.14
Real estate	4.84	5.88	5.78	4.93	4.67	5.94	5.98
Backward agglomeration index							
Rubber and plastics	-	0.89	0.97	1.42	1.58	3.40	2.47
Refined fuels	-	0.97	0.99	1.58	1.53	1.35	1.77
Chemicals	-	1.23	1.18	1.14	1.23	1.78	1.76
Forward agglomeration index							
Manufacturing, NEC	-	1.38	1.49	1.60	1.52	1.87	1.73
Electricals	-	2.50	2.24	2.20	1.96	1.40	1.63
Textiles	-	1.19	1.52	1.55	1.60	1.15	1.46

CIF = cost, insurance, and freight; FOB = free on board; GVC = global value chain; NEC = not elsewhere classified; NPISHs = nonprofit institutions serving households.
Source: Calculations using the Asian Development Bank Multiregional Input-Output Table. https://mrio.adbx.online/ (accessed July 2021).

continued on next page.

continued.

Mongolia

East Asia

The four select sectors are chosen based on their gross outputs in the economy as of 2019.

Economy Ranking out of 25 Economies

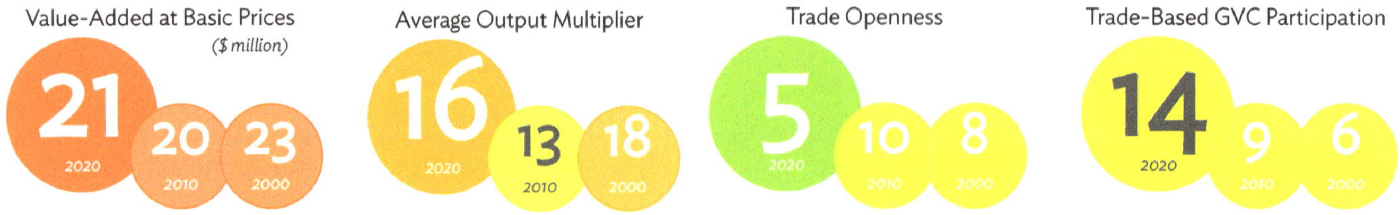

Share of Intermediate Consumption and Gross Value-Added in Output

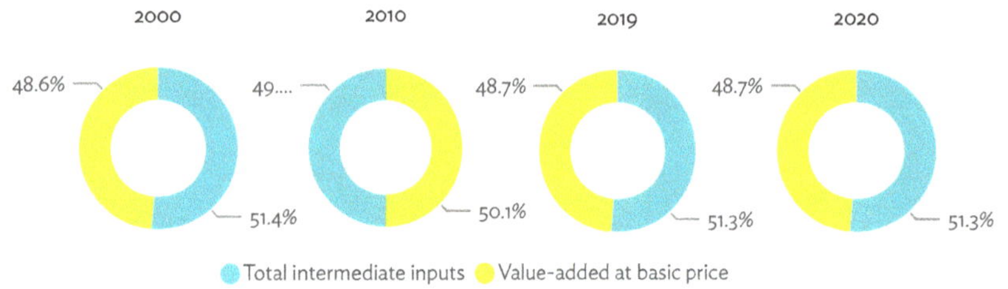

Imports and Exports, 2019-2020

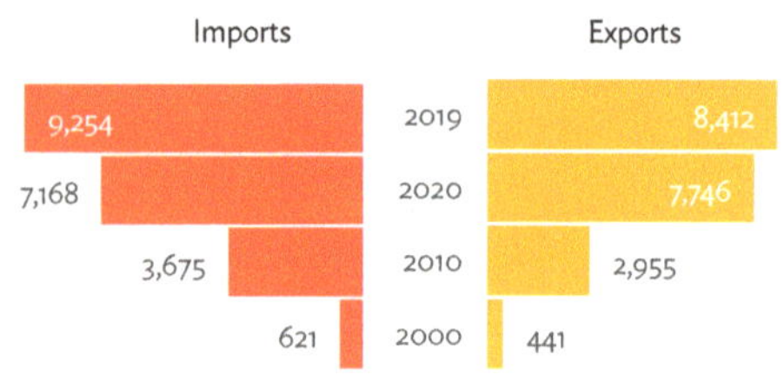

Domestic Linkages

Normalized Linkages

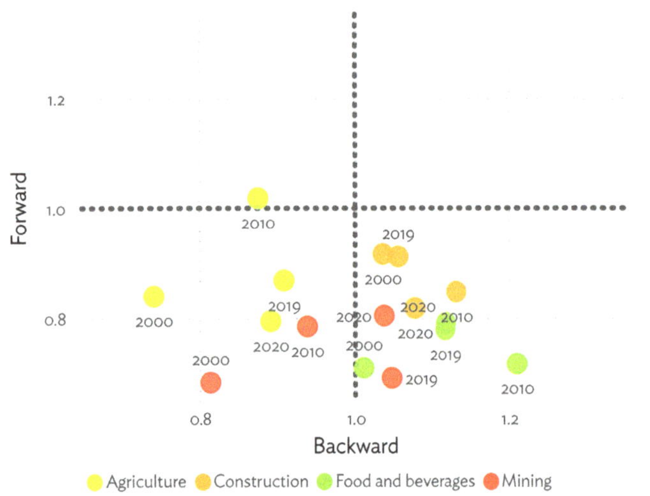

Net Linkages

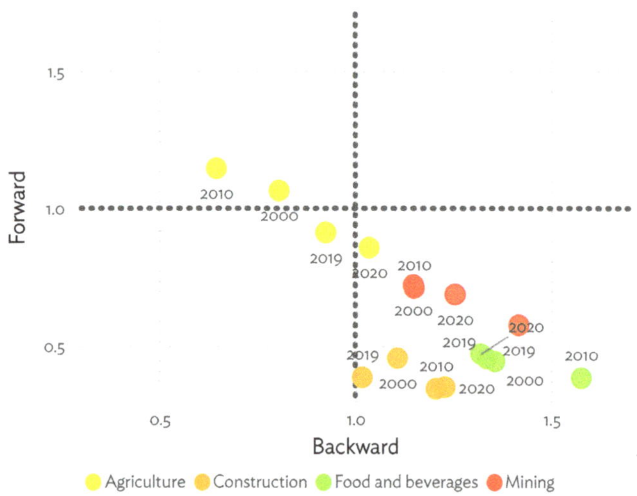

Value-Added Multipliers

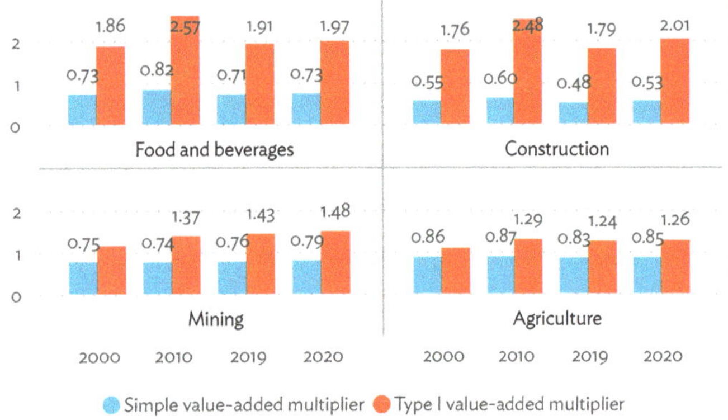

Production-Induced Effect

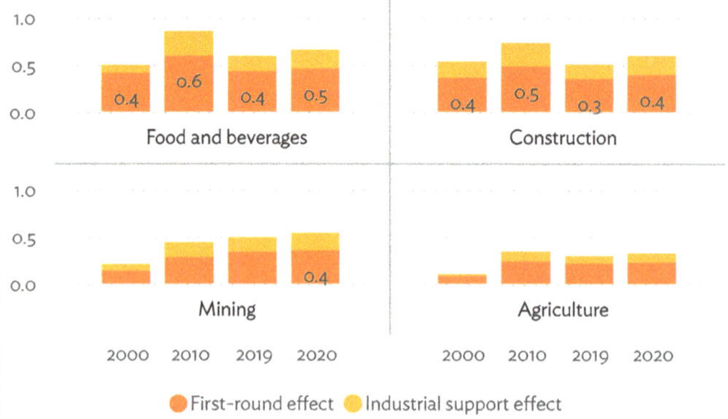

continued on next page.

Click here for figure data

continued.

Mongolia
East Asia

International Linkages

Change in Exports, by Value-Added Components, 2019-2020
($ million)

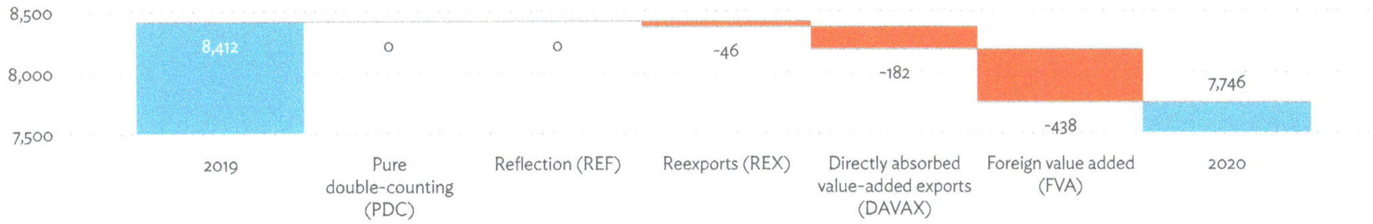

Import Multipliers

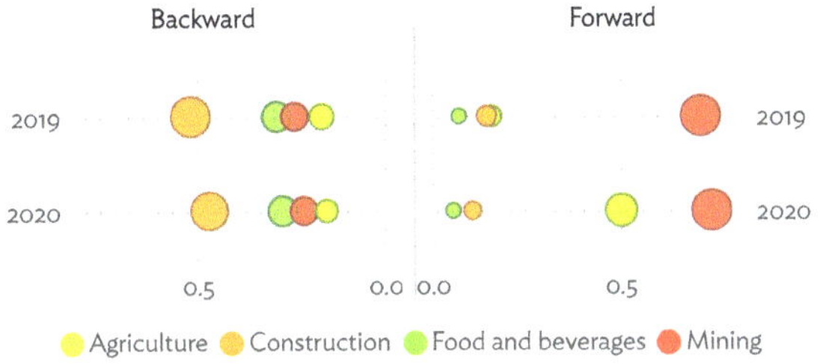

GVC Participation Rates

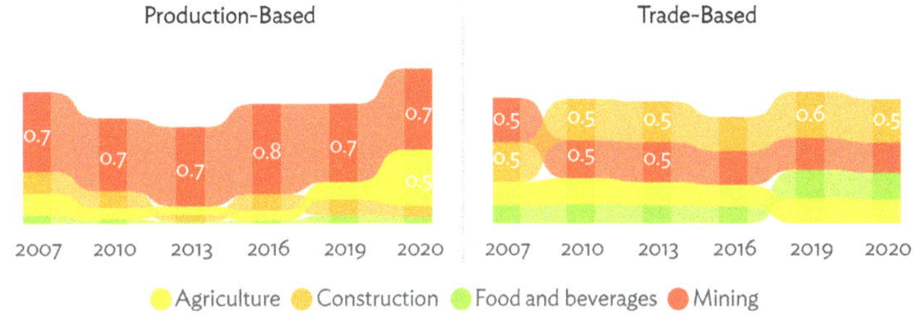

Average Production Length

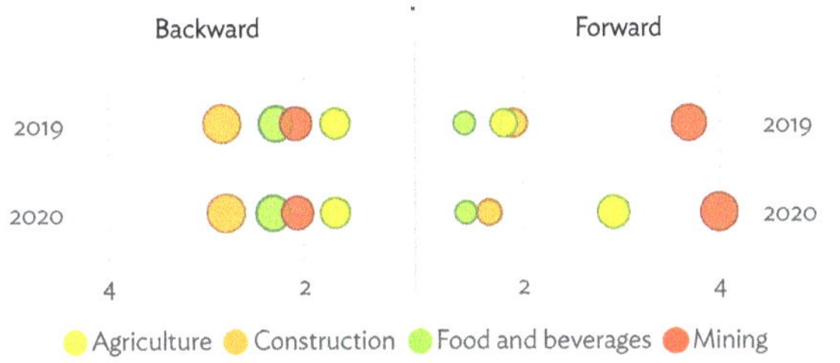

New Revealed Comparative Advantage

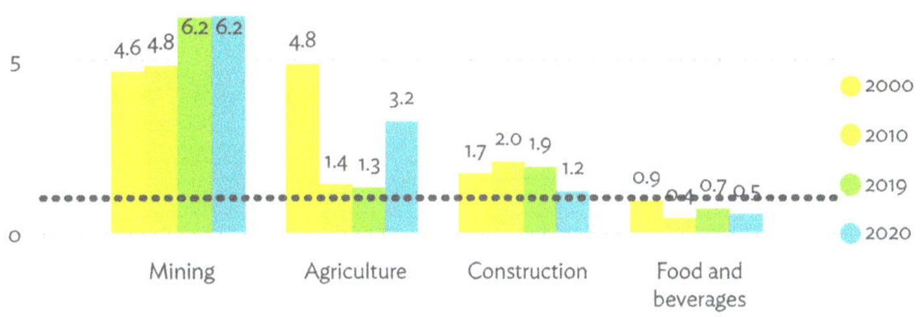

Trade Orientation

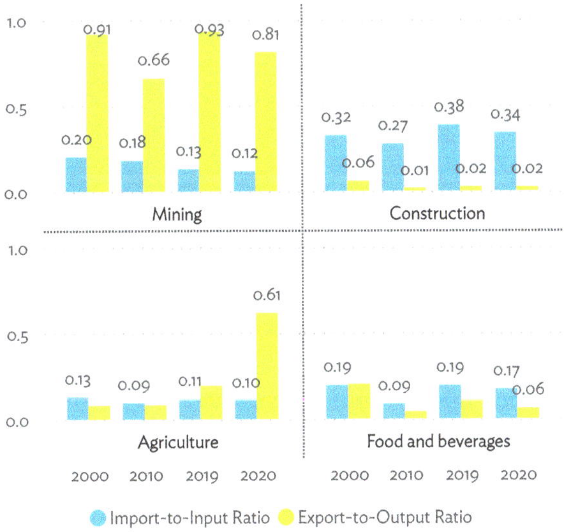

Agglomeration Indices

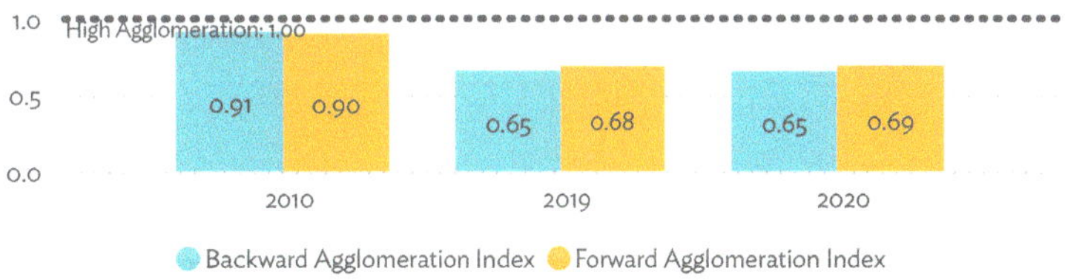

Domestic Transfer Effects and International Spillover Effects
($ million)

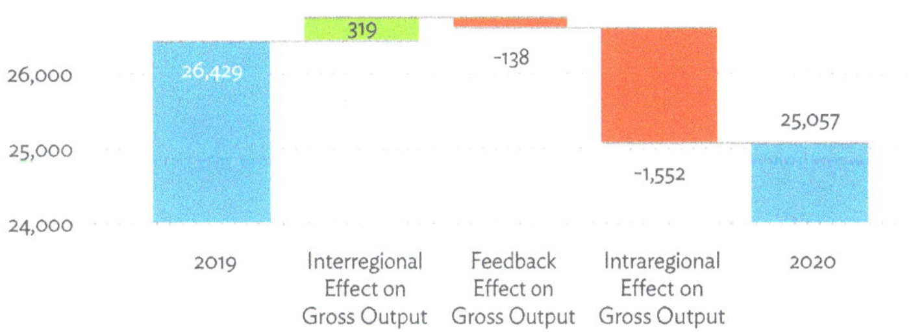

GVC = global value chain; NEC = not elsewhere classified.
Source: Calculations using the Asian Development Bank Multiregional Input-Output Table. https://mrio.adbx.online/ (accessed July 2021).

Click here for figure data

Nepal

South and Central Asia

Basic Economic Indicators

Economic Aggregates ($ million)	2000	2007	2010	2013	2016	2019	2020
Value-added at basic price	4,836	9,835	14,274	16,401	18,447	29,683	29,410
Gross output	9,350	17,263	24,532	26,552	29,426	53,377	51,388
Total intermediate inputs	4,380	7,156	9,762	9,537	10,090	21,920	20,531
Taxes less subsidies on products	135	271	495	614	888	1,774	1,447
International transport margins	0	0	0	0	0	0	0
CIF/FOB adjustment	0	0	0	0	0	0	0
Direct purchases abroad by residents	0	0	0	0	0	0	0
Purchases by nonresidents on the domestic territory	0	0	0	0	0	0	0
Household final consumption expenditure	3,161	6,859	9,314	9,964	11,958	18,698	20,953
Final consumption expenditure by NPISHs	56	178	257	282	340	441	486
Government final consumption expenditure	494	1,061	1,739	1,776	2,372	2,730	2,940
Gross fixed capital formation	837	1,872	2,902	3,498	5,151	9,095	8,701
Changes in inventories	197	604	1,857	2,599	863	5,150	1,389
Total final demand	4,745	10,574	16,069	18,119	20,684	36,115	34,469
Exports	984	1,031	1,067	1,126	1,100	2,666	2,234
Imports	1,352	2,932	5,282	6,090	7,181	14,211	11,194

Economic Aggregates, Top 3 Sectors ($ million)	2000	2007	2010	2013	2016	2019	2020
Value-added at basic price							
Agriculture	1,631	3,029	4,793	5,569	5,884	7,396	7,650
Retail trade	616	1,060	1,671	1,946	2,178	3,957	3,602
Real estate	288	729	875	1,007	1,350	2,626	2,679
Gross output							
Agriculture	2,571	4,234	6,578	7,307	7,753	9,788	10,148
Construction	820	1,398	2,193	2,377	2,590	5,770	5,216
Retail trade	910	1,413	2,239	2,396	2,613	5,032	4,626
Total intermediate inputs							
Construction	368	737	1,145	1,151	1,178	3,338	3,078
Agriculture	914	1,161	1,698	1,626	1,707	2,199	2,320
Food and beverages	590	838	1,015	1,063	1,074	2,184	1,973
Total final demand							
Agriculture	1,496	2,895	4,852	5,704	5,841	6,574	6,623
Construction	594	1,063	1,722	1,979	2,233	4,926	4,407
Retail trade	388	748	1,364	1,630	1,889	3,404	3,314
Exports							
Food and beverages	118	71	66	52	50	529	437
Inland transport	60	90	80	121	105	387	311
Personal services, NEC	106	191	228	250	243	342	269
Imports							
Refined fuels	105	501	740	1,041	1,200	2,278	1,835
Metals	188	333	673	777	804	1,992	1,620
Electricals	127	270	495	608	773	1,667	1,349

Domestic Linkages

Indicator and Top 3 Sectors, 2020	2000	2007	2010	2013	2016	2019	2020
First-round effect							
Personal services, NEC	0.31	0.27	0.25	0.24	0.25	0.65	0.64
Food and beverages	0.71	0.65	0.62	0.63	0.61	0.61	0.64
Hotels and restaurants	0.54	0.52	0.49	0.54	0.61	0.60	0.64
Industrial support effect							
Personal services, NEC	0.20	0.13	0.12	0.10	0.10	0.28	0.29
Transport activities, NEC	0.40	0.27	0.24	0.20	0.20	0.23	0.27
Hotels and restaurants	0.34	0.25	0.21	0.22	0.24	0.23	0.26
Production-induced effect							
Personal services, NEC	0.52	0.40	0.38	0.34	0.36	0.92	0.93
Hotels and restaurants	0.89	0.77	0.70	0.76	0.85	0.83	0.90
Food and beverages	1.13	0.95	0.86	0.85	0.82	0.78	0.85

continued on next page.

continued.

Nepal

South and Central Asia

Domestic Linkages

Indicator and Top 3 Sectors, 2020	2000	2007	2010	2013	2016	2019	2020
Simple value-added multiplier							
Wholesale trade	0.94	0.96	0.96	0.97	0.97	0.96	0.97
Education	0.93	0.93	0.92	0.94	0.95	0.94	0.95
Sale of motor vehicles	0.94	0.95	0.94	0.96	0.96	0.94	0.95
Type I value-added multiplier							
Food and beverages	3.53	3.10	2.92	2.87	2.73	2.98	3.15
Hotels and restaurants	2.15	2.09	2.00	2.25	2.74	2.67	2.91
Personal services, NEC	1.41	1.32	1.30	1.27	1.29	2.84	2.89
Direct backward linkage							
Personal services, NEC	0.31	0.27	0.25	0.24	0.25	0.65	0.64
Food and beverages	0.71	0.65	0.62	0.63	0.61	0.61	0.64
Hotels and restaurants	0.54	0.52	0.49	0.54	0.61	0.60	0.64
Complete hypothetical extraction (backward)							
Personal services, NEC	1.48	1.40	1.37	1.34	1.36	1.92	1.93
Hotels and restaurants	1.82	1.72	1.65	1.70	1.78	1.70	1.81
Transport activities, NEC	1.96	1.76	1.69	1.63	1.61	1.68	1.75
Partial hypothetical extraction (backward)							
Personal services, NEC	0.50	0.40	0.38	0.34	0.36	0.92	0.93
Hotels and restaurants	0.85	0.75	0.68	0.74	0.82	0.77	0.85
Food and beverages	0.98	0.84	0.78	0.76	0.73	0.75	0.79
Total backward linkage							
Personal services, NEC	1.52	1.40	1.38	1.34	1.36	1.92	1.93
Hotels and restaurants	1.89	1.77	1.70	1.76	1.85	1.83	1.90
Food and beverages	2.13	1.95	1.86	1.85	1.82	1.78	1.85
Direct forward linkage							
Minerals, NEC	0.67	0.75	0.75	0.79	0.84	0.72	0.85
Utilities	0.85	0.66	0.73	0.72	0.72	0.79	0.79
Refined fuels	0.86	0.91	0.78	0.74	0.77	0.70	0.73
Complete hypothetical extraction (forward)							
Mining	2.51	2.47	2.32	2.22	2.18	1.97	2.14
Refined fuels	2.61	2.46	2.27	2.16	2.16	2.05	2.12
Utilities	2.36	1.95	2.01	1.97	1.94	2.00	2.00
Partial hypothetical extraction (forward)							
Mining	1.51	1.47	1.32	1.22	1.18	0.97	1.14
Refined fuels	1.61	1.47	1.28	1.16	1.16	1.06	1.12
Utilities	1.39	0.99	1.05	1.01	0.98	1.06	1.07
Total forward linkage							
Minerals, NEC	2.12	2.21	2.16	2.18	2.24	2.00	2.26
Utilities	2.43	2.03	2.09	2.05	2.02	2.13	2.16
Metals	2.17	2.20	1.98	2.32	2.32	1.68	2.15
Normalized backward linkage							
Personal services, NEC	0.91	0.90	0.92	0.92	0.94	1.39	1.34
Hotels and restaurants	1.13	1.14	1.14	1.20	1.29	1.32	1.31
Food and beverages	1.28	1.25	1.24	1.26	1.26	1.29	1.28
Normalized forward linkage							
Minerals, NEC	1.31	1.43	1.44	1.45	1.51	1.43	1.54
Utilities	1.50	1.31	1.39	1.37	1.37	1.53	1.47
Metals	1.34	1.42	1.32	1.54	1.57	1.20	1.46
Net backward linkage							
Personal services, NEC	1.29	1.31	1.29	1.28	1.31	1.81	1.79
Leather	1.90	1.77	1.70	1.64	1.62	1.55	1.61
Hotels and restaurants	1.32	1.31	1.29	1.38	1.48	1.38	1.48
Net forward linkage							
Mining	1.67	1.83	1.72	1.77	1.77	1.58	1.72
Agriculture	1.02	1.04	1.00	1.01	1.03	1.10	1.13
Retail trade	1.20	1.23	1.15	1.18	1.13	1.14	1.11

continued on next page.

continued.

Nepal

South and Central Asia *International Linkages*

Indicator and Top 3 Sectors, 2020	2000	2007	2010	2013	2016	2019	2020
Self-sufficiency ratio							
Personal services, NEC	1.75	1.64	1.36	1.39	1.30	1.89	1.64
Air transport	0.94	0.98	0.98	0.98	0.98	1.33	1.31
Business activities, NEC	1.02	1.00	0.99	1.03	0.99	1.22	1.16
Import-to-input ratio							
Electricals	0.34	0.32	0.35	0.32	0.31	0.54	0.47
Transport equipment	0.27	0.25	0.28	0.26	0.26	0.46	0.41
Metals	0.29	0.29	0.33	0.27	0.26	0.45	0.39
Export-to-output ratio							
Water transport	1.00	1.00	1.00	1.00	1.00	1.00	1.00
Transport equipment	0.03	0.02	0.04	0.31	0.03	0.99	0.90
Textiles	0.59	0.42	0.33	0.31	0.29	0.80	0.82
Domestic inputs share to output							
Personal services, NEC	0.31	0.27	0.25	0.24	0.25	0.65	0.64
Food and beverages	0.71	0.65	0.62	0.63	0.61	0.61	0.64
Hotels and restaurants	0.54	0.52	0.49	0.54	0.61	0.60	0.64
Foreign inputs share to output							
Electricals	0.34	0.32	0.35	0.32	0.31	0.54	0.47
Transport equipment	0.27	0.25	0.28	0.26	0.26	0.46	0.41
Metals	0.29	0.29	0.33	0.27	0.26	0.45	0.39
Backward import multipliers							
Electricals	0.47	0.44	0.47	0.43	0.42	0.60	0.57
Metals	0.45	0.45	0.48	0.42	0.40	0.56	0.54
Transport equipment	0.39	0.38	0.40	0.36	0.34	0.50	0.47
Forward import multipliers							
Textiles	0.17	0.09	0.07	0.07	0.07	0.43	0.45
Transport activities, NEC	0.67	0.54	0.48	0.36	0.33	0.27	0.26
Transport equipment	0.02	0.02	0.01	0.02	0.02	0.04	0.22
Intraregional transfer multiplier							
Personal services, NEC	1.52	1.40	1.38	1.34	1.36	1.92	1.93
Hotels and restaurants	1.89	1.77	1.70	1.76	1.85	1.83	1.90
Food and beverages	2.13	1.95	1.86	1.85	1.82	1.78	1.85
Interregional spillover multiplier							
Electricals	1.66	1.63	1.72	1.65	1.68	2.10	2.01
Transport equipment	1.50	1.47	1.54	1.52	1.54	1.87	1.82
Metals	1.55	1.59	1.69	1.53	1.56	1.79	1.74
Interregional feedback multiplier							
Electricals	1.22	1.22	1.25	1.24	1.19	1.36	1.30
Inland transport	1.14	1.19	1.21	1.29	1.19	1.29	1.29
Metals	1.18	1.19	1.22	1.19	1.15	1.35	1.29
Intraregional effect on gross output ($ million)							
Agriculture	2,450.76	4,149.95	6,509.12	7,254.50	7,674.11	9,487.65	9,823.29
Construction	769.46	1,376.47	2,161.39	2,351.88	2,564.95	5,750.51	5,200.13
Retail trade	793.12	1,320.76	2,146.94	2,334.43	2,521.61	4,905.19	4,529.20
Interregional effect on gross output ($ million)							
Food and beverages	47.80	38.94	30.51	25.34	42.02	485.76	408.69
Agriculture	108.86	73.72	59.67	43.84	69.57	270.74	293.47
Inland transport	69.54	82.31	78.24	97.42	100.53	291.20	227.68
Feedback effect on gross output ($ million)							
Inland transport	10.86	15.57	16.58	19.68	16.23	83.87	62.78
Food and beverages	5.12	5.48	5.09	4.51	6.97	40.23	35.16
Business activities, NEC	3.33	5.15	4.75	9.29	4.13	40.85	33.04
Directly absorbed value-added exports (DAVAX) ($ million)							
Food and beverages	100.61	60.08	53.96	44.32	38.78	364.01	308.20
Personal services, NEC	81.55	142.51	172.21	193.29	192.22	238.19	192.73
Inland transport	38.47	54.69	47.64	67.93	59.89	171.67	139.11
Reflection (REF) ($ million)							
Food and beverages	0.02	0.02	0.02	0.02	0.02	0.73	0.56
Inland transport	0.01	0.02	0.03	0.05	0.05	0.38	0.30
Textiles	0.00	0.00	0.01	0.01	0.01	0.09	0.09

continued on next page.

continued.

Nepal

South and Central Asia *International Linkages*

Indicator and Top 3 Sectors, 2020	2000	2007	2010	2013	2016	2019	2020
Reexports (REX) ($ million)							
Food and beverages	3.78	2.04	1.88	1.55	4.91	66.74	57.59
Inland transport	5.47	8.03	8.68	13.67	10.94	65.44	50.68
Business activities, NEC	1.71	2.61	2.00	8.96	1.90	42.25	35.12
Foreign value added (FVA) ($ million)							
Inland transport	15.66	26.97	24.06	38.97	34.23	149.05	120.48
Textiles	14.35	15.41	16.28	15.53	14.67	102.98	85.33
Food and beverages	13.43	9.12	10.44	6.59	6.00	97.31	70.30
Pure double-counting (PDC) ($ million)							
Inland transport	0.00	0.00	0.00	0.00	0.00	0.03	0.03
Textiles	0.00	0.00	0.00	0.00	0.00	0.02	0.02
Food and beverages	0.00	0.00	0.00	0.00	0.00	0.03	0.02
Trade-based GVC participation rate							
Electricals	0.51	0.49	0.48	0.45	0.44	0.69	0.64
Construction	0.33	0.33	0.39	0.35	0.37	0.65	0.64
Refined fuels	0.42	0.44	0.50	0.37	0.35	0.81	0.61
Production-based GVC participation rate							
Textiles	0.17	0.09	0.07	0.07	0.07	0.43	0.45
Transport activities, NEC	0.67	0.54	0.48	0.36	0.33	0.27	0.26
Transport equipment	0.02	0.02	0.01	0.02	0.02	0.04	0.22
Trade-based backward GVC participation rate							
Electricals	0.47	0.44	0.47	0.43	0.42	0.60	0.57
Metals	0.45	0.45	0.48	0.42	0.40	0.56	0.54
Transport equipment	0.39	0.38	0.40	0.36	0.34	0.50	0.47
Trade-based forward GVC participation rate							
Wholesale trade	0.26	0.33	0.33	0.34	0.34	0.33	0.32
Transport activities, NEC	0.18	0.20	0.19	0.17	0.12	0.30	0.29
Sale of motor vehicles	0.28	0.33	0.32	0.34	0.35	0.26	0.25
Traditional revealed comparative advantage							
Inland transport	3.42	4.71	3.87	5.77	5.03	10.52	11.29
Telecommunications	3.81	5.27	5.27	4.59	5.02	10.98	10.86
Personal services, NEC	8.39	16.13	18.69	19.76	17.16	8.76	9.37
New revealed comparative advantage							
Air transport	0.75	0.94	0.95	1.09	0.96	12.41	13.53
Education	0.68	0.88	1.02	3.90	0.89	5.08	5.51
Inland transport	2.10	2.85	2.71	3.39	3.07	4.58	4.21
Backward production length							
Metals	3.07	3.05	2.96	2.94	2.81	2.85	3.00
Electricals	2.96	2.93	2.88	2.87	2.76	2.90	2.99
Manufacturing, NEC	2.82	2.74	2.68	2.66	2.57	2.65	2.77
Forward production length							
Transport activities, NEC	2.78	2.68	2.51	2.31	2.20	2.34	2.31
Refined fuels	2.88	2.62	2.38	2.28	2.27	2.21	2.29
Minerals, NEC	2.66	2.45	2.28	2.36	2.31	2.01	2.29
Backward production length of GVC segment							
Real estate	5.02	5.11	5.00	5.15	5.15	4.80	4.96
Wholesale trade	4.49	4.58	4.54	4.41	4.16	4.43	4.79
Sale of motor vehicles	4.46	4.49	4.42	4.47	4.41	4.47	4.69
Forward production length of GVC segment							
Construction	3.57	4.13	3.90	3.78	3.60	5.12	5.22
Mining	4.50	4.49	4.62	4.66	4.51	5.18	5.05
Wood	4.08	4.21	4.35	4.02	4.17	4.46	4.70
Backward agglomeration index							
Rubber and plastics	-	1.23	1.27	1.56	1.54	2.71	2.46
Leather	-	1.89	1.63	1.65	1.55	1.63	1.82
Electricals	-	1.90	1.86	2.02	1.83	1.42	1.54
Forward agglomeration index							
Mining	-	2.23	2.16	2.19	1.98	2.53	2.35
Electricals	-	2.82	2.62	2.50	2.28	2.30	2.20
Manufacturing, NEC	-	1.41	1.54	1.60	1.62	2.25	2.14

CIF = cost, insurance, and freight; FOB = free on board; GVC = global value chain; NEC = not elsewhere classified; NPISHs = nonprofit institutions serving households.
Source: Calculations using the Asian Development Bank Multiregional Input-Output Table. https://mrio.adbx.online/ (accessed July 2021).

continued on next page.

continued.

Nepal

South and Central Asia

The four select sectors are chosen based on their gross outputs in the economy as of 2019.

Economy Ranking out of 25 Economies

	2020	2010	2000
Value-Added at Basic Prices (*$ million*)	17	17	18
Average Output Multiplier	19	15	9
Trade Openness	18	21	20
Trade-Based GVC Participation	13	23	21

Share of Intermediate Consumption and Gross Value-Added in Output

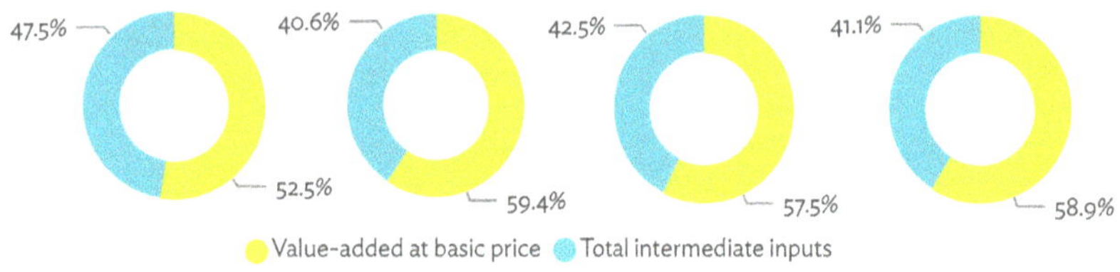

Imports and Exports, 2019-2020

($ million)

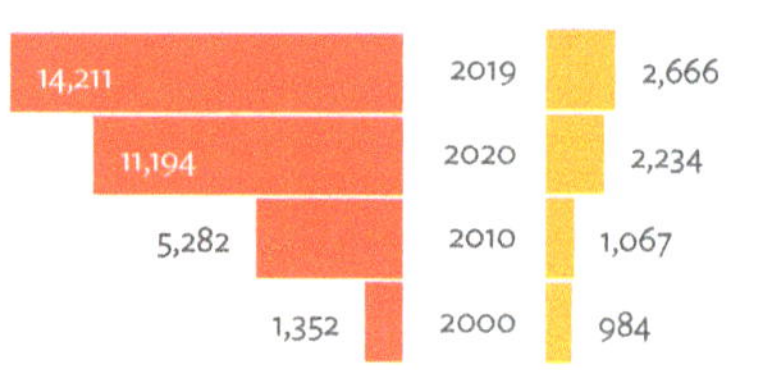

Domestic Linkages

Normalized Linkages

Net Linkages

Value-Added Multipliers

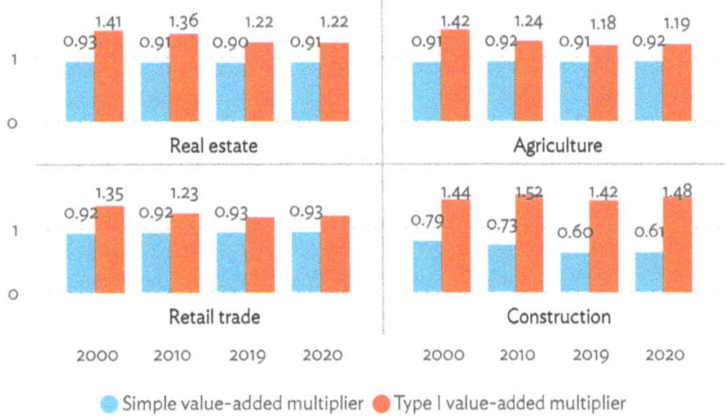

Production-Induced Effect

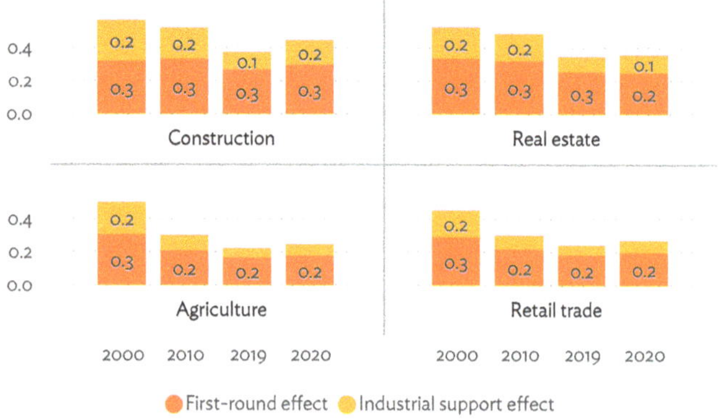

continued on next page.

Click here for figure data

continued.

Nepal

South and Central Asia

International Linkages

Change in Exports, by Value-Added Components, 2019-2020

($ million)

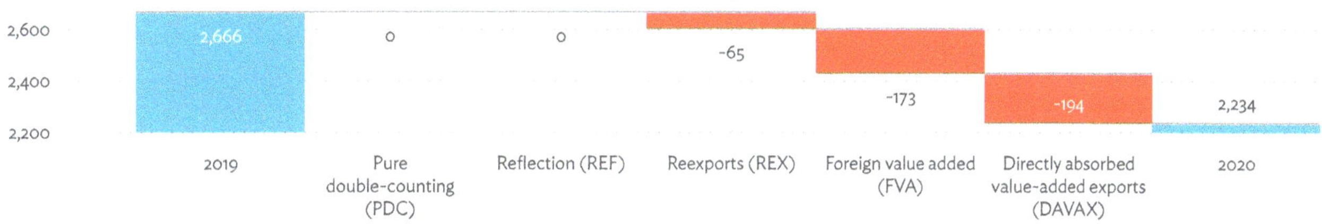

Import Multipliers

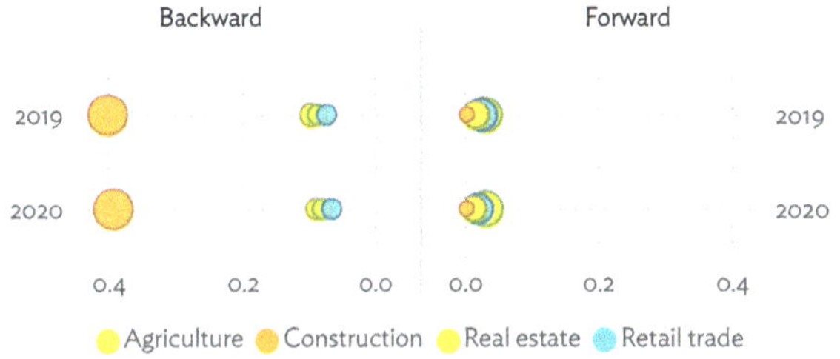

GVC Participation Rates

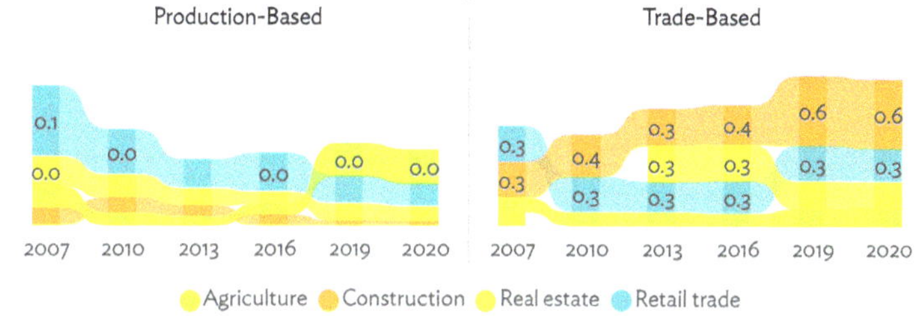

Average Production Length

New Revealed Comparative Advantage

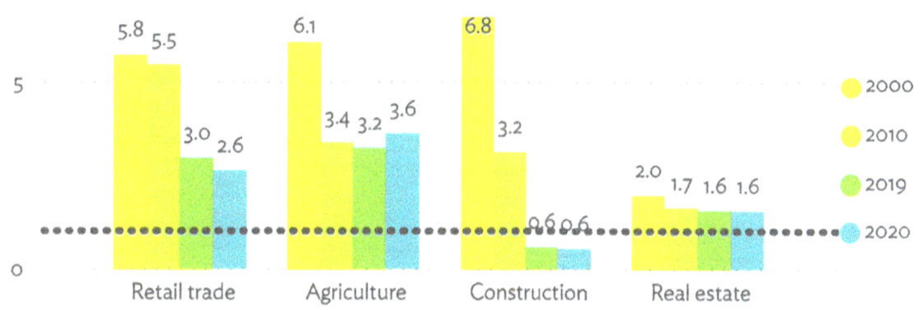

Trade Orientation

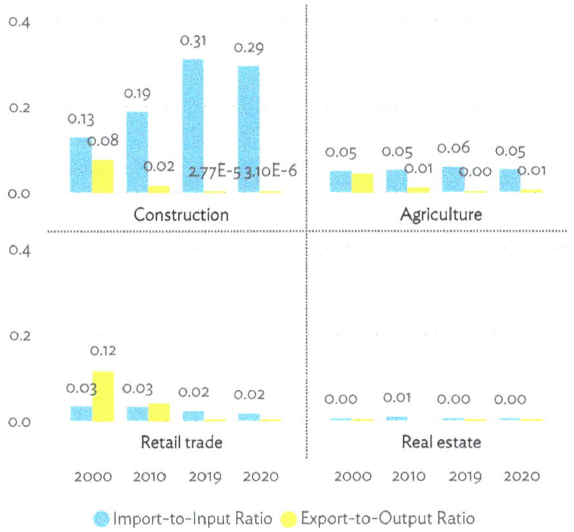

Agglomeration Indices

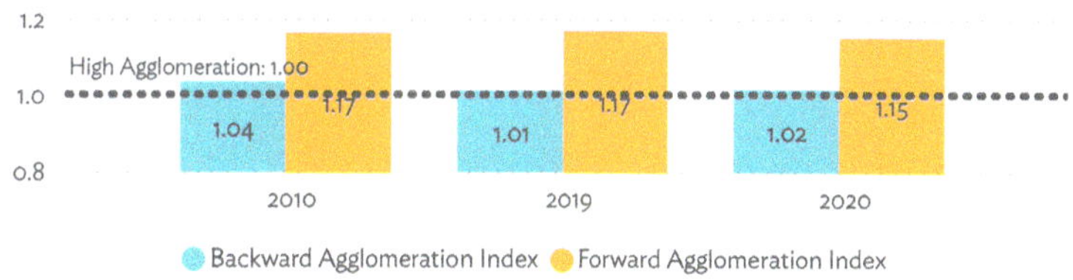

Domestic Transfer Effects and International Spillover Effects

($ million)

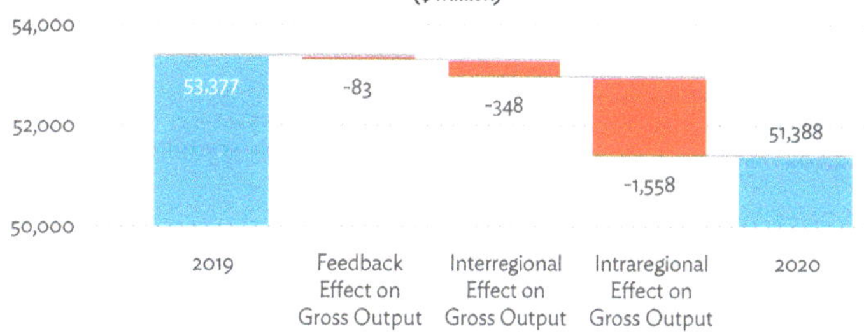

GVC = global value chain; NEC = not elsewhere classified.

Source: Calculations using the Asian Development Bank Multiregional Input-Output Table. https://mrio.adbx.online/ (accessed July 2021).

Click here for figure data

Pakistan

South and Central Asia

Basic Economic Indicators

Economic Aggregates ($ million)	2000	2007	2010	2013	2016	2019	2020
Value-added at basic price	66,396	143,826	167,249	211,587	262,877	238,498	240,230
Gross output	132,904	268,224	311,415	397,278	489,334	436,051	436,997
Total intermediate inputs	63,993	120,158	140,457	181,255	217,996	189,890	187,916
Taxes less subsidies on products	2,515	4,240	3,709	4,436	8,460	7,664	8,851
International transport margins	0	0	0	0	0	0	0
CIF/FOB adjustment	0	0	0	0	0	0	0
Direct purchases abroad by residents	0	0	0	0	0	0	0
Purchases by nonresidents on the domestic territory	0	0	0	0	0	0	0
Household final consumption expenditure	49,552	108,204	128,061	163,768	205,511	195,779	189,594
Final consumption expenditure by NPISHs	0	0	0	0	0	0	0
Government final consumption expenditure	5,921	14,344	17,250	23,254	30,227	28,292	32,620
Gross fixed capital formation	9,412	21,241	19,576	22,721	29,744	25,075	25,598
Changes in inventories	772	1,961	2,289	2,877	3,641	3,340	3,406
Total final demand	65,657	145,750	167,175	212,620	269,124	252,487	251,217
Exports	8,647	17,741	21,099	26,054	25,510	25,610	24,694
Imports	9,925	28,378	31,857	41,673	45,076	51,425	42,884

Economic Aggregates, Top 3 Sectors ($ million)	2000	2007	2010	2013	2016	2019	2020
Gross output							
Agriculture	23,961	46,495	56,809	73,412	90,400	77,877	81,685
Inland transport	11,662	28,029	33,657	36,218	46,685	40,303	36,705
Food and beverages	9,847	20,994	23,690	31,015	34,907	32,130	35,236
Total intermediate inputs							
Food and beverages	7,511	16,083	18,175	23,805	26,680	24,562	26,863
Utilities	13,455	10,605	14,769	21,240	28,983	19,870	23,619
Agriculture	6,676	13,216	16,080	20,796	25,415	21,898	22,910
Total final demand							
Food and beverages	8,075	16,691	19,000	25,059	28,888	27,224	30,227
Inland transport	7,169	22,974	25,903	27,794	35,230	31,744	28,492
Agriculture	8,095	14,162	16,927	21,846	28,535	25,515	26,785
Exports							
Textiles	3,009	8,775	9,915	12,400	11,051	14,020	14,116
Food and beverages	768	1,945	2,355	2,948	2,658	2,202	1,907
Metals	35	81	107	142	186	940	1,075
Imports							
Metals	227	4,935	5,504	7,215	7,253	8,559	7,123
Chemicals	411	3,784	4,358	5,527	6,392	7,625	6,729
Refined fuels	429	2,573	3,965	5,476	5,065	6,055	5,145
Value-added at basic price							
Agriculture	17,216	33,164	40,628	52,495	64,754	55,784	58,511
Retail trade	6,129	14,976	17,528	22,733	28,111	24,061	22,875
Business activities, NEC	1,655	6,821	8,010	10,814	15,146	17,009	18,314

Domestic Linkages

Indicator and Top 3 Sectors, 2020	2000	2007	2010	2013	2016	2019	2020
First-round effect							
Food and beverages	0.74	0.73	0.73	0.74	0.74	0.72	0.72
Utilities	0.78	0.65	0.69	0.70	0.74	0.68	0.70
Textiles	0.69	0.69	0.69	0.69	0.69	0.67	0.68
Industrial support effect							
Utilities	1.15	0.45	0.58	0.67	0.85	0.52	0.59
Hotels and restaurants	0.43	0.40	0.37	0.39	0.42	0.31	0.33
Textiles	0.39	0.31	0.34	0.35	0.37	0.29	0.30
Production-induced effect							
Utilities	1.93	1.10	1.26	1.37	1.59	1.20	1.28
Food and beverages	1.04	1.02	1.02	1.03	1.03	0.98	0.99
Textiles	1.08	1.00	1.03	1.03	1.06	0.96	0.98

continued on next page.

continued.

Pakistan

South and Central Asia | *Domestic Linkages*

Indicator and Top 3 Sectors, 2020	2000	2007	2010	2013	2016	2019	2020
Simple value-added multiplier							
Real estate	1.00	1.00	1.00	1.00	1.00	1.00	1.00
Business activities, NEC	0.98	0.98	0.98	0.98	0.99	0.98	0.98
Mining	0.99	0.98	0.98	0.98	0.98	0.98	0.98
Type I value-added multiplier							
Utilities	5.16	4.94	4.94	4.87	5.06	4.59	4.71
Food and beverages	4.01	3.99	4.02	4.03	4.01	3.89	3.90
Textiles	3.36	3.30	3.29	3.29	3.35	3.24	3.29
Direct backward linkage							
Food and beverages	0.74	0.73	0.73	0.74	0.74	0.72	0.72
Utilities	0.78	0.65	0.69	0.70	0.74	0.68	0.70
Textiles	0.69	0.69	0.69	0.69	0.69	0.67	0.68
Complete hypothetical extraction (backward)							
Food and beverages	1.97	1.95	1.96	1.96	1.97	1.93	1.93
Hotels and restaurants	2.03	2.00	1.97	1.99	2.02	1.90	1.93
Textiles	1.97	1.92	1.93	1.93	1.96	1.89	1.92
Partial hypothetical extraction (backward)							
Food and beverages	1.01	0.98	0.99	0.99	1.00	0.95	0.96
Textiles	1.02	0.96	0.98	0.98	1.01	0.93	0.95
Hotels and restaurants	1.04	1.01	0.98	1.00	1.03	0.91	0.93
Total backward linkage							
Utilities	2.93	2.10	2.26	2.37	2.59	2.20	2.28
Food and beverages	2.04	2.02	2.02	2.03	2.03	1.98	1.99
Textiles	2.08	2.00	2.03	2.03	2.06	1.96	1.98
Direct forward linkage							
Transport activities, NEC	0.95	0.95	0.96	0.95	0.94	0.89	0.89
Mining	0.94	0.85	0.78	0.82	0.85	0.86	0.87
Wood	0.80	0.82	0.82	0.85	0.84	0.83	0.82
Complete hypothetical extraction (forward)							
Mining	3.07	2.54	2.45	2.61	2.80	2.52	2.57
Wood	2.24	2.23	2.23	2.25	2.23	2.16	2.17
Transport activities, NEC	2.28	2.06	2.11	2.13	2.13	2.00	2.03
Partial hypothetical extraction (forward)							
Mining	2.07	1.54	1.45	1.61	1.81	1.52	1.58
Wood	1.29	1.29	1.29	1.30	1.28	1.20	1.20
Transport activities, NEC	1.45	1.22	1.28	1.30	1.30	1.17	1.20
Total forward linkage							
Mining	3.09	2.56	2.47	2.63	2.82	2.53	2.59
Transport activities, NEC	2.74	2.46	2.55	2.56	2.57	2.41	2.44
Wood	2.37	2.36	2.36	2.38	2.35	2.27	2.24
Normalized backward linkage							
Utilities							
Food and beverages							
Textiles							
Normalized forward linkage							
Mining							
Transport activities, NEC							
Wood							
Net backward linkage							
Hotels and restaurants							
Food and beverages							
Leather							
Net forward linkage							
Mining							
Transport activities, NEC							
Real estate							

continued on next page.

continued.

Pakistan

South and Central Asia *International Linkages*

Indicator and Top 3 Sectors, 2020	2000	2007	2010	2013	2016	2019	2020
Self-sufficiency ratio							
Leather	1.21	1.24	1.32	1.29	1.20	2.46	2.23
Textiles	1.35	1.63	1.66	1.61	1.41	1.76	2.00
Health and social work	1.04	1.18	1.11	1.11	1.08	1.20	1.16
Import-to-input ratio							
Transport equipment	0.20	0.27	0.27	0.27	0.23	0.36	0.31
Electricals	0.17	0.22	0.22	0.22	0.19	0.30	0.25
Refined fuels	0.15	0.20	0.21	0.22	0.16	0.27	0.21
Export-to-output ratio							
Water transport	0.40	0.03	0.04	0.04	0.04	0.89	0.69
Leather	0.23	0.26	0.30	0.29	0.23	0.66	0.61
Textiles	0.31	0.44	0.44	0.42	0.33	0.47	0.53
Domestic inputs share to output							
Food and beverages	0.74	0.73	0.73	0.74	0.74	0.72	0.72
Utilities	0.78	0.65	0.69	0.70	0.74	0.68	0.70
Textiles	0.69	0.69	0.69	0.69	0.69	0.67	0.68
Foreign inputs share to output							
Transport equipment	0.20	0.27	0.27	0.27	0.23	0.36	0.31
Electricals	0.17	0.22	0.22	0.22	0.19	0.30	0.25
Refined fuels	0.15	0.20	0.21	0.22	0.16	0.27	0.21
Backward import multipliers							
Transport equipment	0.27	0.36	0.37	0.37	0.30	0.44	0.37
Electricals	0.22	0.30	0.30	0.31	0.25	0.37	0.31
Utilities	0.16	0.31	0.28	0.28	0.22	0.29	0.27
Forward import multipliers							
Water transport	0.35	0.03	0.04	0.04	0.04	0.70	0.53
Leather	0.15	0.17	0.21	0.20	0.16	0.49	0.44
Metals	0.02	0.03	0.04	0.04	0.04	0.21	0.30
Intraregional transfer multiplier							
Utilities	2.93	2.10	2.26	2.37	2.59	2.20	2.28
Food and beverages	2.04	2.02	2.02	2.03	2.03	1.98	1.99
Textiles	2.08	2.00	2.03	2.03	2.06	1.96	1.98
Interregional spillover multiplier							
Transport equipment	1.37	1.55	1.56	1.59	1.51	1.83	1.71
Electricals	1.29	1.45	1.46	1.49	1.42	1.68	1.59
Refined fuels	1.22	1.35	1.37	1.38	1.32	1.59	1.50
Interregional feedback multiplier							
Transport equipment	1.12	1.16	1.17	1.18	1.13	1.17	1.15
Electricals	1.07	1.13	1.14	1.13	1.10	1.14	1.12
Rubber and plastics	1.05	1.09	1.08	1.09	1.07	1.11	1.09
Intraregional effect on gross output ($ million)							
Agriculture	22,438.64	42,316.17	51,704.50	67,007.12	84,086.99	74,700.44	78,398.68
Inland transport	10,837.49	27,337.60	32,591.11	35,115.65	45,380.26	39,794.10	36,233.12
Food and beverages	9,371.65	19,853.83	22,324.07	29,328.06	33,401.21	30,906.58	34,202.35
Interregional effect on gross output ($ million)							
Textiles	1,321.18	3,795.76	4,627.13	5,845.51	4,966.17	2,744.56	3,074.68
Agriculture	1,296.06	3,516.10	4,317.86	5,360.32	5,314.86	2,587.53	2,767.51
Food and beverages	400.31	976.50	1,163.50	1,424.77	1,263.82	1,025.19	867.34
Feedback effect on gross output ($ million)							
Textiles	241.83	776.08	887.61	1,196.86	998.43	683.31	577.17
Agriculture	226.50	663.08	787.04	1,044.19	997.75	589.13	518.34
Business activities, NEC	39.42	68.10	78.58	111.86	134.30	218.72	192.32
Directly absorbed value-added exports (DAVAX) ($ million)							
Textiles	2,162.57	6,057.23	6,798.22	8,419.25	7,941.67	11,062.65	11,376.71
Food and beverages	604.22	1,528.97	1,845.99	2,324.61	2,119.30	1,657.94	1,446.68
Business activities, NEC	94.78	86.47	116.75	174.34	236.92	798.97	697.02
Reflection (REF) ($ million)							
Textiles	1.26	5.62	5.85	8.33	9.72	1.94	1.99
Metals	0.01	0.03	0.04	0.04	0.09	0.87	0.94
Mining	0.03	0.07	0.09	0.12	0.23	0.66	0.74

continued on next page.

continued.

Pakistan

South and Central Asia

International Linkages

Indicator and Top 3 Sectors, 2020	2000	2007	2010	2013	2016	2019	2020
Reexports (REX) ($ million)							
Textiles	674.71	1,996.83	2,298.60	2,950.99	2,335.25	1,568.12	1,494.45
Food and beverages	126.54	286.73	358.60	432.88	392.94	360.87	321.86
Business activities, NEC	40.42	69.75	72.52	106.41	130.35	266.07	226.40
Foreign value added (FVA) ($ million)							
Textiles	170.76	714.68	811.88	1,020.88	764.04	1,387.26	1,242.41
Metals	5.31	16.91	22.39	30.20	31.80	233.17	222.97
Food and beverages	36.62	128.09	149.01	188.06	143.27	181.99	137.47
Pure double-counting (PDC) ($ million)							
Textiles	0.07	0.26	0.26	0.35	0.28	0.18	0.17
Metals	0.00	0.00	0.01	0.01	0.01	0.03	0.03
Transport equipment	0.00	0.01	0.02	0.03	0.02	0.03	0.02
Trade-based GVC participation rate							
Water transport	0.40	0.34	0.41	0.41	0.42	0.52	0.48
Chemicals	0.40	0.42	0.41	0.42	0.40	0.49	0.43
Metals	0.31	0.39	0.34	0.33	0.36	0.44	0.42
Production-based GVC participation rate							
Water transport	0.35	0.03	0.04	0.04	0.04	0.70	0.53
Leather	0.15	0.17	0.21	0.20	0.16	0.49	0.44
Metals	0.02	0.03	0.04	0.04	0.04	0.21	0.30
Trade-based backward GVC participation rate							
Transport equipment	0.27	0.36	0.37	0.37	0.30	0.44	0.37
Electricals	0.22	0.30	0.30	0.31	0.25	0.37	0.31
Utilities	0.16	0.31	0.28	0.28	0.22	0.29	0.27
Trade-based forward GVC participation rate							
Transport activities, NEC	0.37	0.36	0.36	0.37	0.16	0.38	0.36
Water transport	0.31	0.22	0.29	0.28	0.32	0.36	0.35
Leather	0.29	0.30	0.30	0.29	0.30	0.36	0.34
Traditional revealed comparative advantage							
Textiles	7.71	14.23	14.73	14.45	13.09	17.87	16.72
Health and social work	6.37	15.00	7.11	7.05	6.54	10.92	10.63
Education	5.92	14.05	7.51	7.24	7.37	8.47	8.09
New revealed comparative advantage							
Textiles	4.36	8.08	8.64	8.24	7.08	10.57	10.19
Agriculture	7.23	8.88	8.31	7.66	7.54	7.01	6.35
Health and social work	3.43	5.73	3.74	3.91	3.78	5.93	5.58
Backward production length							
Utilities	3.26	2.84	2.96	3.10	3.17	2.96	3.04
Transport equipment	2.41	2.70	2.77	2.83	2.62	2.72	2.56
Rubber and plastics	2.25	2.43	2.44	2.48	2.38	2.51	2.45
Forward production length							
Mining	3.20	2.64	2.56	2.73	2.94	2.77	2.84
Transport activities, NEC	2.90	2.56	2.66	2.69	2.67	2.60	2.62
Water transport	2.21	1.26	1.36	1.43	1.49	2.89	2.57
Backward production length of GVC segment							
Hotels and restaurants	4.13	4.43	4.48	4.65	4.65	4.40	4.56
Utilities	4.57	3.86	4.13	4.41	4.64	4.30	4.54
Leather	4.08	4.40	4.39	4.58	4.50	4.41	4.48
Forward production length of GVC segment							
Utilities	5.31	4.57	4.75	5.11	5.22	4.76	4.89
Refined fuels	4.18	4.05	4.17	4.31	4.25	4.70	4.73
Real estate	4.29	4.41	4.46	4.62	4.56	4.58	4.65
Backward agglomeration index							
Rubber and plastics	-	1.66	1.74	1.98	2.04	3.22	2.96
Manufacturing, NEC	-	1.66	1.60	1.78	1.86	2.36	2.17
Electricals	-	2.33	2.34	2.41	2.29	1.85	2.04
Forward agglomeration index							
Manufacturing, NEC	-	1.48	1.47	1.59	1.63	2.17	2.12
Mining	-	2.29	2.12	2.17	1.90	2.25	2.08
Electricals	-	2.75	2.48	2.41	2.20	2.01	1.90

CIF = cost, insurance, and freight; FOB = free on board; GVC = global value chain; NEC = not elsewhere classified; NPISHs = nonprofit institutions serving households.
Source: Calculations using the Asian Development Bank Multiregional Input-Output Table. https://mrio.adbx.online/ (accessed July 2021).

continued on next page.

continued.

Pakistan

South and Central Asia

The four select sectors are chosen based on their gross outputs in the economy as of 2019.

Economy Ranking out of 25 Economies

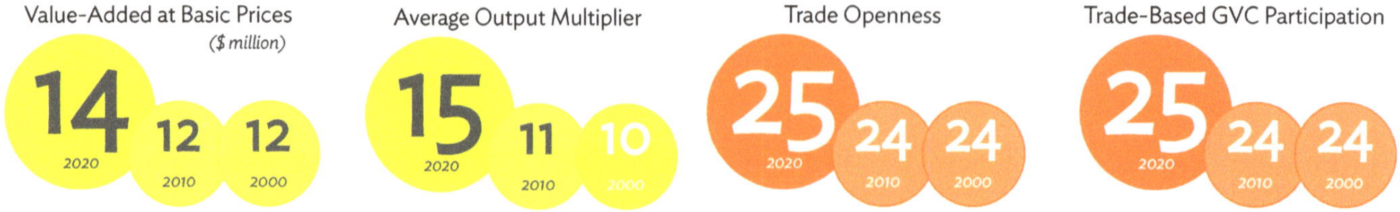

Share of Intermediate Consumption and Gross Value-Added in Output

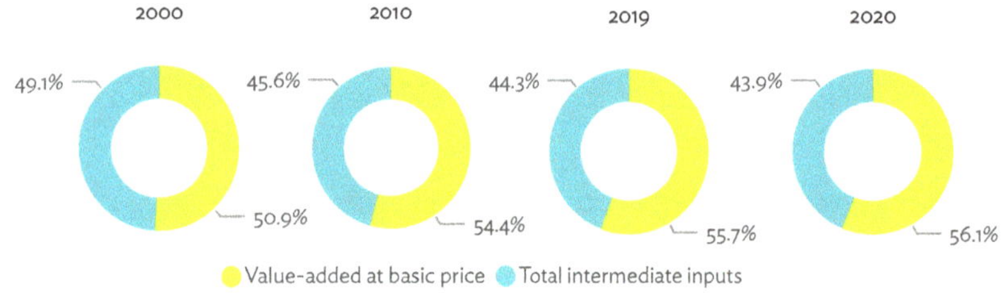

Imports and Exports, 2019-2020

($ million)

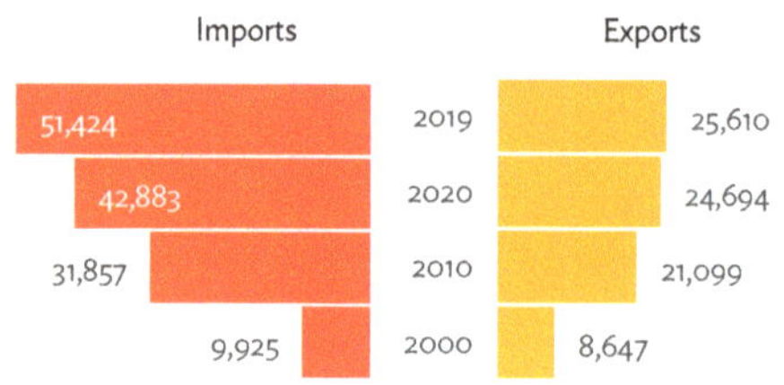

Domestic Linkages

Normalized Linkages

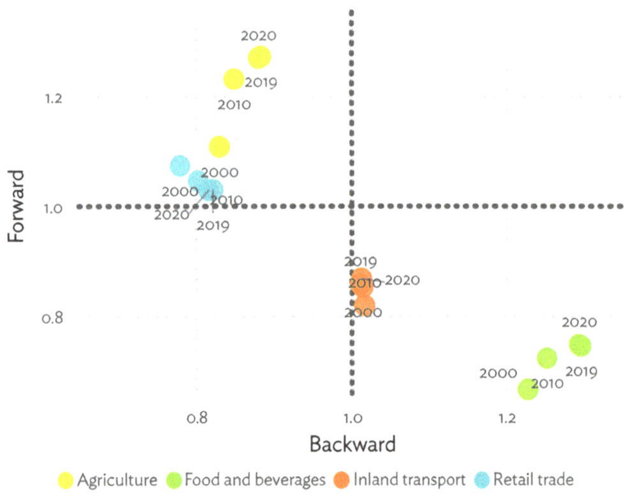

Net Linkages

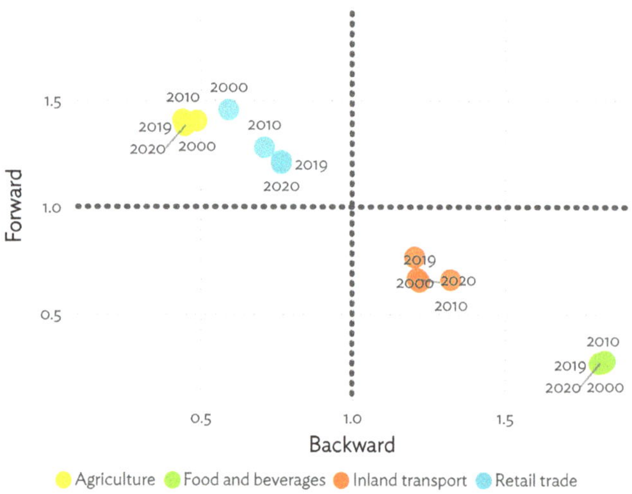

Value-Added Multipliers

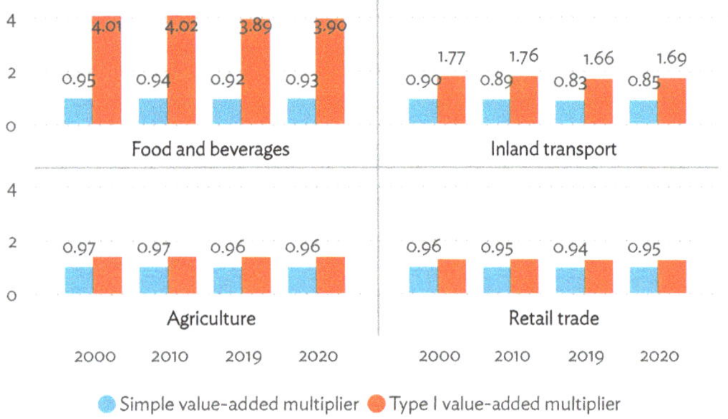

Production-Induced Effect

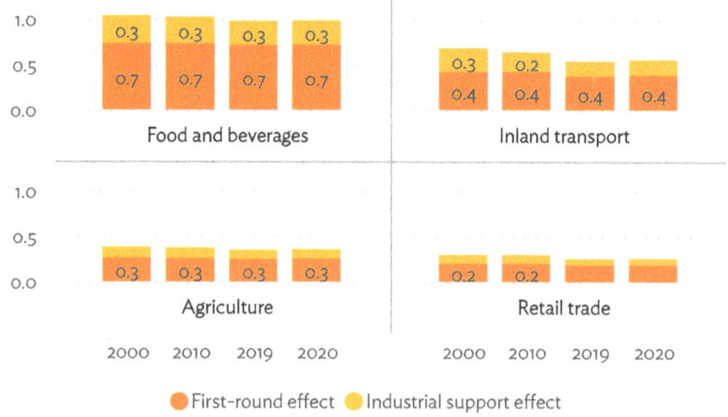

continued on next page.

Click here for figure data

continued.

Pakistan

South and Central Asia

International Linkages

Change in Exports, by Value-Added Components, 2019-2020

($ million)

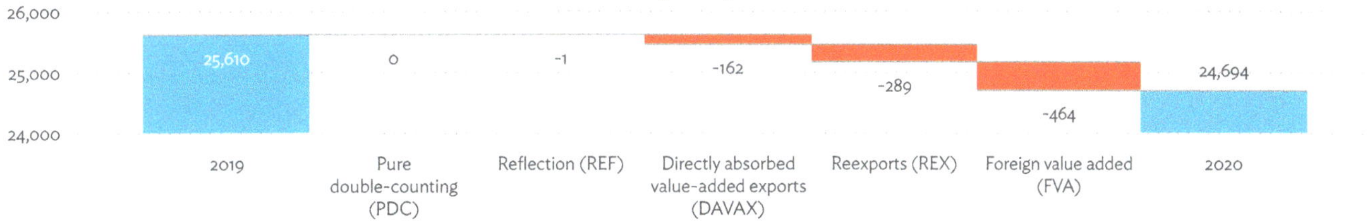

Import Multipliers

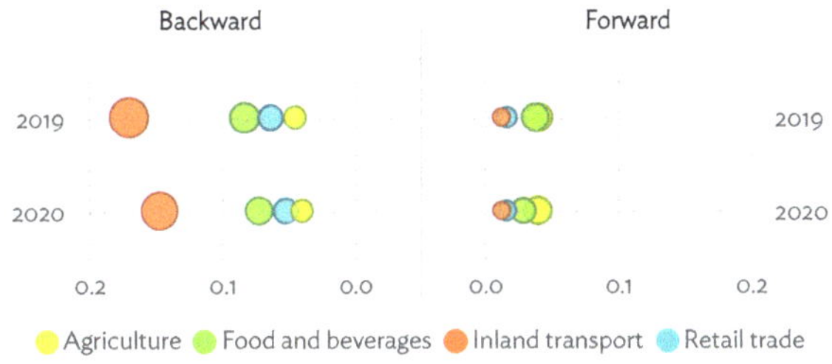

GVC Participation Rates

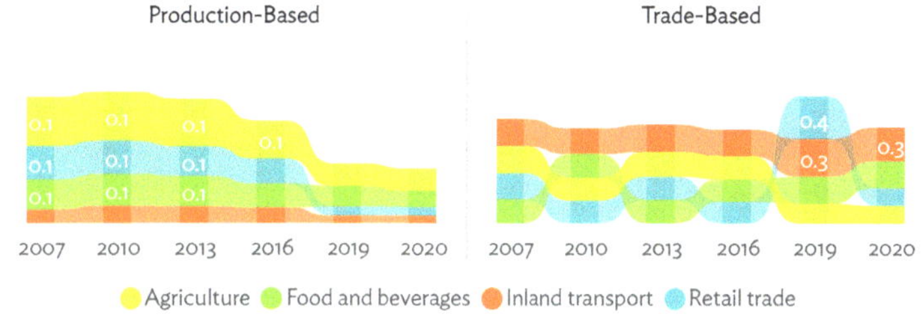

Average Production Length

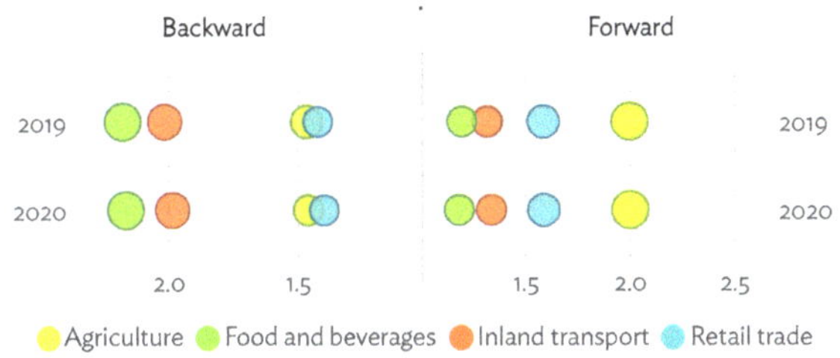

New Revealed Comparative Advantage

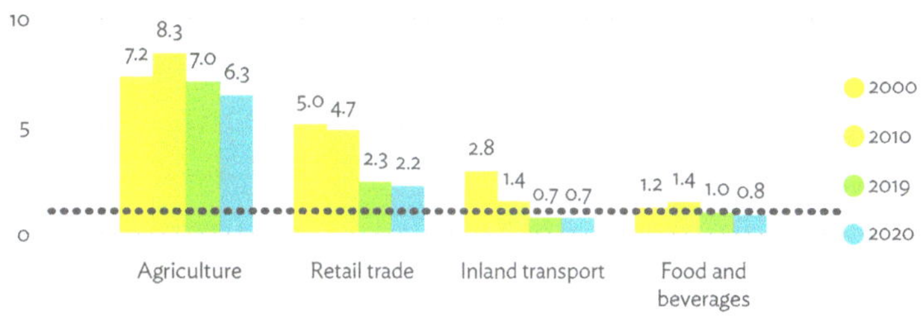

Trade Orientation

Agglomeration Indices

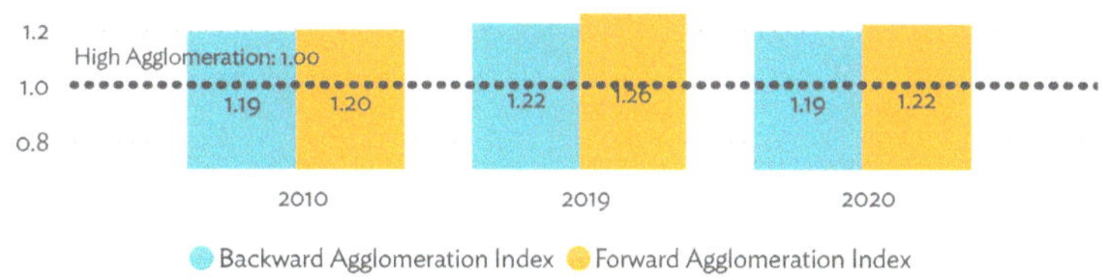

Domestic Transfer Effects and International Spillover Effects

($ million)

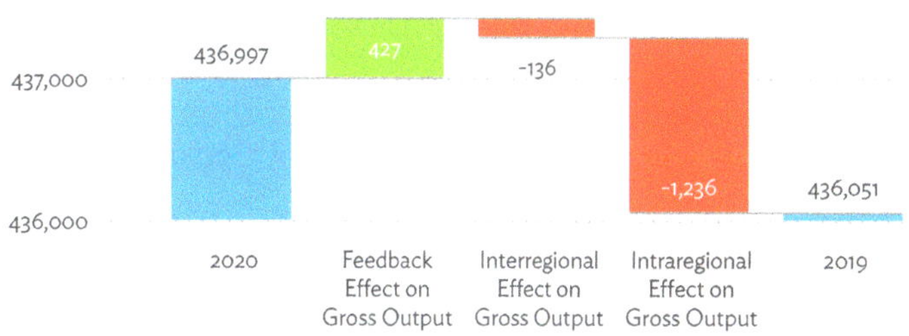

GVC = global value chain; NEC = not elsewhere classified.

Source: Calculations using the Asian Development Bank Multiregional Input-Output Table. https://mrio.adbx.online/ (accessed July 2021).

Click here for figure data

Philippines

Southeast Asia and the Pacific

Basic Economic Indicators

Economic Aggregates ($ million)	2000	2007	2010	2013	2016	2019	2020
Value-added at basic price	91,916	149,360	199,591	271,836	304,889	359,773	345,133
Gross output	170,188	301,496	397,306	529,886	592,060	694,378	647,899
Total intermediate inputs	78,272	152,136	197,716	258,050	287,170	334,605	302,767
Taxes less subsidies on products	0	0	0	0	0	0	0
International transport margins	0	0	0	0	0	0	0
CIF/FOB adjustment	0	0	0	0	0	0	0
Direct purchases abroad by residents	0	0	0	0	0	0	0
Purchases by nonresidents on the domestic territory	0	0	0	0	0	0	0
Household final consumption expenditure	56,244	95,888	129,790	181,257	201,848	235,184	239,302
Final consumption expenditure by NPISHs	2,960	0	0	0	0	0	0
Government final consumption expenditure	9,919	13,030	18,351	27,969	31,462	41,079	48,838
Gross fixed capital formation	11,212	22,412	35,133	47,564	60,495	74,750	55,483
Changes in inventories	1,160	-6,118	-2,065	-1,051	-2,100	-4,931	-13,999
Total final demand	81,495	125,213	181,208	255,740	291,705	346,083	329,624
Exports	26,395	64,540	52,542	57,568	65,588	82,158	69,913
Imports	25,625	64,687	56,161	69,012	90,052	121,939	95,456

Economic Aggregates, Top 3 Sectors ($ million)	2000	2007	2010	2013	2016	2019	2020
Value-added at basic price							
Retail trade	8,156	18,605	26,603	37,472	43,199	52,221	52,202
Finance	4,460	9,744	13,798	20,509	24,456	31,730	35,725
Business activities, NEC	2,223	12,501	17,739	25,053	32,783	35,030	34,222
Gross output							
Food and beverages	20,311	43,929	61,168	85,458	96,104	103,541	103,224
Retail trade	12,280	26,282	38,515	54,147	62,661	75,770	75,741
Business activities, NEC	3,964	20,098	28,520	40,205	52,482	56,097	54,803
Total intermediate inputs							
Food and beverages	13,811	29,613	41,234	57,601	65,001	70,051	69,837
Electricals	7,530	23,385	28,868	29,223	28,132	33,405	27,831
Retail trade	4,123	7,676	11,913	16,676	19,463	23,548	23,540
Total final demand							
Food and beverages	12,309	23,974	34,200	48,553	52,218	62,642	64,714
Construction	6,012	13,138	21,751	29,644	38,077	51,697	41,233
Retail trade	7,245	10,978	16,960	22,199	26,113	35,632	36,632
Exports							
Electricals	9,756	23,911	15,773	15,400	14,307	25,891	22,364
Business activities, NEC	401	8,464	10,815	12,863	16,716	19,973	15,595
Hotels and restaurants	1,611	2,520	3,412	4,401	5,204	4,848	3,884
Imports							
Electricals	3,677	19,795	12,168	13,975	19,904	22,845	20,283
Refined fuels	711	3,444	3,859	8,129	11,477	16,395	13,496
Food and beverages	1,750	4,132	4,705	7,003	8,436	12,835	9,764

Domestic Linkages

Indicator and Top 3 Sectors, 2020	2000	2007	2010	2013	2016	2019	2020
First-round effect							
Paper	0.50	0.58	0.58	0.66	0.66	0.65	0.66
Wood	0.51	0.57	0.60	0.63	0.63	0.63	0.64
Food and beverages	0.62	0.62	0.63	0.63	0.63	0.62	0.63
Industrial support effect							
Hotels and restaurants	0.46	0.45	0.51	0.53	0.54	0.53	0.53
Paper	0.36	0.32	0.36	0.50	0.52	0.50	0.47
Food and beverages	0.32	0.36	0.40	0.43	0.44	0.44	0.43
Production-induced effect							
Paper	0.86	0.90	0.95	1.16	1.18	1.15	1.13
Hotels and restaurants	1.04	1.02	1.09	1.10	1.11	1.10	1.10
Food and beverages	0.94	0.98	1.03	1.06	1.07	1.06	1.05

continued on next page.

continued.

Philippines

Southeast Asia and the Pacific

Domestic Linkages

Indicator and Top 3 Sectors, 2020	2000	2007	2010	2013	2016	2019	2020
Simple value-added multiplier							
Real estate	0.97	0.96	0.96	0.97	0.97	0.96	0.97
Public administration	0.92	0.95	0.96	0.96	0.96	0.95	0.96
Finance	0.90	0.94	0.95	0.96	0.95	0.95	0.96
Type I value-added multiplier							
Transport equipment	2.19	3.09	3.40	3.39	3.29	3.23	3.34
Paper	2.05	2.93	2.98	3.28	3.24	3.17	3.16
Wood	2.03	2.62	2.72	2.87	2.90	2.85	2.86
Direct backward linkage							
Paper	0.50	0.58	0.58	0.66	0.66	0.65	0.66
Wood	0.51	0.57	0.60	0.63	0.63	0.63	0.64
Food and beverages	0.62	0.62	0.63	0.63	0.63	0.62	0.63
Complete hypothetical extraction (backward)							
Hotels and restaurants	2.04	1.98	2.04	2.05	2.05	2.03	2.04
Wood	1.47	1.82	1.87	1.97	1.98	1.97	1.96
Manufacturing, NEC	1.57	1.45	1.70	1.96	1.94	1.91	1.91
Partial hypothetical extraction (backward)							
Hotels and restaurants	1.04	1.00	1.06	1.08	1.08	1.06	1.07
Wood	0.68	0.83	0.89	0.99	0.99	0.98	0.96
Paper	0.60	0.79	0.83	0.99	0.98	0.97	0.94
Total backward linkage							
Paper	1.86	1.90	1.95	2.16	2.18	2.15	2.13
Hotels and restaurants	2.04	2.02	2.09	2.10	2.11	2.10	2.10
Food and beverages	1.94	1.98	2.03	2.06	2.07	2.06	2.05
Direct forward linkage							
Refined fuels	0.77	0.75	0.82	0.80	0.79	0.88	0.97
Minerals, NEC	0.87	0.28	0.59	0.63	0.71	0.92	0.97
Sale of motor vehicles	0.28	0.91	0.82	0.81	0.75	0.94	0.93
Complete hypothetical extraction (forward)							
Refined fuels	2.18	1.98	2.24	2.18	2.29	2.40	2.44
Mining	3.03	2.57	3.10	3.07	2.90	2.39	2.26
Sale of motor vehicles	1.39	2.09	2.00	1.97	1.88	2.14	2.16
Partial hypothetical extraction (forward)							
Refined fuels	1.25	1.10	1.35	1.30	1.33	1.45	1.56
Sale of motor vehicles	0.40	1.27	1.20	1.17	1.07	1.34	1.35
Paper	1.07	0.88	1.08	1.24	1.24	1.24	1.28
Total forward linkage							
Refined fuels	2.35	2.24	2.51	2.46	2.40	2.53	2.76
Sale of motor vehicles	1.41	2.55	2.49	2.47	2.32	2.66	2.66
Paper	2.51	2.00	2.23	2.45	2.49	2.48	2.52
Normalized backward linkage							
Paper	1.16	1.21	1.17	1.28	1.32	1.33	1.30
Hotels and restaurants	1.28	1.28	1.25	1.24	1.28	1.30	1.29
Food and beverages	1.22	1.26	1.22	1.22	1.26	1.27	1.26
Normalized forward linkage							
Refined fuels	1.39	1.41	1.47	1.48	1.45	1.58	1.72
Sale of motor vehicles	0.83	1.61	1.47	1.48	1.40	1.66	1.65
Paper	1.49	1.27	1.31	1.47	1.51	1.54	1.57
Net backward linkage							
Transport equipment	1.27	1.80	1.98	1.96	1.89	1.83	1.87
Leather	0.96	0.55	0.81	0.94	1.03	1.66	1.77
Machinery, NEC	1.34	1.87	1.82	1.66	1.68	1.64	1.72
Net forward linkage							
Mining	1.96	1.79	2.18	2.14	2.04	1.68	1.59
Utilities	1.48	1.82	1.62	1.62	1.62	1.62	1.56
Sale of motor vehicles	0.78	1.48	1.44	1.43	1.34	1.54	1.54

continued on next page.

continued.

Philippines

Southeast Asia and the Pacific

International Linkages

Indicator and Top 3 Sectors, 2020	2000	2007	2010	2013	2016	2019	2020
Self-sufficiency ratio							
Water transport	0.43	0.47	0.52	0.67	0.62	1.38	4.81
Business activities, NEC	0.90	1.65	1.57	1.41	1.42	1.50	1.36
Hotels and restaurants	1.33	1.10	1.32	1.24	1.20	1.08	1.19
Import-to-input ratio							
Metals	0.19	0.31	0.27	0.29	0.37	0.41	0.37
Electricals	0.15	0.47	0.22	0.26	0.33	0.36	0.33
Refined fuels	0.49	0.43	0.39	0.40	0.51	0.56	0.27
Export-to-output ratio							
Water transport	0.15	0.18	0.11	0.06	0.06	0.99	1.00
Leather	0.28	0.83	0.70	0.17	0.20	0.92	1.00
Air transport	0.08	0.11	0.08	0.06	0.06	0.27	0.70
Domestic inputs share to output							
Paper	0.50	0.58	0.58	0.66	0.66	0.65	0.66
Wood	0.51	0.57	0.60	0.63	0.63	0.63	0.64
Food and beverages	0.62	0.62	0.63	0.63	0.63	0.62	0.63
Foreign inputs share to output							
Metals	0.19	0.31	0.27	0.29	0.37	0.41	0.37
Electricals	0.15	0.47	0.22	0.26	0.33	0.36	0.33
Refined fuels	0.49	0.43	0.39	0.40	0.51	0.56	0.27
Backward import multipliers							
Metals	0.28	0.44	0.40	0.42	0.48	0.53	0.48
Electricals	0.22	0.57	0.38	0.43	0.50	0.50	0.48
Chemicals	0.22	0.35	0.32	0.24	0.22	0.24	0.39
Forward import multipliers							
Water transport	0.06	0.09	0.06	0.03	0.04	0.84	0.86
Electricals	0.65	0.76	0.47	0.47	0.41	0.56	0.61
Mining	0.22	0.45	0.23	0.21	0.21	0.43	0.54
Intraregional transfer multiplier							
Paper	1.86	1.90	1.95	2.16	2.18	2.15	2.13
Hotels and restaurants	2.04	2.02	2.09	2.10	2.11	2.10	2.10
Food and beverages	1.94	1.98	2.03	2.06	2.07	2.06	2.05
Interregional spillover multiplier							
Metals	1.34	1.55	1.50	1.57	1.76	1.84	1.83
Electricals	1.27	1.84	1.40	1.48	1.63	1.72	1.67
Chemicals	1.23	1.41	1.37	1.22	1.20	1.22	1.60
Interregional feedback multiplier							
Electricals	1.09	1.35	1.17	1.20	1.25	1.20	1.18
Metals	1.07	1.15	1.13	1.16	1.21	1.18	1.16
Chemicals	1.06	1.12	1.11	1.07	1.06	1.06	1.13
Intraregional effect on gross output ($ million)							
Food and beverages	19,184.16	37,835.48	54,879.42	78,108.84	88,264.42	100,028.65	100,159.08
Retail trade	10,223.56	21,689.09	34,418.87	48,656.58	56,793.18	70,410.37	70,691.59
Finance	6,423.90	12,414.23	17,959.33	27,166.85	32,699.11	42,286.04	48,201.34
Interregional effect on gross output ($ million)							
Electricals	6,017.65	14,736.88	11,025.46	10,839.62	9,211.37	17,365.79	15,965.32
Business activities, NEC	544.00	6,565.18	8,523.50	10,638.27	13,843.80	14,964.34	12,163.97
Retail trade	1,513.95	3,484.86	3,045.16	4,087.26	4,429.00	4,090.62	3,911.39
Feedback effect on gross output ($ million)							
Electricals	2,987.19	8,130.83	6,228.58	6,675.41	5,449.45	6,084.34	5,410.20
Business activities, NEC	138.93	1,728.91	2,254.74	3,065.33	4,126.40	5,376.50	4,074.54
Retail trade	542.24	1,107.78	1,051.38	1,403.42	1,439.25	1,268.63	1,138.34
Directly absorbed value-added exports (DAVAX) ($ million)							
Business activities, NEC	265.75	5,547.97	7,200.29	8,532.88	10,881.75	12,395.25	9,886.04
Electricals	4,079.47	5,073.24	5,444.36	4,925.33	4,248.70	8,350.32	7,662.64
Hotels and restaurants	1,317.48	2,024.56	2,796.06	3,609.97	4,212.99	3,872.64	3,146.04
Reflection (REF) ($ million)							
Business activities, NEC	0.72	10.92	13.07	15.56	28.76	31.70	23.82
Electricals	13.00	25.33	29.86	20.86	25.16	25.80	21.94
Mining	0.18	1.40	0.54	0.63	0.81	5.26	4.42

continued on next page.

continued.

Philippines

Southeast Asia and the Pacific | *International Linkages*

Indicator and Top 3 Sectors, 2020	2000	2007	2010	2013	2016	2019	2020
Reexports (REX) ($ million)							
Business activities, NEC	86.58	2,267.59	2,924.22	3,558.46	4,749.05	6,185.12	4,764.71
Electricals	3,479.68	5,127.70	4,264.56	3,802.64	2,884.79	4,453.61	3,943.50
Metals	130.48	471.97	249.12	311.09	376.89	451.51	471.38
Foreign value added (FVA) ($ million)							
Electricals	2,174.05	13,566.24	5,994.34	6,619.15	7,113.66	13,018.46	10,703.97
Metals	163.82	1,210.52	558.14	689.11	1,033.35	1,282.70	1,206.55
Business activities, NEC	48.16	635.76	676.02	755.36	1,054.66	1,358.45	919.58
Pure double-counting (PDC) ($ million)							
Electricals	10.29	118.01	39.95	32.41	34.75	42.49	32.21
Metals	0.15	1.31	0.38	0.47	0.98	1.35	1.33
Business activities, NEC	0.06	1.57	1.12	1.13	1.85	1.98	1.31
Trade-based GVC participation rate							
Refined fuels	0.73	0.67	0.71	0.70	0.74	0.78	0.69
Metals	0.51	0.61	0.58	0.61	0.66	0.71	0.67
Electricals	0.58	0.79	0.65	0.68	0.70	0.68	0.66
Production-based GVC participation rate							
Water transport	0.06	0.09	0.06	0.03	0.04	0.84	0.86
Electricals	0.65	0.76	0.47	0.47	0.41	0.56	0.61
Mining	0.22	0.45	0.23	0.21	0.21	0.43	0.54
Trade-based backward GVC participation rate							
Metals	0.28	0.44	0.40	0.42	0.48	0.53	0.48
Electricals	0.22	0.57	0.38	0.43	0.50	0.50	0.48
Chemicals	0.22	0.35	0.32	0.24	0.22	0.24	0.39
Trade-based forward GVC participation rate							
Water transport	0.06	0.12	0.12	0.13	0.20	0.36	0.39
Transport activities, NEC	0.30	0.24	0.30	0.32	0.31	0.39	0.37
Refined fuels	0.18	0.15	0.24	0.22	0.18	0.17	0.34
Traditional revealed comparative advantage							
Hotels and restaurants	4.95	3.97	6.00	7.44	6.31	3.55	4.17
Telecommunications	0.92	1.06	2.10	1.74	1.35	3.43	3.41
Business activities, NEC	0.28	2.28	3.21	3.36	3.43	3.05	2.85
New revealed comparative advantage							
Retail trade	3.24	3.96	4.51	5.18	4.91	4.17	4.43
Telecommunications	0.84	1.43	2.07	1.62	1.32	2.40	2.54
Hotels and restaurants	2.18	2.00	2.74	3.31	3.00	1.96	2.20
Backward production length							
Electricals	2.15	3.03	3.10	3.19	3.23	3.07	3.07
Metals	2.32	2.78	2.84	2.93	2.99	2.94	2.98
Machinery, NEC	2.12	3.03	2.75	2.80	2.89	2.86	2.84
Forward production length							
Mining	3.59	3.81	3.75	3.68	3.49	3.74	4.02
Water transport	1.39	1.33	1.35	1.18	1.21	3.25	3.33
Refined fuels	2.75	2.84	2.94	2.79	2.73	2.92	3.27
Backward production length of GVC segment							
Agriculture	4.07	4.27	4.42	4.62	4.64	4.55	4.65
Health and social work	3.98	4.13	4.29	4.57	4.64	4.57	4.65
Paper	4.07	4.05	4.10	4.56	4.60	4.54	4.64
Forward production length of GVC segment							
Utilities	4.88	4.87	5.08	5.15	5.11	5.04	5.14
Retail trade	4.16	4.51	4.79	4.75	4.61	5.02	5.09
Sale of motor vehicles	4.64	4.99	5.39	5.28	5.37	4.96	4.97
Backward agglomeration index							
Rubber and plastics	-	1.13	1.46	1.75	1.67	3.09	2.76
Manufacturing, NEC	-	1.02	1.40	1.70	1.64	1.84	1.72
Textiles	-	1.25	1.55	1.58	1.43	1.54	1.42
Forward agglomeration index							
Manufacturing, NEC	-	1.30	1.51	1.55	1.58	1.83	1.83
Transport equipment	-	1.23	1.55	1.41	1.22	1.60	1.43
Chemicals	-	1.14	1.40	1.56	1.47	1.40	1.41

CIF = cost, insurance, and freight; FOB = free on board; GVC = global value chain; NEC = not elsewhere classified; NPISHs = nonprofit institutions serving households.
Source: Calculations using the Asian Development Bank Multiregional Input-Output Table. https://mrio.adbx.online/ (accessed July 2021).

continued on next page.

continued.

Philippines

Southeast Asia and the Pacific

The four select sectors are chosen based on their gross outputs in the economy as of 2019.

Economy Ranking out of 25 Economies

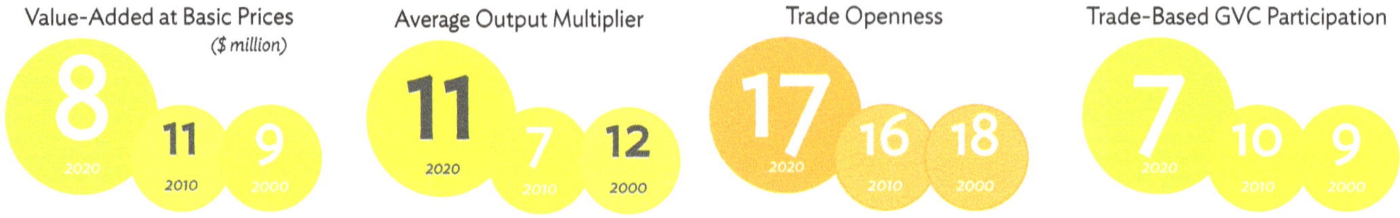

Share of Intermediate Consumption and Gross Value-Added in Output

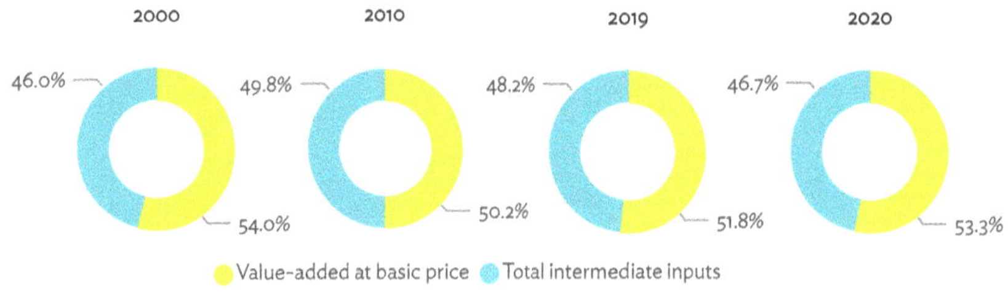

Imports and Exports, 2019-2020

($ million)

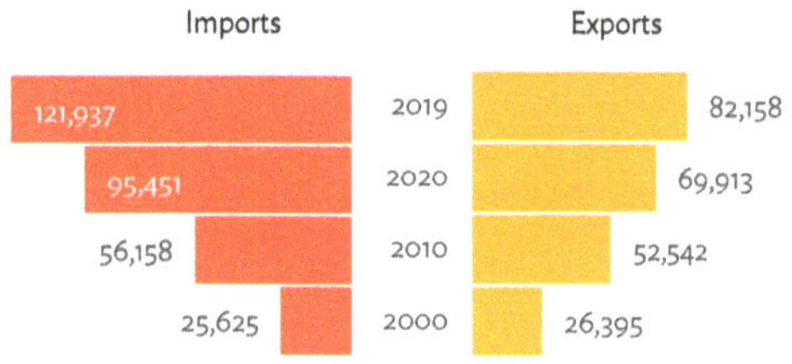

Domestic Linkages

Normalized Linkages

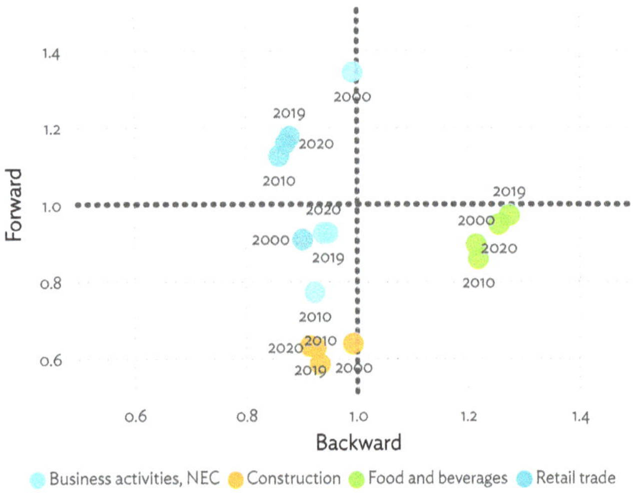

Net Linkages

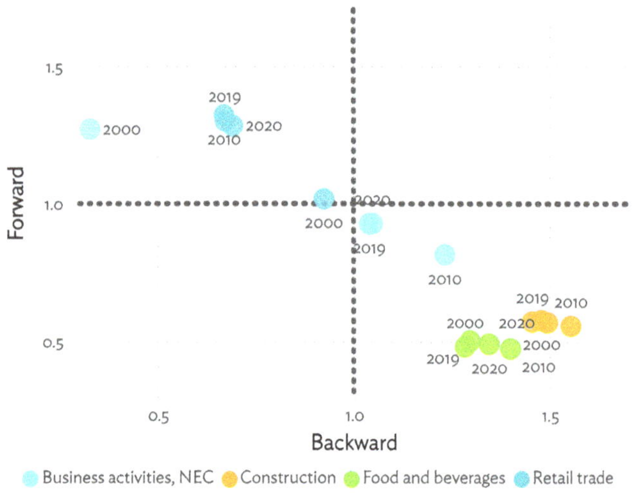

Value-Added Multipliers

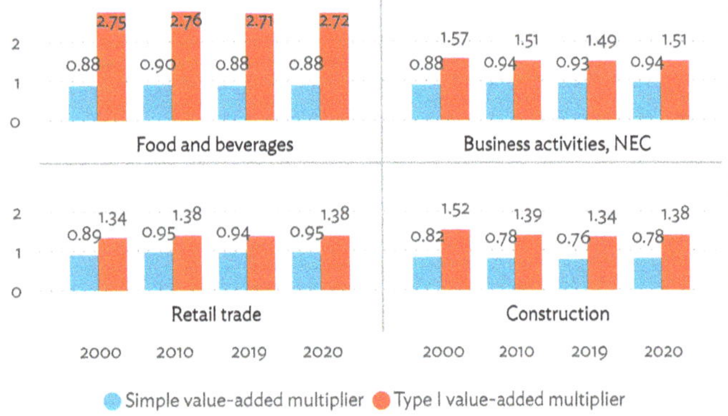

Production-Induced Effect

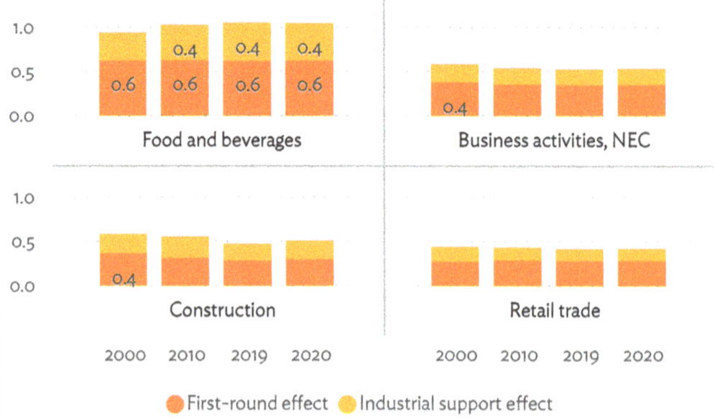

continued on next page.

Click here for figure data

continued.

Philippines

Southeast Asia and the Pacific

International Linkages

Change in Exports, by Value-Added Components, 2019-2020

($ million)

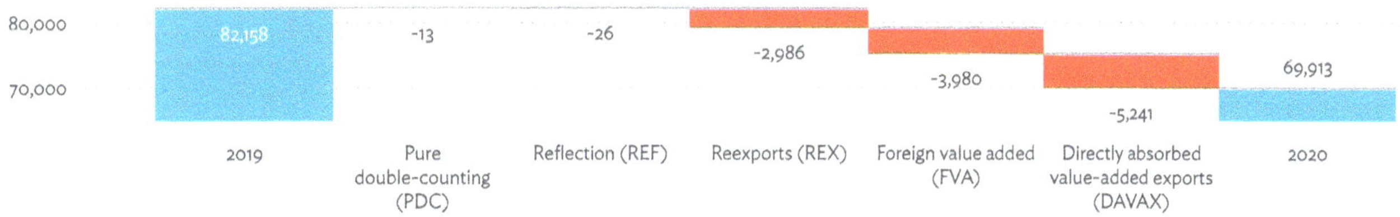

Import Multipliers

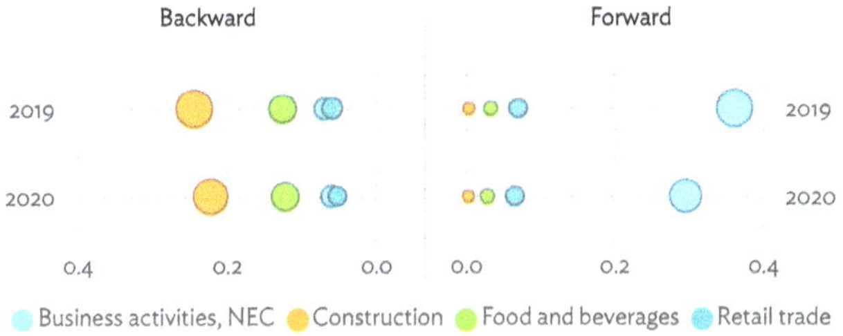

GVC Participation Rates

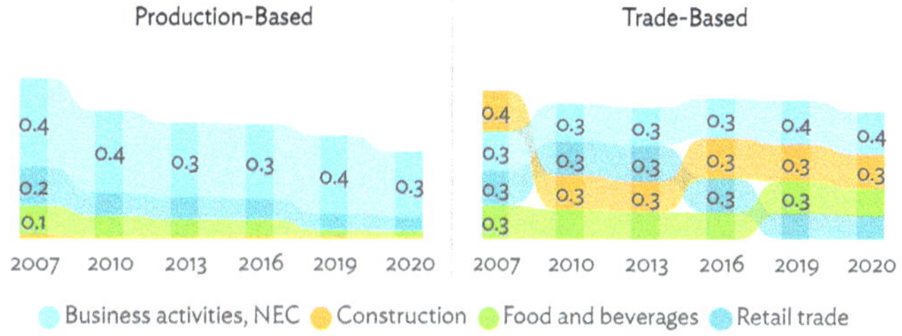

Average Production Length

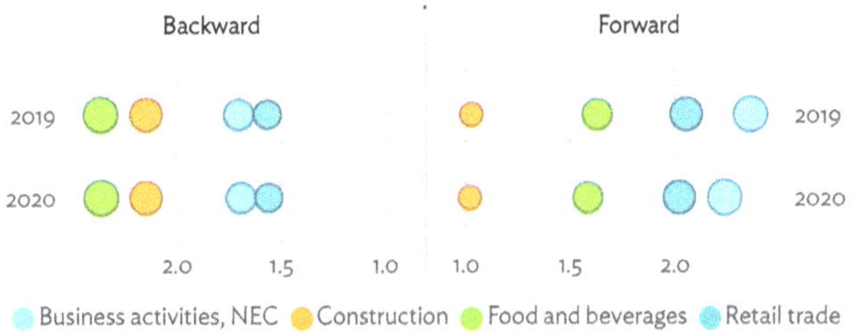

New Revealed Comparative Advantage

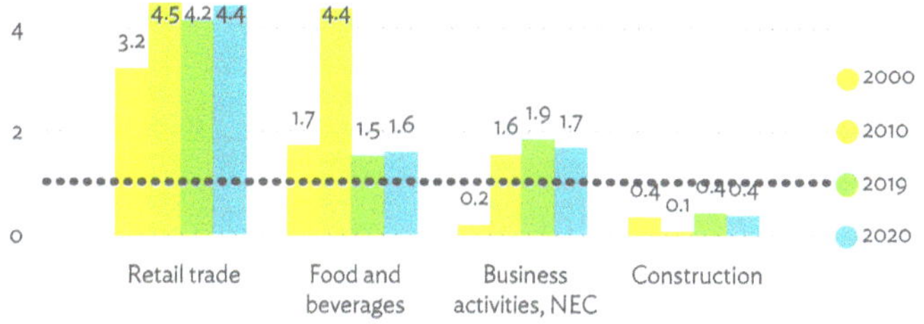

Trade Orientation

Agglomeration Indices

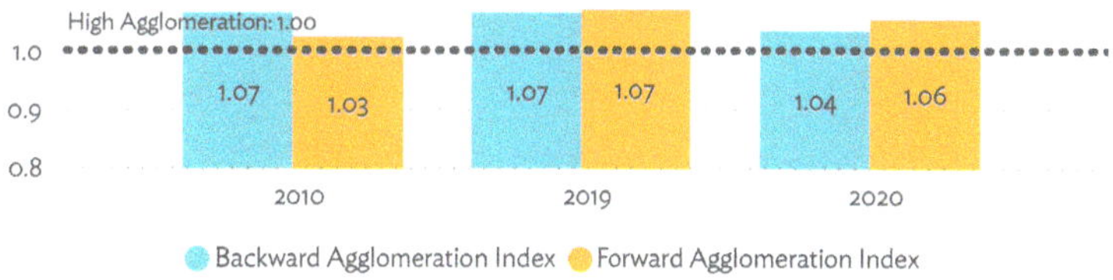

Domestic Transfer Effects and International Spillover Effects

($ million)

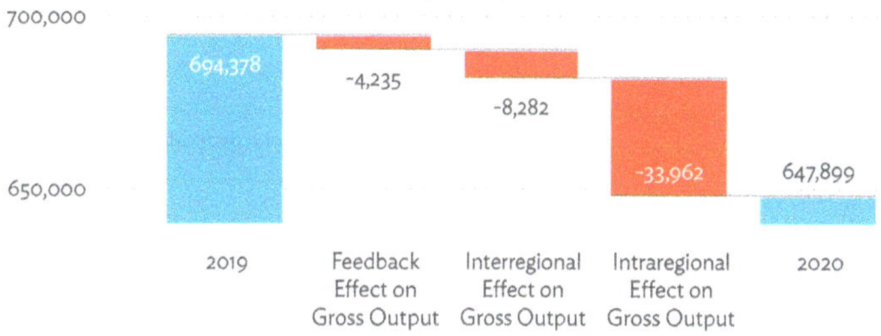

GVC = global value chain; NEC = not elsewhere classified.

Source: Calculations using the Asian Development Bank Multiregional Input-Output Table. https://mrio.adbx.online/ (accessed July 2021).

Click here for figure data

Singapore

Southeast Asia and the Pacific

Basic Economic Indicators

Economic Aggregates ($ million)	2000	2007	2010	2013	2016	2019	2020
Value-added at basic price	89,321	167,258	223,268	286,736	290,558	355,357	324,163
Gross output	252,981	460,843	612,758	799,744	818,163	944,898	849,841
Total intermediate inputs	163,423	293,149	388,829	512,329	526,794	588,430	524,740
Taxes less subsidies on products	238	435	660	679	811	1,111	938
International transport margins	0	0	0	0	0	0	0
CIF/FOB adjustment	0	0	0	0	0	0	0
Direct purchases abroad by residents	0	0	0	0	0	0	0
Purchases by nonresidents on the domestic territory	0	0	0	0	0	0	0
Household final consumption expenditure	26,790	43,677	61,015	82,635	84,131	80,335	66,624
Final consumption expenditure by NPISHs	0	0	0	0	0	0	0
Government final consumption expenditure	10,431	16,985	24,083	30,456	33,082	38,564	42,212
Gross fixed capital formation	17,002	23,279	42,918	56,450	58,597	50,597	44,116
Changes in inventories	601	-1,257	751	1,185	434	3,395	841
Total final demand	54,824	82,684	128,767	170,726	176,244	172,891	153,792
Exports	112,950	231,817	284,178	372,887	345,107	452,607	395,395
Imports	96,657	177,226	221,720	304,352	264,175	346,776	286,877

Economic Aggregates, Top 3 Sectors ($ million)	2000	2007	2010	2013	2016	2019	2020
Value-added at basic price							
Wholesale trade	9,016	29,239	38,283	49,498	43,439	56,503	53,014
Finance	9,003	19,185	24,286	34,014	34,939	49,971	50,950
Business activities, NEC	6,375	14,589	25,133	29,296	45,275	47,329	42,342
Gross output							
Electricals	46,107	58,229	87,509	85,336	82,388	145,299	139,278
Wholesale trade	17,243	54,640	73,043	100,202	97,195	126,426	118,619
Finance	19,769	36,628	46,928	65,766	67,997	100,150	102,112
Total intermediate inputs							
Electricals	34,327	44,248	66,957	66,251	63,436	111,290	106,678
Wholesale trade	8,218	25,379	34,745	50,696	53,745	69,910	65,594
Business activities, NEC	10,441	20,346	28,489	29,870	46,006	60,882	54,468
Total final demand							
Public administration	10,798	18,601	19,779	24,617	26,509	31,619	29,138
Finance	2,288	5,663	5,895	8,489	10,951	16,275	21,281
Construction	12,319	11,865	21,134	27,368	28,698	24,708	17,008
Exports							
Electricals	41,114	46,491	62,507	68,018	57,240	118,832	100,911
Wholesale trade	10,838	39,719	57,602	79,803	70,455	72,303	72,464
Refined fuels	8,949	39,488	38,338	43,781	43,517	50,510	42,649
Imports							
Business activities, NEC	12,458	22,348	35,144	45,444	44,735	67,622	58,638
Electricals	23,485	27,059	35,522	44,471	34,417	38,084	31,964
Water transport	1,661	10,279	14,615	28,103	27,727	36,768	29,919

Domestic Linkages

Indicator and Top 3 Sectors, 2020	2000	2007	2010	2013	2016	2019	2020
First-round effect							
Public administration	0.37	0.52	0.52	0.51	0.57	0.61	0.62
Construction	0.62	0.59	0.59	0.61	0.63	0.61	0.62
Paper	0.31	0.27	0.30	0.29	0.32	0.51	0.52
Industrial support effect							
Construction	0.71	0.56	0.51	0.56	0.66	0.55	0.53
Paper	0.16	0.12	0.14	0.12	0.16	0.25	0.28
Public administration	0.21	0.28	0.24	0.23	0.30	0.26	0.27
Production-induced effect							
Construction	1.33	1.15	1.09	1.16	1.28	1.16	1.15
Public administration	0.59	0.80	0.77	0.74	0.87	0.87	0.89
Paper	0.47	0.39	0.44	0.41	0.49	0.76	0.80

continued on next page.

continued.

Singapore

Southeast Asia and the Pacific

Domestic Linkages

Indicator and Top 3 Sectors, 2020	2000	2007	2010	2013	2016	2019	2020
Simple value-added multiplier							
Education	0.88	0.86	0.90	0.88	0.89	0.88	0.88
Real estate	0.91	0.87	0.89	0.88	0.90	0.87	0.88
Retail trade	0.84	0.85	0.85	0.85	0.84	0.82	0.83
Type I value-added multiplier							
Public administration	1.58	1.97	2.46	2.26	2.41	2.57	2.60
Refined fuels	1.58	2.66	3.57	11.45	4.17	2.71	2.49
Minerals, NEC	1.68	1.73	1.85	1.97	2.11	2.24	2.49
Direct backward linkage							
Public administration	0.37	0.52	0.52	0.51	0.57	0.61	0.62
Construction	0.62	0.59	0.59	0.61	0.63	0.61	0.62
Paper	0.31	0.27	0.30	0.29	0.32	0.51	0.52
Complete hypothetical extraction (backward)							
Public administration	1.57	1.79	1.73	1.71	1.84	1.83	1.88
Retail trade	1.65	1.67	1.66	1.68	1.68	1.68	1.69
Sale of motor vehicles	1.59	1.33	1.42	1.47	1.55	1.64	1.67
Partial hypothetical extraction (backward)							
Public administration	0.58	0.79	0.75	0.72	0.86	0.85	0.88
Construction	0.70	0.67	0.69	0.70	0.73	0.71	0.76
Retail trade	0.67	0.68	0.68	0.69	0.71	0.68	0.69
Total backward linkage							
Construction	2.33	2.15	2.09	2.16	2.28	2.16	2.15
Public administration	1.59	1.80	1.77	1.74	1.87	1.87	1.89
Paper	1.47	1.39	1.44	1.41	1.49	1.76	1.80
Direct forward linkage							
Utilities	0.78	0.82	0.77	0.78	0.77	0.77	0.90
Minerals, NEC	0.66	0.77	0.84	0.87	0.91	0.86	0.86
Leather	0.16	0.28	0.41	0.00	0.00	0.74	0.82
Complete hypothetical extraction (forward)							
Sale of motor vehicles	1.66	2.15	2.18	1.26	2.22	2.17	2.21
Leather	1.03	1.04	1.28	1.00	1.00	2.09	2.17
Minerals, NEC	2.05	2.16	2.06	2.28	2.27	2.19	2.11
Partial hypothetical extraction (forward)							
Minerals, NEC	1.13	1.29	1.28	1.42	1.47	1.32	1.26
Sale of motor vehicles	0.68	1.18	1.20	0.26	1.23	1.19	1.24
Leather	0.17	0.29	0.51	0.00	0.00	1.14	1.22
Total forward linkage							
Minerals, NEC	2.23	2.49	2.64	2.66	2.82	2.51	2.49
Utilities	2.29	2.35	2.29	2.22	2.27	2.12	2.38
Leather	1.20	1.40	1.66	1.00	1.00	2.19	2.29
Normalized backward linkage							
Construction	1.55	1.47	1.40	1.49	1.48	1.43	1.39
Public administration	1.05	1.23	1.18	1.19	1.21	1.23	1.22
Paper	0.98	0.95	0.96	0.97	0.96	1.16	1.16
Normalized forward linkage							
Minerals, NEC	1.41	1.58	1.63	1.74	1.75	1.61	1.57
Utilities	1.44	1.50	1.42	1.45	1.41	1.36	1.50
Leather	0.75	0.89	1.03	0.65	0.62	1.41	1.45
Net backward linkage							
Public administration	1.42	1.68	1.65	1.62	1.74	1.72	1.83
Retail trade	0.91	1.38	1.34	1.48	1.47	1.68	1.69
Refined fuels	1.12	1.12	1.06	0.95	1.04	1.65	1.62
Net forward linkage							
Real estate	1.20	0.96	0.99	0.96	0.98	1.21	1.23
Inland transport	0.88	0.81	0.93	0.94	0.94	0.95	0.99
Sale of motor vehicles	0.87	0.78	0.76	0.51	0.95	0.94	0.96

continued on next page.

continued.

Singapore

Southeast Asia and the Pacific *International Linkages*

Indicator and Top 3 Sectors, 2020	2000	2007	2010	2013	2016	2019	2020
Self-sufficiency ratio							
Retail trade	1.02	1.04	1.05	1.04	1.03	36.92	38.98
Chemicals	1.64	2.64	1.75	1.73	1.74	2.36	2.62
Refined fuels	0.57	1.04	0.91	0.81	0.97	1.87	2.01
Import-to-input ratio							
Water transport	0.50	0.61	0.58	0.55	0.55	0.78	0.72
Refined fuels	0.78	0.63	0.66	0.69	0.56	0.38	0.38
Air transport	0.48	0.32	0.40	0.39	0.33	0.41	0.38
Export-to-output ratio							
Mining	1.00	1.00	1.00	1.00	1.00	1.00	1.00
Retail trade	0.02	0.04	0.05	0.04	0.03	0.99	0.99
Refined fuels	0.94	0.77	0.72	0.63	0.62	1.00	0.99
Domestic inputs share to output							
Public administration	0.37	0.52	0.52	0.51	0.57	0.61	0.62
Construction	0.62	0.59	0.59	0.61	0.63	0.61	0.62
Paper	0.31	0.27	0.30	0.29	0.32	0.51	0.52
Foreign inputs share to output							
Water transport	0.50	0.61	0.58	0.55	0.55	0.78	0.72
Refined fuels	0.78	0.63	0.66	0.69	0.56	0.38	0.38
Air transport	0.48	0.32	0.40	0.39	0.33	0.41	0.38
Backward import multipliers							
Water transport	0.65	0.69	0.71	0.73	0.71	0.84	0.82
Minerals, NEC	0.57	0.56	0.50	0.62	0.58	0.63	0.59
Refined fuels	0.82	0.81	0.85	0.93	0.84	0.57	0.55
Forward import multipliers							
Chemicals	0.78	0.79	0.76	0.77	0.68	0.78	0.79
Metals	0.57	0.62	0.64	0.54	0.56	0.78	0.79
Refined fuels	0.63	0.61	0.59	0.54	0.56	0.75	0.76
Intraregional transfer multiplier							
Construction	2.33	2.15	2.09	2.16	2.28	2.16	2.15
Public administration	1.59	1.80	1.77	1.74	1.87	1.87	1.89
Paper	1.47	1.39	1.44	1.41	1.49	1.76	1.80
Interregional spillover multiplier							
Water transport	1.81	2.05	1.99	1.94	1.99	2.43	2.40
Refined fuels	2.34	2.18	2.19	2.21	2.16	1.77	1.83
Air transport	1.81	1.58	1.70	1.69	1.59	1.75	1.71
Interregional feedback multiplier							
Water transport	1.20	1.28	1.30	1.33	1.29	1.37	1.33
Refined fuels	1.56	1.45	1.50	1.61	1.39	1.20	1.21
Metals	1.21	1.27	1.27	1.29	1.24	1.18	1.16
Intraregional effect on gross output ($ million)							
Electricals	18,745.01	25,459.97	38,668.07	34,827.15	36,376.16	85,851.38	72,808.20
Finance	9,739.69	20,689.71	23,733.98	31,667.40	34,684.62	50,550.48	61,662.56
Wholesale trade	7,044.14	16,842.84	18,168.74	30,237.28	33,338.29	54,679.58	49,277.12
Interregional effect on gross output ($ million)							
Wholesale trade	7,913.07	29,421.50	43,650.83	56,185.71	51,029.99	57,496.92	55,933.77
Electricals	19,130.21	22,409.73	34,070.87	34,077.61	30,955.42	41,119.24	47,726.52
Business activities, NEC	7,137.61	14,436.67	20,824.29	23,358.00	36,192.85	41,102.88	38,763.31
Feedback effect on gross output ($ million)							
Electricals	8,232.21	10,359.41	14,770.42	16,431.60	15,056.33	18,328.57	18,743.28
Wholesale trade	2,285.85	8,375.50	11,223.01	13,779.20	12,826.97	14,249.17	13,408.50
Finance	2,125.98	3,495.25	4,799.55	6,872.12	6,954.65	10,800.86	9,439.29
Directly absorbed value-added exports (DAVAX) ($ million)							
Electricals	10,406.94	11,413.88	15,498.09	14,204.02	14,411.84	43,413.06	37,318.71
Wholesale trade	5,819.15	20,591.17	29,027.01	40,220.31	34,524.43	34,294.67	35,692.09
Business activities, NEC	3,058.43	5,197.97	8,064.47	9,590.49	13,593.91	15,233.17	18,102.93
Reflection (REF) ($ million)							
Electricals	78.35	48.46	91.88	100.93	84.89	89.94	90.16
Wholesale trade	28.02	48.86	64.08	113.77	82.88	60.07	61.99
Refined fuels	19.59	17.63	15.28	9.18	13.74	56.70	40.57

continued on next page.

continued.

Singapore

Southeast Asia and the Pacific

International Linkages

Indicator and Top 3 Sectors, 2020	2000	2007	2010	2013	2016	2019	2020
Foreign value added (FVA) ($ million)							
Electricals	25,171.80	28,773.48	38,471.34	45,179.72	34,412.62	62,892.26	50,982.20
Wholesale trade	2,825.03	12,181.32	18,842.98	27,633.39	26,365.78	29,357.41	27,644.73
Reexports (REX) ($ million)							
Electricals	4,876.04	5,894.41	7,915.70	7,823.30	7,867.86	11,687.19	11,898.99
Wholesale trade	2,120.99	6,753.74	9,403.11	10,933.27	8,837.37	8,210.11	8,751.72
Refined fuels	497.85	2,166.76	1,687.23	751.10	1,597.12	5,612.86	4,997.38
Pure double-counting (PDC) ($ million)							
Electricals	580.70	360.53	530.48	709.60	462.39	749.83	621.02
Wholesale trade	44.59	143.90	264.85	902.33	644.85	380.92	313.25
Water transport	107.84	184.18	509.07	1,060.63	660.26	371.97	237.50
Trade-based GVC participation rate							
Water transport	0.81	0.78	0.82	0.81	0.80	0.89	0.88
Refined fuels	0.88	0.86	0.90	0.95	0.88	0.68	0.67
Minerals, NEC	0.65	0.66	0.62	0.73	0.70	0.72	0.65
Production-based GVC participation rate							
Chemicals	0.78	0.79	0.76	0.77	0.68	0.78	0.79
Metals	0.57	0.62	0.64	0.54	0.56	0.78	0.79
Refined fuels	0.63	0.61	0.59	0.54	0.56	0.75	0.76
Trade-based backward GVC participation rate							
Water transport	0.65	0.69	0.71	0.73	0.71	0.84	0.82
Minerals, NEC	0.57	0.56	0.50	0.62	0.58	0.63	0.59
Refined fuels	0.82	0.81	0.85	0.93	0.84	0.57	0.55
Trade-based forward GVC participation rate							
Transport activities, NEC	0.16	0.16	0.19	0.18	0.17	0.25	0.23
Rubber and plastics	0.18	0.16	0.19	0.15	0.18	0.25	0.22
Chemicals	0.14	0.19	0.16	0.19	0.18	0.20	0.21
Traditional revealed comparative advantage							
Water transport	3.32	3.73	5.18	6.50	7.16	7.94	7.16
Wholesale trade	1.75	3.35	3.18	3.34	3.09	3.67	4.65
Retail trade	0.06	0.13	0.14	0.12	0.09	3.77	4.50
New revealed comparative advantage							
Water transport	4.85	4.14	4.03	5.11	5.78	4.37	3.65
Wholesale trade	1.64	3.02	2.92	2.91	2.42	2.61	2.72
Refined fuels	1.94	2.00	0.98	0.14	1.10	2.44	2.60
Backward production length							
Water transport	2.76	2.82	3.09	3.27	3.21	3.20	3.25
Refined fuels	3.29	3.61	3.73	4.06	4.08	3.09	3.10
Minerals, NEC	2.83	3.00	2.99	3.29	3.35	3.04	3.09
Forward production length							
Water transport	3.89	3.28	3.55	3.50	3.49	3.45	3.58
Transport activities, NEC	3.07	3.29	3.43	3.60	3.54	3.56	3.49
Rubber and plastics	2.82	3.07	3.44	3.27	3.40	3.48	3.45
Backward production length of GVC segment							
Construction	4.69	4.80	4.81	5.02	5.16	4.56	4.63
Retail trade	4.45	4.73	4.64	4.80	4.82	4.47	4.48
Inland transport	4.23	4.80	4.72	4.70	4.82	4.38	4.43
Forward production length of GVC segment							
Sale of motor vehicles	4.76	4.76	4.90	3.20	4.95	5.02	5.06
Utilities	4.77	4.95	4.88	4.89	5.05	4.76	4.99
Hotels and restaurants	4.63	4.57	4.64	4.64	4.72	4.83	4.90
Backward agglomeration index							
Leather	-	0.19	0.28	0.00	0.00	1.48	1.69
Rubber and plastics	-	0.23	0.29	0.29	0.53	1.40	1.00
Inland transport	-	0.88	0.97	0.90	0.92	0.99	0.97
Forward agglomeration index							
Leather	-	0.34	0.59	0.00	0.00	1.39	1.28
Personal services, NEC	-	0.81	1.06	1.06	1.07	1.08	1.07
Public administration	-	0.98	0.98	0.98	0.98	0.98	0.99

CIF = cost, insurance, and freight; FOB = free on board; GVC = global value chain; NEC = not elsewhere classified; NPISHs = nonprofit institutions serving households.
Source: Calculations using the Asian Development Bank Multiregional Input-Output Table. https://mrio.adbx.online/ (accessed July 2021).

continued on next page.

continued.

Singapore

Southeast Asia and the Pacific

The four select sectors are chosen based on their gross outputs in the economy as of 2019.

Economy Ranking out of 25 Economies

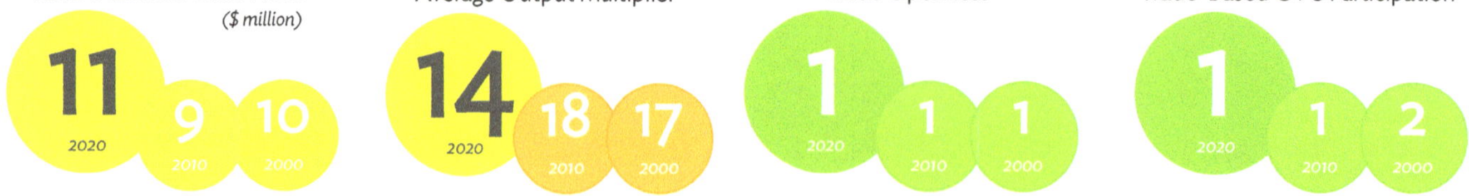

Share of Intermediate Consumption and Gross Value-Added in Output

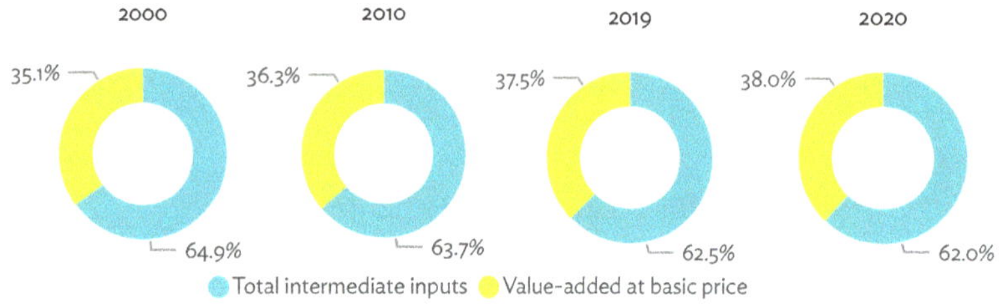

Imports and Exports, 2019-2020

($ million)

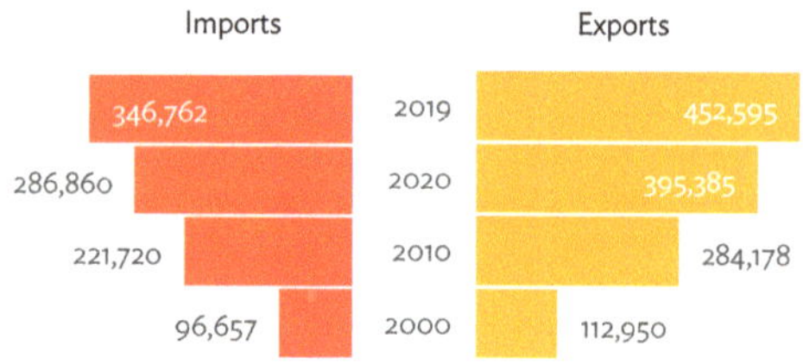

Domestic Linkages

Normalized Linkages

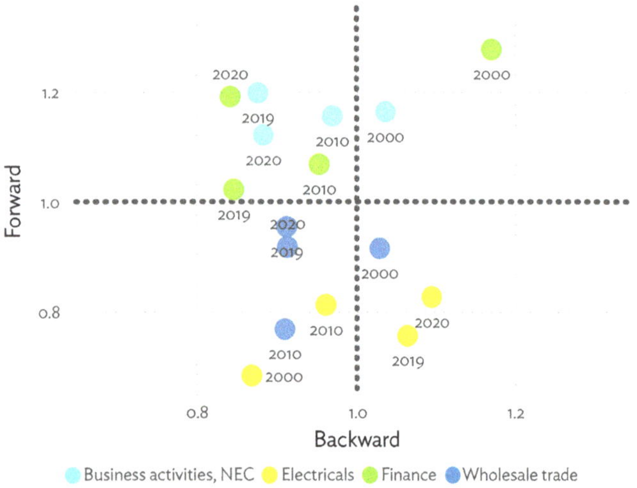

Net Linkages

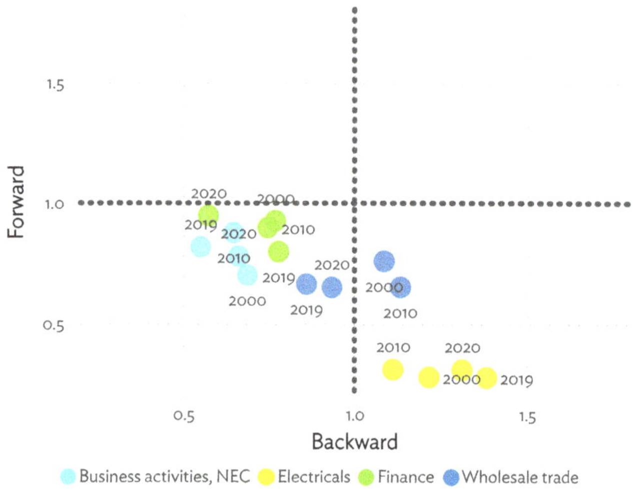

Value-Added Multipliers

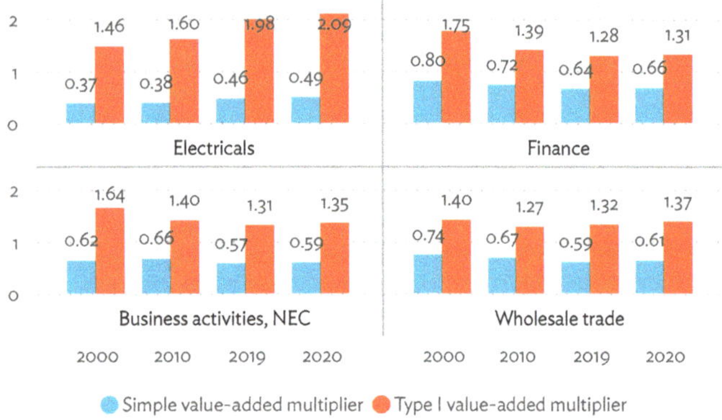

Production-Induced Effect

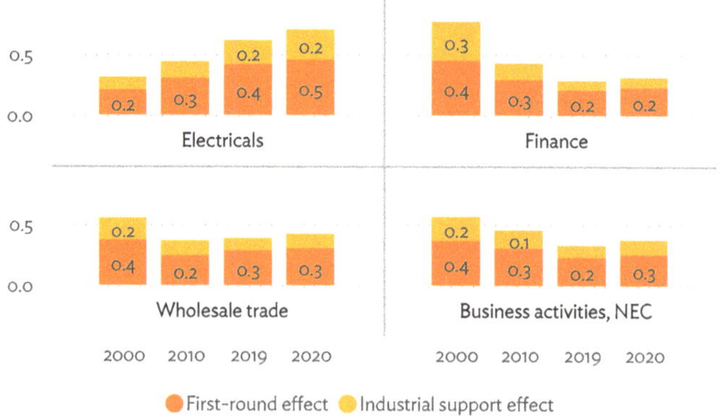

continued on next page.

Click here for figure data

continued.

Singapore

Southeast Asia and the Pacific

International Linkages

Change in Exports, by Value-Added Components, 2019-2020

($ million)

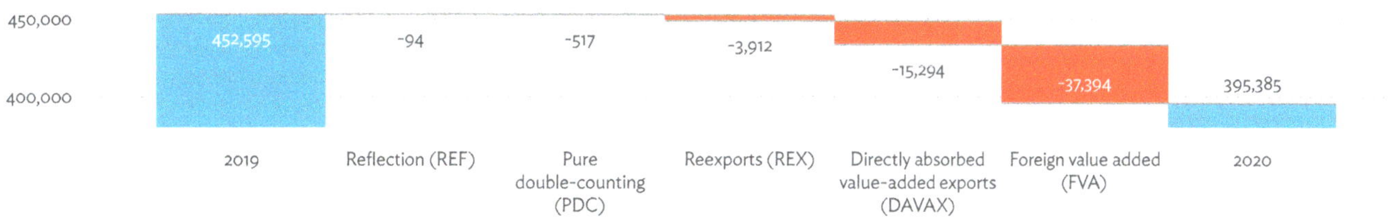

Import Multipliers

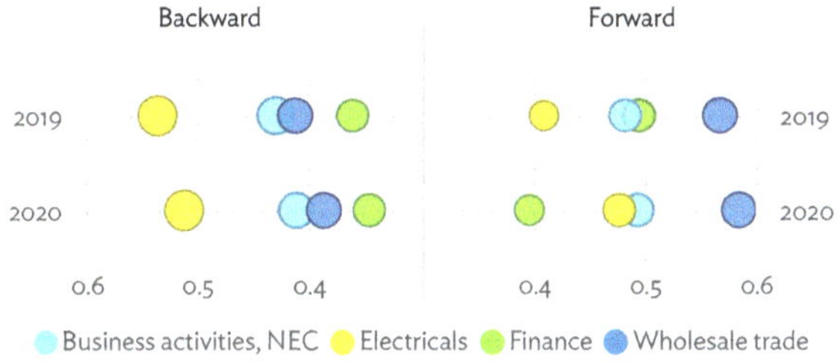

GVC Participation Rates

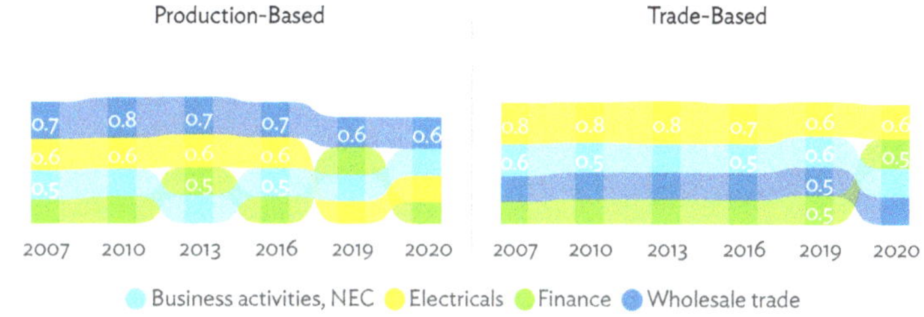

Average Production Length

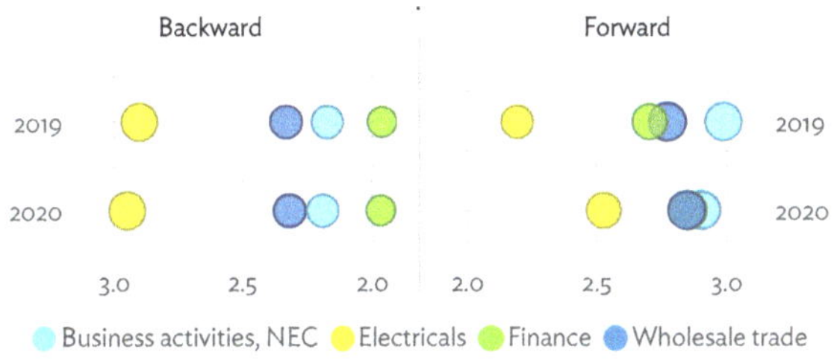

New Revealed Comparative Advantage

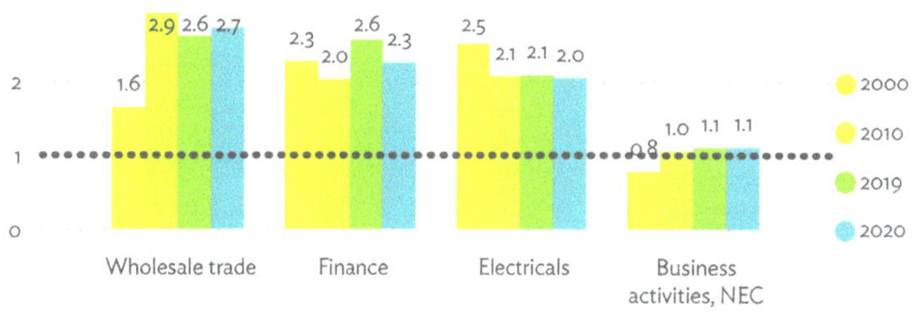

Trade Orientation

Agglomeration Indices

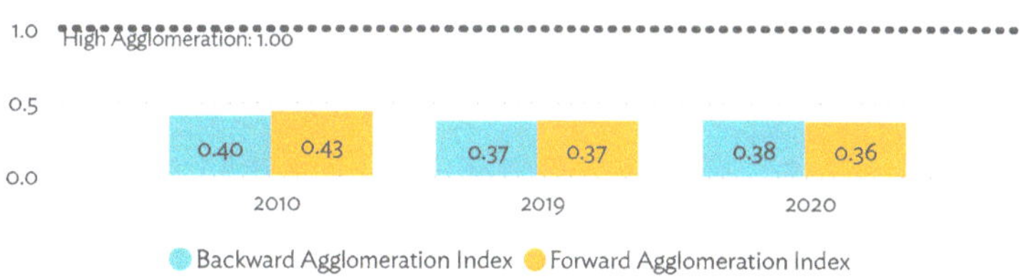

Domestic Transfer Effects and International Spillover Effects

($ million)

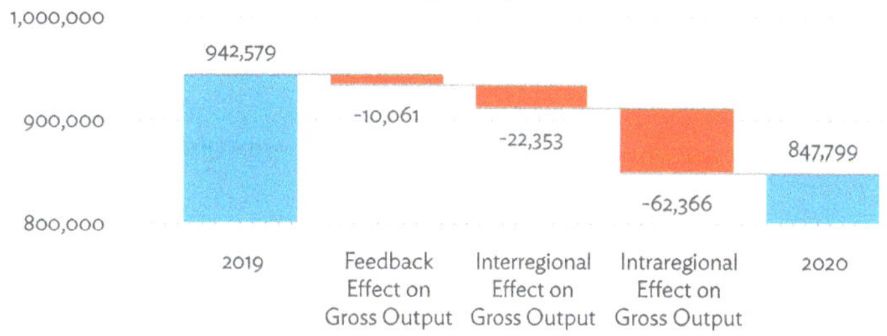

GVC = global value chain; NEC = not elsewhere classified.

Source: Calculations using the Asian Development Bank Multiregional Input-Output Table. https://mrio.adbx.online/ (accessed July 2021).

Click here for figure data

Sri Lanka

South and Central Asia

Basic Economic Indicators

Economic Aggregates ($ million)	2000	2007	2010	2013	2016	2019	2020
Value-added at basic price	14,612	33,083	50,928	69,286	74,506	78,153	76,057
Gross output	23,194	58,429	86,741	126,019	124,339	130,241	124,716
Total intermediate inputs	8,018	23,724	33,935	54,946	47,417	49,969	46,997
Taxes less subsidies on products	564	1,623	1,878	1,786	2,417	2,120	1,661
International transport margins	0	0	0	0	0	0	0
CIF/FOB adjustment	0	0	0	0	0	0	0
Direct purchases abroad by residents	0	0	0	0	0	0	0
Purchases by nonresidents on the domestic territory	0	0	0	0	0	0	0
Household final consumption expenditure	10,160	19,664	33,850	44,580	48,250	51,479	51,740
Final consumption expenditure by NPISHs	0	0	0	0	0	0	0
Government final consumption expenditure	1,684	5,270	4,760	5,700	6,853	7,787	8,263
Gross fixed capital formation	2,529	7,386	9,652	16,120	15,908	17,957	16,651
Changes in inventories	2	864	2,425	2,236	2,470	-171	-133
Total final demand	14,375	33,184	50,687	68,636	73,481	77,052	76,522
Exports	4,661	7,518	10,245	12,231	14,365	14,620	10,069
Imports	6,532	10,566	14,718	19,034	20,923	19,764	15,197

Economic Aggregates, Top 3 Sectors ($ million)	2000	2007	2010	2013	2016	2019	2020
Value-added at basic price							
Inland transport	1,595	3,246	5,507	8,592	9,226	9,031	8,198
Personal services, NEC	1,410	2,571	5,378	7,403	8,036	8,397	7,912
Agriculture	2,908	2,860	4,820	5,760	6,120	6,333	6,746
Gross output							
Personal services, NEC	2,661	6,596	9,822	14,614	15,416	16,106	15,177
Inland transport	2,658	5,797	9,507	15,814	16,689	16,334	14,827
Construction	5,414	4,308	7,000	12,270	12,738	12,476	10,881
Total intermediate inputs							
Personal services, NEC	1,154	3,737	4,196	6,932	7,003	7,377	7,002
Inland transport	998	2,306	3,683	7,001	7,163	7,056	6,441
Construction	2,659	2,254	3,756	6,382	5,919	5,860	5,159
Total final demand							
Personal services, NEC	1,190	3,687	7,894	10,847	11,868	12,764	12,055
Construction	5,251	3,999	6,488	11,167	11,626	11,721	10,116
Inland transport	1,361	3,296	5,719	7,839	8,441	10,213	9,474
Exports							
Textiles	126	1,891	2,978	2,927	3,097	4,577	3,750
Business activities, NEC	89	140	236	149	212	2,617	1,871
Food and beverages	92	925	1,527	2,220	2,281	960	784
Imports							
Refined fuels	633	1,297	2,059	2,214	2,075	1,853	1,678
Transport equipment	835	722	1,453	2,568	2,663	1,965	1,647
Chemicals	629	631	1,110	1,787	2,073	1,862	1,620

Domestic Linkages

Indicator and Top 3 Sectors, 2020	2000	2007	2010	2013	2016	2019	2020
First-round effect							
Paper	0.03	0.30	0.29	0.53	0.58	0.59	0.61
Textiles	0.09	0.30	0.34	0.49	0.46	0.47	0.49
Leather	0.07	0.38	0.44	0.53	0.44	0.45	0.47
Industrial support effect							
Paper	0.01	0.12	0.11	0.41	0.42	0.43	0.45
Textiles	0.02	0.12	0.13	0.34	0.27	0.27	0.29
Leather	0.01	0.18	0.22	0.39	0.24	0.24	0.26
Production-induced effect							
Paper	0.03	0.42	0.40	0.94	1.00	1.02	1.06
Textiles	0.11	0.42	0.47	0.83	0.73	0.74	0.78
Leather	0.09	0.56	0.66	0.92	0.68	0.68	0.73

continued on next page.

continued.

Sri Lanka

South and Central Asia *Domestic Linkages*

Indicator and Top 3 Sectors, 2020	2000	2007	2010	2013	2016	2019	2020
Simple value-added multiplier							
Education	0.99	0.97	0.97	0.99	0.99	0.99	0.99
Public administration	0.97	0.92	0.98	0.97	0.98	0.98	0.98
Real estate	0.91	0.96	0.95	0.95	0.95	0.95	0.96
Type I value-added multiplier							
Paper	1.03	1.52	1.49	2.34	2.62	2.66	2.81
Refined fuels	1.34	1.99	1.52	6.29	5.10	2.09	2.37
Textiles	1.13	1.51	1.65	2.00	1.92	1.95	2.01
Direct backward linkage							
Paper	0.03	0.30	0.29	0.53	0.58	0.59	0.61
Textiles	0.09	0.30	0.34	0.49	0.46	0.47	0.49
Leather	0.07	0.38	0.44	0.53	0.44	0.45	0.47
Complete hypothetical extraction (backward)							
Water transport	1.52	1.18	1.02	1.66	1.68	1.67	1.68
Hotels and restaurants	1.37	1.56	1.59	1.72	1.62	1.61	1.64
Telecommunications	1.37	1.50	1.64	1.73	1.53	1.51	1.61
Partial hypothetical extraction (backward)							
Paper	0.03	0.37	0.34	0.67	0.69	0.69	0.73
Water transport	0.52	0.18	0.02	0.66	0.68	0.67	0.68
Telecommunications	0.40	0.51	0.66	0.77	0.57	0.54	0.64
Total backward linkage							
Paper	1.03	1.42	1.40	1.94	2.00	2.02	2.06
Textiles	1.11	1.42	1.47	1.83	1.73	1.74	1.78
Leather	1.09	1.56	1.66	1.92	1.68	1.68	1.73
Direct forward linkage							
Refined fuels	0.78	0.56	0.62	0.79	0.72	0.90	0.89
Utilities	0.49	0.71	0.80	0.87	0.83	0.79	0.78
Paper	0.69	0.75	0.79	0.98	0.79	0.77	0.77
Complete hypothetical extraction (forward)							
Utilities	1.57	1.96	2.10	2.31	2.14	2.08	2.11
Refined fuels	1.97	1.81	1.92	1.60	1.78	2.00	2.02
Chemicals	1.85	1.76	1.93	2.41	2.07	1.94	1.95
Partial hypothetical extraction (forward)							
Refined fuels	0.97	0.82	0.93	1.01	0.96	1.20	1.21
Utilities	0.65	1.05	1.17	1.38	1.21	1.13	1.16
Chemicals	0.85	0.90	1.03	1.50	1.12	0.99	1.00
Total forward linkage							
Refined fuels	1.97	1.82	1.93	2.72	2.18	2.51	2.50
Paper	1.95	2.30	2.31	2.99	2.48	2.42	2.45
Utilities	1.70	2.14	2.26	2.47	2.29	2.19	2.23
Normalized backward linkage							
Paper	0.85	1.01	1.01	1.25	1.45	1.46	1.45
Textiles	0.91	1.01	1.07	1.18	1.25	1.26	1.25
Leather	0.89	1.11	1.21	1.24	1.22	1.22	1.22
Normalized forward linkage							
Refined fuels	1.40	1.22	1.27	1.61	1.43	1.73	1.67
Paper	1.39	1.54	1.53	1.77	1.63	1.67	1.64
Utilities	1.21	1.43	1.49	1.46	1.50	1.51	1.49
Net backward linkage							
Water transport	1.52	0.70	0.61	1.22	1.41	1.66	1.68
Hotels and restaurants	1.28	1.04	1.43	1.59	1.51	1.54	1.53
Construction	1.26	1.51	1.58	1.47	1.35	1.40	1.42
Net forward linkage							
Wholesale trade	1.21	1.29	1.45	1.51	1.29	1.48	1.52
Finance	1.39	1.56	1.57	1.49	1.34	1.33	1.34
Mining	1.23	1.84	1.75	1.35	1.25	1.32	1.32

continued on next page.

continued.

Sri Lanka

South and Central Asia *International Linkages*

Indicator and Top 3 Sectors, 2020	2000	2007	2010	2013	2016	2019	2020
Self-sufficiency ratio							
Business activities, NEC	1.07	0.82	0.93	0.99	1.01	6.92	2.55
Rubber and plastics	0.11	1.12	1.20	1.12	1.21	1.49	1.46
Textiles	0.66	1.42	1.42	1.35	1.44	1.52	1.43
Import-to-input ratio							
Metals	0.23	0.31	0.28	0.38	0.52	0.52	0.50
Electricals	0.53	0.22	0.18	0.33	0.43	0.41	0.37
Refined fuels	0.62	0.46	0.67	0.16	0.52	0.40	0.36
Export-to-output ratio							
Water transport	1.00	0.44	0.15	0.11	0.10	0.99	1.00
Machinery, NEC	0.44	0.25	0.35	0.06	0.06	0.99	0.74
Business activities, NEC	0.21	0.13	0.14	0.06	0.09	0.99	0.71
Domestic inputs share to output							
Paper	0.03	0.30	0.29	0.53	0.58	0.59	0.61
Textiles	0.09	0.30	0.34	0.49	0.46	0.47	0.49
Leather	0.07	0.38	0.44	0.53	0.44	0.45	0.47
Foreign inputs share to output							
Metals	0.23	0.31	0.28	0.38	0.52	0.52	0.50
Electricals	0.53	0.22	0.18	0.33	0.43	0.41	0.37
Refined fuels	0.62	0.46	0.67	0.16	0.52	0.40	0.36
Backward import multipliers							
Metals	0.23	0.38	0.35	0.44	0.52	0.53	0.52
Refined fuels	0.64	0.49	0.69	0.35	0.68	0.53	0.48
Machinery, NEC	0.11	0.27	0.26	0.41	0.47	0.47	0.42
Forward import multipliers							
Water transport	0.76	0.41	0.17	0.12	0.10	0.72	0.72
Business activities, NEC	0.29	0.17	0.16	0.07	0.11	0.81	0.59
Rubber and plastics	0.20	0.42	0.26	0.18	0.22	0.46	0.38
Intraregional transfer multiplier							
Paper	1.03	1.42	1.40	1.94	2.00	2.02	2.06
Textiles	1.11	1.42	1.47	1.83	1.73	1.74	1.78
Leather	1.09	1.56	1.66	1.92	1.68	1.68	1.73
Interregional spillover multiplier							
Metals	1.40	1.58	1.53	1.76	2.13	2.13	2.13
Electricals	1.94	1.40	1.34	1.70	1.93	1.88	1.82
Transport equipment	1.90	1.41	1.44	1.71	1.92	1.81	1.79
Interregional feedback multiplier							
Metals	1.16	1.22	1.23	1.30	1.36	1.31	1.31
Electricals	1.34	1.16	1.13	1.24	1.28	1.24	1.21
Machinery, NEC	1.07	1.17	1.16	1.26	1.27	1.22	1.19
Intraregional effect on gross output ($ million)							
Personal services, NEC	2,022.47	6,333.92	9,697.95	14,194.36	14,901.75	15,821.51	15,009.10
Inland transport	2,111.59	5,086.83	8,527.20	14,199.31	14,346.40	15,757.88	14,558.34
Construction	5,383.59	4,231.14	6,857.15	12,215.70	12,671.71	12,443.88	10,865.44
Interregional effect on gross output ($ million)							
Business activities, NEC	105.25	144.35	197.19	148.60	180.43	1,703.38	1,257.12
Agriculture	573.72	311.19	382.58	456.11	437.34	615.35	490.67
Rubber and plastics	3.42	207.75	243.18	212.61	265.55	466.96	355.87
Feedback effect on gross output ($ million)							
Business activities, NEC	17.54	47.60	66.63	44.27	56.49	426.84	281.73
Agriculture	89.47	63.04	90.42	96.44	90.44	151.23	102.85
Rubber and plastics	0.77	66.94	85.55	60.27	68.49	139.69	101.18
Directly absorbed value-added exports (DAVAX) ($ million)							
Textiles	74.81	1,211.56	1,923.16	2,204.10	2,309.17	3,711.84	3,133.17
Business activities, NEC	57.15	75.99	141.47	97.13	135.88	1,719.05	1,288.82
Food and beverages	65.82	705.26	1,184.14	1,761.65	1,798.77	710.90	627.37
Reflection (REF) ($ million)							
Business activities, NEC	0.02	0.07	0.13	0.06	0.08	0.69	0.42
Food and beverages	0.02	0.12	0.13	0.24	0.30	0.34	0.26
Agriculture	0.23	0.31	0.15	0.14	0.15	0.16	0.15

continued on next page.

continued.

Sri Lanka

South and Central Asia — *International Linkages*

Indicator and Top 3 Sectors, 2020	2000	2007	2010	2013	2016	2019	2020
Reexports (REX) ($ million)							
Business activities, NEC	15.21	46.29	73.38	34.05	50.27	579.90	390.82
Rubber and plastics	0.34	109.19	120.37	84.19	91.84	184.97	142.11
Agriculture	172.63	70.19	74.16	70.15	72.37	158.37	118.98
Foreign value added (FVA) ($ million)							
Textiles	43.67	500.81	839.89	511.44	556.70	789.18	562.10
Business activities, NEC	16.45	17.64	20.93	18.06	25.29	317.62	190.99
Rubber and plastics	0.76	47.58	75.59	61.77	97.93	109.43	86.52
Pure double-counting (PDC) ($ million)							
Textiles	0.01	1.15	0.40	0.14	0.16	0.13	0.07
Business activities, NEC	0.00	0.00	0.00	0.00	0.01	0.05	0.02
Electricals	0.00	0.01	0.01	0.00	0.01	0.01	0.01
Trade-based GVC participation rate							
Metals	0.36	0.50	0.43	0.51	0.58	0.62	0.61
Electricals	0.63	0.46	0.32	0.42	0.52	0.63	0.60
Machinery, NEC	0.28	0.30	0.28	0.45	0.53	0.60	0.54
Production-based GVC participation rate							
Water transport	0.76	0.41	0.17	0.12	0.10	0.72	0.72
Business activities, NEC	0.29	0.17	0.16	0.07	0.11	0.81	0.59
Rubber and plastics	0.20	0.42	0.26	0.18	0.22	0.46	0.38
Trade-based backward GVC participation rate							
Metals	0.23	0.38	0.35	0.44	0.52	0.53	0.52
Refined fuels	0.64	0.49	0.69	0.35	0.68	0.53	0.48
Machinery, NEC	0.11	0.27	0.26	0.41	0.47	0.47	0.42
Trade-based forward GVC participation rate							
Transport activities, NEC	0.17	0.22	0.00	0.32	0.29	0.28	0.39
Leather	0.10	0.02	0.04	0.05	0.04	0.45	0.35
Water transport	0.12	0.36	0.36	0.33	0.34	0.36	0.33
Traditional revealed comparative advantage							
Textiles	0.60	7.24	9.11	7.27	6.51	10.22	10.89
Real estate	0.15	0.00	0.00	0.08	0.08	6.07	3.25
Hotels and restaurants	2.75	0.02	0.02	4.37	3.39	5.20	3.15
New revealed comparative advantage							
Textiles	0.82	8.59	10.41	8.66	7.40	12.43	13.79
Food and beverages	1.09	3.96	4.53	5.73	5.40	2.58	2.60
Air transport	0.15	1.69	0.88	1.56	1.70	3.60	2.18
Backward production length							
Refined fuels	2.44	2.55	2.59	3.41	3.29	2.73	2.86
Machinery, NEC	1.31	2.11	2.18	2.72	2.76	2.67	2.67
Metals	1.67	2.43	2.46	2.70	2.61	2.57	2.62
Forward production length							
Water transport	2.84	2.65	1.95	1.72	1.49	2.94	2.94
Paper	2.72	2.90	2.76	3.11	2.99	2.78	2.74
Refined fuels	2.64	2.27	2.53	3.04	2.41	2.61	2.58
Backward production length of GVC segment							
Water transport	3.64	3.90	3.73	5.42	4.88	4.63	4.96
Education	4.19	4.21	3.90	5.23	4.88	4.52	4.78
Transport activities, NEC	3.71	4.01	3.91	4.84	4.73	4.39	4.66
Forward production length of GVC segment							
Health and social work	4.15	4.55	5.21	4.83	4.62	4.72	4.82
Refined fuels	3.72	3.52	3.45	4.52	4.10	4.87	4.78
Construction	3.74	3.22	3.13	4.18	3.97	4.21	4.65
Backward agglomeration index							
Leather	-	1.65	1.88	1.93	1.69	2.19	2.43
Rubber and plastics	-	1.33	1.20	1.58	1.36	2.96	2.22
Manufacturing, NEC	-	1.43	1.47	1.88	1.67	1.72	1.77
Forward agglomeration index							
Mining	-	1.95	2.09	2.02	1.91	2.48	2.28
Leather	-	1.64	1.83	1.84	1.67	1.76	2.00
Manufacturing, NEC	-	1.19	1.32	1.75	1.63	1.56	1.74

CIF = cost, insurance, and freight; FOB = free on board; GVC = global value chain; NEC = not elsewhere classified; NPISHs = nonprofit institutions serving households.
Source: Calculations using the Asian Development Bank Multiregional Input-Output Table. https://mrio.adbx.online/ (accessed July 2021).

continued on next page.

continued.

Sri Lanka

South and Central Asia

The four select sectors are chosen based on their gross outputs in the economy as of 2019.

Economy Ranking out of 25 Economies

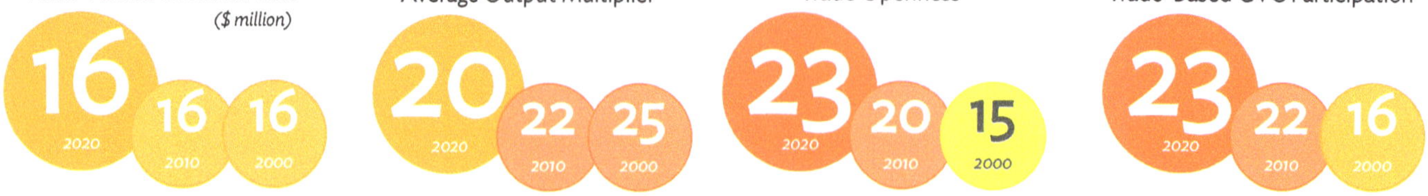

Share of Intermediate Consumption and Gross Value-Added in Output

Imports and Exports, 2019-2020

($ million)

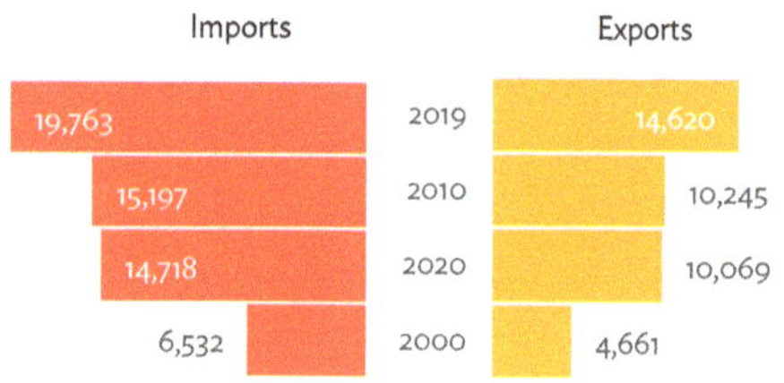

Domestic Linkages

Normalized Linkages

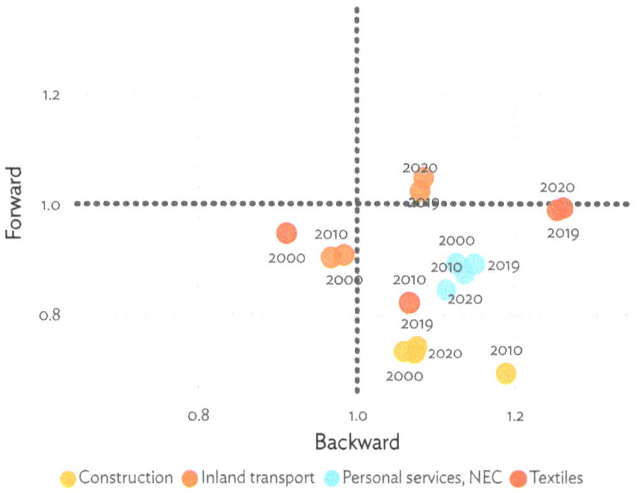

Net Linkages

Value-Added Multipliers

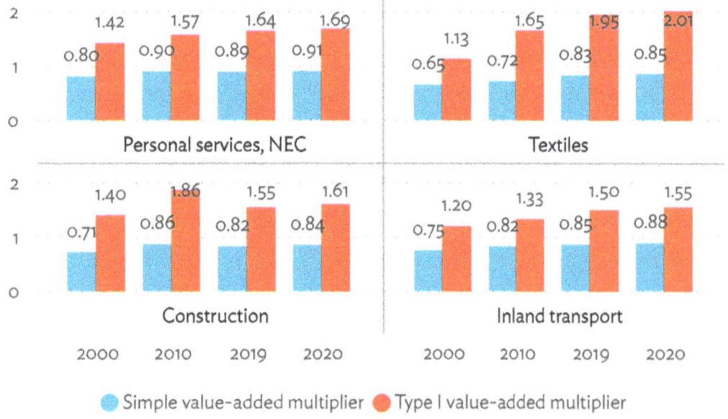

Production-Induced Effect

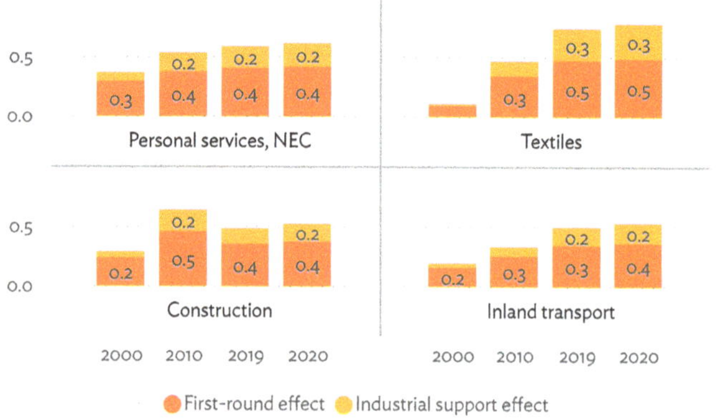

continued on next page.

Click here for figure data

continued.

Sri Lanka
South and Central Asia

International Linkages

Change in Exports, by Value-Added Components, 2019-2020
($ million)

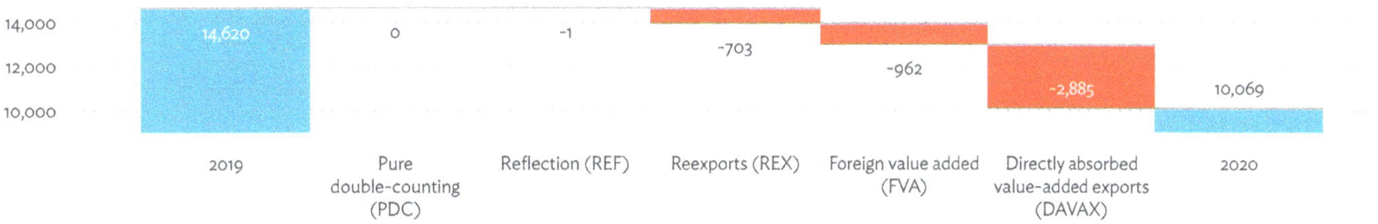

Import Multipliers

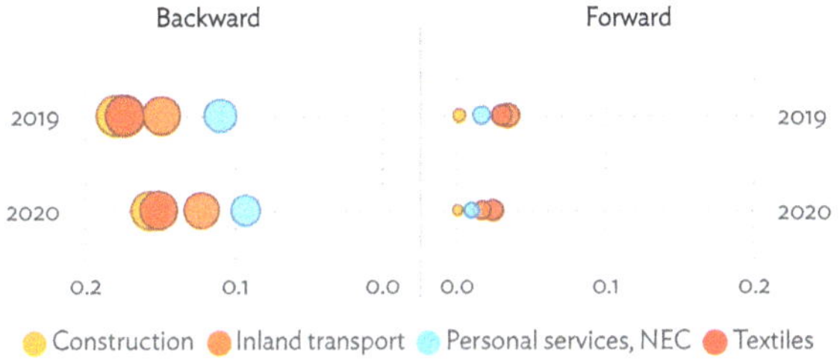

GVC Participation Rates

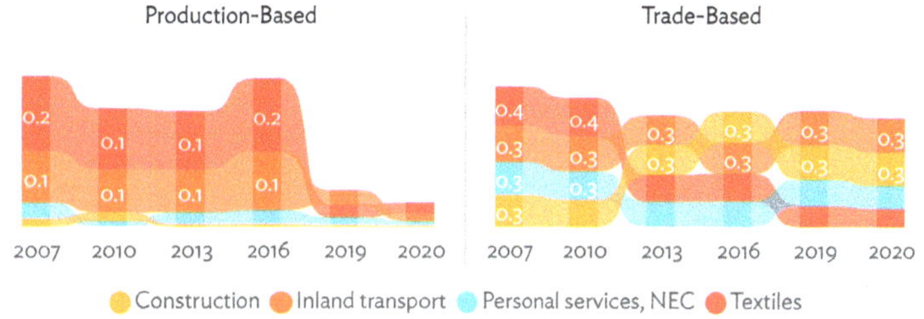

Average Production Length

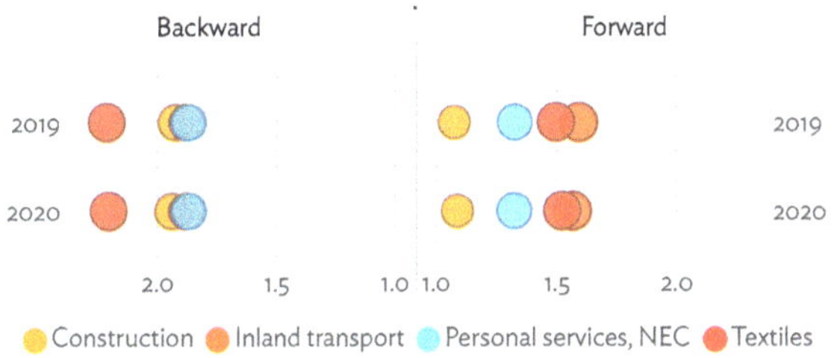

New Revealed Comparative Advantage

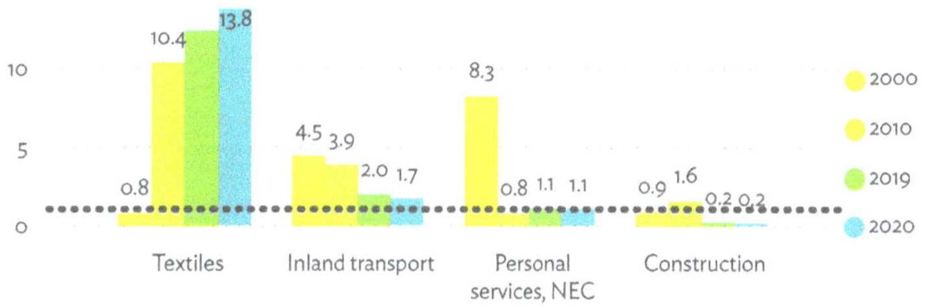

Trade Orientation

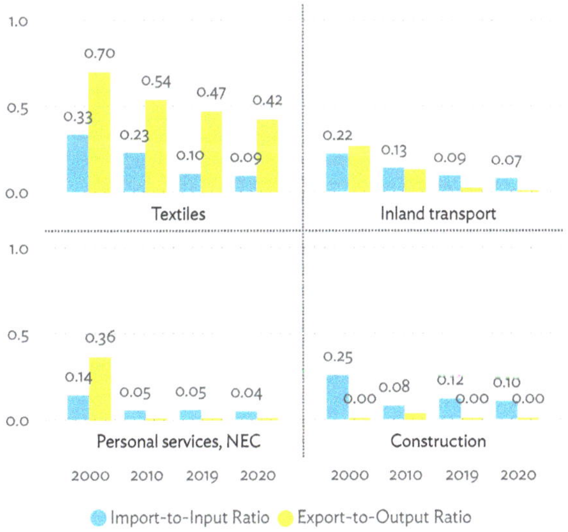

Agglomeration Indices

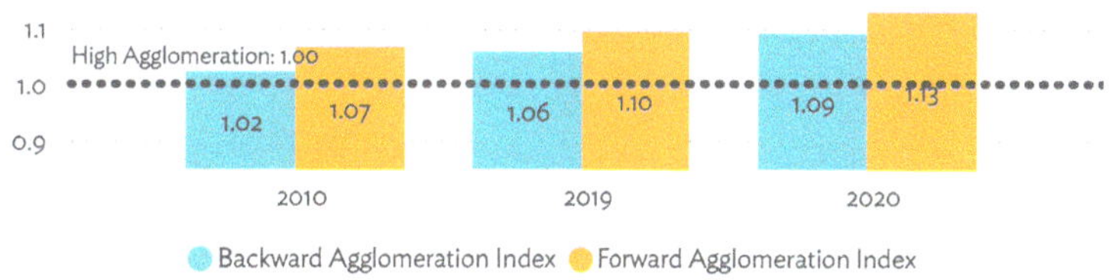

Domestic Transfer Effects and International Spillover Effects
($ million)

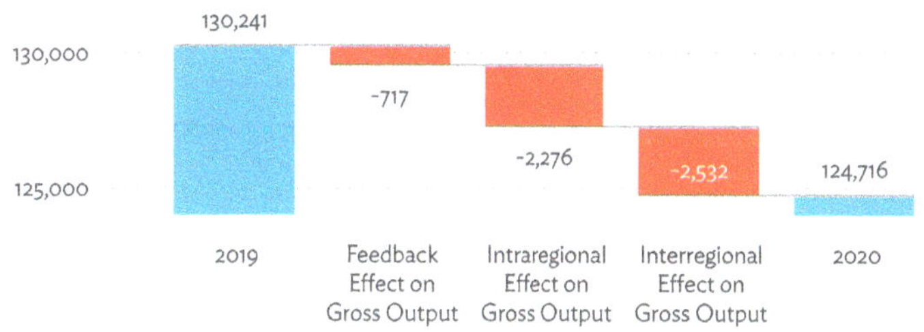

GVC = global value chain; NEC = not elsewhere classified.
Source: Calculations using the Asian Development Bank Multiregional Input-Output Table. https://mrio.adbx.online/ (accessed July 2021).

Click here for figure data

Taipei,China

East Asia

Basic Economic Indicators

Economic Aggregates ($ million)	2000	2007	2010	2013	2016	2019	2020
Value-added at basic price	321,951	391,994	432,114	494,432	514,891	594,468	650,161
Gross output	682,643	937,701	1,059,650	1,193,656	1,100,377	1,291,601	1,356,572
Total intermediate inputs	350,688	528,373	607,800	676,281	581,590	692,907	698,677
Taxes less subsidies on products	2,092	2,656	3,027	3,553	3,895	4,226	4,810
International transport margins	7,912	14,678	16,709	19,390	0	0	0
CIF/FOB adjustment	0	0	0	0	0	0	0
Direct purchases abroad by residents	0	0	0	0	0	0	0
Purchases by nonresidents on the domestic territory	0	0	0	0	0	0	0
Household final consumption expenditure	156,364	181,571	197,514	230,575	219,008	260,789	272,086
Final consumption expenditure by NPISHs	1,811	2,224	2,826	2,742	2,603	0	3,232
Government final consumption expenditure	51,590	56,775	65,037	73,313	71,668	83,881	92,194
Gross fixed capital formation	55,250	66,755	72,323	88,187	82,749	90,849	108,571
Changes in inventories	1,035	-130	2,989	-1,638	444	-2,356	-168
Total final demand	266,050	307,195	340,689	393,180	376,471	433,163	475,915
Exports	171,251	283,077	315,574	354,668	336,477	388,731	388,430
Imports	153,848	232,881	263,832	286,211	253,096	326,408	299,929

Economic Aggregates, Top 3 Sectors ($ million)	2000	2007	2010	2013	2016	2019	2020
Value-added at basic price							
Electricals	29,429	52,585	59,841	72,247	81,874	94,515	105,180
Wholesale trade	30,092	39,625	45,008	52,225	51,449	55,503	58,066
Real estate	27,791	33,203	37,570	43,275	43,890	50,324	54,872
Gross output							
Electricals	107,039	167,433	194,508	210,579	205,857	252,578	291,721
Metals	41,653	76,737	89,611	91,950	73,120	89,496	89,319
Chemicals	31,353	74,059	91,686	100,093	74,927	81,343	75,293
Total intermediate inputs							
Electricals	74,495	110,659	129,853	133,247	123,730	157,761	165,252
Metals	29,526	61,438	72,596	74,352	58,278	68,600	66,518
Chemicals	23,265	62,216	75,528	85,820	59,807	63,279	55,314
Total final demand							
Real estate	29,275	33,443	38,675	45,870	44,081	53,694	58,829
Construction	29,510	34,801	35,604	40,749	36,177	44,250	51,344
Public administration	37,131	36,619	39,742	42,570	42,243	44,553	48,877
Exports							
Electricals	77,016	118,726	134,799	143,139	142,265	205,091	196,852
Chemicals	9,874	28,422	34,858	38,112	29,882	34,373	39,520
Metals	12,833	25,320	26,473	27,175	24,373	29,817	31,540
Imports							
Electricals	49,968	56,710	59,911	68,131	61,983	83,231	80,765
Mining	9,558	29,379	36,972	46,826	25,791	35,174	34,156
Chemicals	15,092	26,948	31,902	27,827	27,155	27,093	25,345

Domestic Linkages

Indicator and Top 3 Sectors, 2020	2000	2007	2010	2013	2016	2019	2020
First-round effect							
Manufacturing, NEC	0.51	0.53	0.54	0.55	0.53	0.55	0.56
Water transport	0.63	0.56	0.58	0.56	0.55	0.51	0.56
Paper	0.54	0.53	0.53	0.54	0.53	0.56	0.55
Industrial support effect							
Metals	0.37	0.44	0.50	0.50	0.41	0.39	0.41
Textiles	0.38	0.51	0.56	0.52	0.43	0.50	0.41
Manufacturing, NEC	0.36	0.41	0.44	0.45	0.38	0.37	0.39
Production-induced effect							
Textiles	0.90	1.08	1.17	1.10	0.98	1.09	0.96
Metals	0.88	0.97	1.06	1.07	0.94	0.91	0.95
Manufacturing, NEC	0.87	0.94	0.99	1.00	0.91	0.92	0.95

continued on next page.

continued.

Taipei,China

East Asia

Domestic Linkages

Indicator and Top 3 Sectors, 2020	2000	2007	2010	2013	2016	2019	2020
Simple value-added multiplier							
Real estate	0.97	0.96	0.95	0.95	0.96	0.95	0.96
Finance	0.96	0.94	0.93	0.93	0.93	0.93	0.96
Education	0.94	0.92	0.92	0.92	0.93	0.93	0.94
Type I value-added multiplier							
Water transport	3.07	3.66	4.24	6.21	11.35	3.52	3.21
Manufacturing, NEC	2.23	2.31	2.36	2.40	2.27	2.47	2.59
Metals	2.23	2.48	2.60	2.63	2.50	2.40	2.50
Direct backward linkage							
Manufacturing, NEC	0.51	0.53	0.54	0.55	0.53	0.55	0.56
Water transport	0.63	0.56	0.58	0.56	0.55	0.51	0.56
Paper	0.54	0.53	0.53	0.54	0.53	0.56	0.55
Complete hypothetical extraction (backward)							
Manufacturing, NEC	1.73	1.85	1.88	1.89	1.79	1.92	1.83
Construction	1.86	1.86	1.86	1.85	1.78	1.81	1.81
Water transport	1.54	1.61	1.62	1.68	1.71	1.19	1.76
Partial hypothetical extraction (backward)							
Manufacturing, NEC	0.80	0.90	0.93	0.94	0.85	0.92	0.89
Construction	0.86	0.87	0.87	0.86	0.79	0.81	0.82
Water transport	0.78	0.71	0.74	0.74	0.72	0.56	0.79
Total backward linkage							
Textiles	1.90	2.08	2.17	2.10	1.98	2.09	1.96
Metals	1.88	1.97	2.06	2.07	1.94	1.91	1.95
Manufacturing, NEC	1.87	1.94	1.99	2.00	1.91	1.92	1.95
Direct forward linkage							
Mining	0.99	0.95	0.91	0.94	0.63	0.52	0.92
Wood	0.60	0.75	0.78	0.82	0.79	0.89	0.82
Utilities	0.79	0.82	0.82	0.82	0.81	0.82	0.81
Complete hypothetical extraction (forward)							
Mining	3.36	3.07	3.06	3.03	2.35	2.18	2.96
Utilities	2.14	2.20	2.23	2.22	2.17	2.12	2.13
Transport activities, NEC	2.19	1.82	1.86	1.82	1.74	1.88	1.93
Partial hypothetical extraction (forward)							
Mining	2.37	2.08	2.07	2.04	1.35	1.18	1.96
Utilities	1.26	1.32	1.34	1.33	1.28	1.25	1.26
Wood	0.78	0.97	1.04	1.08	1.02	1.16	1.05
Total forward linkage							
Mining	3.42	3.09	3.08	3.04	2.36	2.18	2.96
Utilities	2.42	2.50	2.52	2.49	2.43	2.44	2.44
Wood	1.88	2.14	2.22	2.28	2.21	2.38	2.24
Normalized backward linkage							
Textiles	1.18	1.29	1.34	1.28	1.24	1.31	1.22
Metals	1.17	1.22	1.27	1.26	1.22	1.20	1.22
Manufacturing, NEC	1.16	1.20	1.22	1.22	1.20	1.20	1.22
Normalized forward linkage							
Mining	2.02	1.86	1.85	1.83	1.46	1.32	1.79
Utilities	1.43	1.51	1.51	1.50	1.50	1.47	1.47
Wood	1.11	1.29	1.34	1.37	1.36	1.44	1.35
Net backward linkage							
Water transport	1.35	1.57	1.58	1.66	1.70	1.05	1.76
Manufacturing, NEC	1.61	1.73	1.73	1.73	1.62	1.92	1.68
Construction	1.67	1.65	1.60	1.60	1.55	1.50	1.53
Net forward linkage							
Mining	2.28	1.90	1.93	1.69	1.40	1.31	1.80
Finance	1.44	1.32	1.28	1.27	1.27	1.30	1.34
Wholesale trade	1.13	1.10	1.12	1.09	1.03	1.37	1.29

continued on next page.

continued.

Taipei,China

East Asia

International Linkages

Indicator and Top 3 Sectors, 2020	2000	2007	2010	2013	2016	2019	2020
Self-sufficiency ratio							
Electricals	1.34	1.59	1.63	1.55	1.64	1.93	1.66
Water transport	2.05	4.58	3.91	6.07	12.09	1.82	1.47
Rubber and plastics	1.33	1.31	1.27	1.28	1.29	1.24	1.35
Import-to-input ratio							
Refined fuels	0.47	0.61	0.65	0.68	0.60	0.65	0.55
Utilities	0.16	0.37	0.42	0.44	0.38	0.40	0.34
Water transport	0.13	0.29	0.30	0.37	0.41	0.41	0.27
Export-to-output ratio							
Electricals	0.72	0.71	0.69	0.68	0.69	0.81	0.67
Manufacturing, NEC	0.54	0.63	0.61	0.60	0.62	1.00	0.67
Leather	0.48	0.31	0.85	0.31	0.31	0.59	0.54
Domestic inputs share to output							
Sale of motor vehicles	0.42	0.40	0.38	0.38	0.39	0.18	0.59
Metals	0.51	0.53	0.56	0.57	0.53	0.53	0.53
Manufacturing, NEC	0.51	0.53	0.54	0.55	0.53	0.55	0.51
Foreign inputs share to output							
Refined fuels	0.47	0.61	0.65	0.68	0.60	0.65	0.55
Utilities	0.16	0.37	0.42	0.44	0.38	0.40	0.34
Water transport	0.13	0.29	0.30	0.37	0.41	0.41	0.27
Backward import multipliers							
Refined fuels	0.53	0.68	0.73	0.75	0.65	0.75	0.69
Water transport	0.26	0.48	0.51	0.56	0.55	0.71	0.58
Utilities	0.26	0.53	0.54	0.56	0.47	0.52	0.48
Forward import multipliers							
Mining	0.31	0.56	0.56	0.53	0.38	0.61	0.81
Electricals	0.51	0.69	0.65	0.71	0.75	0.78	0.76
Chemicals	0.62	0.76	0.76	0.76	0.76	0.72	0.66
Intraregional transfer multiplier							
Water transport	2.01	1.79	1.84	1.78	1.73	1.89	2.38
Agriculture	1.75	1.75	1.73	1.79	1.64	1.61	2.26
Textiles	1.90	2.08	2.17	2.10	1.98	2.09	2.25
Interregional spillover multiplier							
Refined fuels	1.67	2.00	2.09	2.12	2.09	2.15	1.96
Utilities	1.23	1.60	1.69	1.73	1.69	1.71	1.59
Wood	1.51	1.56	1.54	1.56	1.57	1.55	1.49
Interregional feedback multiplier							
Refined fuels	1.13	1.24	1.17	1.22	1.22	1.17	1.14
Electricals	1.21	1.20	1.19	1.20	1.17	1.17	1.12
Water transport	1.04	1.11	1.13	1.20	1.22	1.15	1.11
Intraregional effect on gross output ($ million)							
Electricals	52,721.48	52,708.83	67,605.11	62,073.62	52,063.92	55,377.67	67,891.95
Real estate	35,110.93	40,072.70	45,322.79	53,457.71	51,636.87	62,593.59	67,629.54
Construction	32,476.21	38,561.07	40,452.25	46,254.74	40,618.51	52,121.35	62,795.03
Interregional effect on gross output ($ million)							
Electricals	40,336.36	82,955.16	91,933.67	107,254.04	113,442.88	155,204.58	171,422.85
Chemicals	15,676.59	43,485.97	54,448.12	59,463.79	44,361.63	47,064.88	45,103.68
Metals	15,981.21	35,236.75	40,428.24	40,317.10	32,207.86	40,263.77	37,759.25
Feedback effect on gross output ($ million)							
Electricals	13,980.68	31,769.15	34,968.78	41,250.94	40,349.69	41,995.47	44,145.70
Metals	3,719.68	10,152.01	11,280.77	11,865.54	10,334.23	13,035.50	11,126.00
Chemicals	3,827.64	12,638.01	15,218.95	16,691.91	12,453.96	11,606.91	10,834.49
Directly absorbed value-added exports (DAVAX) ($ million)							
Electricals	28,865.30	38,334.23	47,322.40	50,610.31	53,449.53	81,522.85	92,897.80
Chemicals	3,748.28	6,905.26	9,289.84	9,229.37	9,243.00	11,834.37	12,359.66
Machinery, NEC	6,792.06	9,082.86	9,553.55	10,950.93	11,125.57	11,334.44	10,854.06
Reflection (REF) ($ million)							
Electricals	260.33	349.90	363.37	401.67	412.45	458.08	744.14
Metals	45.68	52.28	52.56	45.25	41.55	73.81	75.80
Chemicals	32.08	50.94	59.20	47.89	49.41	43.76	58.26

continued on next page.

continued.

Taipei,China

East Asia

International Linkages

Indicator and Top 3 Sectors, 2020	2000	2007	2010	2013	2016	2019	2020
Reexports (REX) ($ million)							
Electricals	10,694.37	27,459.07	27,670.91	31,686.74	33,010.94	45,552.78	47,827.21
Metals	2,089.41	4,211.64	4,196.42	4,432.87	4,348.90	6,380.75	5,861.94
Chemicals	1,688.80	4,471.71	4,972.35	4,570.29	4,396.41	4,807.89	4,906.50
Foreign value added (FVA) ($ million)							
Electricals	36,415.68	51,321.11	58,117.63	59,070.92	54,092.26	76,453.94	70,891.94
Chemicals	4,377.41	16,863.83	20,393.00	24,110.01	16,089.67	17,626.05	15,065.33
Metals	4,478.59	12,716.26	13,344.00	13,428.17	11,928.91	13,043.95	10,420.79
Pure double-counting (PDC) ($ million)							
Electricals	780.27	1,262.03	1,324.39	1,369.09	1,299.58	1,103.32	1,621.32
Machinery, NEC	41.54	93.23	90.55	97.14	99.63	61.58	67.97
Chemicals	27.76	130.66	143.49	154.82	103.61	61.41	64.37
Trade-based GVC participation rate							
Refined fuels	0.67	0.82	0.86	0.87	0.83	0.82	0.79
Water transport	0.45	0.70	0.71	0.75	0.74	0.87	0.78
Textiles	0.52	0.61	0.61	0.60	0.58	0.66	0.64
Production-based GVC participation rate							
Mining	0.31	0.56	0.56	0.53	0.38	0.61	0.81
Electricals	0.51	0.69	0.65	0.71	0.75	0.78	0.76
Chemicals	0.62	0.76	0.76	0.76	0.76	0.72	0.66
Trade-based backward GVC participation rate							
Refined fuels	0.53	0.68	0.73	0.75	0.65	0.75	0.69
Water transport	0.26	0.48	0.51	0.56	0.55	0.71	0.58
Utilities	0.26	0.53	0.54	0.56	0.47	0.52	0.48
Trade-based forward GVC participation rate							
Transport activities, NEC	0.34	0.32	0.40	0.30	0.26	0.42	0.36
Textiles	0.20	0.19	0.21	0.20	0.21	0.30	0.33
Finance	0.22	0.22	0.22	0.21	0.20	0.29	0.26
Traditional revealed comparative advantage							
Electricals	2.77	3.09	3.19	3.22	3.40	4.31	4.21
Air transport	0.76	1.13	1.17	1.28	1.31	1.52	1.90
Water transport	0.90	1.12	1.00	1.11	1.20	1.37	1.51
New revealed comparative advantage							
Electricals	3.09	4.84	4.97	5.43	5.52	5.81	5.67
Air transport	0.61	0.75	1.09	0.91	1.07	1.12	1.38
Metals	1.38	1.20	1.35	1.28	1.10	1.49	1.32
Backward production length							
Water transport	2.52	2.83	2.90	3.06	2.98	3.47	3.72
Chemicals	2.85	3.54	3.50	3.75	3.42	3.16	3.19
Textiles	2.65	3.16	3.19	3.16	2.96	2.96	3.05
Forward production length							
Mining	4.13	4.55	4.56	4.49	3.40	3.98	4.17
Chemicals	3.75	4.27	4.34	4.43	4.36	4.10	4.03
Water transport	2.72	3.27	3.34	3.22	3.18	3.94	4.03
Backward production length of GVC segment							
Real estate	4.46	4.75	4.73	4.81	4.71	4.53	4.85
Leather	4.31	4.77	4.11	4.92	4.73	4.46	4.77
Hotels and restaurants	4.28	4.48	4.44	4.68	4.48	4.35	4.76
Forward production length of GVC segment							
Utilities	5.05	5.43	5.49	5.55	5.51	5.44	5.63
Real estate	5.03	5.31	5.30	5.29	5.22	5.49	5.61
Refined fuels	5.02	4.55	4.65	4.57	4.66	5.24	5.33
Backward agglomeration index							
Textiles	-	0.39	0.81	0.64	0.55	1.25	1.34
Leather	-	1.13	0.11	1.11	1.03	1.00	1.29
Rubber and plastics	-	0.32	0.49	0.52	0.63	0.43	1.10
Forward agglomeration index							
Agriculture	-	1.10	1.03	1.05	1.02	1.11	1.15
Food and beverages	-	1.11	1.07	1.05	1.03	1.01	1.05
Education	-	1.03	1.02	1.02	1.02	1.02	1.01

CIF = cost, insurance, and freight; FOB = free on board; GVC = global value chain; NEC = not elsewhere classified; NPISHs = nonprofit institutions serving households.
Source: Calculations using the Asian Development Bank Multiregional Input-Output Table. https://mrio.adbx.online/ (accessed July 2021).

continued on next page.

continued.

Taipei,China

East Asia

The four select sectors are chosen based on their gross outputs in the economy as of 2019.

Economy Ranking out of 25 Economies

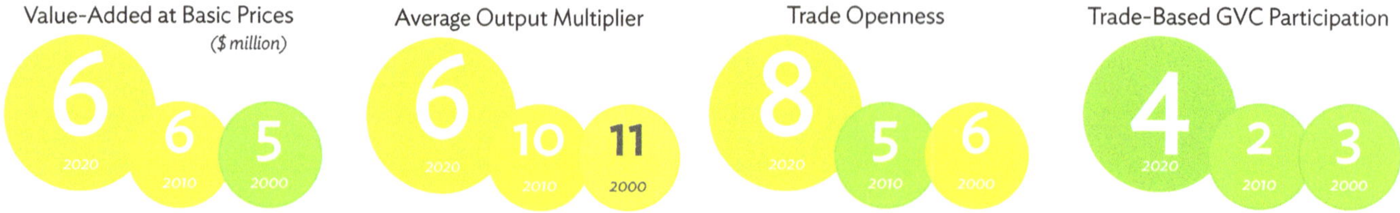

Share of Intermediate Consumption and Gross Value-Added in Output

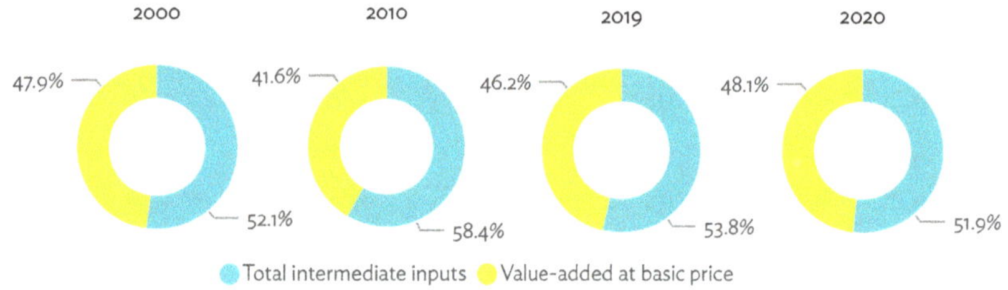

Imports and Exports, 2019-2020

($ million)

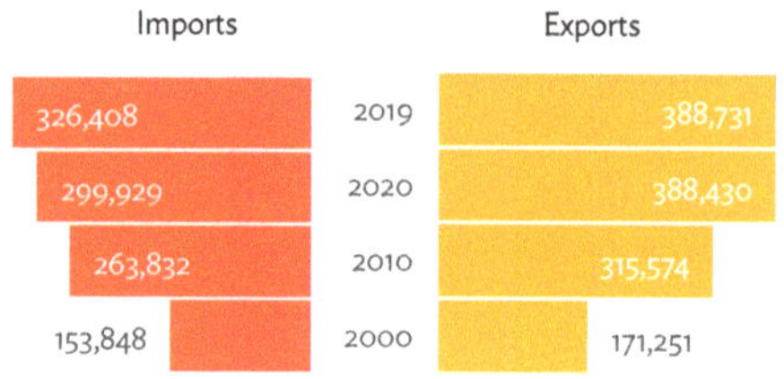

Domestic Linkages

Normalized Linkages

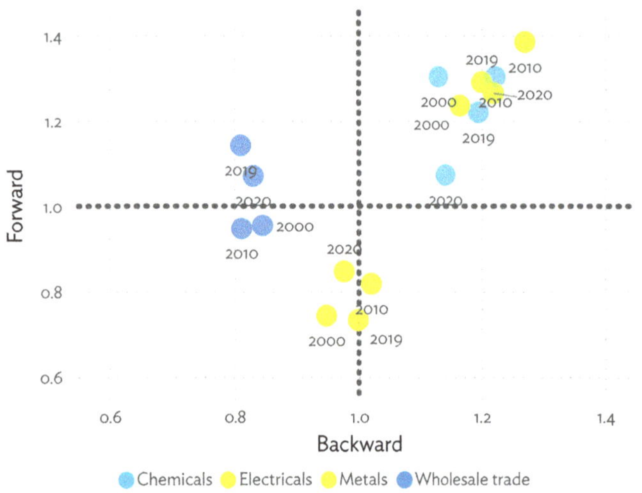

Net Linkages

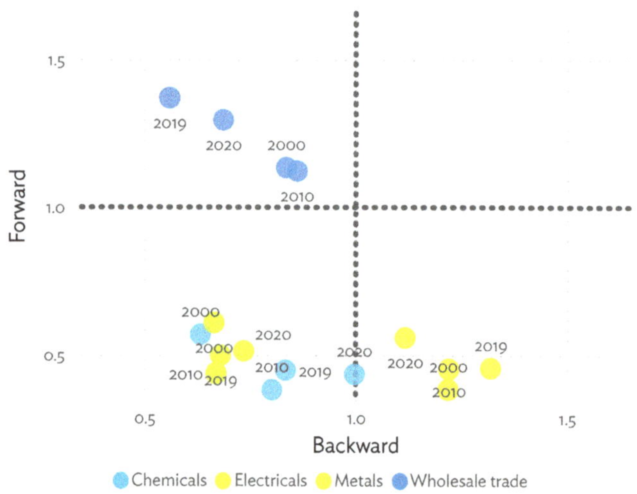

Value-Added Multipliers

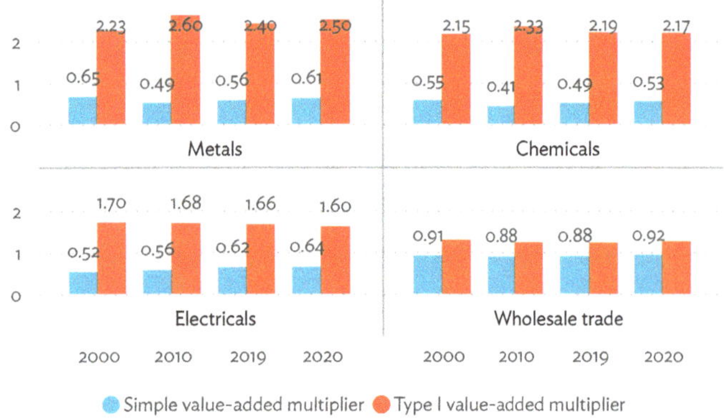

Production-Induced Effect

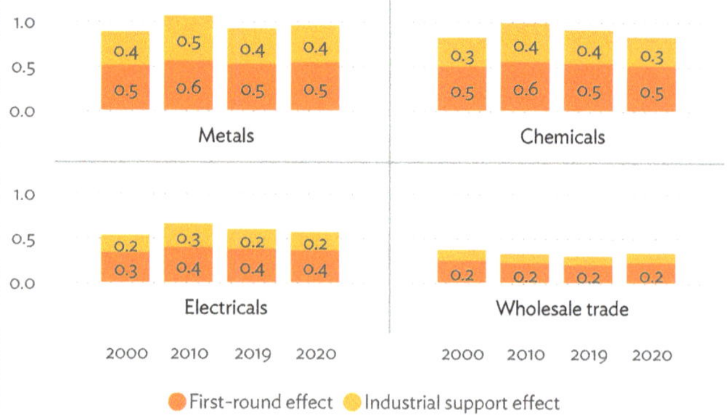

continued on next page.

Click here for figure data

continued.

Taipei,China

East Asia

International Linkages

Change in Exports, by Value-Added Components, 2019-2020

($ million)

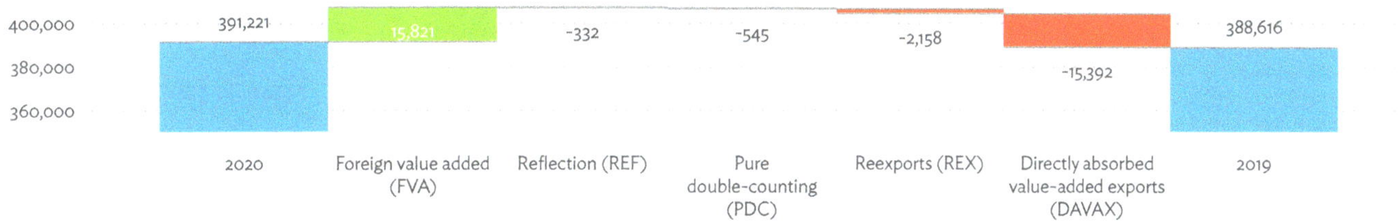

Import Multipliers

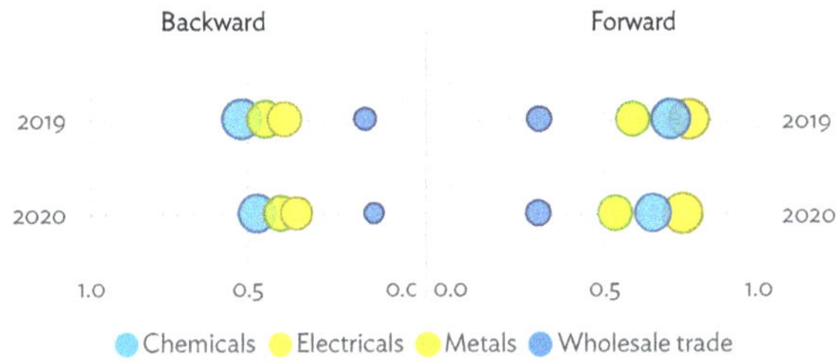

GVC Participation Rates

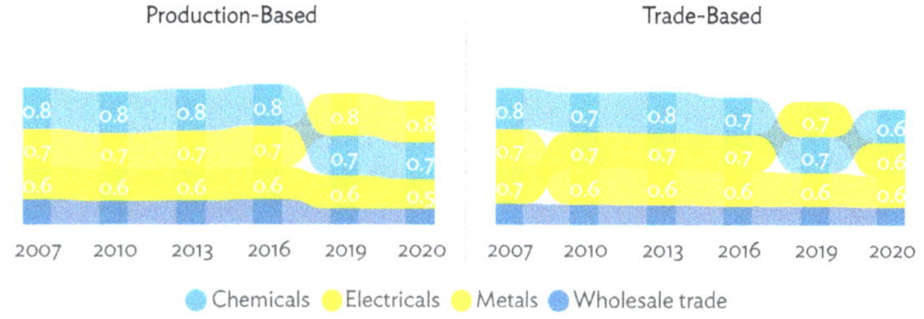

Average Production Length

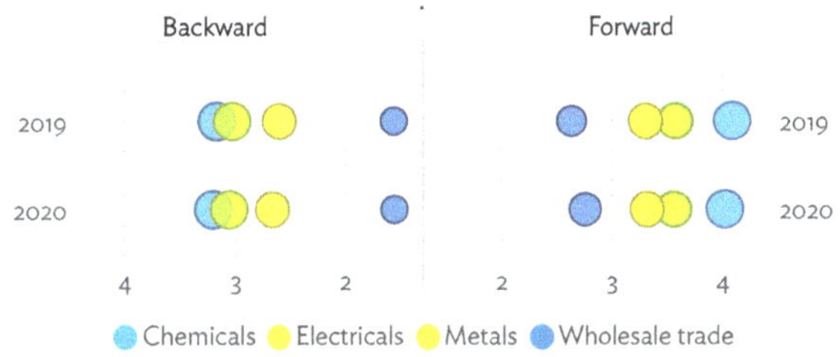

New Revealed Comparative Advantage

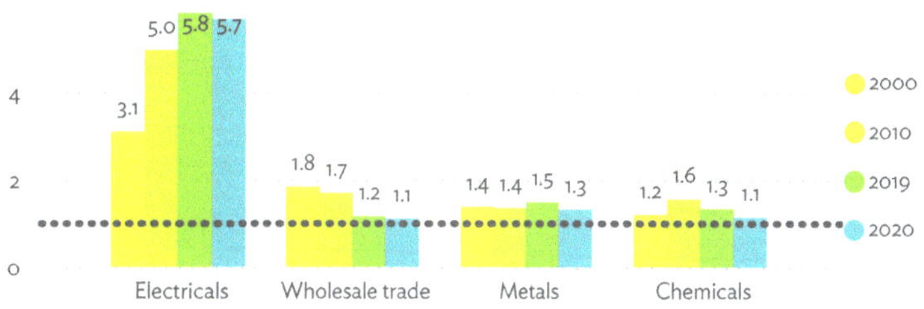

Trade Orientation

Agglomeration Indices

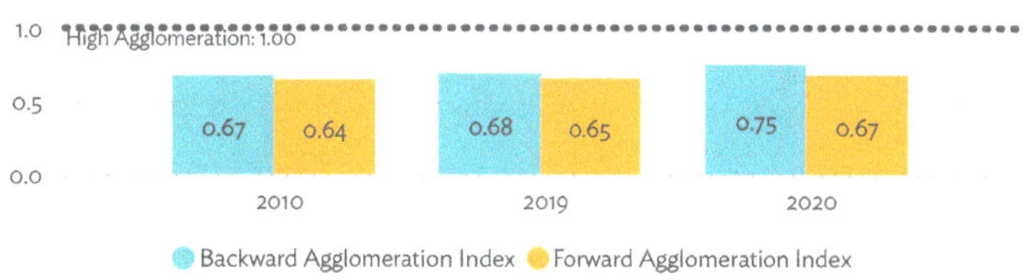

Domestic Transfer Effects and International Spillover Effects

($ million)

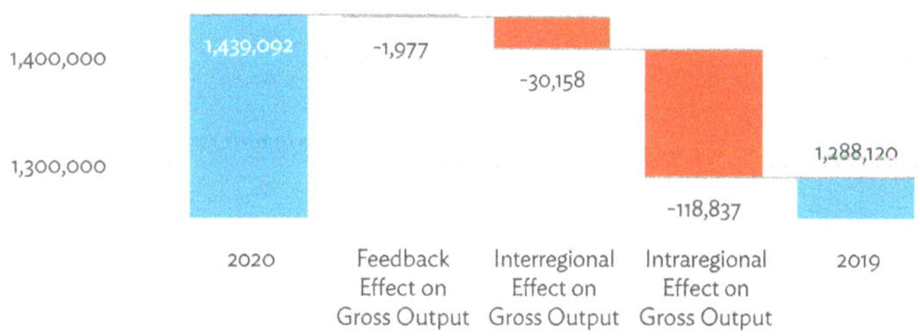

GVC = global value chain; NEC = not elsewhere classified.

Source: Calculations using the Asian Development Bank Multiregional Input-Output Table. https://mrio.adbx.online/ (accessed July 2021).

Click here for figure data

Thailand

Southeast Asia and the Pacific

Basic Economic Indicators

Economic Aggregates ($ million)	2000	2007	2010	2013	2016	2019	2020
Value-added at basic price	112,386	241,187	303,725	397,580	402,436	493,739	451,375
Gross output	287,499	710,145	908,025	1,030,490	1,041,300	1,270,191	1,130,804
Total intermediate inputs	168,139	455,866	586,257	612,657	611,863	741,484	645,905
Taxes less subsidies on products	6,975	13,093	18,043	20,253	27,001	34,969	33,524
International transport margins	0	0	0	0	0	0	0
CIF/FOB adjustment	0	0	0	0	0	0	0
Direct purchases abroad by residents	0	0	0	0	0	0	0
Purchases by nonresidents on the domestic territory	0	0	0	0	0	0	0
Household final consumption expenditure	63,366	136,618	166,911	208,298	200,633	210,979	209,926
Final consumption expenditure by NPISHs	1	2	3	4	4	4	4
Government final consumption expenditure	18,292	40,825	55,857	69,155	69,871	89,088	90,145
Gross fixed capital formation	21,683	59,302	68,352	77,922	76,366	90,984	87,899
Changes in inventories	610	216	3,671	2,753	-21,057	10,788	6,564
Total final demand	103,952	236,964	294,793	358,131	325,817	401,844	394,538
Exports	55,962	121,118	152,231	213,641	219,491	323,769	258,073
Imports	54,968	132,271	158,942	203,040	152,615	272,917	233,333

Economic Aggregates, Top 3 Sectors ($ million)	2000	2007	2010	2013	2016	2019	2020
Value-added at basic price							
Wholesale trade	12,187	22,054	28,711	37,081	40,390	52,925	50,636
Retail trade	9,902	17,919	23,327	30,128	32,816	43,002	41,142
Agriculture	8,478	20,406	29,786	40,537	30,368	37,192	36,528
Gross output							
Metals	30,133	131,106	137,243	143,867	138,309	155,707	140,128
Hotels and restaurants	15,079	25,438	32,360	43,453	90,976	140,767	85,504
Wholesale trade	22,345	38,813	52,568	61,583	67,540	87,702	82,976
Total intermediate inputs							
Metals	20,079	106,767	112,389	115,251	110,577	124,393	111,444
Food and beverages	22,549	37,019	62,941	65,457	62,629	65,491	58,522
Hotels and restaurants	8,903	15,218	19,744	24,664	51,134	79,407	47,479
Total final demand							
Hotels and restaurants	10,756	21,003	24,383	30,955	61,338	87,945	58,815
Public administration	10,219	21,143	28,633	36,124	35,716	41,658	42,947
Construction	9,591	26,066	33,713	30,395	31,524	31,741	33,373
Exports							
Food and beverages	7,510	9,068	15,291	21,743	20,568	37,553	35,953
Transport equipment	1,767	14,414	16,465	13,834	16,704	38,304	34,803
Agriculture	986	2,881	4,726	11,003	8,349	18,291	28,230
Imports							
Metals	14,671	47,907	57,466	70,143	50,495	80,174	69,605
Mining	2,957	9,891	10,305	34,472	22,869	46,411	39,949
Water transport	8,309	18,682	20,109	21,582	16,140	25,117	26,593

Domestic Linkages

Indicator and Top 3 Sectors, 2020	2000	2007	2010	2013	2016	2019	2020
First-round effect							
Food and beverages	0.68	0.68	0.70	0.72	0.74	0.71	0.71
Sale of motor vehicles	0.63	0.61	0.62	0.59	0.62	0.58	0.59
Textiles	0.38	0.55	0.56	0.58	0.60	0.58	0.58
Industrial support effect							
Food and beverages	0.50	0.54	0.61	0.52	0.59	0.44	0.46
Metals	0.32	0.57	0.60	0.45	0.59	0.40	0.42
Textiles	0.30	0.56	0.61	0.50	0.59	0.42	0.41
Production-induced effect							
Food and beverages	1.19	1.23	1.31	1.24	1.33	1.15	1.17
Textiles	0.68	1.12	1.17	1.08	1.19	1.00	0.99
Sale of motor vehicles	1.10	1.13	1.19	1.00	1.10	0.95	0.95

continued on next page.

continued.

Thailand

Southeast Asia and the Pacific — *Domestic Linkages*

Indicator and Top 3 Sectors, 2020	2000	2007	2010	2013	2016	2019	2020
Simple value-added multiplier							
Finance	0.92	0.92	0.91	0.93	0.94	0.93	0.93
Real estate	0.95	0.92	0.91	0.92	0.93	0.89	0.90
Public administration	0.87	0.88	0.87	0.89	0.91	0.89	0.90
Type I value-added multiplier							
Food and beverages	4.55	4.04	4.27	4.33	4.40	4.11	4.02
Chemicals	3.24	3.21	3.28	2.82	3.10	2.95	2.96
Mining	3.38	3.21	3.33	3.14	3.27	2.83	2.85
Direct backward linkage							
Food and beverages	0.68	0.68	0.70	0.72	0.74	0.71	0.71
Sale of motor vehicles	0.63	0.61	0.62	0.59	0.62	0.58	0.59
Textiles	0.38	0.55	0.56	0.58	0.60	0.58	0.58
Complete hypothetical extraction (backward)							
Sale of motor vehicles	2.09	2.13	2.19	2.00	2.10	1.95	1.95
Air transport	1.80	1.75	1.86	1.78	1.94	1.92	1.93
Electricals	1.86	1.89	1.92	1.83	1.95	1.91	1.91
Partial hypothetical extraction (backward)							
Food and beverages	0.97	1.02	1.04	1.01	1.06	1.01	1.02
Sale of motor vehicles	1.10	1.13	1.19	1.00	1.10	0.95	0.95
Air transport	0.99	0.95	1.03	0.92	1.06	0.92	0.93
Total backward linkage							
Food and beverages	2.19	2.23	2.31	2.24	2.33	2.15	2.17
Textiles	1.68	2.12	2.17	2.08	2.19	2.00	1.99
Sale of motor vehicles	2.10	2.13	2.19	2.00	2.10	1.95	1.95
Direct forward linkage							
Mining	0.91	0.98	0.99	0.97	0.96	0.91	0.89
Business activities, NEC	0.91	0.93	0.91	0.84	0.85	0.70	0.84
Utilities	0.84	0.85	0.86	0.79	0.87	0.87	0.80
Complete hypothetical extraction (forward)							
Mining	2.83	3.24	3.35	2.83	3.13	2.55	2.55
Business activities, NEC	2.48	2.53	2.56	2.32	2.41	2.02	2.20
Finance	2.52	2.55	2.55	2.12	2.29	2.20	2.14
Partial hypothetical extraction (forward)							
Mining	1.85	2.26	2.37	1.85	2.14	1.56	1.55
Business activities, NEC	1.58	1.69	1.72	1.45	1.53	1.11	1.32
Finance	1.56	1.60	1.60	1.18	1.36	1.26	1.21
Total forward linkage							
Mining	2.88	3.29	3.42	2.89	3.19	2.57	2.57
Business activities, NEC	2.75	2.99	3.02	2.66	2.75	2.23	2.49
Utilities	2.49	2.68	2.75	2.40	2.60	2.45	2.35
Normalized backward linkage							
Food and beverages	1.23	1.15	1.16	1.26	1.24	1.26	1.27
Textiles	0.94	1.09	1.09	1.17	1.17	1.17	1.17
Sale of motor vehicles	1.18	1.10	1.10	1.13	1.12	1.14	1.14
Normalized forward linkage							
Mining	1.56	1.64	1.65	1.59	1.63	1.61	1.61
Business activities, NEC	1.48	1.48	1.46	1.46	1.40	1.39	1.56
Utilities	1.35	1.33	1.33	1.31	1.33	1.53	1.47
Net backward linkage							
Electricals	1.08	0.84	0.61	0.67	0.61	1.90	1.91
Air transport	0.79	0.70	0.74	0.92	0.93	1.91	1.90
Machinery, NEC	0.68	0.68	0.60	0.74	0.76	1.84	1.86
Net forward linkage							
Finance	1.85	1.91	1.85	1.62	1.77	1.67	1.65
Wholesale trade	1.08	1.23	1.20	1.10	1.16	1.33	1.33
Retail trade	1.14	1.35	1.32	1.27	1.38	1.34	1.29

continued on next page.

continued.

Thailand

Southeast Asia and the Pacific *International Linkages*

Indicator and Top 3 Sectors, 2020	2000	2007	2010	2013	2016	2019	2020
Self-sufficiency ratio							
Wood	1.42	1.29	1.24	1.39	1.37	1.79	3.80
Chemicals	0.99	0.99	1.04	0.96	0.94	2.01	2.23
Manufacturing, NEC	1.16	1.05	1.05	1.02	1.05	1.99	2.08
Import-to-input ratio							
Refined fuels	0.25	0.22	0.21	0.50	0.38	0.59	0.57
Minerals, NEC	0.27	0.23	0.22	0.40	0.31	0.45	0.43
Metals	0.24	0.27	0.26	0.28	0.22	0.30	0.29
Export-to-output ratio							
Machinery, NEC	0.34	0.31	0.27	0.36	0.34	0.99	1.00
Electricals	0.43	0.25	0.15	0.16	0.15	0.99	1.00
Leather	0.49	0.17	0.19	0.19	0.21	0.84	0.92
Domestic inputs share to output							
Food and beverages	0.68	0.68	0.70	0.72	0.74	0.71	0.71
Sale of motor vehicles	0.63	0.61	0.62	0.59	0.62	0.58	0.59
Textiles	0.38	0.55	0.56	0.58	0.60	0.58	0.58
Foreign inputs share to output							
Refined fuels	0.25	0.22	0.21	0.50	0.38	0.59	0.57
Minerals, NEC	0.27	0.23	0.22	0.40	0.31	0.45	0.43
Metals	0.24	0.27	0.26	0.28	0.22	0.30	0.29
Backward import multipliers							
Refined fuels	0.47	0.52	0.46	0.69	0.61	0.75	0.75
Minerals, NEC	0.43	0.42	0.42	0.58	0.48	0.63	0.60
Metals	0.37	0.49	0.48	0.48	0.40	0.52	0.49
Forward import multipliers							
Wood	0.55	0.47	0.42	0.51	0.51	0.67	0.85
Chemicals	0.40	0.33	0.33	0.44	0.42	0.84	0.83
Water transport	0.28	0.30	0.27	0.31	0.33	0.81	0.60
Intraregional transfer multiplier							
Food and beverages	2.19	2.23	2.31	2.24	2.33	2.15	2.17
Textiles	1.68	2.12	2.17	2.08	2.19	2.00	1.99
Sale of motor vehicles	2.10	2.13	2.19	2.00	2.10	1.95	1.95
Interregional spillover multiplier							
Refined fuels	1.38	1.37	1.38	1.94	1.73	2.06	2.07
Minerals, NEC	1.41	1.38	1.37	1.75	1.60	1.81	1.81
Metals	1.46	1.55	1.56	1.60	1.48	1.67	1.66
Interregional feedback multiplier							
Refined fuels	1.09	1.10	1.09	1.19	1.15	1.16	1.17
Metals	1.10	1.16	1.16	1.18	1.13	1.17	1.16
Minerals, NEC	1.10	1.10	1.10	1.16	1.13	1.14	1.15
Intraregional effect on gross output ($ million)							
Metals	18,486.16	70,814.52	77,733.71	78,280.99	73,598.16	114,365.79	104,427.81
Hotels and restaurants	14,305.94	24,577.41	30,813.80	41,029.99	84,726.43	128,793.06	79,017.17
Wholesale trade	15,095.13	29,104.70	36,559.47	38,749.02	41,888.12	67,017.03	67,094.41
Interregional effect on gross output ($ million)							
Metals	8,965.58	45,556.73	45,790.51	50,872.57	49,266.34	30,763.41	27,160.85
Chemicals	2,331.36	4,494.42	6,493.81	9,292.61	8,461.09	22,003.54	20,078.33
Agriculture	1,802.71	3,780.66	6,446.94	12,064.51	9,275.22	14,951.66	18,599.79
Feedback effect on gross output ($ million)							
Metals	2,681.06	14,734.93	13,718.78	14,713.60	15,444.61	10,577.59	8,539.01
Chemicals	780.24	1,505.31	2,048.34	2,719.64	2,673.88	6,159.26	4,988.96
Business activities, NEC	576.11	2,078.45	2,574.49	3,833.39	3,894.86	6,513.17	3,605.51
Directly absorbed value-added exports (DAVAX) ($ million)							
Food and beverages	4,655.05	5,908.24	9,890.46	15,198.09	14,751.51	27,494.91	26,665.24
Agriculture	620.67	1,889.36	3,022.61	7,596.03	5,954.41	13,325.10	21,514.12
Transport equipment	976.10	6,733.42	7,724.55	7,875.35	10,462.56	20,890.74	19,842.67
Reflection (REF) ($ million)							
Metals	28.64	113.53	115.08	140.26	132.05	85.68	76.49
Chemicals	5.08	5.62	8.94	9.80	10.70	71.39	54.60
Transport equipment	2.35	19.78	25.37	14.28	14.66	58.43	50.34

continued on next page.

continued.

Thailand

Southeast Asia and the Pacific *International Linkages*

Indicator and Top 3 Sectors, 2020	2000	2007	2010	2013	2016	2019	2020
Reexports (REX) ($ million)							
Chemicals	331.91	483.45	800.60	919.93	1,064.70	5,142.01	4,485.90
Agriculture	219.51	644.85	1,101.85	2,104.30	1,531.14	2,755.23	3,544.59
Rubber and plastics	599.97	1,787.77	1,863.24	2,624.27	2,548.37	3,487.93	3,017.10
Foreign value added (FVA) ($ million)							
Transport equipment	660.26	5,681.75	6,465.44	4,596.74	4,572.48	13,996.05	12,049.40
Chemicals	639.89	748.01	1,363.72	2,283.67	1,694.98	12,299.38	10,551.28
Metals	3,509.26	19,382.83	19,981.61	22,877.49	17,224.95	9,236.86	8,227.18
Pure double-counting (PDC) ($ million)							
Transport equipment	2.54	32.11	35.28	25.04	28.17	86.62	66.50
Metals	13.58	112.41	109.72	123.38	100.25	56.05	44.70
Chemicals	1.71	2.63	4.82	7.33	6.03	55.04	41.20
Trade-based GVC participation rate							
Refined fuels	0.60	0.71	0.69	0.81	0.71	0.82	0.82
Metals	0.56	0.65	0.63	0.63	0.58	0.70	0.68
Minerals, NEC	0.52	0.53	0.53	0.66	0.57	0.69	0.66
Production-based GVC participation rate							
Wood	0.55	0.47	0.42	0.51	0.51	0.67	0.85
Chemicals	0.40	0.33	0.33	0.44	0.42	0.84	0.83
Water transport	0.28	0.30	0.27	0.31	0.33	0.81	0.60
Trade-based backward GVC participation rate							
Refined fuels	0.47	0.52	0.46	0.69	0.61	0.75	0.75
Minerals, NEC	0.43	0.42	0.42	0.58	0.48	0.63	0.60
Metals	0.37	0.49	0.48	0.48	0.40	0.52	0.49
Trade-based forward GVC participation rate							
Transport activities, NEC	0.24	0.31	0.31	0.31	0.33	0.24	0.29
Paper	0.25	0.24	0.24	0.23	0.24	0.26	0.25
Business activities, NEC	0.23	0.23	0.23	0.25	0.26	0.26	0.25
Traditional revealed comparative advantage							
Hotels and restaurants	4.22	1.79	2.75	4.08	6.31	7.03	4.39
Agriculture	0.82	1.17	1.38	2.19	1.62	1.96	3.55
Rubber and plastics	2.07	2.43	2.23	2.24	1.93	2.29	2.59
New revealed comparative advantage							
Hotels and restaurants	2.64	1.21	1.75	2.53	4.39	4.78	3.19
Retail trade	2.44	2.47	3.10	2.85	3.13	3.04	3.00
Agriculture	1.98	1.80	2.08	2.53	1.93	2.29	2.70
Backward production length							
Metals	2.67	3.45	3.51	3.35	3.33	3.37	3.37
Refined fuels	3.11	3.79	3.63	3.47	3.58	3.16	3.27
Minerals, NEC	2.88	3.32	3.40	3.27	3.27	3.11	3.15
Forward production length							
Mining	3.82	4.21	4.19	3.85	4.30	3.61	3.62
Chemicals	3.47	3.55	3.57	3.86	3.74	3.53	3.56
Wood	3.03	3.50	3.54	3.47	3.56	3.35	3.38
Backward production length of GVC segment							
Hotels and restaurants	4.48	4.83	4.89	4.85	4.97	4.71	4.77
Wood	4.06	4.74	4.81	4.68	4.78	4.64	4.69
Food and beverages	4.13	4.47	4.53	4.67	4.80	4.56	4.67
Forward production length of GVC segment							
Real estate	4.68	5.79	5.71	5.41	5.52	5.16	5.40
Telecommunications	4.46	4.98	4.55	4.16	4.20	4.85	5.25
Utilities	4.85	5.38	5.40	5.11	5.29	5.07	5.13
Backward agglomeration index							
Textiles	-	1.35	1.14	1.11	1.00	0.98	1.16
Metals	-	0.74	0.61	0.77	0.89	1.07	1.07
Wholesale trade	-	0.91	0.83	0.73	0.63	1.01	1.05
Forward agglomeration index							
Metals	-	0.86	0.76	0.78	0.72	1.12	1.10
Mining	-	1.28	1.31	1.23	0.31	1.17	1.08
Education	-	1.03	1.02	1.02	1.02	1.00	1.02

CIF = cost, insurance, and freight; FOB = free on board; GVC = global value chain; NEC = not elsewhere classified; NPISHs = nonprofit institutions serving households.
Source: Calculations using the Asian Development Bank Multiregional Input-Output Table. https://mrio.adbx.online/ (accessed July 2021).

continued on next page.

continued.

Thailand

Southeast Asia and the Pacific

The four select sectors are chosen based on their gross outputs in the economy as of 2019.

Economy Ranking out of 25 Economies

Share of Intermediate Consumption and Gross Value-Added in Output

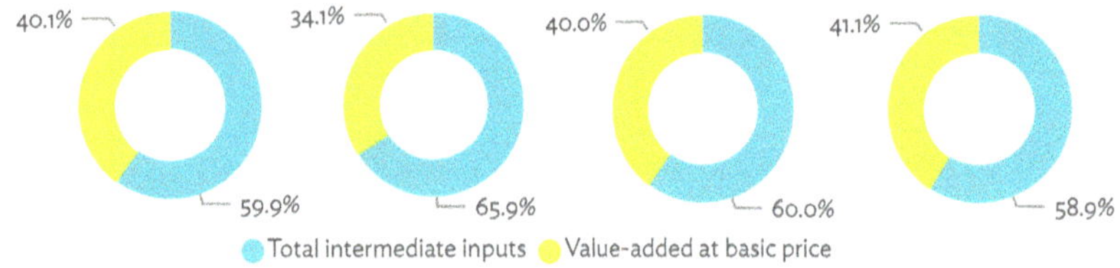

Imports and Exports, 2019-2020

($ million)

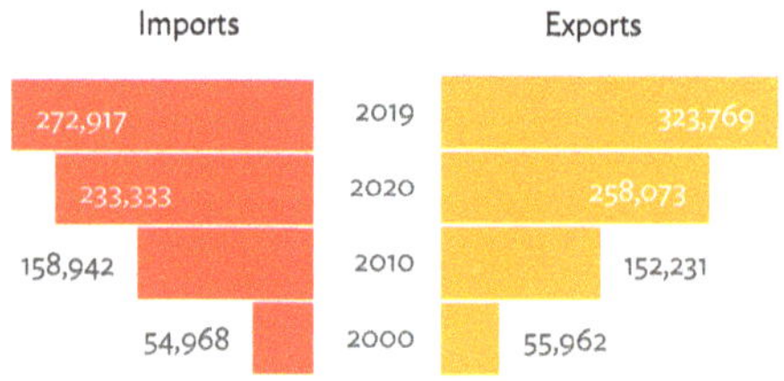

Domestic Linkages

Normalized Linkages

Net Linkages

Value-Added Multipliers

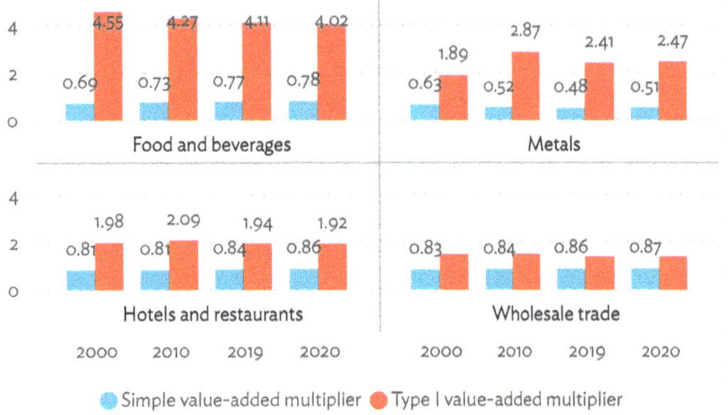

Production-Induced Effect

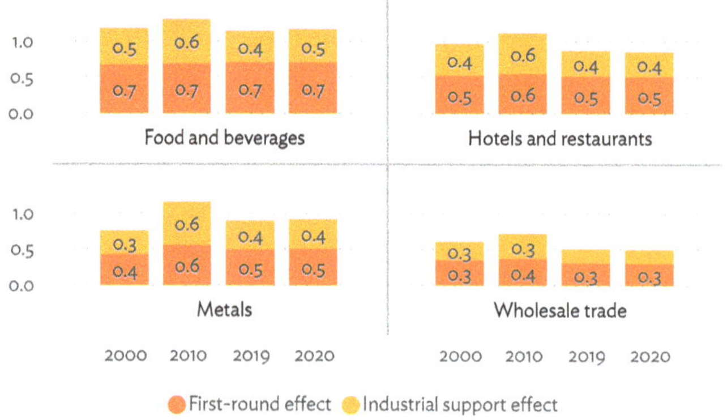

continued on next page.

Click here for figure data

continued.

Thailand

Southeast Asia and the Pacific

International Linkages

Change in Exports, by Value-Added Components, 2019-2020

($ million)

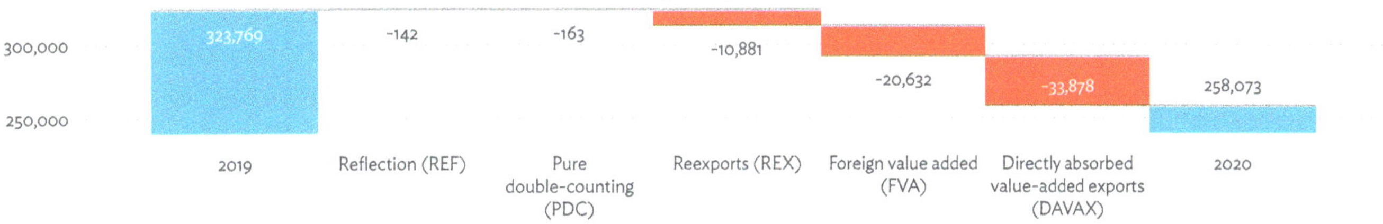

Import Multipliers

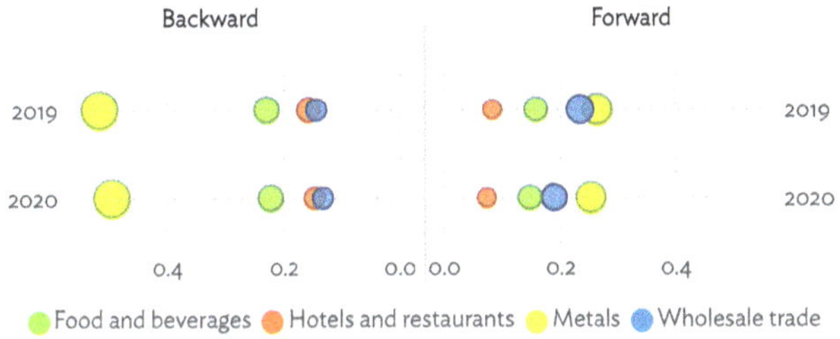

GVC Participation Rates

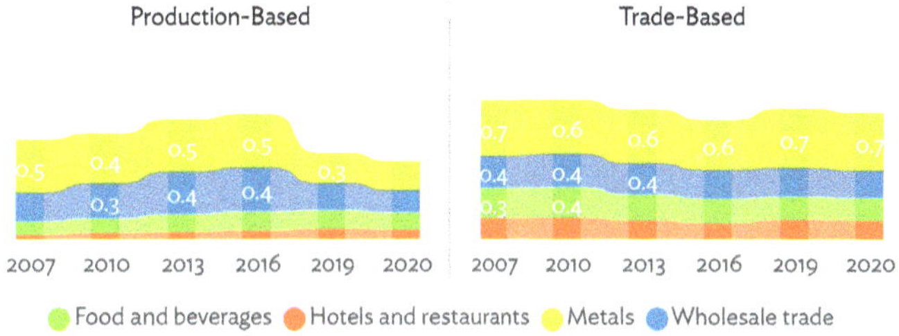

Average Production Length

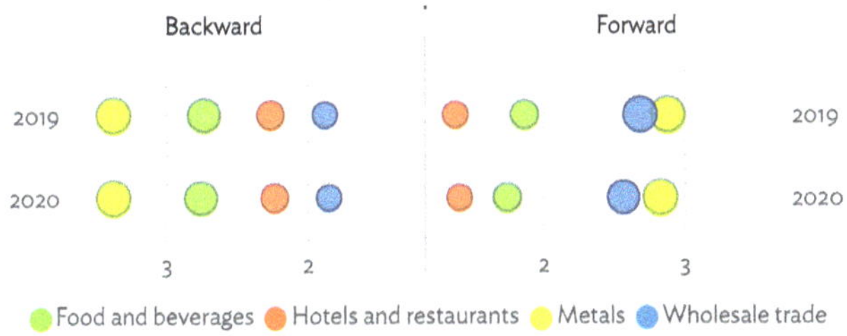

New Revealed Comparative Advantage

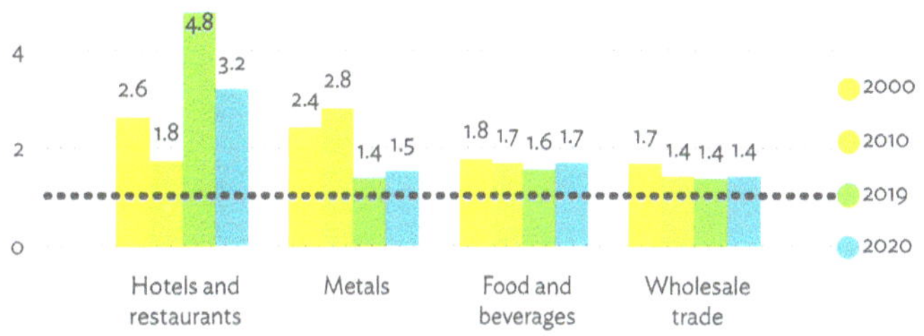

Trade Orientation

Agglomeration Indices

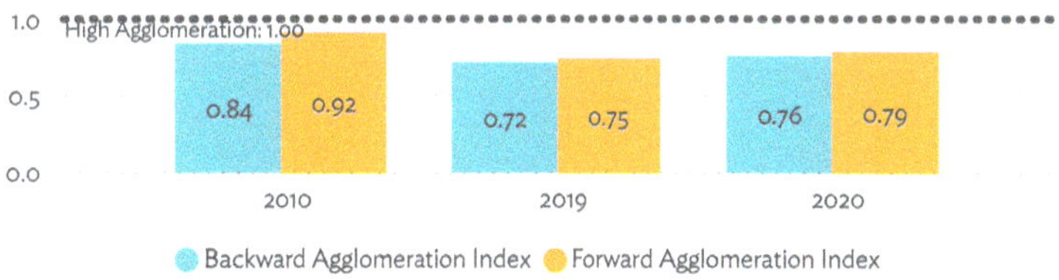

Domestic Transfer Effects and International Spillover Effects

($ million)

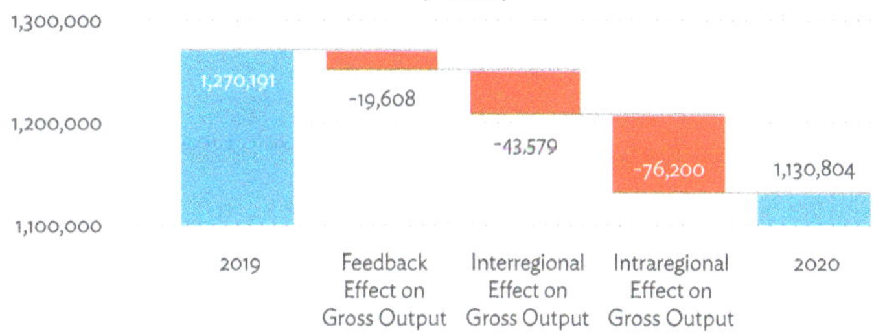

GVC = global value chain; NEC = not elsewhere classified.
Source: Calculations using the Asian Development Bank Multiregional Input-Output Table. https://mrio.adbx.online/ (accessed July 2021).

Click here for figure data

Viet Nam

Southeast Asia and the Pacific

Basic Economic Indicators

Economic Aggregates ($ million)	2000	2007	2010	2013	2016	2019	2020
Value-added at basic price	31,126	69,772	101,386	153,911	184,665	235,951	244,592
Gross output	66,977	179,046	314,784	462,435	557,872	726,773	753,263
Total intermediate inputs	35,851	105,478	206,588	300,418	363,556	478,595	496,180
Taxes less subsidies on products	0	3,795	6,811	8,106	9,651	12,227	12,491
International transport margins	0	0	0	0	0	0	0
CIF/FOB adjustment	0	0	0	0	0	0	0
Direct purchases abroad by residents	0	0	0	0	0	0	0
Purchases by nonresidents on the domestic territory	0	0	0	0	0	0	0
Household final consumption expenditure	15,503	35,831	58,048	85,035	102,135	136,245	143,722
Final consumption expenditure by NPISHs	0	0	0	0	0	0	0
Government final consumption expenditure	1,421	3,419	6,317	9,924	12,942	15,819	17,346
Gross fixed capital formation	7,358	21,222	30,350	32,974	35,866	30,055	32,154
Changes in inventories	-111	-2,016	2,112	1,851	-2,983	-6,214	-6,723
Total final demand	24,172	58,456	96,826	129,784	147,959	175,905	186,499
Exports	17,155	55,038	83,474	143,186	192,188	279,720	274,571
Imports	17,970	65,543	92,995	139,491	186,929	271,363	266,645

Economic Aggregates, Top 3 Sectors ($ million)	2000	2007	2010	2013	2016	2019	2020
Value-added at basic price							
Wholesale trade	4,038	7,925	9,091	15,330	19,322	26,808	28,743
Agriculture	5,708	9,731	15,736	22,956	24,124	25,147	27,510
Construction	1,669	4,286	7,282	9,080	11,485	14,815	15,864
Gross output							
Food and beverages	5,719	19,998	40,955	60,935	76,455	97,803	101,833
Agriculture	11,892	20,932	41,979	61,348	63,227	66,082	72,289
Construction	5,488	14,098	25,150	31,237	38,962	50,257	53,815
Total intermediate inputs							
Food and beverages	4,087	15,033	34,946	51,908	65,323	83,603	87,064
Agriculture	6,184	10,927	25,657	37,694	38,272	40,268	44,061
Electricals	3,812	11,926	13,869	20,464	25,720	38,347	39,942
Total final demand							
Food and beverages	1,456	3,286	11,792	15,352	13,695	35,833	42,953
Construction	4,777	13,231	23,370	28,127	33,343	36,444	38,377
Health and social work	547	1,587	3,084	5,659	10,199	16,443	18,282
Exports							
Electricals	972	3,267	7,476	25,472	30,854	48,340	50,342
Textiles	2,006	6,742	13,371	21,394	24,879	43,646	45,509
Leather	1,938	6,515	7,609	12,641	18,227	23,589	24,056
Imports							
Electricals	1,295	5,527	8,724	30,262	30,679	47,697	48,036
Chemicals	2,485	7,683	11,968	18,485	29,024	36,152	36,390
Metals	1,057	9,831	11,406	14,639	23,661	35,307	35,017

Domestic Linkages

Indicator and Top 3 Sectors, 2020	2000	2007	2010	2013	2016	2019	2020
First-round effect							
Wood	0.60	0.58	0.69	0.71	0.71	0.72	0.73
Refined fuels	0.21	0.15	0.54	0.61	0.69	0.71	0.72
Food and beverages	0.60	0.65	0.71	0.69	0.67	0.62	0.63
Industrial support effect							
Refined fuels	0.12	0.05	0.34	0.42	0.47	0.55	0.63
Food and beverages	0.40	0.46	0.70	0.60	0.51	0.52	0.55
Wood	0.37	0.41	0.64	0.64	0.60	0.52	0.53
Production-induced effect							
Refined fuels	0.32	0.20	0.88	1.03	1.16	1.27	1.35
Wood	0.97	0.99	1.33	1.35	1.32	1.24	1.26
Food and beverages	0.99	1.10	1.40	1.29	1.18	1.14	1.18

continued on next page.

continued.

Viet Nam

Southeast Asia and the Pacific

Domestic Linkages

Indicator and Top 3 Sectors, 2020	2000	2007	2010	2013	2016	2019	2020
Simple value-added multiplier							
Utilities	0.80	0.83	0.86	0.86	0.88	0.90	0.91
Education	0.87	0.91	0.90	0.93	0.92	0.90	0.90
Public administration	0.86	0.84	0.86	0.90	0.89	0.87	0.88
Type I value-added multiplier							
Wood	2.61	2.47	4.47	4.65	4.67	4.67	4.81
Refined fuels	1.82	1.49	3.22	3.98	4.31	4.38	4.49
Food and beverages	2.66	3.02	4.16	4.04	3.96	3.52	3.64
Direct backward linkage							
Wood	0.60	0.58	0.69	0.71	0.71	0.72	0.73
Refined fuels	0.21	0.15	0.54	0.61	0.69	0.71	0.72
Food and beverages	0.60	0.65	0.71	0.69	0.67	0.62	0.63
Complete hypothetical extraction (backward)							
Wood	1.90	1.75	1.87	1.86	1.82	1.98	2.06
Manufacturing, NEC	1.52	1.78	1.99	1.99	1.92	1.92	1.94
Hotels and restaurants	1.58	1.47	1.83	1.79	1.73	1.72	1.75
Partial hypothetical extraction (backward)							
Wood	0.94	0.87	1.07	1.07	1.04	1.10	1.15
Manufacturing, NEC	0.66	0.78	1.01	1.02	0.94	0.92	0.94
Refined fuels	0.32	0.19	0.69	0.83	0.88	0.87	0.88
Total backward linkage							
Refined fuels	1.32	1.20	1.88	2.03	2.16	2.27	2.35
Wood	1.97	1.99	2.33	2.35	2.32	2.24	2.26
Food and beverages	1.99	2.10	2.40	2.29	2.18	2.14	2.18
Direct forward linkage							
Refined fuels	0.91	0.66	0.96	0.96	0.89	0.84	0.85
Transport activities, NEC	0.00	0.42	0.64	0.79	0.79	0.86	0.84
Wholesale trade	0.50	0.48	0.61	0.65	0.67	0.80	0.83
Complete hypothetical extraction (forward)							
Mining	1.57	1.17	1.80	1.95	2.27	2.53	2.62
Wholesale trade	1.77	1.78	2.02	2.02	2.01	2.11	2.18
Utilities	2.07	1.90	2.28	2.25	2.14	2.13	2.16
Partial hypothetical extraction (forward)							
Mining	0.62	0.19	0.91	1.12	1.39	1.67	1.75
Transport activities, NEC	0.00	0.63	1.00	1.24	1.24	1.29	1.29
Utilities	1.13	1.00	1.33	1.31	1.21	1.22	1.26
Total forward linkage							
Mining	1.65	1.19	2.03	2.35	2.58	2.94	3.00
Refined fuels	2.46	2.07	2.87	2.94	2.82	2.79	2.89
Transport activities, NEC	1.00	1.65	2.23	2.62	2.59	2.64	2.63
Normalized backward linkage							
Refined fuels	0.87	0.81	1.15	1.25	1.37	1.49	1.51
Wood	1.30	1.35	1.43	1.44	1.46	1.47	1.45
Food and beverages	1.31	1.43	1.48	1.40	1.38	1.41	1.40
Normalized forward linkage							
Mining	1.01	0.74	1.20	1.36	1.53	1.84	1.82
Refined fuels	1.50	1.29	1.69	1.71	1.67	1.74	1.76
Transport activities, NEC	0.61	1.03	1.31	1.53	1.54	1.65	1.60
Net backward linkage							
Manufacturing, NEC	0.78	1.72	1.63	1.66	1.62	1.91	1.94
Wood	0.91	0.76	0.76	0.73	0.74	1.41	1.59
Textiles	1.14	1.14	1.19	1.23	1.22	1.47	1.51
Net forward linkage							
Utilities	1.26	1.28	1.76	1.74	1.71	1.73	1.77
Finance	1.54	1.07	1.25	1.44	1.37	1.38	1.53
Real estate	1.65	1.05	1.15	1.28	1.29	1.33	1.43

continued on next page.

continued.

Viet Nam

Southeast Asia and the Pacific — *International Linkages*

Indicator and Top 3 Sectors, 2020	2000	2007	2010	2013	2016	2019	2020
Self-sufficiency ratio							
Leather	4.67	3.33	3.89	6.19	8.23	7.71	7.18
Manufacturing, NEC	1.08	1.38	1.44	1.54	1.76	5.95	6.89
Textiles	1.44	1.53	2.18	1.92	1.86	3.01	3.14
Import-to-input ratio							
Electricals	0.21	0.45	0.33	0.58	0.60	0.58	0.55
Machinery, NEC	0.20	0.15	0.36	0.45	0.49	0.56	0.53
Water transport	0.32	0.56	0.30	0.29	0.32	0.54	0.52
Export-to-output ratio							
Electricals	0.19	0.22	0.43	0.98	0.95	1.00	1.00
Textiles	0.63	0.69	0.84	0.91	0.85	1.00	1.00
Manufacturing, NEC	0.39	0.61	0.50	0.56	0.65	1.00	1.00
Domestic inputs share to output							
Wood	0.60	0.58	0.69	0.71	0.71	0.72	0.73
Refined fuels	0.21	0.15	0.54	0.61	0.69	0.71	0.72
Food and beverages	0.60	0.65	0.71	0.69	0.67	0.62	0.63
Foreign inputs share to output							
Electricals	0.21	0.45	0.33	0.58	0.60	0.58	0.55
Machinery, NEC	0.20	0.15	0.36	0.45	0.49	0.56	0.53
Water transport	0.32	0.56	0.30	0.29	0.32	0.54	0.52
Backward import multipliers							
Electricals	0.37	0.63	0.56	0.66	0.68	0.66	0.64
Machinery, NEC	0.35	0.42	0.54	0.57	0.61	0.64	0.62
Metals	0.09	0.52	0.56	0.56	0.62	0.63	0.61
Forward import multipliers							
Wood	0.24	0.40	0.39	0.40	0.46	0.63	0.68
Metals	0.25	0.24	0.38	0.47	0.55	0.65	0.60
Rubber and plastics	0.34	0.51	0.56	0.56	0.71	0.57	0.52
Intraregional transfer multiplier							
Refined fuels	1.32	1.20	1.88	2.03	2.16	2.27	2.35
Wood	1.97	1.99	2.33	2.35	2.32	2.24	2.26
Food and beverages	1.99	2.10	2.40	2.29	2.18	2.14	2.18
Interregional spillover multiplier							
Electricals	1.40	1.87	1.66	2.14	2.25	2.28	2.24
Machinery, NEC	1.38	1.30	1.75	1.93	2.07	2.27	2.23
Metals	1.08	1.68	1.79	1.83	2.09	2.14	2.11
Interregional feedback multiplier							
Water transport	1.22	1.41	1.20	1.22	1.21	1.37	1.35
Electricals	1.10	1.36	1.24	1.50	1.49	1.31	1.29
Air transport	1.06	1.13	1.22	1.26	1.23	1.30	1.28
Intraregional effect on gross output ($ million)							
Food and beverages							
Agriculture							
Construction							
Interregional effect on gross output ($ million)							
Electricals							
Metals							
Agriculture							
Feedback effect on gross output ($ million)							
Electricals							
Metals							
Agriculture							
Directly absorbed value-added exports (DAVAX) ($ million)							
Textiles							
Electricals							
Leather							
Reflection (REF) ($ million)							
Electricals							
Metals							
Refined fuels							

continued on next page.

continued.

Viet Nam

Southeast Asia and the Pacific

International Linkages

Indicator and Top 3 Sectors, 2020	2000	2007	2010	2013	2016	2019	2020
Reexports (REX) ($ million)							
Electricals	153.69	479.44	1,373.54	3,444.43	3,924.89	3,820.70	3,692.00
Metals	76.07	211.91	378.14	772.89	1,316.71	2,629.68	2,217.89
Textiles	158.84	269.74	532.08	930.48	1,388.84	1,437.01	1,577.09
Foreign value added (FVA) ($ million)							
Electricals	362.60	2,062.90	4,189.00	16,859.58	20,955.01	31,811.09	32,153.53
Textiles	453.40	2,623.88	7,495.91	12,146.48	13,203.08	21,205.67	21,304.22
Metals	41.76	785.57	1,382.19	2,897.53	6,455.85	11,393.84	10,438.36
Pure double-counting (PDC) ($ million)							
Electricals	0.34	2.50	9.29	70.11	149.21	157.84	165.35
Textiles	0.49	3.94	18.66	47.26	68.62	117.76	111.73
Leather	0.61	4.05	10.81	25.16	67.33	46.14	43.63
Trade-based GVC participation rate							
Metals	0.26	0.67	0.72	0.71	0.75	0.77	0.75
Electricals	0.53	0.78	0.75	0.80	0.81	0.74	0.72
Rubber and plastics	0.64	0.68	0.74	0.73	0.76	0.74	0.70
Production-based GVC participation rate							
Wood	0.24	0.40	0.39	0.40	0.46	0.63	0.68
Metals	0.25	0.24	0.38	0.47	0.55	0.65	0.60
Rubber and plastics	0.34	0.51	0.56	0.56	0.71	0.57	0.52
Trade-based backward GVC participation rate							
Electricals	0.37	0.63	0.56	0.66	0.68	0.66	0.64
Machinery, NEC	0.35	0.42	0.54	0.57	0.61	0.64	0.62
Metals	0.09	0.52	0.56	0.56	0.62	0.63	0.61
Trade-based forward GVC participation rate							
Transport activities, NEC	0.07	0.33	0.37	0.39	0.40	0.34	0.32
Mining	0.18	0.16	0.17	0.19	0.18	0.22	0.21
Finance	0.16	0.16	0.16	0.19	0.21	0.21	0.21
Traditional revealed comparative advantage							
Leather	11.80	14.44	12.34	11.47	11.75	10.34	10.25
Textiles	2.59	3.53	5.02	4.54	3.91	5.09	4.85
Wood	0.96	1.18	2.32	1.91	1.94	3.48	4.08
New revealed comparative advantage							
Leather	19.13	20.26	19.17	18.35	17.78	19.04	18.67
Textiles	4.21	5.05	5.63	4.95	4.58	5.63	5.54
Agriculture	3.47	5.11	3.75	3.58	3.50	2.19	1.95
Backward production length							
Refined fuels	3.09	3.08	3.33	3.37	3.40	3.42	3.48
Food and beverages	2.57	2.78	3.37	3.38	3.32	3.33	3.35
Transport equipment	2.79	3.36	3.35	3.43	3.46	3.25	3.33
Forward production length							
Mining	3.40	3.88	3.86	3.91	3.99	4.13	4.21
Transport activities, NEC	1.13	2.64	3.68	3.77	3.77	3.55	3.58
Refined fuels	2.87	2.57	3.48	3.53	3.36	3.41	3.52
Backward production length of GVC segment							
Refined fuels	3.73	3.69	4.26	4.58	4.85	4.80	4.90
Utilities	4.23	4.66	4.47	4.61	4.72	4.63	4.68
Wood	4.26	4.66	4.59	4.95	4.80	4.61	4.66
Forward production length of GVC segment							
Finance	4.20	4.44	4.86	5.20	5.14	5.05	5.20
Real estate	4.85	4.82	5.16	5.35	5.31	4.98	5.19
Refined fuels	4.76	4.97	5.40	5.51	5.42	5.00	5.09
Backward agglomeration index							
Utilities	-	1.09	1.09	1.13	1.13	1.18	1.15
Minerals, NEC	-	0.48	0.00	0.00	0.54	0.96	1.14
Mining	-	0.00	0.80	0.93	0.59	1.03	1.05
Forward agglomeration index							
Sale of motor vehicles	-	0.87	1.00	1.05	1.04	1.01	1.03
Public administration	-	1.02	1.02	1.02	1.02	1.01	1.00
Health and social work	-	0.96	0.97	0.98	0.98	1.00	1.00

CIF = cost, insurance, and freight; FOB = free on board; GVC = global value chain; NEC = not elsewhere classified; NPISHs = nonprofit institutions serving households.
Source: Calculations using the Asian Development Bank Multiregional Input-Output Table. https://mrio.adbx.online/ (accessed July 2021).

continued on next page.

continued.

Viet Nam

Southeast Asia and the Pacific

The four select sectors are chosen based on their gross outputs in the economy as of 2019.

Economy Ranking out of 25 Economies

Share of Intermediate Consumption and Gross Value-Added in Output

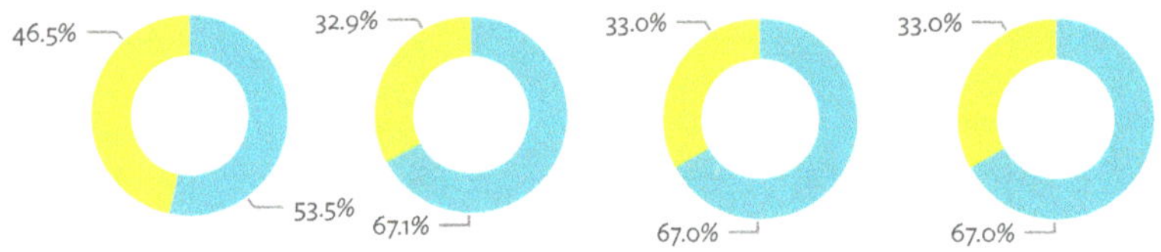

Total intermediate inputs Value-added at basic price

Imports and Exports, 2019-2020

($ million)

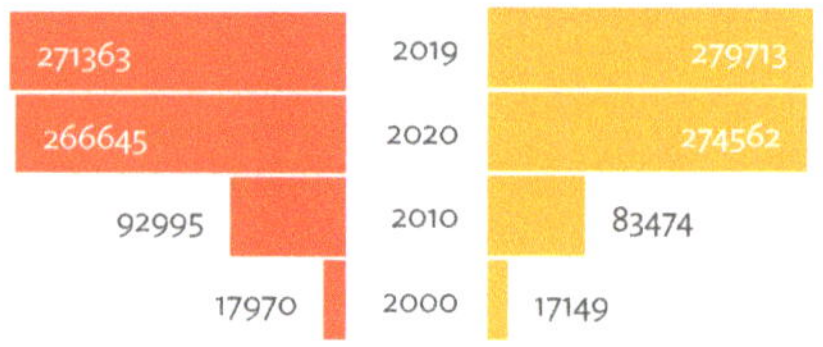

Domestic Linkages

Normalized Linkages

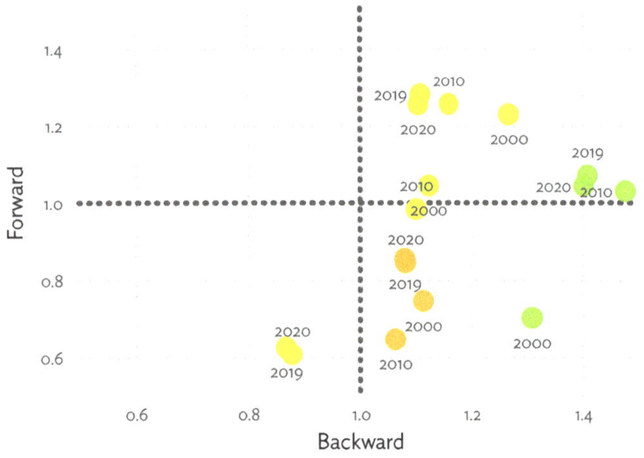

Agriculture Construction Electricals Food and beverages

Net Linkages

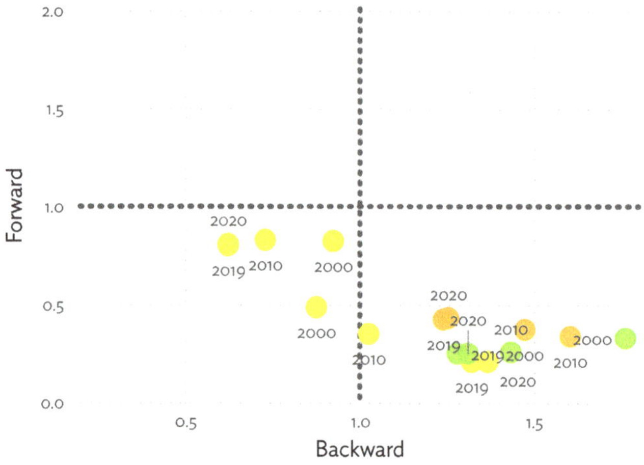

Agriculture Construction Electricals Food and beverages

Value-Added Multipliers

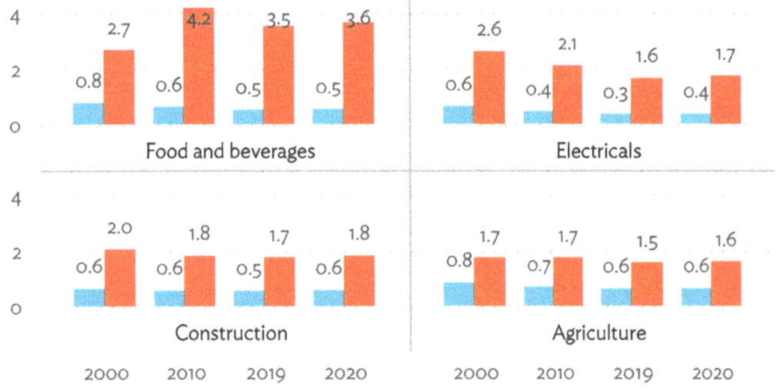

Simple value-added multiplier Type I value-added multiplier

Production-Induced Effect

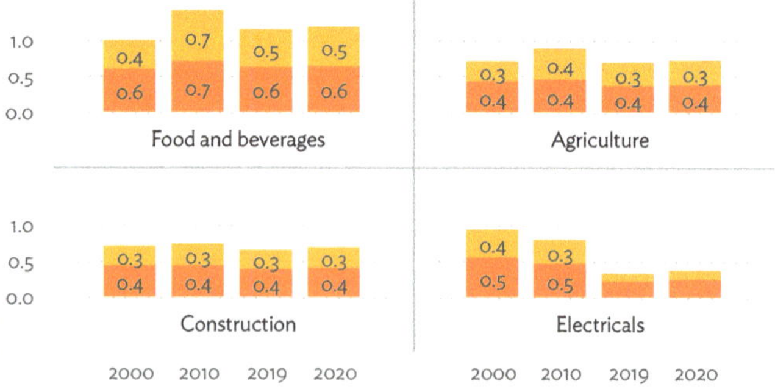

First-round effect Industrial support effect

continued on next page.

Click here for figure data

continued.

Viet Nam

Southeast Asia and the Pacific

International Linkages

Change in Exports, by Value-Added Components, 2019-2020

($ million)

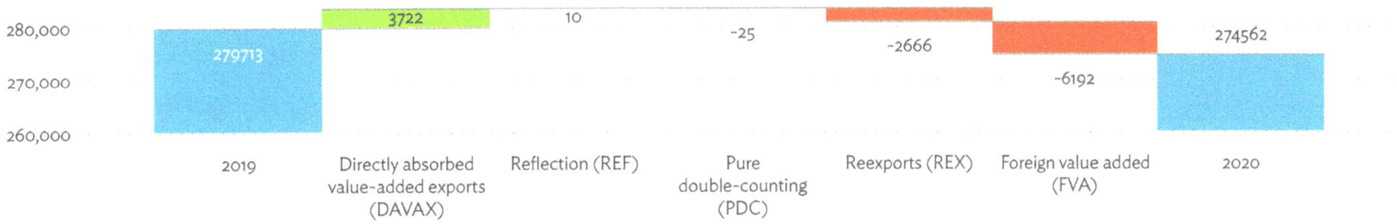

Import Multipliers

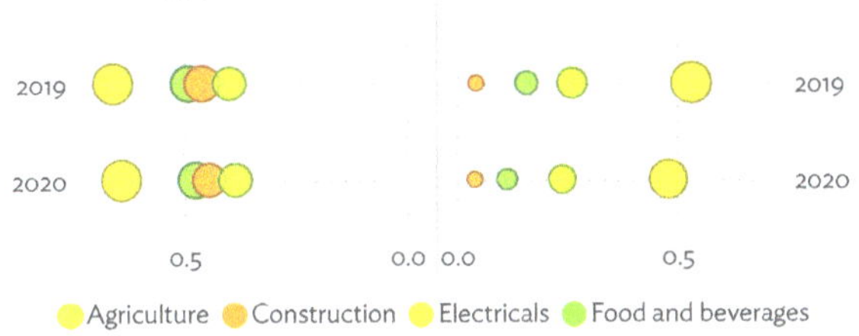

GVC Participation Rates

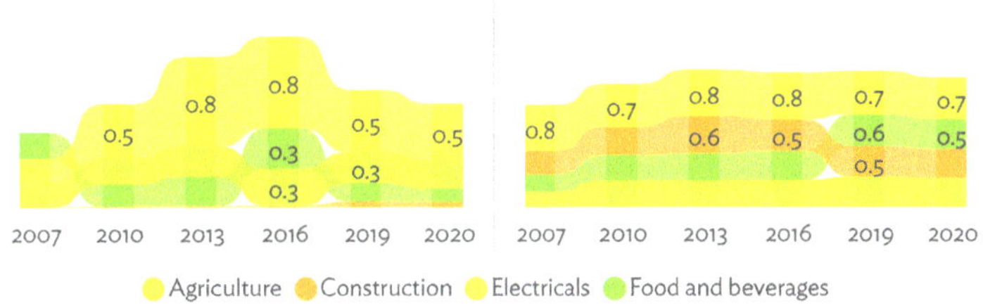

Average Production Length

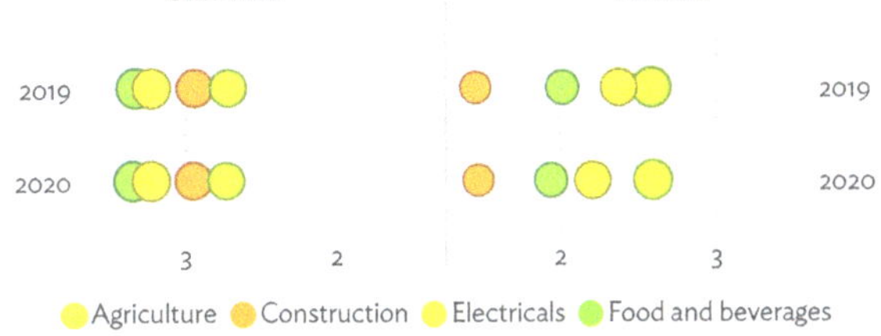

New Revealed Comparative Advantage

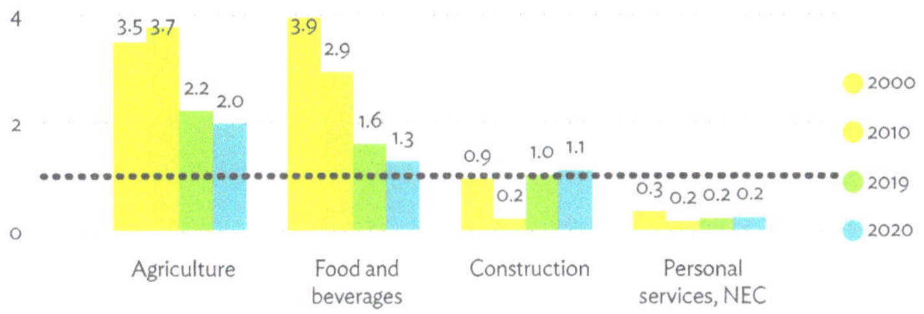

Trade Orientation

Agglomeration Indices

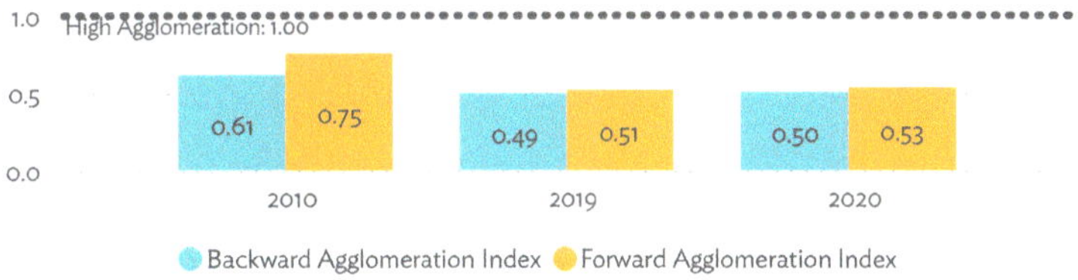

Domestic Transfer Effects and International Spillover Effects

($ million)

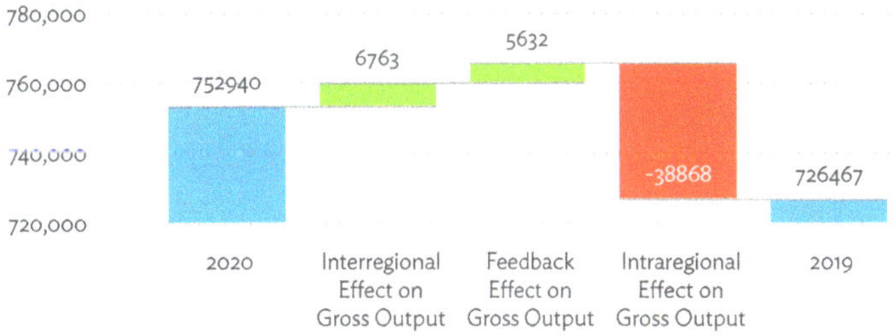

GVC = global value chain; NEC = not elsewhere classified.

Source: Calculations using the Asian Development Bank Multiregional Input-Output Table. https://mrio.adbx.online/ (accessed July 2021).

Click here for figure data

References

A. Borin and M. Mancini. 2019. Measuring What Matters in Global Value Chains and Value-Added Trade. *Policy Research Working Paper*. No. 8804. Washington, DC: World Bank.

R. Miller and P. Blair. 2009. *Input–Output Analysis: Foundations and Extensions*. Second edition. Cambridge: Cambridge University Press.

J. Oosterhaven. 2019. *Rethinking Input–Output Analysis: A Spatial Perspective*. SpringerBriefs in Regional Science. Springer, Cham.

Z. Wang, S. J. Wei, X. Yu, and K. Zhu. 2017a. Measures of Participation in Global Value Chains and Global Business Cycles. *NBER Working Paper*. No. 23222. Cambridge, MA: National Bureau of Economic Research.

Z. Wang, S. Wei, X. Yu, and K. Zhu. 2017b. Characterizing Global Value Chains: Production Length and Upstreamness. *NBER Working Paper*. No. 23261. Cambridge, MA: National Bureau of Economic Research.

Technical Notes

8

This chapter provides an overview of the methodologies implemented throughout the publication, beginning with the structure of multiregional input-output tables. The technical derivations of each indicator are briefly documented to serve as guide for users and researchers.

8.1 Input–Output Tables

A traditional input–output framework analyzes the interdependence of sectors in an economy by looking at the goods and services they produce (outputs) and consume (inputs) in the process of producing their own output.

An economy with N sectors has an input–output table (IOT) comprised of four major parts (Table 8.1). The "intermediate uses" matrix Z illustrates the volume of goods and services consumed by sector j that are produced by sector i. Adding imports and value-added of sector j produces the total inputs x_j for the sector.

Meanwhile, the "final uses" section contains information on consumption of households (y_{i1}), nonprofit organizations and institutions serving households (y_{i2}), government (y_{i3}), gross fixed capital formation (y_{i4}), changes in inventories (y_{i5}), and exports (e_i) of sector i. Imports consumed as final products are denoted as (y_{mj}).

Table 8.1: Basic Structure of a National Input-Output Table

		Intermediate Uses				Final Uses						
		Sector 1	Sector 2	...	Sector N	Households	NPISHs	Government	GFCF	CIIs	Export	Gross Output
Domestic	1	z_{11}	z_{12}	...	z_{1N}	y_{11}	y_{12}	y	y_{14}	y_{15}	e_1	x_1
	2	z_{21}	z_{22}	...	z_{2N}	y_{21}	y_{22}	y_{23}	y_{24}	y_{24}	e_2	x_2
	...	...	...	...	...	...	...	...	...	...	...	...
	N	z_{N1}	z_{N1}	...	z_{N1}	y_{N1}	y_{N2}	y_{N3}	y_{N3}	y_{N4}	e_N	x_N
Imports		m_1	m_2	...	m_N	m_{Y1}	m_{Y2}	m_{Y3}	m_{Y3}	m_{Y4}		
Value-added		v_1	v_2	...	v_N							
Total inputs		x_1	x_2	...	x_N							

CII = changes in inventories and acquisitions less disposal of valuables; Households = final consumption expenditure of households; government = government final consumption expenditure; NPISHs = final consumption expenditure of nonprofit institutions serving households; GFCF = gross fixed capital formation.
Source: Asian Development Bank Multiregional Input–Output Database Team.

The multiregional input-output table (MRIOT) retains the structure of the traditional IOT depicted in Table 8.1, but expands row and column dimensions to include information on G economies. Thus, the intermediate uses matrix Z expands to a $GN \times GN$ matrix. Meanwhile, the final uses matrix Y includes the same components as a typical IOT, but excludes the export column in Table 8.1. Thus, the final uses matrix becomes $GN \times 5G$ matrix. Value-added, total inputs, and gross output vectors expand to become a $GN \times 1$ vector.

8.2 Core Concepts in Input-Output Analysis

Any input-output framework starts with the core concepts from an economy's national accounts. At the helm is gross domestic product (GDP), which measures the values of final goods and services produced within an economy over a given period (European Commission 2008). Different estimation approaches of GDP make use of the following concepts:

- **Exports and imports** (e & m). Goods and services that leave an economy are referred to as exports (e), while those that enter an economy from an external source are defined as imports (m).

- **Total final demand** (Y) includes the components of domestic demand and net exports, which is the difference between exports and imports. This is comprised of household final consumption expenditure, final consumption expenditure by nonprofit institutions serving households (NPISHs), government final consumption expenditure, gross fixed capital formation, and changes in inventories.

- **Intermediate consumption** (Z) describes the value of inputs that go into a given product or service (Lequiller and Blades 2014). These include raw materials, components, partly manufactured goods, and other services used in production. This can be disaggregated into domestic inputs, which refers to domestically sourced intermediates, and foreign inputs, which refers to externally sourced intermediates (UN 2018).

- **Gross value-added** (GVA) describes the additional contribution by an individual, producer, or sector, to the total GDP. This is derived by subtracting intermediate consumption from the total gross output. Alternatively, the GVA can be calculated as the sum of the following: taxes less subsidies on products, cost-insurance-freight (CIF) and/or free-on-board (FOB) adjustment, direct purchases abroad by residents, purchases on the domestic territory by nonresidents, value-added at basic price, and international transport margins (UN 2018; European Commission 2008).

- **Gross output** (x) refers to the total output required to satisfy final demand. This obtained by taking the sum of intermediate consumption and GVA. The gross output for sector j is denoted as x_j. In the standard IOT analysis, gross output equals gross input.

Most analyses on national accounts and input–output analysis revolve around the composition, trends, and changes of these core concepts. Going further, these concepts give rise to five sets of matrixes that form the basis for several indicators in input–output analysis and global value chain (GVC) analysis. These matrixes are defined as follows:

- **The technical coefficients matrix** (A) describes the share of costs for goods, services, and primary inputs to gross output. This is calculated by dividing every element of Z with the corresponding sectoral output. Mathematically, $A = Z\hat{x}^{-1}$.[1]

- **The Leontief inverse matrix** (B), otherwise known as the total requirements matrix, describes how much additional output is needed to satisfy the increase in final demand in an economy sector (Miller and Blair 2009). It is derived as follows: $B = (I - A)^{-1}$, where I is the identity matrix.

- **The output coefficients matrix** (O), otherwise known as the allocation coefficients matrix, illustrates how output in sector j is allocated across sectors. To calculate, each row of the intermediate consumption matrix Z is divided by the gross output corresponding to that row. Mathematically, $O = \hat{x}^{-1}Z$.

- **The Ghosh matrix** (G) presents an alternative to the Leontief inverse. Instead of looking at what leaves the intersectoral system, the Ghosh matrix describes how much primary inputs goes into intersectoral production (Miller and Blair 2009). Mathematically, the Ghosh matrix is defined as $B = (I - O)^{-1}$.

- **The VBY matrix** serves as the basis for many indicators associated with GVCs. Each element in the VBY matrix describes the direct and indirect value-added from an economy-sector (source) that is embodied in the final goods or services of another economy-sector (Wang et al. 2017b). It is calculated as $VBY = \hat{V} \times B \times \hat{Y}$, where $\hat{V}$ is a diagonal matrix whose diagonal entry $v_j = {}^{va_j}/_{x_j}$ refers to the value-added (va_j) per unit of output in sector j, and $\hat{Y}$ is a diagonal matrix whose diagonal elements correspond to the elements in the final use matrix, Y.

1 For the rest of the text, a matrix denoted with a hat, i.e., $\hat{x}$, represents a diagonal matrix whose diagonal elements correspond to the elements of its source vector. Thus, $x_{N \times 1}$ becomes $\hat{x}_{N \times N}$.

Thus, any input–output structure can be represented mathematically as a system of linear equations:

$$\begin{aligned} x &= Zi + Yi \\ &= Ax + Yi \end{aligned} \tag{1}$$

where **i** is a vector of ones.

In general, the concepts discussed previously will serve as the basis for the other indicators discussed in the remainder of this chapter.

8.3 Multipliers and Linkages

Multipliers examine how exogenous changes in the system translate to changes in macroeconomic variables of interest. Exogenous changes are typically assumed to take the form of changes in final demand, implying a demand-driven input-output model. Macroeconomic variables determined in the system include output and income, and may be expanded to include employment and value-added. (Miller and Blair 2009).

Output multipliers represent the basic structure for multipliers. Using Equation 1, output is related to final demand using the following equation:

$$\begin{aligned} x &= (I - A)^{-1}Y \\ &= BY \end{aligned} \tag{2}$$

Taking the column sum of the Leontief inverse gives the simple output multiplier for sector *j* in economy *r*. Mathematically, this is denoted as

$$mo_{(j,r)} = \sum_{i=1}^{N} b_{(i,j,r)} \tag{3}$$

close to the concept of multipliers are linkages. This takes advantage of the structure of IOTs to highlight interconnectedness across economies and sectors. Specifically, it maps how an exogenous change in one economy-sector affects other economy-sectors. Backward linkages represent how a change in output of one sector affects the input requirements from other sectors. Simply put, it represents the relationship of a sector with its suppliers. The backward linkage of sector j in economy r equals the simple output multiplier, that is,

$$bl_{(j,r)} = \sum_{i=1}^{N} b_{(i,j,r)} \tag{4}$$

Meanwhile, forward linkages map how changes in the output of sector j affect sectors consuming j's output for their own respective production. This relies on a supply-driven input–output analysis and makes use of the Ghosh inverse. The forward linkage of sector i in economy r is calculated by taking the row sum of the Ghosh inverse matrix, denoted as

$$fl_{(i,r)} = \sum_{j=1}^{N} g_{(i,j,r)} \tag{5}$$

Equations 2 to 5 form the basic structure for multipliers and linkages used in input-output analysis. Overall, multipliers provide a useful picture of how changes in one portion of the economy translate into increases in output. Analogously, this concept can be extended to other economic variables. To measure the aggregate income generated by an exogenous increase in final demand, one can calculate for the simple value-added multiplier

$$vb_{(j,r)} = \sum_{i=1}^{N} v_{(j,r)} b_{(i,j,r)} \tag{6}$$

where $v_{(j,r)}$ is a vector of value-added per unit of output in economy r sector j. By multiplying elements of the Leontief inverse to the value-added vector, one derives the value-added produced by exogenous changes in final demand (Miller and Blair 2009; Ten Raa 2006; Oosterhaven 2019). Analogously, employment generated by increases in final demand is captured by employment multipliers,

$$eb_{(j,r)} = \sum_{i=1}^{N} e_{(j,r)} b_{(i,j,r)} \tag{7}$$

where $e_{(j,r)}$ is vector containing the labor per unit of output produced in economy r sector j (Oosterhaven 2019; Ten Raa 2006).

In an interregional context, changes in one sector in a given economy results in changes not just in the economy in question but can have resulting effects in other regions. Hence, the concept of linkages and multipliers can be analyzed in a global context by looking at the intraregional transfer multiplier, interregional spillover multiplier, and interregional feedback multiplier. Assuming a two-region global economy denoted by r and s, the Leontief inverse matrix B is redefined as the product of three matrixes:

$$B = M_3 \times M_2 \times M_1 \tag{8}$$

Here, the intraregional transfer multiplier is denoted by M_1. This represents the amount of output that the domestic sectors should produce in order to satisfy any increase in final demand for any commodity anywhere in the global economy. Meanwhile, the interregional spillover multiplier, denoted by M_2

captures the direct and indirect changes in output in other regions resulting from an increase in final demand in any given economy-sector. The final matrix, M_3, measures the interregional feedback multiplier. This accounts for the demand of an economy-sector for its own product arising from the production of commodities that the economy-sector in question requires for its own production process (Miller and Blair 2009). Denoting I as the identity matrix and O as the zero matrix, these matrixes are constructed as follows:

$$M_1 = \begin{bmatrix} \left(I - A_{(r,r)}\right)^{-1} & 0 \\ 0 & \left(I - A_{(s,s)}\right)^{-1} \end{bmatrix} \tag{9}$$

$$M_2 = \begin{bmatrix} I & \left(I - A_{(r,r)}\right)^{-1} A_{(r,s)} \\ \left(I - A_{(s,s)}\right)^{-1} A_{(s,r)} & I \end{bmatrix} \tag{10}$$

$$M_3 = \begin{bmatrix} \left(I - \left(I - A_{(r,r)}\right)^{-1} A_{(r,s)} \left(I - A_{(s,s)}\right)^{-1} A_{(s,r)}\right)^{-1} & 0 \\ 0 & \left(I - \left(I - A_{(s,s)}\right)^{-1} A_{(s,r)} \left(I - A_{(r,r)}\right)^{-1} A_{(r,s)}\right)^{-1} \end{bmatrix} \tag{11}$$

One can use Equations 9 to 11 to decompose gross output. Redefining the Leontief inverse as

$$B = I + (M_2 - I) + (M_2M_1 - M_1) + (M_3M_2M_1 - M_2M_1) \tag{12}$$

gross output can be decomposed as

$$\begin{aligned} x &= BY \\ &= IY + (M_1 - I)Y + (M_2M_1 - M_1)Y + (M_3M_2M_1 - M_2M_1)Y \end{aligned} \tag{13}$$

By construction, the first two terms capture the direct and indirect intraregional effects, respectively. The term $(M_2M_1 - M_1)Y$ captures the gross output coming from the net interregional effect, while the term $(M_3M_2M_1 - M_2M_1)Y$ denotes the net feedback effect. Overall, the last two terms measure how integrated an economy-sector is to economy-sectors in other regions. This decomposition also extends the concept of output multipliers in a global context, as it can be used to identify where the increase in output happens for any given increase in final demand.

Other indicators associated with multipliers and linkages are listed in Table 8.2.

8.4 International trade and global value chains

GVCs are characterized by fragmentation of different parts of production processes into different economy-sectors across the globe. GVCs have been an integral part of global trade since the 1990s, creating a need for a set of indicators that analyze their movement and evolution over time. This section discusses indicators typically used to measure different aspects of GVCs and international trade.

8.4.1 *Value-Added Trade Accounting*

Understanding the interconnected production process across the globe implies the need to disentangle direct trading from indirect trading. A way to do so is by decomposing value-added and final demand into activities that can be attributed to domestic sectors, traditional trade, and, finally, simple and complex GVC activities. Wang et al. (2017a) splits Equation 1 into its domestic and foreign component, so that

$$\begin{aligned} x &= A^d x + Y^d + A^f x \\ &= A^d x + Y^d + e \end{aligned} \tag{14}$$

where A^d contains the domestic elements of the technical coefficient matrix, and A^f denotes the imported intermediates, captured by the off-diagonal matrixes of A. Denoting $L \equiv (I - A^d)$

$$\begin{aligned} x &= (I - A^d)Y^d + (I - A^d)e \\ &= LY^d + Le \\ &= LY^d + LY^f + LA^f x \end{aligned} \tag{15}$$

Here, Y^d is the vector of final goods associated with domestic consumption, while Y^f is that of foreign consumption. Replacing x in equation 15 with BY from Equation 2 and multiplying both sides of the equation by a diagonal matrix whose diagonal entries correspond to the value-added per unit of output for the relevant economy-sectors $(\hat{V})$, we obtain the key equations from Wang et al. (2017a):

$$\begin{aligned} \hat{V}B\hat{Y} &= \hat{V}L\hat{Y}^d + \hat{V}L\hat{Y}^f + \hat{V}LA^f B\hat{Y}^f \\ &= \hat{V}L\hat{Y}^d + \hat{V}L\hat{Y}^f + \hat{V}LA^f L\hat{Y}^d + \hat{V}LA^f(B\hat{Y} - L\hat{Y}^d) \end{aligned} \tag{16}$$

Value added that does not involve cross-border trade is captured by the term $\hat{V}L\hat{Y}^d$ and is denoted as value-added from pure domestic production. Meanwhile, activities associated with traditional trade activities, i.e., value-added contained in exports of final product, are captured by $\hat{V}L\hat{Y}^f$. GVC-related activities are captured by the last two terms. Domestic and/or final value-added that cross national borders only once are simple GVCs and are captured by $\hat{V}LA^f L\hat{Y}^d$. Meanwhile, activities involving several cross-border production processes involve value-added from complex GVCs and are captured by $\hat{V}LA^f (B\hat{Y} - L\hat{Y}^d)$.

Obtaining the sum of the rows of Equation 16 traces where value-added is absorbed through upstream activities. Replacing the diagonal matrix $\hat{Y}$ with a vector Y, Equation 16 can be expressed as

$$Va^T = \hat{V}BY \quad = \quad \hat{V}LY^d + \hat{V}LY^f + \hat{V}LA^fLY^d + \hat{V}LA^f(BY - LY^d) \tag{17}$$

where an element of $Va = \{Va_j\}_{j=1}^{N}$ corresponds to the gross value-added of sector j. Thus, where value added is absorbed can be decomposed into pure domestic, traditional trade, and GVC activities, as illustrated in Figure 8.1. The term $\hat{V}LA^fLY^d$ captures simple GVCs based on forward linkages (V_GVC_S) while the term $\hat{V}LA^f(B\hat{Y} - L\hat{Y}^d)$ corresponds to complex GVCs based on forward linkages (V_GVC_C).

Figure 8.1: Decomposition of Value-Added by Sector Based on Forward Linkages

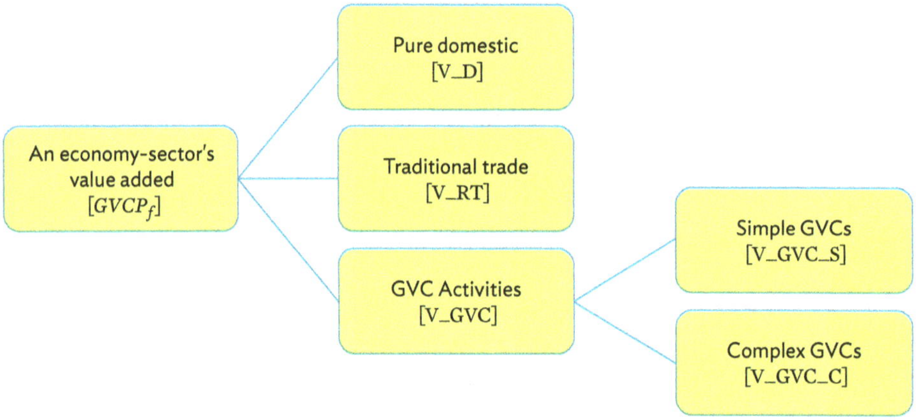

GVC = global value chain.
Source: Z. Wang, S. J. Wei, X. Yu, and K. Zhu. 2017. Measures of Participation in Global Value Chains and Global Business Cycles. *NBER Working Paper*. No. 23222. Cambridge, MA: National Bureau of Economic Research.

Meanwhile, taking the sum for each column of Equation 16 gives the final demand for each sector. By replacing $\hat{V}$ with the vector V, one can decompose final demand by the source of value-added. Thus,

$$Y = VB\hat{Y} \quad = \quad VL\hat{Y}^d + VL\hat{Y}^f + VLA^fL\hat{Y}^d + VLA^f(B\hat{Y} - L\hat{Y}^d) \tag{18}$$

Equation 18 decomposes final goods into pure domestic, traditional trade, and GVC activities, according to where its value-added comes from. This is illustrated in Figure 8.2. As with the previous figure, the term $\hat{V}LA^fL\hat{Y}^d$ depicts simple GVCs based on backward linkages (Y_GVC_S) while $\hat{V}LA^f(B\hat{Y} - L\hat{Y}^d)$ captures complex GVCs based on backward linkages (Y_GVC_C).

Figure 8.2: Decomposition of Value-Added by Sector Based on Backward Linkages

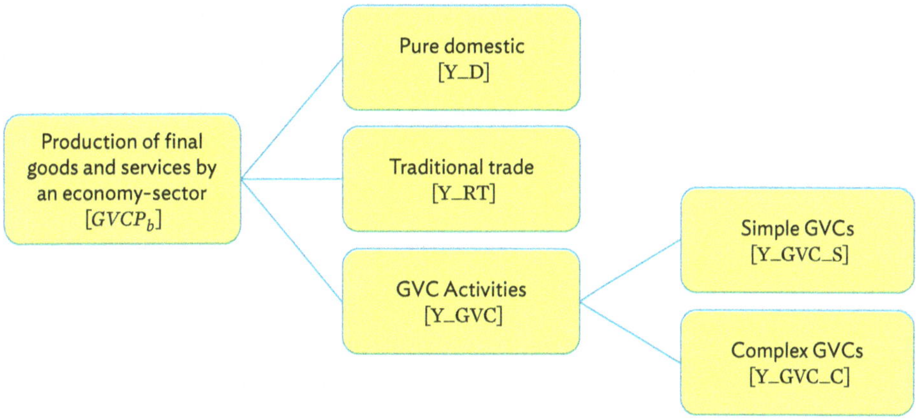

GVC = global value chain.
Source: Z. Wang, S. J. Wei, X. Yu, and K. Zhu. 2017. Measures of Participation in Global Value Chains and Global Business Cycles. *NBER Working Paper*. No. 23222. Cambridge, MA: National Bureau of Economic Research.

8.4.2 Export Decomposition

Measures of international trade form the baseline in any GVC analysis. At the core are measures of exports and imports in any economy, which take on various forms:

- Gross imports and exports (in millions of United States dollars), which indicate the size of foreign trade in absolute terms (UN 2018)
- Exports and imports as a percentage of GDP, which measure the relative size of international trade to other macroeconomic variables (UN 2018)
- Export and import activity by end-use category, which disaggregate export and import levels into intermediate use and final use (UN 2018).

The specification of these and other trade-based indicators are listed in Table 8.2.

Traditional measures of exports, however, do not take into account production sharing networks and hence are not adjusted to account for double-counting. This inflates the size of exports and consequently overstates the importance of exports in any economy. Addressing this issue involves using a value-added approach to decompose gross exports. Wang et al. (2018) extended the work of Koopman et al. (2014) and decomposed exports into domestic value-added (DVA), foreign value-added (FVA), and pure double-counting. Their framework is presented in Figure 8.3. DVA is further decomposed into value-added that is directly absorbed by the importer and value-added that is later reexported. These are also decomposed according to the destination of value-added.

Figure 8.3: Export Decomposition Framework

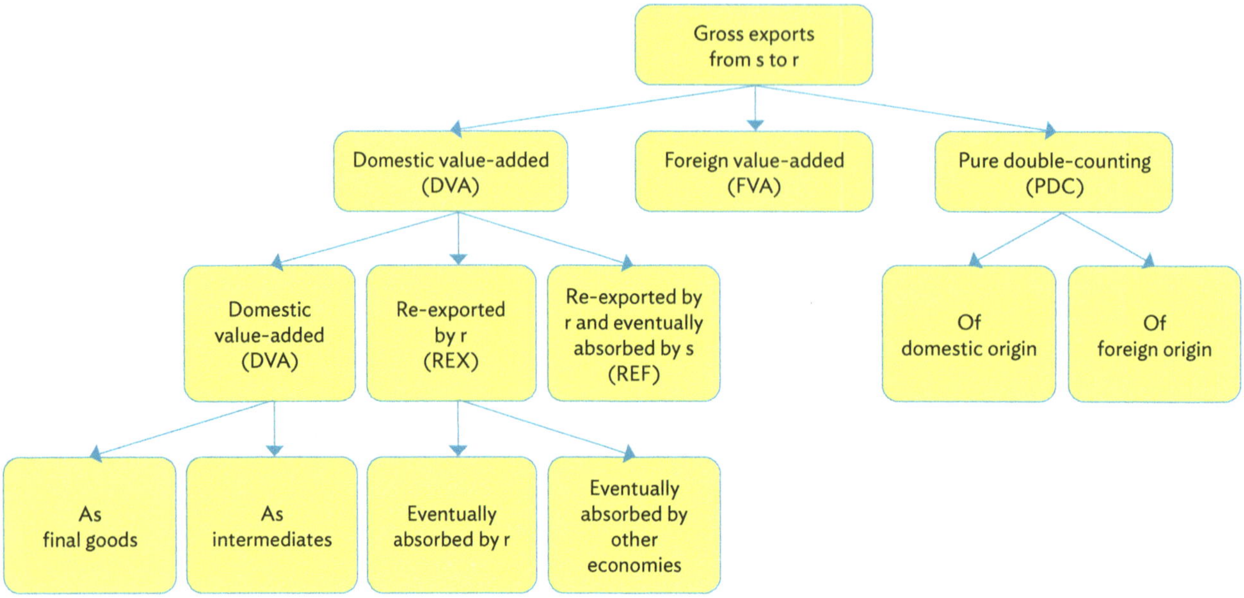

Sources: Adapted from A. Borin and M. Mancini. 2019. Measuring What Matters in Global Value Chains and Value-Added Trade. *Policy Research Working Paper*. No. 8804. Washington, DC: World Bank.; and Asian Development Bank. 2021. *Key Indicators for Asia and the Pacific 2021*. Manila.

Denoting B^d as a square matrix whose N × N blocked diagonal elements correspond to the domestic components of B, the matrix $B^{\sim s} \equiv (I - A^{\sim s})^{-1}$ is a modified version of B^d. Specifically, $B^{\sim s}$ assumes that the use of intermediate inputs from economy s is limited to economy s; however, economy s can use inputs from other economies. Thus, the tth block matrix in column s of the Leontief inverse can be expressed as

$$B_{(t,s)} = B^{\sim s}_{(t,s)} + B^{\sim s}_{(t,s)} \sum_{s \neq u} A_{(s,u)} B_{(u,s)} \quad (19)$$

The previous can be used to disaggregate exports from economy s to economy r as

$$\begin{aligned} E_{(s,r)} &= v_s B^{\sim s}_{(s,s)} e_{(s,r)} + \sum_{t \neq s} v_t B^{\sim s}_{(s,s)} e_{(s,r)} + \sum_{t} v_t B^{\sim s}_{(s,s)} A_{(s,u)} B_{(u,s)} e_{(s,r)} \\ &= DVA_{(s,r)} + FVA_{(s,r)} + PDC_{(s,r)} \end{aligned} \quad (20)$$

The first term, DVA, can be decomposed into exports to economy r directly absorbed in the same economy, denoted as $DAVAX_{(s,r)}$ and reexports from economy r that eventually end up somewhere else. Mathematically, this is calculated as

$$\begin{aligned} DVA_{(s,r)} &= v_s B^{\sim s}_{(s,s)} \left(y_{(s,r)} + A_{(s,r)} B^d_{(r,r)} y_{(r,r)} + A_{(s,r)} B^d_{(r,r)} ye_{(r,*)} \right) \\ &= DAVAX_{(s,r)} + \text{reexports} \end{aligned} \quad (21)$$

The last term can further be disaggregated into exports that end up back in economy s, denoted as $\mathrm{REF}_{(s,r)}$, and exports that end up elsewhere, denoted as $\mathrm{REF}_{(s,r)}$. Thus, the previous equation can be reexpressed as

$$\begin{aligned}
\mathrm{DVA}_{(s,r)} &= v_s B^{\sim s}_{(s,s)} \left(y_{(s,r)} + A_{(s,r)} B^{d}_{(r,r)} y_{(r,r)} \right) \\
&\quad + v_s B^{\sim s}_{(s,s)} A_{(s,r)} B^{d}_{(r,r)} \left(\sum_{u \neq r,s} y_{(r,u)} \right. \\
&\qquad \left. + \sum_{u \neq r} A_{(r,u)} \left(\sum_{k} \sum_{l \neq s,r} B_{(u,k)} y_{(k,l)} + \sum_{k} B_{(u,k)} y_{(k,r)} \right) \right) \\
&\quad + v_s B^{\sim s}_{(s,s)} A_{(s,r)} B^{d}_{(r,r)} \left[y_{(r,s)} + \sum_{u \neq r} A_{(r,u)} \sum_{k} B_{(u,k)} y_{(k,s)} \right] \\
&= \mathrm{DAVAX}_{(s,r)} + \mathrm{REX}_{(s,r)} + \mathrm{REF}_{(s,r)}
\end{aligned} \tag{22}$$

Here, each component is further subdivided into two i.e., $\mathrm{DAVAX1}$, $\mathrm{DAVAX2}$, etc. Decomposing the FVA is analogous and is omitted in this note. Further details are provided in Borin and Mancini (2019).

8.4.3 Global Value Chain Participation

The results from export decomposition can be used to define other GVC indicators. One of these indicators includes the GVC participation rate. From its name, this measures the extent to which different economy-sectors are participating in GVCs. Two measures are used in this publication. First, the trade-based GVC participation is rooted in cross-border trade and defines GVC-related activities as those involving products that cross at least two borders prior to final consumption (Yi 2003). Using the approach of Borin and Mancini (2019), the backward measure of GVC exports, ($\mathrm{GVCX}^{\mathrm{backward}}$), captures the import content of export, while the forward measure of GVC exports, ($\mathrm{GVCX}^{\mathrm{forward}}$), captures exports reexported by partners. Mathematically, this is calculated as

$$\begin{aligned}
\mathrm{GVCX}^{\mathrm{backward}}_{(s,r)} &= \mathrm{FVA}_{(s,r)} + \mathrm{PDC}_{(s,r)} \\
\mathrm{GVCX}^{\mathrm{forward}}_{(s,r)} &= \mathrm{REX}_{(s,r)} + \mathrm{REF}_{(s,r)}
\end{aligned} \tag{23}$$

Hence, the trade-based GVC participation can be expressed as

$$\mathrm{GVCX}^{\mathrm{trade}}_{(s,r)} = \frac{\mathrm{GVCX}^{\mathrm{backward}}_{(s,r)}}{e_{(s,r)}} + \frac{\mathrm{GVCX}^{\mathrm{forward}}_{(s,r)}}{e_{(s,r)}} \tag{24}$$

The second measure is based on Wang et al. (2017b), who suggested the production-based GVC participation, rooted in value-added associated with intermediate goods. It is defined as

$$GVCX^{production}_{(s,r)} = \frac{\sum_{r \neq s} DAVAX2_{(s,r)} + REX_{(s,r)} + REF_{(s,r)}}{e_{(s,r)}} \tag{25}$$

8.4.4 Revealed Comparative Advantage

The export decomposition framework can also be used to obtain indicators associated with trade specialization. Comparative advantage from Ricardian theory posits differences in productivity as the main driver of patterns of trade across economies (UNCTAD 2019). A commonly used measure is the traditional revealed comparative advantage ($RCA^{Traditional}$),

$$RCA^{traditional}_{(s,r)} = \frac{e_{(j,r*)} \Big/ \sum_{j=1}^{N} e_{(j,r*)}}{\sum_{t=1}^{G} e_{(j,t*)} \Big/ \sum_{j=1}^{N} \sum_{t=1}^{G} e_{(j,t*)}} \tag{26}$$

where the numerator refers to the export share of total exports in sector j to the total exports of economy r, and the denominator represents the export share of sector j to world exports.

An alternative measure (also referred in previous chapters as new revealed comparative advantage) arises from the export decomposition framework previously discussed. Defining value-added exports (VAX) as exports of domestic value-added eventually absorbed abroad as

$$VAX_{(s,r)} = DAVAX_{(s,r)} + REX_{(s,r)} \tag{27}$$

the value-added adjusted revealed comparative advantage ($RCA^{va}_{(s,r)}$) becomes

$$RCA^{va}_{(s,r)} = \frac{VAX_{(j,r)} \Big/ VAX_{r}}{\sum_{r=1}^{G} VAX_{(j,r)} \Big/ \sum_{r=1}^{G} VAX_{r}} \tag{28}$$

8.4.5 Position in Global Value Chains

Other indicators describe an economy-sector's position in GVCs. Defining upstreamness by a sector's tendency to undergo several stages of production before the product is consumed in its final use, a measure of upstreamness describes the distance of a sector from its final use (Miller and Temurshoev 2017). A basic measure of upstreamness involves looking at the share of gross output absorbed as final use. Antras and Chor (2018) provide an alternative measure of upstreamness ($U_{(j,r)}$) by taking the average distance of a sector from its final use, which is calculated as follows:

$$U_{(j,r)} = \frac{Y_{(j,r)}}{x_{(j,r)}} + 2\frac{\sum_{s=1}^{G}\sum_{i=1}^{N} a_{(i,j,s,r)}\,Y_{(j,r)}}{x_{(j,r)}} + 3\frac{\sum_{s=1}^{G}\sum_{i=1}^{N}\sum_{t=1}^{G}\sum_{k=1}^{N}\sum_{i=1}^{N} a_{(i,j,s,r)}a_{(i,k,s,t)}Y_{(k,t)}}{x_{(j,r)}} + \cdots \quad (29)$$

where $a_{(i,j,s,r)}$ is an element from the technical coefficient matrix and describes how much output from economy s's sector $\mathbf{i}$ is required to produce \$1 worth of output in economy $\mathbf{r}$ sector $\mathbf{j}$. Apart from upstreamness, position in GVCs can also be described by looking at production lengths. Antras and Chor (2013) pioneered the use of IOTs in measuring production lengths. Their approach was further developed by Wang et al. (2017b). Using the latter, backward measures of average production length capture the relative downstreamness of an economy by looking at the average number of upstream processes prior to the final product's absorption in the economy. Mathematically, this is calculated as

$$PL_y = \frac{VBB\hat{Y}}{VB\hat{Y}} = uB \quad (30)$$

An analogous measure based on forward linkages can be constructed as

$$PL_u = \frac{\hat{V}BBY}{\hat{V}BY} = Gu^T \quad (31)$$

The forward measure of average production length captures the number of downstream processes that are incorporated in an economy's gross output. As such, this measures the relative upstreamness of an economy-sector. Related indicators are listed in Table 8.2.

8.5 Domestic Agglomeration

The concept of agglomeration, often used in economic geography, can be used to measure the extent to which economic activities cluster in the domestic economy. The framework builds on the value- added decomposition framework discussed in Section 8.4.1. Denote $\Theta_{(j,r,t)} = Y^{D}_{(j,r,t)}/Y_{(j,r,t)}$ as the share of the domestic sectors to the total value of final goods production in economy r sector j at time t. The backward agglomeration index of sector j in economy r, $AGG^{B}_{(j,r,t)}$, captures domestic production for domestic consumption and is defined as

$$AGG^{B}_{(j,r,t)} = \frac{\Theta_{(j,r,t)}}{\sum_{\tau=t-1}^{t}\sum_{r=1}^{G} 0.5\gamma_{(j,r,\tau)}\Theta_{(j,r,\tau)}} \quad (32)$$

where $\gamma_{(j,r,\tau)} \in (0,1)$ is the share of economy r to the total global output of sector j. The numerator is the share of final goods consumed domestically in (j,r) whose value-added comes from the domestic sectors in the total final demand for (j,r). By construction, the backward agglomeration index captures the share of Y^D to Y against the global average for that sector. A value of $AGG^{B}_{(j,r,t)} > 1$ implies that the value-added coming from the domestic sectors in the final goods production of sector j in economy r is higher than the world average, implying high backward agglomeration.

The forward agglomeration index has a similar structure. Let $\Phi_{(j,r,t)} = V^{D}_{(j,r,t)}/Va_{(j,r,t)}$ be the share of value-added generated in (j,r) that is absorbed domestically as final goods. The forward agglomeration index of sector j in economy r, $AGG^{F}_{(j,r,t)}$ is defined as

$$AGG^{F}_{(j,r,t)} = \frac{\Phi_{(j,r,t)}}{\sum_{\tau=t-1}^{t}\sum_{r=1}^{G} 0.5\gamma_{(j,r,\tau)}\Phi_{(j,r,\tau)}} \quad (33)$$

A value of $AGG^{F}_{(j,r,t)} > 1$ implies that the final goods of economy-sector (j,r) generates more value-added to the domestic sectors relative to the global average for that sector. Consequently, this indicates high forward agglomeration.

8.6 Supplementary Indicators

Other indicators that can be modeled from national and multiregional input-output tables are specified in Table 8.2. For more in-depth discussion, readers are encouraged to review the papers and documentation from each corresponding author(s) of these analytical indicators.

Table 8.2: Supplementary Input–Output Indicators

Indicator	Description	Notation
	Multiplier Effects	
Sectoral output multiplier	This shows the impact of a dollar's worth of a sectors final demand (row sector i) for another sectors output (column sector j). It is the Leontief inverse matrix itself (Miller and Blair 2009).	$B = (I - A)^{-1}$
Type 1 value-added multiplier	This is calculated as the sum of the ratio of the total value-added and total output of a sector divided by the simple value-added multiplier. Intuitively, this captures how much the initial effects on value-added are expanded when direct and indirect effects of a change in final demand are considered (Miller and Blair 2009).	$vb^{I}_{(j,r)} = \frac{\sum_{i=1}^{N} va_{(j,r)} b_{(i,j,r)}}{va_{(j,r)}}$
First-round effects	This captures the increase in intermediate input requirements for a unit increase in the production of output. It is calculated as just the column sum of the technical coefficients matrix $A = \{a_{ij}\}_{i,j \in N}$. Direct effects for sector j are denoted as d_j (Miller and Blair 2009; Oosterhaven 2019).	$d_j = \sum_{i=1}^{N} a_{(i,j)}$
Industrial support effects	This measures the indirect effects and the effects of induced production. It is calculated as the difference between the simple output multiplier, the initial effect (usually set equal to 1), and the first-round effects (Oosterhaven 2019).	
Production-induced effects	This measures additional output required from other sectors to produce the initial unit of extra output to meet the increase in final demand and all subsequent induced output. To calculate, take the sum of the first-round and industrial support effect, or the difference of the simple output multiplier and the initial effect (Oosterhaven 2019).	
	Linkages	
Direct backward linkage	This provides a direct measure of a sector's dependence on the supply of inputs across several sectors. This captures the first-round effects on gross output and an increase in a sector's final demand.	
Direct forward linkage	This provides a direct measure of a sector's dependence on the intersectoral demand for inputs. This represents the supply-side analog of the direct backward linkage.	
Complete hypothetical extraction backward linkage	This adjusts the backward linkage measure for self-dependency. Sectors with high backward linkages and high self-dependence will result in smaller overall effects in the economy, given an exogenous change in final demand. It is the ratio of the total backward linkage and the corresponding diagonal element in the Leontief inverse B (Miller and Blair 2009).	$bl^{HC}_{(j,r)} = \frac{bl_{(j,r)}}{b_{(j,j)}}$
Complete hypothetical extraction forward linkage	This adjusts the forward linkage measure for self-dependency. Sectors with high forward linkages and high self-dependence will result in smaller overall effects in the economy, given an exogenous change in production. It is the ratio of the total forward linkage and the corresponding diagonal element in the Ghosh inverse G (Miller and Blair 2009).	$fl^{HC}_{(i,r)} = \frac{fl_{(i,r)}}{g_{(i,i)}}$
Partial hypothetical extraction backward linkage	This indicator adjusts total backward linkages for self-dependency to isolate upstream linkages. Specifically, it sets apart the input column of sector *j* from the technical coefficient matrix, as well as sector *j*'s final demand (Oosterhaven 2019).	$bl^{HP}_{(j,r)} = \frac{bl_{(j,r)} - 1}{b_{(j,j)}}$

continued on next page.

Table 8.2 *continued.*

Indicator	Description	Notation
Partial hypothetical extraction forward linkage	This indicator adjusts total forward linkages for self-dependency to isolate downstream linkages. Specifically, it sets apart the input row of sector *i* from the technical coefficient matrix, as well as sector *i*'s value-added (Oosterhaven 2019).	$\mathrm{fl}_{(i,\mathrm{r})}^{\mathrm{HP}} = \frac{\mathrm{fl}_{(\mathrm{i,r})} - 1}{\mathrm{g}_{(\mathrm{i,i})}}$
Absolute impact of sector's hypothetical extraction	This measures the economic impact (loss) from hypothetical extraction of sector j's sales and purchases from the input-output table (Miller and Blair 2009). The respective columns and rows of sector j is nullified (or replaced with zeroes) in the technical coefficients matrix, yielding $\mathrm{A}^{(\mathrm{j})}$. Similarly, this nullifying of respective entries corresponding to sector j is performed for the value-added coefficients matrix, $\mathrm{V}^{(\mathrm{j})}$, and final demand vector, $\mathrm{Y}^{(\mathrm{j})}$. Using these input-output components, hypothetical value-added $\overline{\mathbf{va}}_{(j)}$ in the economy without sector *j* is evaluated. The absolute difference between actual **va** and hypothetical gross value-added $\overline{\mathbf{va}}_{(j)}$ is considered an absolute measure of sector j's linkages with the economy.	Sector's total linkage impact is the absolute difference of $\mid \mathbf{va} - \overline{\mathbf{va}}_{(j)} \mid$ where $\overline{\mathbf{va}}_{(j)} = \mathbf{V}^{(\mathrm{j})}(\mathbf{I} - \mathbf{A}^{(\mathrm{j})})^{-1}\mathbf{Y}^{(\mathrm{j})}$
Relative impact of sector's hypothetical extraction	From above, the relative impact of sector's hypothetical extraction is simply the absolute difference divided by the baseline economy-wide gross value-added (Miller and Blair 2009).	Sector's relative linkage impact is given as $\frac{\lvert \mathbf{va} - \overline{\mathbf{va}}_{(j)} \rvert}{\mathbf{va}}$
Net backward linkage	The net backward linkage adjusts the original measure of backward linkages to account for the "two-sided nature of sectoral dependence." This is done by multiplying total backward linkages of sector *j* ($\mathrm{bl}_{(\mathrm{j,r})}$) with its final output ratio ($\frac{y_{(\mathrm{j,r})}}{x_{(\mathrm{j,r})}}$) (Oosterhaven 2019).	$\mathrm{bl}_{(\mathrm{j,r})}^{net} = (\mathrm{bl}_{(\mathrm{j,r})})\frac{y_{(\mathrm{j,r})}}{x_{(\mathrm{j,r})}}$
Net forward linkage	The net forward linkage adjusts the original measure of forward linkages to account for the "two-sided nature of sectoral dependence." This is done by multiplying total forward linkages of sector *i* ($\mathrm{fl}_{(\mathrm{i,r})}$) with its primary input ratio ($\frac{va_{(\mathrm{i,r})}}{x_{(\mathrm{i,r})}}$) (Oosterhaven 2019).	$\mathrm{fl}_{(\mathrm{i,r})}^{net} = (\mathrm{fl}_{(\mathrm{i,r})})\frac{va_{(\mathrm{i,r})}}{x_{(\mathrm{i,r})}}$
Backward import multiplier	This measures how much production is attributed to activities outside the economy r due to an exogenous change in final demand in sector j in economy r. It is calculated from the column sums of the matrix $\mathrm{A}^{\mathrm{f}}(\mathrm{I} - \mathrm{A}^{\mathrm{d}})^{-1}$, where A^{f} corresponds to the imported intermediates in matrix A, while A^{d} refers to the domestic components of matrix A (Miller and Blair 2009).	Column sums of $\mathrm{A}^{\mathrm{f}}(\mathrm{I} - \mathrm{A}^{\mathrm{d}})^{-1}$
Forward import multiplier	This measures how much production is attributed to activities outside the economy r due to an exogenous change in primary inputs available for sector j in economy r. It is calculated from the row sums of the matrix $(\mathrm{I} - \mathrm{O}^{\mathrm{d}})^{-1}\mathrm{O}^{\mathrm{f}}$, where O^{f} corresponds to the allocation coefficients from the imported intermediates in matrix, while O^{d} refers to the domestic components of the allocation coefficient matrix O (Miller and Blair 2009).	Row sums of $(\mathrm{I} - \mathrm{O}^{\mathrm{d}})^{-1}\mathrm{O}^{\mathrm{f}}$
	International Trade Indicators	
Self-sufficiency ratio	This measures the ratio of internal demand for product *i* to total output of domestic sector *i*. This is calculated by taking the sum of the intermediate inputs purchased by sector *i* from sector *j* (irrespective of origin) ($\sum_{j=1}^{N} z_{(i,j,r*)}$), the final consumption of sector *i*'s products within *r* ($y_{(i,r*)}$), and the total exports of sector *i* ($e_{(i)}$), and obtaining its share of the total gross output of sector *i*.	$\frac{\sum_{j=1}^{N} z_{(i,j,r*)} + y_{(i,r*)} - e_{(i)}}{x_i}$

continued on next page.

Table 8.2 *continued.*

Indicator	Description	Notation
Export-to-output ratio	This is a measure of the export orientation of a producing sector. It is the ratio of sector *i*'s exported output to its total output.	$\frac{e_{(i,r)}}{x_{(i,r)}}$
	Aggregation on an economy level can be undertaken by taking the sum of all sectoral exported outputs and dividing it by economy-wide output.	$\frac{\sum_{i=1}^{N} e_{(i,r)}}{\sum_{i=1}^{N} x_{(i,r)}}$
Import-to-input ratio	This is a measure of the import dependence of a purchasing sector's production. It is the ratio of sector *j*'s imported inputs of all products *i* to *n* from all partners *s* to *G* to its total inputs or outlays.	$\frac{\sum_{i=1}^{N} z_{(i,j,r,s)}}{x_{(i,r)}}$
	Aggregation on an economy level can be undertaken by taking the sum of all sectoral imported inputs and dividing it by economy-wide output.	$\frac{\sum_{i=1}^{N} z_{(i,r,s)}}{\sum_{i=1}^{N} x_{(i,r)}}$
Trade openness	This measure is simply derived as the sum of export and imports divided by the total gross domestic product of an economy.	$\frac{\sum_{i=1}^{N} e_{(i,r)} + \sum_{j=1}^{N} m_{(j,r)}}{GDP}$
Domestic input share in intermediate inputs	This captures the domestic component of a sector's intermediate inputs.	$\frac{z_{(i,j,r)}}{x_{(i,r)}}$
	Aggregation on an economy level can be undertaken by taking the sum of the domestically sourced inputs of all sectors and dividing it by economy-wide intermediate inputs.	$\frac{\sum_{i=1}^{N} z_{(i,j,r)}}{\sum_{i=1}^{N} x_{(i,r)}}$
Foreign input share in intermediate inputs	This captures the foreign component of a sector's intermediate inputs. It is equivalent to the import-to-input ratio.	$\frac{\sum_{s\neq r}\sum_{i=1}^{N} z_{(i,j,s,r)}}{x_{(i,r)}}$
	Aggregation on an economy level can be undertaken by taking the sum of the foreign-sourced inputs of all sectors and dividing it by economy-wide intermediate inputs.	$\frac{\sum_{s\neq r}\sum_{i=1}^{N} z_{(i,j,s,r)}}{\sum_{i=1}^{N} x_{(i,r)}}$
	Global Value Chains	
Backward production length, domestic segment	This captures the intermediate inputs generated by a unit increase in final demand of a sector throughout all the upstream sectors of the economy that does not involve any cross-border trade (Wang et al. 2017).	$\mathrm{PL_y^d} = \frac{\mathrm{VBB\hat{Y}^d}}{\mathrm{VB\hat{Y}^d}}$
Backward production length, GVC segment	This captures the intermediate inputs generated by a unit increase in final demand of a sector throughout the upstream sectors of all importing partners (Wang et al. 2017).	$\mathrm{PL_y^{GVC}} = \frac{\mathrm{VLLA^fB\hat{Y}}}{\mathrm{VLA^fB\hat{Y}}} + \frac{\mathrm{VLLA^fBB\hat{Y}}}{\mathrm{VLA^fB\hat{Y}}}$
Forward production length, domestic segment	This captures the gross output generated by a unit increase in the primary inputs of a sector throughout all the downstream sectors of the economy that does not involve any cross-border trade (Wang et al. 2017).	$\mathrm{PL_v^d} = \mathrm{\hat{V}BBY^d}/\mathrm{\hat{V}BY^d}$
Forward production length, GVC segment	This captures the gross output generated by a unit increase in the primary inputs of a sector throughout the downstream sectors of all importing partners (Wang et al. 2017).	$\mathrm{PL_v^{GVC}} = \frac{\mathrm{\hat{V}LLA^fBY}}{\mathrm{\hat{V}LA^fBY}} + \frac{\mathrm{\hat{V}LLA^fBBY}}{\mathrm{\hat{V}LA^fBY}}$

GVC = global value chain.

Sources: Compilation of the Asian Development Bank Input–Output Study Team; R.E. Miller and P.D. Blair. 2009. *Input–Output Analysis: Foundations and Extensions* (second edition). Cambridge, UK: Cambridge University Press; J. Oosterhaven. 2019. *Rethinking Input–Output Analysis: A Spatial Perspective.* SpringerBriefs in Regional Science. Springer, Cham.; and Z. Wang, S. J. Wei, X. Yu, and K. Zhu. 2017. Measures of Participation in Global Value Chains and Global Business Cycles. *NBER Working Paper.* No. 23222. Cambridge, MA: National Bureau of Economic Research.

continued on next page.

Appendix

Reference Guide to Mathematical Notations

Table A8.1: List of Mathematical Notations for Input-Output Indicators

Indicator Name	Mathematical Notation
Exports	e
Total final demand	Y
Gross output	x
Gross value-added	GVA
Imports	m
Intermediate consumption	Z
Technical coefficients matrix	A
Domestic elements of the technical coefficients matrix	A^{d}
Imported elements of the technical coefficients matrix	A^{f}
Leontief inverse matrix	B
Allocation coefficients matrix	O
Domestic elements of the allocation coefficients matrix	O^{d}
Imported elements of the allocation coefficients matrix	O^{f}
Ghosh matrix	G
VBY matrix	VBY
Value-added of a sector	va_{j}
Simple output multiplier	$\mathrm{mo}_{(\mathrm{j,r})}$
Backward linkage	$\mathrm{bl}_{(\mathrm{j,r})}$
Forward linkage	$\mathrm{fl}_{(\mathrm{i,r})}$
Complete hypothetical extraction backward linkage	$\mathrm{bl}^{\mathrm{HC}}_{(\mathrm{j,r})}$
Complete hypothetical extraction forward linkage	$\mathrm{fl}^{\mathrm{HC}}_{(\mathrm{j,r})}$
Partial hypothetical extraction backward linkage	$\mathrm{bl}^{\mathrm{HP}}_{(\mathrm{j,r})}$
Partial hypothetical extraction forward linkage	$i\mathrm{l}^{\mathrm{HP}}_{(\mathrm{jir})}$
Absolute impact of sector's hypothetical extraction	$\overline{\mathrm{va}}_{(j)}$
Net backward linkage	$\mathrm{bl}^{net}_{(\mathrm{j,r})}$
Net forward linkage	$\mathrm{fl}^{net}_{(i,\mathrm{r})}$
Simple value-added multiplier	$\mathrm{vb}_{(\mathrm{j,r})}$
Employment multiplier	$\mathrm{eb}_{(\mathrm{j,r})}$

continued on next page.

Table A8.1 *continued.*

Indicator Name	Mathematical Notation
Intraregional transfer multiplier	M_1
Interregional spillover multiplier	M_2
Interregional feedback multiplier	M_3
Type 1 value-added multiplier	$vb^{I}_{(j,r)}$
First-round effects	d_j
Domestic value-added	DVA
Foreign value-added	FVA
Pure double-counting	PDC
Value-added directly absorbed by economy r	DAVAX
Value-added reexported by economy r	REX
Value-added reexported by economy r and eventually absorbed by s	REF
Trade-based backward GVC participation	$GVCX^{backward}_{(s,r)}$
Trade-based forward GVC participation	$GVCX^{forward}_{(s,r)}$
Trade-based GVC participation	$GVCX^{trade}_{(s,r)}$
Production-based GVC participation	$GVCX^{production}_{(s,r)}$
Value-added exports	$VAX_{(s,r)}$
Value-added adjusted revealed comparative advantage	$RCA^{va}_{(s,r)}$
Traditional revealed comparative advantage	$RCA^{traditional}_{(s,r)}$
Upstreamness	$U_{(j,r)}$
Backward measure of average production length	PL_y
Forward measure of average production length	PL_u
Backward production length, domestic segment	PL^{d}_{y}
Backward production length, GVC segment	PL^{GVC}_{y}
Forward production length, domestic segment	PL^{d}_{v}
Forward production length, GVC segment	PL^{GVC}_{v}
Backward agglomeration index	$AGG^{B}_{(j,r,t)}$
Forward agglomeration index	$AGG^{F}_{(j,r,t)}$

GVC = global value chain;
Source: Compiled by the Asian Development Bank Input–Output Study Team.

References

P. Antràs and D. Chor. 2013. Organizing the Global Value Chain. *Econometrica*. 81(6). pp. 2127–2204.

P. Antràs and D. Chor. 2018. On the Measurement of Upstreamness and Downstreamness in Global Value Chains. *NBER Working Paper*. No. 24185. Cambridge, MA: National Bureau of Economic Research.

Asian Development Bank (ADB). 2021. *Key Indicators for Asia and the Pacific 2021*. Manila: ADB.

R. Bems and R. C. Johnson. 2017. Demand for Value Added and Value-Added Exchange Rates. *American Economic Journal: Macroeconomics*. 9 (4). pp. 45–90.

A. Borin and M. Mancini. 2019. Measuring What Matters in Global Value Chains and Value-Added Trade. *Policy Research Working Paper*. No. 8804. Washington, DC: World Bank.

K. Dervis, J. De Melo, and S. Robinson. 1982. *General Equilibrium Models for Development Policy*. Washington, D.C.: World Bank.

European Commission. 2018. *Eurostat Manual of Supply, Use and Input–Output Tables*. Luxembourg: Office for Official Publications of the European Communities.

R. Koopman, Z. Wang, and S. J. Wei. 2014. Tracing Value-Added and Double Counting in Gross Exports. *American Economic Review*. 104 (2). pp. 459–94.

F. Lequiller and D. Blades. 2014. *Understanding National Accounts* (second edition). Paris: Organisation for Economic Co-operation and Development (OECD) Publishing.

R.E. Miller and P.D. Blair. 2009. *Input–Output Analysis: Foundations and Extensions* (second edition). Cambridge, UK: Cambridge University Press.

R. E. Miller and U. Temurshoev. 2017. Output Upstreamness and Input Downstreamness of Industries/Countries in World Production. *International Regional Science Review*. 40 (5). pp. 443–475.

J. Oosterhaven. 2019. *Rethinking Input–Output Analysis: A Spatial Perspective*. SpringerBriefs in Regional Science. Springer, Cham.

T. Ten Raa. 2006. *The Economics of Input–Output Analysis*. Cambridge University Press.

J. Teng. 1996. Input–Output Analysis of Economic Growth and Structural Changes in China. *Journal of Applied Input–Output Analysis*. 3. Pan Pacific Association of Input–Output studies.

United Nations (UN). 2018. *Handbook on Supply, Use and Input–Output Tables with Extensions and Applications*. Studies in Methods. New York: United Nations.

United Nations Conference on Trade and Development (UNCTAD). 2019. Revealed Comparative Advantage. https://unctadstat.unctad.org/en/ RcaRadar.html.

Z. Wang, S. J. Wei, X. Yu, and K. Zhu. 2017a. Measures of Participation in Global Value Chains and Global Business Cycles. *NBER Working Paper*. No. 23222. Cambridge, MA: National Bureau of Economic Research.

Z. Wang, S. J. Wei, X. Yu, and K. Zhu. 2017b. Characterizing Global Value Chains: Production Length and Upstreamness. *NBER Working Paper*. No. 23261. Cambridge, MA: National Bureau of Economic Research.

Z. Wang, S. J. Wei, and K. Zhu. 2018. Quantifying International Production Sharing at the Bilateral and Sector Levels. *NBER Working Paper*. No 19677. Cambridge, MA: National Bureau of Economic Research.

K. M. Yi. 2003. Can Vertical Specialization Explain the Growth of World Trade? *Journal of Political Economy*. 111 (1). pp. 52–102.

www.ingramcontent.com/pod-product-compliance
Lightning Source LLC
Chambersburg PA
CBHW041751220926
51847CB00014B/169
9789292696368